FROM

MANASSAS TO APPOMATTOX

MEMOIRS OF THE CIVIL WAR IN AMERICA

BY

JAMES LONGSTREET

LIEUTENANT-GENERAL CONFEDERATE ARMY

ILLUSTRATED WITH NUMEROUS PORTRAITS, ENGRAVINGS, AND COLORED MAPS SPECIALLY PREPARED FOR THIS WORK

SKYHORSE PUBLISHING

THIS WORK IS RESPECTFULLY DEDICATED

TO THE

OFFICERS AND SOLDIERS OF THE FIRST CORPS OF THE ARMY OF NORTHERN VIRGINIA

TO THE LIVING AND THE DEAD

In Memory of

THEIR BRAVE DEEDS, THEIR TOILS, THEIR TRIBULATIONS. AND THEIR TRIUMPHS

Skyhorse Publishing books may be purchased in bulk at special discounts for sales promotion, corporate gifts, fund-raising, or educational purposes. Special editions can also be created to specifications. For details, contact the Special Sales Department, Skyhorse Publishing, 307 West 36th Street, 11th Floor, New York, NY 10018 or info@skyhorsepublishing.com.

Skyhorse® and Skyhorse Publishing® are registered trademarks of Skyhorse Publishing, Inc.®, a Delaware corporation.

Visit our website at www.skyhorsepublishing.com.

10 9 8 7 6 5 4

Library of Congress Cataloging-in-Publication Data is available on file.
ISBN: 978-1-62087-470-7

Printed in the United States of America

PREFACE.

After the surrender of the Confederate armies engaged in the war between the States, General Lee undertook to write of the campaigns of the Army of Northern Virginia while under his command, and asked such assistance as I could give in supplying reports, despatches, and letters of his, the originals of which had been lost or destroyed. Under the impression that they could not be put to better use, such as were in hand were packed and sent. He gave up the work, and after a few years his death made it impossible that the world should receive the story of the Confederate campaigns in Virginia from the noble mind that controlled them.

Possibly, had I not expected our commander to write, I should have written myself a decade or so earlier. But the world is now better prepared to receive the account of events as the records show them.

While I am so constituted, temperamentally, as to have viewed the great struggle then as I view it now, I do not know that others might have so regarded it at the earlier periods to which I refer.

I believe that now, more fully than then, the public is ready to receive, in the spirit in which it is written, the story which I present.

It is not my purpose to philosophize upon the war, but I cannot refrain from expressing my profound thankfulness that Providence has spared me till such time as I can see the asperities of the great conflict softened, its passions entering upon the sleep of oblivion, only its nobler—if less immediate—results springing into virile and vast life. I believe there is to-day, *because of the war*, a broader and deeper patriotism in all Americans; that patriotism throbs the heart and pulses the being as ardently of the South Carolinian as of the Massachusetts Puritan; that the Liberty Bell, even now, as I write, on its Southern pilgrimage, will be as reverently received and as devotedly loved in Atlanta and Charleston as in Philadelphia and Boston. And to stimulate and evolve this noble sentiment all the more, what we need is the resumption of fraternity, the hearty restoration and cordial cultivation of neighborly, brotherly relations, faith in Jehovah, and respect for each other; and God grant that the happy vision that delighted the soul of the sweet singer of Israel may rest like a benediction upon the North and the South, upon the Blue and the Gray.

The spirit in which this work has been conceived, and in which I have conscientiously labored to carry it out, is one of sincerity and fairness. As an actor in, and an eye-witness of, the events of 1861–65, I have endeavored to perform my humble share of duty in passing the materials of history to those who may give them place in the records of the nation,—not of the South nor of the North,—but in the history of the United Nation. It is with such magnified view of the responsibility of saying the truth that I have written.

I yield to no one as a champion of the Southern soldier wherever he may have fought and in whatever army, and I do not think I shall be charged more now than in war-time with "underestimating the enemy." Honor to all! If I speak with some particularity of the First Corps of the Army of Northern Virginia, it must be ascribed in part to the affection of a commander, and in part to my desire to relieve its brave officers and men in the ranks from unjust aspersions. After General Lee's death, various writers on the Southern cause combined with one accord to hold the First Corps and its commander responsible for all adversity that befell the army. I being under the political ban, and the political passions and prejudices of the times running high, they had no difficulty in spreading their misrepresentations South and North until some people, through their mere reiteration, came to accept them as facts. I simply present the facts concerning the First Corps in all fulness and fairness, attested by indisputable authorities, that the public may judge between it and its detractors.

That the South had just cause for war in protecting and defending lawful property is proved by the sequel. This narrative will show that its chances of success were fair.

In the accounts of battles and movements, the official War Records supply in a measure the place of lost papers, and afford a great mass of most trustworthy statistics. I am under obligations to General E. P. Alexander, General G. M. Sorrel, Colonel Osmun Latrobe, Colonel J. W. Fairfax, Colonel T. J. Goree, Colonel Erasmus Taylor, and Colonel J. C. Haskell for many interesting suggestions.

To Major George B. Davis and Mr. L. J. Perry, of the War Records office, I am under obligations for invaluable assistance; as also to Mr. Alfred Mathews, of Philadelphia, for material aid in revising the manuscript of these memoirs.

THE AUTHOR.

Respectfully
Your Obt Servt
James Longstreet

CONTENTS.

CHAPTER I.

THE ANTE-BELLUM LIFE OF THE AUTHOR.

CHAPTER II.

FROM NEW MEXICO TO MANASSAS.

CHAPTER III.

BATTLE OF MANASSAS, OR BULL RUN.

CHAPTER IV.

THE CONFEDERATES HOVERING AROUND WASHINGTON.

CHAPTER XIV.

SECOND BATTLE OF MANASSAS (BULL RUN).

CHAPTER XV.

THE MARYLAND CAMPAIGN.

CHAPTER XVI.

"THE LOST ORDER"—SOUTH MOUNTAIN.

CHAPTER XVII.

PRELIMINARIES OF THE GREAT BATTLE.

CHAPTER XVIII.

BATTLE OF SHARPSBURG, OR ANTIETAM.

CHAPTER XIX.

BATTLE OF SHARPSBURG, OR ANTIETAM (CONTINUED).

CHAPTER XX.

REVIEW OF THE MARYLAND CAMPAIGN.

CHAPTER XXI.

REORGANIZATION AND REST FOR BOTH ARMIES.

CHAPTER XXXIV.

BESIEGING KNOXVILLE.

CHAPTER XXXV.

CUT OFF FROM EAST AND WEST.

CHAPTER XXXVI.

STRATEGIC IMPORTANCE OF THE FIELD.

CHAPTER XXXVII.

LAST DAYS IN TENNESSEE.

LIST OF ILLUSTRATIONS.

LIST OF MAPS.

FROM
MANASSAS TO APPOMATTOX.

CHAPTER I.

THE ANTE-BELLUM LIFE OF THE AUTHOR.

Birth—Ancestry—School-Boy Days—Appointment as Cadet at the United States Military Academy—Graduates of Historic Classes—Assignment as Brevet Lieutenant—Gay Life of Garrison at Jefferson Barracks—Lieutenant Grant's Courtship—Annexation of Texas—Army of Observation—Army of Occupation—Camp Life in Texas—March to the Rio Grande—Mexican War.

I WAS born in Edgefield District, South Carolina, on the 8th of January, 1821. On the paternal side the family was from New Jersey; on my mother's side, from Maryland. My earliest recollections were of the Georgia side of Savannah River, and my school-days were passed there, but the appointment to West Point Academy was from North Alabama. My father, James Longstreet, the oldest child of William Longstreet and Hannah Fitzrandolph, was born in New Jersey. Other children of the marriage, Rebecca, Gilbert, Augustus B., and William, were born in Augusta, Georgia, the adopted home. Richard Longstreet, who came to America in 1657 and settled in Monmouth County, New Jersey, was the progenitor of the name on this continent. It is difficult to determine whether the name sprang from France, Germany, or Holland. On the maternal side, Grandfather Marshall Dent was first cousin of John Marshall, of the Supreme Court. That branch claimed to trace their line back to the Conqueror. Marshall Dent married Ann Magruder, when they migrated to Augusta, Georgia. Father married the eldest daughter, Mary Ann.

Grandfather William Longstreet first applied steam as a motive power, in 1787, to a small boat on the Savannah River at Augusta, and spent all of his private means upon that idea, asked aid of his friends in Augusta and elsewhere, had no encouragement, but, on the contrary, ridicule of his proposition to move a boat without a pulling or other external power, and especially did they ridicule the thought of expensive steam-boilers to be made of iron. To obviate costly outlay for this item, he built boilers of heavy oak timbers and strong iron bands, but the Augusta marines were incredulous, as the following from the city papers of the times will indicate:

"Can you row the boat ashore,
Billy boy, Billy boy;
Can you row the boat ashore,
Gentle Billy?
Can you row the boat ashore,
Without paddle or an oar,
Billy boy?"

Full of confidence, the inventor thought to appeal to the governor, and his letter is still preserved in the State archives:

"Augusta, Georgia, September 26, 1790.

"Sir,—I make no doubt but you have often heard of my steamboat, and as often heard it laughed at, but in this I have only shared the fate of other projectors, for it has uniformly been the custom of every country to ridicule the greatest inventions until they had proved their utility. In not reducing my scheme to active use it has been unfortunate for me, I confess, and perhaps the people in general; but, until very lately, I did not think that artists or material could be had in the place sufficient. However, necessity, that grand mother of invention, has furnished me with an idea of perfecting my plan almost entirely of wooden material, and by such workmen as may be had here; and, from a thorough confidence of its success, I have presumed to ask your assistance and patronage. Should it succeed agreeably to my expectations, I hope I shall discover that sense of duty which such favors always merit; and should it not succeed, your reward must lay with other unlucky adventures.

"For me to mention all of the advantages arising from such a machine would be tedious, and, indeed, quite unnecessary. Therefore I have taken the liberty to state, in this plain and humble manner, my wish and opinion, which I hope you will excuse, and I shall remain, either with or without your approbation,

"Your Excellency's most obedient and humble servant,

"WM. LONGSTREET.

"GOVERNOR TELFAIR."

He failed to secure the necessary aid, and the discovery passed into the possession of certain New Yorkers, who found the means for practicable application, and now steam is the goddess that enlightens the world.

My father was a planter. From my early boyhood he conceived that he would send me to West Point for army service, but in my twelfth year he passed away during the cholera epidemic at Augusta. Mother moved to North Alabama with her children, whence in my sixteenth year I made application through a kinsman, Congressman Reuben Chapman, for appointment as cadet, received the coveted favor, and entered with the class that was admitted in 1838.

As cadet I had more interest in the school of the soldier, horsemanship, sword exercise, and the outside game of foot-ball than in the academic courses. The studies were successfully passed, however, until the third year, when I failed in mechanics. When I came to the problem of the pulleys, it seemed to my mind that a soldier could not find use for such appliances, and the pulleys were passed by. At the January examination I was called to the blackboard and given the problem of the pulleys. The drawing from memory of recitation of classmates was good enough, but the demonstration failed to satisfy the sages of the Academic Board. It was the custom, however, to give those who failed in the general examination a second hearing, after all of the classes were examined. This gave me two days to "cram" mechanics, and particularly on pulleys. But the professors were too wily to introduce them a second time, and took me through a searching examination of the six months' course. The bridge was safely passed, however, and mechanics left behind. At the June examination, the end of the academic year, I was called to demonstrate the pulleys. The professor thought that I had forgotten my old friend the enemy, but I smiled, for he had become dear to me,—in waking hours and in dreams,—and the cadet passed easily enough for a maximum mark.

The cadets had their small joys and sometimes little troubles. On one occasion a cadet officer reported me for disobedience of orders. As the report was not true, I denied it and sent up witnesses of the occasion. Dick Garnett, who fell in the assault of the 3d, at Gettysburg, was one witness, and Cadet Baker, so handsome and lovable that he was called Betsy, was the other. Upon overlooking the records I found the report still there, and went to ask the superintendent if other evidence was necessary to show that the report was not true. He was satisfied of that, but said that the officer complained that I smiled contemptuously. As that could only be rated as a single demerit, I asked the benefit of the smile; but the report stands to this day, Disobedience of orders and *three* demerits. The cadet had his revenge, however, for the superintendent was afterwards known as *The Punster*.

There were sixty-two graduating members of the class of 1842, my number being sixty. I was assigned to the Fourth United States Infantry as brevet lieutenant, and found my company with seven others of the regiment at Jefferson Barracks, Missouri, in the autumn of 1842.

Of the class graduating the year that we entered were G. T. Beauregard and Irvin McDowell, who, twenty-three years later, commanded the hostile armies on the plains of Manassas, in Virginia. Braxton Bragg and W. J. Hardee were of that class.

The head man of the next class (1839) was I. I. Stevens, who resigned from the army, and, after being the first governor of Washington Territory, returned to military service, and fell on the sanguinary field of Chantilly on the 1st of September, 1862. Next on the class roll was Henry Wager Halleck, who was commander-in-chief of the United States armies from July, 1862, to March, 1864. W. T. Sherman and George H. Thomas, of the Union army, and R. S. Ewell, of the Confederate army, were of the same class (1840). The class of 1841 had the largest list of officers killed in action. Irons, Ayers, Ernst, Gantt, Morris, and Burbank were killed in the Mexican War. N. Lyon, R. S. Garnett, J. F. Reynolds, R. B. Garnett, A. W. Whipple, J. M. Jones, I. B. Richardson, and J. P. Garesché fell on the fields of the late war.

Of the class of 1842 few were killed in action, but several rose to distinguished positions,—Newton, Eustis, Rosecrans, Lovell, Van Dorn, Pope, Sykes, G. W. Smith, M. L. Smith, R. H. Anderson, L. McLaws, D. H. Hill, A. P. Stewart, B. S. Alexander, N. J. T. Dana, and others.

But the class next after us (1843) was destined to furnish the man who was to eclipse all,—to rise to the rank of general, an office made by Congress to honor his services; who became President of the United States, and for a second term; who received the salutations of all the powers of the world in his travels as a private citizen around the earth; of noble, generous heart, a lovable character, a valued friend,—Ulysses S. Grant.

I was fortunate in the assignment to Jefferson Barracks, for in those days the young officers were usually sent off among the Indians or as near the borders as they could find habitable places. In the autumn of 1842 I reported to the company commander, Captain Bradford R. Alden, a most exemplary man, who proved a lasting, valued friend. Eight companies of the Third Infantry were added to the garrison during the spring of 1843, which made garrison life and society gay for the young people and interesting for the older classes. All of the troops were recently from service in the swamps and Everglades of Florida, well prepared to enjoy the change from the war-dance of the braves to the hospitable city of St. Louis; and the graceful step of its charming belles became a joy forever.

Of the class of 1843, Ulysses S. Grant joined the Fourth Regiment as brevet lieutenant, and I had the pleasure to ride with him on our first visit to Mr. Frederick Dent's home, a few miles from the garrison, where we first met Miss Julia Dent, the charming woman who, five years later, became Mrs. Grant. Miss Dent was a frequent visitor at the garrison balls and hops, where Lieutenant Hoskins, who was something of a tease, would inquire of her if she could tell where he might find "the small lieutenant with the large epaulettes."

In May, 1844, all of our pleasures were broken by orders sending both regiments to Louisiana, near Fort Jessup, where with other troops we were organized as "The Army of Observation," under General Zachary Taylor.

In March, 1845, I was assigned as lieutenant in the Eighth Regiment, and joined my company at St. Augustine, Florida. The soldier's life of those days was not encouraging to those of active aspirations; but influences were then at work that were beginning to brighten the horizon a little. The new republic of Texas was seeking annexation with the United States, which would endanger the peace between them and the republic of Mexico. Annexation of Texas became the supreme question of the canvass of 1844. James K. Polk was the nominee of the Democratic and annexation party, and Henry Clay was on the other side as the Whig nominee. Polk was elected, and his party prepared to signalize its triumph by annexation as soon as it came into power; but in the last days of President Tyler's administration, through skilful management of Secretary of State John C. Calhoun, joint resolutions of annexation were passed by both houses of Congress, subject to concurrence of the Congress of the new republic. Strange as it may seem, the resolutions that added to the territory of the United States more than the New England and Middle States combined, and which eventually led to extension to the Pacific coast and hundreds of miles north, only passed the lower house by twenty-two majority, and the Senate by a majority of two.

When the resolution was passed, the minister from Mexico to our government, General Almonte, demanded his passports, and diplomatic relations between the governments ceased. On July 4, 1845, the Texas Congress accepted and ratified the resolutions of annexation by unanimous vote, and Texas was a State of the Union.

General Taylor's little army of observation was ordered to Corpus Christi, Texas, and became "The Army of Occupation." All other available forces were ordered to join him, including General Worth and his forces in Florida. At the time there were in the line of the army eight regiments of infantry, four of artillery, and two of dragoons, stationed along the northern frontier from Fort Kent in the northeast of Maine to the west end of Lake Superior, and along the western frontier from Fort Snelling to Fort Leavenworth, and southward to Fort Jessup in Louisiana.

By the middle of October, 1846, three thousand eight hundred and sixty men of all arms had concentrated at Corpus Christi. Seven companies of the Second Dragoons had marched from Fort Jessup to San Patricio on the Nueces River, about twenty-eight miles up from Corpus Christi; the other three companies were halted at San Antonio, Texas. Near our camps were extensive plains well adapted to military manœuvres, which were put to prompt use for drill and professional instruction. There were many advantages too in the way of amusement, game on the wild prairies and fish in the broad gulf were plentiful, and there was the salt water for bathing. On one occasion during the winter a violent north wind forced the waters over the beach, in some places far enough to disturb our camps, and when they receded, quantities of fish were found in the little puddles left behind, and turtles more than enough to supply the army.

The officers built a theatre, depending upon their own efforts to reimburse them. As there was no one outside the army except two rancheros within a hundred miles, our dramatic company was organized from among the officers, who took both male and female characters. In farce and comedy we did well enough, and soon collected funds to pay for the building and incidental expenses. The house was filled every night. General Worth always encouraging us, General Taylor sometimes, and General Twiggs occasionally, we found ourselves in funds sufficient to send over to New Orleans for costumes, and concluded to try tragedy. The "Moor of Venice" was chosen, Lieutenant Theoderic Porter* to be the Moor, and Lieutenant U. S. Grant to be the daughter of Brabantio. But after rehearsal Porter protested that male heroines could not support the character nor give sentiment to the hero, so we sent over to New Orleans and secured Mrs. Hart, who was popular with the garrisons in Florida. Then all went well, and life through the winter was gay.

Formal diplomatic relations between the republics were suspended, but quasi negotiations were continued, seeking a course by which war might be averted. The authorities of Mexico were not averse to the settlement according to the claims of Texas,—the Rio Grande fron-

* Brother of the rear-admiral.

tier,—but the political affairs of the country were such that they could not agree. Excitement in the United States increased as the suspense continued. But the authorities, having confidence in their negotiations or wishing to precipitate matters, ordered General Taylor to march across to the Rio Grande at Matamoras in the spring of 1846. The execution of the order precipitated war.

The move from Corpus Christi to the Rio Grande made necessary a change of base from St. Joseph's Island to Point Isabel and Brazos Santiago, near the mouth of the Rio Grande. Supplies were sent by sea, under charge of Major Munroe, with a siege train and field battery, and the army took up its march on the 9th of March, 1846, the advance under General Twiggs, consisting of the dragoons and Ringgold's field battery. The army was well instructed, under good discipline, and fully prepared for field work, the weather was fine, and the firm turf of the undulating prairies made the march easy. Wild horses and cattle, and deer and antelope, were often seen in the distance as they scampered away to hide themselves. On the 19th the head of the column approached Arroyo Colorado, one hundred and thirty miles from Corpus Christi. The arroyo was about three feet deep, of salt water. Mexican lancers were on the southern side, and gave notice that they had orders to resist our further advance. On the 21st the army was up and deployed along the high banks of the arroyo, the field batteries in position. General Worth was ordered to make the crossing, and rode at the head of the column. We looked with confidence for a fight and the flow of blood down the salt water before we could cross, but the Mexicans had no artillery, and could not expose their cavalry to the fire of our batteries; they made their formal protest, however, that the crossing would be regarded as a declaration of war.

On the 24th of March the column reached the road leading from Point Isabel to Matamoras. General Taylor ordered Worth to march the greater part of the army towards Matamoras and halt at the first good camping-ground, and rode towards Point Isabel to meet the detachment ordered there under Major Munroe. He found them already landed, and the Mexicans fired their little hamlets and fled. After ordering construction of protection for his supplies and defensive works for the troops, General Taylor returned to the army, and rode with General Worth towards the Rio Grande. As the army approached the river the Mexicans on the Matamoras side made some display of forces, manned their works on that side, and prepared to resist us, under the impression that we would cross at once. General Worth was sent over, and was met by General La Vega, on the part of General Mejia, commanding on that side. He was told that Mexico had not declared war, that the American consul was in the exercise of his functions; but Worth's request to see the consul was refused, which was denounced as a belligerent act, and he cautioned General La Vega against passing Mexicans to the north side of the river.

Camps were pitched in range of the Mexican works about Matamoras, grounds staked for constructing defensive works, and large details put out to work on them. The Mexican forces at this time were three thousand, and they were soon joined by two thousand more.

Political affairs with them were confused. President Herrera was thought to favor the claims of Texas to the Rio Grande border. General Paredes made pronunciamento, overthrew the president's government, and had authority as war president. He sent General Ampudia to the frontier to take charge, but the appointment was not satisfactory on the border, and General Arista was assigned. There was discord over there between the authorities and the generals, while General Taylor was too far from his government to be bothered. His army was all that he could wish, except in numbers.

Marauding parties came over occasionally and made trouble about the ranches on the American side. One party killed Colonel Cross, our chief quartermaster, on the 10th of April. Scouting parties were sent out to look for the intruders. Lieutenant Theoderic Porter, in command of one party, and one of his men were caught in ambush and killed. Captain Walker, of the Texan Rangers, while out on a scout lost his camp guard of five men, surprised and killed, and later Captains Thornton and Hardee, of the dragoons, were met at Rancho Carricitos by a large cavalry force and some infantry under General Torrijon, who took captive or killed the entire party. Captains Thornton and Hardee and Lieutenant Kane were made prisoners. The other commissioned officer of the command, George T. Mason, of my class, refused to surrender; being a superior swordsman, he tried to cut his way out, and was killed. This affair was taken as open war, and General Taylor called on the governors of Texas and Louisiana—under his authority from Washington—for volunteers of infantry and cavalry.

The capture of Thornton and Hardee created great excitement with the people at home. Fanning's massacre and the Alamo at San Antonio were remembered, and it was reported of General Ampudia, who on a recent occasion had captured a general in Yucatan, that he boiled his head in oil. So it was thought he would give no quarter; but in a day or two we heard from the officers that they received great kindness from their captors, and that General Ampudia had ordered that his government should allow them their full pay and every liberty consistent with their safe-keeping. They declined, however, to accept pay, and were held as the guests of Generals Arista and Ampudia.

On the 1st of May our tents were struck, wagons packed, assembly sounded, and the troops were under arms at three A.M., marched at four o'clock, and bivouacked within ten miles of Point Isabel. No one was advised of the cause of movements, but all knew that our general understood his business. He had been informed that General Arista, with his movable forces, had marched to Rancho de Longoreno, some leagues below us on the river, intending to cross and cut us off from the base at Point Isabel. Major Jacob Brown was left in charge of the works opposite Matamoras with the Seventh Regiment of Infantry, Captain Lowd's company of artillery, and Bragg's field battery.

By some accident provision was not made complete for Arista to make prompt crossing of the river, and that gave General Taylor time to reach his base, reinforce it, and draw sufficient supplies. Advised of our move by General Mejia, at Matamoras, General Arista was thrown into doubt as to whether our move was intended for Matamoras, and sent back part of his forces for its defence. Finding, however, that Taylor had gone to Point Isabel, Arista crossed the river and put his line athwart our return march at Palo Alto. To hasten Taylor's return, he ordered General Mejia, at Matamoras, to open his batteries on our troops at Fort Brown, and make serious demonstrations against them.

General Taylor started on his return on the 7th of May. We had heard the artillery-fire upon comrades left at the forts, and were anxiously looking for the order. It was received with cheers, and a good march was made, but the night was awful. The mosquitoes seemed as thick as the blades of grass on the prairie, and swarmed and buzzed in clouds, and packs of half-famished wolves prowled and howled about us. There was no need for the sound of reveille. The wolves and mosquitoes, and perhaps some solemn thoughts, kept us on the *qui vive.* Arista's army was known to be in line of battle only a few miles off. About one o'clock we halted to fill the canteens, and marched to meet the enemy. The columns were deployed,

—Fifth Infantry on the right, Ringgold's battery, Third Infantry, a two-gun battery of eighteen-pounders, the Fourth Infantry, battalion of artillery acting as infantry, Duncan's field battery and Eighth Infantry, Captains Charles May and Croghan Ker, with squadrons of dragoons, looking to the trains; the Third and Fourth Infantry, the Third Brigade, under Colonel John Garland. That brigade, with the Fifth Regiment, the heavy guns, and Ringgold's, were of the right wing, General Twiggs commanding. Other forces of the left were under Colonel William G. Belknap, Eighth Infantry, and Duncan's Battery.

As the lines deployed, Lieutenant J. E. Blake, of the Topographical Engineers, dashed forward alone, made a close inspection of the enemy's line with such lightning speed that his work was accomplished before the enemy could comprehend his purpose, rode back and reported to the commanding general. He was one of the heroes of the day, but his laurels were enjoyed only a few hours. As he took his pistol off at night he threw it upon the ground, and an accidental explosion of one of the charges gave him a mortal wound.

The line advanced until the puff of smoke from one of the enemy's guns rose, and the ball bounded over the prairie, passed over our heads, and wounded a teamster far in our rear. Our infantry was ordered down and our artillery into practice. It was an artillery combat more than a battle, and held until night. The Mexican cavalry made a charge against the Fifth Regiment, and finding our front of square too strong repeated on another front, but were repulsed. Presently the grass took fire, and the winds so far favored us as to sweep the smoke in the enemy's faces, and when it passed we found the Mexican line had been drawn back a little. May's squadron was sent there, and General Taylor advanced the right of his line, but night closed in before decisive work could be done. The armies were near enough during the night to hear the moans of the wounded. Major Ringgold was mortally wounded, also Captain John Page, of the Fourth Infantry, but less than fifty of our troops were lost.

Early the next morning a few of the Mexican troops could be seen, but when the sun rose to light the field it was found vacant. A careful reconnoissance revealed that the enemy was in retreat, and the dragoons reported them in march towards our comrades at Fort Brown.

General Taylor remained on the field a few hours to have the killed and wounded of both sides cared for, but sent the dragoons, light infantry, and Ringgold's battery in pursuit, the latter under Lieutenant Randolph Ridgely. The light infantry was of two battalions, under Captain George A. McCall and Captain C. F. Smith. The route of march was through a dense chaparral on both sides of the road, the infantry finding their way as best they could through the chaparral, the dragoons and Texas Rangers moving on the road, and far off from our flanks, wherever they could find ways of passage. The company to which I was attached was of Smith's battalion, on the right of the road. After a considerable march the battalion came to the body of a young Mexican woman. She had ceased to breathe, but blood heat was still in her body, and her expression life-like. A profusion of black hair covered her shoulders and person, the only covering to her waist. This sad spectacle, so unlike our thoughts of battle, unnerved us a little, but the crush through the thorny bushes soon brought us back to thoughts of heavy work, and then came reports of several guns and of grape-shot flying over our heads and tearing through the wood. A reconnoissance found General Arista's army on the south bank of a stream, Resaca de la Palma, which at this season had dried into lagoons with intervening passes. The road crossed at a wide gap between two extensive lagoons. The most of the enemy's artillery was near the road, the infantry behind the lagoons, with improvised breast defences of pack-saddles and other articles that could be found to stop musket-balls. The lagoons were about a hundred feet wide and from two to three feet deep.

The position was so strong that General Arista thought it would not be attacked. He left General La Vega in command at the road, and made his head-quarters some distance in rear, holding his cavalry in hand to look for any flank move, unpacked his mule-train, and turned the animals out to graze. General Taylor received reports of our adventures and reconnoissance when he rode up, deployed his army for battle, and ordered it forward. In the dense chaparral it was not possible to hold the regiments to their lines, and in places the companies were obliged to break files to get along. All of the enemy's artillery opened, and soon his musketry. The lines closed in to short work, even to bayonet work at places. Lieutenant-Colonel McIntosh had a bayonet thrust through his mouth and neck.* Lieutenant R. M. Cochran, Fourth Regiment, and T. L. Chadbourne, of the Eighth, were killed; C. R. Gates and C. D. Jordan, of the Eighth, were severely wounded. The latter, a classmate, was overpowered and about to be slaughtered when rescued by Lieutenant George Lincoln, of the Eighth, who slew with his sword one of the assailants.

Finding the enemy's strong fight, in defence, by his artillery, General Taylor ordered Captain May to charge and capture the principal battery. The squadron was of his own and L. P. Graham's troops. The road was only wide enough to form the dragoons in column of fours. When in the act of springing to their work, Ridgely called, "Hold on, Charlie, till I draw their fire," and loosed his six guns upon the battery at the road.

---

* He had a similar wound in the war of 1812.

The return was prompt, but General Taylor, not noting the cause of delay, repeated the order. Ridgely's work, however, was done, and May's spurs pressing his horses had them on the leap before the order reached his ears. In a minute he was at the guns sabring the gunners, and wheeling right and left got possession of the batteries. General La Vega was found at one of his batteries trying to defend it with his sword against one of May's dragoons, but was forced to get in between the wheels of his guns to avoid the horse's heels as they pressed him, when his rank was recognized and he was called to surrender.

As May made his dash the infantry on our right was wading the lagoon. A pause was made to dip our cups for water, which gave a moment for other thoughts; mine went back to her whom I had left behind. I drew her daguerreotype from my breast-pocket, had a glint of her charming smile, and with quickened spirit mounted the bank in time to send some of the mixed infantry troops to relieve May of his charge of the captive knight.

As a dragoon and soldier May was splendid. He stood six feet four without boots, wore his beard full and flowing, his dark-brown locks falling well over his shoulders. His appearance as he sat on his black horse Tom, his heavy sabre over General La Vega, was grand and picturesque. He was amiable of disposition, lovable and genial in character.

Not so grand of stature, or beard, or flowing locks, Randolph Ridgely was as accomplished a soldier and as charming a companion,—a fitting counterpart in spirit and dash.

I have gone thus far into the Mexican War for the opportunity to mention two valued friends, whose memory returning refreshes itself. Many gallant, courageous deeds have since been witnessed, but none more interesting than Ridgely's call for the privilege to draw upon himself the fire that was waiting for May.

CHAPTER II.

FROM NEW MEXICO TO MANASSAS.

The War-Cloud—The Journey Northward—Appointed Brigadier-General—Report to General Beauregard—Assigned to Command at the Scene of the First Conflict—Personnel of the Confronting Forces—Description of the Field of Manassas, or Bull Run—Beauregard and McDowell of the same West Point Class—Battle of Blackburn's Ford—Early's Mistake—Under Fire of Friend and Foe.

I WAS stationed at Albuquerque, New Mexico, as paymaster in the United States army when the war-cloud appeared in the East. Officers of the Northern and Southern States were anxious to see the portending storm pass by or disperse, and on many occasions we, too, were assured, by those who claimed to look into the future, that the statesman would yet show himself equal to the occasion, and restore confidence among the people. Our mails were due semi-monthly, but during winter seasons we were glad to have them once a month, and occasionally had to be content with once in six weeks. When mail-day came the officers usually assembled on the flat roof of the quartermaster's office to look for the dust that in that arid climate announced the coming mail-wagon when five or ten miles away; but affairs continued to grow gloomy, and eventually came information of the attack upon and capture of Fort Sumter by the Confederate forces, which put down speculation and drew the long-dreaded line.

A number of officers of the post called to persuade me to remain in the Union service. Captain Gibbs, of the Mounted Rifles, was the principal talker, and after a long but pleasant discussion, I asked him what course he would pursue if his State should pass ordinances of secession and call him to its defence. He confessed that he would obey the call.

It was a sad day when we took leave of lifetime comrades and gave up a service of twenty years. Neither Union officers nor their families made efforts to conceal feelings of deepest regret. When we drove out from the post, a number of officers rode with us, which only made the last farewell more trying.

Passing Fort Craig, on the opposite side of the Rio Grande, we pitched our camp for the night. A sergeant of the Mounted Rifle Regiment came over to see me, and stated that he was from Virginia, and thought that he could go with us to his native State, and at the same time asked that several other soldiers who wished to return to their States might go as my escort. I explained that private soldiers could not go without authority from the War Department; that it was different with commissioned officers, in that the latter could resign their commissions, and when the resignations were accepted they were independent of military authority, and could, as other citizens, take such action as they might choose, but that he and his comrades had enlisted for a specified term of years, and by their oaths were bound to the term of enlistment; that I could not entertain the proposition.

We stayed overnight at Fort Fillmore, in pleasant meeting with old comrades, saddened by the reflection that it was the last, and a prelude to occurrences that must compel the ignoring of former friendships with the acceptance of opposing service.

Speaking of the impending struggle, I was asked as to the length of the war, and said, "At least three years, and if it holds for five you may begin to look for a dictator," at which Lieutenant Ryan, of the Seventh Infantry, said, "If we are to have a dictator, I hope that you may be the man."

My mind was relieved by information that my resignation was accepted, to take effect on the 1st of June. In our travel next day we crossed the line into the State of

Texas. From the gloomy forebodings of old friends, it seemed at El Paso that we had entered into a different world. All was enthusiasm and excitement, and songs of "Dixie and the South" were borne upon the balmy air. But the Texas girl did not ascend to a state of incandescent charm until the sound of the first notes of "The Bonny Blue Flag" reached her ear. Then her feet rose in gleeful springs, her limbs danced, her hands patted, her eyes glowed, her lips moved, though she did not care to speak, or listen to any one. She seemed lifted in the air, thrilled and afloat, holding to the "Single Star" in joyful hope of Southern rights.

Friends at El Paso persuaded me to leave my family with them to go by a train that was to start in a few days for San Antonio, and to take the faster route by stage for myself.

Our travelling companions were two young men, returning to their Northern homes. The ride of our party of four (including the driver) through the Indian country was attended with some risk, and required vigilance, to be assured against surprise. The constant watchfulness and possible danger over a five-hundred-miles travel drew us near together, and in closer communion as to our identity and future movements, and suggested to the young men that it would be best to put themselves under my care, trusting that I would see them safely through the Confederate lines. They were of the laboring class, and had gone South to find employment. They were advised to be careful, and talk but little when among strangers. Nothing occurred to cause apprehension until we reached Richmond, Texas, where, at supper, I asked for a glass of milk, and was told there was none.

"What!" said one of my companions, "haven't the keows come up?"

Signal was telegraphed under the table to be on guard. The *nom de plume* of the Texas bovine escaped attention, and it passed as an enjoyable *lapsus linguæ*.

At Galveston we took a small inland sailing-craft, but were a little apprehensive, as United States ships were reported cruising outside in search of all vessels not flying the Stars and Stripes. Our vessel, however, was only boarded once, and that by a large Spanish mackerel that made a misleap, fell amidships, and served our little company with a pleasant dinner. Aboard this little vessel I first met T. J. Goree, an intelligent, clever Texan, who afterwards joined me at Richmond, and served in faithful duty as my aide-de-camp from Bull Run to Appomattox Court-House.

At New Orleans, my companions found safe-conduct to their Northern lines, and I journeyed on to Richmond. Relatives along the route, who heard of my approach, met me at the stations, though none suggested a stop overnight, or for the next train, but after affectionate salutations waved me on to join "Jeff Davis, for Dixie and for Southern rights."

At every station old men, women, and children assembled, clapping hands and waving handkerchiefs to cheer the passengers on to Richmond. On crossing the Virginia line, the feeling seemed to culminate. The windows and doors of every farm-house and hamlet were occupied, and from them came hearty salutations that cheered us on to Richmond. The spirit electrified the air, and the laborers of the fields, white and black, stopped their ploughs to lift their hats and wave us on to speedy travel. At stations where meals were served, the proprietors, in response to offers to settle, said, "Meals for those going on to join Jeff Davis are paid."

On the 29th of June, 1861, I reported at the War Department at Richmond, and asked to be assigned for service in the pay department, in which I had recently served (for when I left the line service, under appointment as paymaster, I had given up all aspirations of military honor, and thought to settle down into more peaceful pursuits). On the 1st of July I received notice of my appointment as brigadier-general, with orders to report at Manassas Junction, to General Beauregard.

I reported on the 2d, and was assigned to command of the First, Eleventh, and Seventeenth Regiments of Virginia Volunteers, to be organized as a brigade. The regiments were commanded respectively by Colonels —— Moore, Samuel Garland, and M. D. Corse, all active, energetic, and intelligent officers, anxious to acquire skill in the new service in which they found themselves. Lieutenant Frank Armstead was assigned to duty at brigade head-quarters, as acting assistant adjutant-general, and Lieutenant Peyton T. Manning as aide-de-camp. Dr. J. S. D. Cullen, surgeon of the First Virginia Regiment, became medical director. The regiments were stationed at Manassas Junction.

On the 6th they were marched out, formed as a brigade, and put through the first lessons in evolutions of the line, and from that day to McDowell's advance had other opportunities to learn more of the drill and of each other. General Beauregard had previously settled upon the stream of Bull Run as his defensive-aggressive line, and assigned his forces accordingly. A brigade under Brigadier-General R. S. Ewell was posted at Union Mills Ford, on the right of the Confederate lines; one under Brigadier-General D. R. Jones at McLean's Ford; Brigadier-General Bonham's brigade was placed on outpost duty at Fairfax Court-House with orders to retire, at the enemy's approach, to Mitchell's Ford, and Brigadier-General P. St. George Cocke was to hold the fords between Mitchell's and the Stone Bridge, the latter point to be defended by a regiment and a battalion of infantry, and a battery, under Brigadier-General N. G. Evans.

Between Mitchell's and McLean's Fords, and about half a mile from each, is Blackburn's Ford. The guard at that point was assigned to my command,—the Fourth

Brigade,—which was ordered to be ready, at a moment's warning, to march to position, and prepare for battle. In the mean time I was to study the ground and familiarize myself with the surroundings and avenues of approach and retreat. Bull Run rises from the foot-hills of the Blue Ridge and flows southeast through deeps and shallows into the Potomac, about forty miles south of Alexandria. The swell of the tide-waters up to Union Mills gives it the depth and volume of water of a river. Blackburn's Ford is in a great bend of the river, the north bank holding the concave of the turn. On the convex side was a strip of alluvial soil about seventy feet wide, covered by large forest-trees and some tangled undergrowth. Outside and extending some three hundred yards from the edge of the woodland was an arable field upon a pretty ascending plain, beyond which was a second growth of pine and oak. On the north bank stood a bluff of fifteen feet, overhanging the south side and ascending towards the heights of Centreville. Below Blackburn's Ford the bluff extended, in more or less ragged features, far down to the southeast. Just above my position the bluff graded down in even decline to Mitchell's Ford, the position assigned for Bonham's brigade, the latter being on the concave of the river, six hundred yards retired from my left and at the crossing of the direct road between Centreville and Manassas Junction. At the Junction well-constructed battery epaulements were prepared for defence.

The bluff of the north bank was first designated as my most suitable ground, and I was ordered to open the front, lay out and construct trenches, to be concealed by green pine-boughs. The regiments were from Richmond, Lynchburg, and Alexandria,—more familiar with the amenities of city life than with the axe, pick, spade, or shovel. They managed, however, to bring down as many as half a dozen spreading second-growth pines in the course of two days' work, when General Beauregard concluded that the advanced position of the brigade would mar his general plan, and ordered the line to be taken along the river bank of the south side, under the woodland, and close under the bluff, a position only approvable as temporary under accepted rules of warfare, but this proved a favorable exception between the raw forces of the contending armies. In addition to the two brigades on my right, the Sixth Brigade, under Colonel Jubal A. Early, was posted (with artillery) near the fords. As proximate but separate commands, stood General Theo. Holmes, thirty miles off to the right, with a brigade, a battery, and cavalry, at and about Acquia Creek, and General J. E. Johnston, sixty miles away, over the Blue Ridge Mountains. Holmes's should have been an outpost, but he had ranked Beauregard in the old service, and as a point of etiquette was given a separate command. Johnston's command should have been an outlying contingent, but he had been assigned to the Shenandoah Valley when, because threatened with immediate invasion, it was of first importance. Beauregard was subsequently assigned to Manassas Junction, which, under later developments, became the strategic point. As Johnston was his senior, another delicate question arose, that was not solved until the tramp of McDowell's army was heard on the Warrenton Turnpike.

The armies preparing for the first grand conflict were commanded by West Point graduates, both of the class of 1838,—Beauregard and McDowell. The latter had been assigned to command of the Federal forces at Washington, south of the Potomac, in the latter part of May, 1861. The former had assumed command of the Confederates at Manassas Junction about the 1st of June.

McDowell marched on the afternoon of the 16th of July at the head of an army of five divisions of infantry, supplemented by nine field batteries of the regular service, one of volunteers, besides two guns operating separately, and seven companies of regular cavalry. In his infantry columns were eight companies of regulars and a battalion of marines, an aggregate of thirty-five thousand men.

Beauregard stood behind Bull Run with seven brigades, including Holmes, who joined on the 19th, twenty-nine guns, fourteen hundred cavalry,—an aggregate of twenty-one thousand nine hundred men, all volunteers. To this should be added, for the battle of the 21st, reinforcements aggregating eight thousand five hundred men, under General Johnston, making the sum of the aggregate, thirty thousand four hundred.

The line behind Bull Run was the best between Washington and the Rapidan for strategy, tactics, and army supplies.

General Beauregard gave minute instructions to his brigade commanders of his position and general plan, which in itself was admirable. Bonham was to retire from Fairfax Court-House, as the enemy advanced, and take his place behind Mitchell's Ford on the Centreville and Manassas Junction road. It was proposed that he should engage his rear-guard so as to try to bring on the battle against him, as he approached his crossing of Bull Run, when the brigades along the Run on his right should cross, wheel to the left and attack on the enemy's left and rear.

We had occasional glimpses behind the lines about Washington, through parties who managed to evade the eyes of guards and sentinels, which told of McDowell's work since May, and heard on the 10th of July that he was ready to march. Most of us knew him and of his attainments, as well as of those of Beauregard, to the credit of the latter, so that on that point we were quite satisfied. But the backing of an organized government, and an army led by the foremost American war-chief, that consummate strategist, tactician, and organizer, General Scott, together with the splendid equipment of the field batteries, and the presence of the force of regulars of infantry, gave serious apprehension.

On the 16th of July notice came that the advance of McDowell's army was under definite orders for the next day. My brigade was at once ordered into position at Blackburn's Ford, and all others were ordered on the alert. Cocke's detachments were recalled to the fords between Mitchell's and Stone Bridge, and Evans was left to hold the bridge. Bonham withdrew from Fairfax Court-House as McDowell advanced. He retired behind the Run at Mitchell's Ford, his vedettes following after exchanging shots with the enemy's advance on the 18th. Early that morning a section of the Washington Artillery was posted on a rear line behind Blackburn's Ford, and trailed across towards the left, so as to flank fire against the direct advance upon Bonham at Mitchell's Ford.

At eight o'clock A.M. on the 18th, McDowell's army concentrated about Centreville, his immediate objective being Manassas Junction. From Centreville the Warrenton Turnpike bears off a little south of west, crossing Bull Run at Stone Bridge (four miles). The Manassas Junction road due south crosses at Mitchell's Ford (three miles). Other farm roads turned to the fords above and below Mitchell's. His orders to General Tyler, commanding the advance division, were to look well to the roads on the direct route to Manassas Junction and *via* the Stone Bridge, to impress an advance upon the former, but to have care not to bring on a general engagement. At the same time he rode towards his left to know of the feasibility of a turning move around the Confederates' right. There were three moves by which it was supposed he could destroy the Confederates,—first, by turning their right; second, by direct and forcible march to the Junction; third, by turning their left. McDowell's orders to his leading divisions indicated that he had settled down to a choice of one of the two flanking moves; but to justify either he must first test the feasibility of the direct route. The ride to his left disclosed rough ground, rocky heights cut by streamlets, and covered by heavy forest tangle, as formidable to military manœuvres of raw troops as armed battlements. According to preconceived plans, this eliminated the question of the flanking move by the Confederate right.

Under the instructions, as General Tyler construed them, he followed the Confederates to the heights of Centreville, overlooking the valley of Bull Run, with a squadron of cavalry and two companies of infantry. From the heights to the Run, a mile away, the field was open, and partially disclosed the Confederate position on his right. On the left the view was limited by a sparse growth of spreading pines. On the right was Mitchell's Ford, on the left Blackburn's. To have a better knowledge of the latter, he called up a brigade of infantry under General Richardson, Ayres's battery of six field-guns, and two twenty-pound rifle guns under Benjamin. The artillery was brought into action by the twenty-pound rifle guns, the first shot aimed at the section of the Washington Artillery six-pounders in rear of Blackburn's Ford, showing superior marksmanship, the ball striking close beside the guns, and throwing the dust over the limber and gunners.

It was noticed that the enemy was far beyond our range, his position commanding, as well as his metal, so I ordered the guns withdrawn to a place of safety, till a fairer opportunity was offered them. The guns were limbered and off before a second shot reached them. Artillery practice of thirty minutes was followed by an advance of infantry. The march was made quite up to the bluff overlooking the ford, when both sides opened fire.

The first pouring-down volleys were most startling to

the new troops. Part of my line broke and started at a run. To stop the alarm I rode with sabre in hand for the leading files, determined to give them all that was in the sword and my horse's heels, or stop the break. They seemed to see as much danger in their rear as in front, and soon turned and marched back to their places, to the evident surprise of the enemy. Heavy firing was renewed in ten or fifteen minutes, when the Federals retired. After about twenty minutes a second advance was made to the top of the bluff, when another rousing fusillade followed, and continued about as long as the first, with like result. I reinforced the front line with part of my reserve, and, thinking to follow up my next success, called for one of the regiments of the reserve brigade.

Colonel Hays, of the Seventh Louisiana Regiment, was sent, but was not in time for the next attack. He was in position for the fourth, and did his share in that fight. After the fourth repulse I ordered the advance, and called for the balance of the reserve brigade. The Fourth Brigade, in their drills in evolution, had not progressed as far as the passage of defiles. The pass at the ford was narrow, unused, and boggy. The lagoons above and below were deep, so that the crossing was intricate and slow. Colonel Early came in with his other regiments, formed his line behind my front, and was asked to hurry his troops to the front line, lest the next attack should catch him behind us, when his raw men would be sure to fire on the line in front of them. He failed to comprehend, however, and delayed till the next attack, when his men promptly returned fire at anything and everything before them. I thought to stop the fire by riding in front of his line, but found it necessary to dismount and lie under it till the loads were discharged. With the Federals on the bluff pouring down their fire, and Early's tremendous fire in our rear, soldiers and officers became mixed and a little confused. Part of my men got across the Run and partially up the bluff of the enemy's side; a body of the Union soldiers were met at the crest, where shots were exchanged, but passing the Run, encountering the enemy in front, and receiving fire from our friends in rear were not reassuring, even in handling veterans. The recall was ordered as the few of the enemy's most advanced parties joined issue with Captain Marye of my advance. Federal prisoners were brought in with marks of burnt powder on their faces, and Captain Marye and some of his men of the Seventeenth, who brought them in, had their faces and clothing soiled by like marks. At the first moment of this confusion it seemed that a vigorous pressure by the enemy would force us back to the farther edge of the open field, and, to reach that stronger ground, preparations were considered, but with the aid of Colonels Garland and Corse order was restored, the Federals were driven off, and the troops better distributed. This was the last effort on the part of the infantry, and was followed by the Federal batteries throwing shot and shell through the trees above our heads. As we were under the bluff, the fire was not annoying, except occasionally when some of the branches of the trees were torn off and dropped among us. One shot passed far over, and dropped in the house in which General Beauregard was about to sit down to his dinner. The interruption so annoyed him that he sent us four six-pound and three rifle guns of the Washington Artillery, under Captain Eshleman, to return fire and avenge the loss of his dinner. The guns had good cover under the bluff, by pushing them as close up as would admit of effective fire over it; but under tactical formation the limbers and caissons were so far in rear as to bring them under destructive fire. The men, thinking it unsoldierlike to flinch, or complain of their exposure, worked away very courageously till the limbers and caissons were ordered forward, on the right and left of the guns, to safer cover. The combat lasted about an hour, when the Federals withdrew to their ground about Centreville, to the delight of the Confederates. After this lively affair the report came of a threatened advance off to our right. General Beauregard recalled Early's command to its position in that quarter. He was ordered to march to the right, under the bluff, so that his men could not come within range of the batteries, but he chose to march back on the road leading directly to the rear, when the dust of his columns drew fire of a battery, and several damaging shots were thrown among his troops. The Confederate losses were sixty-eight; Federal, eighty-three. The effect of this little affair was encouraging to the Confederates, and as damaging to the Federals. By the double action of success and failure the Confederate infantry felt themselves christened veterans. The Washington Artillery was equally proud of its even combat against the famed batteries of United States regulars.

McDowell was disposed to ignore this fight as unwarranted under his instructions, and not a necessary adjunct of his plans. His course and that of the officers about him reduced the aggressive spirit of the division commander to its minimum, and had some influence upon the troops of the division. For battle at this time McDowell had 37,300* men and forty-nine guns. Beauregard had 20,500† men and twenty-nine guns.

---

* Rebellion Record, vol. ii. p. 309. Less two regiments and one cavalry troop.

† General Beauregard claims that he was not so strong, but estimates seem to warrant the number given.

CHAPTER III.

BATTLE OF MANASSAS, OR BULL RUN.

Commanders on both Sides generally Veterans of the Mexican War—General Irvin McDowell's Preconceived Plan—Johnston reinforces Beauregard and approves his Plans—General Bernard E. Bee—Analysis of the Fight—Superb Work of the Federal Artillery—Christening of "Stonewall Jackson"—McDowell's Gallant Effort to recover Lost Power—Before he was shorn of his Artillery he was the Samson of the Field—The Rout—Criticism of McDowell—Tyler's Reconnoissance—Ability of the Commanding Generals tested.

Before treating of future operations, I should note the situation of the Confederate contingents in the Shenandoah Valley and at Acquia Creek. The latter was ordered up to reinforce Beauregard as soon as the advance from Washington took definite shape, and arrived as a supporting brigade to his right on the 19th of July. At the same time orders were sent authorizing Johnston's withdrawal from the Valley, to join with Beauregard for the approaching conflict. The use of these contingents was duly considered by both sides some days before the campaign was put on foot.

Opposing Johnston in the Valley was General Robert Patterson, of Philadelphia, a veteran of the war of 1812 and of the Mexican War, especially distinguished in the latter by the prestige of the former service. Johnston was a veteran of the Mexican War, who had won distinction by progressive service and was well equipped in the science of war. Beauregard and McDowell were also veterans of the Mexican War, of staff service, and distinguished for intelligent action and attainments, both remarkable for physical as well as mental power.

Between Johnston and Beauregard the Blue Ridge stretched out from the Potomac southwest far below the

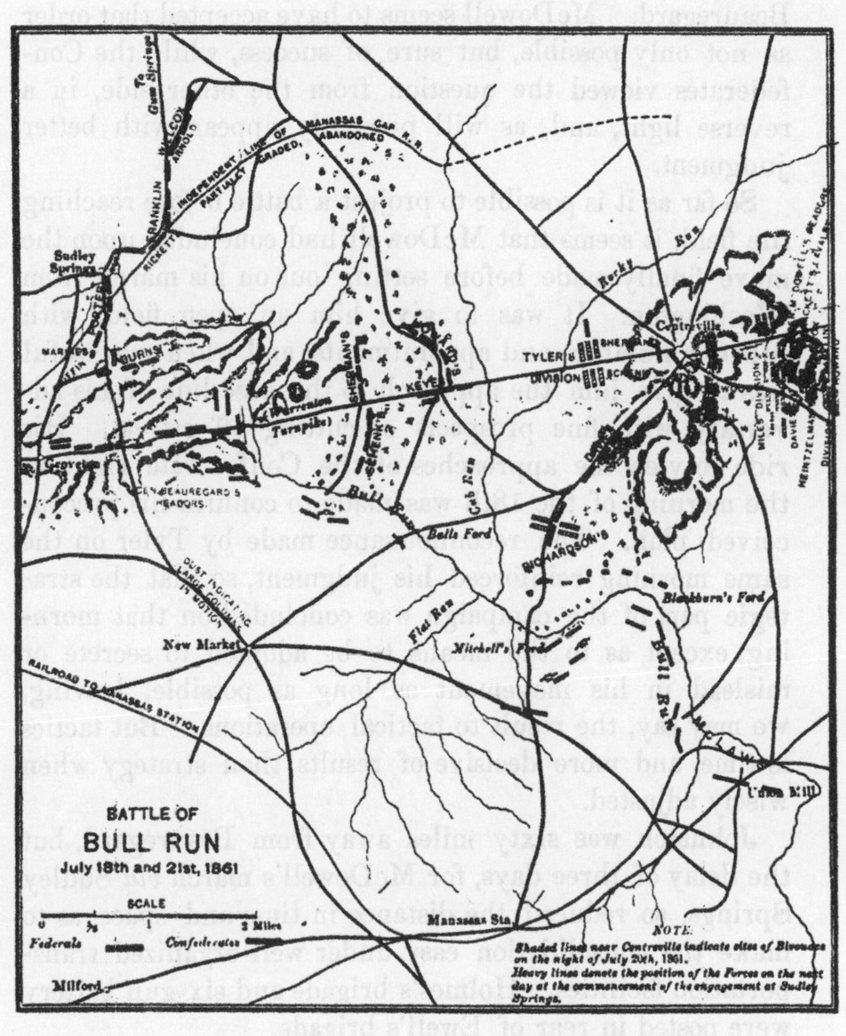
BATTLE OF
BULL RUN
July 18th and 21st, 1861
SCALE
0
½
2 Miles
Federals
Confederates
NOTE.
Shaded lines near Centreville indicate sites of Bivouacs on the night of July 20th, 1861.
Heavy lines denote the position of the Forces on the next day at the commencement of the engagement at Sudley Springs.
Sudley Springs
Groveton
GEN. BEAUREGARD'S HEADQRS.
(Warrenton Turnpike)
DUST INDICATING LARGE COLUMNS IN MOTION
New Market
RAILROAD TO MANASSAS STATION
Manassas Sta.
Milford
Balls Ford
Flat Run
Mitchell's Ford
Blackburn's Ford
Cub Run
Rocky Run
Centreville
Union Mill
TYLER'S DIVISION
RICHARDSON'S
KEYES
SHERMAN'S
MANASSAS GAP R.R.
ABANDONED
PARTIALLY GRADED
FRANKLIN
WILLCOX
ARNOLD
RICKETTS
To Gum Springs

southern line of Virginia, cut occasionally by narrow passes, quite defensible by small bodies of infantry and artillery. Patterson was ordered to hold Johnston in the Valley, while McDowell should direct his strength against Beauregard. McDowell seems to have accepted that order as not only possible, but sure of success, while the Confederates viewed the question from the other side, in a reverse light, and, as will presently appear, with better judgment.

So far as it is possible to project a battle before reaching the field, it seems that McDowell had concluded upon the move finally made before setting out on his march from Washington. It was to give him an open field, with superior numbers and appointments, and when successful was to give him the approach to the base line of his adversary with fine prospects of cutting off retreat. His ride to view the approaches of the Confederate right on the morning of the 18th was made to confirm his preconceived plan. The reconnoissance made by Tyler on the same morning reinforced his judgment, so that the strategic part of the campaign was concluded on that morning, except as to the means to be adopted to secrete or mislead in his movement as long as possible, leaving, we may say, the result to tactical operations. But tactics is time, and more decisive of results than strategy when wisely adjusted.

Johnston was sixty miles away from Beauregard, but the delay of three days, for McDowell's march *via* Sudley Springs, so reduced the distance in time and space as to make the consolidation easy under well-organized transportation facilities. Holmes's brigade and six-gun battery were posted in rear of Ewell's brigade.

General McDowell's order for battle on the 21st of July was issued on the afternoon of the 20th, directing his First Division to march by the Warrenton Turnpike, and make a diversion against the crossing of Bull Run at the

Stone Bridge, while the Second and Third Divisions, following on the turnpike, were to file to the right, along the farm road, about half-way between Centreville and the bridge, cross Bull Run at Sudley Springs, and bear down against the Confederate rear and left; the First Division, under Tyler, to march at two o'clock in the morning, to be closely followed by the others under Hunter and Heintzelman; the turning divisions, after crossing, to march down, clear the bridge, and lift Tyler over the Run, bringing the three into compact battle order.

General Johnston came in from the Shenandoah Valley on the 20th with the brigades of Bee, Bartow, and Jackson. The brigades were assigned by Beauregard, the former two in reserve near the right of Blackburn's Ford, the latter near its left.

Beauregard's order for battle, approved by General Johnston, was issued at five A.M. on the 21st,—the brigades at Union Mills Ford to cross and march by the road leading towards Centreville, and in rear of the Federal reserve at that point; the brigades at McLean's Ford to follow the move of those on their right, and march on a converging road towards Centreville; those at and near Blackburn's to march in co-operative action with the brigades on the right; the reserve brigades and troops at Mitchell's Ford to be used as emergency called, but in the absence of special orders to seek the most active point of battle.

This order was only preliminary, coupled with the condition that the troops were to be held ready to move, but to wait for the special order for action. The brigade at Blackburn's Ford had been reinforced by the Fifth North Carolina and Twenty-fourth Virginia Regiments, under Lieutenant-Colonel Jones and Colonel Kemper. I crossed the Run under the five o'clock order, adjusted the regiments to position for favorable action, and gave instructions for their movements on the opening of the battle.

While waiting for the order to attack, a clever reconnoissance was made by Colonels Terry and Lubbock, Texans, on the brigade staff, which disclosed the march of the heavy columns of the Federals towards our left. Their report was sent promptly to head-quarters, and after a short delay the brigade was ordered back to its position behind the Run.

Tyler's division moved early on the 21st towards the Stone Bridge. The march was not rapid, but timely. His first shells went tearing through the elements over the heads of the Confederates before six o'clock. The Second and Third Divisions followed his column till its rear cleared the road leading up to the ford at Sudley Springs, when they filed off on that route. McDowell was with them, and saw them file off on their course, and followed their march. His Fifth Division and Richardson's brigade of the First were left in reserve at Centreville, and the Fourth Division was left in a position farther rearward. The march of the columns over the single track of the farm road leading up to Sudley Springs was not only fatiguing, but so prolonged the diversion of Tyler's division at the bridge as to expose its real intent, and cause his adversary to look elsewhere for the important work. Viewing the zone of operations as far as covered by the eye, Evans discovered a column of dust rising above the forest in the vicinity of Sudley Springs. This, with the busy delay of Tyler in front of the bridge, exposed the plans, and told of another quarter for the approaching battle; when Evans, leaving four companies of infantry and two pieces of artillery to defend the bridge, moved with the rest of his command to meet the approaching columns off his left. Bearing in mind his care of the bridge, it was necessary to occupy grounds north of the pike. The position chosen was the plateau near the Matthews House, about a thousand yards north of the pike, and about the same distance from Bull Run, commanding the road by which the turning divisions of the enemy were to approach. His artillery (two six-pound guns) was posted to his right and left, somewhat retired. Meanwhile, Tyler's batteries maintained their position at and below the Stone Bridge, as did those near the lower fords. McDowell's column crossed at Sudley's Ford at nine o'clock, and approached Evans a few minutes before ten. The leading division under Hunter, finding Evans's command across its route, advanced the Second Rhode Island Regiment and battery of six guns of Burnside's brigade to open the way. Evans's infantry and artillery met the advance, and after a severe fight drove it back * to the line of woodland, when Burnside, reinforced by his other three regiments, with them advanced eight guns. This attack was much more formidable, and pressed an hour or more before their forces retired to the woodland. The fight, though slackened, continued, while the brigade under Porter advanced to Burnside's support.

Waiting some time to witness the opening of his aggressive fight towards Centreville, Beauregard found at last that his battle order had miscarried. While yet in doubt as to the cause of delay, his attention was drawn to the fight opened by McDowell against Evans. This affair, increasing in volume, drew him away from his original point and object of observation. He reconsidered the order to attack at Centreville, and rode for the field just opening to severe work. The brigades of Bee and Bartow,—commanded by Bee,—and Jackson's, had been drawn towards the left, the former two near Cocke's position, and Jackson from the right to the left of Mitchell's Ford. They were to await orders, but were instructed, and intrusted, in the absence of orders, to seek the place where the fight was thickest. About twelve o'clock that splendid soldier, Bernard E. Bee, under orders to find the

* In that attack the division commander, General David Hunter, was wounded.

point of danger, construed it as calling him to Evans's support, and marched, without other notice than the noise of increasing battle, with his own and Bartow's brigades and Imboden's battery. The move against the enemy's reserve at Centreville suspended, Colonels Terry and Lubbock, volunteer aides, crossed the Run to make another reconnoissance of the positions about Centreville. Captain Goree, of Texas, and Captain Sorrel, of Georgia, had also joined the brigade staff. As Bee approached Evans he formed line upon the plateau at the Henry House, suggesting to Evans to withdraw to that as a better field than the advance ground held by the latter; but in deference to Evans's care for the bridge, which involved care for the turnpike, Bee yielded, and ordered his troops to join Evans's advance. Imboden's artillery, however, failed to respond, remaining on the Henry plateau; leaving Bee and Evans with two six-pounder smooth-bore guns to combat the enemy's formidable batteries of eight to twelve guns of superior metal, as well as the accumulating superior infantry forces, Imboden's battery making a show of practice with six-pounders at great range. Bee's infantry crossed Young's Branch under severe fire, and were posted on the line of Evans's battle.

Burnside was reinforced by Porter's brigade, and afterwards by a part of Heintzelman's division. Ricketts's battery, and subsequently the battery under Griffin, pressed their fight with renewed vigor. The batteries, particularly active and aggressive, poured incessant fire upon the Confederate ranks, who had no artillery to engage against them except Imboden's, far off to the rear, and the section of Latham's howitzers. The efforts of the Federal infantry were cleverly met and resisted, but the havoc of those splendid batteries was too severe, particularly Griffin's, that had an oblique fire upon the Confederates. It was the fire of this battery that first disturbed our ranks on their left, and the increasing pounding of that and Ricketts's eventually unsettled the line. At this juncture two brigades of Tyler's division, with General W. T. Sherman and General Keyes, crossed the Run at a ford some distance above the bridge and approached the Confederate right, making more unsettled their position. At the same time the attacking artillery and infantry followed up their opportunity in admirable style, pushed the Confederates back, and pursued down to the valley of Young's Branch.

At one P.M., Colonels Terry and Lubbock returned from their reconnoissance of the ground in front of Centreville, with a diagram showing points of the Union lines and troops there posted. I sent it up to head-quarters, suggesting that the brigades at the lower fords be put across the Run, and advance against the reserves as designed by the order of the morning. Colonel Terry returned with the suggestion approved, and we communicated the same to the brigades at McLean's and Union Mills Fords, commanded by officers of senior dates to myself. The brigades were prepared, however, for concert of action. Bee, Bartow, and Evans made valorous efforts, while withdrawing from their struggle on the Matthews plateau, to maintain the integrity of their lines, and with some success, when General Wade Hampton came with his brigade to their aid, checked the progress of pursuit, and helped to lift their broken ranks to the plateau at the Henry House. The fight assumed proportions which called for the care of both General Johnston and General Beauregard, who, with the movements of their right too late to relieve the pressure of the left, found it necessary to draw their forces to the point at which the battle had been forced by the enemy. At the same time the reserve brigades of their right were called to the left. General Thomas J. Jackson also moved to that quarter, and reached the rear crest of the plateau at the Henry House while yet Bee, Bartow, Evans, and Hampton were climbing to the forward crest. Quick to note a proper ground, Jackson deployed on the crest at the height, leaving the open of the plateau in front. He was in time to secure the Imboden battery before it got off the field, and put it into action. Stanard's battery, Pendleton's, and Pelham's, and part of the Washington Artillery were up in time to aid Jackson in his new formation and relieve our discomfited troops rallying on his flank. As they rose on the forward crest, Bee saw, on the farther side, Jackson's line, serene as if in repose, affording a haven so promising of cover that he gave the christening of "Stonewall" for the immortal Jackson.

"There," said he, "is Jackson, standing like a stone wall."

General Johnston and General Beauregard reached the field, and busied themselves in getting the troops together and in lines of defence. Other reinforcements were ordered from the right, including the reserve brigades at McLean's and Union Mills Fords, and a number of batteries. Bee and Evans reformed their lines upon Jackson's. After permitting Burnside's brigade to retire for rest, McDowell pushed his battle by his strong artillery arm, advancing against and turning the Confederate left, only giving some little time to select positions for his batteries to plunge more effective fire into the Confederate ranks. This time, so necessary for McDowell's renewal, was as important to the Confederates in getting their reinforcements of infantry and artillery in position, and proved of even greater value in lengthening out the fight, so as to give Kirby Smith and Elzey, just off the train from the Shenandoah Valley, time to appear at the last moment.

After arranging the new position of the troops about Jackson, General Johnston rode back to the Lewis House, where he could better comprehend the entire field, leaving Beauregard in charge of the troops engaged on his left.

McDowell gave especial care to preparing his batteries for renewal against the Confederate left. He massed Ricketts's and Griffin's batteries, and made their practice grand. So well executed was it that the Confederate left was again in peril, and, seeing reinforcements approaching towards their rear, General Johnston sent orders to the brigades at the lower fords revoking authority given them to advance against Centreville, and ordering their return to the south side, and the brigade at Union Mills was ordered to reinforce the Confederate left. The brigade at Blackburn's Ford received the recall order in ample time, but that at McLean's,—Jones's,—being a little farther away, became partially engaged before the recall reached it. The brigades resumed their former position, however, without serious trouble.

With this order came a message to me, saying that the Federals were pressing severely on our left, and to the limit of its tension, that reinforcements were in sight, approaching their right, which might prove too heavy for our brave men, and force us back, for which emergency our brigades should be held ready to cover retreat. These anxious moments were soon relieved by the approach of General Kirby Smith's command, that had been mistaken as reinforcements for the enemy. General Smith was wounded, but was succeeded in command by the gallant Elzey, who by a well-timed attack approached the rear of the massed batteries. At the same time a brave charge on the part of Beauregard, in co-operation with this fortunate attack of Smith and Elzey, captured the greater part of the batteries and turned some of the guns upon the brave men who had handled them so well.

McDowell made a gallant effort to recover his lost power, riding with his troops and urging them to brave efforts, but our convex line, that he was just now pressing back upon itself, was changed. Though attenuated, it had become concave by reinforcement, and in elliptical curve was delivering a concentrated fire upon its adversary. Before the loss of his artillery he was the Samson of the field; now he was not only shorn of his power, but some of his mighty strength was transferred to his adversary, leaving him in desperate plight and exposed to blows increasing in force and effectiveness. Although his renewed efforts were brave, his men seemed to have given confidence over to despair. Still a show of battle was made until General Johnston directed the brigades of Holmes and Early to good positions for attack, when fight was abandoned and flight ensued.

The regulars under Sykes maintained order, and with the regular cavalry covered the confused retreat. The Confederates in the field and approaching at the moment were ordered in pursuit. At the same time another order was sent the brigades at the lower fords, explaining that the reinforcements, supposed to be Federals, proved to be Confederates, and that the former were not only forced back, but were then in full retreat, directing our brigades to cross again and strike the retreating line on the turnpike. All of D. R. Jones's brigade that had crossed at McLean's Ford under the former order had not yet returned to its position under the order to that effect, and Ewell had gone from Union Mills Ford to the battle on the extreme left, so that neither of them came in position ready to take part in the pursuit. Those at Mitchell's and Blackburn's Fords advanced, the former, under General Bonham, with orders to strike at Cub Run, the latter at Centreville. Finding some obstruction to his march, General Bonham kept the Centreville road, and joined the brigade from Blackburn's, taking the lead as the ranking officer.

Through the abandoned camps of the Federals we found their pots and kettles over the fire, with food cooking; quarters of beef hanging on the trees, and wagons by the roadside loaded, some with bread and general provisions, others with ammunition. When within artillery range of the retreating column passing through Centreville, the infantry was deployed on the sides of the road, under cover of the forest, so as to give room for the batteries ordered into action in the open, Bonham's brigade on the left, the other on the right.

As the guns were about to open, there came a message that the enemy, instead of being in precipitate retreat, was marching around to attack the Confederate right. With this report came orders, or reports of orders, for the brigades to return to their positions behind the Run. I denounced the report as absurd, claimed to know a retreat, such as was before me, and ordered that the batteries open fire, when Major Whiting, of General Johnston's staff, rising in his stirrups, said,—

"In the name of General Johnston, I order that the batteries shall not open."

I inquired, "Did General Johnston send you to communicate that order?"

Whiting replied, "No; but I take the responsibility to give it."

I claimed the privilege of responsibility under the circumstances, and when in the act of renewing the order to fire, General Bonham rode to my side and asked that the batteries should not open. As the ranking officer present, this settled the question. By that time, too, it was near night. Colonel G. W. Lay, of Johnston's staff, supported my views, notwithstanding the protest of Major Whiting.

Soon there came an order for the brigades to withdraw and return to their positions behind the Run. General Bonham marched his brigade back, but, thinking that there was a mistake somewhere, I remained in position until the order was renewed, about ten o'clock. My brigade crossed and recrossed the Run six times during the day and night.

It was afterwards found that some excitable person, seeing Jones's brigade recrossing the Run, from its advance, under previous orders, took them for Federal troops crossing at McLean's Ford, and, rushing to head-quarters at the Junction, reported that the Federals were crossing below and preparing for attack against our right. And upon this report one of the staff-officers sent orders, in the names of the Confederate chiefs, revoking the orders for pursuit.

From the effective service of the two guns of Latham's battery, *at short range,* against the odds brought against them, the inference seems fair that the Imboden battery, had it moved under Bee's orders, could have so strengthened the position on the Matthews plateau as to hold it and give time for them to retire and meet General Jackson on the Henry plateau. Glorious Victory spread her generous wings alike over heroes and delinquents.

The losses of the Confederates in all arms were 1982. Federal losses in all arms, 3333* officers and soldiers, twenty-five cannon.†

On the 22d the cavalry troop of Captain Whitehead was sent forward with Colonel Terry, volunteer aide, on a ride of observation. They picked up a number of prisoners, and Colonel Terry cut the lanyards of the Federal flag over the court-house at Fairfax by a shot from his six-shooter, and sent the bunting to head-quarters.

The plan of the Union campaign was that their army in the Valley of the Shenandoah, under General Patterson, should stand so surely against the Confederates in that field, under General Johnston, as to prevent the withdrawal of the latter through the Blue Ridge, which goes to show that the concentration was considered, and thought possible, and that McDowell was, therefore, under some pressure to act in time to gain his battle before Johnston could have time for his swoop from the mountains. At

* Rebellion Record, vol. ii. pp. 351, 387, 405, 426.
† Ibid., 328.

Centreville on the 18th, McDowell was within five miles of his immediate objective,—Manassas Junction,—by the route of Tyler's reconnoissance. The Sudley Ford route involved a march of twenty miles and drew him nearer the reach of Johnston's forces. So, if Tyler's reconnoissance proved the route by Blackburn's Ford practicable, it was imperative on McDowell to adopt it. If it was proved impracticable, the route by Sudley's Ford was necessary and justified the delay. But it has been claimed that the Union commander did not intend to have the reconnoissance, and that he could have made his move a success by that route if he had adopted it; which, if true, would put him in a more awkward position than his defeat. He was right in his conclusion that the Confederates were prepared for him on that route, but it would have been a grave error to leave the shorter, more direct line for the circuitous route without first so testing the former as to know if it were practicable, knowing as he did that the Confederate left was in the air, because of leaven looked for from over the Blue Ridge. After the trial of General Tyler on the 18th, and finding the route closed against him, he should have given credit to the division commander and his troops for their courageous work, but instead he disparaged their efforts and put them under criticism. The experiment and subsequent events go to show that the route was not practicable except for seasoned troops.

McDowell's first mistake was his display, and march for a grand military picnic. The leading proverb impressed upon the minds of young soldiers of the line by old commanders is, "Never despise your enemy." So important a part of the soldier's creed is it, that it is enjoined upon subalterns pursuing marauding parties of half a dozen of the aborigines. His over-confidence led him to treat with levity the reconnoissance of General Tyler on the 18th, as not called for under his orders, nor necessary to justify his plans, although they involved a delay of three days, and a circuitous march around the Confederate left. Then, he put upon his division commander the odium of error and uncalled-for exposure of the troops. This broke the confidence between them, and worked more or less evil through the ranks in the after-part of the campaign. Had he recognized the importance of the service, and encouraged the conduct of the division commander, he would have drawn the hearts of his officers and soldiers towards him, and toned up the war spirit and *morale* of his men. Tyler was right in principle, in the construction of duty, under the orders, and in his more comprehensive view of the military zodiac. In no other way than by testing the strength along the direct route could McDowell justify delay, when time was power, and a long march with raw troops in July weather was pending.

The delay gave Beauregard greater confidence in his preconceived plan, and brought out his order of the 21st for advance towards McDowell's reserve at Centreville, but this miscarried, and turned to advantage for the plans of the latter.

Had a prompt, energetic general been in command when, on the 20th, his order of battle was settled upon, the division under Tyler would have been deployed in front of Stone Bridge, as soon after nightfall as darkness could veil the march, and the divisions under Hunter and Heintzelman following would have been stretched along the lateral road in bivouac, so as to be prepared to cross Sudley's Ford and put in a good day's work on the morrow. Had General Tyler's action of the 18th received proper recognition, he would have been confident instead of doubting in his service. McDowell's army posted as it should have been, a march at daylight would have brought the columns to the Henry House before seven o'clock, dislodged Evans, busied by Tyler's display at the bridge, without a chance to fight, and brought the three divisions, reunited in gallant style, along the turnpike with little burning of powder. Thus prepared and organized, the compact battle-order of twenty thousand men would have been a fearful array against Beauregard's fragmentary left, and by the events as they passed, would have assured McDowell of victory hours before Kirby Smith and Elzey, of the Army of the Shenandoah, came upon the field.

Beauregard's mistake was in failing to ride promptly after his five-o'clock order, and handling his columns while in action. As events actually occurred, he would have been in overwhelming numbers against McDowell's reserve and supply depot. His adversary so taken by surprise, his raw troops would not have been difficult to conquer.

As the experience of both commanders was limited to staff service, it is not surprising that they failed to appreciate the importance of prompt and vigorous manœuvre in the hour of battle. Beauregard gave indications of a comprehensive military mind and reserve powers that might, with experience and thorough encouragement from the superior authorities, have brought him into eminence as a field-marshal. His adversary seemed untoward, not adapted to military organization or combinations. Most of his men got back to Washington under the sheltering wings of the small bands of regulars.

The mistake of supposing Kirby Smith's and Elzey's approaching troops to be Union reinforcements for McDowell's right was caused by the resemblance, at a distance, of the original Confederate flag to the colors of Federal regiments. This mishap caused the Confederates to cast about for a new ensign, brought out our battle-flag, led to its adoption by General Beauregard, and afterwards by higher authority as the union shield of the Confederate national flag.

The supplies of subsistence, ammunition, and forage

passed as we marched through the enemy's camps towards Centreville seemed ample to carry the Confederate army on to Washington. Had the fight been continued to that point, the troops, in their high hopes, would have marched in terrible effectiveness against the demoralized Federals. Gaining confidence and vigor in their march, they could well have reached the capital with the ranks of McDowell's men. The brigade at Blackburn's Ford (five regiments), those at McLean's and Mitchell's Fords, all quite fresh, could have been reinforced by all the cavalry and most of the artillery, comparatively fresh, and later by the brigades of Holmes, Ewell, and Early. This favorable aspect for fruitful results was all sacrificed through the assumed authority of staff-officers who, upon false reports, gave countermand to the orders of their chiefs.

On the 21st a regiment and battery were discharged from the Union army, reducing its aggregate to about 34,000. The Confederates had 31,860. McDowell crossed Bull Run with 18,500 of his men, and engaged in battle 18,053 Confederates.

There seem to be no data from which the precise figures can be had. These estimates, though not strictly accurate, are justified by returns so far as they have been officially rendered.

The CONFEDERATE ARMY in this battle was organized as follows:

ARMY OF THE POTOMAC (afterwards called ARMY OF NORTHERN VIRGINIA, FIRST CORPS), under Brig.-Gen. G. T. Beauregard:—*Infantry: First Brigade*, under Brig.-Gen. M. S. Bonham, 11th N. C., 2d, 3d, 7th, and 8th S. C.; *Second Brigade*, Brig.-Gen. R. S. Ewell, 5th and 6th Ala., 6th La.; *Third Brigade*, Brig.-Gen. D. R. Jones, 17th and 18th Miss., 5th S. C.; *Fourth Brigade*, Brig.-Gen. James Longstreet, 5th N. C., 1st, 11th, and 17th Va.; *Fifth Brigade*, Col. P. St. George Cocke, 1st La. Battn., 8th Va. (seven companies), 18th, 19th, 28th, and 49th Va. (three companies); *Sixth Brigade*, Col. J. A. Early, 13th Miss., 4th S. C., 7th and 24th Va.; *Troops not brigaded:* 7th and 8th La., Hampton Legion, S. C., 30th Va. (cav.), Harrison's Battn. (cav.); *Independent companies:* 10th Cav., Washington (La.) Cav.; *Artillery:* Kemper's, Latham's, Loudoun, and Shield's batteries, Camp Pickens companies.

ARMY OF THE SHENANDOAH (JOHNSTON'S DIVISION), Brig.-Gen. Joseph E. Johnston :—*First Brigade*, Col. T. J. Jackson, 2d, 4th, 5th, and 27th Va., Pendleton's Batt. ; *Second Brigade*, Col. F. S. Bartow, 7th, 8th, and 9th Ga., Duncan's and Pope's Ky. Battns., Alburti's Batt. : *Third Brigade*, Brig.-Gen. Bernard E. Bee, 4th Ala., 2d and 11th Miss., 1st Tenn., Imboden's Batt. ; *Fourth Brigade*, Col. A. Elzey, 1st Md. Battn., 3d Tenn., 10th and 13th Va., Grane's Batt. ; *Not brigaded* : 1st Va. Cav., 33d Va. Inf.

The FEDERAL ARMY, commanded by Brigadier-General Irvin McDowell, was organized as follows :

FIRST DIVISION, Brig.-Gen. Daniel Tyler :—*First Brigade*, Col. E. D. Keyes, 2d Me., 1st, 2d, and 3d Conn. ; *Second Brigade*, Brig.-Gen. R. C. Schenck, 2d N. Y., 1st and 2d Ohio, Batt. E, 2d U. S. Art. ; *Third Brigade*, Col. W. T. Sherman, 13th, 69th, and 79th N. Y., 2d Wis., Batt. E, 3d U. S. Art. ; *Fourth Brigade*, Col. I. B. Richardson, 1st Mass., 12th N. Y., 2d and 3d Mich., Batt. G, 1st U. S. Art., Batt. M, 2d U. S. Art.

SECOND DIVISION, (1) Col. David Hunter (wounded) ; (2) Col. Andrew Porter :—*First Brigade*, Col. Andrew Porter, 8th (militia), 14th, and 27th N. Y., Battn. U. S. Inf., Battn. U. S. Marines, Battn. U. S. Cav., Batt. D, 5th U. S. Art. ; *Second Brigade*, Col. A. E. Burnside, 2d N. H., 1st and 2d R. I., 71st N. Y.

THIRD DIVISION, Col. S. P. Heintzelman (wounded) :—*First Brigade*, Col. W. B. Franklin, 5th and 11th Mass., 1st Minn., Batt. I, 1st U. S. Art. ; *Second Brigade*, Col. O. B. Wilcox (wounded and captured), 11th N. Y. (Fire Zouaves), 38th N. Y., 1st and 4th Mich., Batt. D, 2d U. S. Art. ; *Third Brigade*, Col. O. O. Howard, 3d, 4th, and 5th Me., 2d Vt.

FOURTH (RESERVE) DIVISION,* Brig.-Gen. Theodore Runyon, 1st, 2d, 3d, and 4th N. J. (three months), 1st, 2d, and 3d N. J., 41st N. Y. (three years).

FIFTH DIVISION, Col. Dixon S. Miles :—*First Brigade*,† Col. Louis Blenker, 8th N. Y. (Vols.), 29th and 39th N. Y., 27th Penn., Batt. A, 2d U. S. Art., Rookwood's N. Y. Batt. ; *Second Brigade*, Col. Thomas A. Davies, 16th, 18th, 31st, and 32d N. Y., Batt. G, 2d U. S. Art.

*** Not engaged.**

† In reserve at Centreville and not in battle proper.

CHAPTER IV.

THE CONFEDERATES HOVERING AROUND WASHINGTON.

An Early War-Time Amenity—The Author invited to dine with the Enemy—"Stove-pipe Batteries"—J. E. B. Stuart, the Famous Cavalryman—His Bold Dash on the Federals at Lewinsville—Major-General G. W. Smith associated with Johnston and Beauregard in a Council—Longstreet promoted Major-General—Fierce Struggle at Ball's Bluff—Dranesville a Success for the Union Arms—McClellan given the Sobriquet of "The Young Napoleon."

AFTER General McDowell reached Washington my brigade was thrown forward, first to Centreville, then to Fairfax Court-House, and later still to Falls Church and Munson's and Mason's Hills; the cavalry, under Colonel J. E. B. Stuart, constituting part of the command.

We were provokingly near Washington, with orders not to attempt to advance even to Alexandria. Well-chosen and fortified positions, with soldiers to man them, soon guarded all approaches to the capital. We had frequent little brushes with parties pushed out to reconnoitre. Nevertheless, we were neither so busy nor so hostile as to prevent the reception of a cordial invitation to a dinner-party on the other side, to be given to me at the head-quarters of General Richardson. He was disappointed when I refused to accept this amenity, and advised him to be more careful lest the politicians should have him arrested for giving aid and comfort to the enemy. He was a singularly devoted friend and admirer before the war, and had not ceased to be conscious of old-time ties.

The service at Falls Church, Munson's and Mason's Hills was first by my brigade of infantry, a battery, and Stuart's cavalry. During that service the infantry and batteries were relieved every few days, but the cavalry was kept at the front with me. As the authorities allowed me but one battery, and that was needed from time to time to strike out at anything and everything that came outside the fortified lines, we collected a number of old wagon-wheels and mounted on them stove-pipes of different calibre, till we had formidable-looking batteries, some large enough of calibre to threaten Alexandria, and even the National Capitol and Executive Mansion. It is needless to add that Munson's Hill was so safe as not to disturb our profound slumbers. This was before the Federals began to realize all of their advantages by floating balloons above our heads.

One of the most conspicuous and successful of our affairs occurred on the 11th of September. A brigade of the enemy's infantry, with eight pieces of artillery and a detachment of cavalry, escorting a reconnoitring party, advanced to Lewinsville. If they had secured and fortified a position there they would have greatly annoyed us. Colonel Stuart, who from the start had manifested those qualities of daring courage, tempered by sagacity, which so admirably fitted him for outpost service, had his pickets so far to the front that he was promptly informed of the presence of the enemy. He was ordered, with about eight hundred infantry, a section of Rosser's battery, and Captain Patrick's troop of cavalry, to give battle, and so adroitly approached the enemy as to surprise him, and by a bold dash drove him off in confusion, with some loss.

We had a number of small affairs which served to season the troops and teach the importance of discipline and vigilance. It was while at Falls Church that Major-General G. W. Smith reported for duty with the Army of Northern Virginia, and was associated with General Johnston and General Beauregard, the three forming a council for the general direction of the operations of the army. General McClellan had by this time been appointed to superior command on the Federal side.

Despairing of receiving reinforcement to enable him to

GENERAL J. E. B. STUART.

assume the offensive, General Johnston regarded it as hazardous to hold longer the advanced post of Munson's and Mason's Hills, drew the troops back to and near Fairfax Court-House, and later, about the 19th of October, still farther to Centreville, and prepared for winter quarters by strengthening his positions and constructing huts, the line extending to Union Mills on the right. These points were regarded as stronger in themselves and less liable to be turned than the positions at and in advance of Fairfax Court-House. We expected that McClellan would advance against us, but were not disturbed. I was promoted major-general, which relieved me of the outpost service, to which Colonel Stuart was assigned.

The autumn and early winter were not permitted to pass without some stirring incidents in our front. Soon after the battle of July 21, Colonel Eppa Hunton was ordered to reoccupy Leesburg with his regiment, the Eighth Virginia. Later, the Thirteenth, Seventeenth, and Eighteenth Mississippi Regiments were sent to the same vicinity, and with the regiment already there and a battery constituted the Seventh Brigade, Brigadier-General N. G. Evans commanding. To cover a reconnoissance and an expedition to gather supplies made by General McCall's division to Dranesville, General McClellan ordered General C. P. Stone, commanding at Poolesville, Maryland, to make a demonstration in force against Leesburg, and, if practicable, to dislodge the Confederates at that place. Early in the morning of the 21st of October four of General Stone's regiments crossed the Potomac at Edwards's Ferry, and about the same time five other regiments, under the immediate command of Colonel Baker, late United States Senator from Oregon, crossed the river above at Ball's Bluff. Leaving Colonel Barksdale with his Thirteenth Mississippi, with six pieces of artillery as a reserve, to hold in check the force that had crossed at Edwards's Ferry, Evans with his main force assailed the force under Colonel Baker, and after a long and fierce struggle, under a heavy fire of batteries on both sides of the river, drove them down the bluff to the river, many surrendering, others plunging into the river to recross, overcrowding and sinking the boats that had brought them over; some drowning in the Potomac.

Two months later, December 20, there was an affair at Dranesville which for us was by no means so satisfactory as Evans's at Leesburg and Ball's Bluff. It was known that food for men and horses could be found in the vicinity of Dranesville. All of the available wagons of the army were sent to gather and bring it in, and Colonel Stuart, with one hundred and fifty of his cavalry, the Sumter Flying Artillery (Captain A. S. Cutts), and four regiments of infantry detailed from different brigades, was charged with the command of the foraging party. The infantry regiments were the Eleventh Virginia, Colonel Samuel Garland; Tenth Alabama, Colonel Forney; Sixth South Carolina, Lieutenant-Colonel Secrest; and First Kentucky, Colonel Thomas Taylor; the cavalry, Ransom's and Bradford's.

General McCall, commanding the nearest Union division, happened just then to want those supplies, or, as seems more probable, had information through a spy of Stuart's expedition.

He took measures to gather the supplies, or surprise and perhaps capture or destroy Stuart's party. However that may be, when Stuart reached the vicinity of Dranesville he found himself in the presence of General Ord, who had under him his own brigade of five regiments of infantry, Easton's battery, two twenty-four-pound howitzers and two twelve-pound guns, and two squadrons of cavalry. Finding that he was anticipated, and that his only way of saving the train was to order it back to Centreville in all haste, Stuart decided to attack, in order to give it time to get to a place of safety, and despatched a detachment of cavalry on the turnpike towards Leesburg to warn the wagons to hasten back to Centreville, the cavalry to march between them and the enemy. He ordered his artillery and infantry to hasten to the front, and as soon as they came up assailed the enemy vigorously, continuing the engagement until he judged that his wagon-train had passed beyond danger; then he extricated his infantry and artillery from the contest, with a much heavier loss than he had inflicted on the enemy, leaving the killed and some of the wounded. It was the first success that had attended the Union arms in that quarter, and was magnified and enjoyed on that side. This action advanced McClellan considerably in popular estimation and led to the bestowal upon him, by some enthusiast, of the sobriquet "the Young Napoleon."

During the autumn and early winter the weather had been unusually fine. The roads and fields in that section were generally firm and in fine condition for marching and manœuvring armies. With the beginning of the new year winter set in with rain and snow, alternate freezing and thawing, until the roads and fields became seas of red mud.

As no effort of general advance was made during the season of firm roads, we had little apprehension of trouble after the winter rains came to make them too heavy for artillery service.

CHAPTER V.

ROUND ABOUT RICHMOND.

The Defences of the Confederate Capital—Army of Northern Virginia at Centreville—Aggressive Action—Council with the President and Secretary of War—Mr. Davis's High Opinion of McClellan—Operations on the Peninsula—Engagements about Yorktown and Williamsburg—Severe Toil added to the Soldiers' Usual Labors by a Saturated Soil.

Apropos of the attack upon Richmond, apprehended in the winter of 1861–62, it should be borne in mind that there were four routes supposed to be practicable for the advance of the enemy:

1. The original route by Manassas Junction and the Orange and Alexandria Railroad.

2. By crossing the Potomac near Potomac Creek, thence by Fredericksburg to Richmond.

3. By land,—the shortest,—to go down the Potomac to the Lower Rappahannock, landing at or near Urbana, and thence march for the Confederate capital.

4. By transports to Fortress Monroe, thence by the Peninsula, between the James and York Rivers.

General McClellan's long delay to march against General Johnston, when he was so near and accessible at Centreville, indicated that he had no serious thought of advancing by that route. To prepare to meet him on either of the other routes, a line behind the Rapidan was the chosen position.

General Beauregard had been relieved of duty in Virginia and ordered West with General A. S. Johnston.

The withdrawal from Centreville was delayed some weeks, waiting for roads that could be travelled, but was started on the 9th of March, 1862, and on the 11th the troops were south of the Rappahannock.

General Whiting's command from Occoquan joined General Holmes at Fredericksburg. Generals Ewell and Early crossed by the railroad bridge and took positions near it. Generals G. W. Smith's and Longstreet's divisions marched by the turnpike to near Culpeper Court-House. General Stuart, with the cavalry, remained on Bull Run until the 10th, then withdrew to Warrenton Junction.

During the last week of March our scouts on the Potomac reported a large number of steamers, loaded with troops, carrying, it was estimated, about one hundred and forty thousand men, passing down and out of the Potomac, destined, it was supposed, for Fortress Monroe, or possibly for the coast of North Carolina. We were not left long in doubt. By the 4th of April, McClellan had concentrated three *corps d'armée* between Fortress Monroe and Newport News, on the James River. The Confederate left crossed the Rapidan, and from Orange Court-House made connection with the troops on the Rappahannock at Fredericksburg. About the 1st of April, Generals Johnston and G. W. Smith were called to Richmond for conference with the War Department, leaving me in command. On the 3d I wrote General Jackson, in the Shenandoah Valley, proposing to join him with sufficient reinforcements to strike the Federal force in front of him a sudden, severe blow, and thus compel a change in the movements of McClellan's army. I explained that the responsibility of the move could not be taken unless I was with the detachment to give it vigor and action to meet my views, or give time to get back behind the Rapidan in case the authorities ordered its recall.

I had been left in command on the Rapidan, but was not authorized to assume command of the Valley district. As the commander of the district did not care to have an officer there of higher rank, the subject was discontinued.*

* *Vide* General Jackson's letters: Rebellion Record.

General Johnston, assigned to the Department of the Peninsula and Norfolk, made an inspection of his new lines, and on his return recommended that they should be abandoned. Meanwhile, his army had been ordered to Richmond. He was invited to meet the President to discuss military affairs, and asked General G. W. Smith and myself to go with him. The Secretary of War and General R. E. Lee were with the President when we met.

It was the first time that I had been called to such august presence, to deliberate on momentous matters, so I had nothing to say till called on. The views intended to be offered were prefaced by saying that I knew General McClellan; that he was a military engineer, and would move his army by careful measurement and preparation; that he would not be ready to advance before the 1st of May. The President interrupted, and spoke of McClellan's high attainments and capacity in a style indicating that he did not care to hear any one talk who did not have the same appreciation of our great adversary. McClellan had been a special favorite with Mr. Davis when he was Secretary of War in the Pierce administration, and he seemed to take such reflections upon his favorites as somewhat personal. From the hasty interruption I concluded that my opinion had only been asked through polite recognition of my presence, not that it was wanted, and said no more. My intention was to suggest that we leave Magruder to look after McClellan, and march, as proposed to Jackson a few days before, through the Valley of Virginia, cross the Potomac, threaten Washington, and call McClellan to his own capital.

At the time of McClellan's landing on the peninsula, the Confederate army on that line was commanded by Major-General J. Bankhead Magruder, and consisted of eleven thousand men of all arms. The defensive line was pitched behind the Warwick River, a sluggish stream that rises about a mile south of Yorktown, and flows south to its confluence with James River. The Warwick was dammed at different points, thus flooding the intervening low lands as far as Lee's Mills, where the river spreads into marsh lands. The dams were defended by batteries and rifle-trenches. The left rested at Yorktown, which was fortified by continuous earthworks, strong water and land batteries, and rifle-trenches reaching to the right, connecting with those behind the Warwick. Yorktown is on the right bank of York River, which narrows at that point, with Gloucester Point on the opposite bank. This point was also fortified, and held by a strong garrison. On the south side of the James, near its mouth, General Huger held Norfolk, fortified and garrisoned by about ten thousand men, while the James River floated the Confederate vessels "Virginia" ("Merrimac"), "Yorktown," "Jamestown," and "Teaser."

McClellan's army, embarked from Alexandria and moved by transports to the vicinity of Fortress Monroe, as first collected, numbered one hundred and eight thousand of all arms, including the garrison at Fortress Monroe.

Magruder was speedily reinforced by a detachment from Huger's army, and afterwards by Early's brigade of Johnston's army, and after a few days by the balance of Johnston's army, the divisions of G. W. Smith, D. H. Hill, and Longstreet, with Stuart's cavalry, General Johnston in command.

General McClellan advanced towards the Confederate line and made some efforts at the dams, but it was generally understood that his plan was to break the position by regular approaches. After allowing due time for the completion of his battering arrangements, Johnston abandoned his line the night of May 3 and marched back towards Richmond, ordering a corresponding move by the troops at Norfolk; but the Confederate authorities interfered in favor of Norfolk, giving that garrison time to withdraw its army supplies. The divisions of G. W. Smith and D. H. Hill were ordered by the Yorktown and Williamsburg road, Magruder's and Longstreet's by the Hampton and Lee's Mill road, Stuart's cavalry to cover both routes.

Anticipating this move as the possible result of operations against his lower line, General Magruder had constructed a series of earthworks about two miles in front of Williamsburg. The main work, Fort Magruder, was a bastion. On either side redoubts were thrown up reaching out towards the James and York Rivers. The peninsula is about eight miles wide at that point. College Creek on the right flows into James River, and Queen's Creek on the left into the York, both giving some defensive strength, except at mill-dams, which were passable by vehicles. The redoubts on the left of Fort Magruder commanded the dam in Queen's Creek at Sanders's Pond, but the dam in College Creek was beyond protection from the redoubts.

The four redoubts on the right of Fort Magruder had commanding positions of the fort.

Finding the entire line of intrenchments at Yorktown empty on the morning of May 4, McClellan ordered pursuit by his cavalry under its chief, General Stoneman, with four batteries of horse artillery, supported by Hooker's division on the Yorktown road and W. F. Smith's on the Hampton road.

They were followed on the Hampton road by General Heintzelman (Kearny's division), Third Corps, and Couch's and Casey's divisions of Keyes's (Fourth) Corps, Sumner's (Second) Corps on the Yorktown road. Nearing Williamsburg, the roads converge and come together in range of field batteries at Fort Magruder. About eight miles out from Yorktown, on the Hampton road, Stuart, hearing of severe cavalry fight by the part of his command on the Yorktown road, thought to ride across to the enemy's rear and confuse his operations, but presently found a part of the enemy's cavalry and a battery under General Emory marching in his rear by a cross-road from the Yorktown road. He formed and charged in column of fours, gaining temporary success, but fell upon the enemy's battery, and found Benson prompt in getting into action, and in turn, with dismounted troopers, drove him back, cutting his line of retreat and forcing him off to the beach road along the James River. The march of Emory's cavalry across to the Hampton road misled Hooker's division to the same march, and that division, crowding the highway, caused Smith's division to diverge by a cross-road, which led it over into the Yorktown road. These misleadings delayed the advance on both roads. Emory followed Stuart until the latter in turn came upon strong grounds, where pursuit became isolated and hazardous.

The removal of the Confederate cavalry from the Hampton road left Hooker's march free of molestation. But not advised of the opportunity, he took the precautions usual on such occasions. His early approach, however, hurried the movements of the Confederate cavalry on the Yorktown road, and let the enemy in upon us on that road before we were advised of his approach.

General Johnston rode near the rear of his army to receive despatches from his cavalry commander. General Stuart wrote and sent them, but his couriers found the enemy's cavalry in the way and returned to him. The cavalry fight on the Yorktown road was also damaging to the Confederates, and not reported to the commanding general.

About four P.M., General Cook's cavalry and the horse artillery under Gibson debouched from the woodlands on the Yorktown road and began to examine the open ground in front of the Confederate field-works. General Johnston, who was at the rear, hurried Semmes's brigade of

McLaws's division into the nearest redoubts, and ordered McLaws to call back another brigade. Kershaw was ordered, and Manly's battery. The battery had to go at a run to be sure of their cover in the redoubts. Another battery was ordered by McLaws, who rode and took command. When Kershaw got to the fort, part of his men were deployed in the wood beyond, to his left.

Meanwhile, the Federal cavalry was advancing, Gibson's horse artillery and Manly's Confederate battery were in severe combat, the latter having the benefit of gun-proof parapets. Observing the approach of cavalry near his left, McLaws ordered two of Manly's guns into Fort Magruder, which, with the assistance of Kershaw's infantry, drove off that column. Some cavalry, riding near the left redoubt with little concern, were first taken for Confederates, but the next moment were identified as Federals, when the artillery was turned upon them, and, with the Confederate cavalry, pushed them quite away. When the left redoubt, commanding the dam at Sanders's Pond, was occupied by a part of Kershaw's men, McCarthy's battery came into action, and, with the assistance of others, gave Gibson's battery, in the open, serious trouble. McLaws ordered an advance of part of Semmes's brigade, led by Colonel Cummings. This, with the severe artillery fire from the redoubts and guns afield, cleared the open, leaving one of Gibson's guns in the mud, which was secured by McCarthy's men as a trophy of the day's work. Ten horses had been sent back to haul the piece off, but the mud was too heavy for them. Stuart, with the troopers of his immediate following and his section of horse artillery, crossed College Creek near James River, and came in after the action at the redoubts. Emory abandoned the pursuit as not feasible, and bivouacked on the route. Cavalry rencounters of the day were reported, in which both sides claimed success. Stuart reported Lieutenant-Colonel Wickham and four men wounded. Of the other side, Cooke reported thirty-five killed, wounded, and missing. Gibson reported one officer and four men wounded, and one gun abandoned. Emory reported two killed and four wounded, and Sanders one officer wounded. But most of the Federal losses were in the encounters at the redoubts with the artillery and infantry.

The enemy's cavalry reported the redoubt on the Confederate left unoccupied, and Hancock's brigade (Smith's division) was ordered forward to take it, but the woods through which he marched were tangled and swampy, and delayed him until night brought him to bivouac. Meanwhile, the Confederates who drove the cavalry from its reconnoissance had occupied the redoubt.

The corps commanders Sumner, Heintzelman, and Keyes and the cavalry leader Stoneman were together that night in conference. The highways, over flats but little above tide-water, were saturated by the spring rains, cut into deep ruts by the haul of heavy trains, and puddled by the tramp of infantry and cavalry. The wood and fallow lands were bogs, with occasional quicksands, adding severest labor to the usual toils of battle. So no plans were formed, further than to feel the way forward when there was light to see.

The enemy got some of our men who were worn out by the fatigue of the siege and the heavy march of the night and day.

CHAPTER VI.

THE BATTLE OF WILLIAMSBURG.

The Attack on Fort Magruder—Hancock occupies two Redoubts—The Slaughter in Early's Brigade—The Fifth North Carolina Regiment and Twenty-Fourth Virginia mercilessly exposed—A Hard-Fought Engagement—A Confederate Victory—McClellan not on the Field the Greater Part of the Day—Hancock called "The Superb" by McClellan—Johnston pays High Tribute to Longstreet.

BEFORE quitting his trenches at Yorktown, Johnston anticipated a move of part of McClellan's army by transports to the head of York River, to cut his line of march towards Richmond, and conceived it important to have a strong force at that point in time to meet and check the move. To that end he ordered Magruder to march at two A.M. on the 5th of May with D. R. Jones's and McLaws's divisions, to be followed by the divisions of G. W. Smith and D. H. Hill; Longstreet's division to cover the movement of his trains and defend Stuart's cavalry in case of severe pressure. Late in the afternoon of the 4th I was ordered to send a brigade to the redoubts to relieve McLaws's division. The brigades being small, I sent two, R. H. Anderson's and Pryor's, with Macon's battery, under Lieutenant Clopton, two guns under Captain Garrett, and two under Captain McCarthy, to report to General Anderson, the senior brigadier. At the time it was thought that the army would be on the march by daylight in the morning, and that the rear-guard would closely follow; but after nightfall a down-pour of rain came, flooding thoroughfares and by-ways, woodlands and fields, so that parts of our trains were stalled on the ground, where they stood during the night. It was dark when Anderson joined McLaws, who had drawn his men together in readiness to join the advance march. Anticipating an early march himself, Anderson occupied Fort Magruder and advanced his pickets so as to cover with their fire the junction of the Yorktown and Hampton roads. Heavy clouds and darkness settling down upon him, he made no effort at a critical survey of the surroundings; while the steady rain through the night gave signs of serious delay in the movements of the army, but he little thought that by the delay he could be called into battle. In the morning when time grew heavier he was advised to call in the brigades near him, in case he should need them, and instructions were sent them to answer his call.

At daylight he occupied the redoubts on the right of Fort Magruder, and two of those on the left. Two others farther on the left were not seen through the rain, and no one had been left to tell him of them or of the grounds. The field in his front and far off on his right was open. That in the immediate front had been opened by felling trees. On his left were woodland and the swampy creek. General Hooker's division of the Third Corps came to the open on the Hampton road at seven A.M. of the 5th, and engaged by regiments,—the First Massachusetts on his left, preceded by a battalion of skirmishers; the Second New Hampshire on the right, in the same order; Hancock's brigade of W. F. Smith's division of the Fifth Corps threatening on the Yorktown road; supported by part of Davidson's brigade and artillery. After the advance of his infantry in the slashes, General Hooker, with the Eleventh Massachusetts and Thirty-sixth Pennsylvania Regiments of Grover's brigade, cleared the way for communication with the troops on the Yorktown road, and ordered Webber's six-gun battery into action towards the front of the fallen timber. As it burst from the wood our infantry and every gun in reach opened upon it a fire so destructive that it was unmanned before it came into practice. Volunteers to man the battery were called, and with the assistance of men of Osborn's battery the guns were opened. Bramhall's battery was advanced and put into action on the right of Webber's, when the two poured an unceasing fire against our troops about the fort and redoubts. It was not very destructive, however, and we thought to reserve the ammunition.

The Fifth New Jersey Regiment, of Patterson's brigade, was added to the guard of the batteries, and the Sixth, Seventh, and Eighth were deployed on the left in the woodland. Anderson called up Wilcox's brigade, and ordered it to his right, reinforced it by the men of Pryor's brigade not needed at the forts, and presently called for the brigades of A. P. Hill and Pickett, to further support his right.

From the swelling noise of battle I concluded that it would be well to ride to the front, and ordered the remaining brigade (Colston's) and the batteries of Dearing and Stribling to follow. Stuart sent his horse artillery under Pelham into the action on the open field.

Viewing the ground on the left, I thought it not so well protected as Anderson conceived, and sent to D. H. Hill, who was but little advanced on his march, for one of his brigades. Early's was sent, to whose brigade were temporarily attached the Florida regiment and a Mississippi battalion. Anderson had left the fort, and was busy handling the brigades engaged in the woods on the right. Colston's was put in with the other brigades under Anderson, who afterwards called for another regiment. The Florida regiment and the Mississippi battalion were sent. Early, with his brigade, was posted on the field in rear of our left.

When it became evident that the fight was for the day, D. H. Hill was asked to return with the balance of his division. Meanwhile, Hooker was bracing the fight on his left. Emory reported to him with his cavalry and light battery, but as his fight was in the wood, Emory was asked to reconnoitre on his extreme left. The fight growing in the wood, Grover drew off part of his brigade to reinforce against it. The Seventy-second and Seventeenth New York Regiments of Taylor's brigade were also sent; then the Seventy-third and Seventy-fourth New York Regiments of the same brigade; but the Confederates gained ground gradually. They were, however, getting short of ammunition. While holding their line, some of the regiments were permitted to retire a little to fill their cartridge-boxes from those of the fallen of the enemy and of their comrades. This move was misconstrued into an order to withdraw, and the line fell back a little. But the mistake was rectified, and the ground that had been abandoned was recovered.

Hooker ordered the Eleventh Massachusetts and Twenty-sixth Pennsylvania Regiments to the support of the batteries, and the Second New Hampshire Regiment to his left. Anderson, drawing his troops together near the batteries, made a concentrated move upon them, and cleared them of the gunners, securing four of Webber's guns and forty horses. Just then he was reinforced by Colston's brigade, the Florida regiment, and the Mississippi battalion. General Stuart taking it that the enemy was badly broken and in retreat, rode up with his cavalry, insisting upon a charge and pursuit. As he did not recognize authority except of the commander-in-chief, he was cautioned that the break was only of the enemy's front, that he would find reinforcements coming up, and this he began to realize by the clearer ring of their muskets. He speedily encountered them, but in time to get away before meeting serious trouble. About three o'clock Kearny's division arrived, and only a few minutes later D. H. Hill's, of the Confederates. On the approach of Kearny's leading brigades, one regiment was detached from Berry's to reinforce Emory's Cavalry detachment on their left. The other regiments were deployed, the Fifth

Michigan across the road, the Thirty-seventh New York on its left, one company of the New York regiment from left to rear. Six companies of the Michigan regiment were broken to the rear from its right as reserve, leaving its forward battalion partly across the road, while that in rear had three companies on the right and three on the left of the road. Two regiments of Birney's brigade were deployed, the Thirty-eighth on the right of, and the Fortieth across, the road, to relieve some of Hooker's regiments. Then Peck's brigade of Couch's division came, and was put in on the right, the One Hundred and Second Pennsylvania and the Fifty-fifth New York on the left, the Sixty-second New York in the wood, the Ninety-third Pennsylvania on the left, and after a little the Ninety-eighth Pennsylvania.

Before the reinforcements arrived for Hooker's relief, Anderson had established his advance line of skirmishers, so as to cover with their fire Webber's guns that were abandoned. The Federal reinforcing columns drove back his advance line, when, in turn, he reinforced, recovered the ground, and met General Peck, who led the last reinforcing brigade. This advance was so firm that General Peck found it necessary to put in his last regiment, the Ninety-eighth Pennsylvania, but neither our force nor our condition of march could warrant further aggressive work of our right. General Couch, left in command on the Federal left, posted his troops for the night,—General Devens with the Seventh Massachusetts Regiment and Second Rhode Island, General Palmer with two, and General Keim with three other regiments, supporting General Peck. General Peck's ammunition being exhausted, his brigade was relieved by six of the new regiments, and reported that "Every preparation was made to resist a night attack."* On the Confederate side, General

* Rebellion Record, vol. xi. part i. p. 521.

Anderson reported his position safe to hold until the time to withdraw for the march. About noon, General Hancock, in command of his own and Davidson's brigades in front of our left, started with three of his own regiments and two of Davidson's and the six-gun battery under Lieutenant Carson in search of the unoccupied redoubts in that quarter. He approached by the dam at Sanders's Pond, passed the dam, and occupied one of the redoubts, leaving three companies to guard a road crossing on the right of his line of march. He put three companies of infantry in the redoubt and advanced his regiments and battery to the field in front. He then found another redoubt not occupied, and posted three other companies in it. He was reinforced by a four-gun battery under Captain Wheeler, which he posted in rear of his line of battle and awaited developments. When the last engagement on our right had calmed down to exchange of desultory shots, D. H. Hill's division was waiting to know if Anderson would need further support. Meanwhile, some of his officers had made a reconnoissance in front of his ground, and reported a route by which favorable attack could be made upon the Federals at the redoubt under Hancock.

General Johnston had arrived at my head-quarters, near Fort Magruder, when General Hill sent to report the reconnoissance, and to ask that he be allowed to make a move against Hancock, by Early's brigade. General Johnston received the message, and referred the officer to me. I ordered that the move should not be made, explaining that we were only fighting for time to draw off our trains, that aggressive battle was necessary on our right in order to keep the enemy back in the woodland from the open, where, by his superior artillery and numbers, he might deploy beyond our limits, and turn us out of position; that on our left there was no cause for apprehension of such action, and we could not risk being drawn into serious delay by starting new work so late in the day. Very soon General Hill rode over to report of the opportunity: that he thought he could get through before night, and would not be likely to involve delay of our night march. General Johnston referred him to me. I said,—

"The brigade you propose to use is not in safe hands. If you will go with it, and see that the troops are properly handled, you can make the attack, but don't involve us so as to delay the march after night."

In a letter from General Hill, after the war, he wrote of the fight by this brigade,—

"I cannot think of it, till this day, without horror. The slaughter of the Fifth North Carolina Regiment was one of the most awful things I ever saw, and it was caused by a blunder. At your request, I think, I followed Early's brigade, following the right wing."

General Hill was in advance of the brigade with the Fifth and Twenty-third North Carolina Regiments, General Early in rear with the Twenty-fourth and Thirty-eighth Virginia Regiments. General Hill ordered the advance regiments to halt after crossing a streamlet and get under cover of the wood till the brigade could form; but General Early, not waiting for orders or the brigade, rode to the front of the Twenty-fourth Virginia, and with it made the attack. The gallant McRae, of the Fifth North Carolina, seeing the Twenty-fourth Virginia hotly engaged, dashed forward, *nolens volens,* to its relief. The other regiments, seeing the confusion of movements and of orders, failed to go forward. Part of my troops, on Early's right, seeing that a fight was open on that part of the field, started without orders to go to his relief, but found the fight lost before they were engaged. After the brigade was collected on its first position, General Johnston rode to his head-quarters. At dark the Confederates were withdrawn and took up the line of march, the division of D. H. Hill taking the rear of the column, Rains's brigade the rear of the division. On his march, General Rains found, in a broken-down ammunition-wagon, several loaded shells, four of them with sensitive fuse primers, which he placed near some fallen trees, cut down as obstructions. He afterwards heard that some of them were tramped upon by the Federal cavalry and exploded.

The pursuit was not active, hardly annoying. The roads were cut into deep mud by the trains, and the sideways by troops far out on either side, making puddles ankle-deep in all directions, so that the march was slow and trying, but giving almost absolute safe-conduct against pursuit, and our men were allowed to spread their ranks in search of ground strong enough to bear them.

My estimate, made on the field, of the troops engaged was, Confederate, 9000; Union, 12,000. The casualties of the engagement were, Confederate, 1565 aggregate;* Federal, 2288 aggregate.†

General McClellan was at Yorktown during the greater part of the day to see Franklin's, Sedgwick's, and Richardson's divisions aboard the transports for his proposed flanking and rear move up York River, but upon receiving reports that the engagement at Williamsburg was growing serious and not satisfactory, he rode to the battle, and called the divisions of Sedgwick and Richardson to follow him.

The object of the battle was to gain time to haul our trains to places of safety. The effect, besides, was to call two of the divisions from their flanking move to support the battle, and this so crippled that expedition that it gave us no serious trouble. The trophies of the battle were with the Confederates, and they claim the honor to inscribe Williamsburg upon their battle-flags.

* Rebellion Record, vol. xi. part i. p. 568.

† Ibid. p. 450.

The success of General Hancock in holding his position in and about the forts with five regiments and two batteries against the assault of the Fifth North Carolina and Twenty-fourth Virginia Regiments was given heroic proportions by his chief, who christened him "The Superb," to relieve, it is supposed, by the picturesque figure on his right, the discomfiture of his left. But, reading between the lines, the highest compliment was for the two Confederate regiments.

In his official account, General Johnston said,—

> "The action gradually increased in magnitude until about three o'clock, when General Longstreet, commanding the rear, requested that a part of Major-General Hill's troops might be sent to his aid. Upon this I rode upon the field, but found myself compelled to be a spectator, for General Longstreet's clear head and brave heart left no apology for interference."

Franklin's division was taken by transports to the mouth of Pamunkey River, and was supported by the navy. On the 7th a brigade of Sedgwick's division joined Franklin. On the same day, Johnston's army was collected near Barhamville. General Whiting, with Hood's brigade and part of Hampton's, engaged the advance of Franklin's command and forced it back. This cleared our route of march towards Richmond, Smith's and Magruder's divisions by the road to New Kent Court-House, Hill's and Longstreet's nearer the Chickahominy.

General McClellan's plans were laid according to strict rules of strategy, but he was not quick or forcible in handling his troops at Williamsburg or Barhamville.

CHAPTER VII.

SEVEN PINES, OR FAIR OAKS.

A New Line of Defence—Positions of the Confronting Armies—Fitz-John Porter—Terrific Storm on the Eve of Battle—General Johnston's Orders to Longstreet, Smith, and Huger—Lack of Co-operation on the Confederate Side, and Ensuing Confusion—Fatalities among Confederate Officers—Kearny's Action—Serious Wounding of General Johnston at the Close of the Battle—Summary and Analysis of Losses.

On the 9th of May the Confederate army was halted, its right near Long Bridge of the Chickahominy River; its left and cavalry extending towards the Pamunkey through New Kent Court-House. On the 11th the commander of the Confederate ram "Virginia" ("Merrimac"), finding the water of James River not sufficient to float her to the works near Richmond, scuttled and sank the ship where she lay.

On the 15th the Federal navy attacked our works at Chapin's and Drury's Bluffs, but found them too strong for water batteries. That attack suggested to General Johnston that he move nearer Richmond to be in position to lend the batteries assistance in case of need. He crossed the Chickahominy, his right wing at Long Bridge, his left by Bottom's Bridge, and took position from Drury's Bluff on his right, to the Mechanicsville turnpike, with his infantry, the cavalry extending on the left and front to the lower Rappahannock and Fredericksburg. The right wing, D. H. Hill's and Longstreet's divisions, under Longstreet, from James River to White Oak Swamp; the left under G. W. Smith. Smith's division and Magruder's command from White Oak Swamp, extending thence to the Mechanicsville pike, with Jackson a hundred miles away in the Shenandoah Valley.

After careful study of the works and armaments at Drury's Bluff, I ventured the suggestion that we recross the Chickahominy at Mechanicsville and stand behind Beaver Dam Creek, prepared against McClellan's right when he should be ready to march towards Richmond, and call him to relieve his flank before crossing the river.

Although the country between McClellan's landing on the Pamunkey to the Chickahominy was free of all obstacles on the 15th of May, the head of his advance did not reach the banks of the latter river till the 21st. On the 16th he established his permanent depot at the White House, on the Pamunkey, and organized two provisional army corps,—the Fifth, of Fitz-John Porter's division, and Sykes's, under command of Porter; the Sixth, of Franklin's and W. F. Smith's divisions, under Franklin. On the 26th the York River Railroad as far as the bridge across the Chickahominy was repaired and in use. This, with other bridges, was speedily repaired, and new bridges ordered built at such points as should be found necessary to make free communication between the posts of the army.

On the 24th parties were advanced on the Williamsburg road as far as Seven Pines, where a spirited affair occurred between General Naglee's forces and General Hatton's brigade, the latter withdrawing a mile and a half on the Williamsburg road. At the same time two other parties of Federals were sent up the left bank, one under General Davidson, of the cavalry, with artillery and infantry supports, as far as Mechanicsville, where he encountered and dislodged a Confederate cavalry force under Colonel B. H. Robertson and occupied the position. The third party, under Colonel Woodbury, the Fourth Michigan Infantry and a squadron of the Second United States Cavalry, moved up to New Bridge, where the Fifth Louisiana, Colonel Hunt, of Semmes's brigade, was on picket. Finding the bridge well guarded, a party, conducted by Lieutenant Bowen, Topographical Engineers, marched up the river, concealing their movements, crossed to the west bank, and, passing down, surprised the Fifth Louisiana, threw it into disorder, and gained position on the west side.

Pleased at these successes, General McClellan sent a sensational despatch to the President. His position thus masked, rested his right upon Beaver Dam Creek, a stream that flows from the height between the Chickahominy and Pamunkey Rivers south to its confluence with the former a few hundred yards below Mechanicsville Bridge. Its banks are scarped, about six feet high, and eight feet apart, making a strong natural ditch for defensive works.

On commanding ground south of the creek admirably planned field-works were soon constructed, which made that flank unassailable. Two miles out from the river the creek loses its value as a defensive line. From Beaver Dam the line was extended down the river to New Bridge, where it crossed and reached its left out to White Oak Swamp, and there found as defensible guard as the right at Beaver Dam Creek. The swamp is about a quarter of a mile wide at the left, and down to the Chickahominy studded with heavy forest-trees, always wet and boggy, but readily forded by infantry, and at places by cavalry.

Near the middle of the line, back from New Bridge, was Stoneman's cavalry. Fitz-John Porter's corps (Fifth) was posted at Beaver Dam Creek, Franklin's (Sixth) two miles lower down, Sumner's (Second) near the middle of the line, about three miles from the river. The Third and Fourth Corps were on the south side, Kearny's division of the Third at Savage Station of the York River Railroad, Hooker's division at White Oak Swamp Bridge, with entrenched lines. The Fourth Corps was posted on the Williamsburg road, Couch's division about a mile in advance of Hooker's, of the Third, at the junction of the Nine Miles road, entrenched, and field of abatis; Casey's division of the Third half a mile in advance of Couch's, entrenched, and field of abatis. The point occupied by Couch's division is known as Seven Pines. His advanced picket-guard on the Nine Miles road was at Fair Oaks Station of the York River Railroad.

The line, which was somewhat concave towards Richmond, was strengthened at vulnerable points by field-works. General Sumner was senior of the corps commanders, and in command of the right wing; General Heintzelman, the senior of the south side, was in command of the left wing. The Chickahominy is a hundred feet wide as far up as Mechanicsville Bridge, but narrows above to forty and thirty. Along the line of McClellan's deployment its course was through lowlands of tangled woods that fringe its banks, the valley seldom more than a hundred yards wide. Artillery was posted to command all bridges and those ordered for construction. On the 26th, General McClellan ordered General Fitz-John Porter to organize a force to march against a Confederate outpost near Hanover Court-House. Porter took of Morell's division three brigades,—Martindale's, Butterfield's, and McQuade's,—Berdan's Sharp-shooters and three batteries, two regiments of cavalry under General Emory, and Benson's horse battery; Warren's brigade to march up the right bank of the Pamunkey in connection with operations projected for the fighting column. Porter was the most skilful tactician and strongest fighter in the Federal army, thoroughly trained in his profession from boyhood, and of some experience in field work.

The Confederate outpost was commanded by Brigadier-General L. O'B. Branch, six regiments of infantry, one battery, under Captain Latham, and a cavalry regiment, under Colonel Robertson. General Branch was a brigadier from civil life. The result of the affair was the discomfiture of General Branch, with the loss of one gun and about seven hundred prisoners. Losses in action, not including prisoners: Confederates, 265; Federals, 285.

A. P. Hill was promoted to major-general, and assigned to command of a division at that outpost and stationed at Ashland.

On the 27th, General Johnston received information that General McDowell's corps was at Fredericksburg, and on the march to reinforce McClellan's right at Mechanicsville. He prepared to attack McClellan before McDowell could reach him. To this end he withdrew Smith's division from the Williamsburg road, relieving it by the division of D. H. Hill; withdrew Longstreet's division from its position, and A. P. Hill's from Ashland. The fighting column was to be under General G. W. Smith, his next in rank, and General Whiting was assigned command of Smith's division,—the column to consist of A. P. Hill's, Whiting's, and D. R. Jones's divisions. The latter was posted between the Mechanicsville pike and Meadow Bridge road. A. P. Hill was to march direct against McClellan's outpost at Mechanicsville, Whiting to cross the river at Meadow Bridge, and D. R. Jones at Mechanicsville, thus completing the column of attack on the east side.

I was to march by the Mechanicsville road to the vicinity of the bridge, and to strike down against the Federal right, west of the river, the march to be made during the night; D. H. Hill to post a brigade on his right on the Charles City road to guard the field to be left by his division, as well as the line left vacant by Longstreet's division.

At nightfall the troops took up the march for their several assigned positions. Before dark General Johnston called a number of his officers together for instructions,—viz., Smith, Magruder, Stuart, and Longstreet. When we were assembled, General Johnston announced later information: that McDowell's line of march had been changed,—that he was going north. Following the report of this information, General Smith proposed that the plan for battle should be given up, in view of the very strong ground at Beaver Dam Creek.* I urged that the plan laid against the concentrating columns was made stronger by the change of direction of McDowell's column, and should suggest more prompt and vigorous prosecution. In this Magruder and Stuart joined me. The *pros* and *cons* were talked over till a late hour, when at last General Johnston, weary of it, walked aside to a separate seat. I took the opportunity to draw near him, and suggested that the Federal position behind Beaver Dam Creek, so seriously objected to by General Smith, could be turned by marching to and along the high ground between the Chickahominy and Pamunkey Rivers; that the position of the enemy when turned would be abandoned without a severe struggle, and give a fair field for battle; that we should not lose the opportunity to await another possible one.

General Johnston replied that he was aware of all that, but found that he had selected the wrong officer for the work. This ended the talk, and I asked to be allowed to halt my columns as soon as possible. The other movements were arrested, except that of A. P. Hill's division, which was ordered to continue its march, cross the Chickahominy at Meadow Bridge, and take position between the Meadow Bridge road and the Brooke turnpike. The counter-order reinstated my command of the right wing, including D. H. Hill's division on the Williamsburg road and extending to the York River Railroad. Before leaving the conference, I announced that we would fight on the Williamsburg road if we had to find the enemy through bayous.

The order to halt the columns found Smith's division

* Smith's War Papers.

between the Mechanicsville and Meadow Bridge roads, Longstreet's near the city at the Nine Miles road; D. R. Jones had not moved.

On the 29th and 30th, General D. H. Hill sent out reconnoitring parties on the Williamsburg and Charles City roads. On the 30th he received a fair report of Casey's intrenched camp, and the probable strength and extent of the line of his skirmishers reaching out his left front to White Oak Swamp. On the 29th, General Johnston wrote General Whiting, commanding Smith's division, giving notice of a reconnoissance ordered by General Hill, cautioning the former that his division should be drawn towards the right, to be in better position for support of a battle of his right, and adding,—

> "Who knows but that in the course of the morning Longstreet's scheme may accomplish itself? If we get into a fight here, you will have to hurry to help us."

The report of General D. H. Hill's reconnoissance of the 30th was forwarded to head-quarters. I followed it, and found General Johnston ready to talk over plans for battle. General Huger had reported with three of his brigades, and was in camp near the outskirts of Richmond on Gillis Creek. The plan settled upon was that the attack should be made by General D. H. Hill's division on the Williamsburg road, supported by Longstreet's division. Huger's division, just out of garrison duty at Norfolk, was to march between Hill's right and the swamp against the enemy's line of skirmishers, and move abreast of the battle; G. W. Smith's division, under Whiting, to march by the Gaines road to Old Tavern, and move abreast of the battle on its left. The field before Old Tavern was not carefully covered by the enemy's skirmishers north of Fair Oaks, nor by parties in observation.

Experience during the discussion of the battle ordered for the 28th caused me to doubt of effective work from the troops ordered for the left flank, but the plan seemed so simple that it was thought impossible for any one to go dangerously wrong; and General Johnston stated that he would be on that road, the better to receive from his troops along the crest of the Chickahominy information of movements of the enemy on the farther side of the river, and to look to the co-operation of the troops on the Nine Miles road.

To facilitate marches, Huger's division was to have the Charles City road to the head of White Oak Swamp, file across it and march down its northern margin; D. H. Hill to have the Williamsburg road to the enemy's front; Longstreet's division to march by the Nine Miles road and a lateral road leading across the rear of General Hill on the Williamsburg road; G. W. Smith by the Gaines road to Old Tavern on the Nine Miles road.

The tactical handling of the battle on the Williamsburg road was left to my care, as well as the general conduct of affairs south of the York River Railroad, the latter line being the left of the field to which I had been assigned, the right wing.

While yet affairs were under consideration, a terrific storm of vivid lightning, thunderbolts, and rain, as severe as ever known to any climate, burst upon us, and continued through the night more or less severe. In the first lull I rode from General Johnston's to my head-quarters, and sent orders for early march.

For a more comprehensive view of affairs as ordered, it may be well to explain that General Johnston ordered Smith's division by the Gaines road, so that, in case of delay of its march, McLaws's division, on that road and nearer the field of proposed action, could be brought in to the left of the battle, leaving the place of his division to be occupied by Smith's, when the latter reached McLaws's vacated line. There was, therefore, no reason why the orders for march should be misconstrued or misapplied.

I was with General Johnston all of the time that he was engaged in planning and ordering the battle, heard every word and thought expressed by him of it, and received his verbal orders; Generals Huger and Smith his written orders.

General Johnston's order to General Smith was:

"HEAD-QUARTERS DEPARTMENT OF NORTHERN VIRGINIA,
"May 30, 9.15 P.M.

"MAJOR-GENERAL G. W. SMITH:

"GENERAL,—If nothing prevents, we will fall upon the enemy in front of Major-General Hill (who occupies the position on the Williamsburg road from which your troops moved to the neighborhood of Meadow Bridge) early in the morning, as early as practicable. The Chickahominy will be passable only at the bridge, a great advantage to us. Please be ready to move by the Gaines road, coming as early as possible to the point at which the road to New Bridge turns off. Should there be cause for haste, Major-General McLaws, on your approach, will be ordered to leave his ground for you, that he may reinforce General Longstreet.

"Most respectfully your obedient servant,
"J. E. JOHNSTON." *

General Johnston's order for General Huger read:

"HEAD-QUARTERS DEPARTMENT OF NORTHERN VIRGINIA,
"May 30, 1862, 8.30 P.M.

"MAJOR-GENERAL HUGER:

"GENERAL,—The reports of Major-General D. H. Hill give me the impression that the enemy is in considerable strength in his front. It seems to me necessary that we should increase our force also; for that object I wish to concentrate the troops of your division on the Charles City road, and to concentrate the troops of Major-General Hill on the Williamsburg road. To do this it will be necessary for you to move, as early in the morning as possible, to relieve the brigade of General Hill's division now on the Charles City road. I have desired General Hill to send you a guide. The road is the second large one diverging to the right

* Rebellion Record, vol. xi. part iii. p. 563.

from the Williamsburg road. The first turns off near the toll-gate. On reaching your position on the Charles City road, learn at once the route to the main roads, to Richmond on your right and left, especially those to the left, and try to find guides. Be ready, if an action should begin on your left, to fall upon the enemy's left flank.

"Most respectfully your obedient servant,

"J. E. JOHNSTON.

"P.S.—It is necessary to move very early." *

The Nine Miles road takes the name from the distance by that road from Richmond to Seven Pines. The Williamsburg road to the same point was sometimes called the Seven Miles road, because of the distance by that road to Seven Pines.

As expressed and repeated in his orders, General Johnston's wish was to have the battle pitched as early as practicable. When his orders were issued, he was under the impression that I would be the ranking officer on the right of the York Railroad, and would give detailed instructions to govern the later operations of Huger's troops.

Subsequent events seem to call for mention just here that General Smith, instead of moving the troops by the route assigned them, marched back to the Nine Miles road near the city, rode to Johnston's head-quarters about six in the morning, and reported that he was with the division, but not for the purpose of taking command from General Whiting. As General Johnston did not care to order him back to his position as commander of the left wing, he set himself to work to make trouble, complained that my troops were on the Nine Miles road in the way of his march, and presently complained that they had left that road and were over on the Williamsburg road, and induced General Johnston to so far modify the plans as to

* Rebellion Record, vol. xi. part i. p. 938.

order three of my brigades down the Nine Miles road to the New Bridge fork.

The order was sent by Lieutenant Washington, of Johnston's staff, who, unused to campaigning, failed to notice that he was not riding on my line of march, and rode into the enemy's lines. This accident gave the enemy the first warning of approaching danger; it was misleading, however, as it caused General Keyes to look for the attack by the Nine Miles road.

The storms had flooded the flat lands, and the waters as they fell seemed weary of the battle of the elements, and inclined to have a good rest on the soft bed of sand which let them gently down to the substratum of clay; or it may have been the purpose of kind Providence to so intermix the upper and lower strata as to interpose serious barriers to the passing of artillery, and thus break up the battle of men.

My march by the Nine Miles and lateral roads leading across to the Williamsburg road was interrupted by the flooded grounds about the head of Gillis Creek. At the same time this creek was bank full, where it found a channel for its flow into the James. The delay of an hour to construct a bridge was preferred to the encounter of more serious obstacles along the narrow lateral road, flooded by the storm. As we were earlier at the creek, it gave us precedence over Huger's division, which had to cross after us. The division was prepared with cooked rations, had wagons packed at six o'clock, and rested in the rear of General Hill's at nine A.M.

Meanwhile, General G. W. Smith's division had marched by the Nine Miles road and was resting near the fork of the New Bridge road at Old Tavern. Upon meeting General Huger in the morning, I gave him a succinct account of General Johnston's plans and wishes; after which he inquired as to the dates of our commissions, which revealed that he was the ranking officer, when I suggested that it was only necessary for him to take command and execute the orders. This he declined. Then it was proposed that he should send two of his brigades across to join on the right of the column of attack, while he could remain with his other brigade, which was to relieve that of General Hill on the Charles City road. Though he expressed himself satisfied with this, his manner was eloquent of discontent. The better to harmonize, I proposed to reinforce his column by three of my brigades, to be sent under General Wilcox, to lead or follow his division, as he might order. Under this arrangement it seemed that concert of action was assured. I gave especial orders to General Wilcox to have care that the head of his column was abreast the battle when it opened, and rode forward to join General Hill, my other three brigades advancing along the Williamsburg road.

Opposing and in the immediate front of General Hill was the division of General Casey, of the Fourth (Keyes's) Corps. The division stood in an intrenched camp across the Williamsburg road, with a pentagonal redoubt (unfinished) on the left of his line. Half a mile in rear of Casey's division was that of Couch, of the same corps, behind a second trenched line, at its junction of the Nine Miles road, part of Couch's extending along the latter road to Fair Oaks Station of the York River Railroad, and intrenched; farther forward he had a guarded picket station. Between Couch and Casey a skirt of wood stretched from the swamp on their left across the Williamsburg and Nine Miles roads and the railroad. Between the stretch of forest and Couch was an open; spreading across the roads, and at Casey's front, was another open, though more limited, some abatis being arranged along their front lines. These were the only cleared fields on the south side of the railroad within two miles of Casey's picket line, our line of march and attack.

General D. H. Hill stood ready for battle at an early

hour, waiting for his brigade on the Charles City road. Under the delay to relieve that brigade by one of Huger's divisions, I sent orders to General Wilcox to pull off from column on that road and march for the position assigned him near the head of White Oak Swamp.

The detailed instructions for battle were that the advance should be made in columns of brigades two on each side the Williamsburg road, preceded by strong lines of skirmishers; the advance, approaching an open or abatis or trench line, should reinforce the skirmish line to strong engagement, while the lines of battle turned those obstacles by flank or oblique march when the general advance should be resumed. As the wooded field was not convenient for artillery use, we only held the batteries of Bondurant and Carter ready for call. At eleven o'clock, weary of delay, General Hill asked to let loose his signal-gun and engage, but was ordered to wait for his absent brigade.

The reports of the hour of opening battle are more conflicting in this than in most battles, owing possibly to the fact that many are fixed by the beginning of the hot battle about the trenched camp, while others are based on the actual firing of the signal-guns. The weight of evidence seems conclusive of the former attack at one P.M., and this would place the firing of the signal-guns back to noon or a little after. As events occurred, however, the hour is not of especial interest, as it is shown that the battle was in time for a finish before night if it had been promptly followed up. I will say, therefore, that General Hill's second appeal to open the signal-gun was made a little before noon, and that he stated in this appeal that his brigade from the Charles City road was approaching, and would be with him. He was then authorized to march, but to give instructions that the advance should be carefully conducted until all the troops were in place, to give full force to his battle. He had four brigades, and was ordered to advance in columns of brigades, two on each side of the road. Garland's and G. B. Anderson's brigades in columns, preceded by skirmishers, advanced on the left of the road at the sound of the guns, and engaged after a short march from the starting. As Rodes's brigade was not yet in position, some little time elapsed before the columns on the right moved, so that Garland's column encountered more than its share of early fight, but Rodes, supported by Rains's brigade, came promptly to his relief, which steadied the advance. The enemy's front was reinforced and arrested progress of our skirmishers, but a way was found by which the enemy was turned out of position, and by and by the open before the intrenched camp was reached. In the redoubt was a six-gun battery, and on the right another section of two pieces. General Hill ordered Bondurant's battery to the open into action, and presently the battery of Captain Carter.

Garland and G. B. Anderson had severe contention at one o'clock, but by pushing front and flank movements got to the enemy's strong line. R. H. Anderson's brigade was pushed up in support of their left, when a bold move gave us the section of artillery and that end of the line. At the same time Carter's battery was in close practice with five guns within four hundred yards of the redoubt, and the enemy was seriously disturbed; but General Hill was disposed to wait a little for Huger, thought to be between him and the swamp, to get farther in; then, fearing that longer wait might be hazardous of his opportunity, he ordered Rains's brigade past the enemy's left, when Rodes seized the moment, rushed in, and gained the redoubt and the battery. The officers at the battery made a brave effort to spike their guns, but were killed in the act. So Rodes, who had some artillerists acting as infantry, turned them with some effect upon the troops as they retired.

When General Hill reported that he must use Rains's brigade to march around the redoubt, other orders were sent General Wilcox to leave General Huger's column and march to his position on the right of General Hill's battle, directing, in case there were serious obstacles to his march by the Charles City road, to march over to and down the Williamsburg road. A slip of paper was sent General Johnston reporting progress and asking co-operation on our left.

The battle moved bravely on. R. H. Anderson's brigade was ordered to support its left at Fair Oaks, and Pickett's, on the railroad, was drawn near. Hill met Casey's troops rallying, and reinforcements with them coming to recover the lost ground, but they were forced back to the second intrenched line (Couch's), where severe fighting ensued, but the line was carried at two o'clock, cutting Couch with four regiments and two companies of infantry, and Brady's six-gun battery, off at Fair Oaks Station. Finding that he could not cut his way back to his command, Couch stood back from the railroad and presently opened his battery fire across our advancing lines. As he was standing directly in front of Smith's division, we thought that he would soon be attacked and driven off. Nevertheless, it was not prudent to leave that point on our flank unguarded until we found Smith's division in action. The force was shut off from our view by the thick pine wood, so that we could know nothing of its strength, and only knew of its position from its artillery fire. We could not attack it lest we should fall under the fire of the division in position for that attack. Anderson's other regiments, under the gallant Colonel M. Jenkins, were ordered into Hill's forward battle, as his troops were worn. Jenkins soon found himself in the van, and so swiftly led on that the discomfited troops found no opportunity to rally. Reinforcements from the Third Corps came, but in the swampy wood Jenkins was prompt enough to strike their heads as their retreating comrades passed. Right and left and front he applied his beautiful tactics and pushed his battle.

General Kearny, finding that he could not arrest the march, put Berry's brigade off to the swamp to flank and strike it, and took part of Jamison's brigade to follow. They got into the swamp and followed it up to the open near the Couch intrenchment,* but Jenkins knew that there was some one there to meet them, and pushed his onward battle. General Hill ordered Rains's brigade to turn this new force, while Rodes attacked, but the latter's men were worn, and some of them were with the advance. Kemper's brigade was sent to support the forward battle, but General Hill directed it to his right against Berry, in front of Rains, and it seems that the heavy, swampy ground so obstructed operations on both sides as to limit their work to infantry fusillades until six o'clock.

Our battle on the Williamsburg road was in a sack. We were strong enough to guard our flanks and push straight on, but the front was growing heavy. It was time for Wilcox's brigades under his last order, but nothing was heard of them. I asked General Stuart, who had joined me, if there were obstacles to Wilcox's march between the Charles City and Williamsburg roads. He reported that there was nothing more than swamp lands, hardly knee-deep. He was asked for a guide, who was sent with a courier bearing orders for them to remain with General Wilcox until he reported at my headquarters.

Again I reported the cramped condition of our work, owing to the artillery practice from beyond the railroad, and asked General Johnston to have the division that was with him drive that force away and loose our left. This note was ordered to be put into General Johnston's hands.

* General Berry thought that he got up as far as the Casey camp, but mistook Couch's opening for that of Casey.

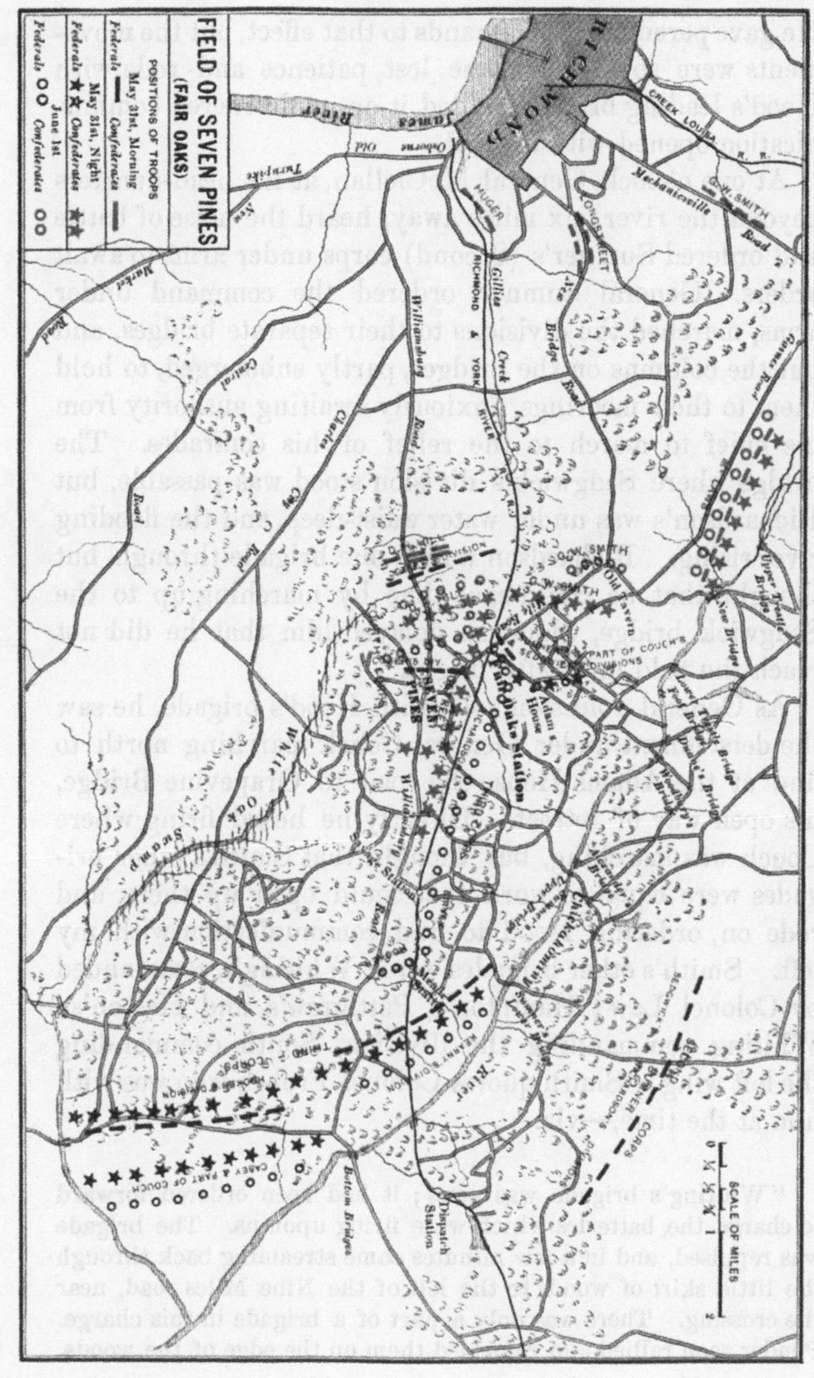
FIELD OF SEVEN PINES
(FAIR OAKS)
POSITIONS OF TROOPS
May 31st, Morning
Federals Confederates
May 31st, Night
Federals Confederates
June 1st
Federals Confederates
RICHMOND
James River
SCALE OF MILES
Mechanicsville Road
Williamsburg Road
Charles City Road
White Oak Swamp
Dispatch Station
Bottom Bridge
Chickahominy

He gave peremptory commands to that effect, but the movements were so slow that he lost patience and rode with Hood's leading brigade, pulled it on, and ordered communication opened with my left.

At one o'clock, General McClellan, at his head-quarters beyond the river, six miles away, heard the noise of battle and ordered Sumner's (Second) corps under arms to await orders. General Sumner ordered the command under arms, marched the divisions to their separate bridges, and put the columns on the bridges, partly submerged, to hold them to their moorings, anxiously awaiting authority from his chief to march to the relief of his comrades. The bridge where Sedgwick's division stood was passable, but Richardson's was under water waist-deep, and the flooding river rising. Richardson waded one brigade through, but thought that he could save time by marching up to the Sedgwick bridge, which so delayed him that he did not reach the field until after night.

As General Johnston rode with Hood's brigade, he saw the detachment under General Couch marching north to find at the Adams House the road to Grapevine Bridge, his open way of retreat. Directly he heard firing where Couch was marching, but thought that Smith's other brigades were equal to work that could open up there, and rode on, ordering Hood to find communication with my left. Smith's other brigades were: Whiting's, commanded by Colonel Law; Hampton's, Pettigrew's, and Hatton's; Whiting commanding the division, Smith commanding the left wing. Smith quotes Colonel Frobel, who was with him at the time,—viz.:

"Whiting's brigade was gone; it had been ordered forward to charge the batteries which were firing upon us. The brigade was repulsed, and in a few minutes came streaming back through the little skirt of woods to the left of the Nine Miles road, near the crossing. There was only a part of a brigade in this charge. Pender soon rallied and reformed them on the edge of the woods.

General Whiting sent an order to him to reconnoitre the batteries, and if he thought they could be taken, to try it again. Before he could do so, some one galloped up, shouting, 'Charge that battery!' The men hurried forward at double-quick, but were repulsed as before." *

It seems that at that moment General Sumner reached the field. He reported:

"On arriving on the field, I found General Couch, with four regiments and two companies of infantry and Brady's battery. These troops were drawn up in line near Adams's House, and there was a pause in the battle."

He received his orders at 2.30 P.M. and marched with Sedgwick's division—three brigades—and Kirby's battery, and reached the ground of Couch's work at 4.30. In less than an hour he had surveyed the ground and placed his troops to receive battle.

General Smith attacked with Hampton's, Pettigrew's, and Hatton's brigades. It seems he made no use of artillery, though on the field right and left the opportunity was fair. The troops fought bravely, as did all Confederate soldiers. We heard the steady, rolling fire of musketry and the boom of cannon that told of deadly work as far as the Williamsburg road, but it did not last. General Hatton was killed, General Pettigrew wounded and a prisoner, and General Hampton wounded. General Smith was beaten.

General Sumner reported:

"I ordered the following regiments, Eighty-second New York, Thirty-fourth New York, Fifteenth Massachusetts, Twentieth Massachusetts, and Seventh Michigan, to move to the front and charge bayonets. There were two fences between us and the enemy, but our men gallantly rushed over them, and the enemy broke and fled, and this closed the battle of Saturday." †

---

* Confederate War Papers, G. W. Smith.

† Rebellion Record, vol. xi. part i. p. 763.

General Smith sent to call Hood's brigade from his right, and posted it, about dark, near Fair Oaks Station. At parting, General Hood said, "Our people over yonder are whipped."

General Wilcox filed his three brigades into the Williamsburg road, followed by two of Huger's division at five o'clock. He was reminded of his orders to be abreast of the battle, and that he was only four hours behind it; but reported that while marching by the first order by the Charles City road, he received orders to try the Williamsburg road; that, marching for that road, he was called by orders to follow a guide, who brought him back to the Charles City road. He confessed that his orders to march with the front of battle were plain and well understood, but his marches did not quite agree with the comprehensive view of his orders.

Two of his regiments—the Eleventh Alabama, under Colonel Sydenham Moore, and the Nineteenth Mississippi, under Major Mullens—were ordered to join Kemper, turn the position of the enemy at that point, and capture or dislodge them. With the other regiments, General Wilcox was ordered by the Williamsburg road to report to General Hill, Pryor's brigade to follow him, Colston's brigade to support the move under Colonel Moore.

Armistead's and Mahone's brigades, of Huger's division, were sent to R. H. Anderson, who was ordered to put them in his position and move his other regiments to the front.

Colonel Moore hurried his leading companies into the turning move against Berry's brigade before his regiment was up, and before the Mississippi regiment was in supporting distance, and fell mortally wounded. General Kearny, seeing the move and other troops marching towards it, ordered his troops out and in retreat through the swamp. He reported of it:

"Although so critically placed, and despite the masses that gathered on and had passed us, checked the enemy in his intent of cutting off against the White Oak Swamp. This enabled the advanced regiments, arrested by orders and this contest in the rear, to return from their hitherto victorious career and retire by a remaining wood-path known to our scouts (the saw-mill road), until they once more arrived at and remained in the impregnable position we had left at noon at our own fortified division camp."*

He states the hour as six P.M.

Birney's brigade of Kearny's division was ordered along the north side of the railroad a little before night, and had several encounters with parts of R. H. Anderson's brigade and some regiments of G. B. Anderson's. Jenkins, nothing daunted, pushed his brave battle forward until the shades of night settled about the wood, and flashes of dark-lanterns began to creep through the pines in search of wounded, friend and foe.

At seven o'clock, General Johnston ordered his troops on the field to sleep on their lines, and be ready to renew operations in the morning, and ordered General Smith to call up other troops of the left wing. At half after seven he was hit by a rifle-ball, then a fragment of shell unhorsed him, and he was borne from the field, so severely wounded that he was for a considerable time incapacitated for duty. The command devolved temporarily upon General G. W. Smith. General Johnston was skilled in the art and science of war, gifted in his quick, penetrating mind and soldierly bearing, genial and affectionate in nature, honorable and winning in person, and confiding in his love. He drew the hearts of those about him so close that his comrades felt that they could die for him. Until his recovery the Confederacy experienced a serious deprivation, and when that occurred he was no longer commander-in-chief, for General Lee was promptly called to the post of honor.

* Rebellion Record, vol. xi. part ii. p. 813.

The brigades were so mixed up through the pines when the battle closed that there was some delay in getting the regiments to their proper commands, getting up supplies, and arranging for the morning. D. H. Hill's was put in good order and in bivouac near the Casey intrenchment; those of Longstreet between the Williamsburg road and railroad. Wilcox's brigade took position on the right, in place of the detachment under Jenkins; Pryor's brigade next on the left; Kemper, Anderson, and Colston near the stage road (Williamsburg). They made blazing fires of pine-knots to dry their clothing and blankets, and these lighted reinforcing Union troops to their lines behind the railroad.

The brigades of Huger's division (Armistead's and Mahone's) were near the left. Pickett was ordered to report to General Hill at daylight, also the batteries of Maurin, Stribling, and Watson. It was past eleven o'clock when all things were made ready and the killed and wounded cared for; then I rode to find the headquarters of our new commander.

SUMMARY OF FORCES AND LOSSES.

Union troops engaged on the Williamsburg road, reported by General Heintzelman, commanding Casey's, Couch's, and Kearny's divisions	18,500
Hooker's division was at hand, but no part of it engaged.	
Confederates engaged on the Williamsburg road, of D. H. Hill's division	8900 *
Two brigades and two regiments of Longstreet's division	5700
	14,600

Two lines of intrenchments were attacked and carried, six pieces of artillery and several thousand small-arms were captured, and the enemy was forced back to his third line of intrenchments by night, a mile and a half from the point of his opening.

* Previous returns give him 11,000, but one of his brigades was absent.

Sedgwick's division is not separately accounted for, but an average of the divisions reported by General Heintzelman will give him	**6080**	
Estimate of Couch's command	**2000**	
Union force against General Smith		**8080**
Smith's division, five brigades	**10,500**	
But Hood's brigade was not engaged	**2,100**	
Of Smith's division in action		**8,400**
Union losses on the Williamsburg road		**4563**
Confederate losses on the Williamsburg road		**3515**
Union losses on the Nine Miles road		**468**
Confederate losses on the Nine Miles road		**1283**

CHAPTER VIII.

SEQUELÆ OF SEVEN PINES.

The Forces under Command of G. W. Smith after Johnston was wounded—The Battle of the 1st—Longstreet requests Reinforcements and a Diversion—Council held—McLaws alone sustains Longstreet's Opposition to retiring—Severe Fighting—Pickett's Brave Stand—General Lee assigned to Command—He orders the withdrawal of the Army—Criticism of General Smith—Confederates should not have lost the Battle—Keyes's Corroboration.

MAJOR-GENERAL G. W. SMITH was of the highest standing of the West Point classes, and, like others of the Engineers, had a big name to help him in the position to which he had been suddenly called by the disabling of the Confederate commander.

I found his head-quarters at one o'clock in the morning, reported the work of the commands on the Williamsburg road on the 31st, and asked for part of the troops ordered up by General Johnston, that we might resume battle at daylight. He was disturbed by reports of pontoon bridges, said to be under construction for the use of other reinforcements to join the enemy from the east side, and was anxious lest the enemy might march his two corps on the east side by the upper river and occupy Richmond. But after a time these notions gave way, and he suggested that we could renew the battle on the Williamsburg road, provided we would send him one of our brigades to help hold his position and make the battle by a wheel on his right as a pivot.

As the commands stood, Smith's division on our left was at right angles to the York River Railroad, facing east, his right near Fair Oaks Station. Besides his division of ten thousand, he had Magruder's and other commands of fresh troops near him,—twenty thousand.

My left lay near Smith's right, the line extending parallel to the railroad for a mile, facing north; thence it broke to the rear, and covered the ground from that point to the swamp, the return front facing the enemy's third intrenched line. Smith's part of the field was open and fine for artillery practice. The field fronting on the railroad was so shut in by heavy pine forest and tangled swamp that we had no place for a single gun. D. H. Hill's division was in reserve near the Casey encampment.

The enemy stood: Sedgwick's division in front of Smith; Richardson's division in column of three brigades parallel to the railroad and behind it, prepared to attack my left; on Richardson's left was Birney's brigade behind the railroad, and under the enemy's third intrenched line were the balance of the Third and all of the Fourth Corps. So the plan to wheel on Smith's right as a pivot, my right stepping out on the wheel, would have left the Third and Fourth Corps to attack our rear as soon as we moved.

Besides, it was evident that our new commander would do nothing, and we must look to accident for such aid as might be drawn to us during the battle.

The plan proposed could only be considered under the hypothesis that Magruder would come in as the pivotal point, and, upon having the enemy's line fully exposed, would find the field fine for his batteries, and put them in practice without orders from his commander, and, breaking the enemy's line by an enfilade fire from his artillery, would come into battle and give it cohesive power.

I left head-quarters at three o'clock, and after an hour's repose rode to the front to find General Hill. Wilcox's brigade was on my right on the return front, Pryor's brigade on his left, and R. H. Anderson, Kemper, Colston, Armistead, and Mahone occupied the line between the Williamsburg road and the railroad. Pickett's brigade was ordered to be with General Hill at daylight, and Maurin's, Stribling's, and Watson's batteries, of Pickett's brigade, to take position on the right of Armistead's.

I found General Hill before he had his breakfast, enjoying the comforts of Casey's camp. Pickett had passed and was in search of his position, which was soon disclosed by a fusillade from the front of Richardson's division. A party of "bummers" from Richmond had found their way into the camp at Fair Oaks, and were getting such things as they could put their hands on. They were taken in the gray of the morning for Confederate troops and fired upon. This made some confusion with our new troops, and part of them opened fire in the wrong direction, putting two or three bullets through General Hill's tent before he got out of it. Hood's brigade of Smith's division, the pivotal point, came under this fire, and was immediately withdrawn. Hood reported his position good, but his orders were to retire.

Our cavalry had established communication with headquarters, and gave prompt notice of movements as they occurred. The pivot was moving to the rear, but battle on the Williamsburg road steadily advanced, with orders to develop the enemy's battle front through its extent along the railroad; not to make the fancied wheel, but to expose his line to the practice of our batteries on the Nine Miles road.

Our infantry moved steadily, engaging French's brigade of Richardson's division, which was led by one of Howard's regiments. French was supported by Howard's brigade, and Howard by Meagher's, and the firing extended along my line as far as the return front of my right. But Magruder was not on the field to seize the opportunity for his artillery. He was nowhere near the battle,—had not been called. General Whiting, however, saw the opportunity so inviting, and reported to his commander at half after six o'clock,—

"I am going to try a diversion for Longstreet, and have found, as reported, a position for artillery. The enemy are in full view and in heavy masses. I have ordered up Lee with four pieces. The musketry firing in advance is tremendous." *

General Smith had parties posted along the heights of the Chickahominy in close observation of the movements of the enemy's forces on the east bank. These parties reported from time to time that the enemy was moving his forces down the east bank and crossing them over to take part in the fight. The accounts proved false, but they continued to come to head-quarters, and were forwarded to my command on the Williamsburg road and gave us some concern. Failing to receive approval of his chief, General Whiting reported at nine o'clock,—

"If I don't receive an answer in half an hour, I shall commence withdrawing my forces." †

The answer he received was to throw back his right and take position a *little* nearer to the New Bridge fork of the Nine Miles road,‡ thus swinging the pivot farther back. General Smith complained that the enemy was getting into the interval between our lines, but position between two fires was not the place the enemy wanted; he could not know that Smith wouldn't shoot. Under this long and severe infantry fight there was no point on my part of the field upon which we could post a single gun. Part of Armistead's new troops gave way, but the gallant brigadier maintained his ground and soon collected his other regiments. Before this I had reported ready, and awaiting a guide, the brigade that was to be sent over to the Nine Miles road. At half after ten o'clock, General Smith sent word that he had heard nothing of the brigade expected to come to his support, and renewed his reports of the enemy crossing over and concentrating against us

* Smith's War Papers. † Ibid. ‡ Ibid.

on the Williamsburg road. He repeated, too, his wish to have his cavalry keep close communication between the wings of the army. This close communication had been established early in the morning and was maintained through the day, and the reports of the enemy's crossing were all false, but our new commander seemed to forget. At the same time he wrote me,—

"I have directed Whiting to take close defensive relations with Magruder. At any rate, that was absolutely necessary to enable a good defence to be made whilst you are pivoting on Whiting's position." *

Whiting's position, instead of being pivotal, began its rearward move at the opening fire at daybreak, and continued in that line of conduct until it reached a point of quiet. General Smith was informed that the brigade called for by him would not be sent over; that his troops were doing nothing, while all of mine were in severe battle, except a single brigade, and the enemy was massing his fighting force against me; that the grounds were so flooded that it was difficult to keep up our supply of ammunition; that with the aid of his troops the battle would be ours.

But just then he held a council with Generals McLaws and Whiting and Chief Engineer Stevens, and submitted the question, "Must the troops be withdrawn, or the attack continued?"

All voted in favor of the former except McLaws. In a letter, since written, he has said,—

"I alone urged that you be reinforced and the attack continued, and the question was reconsidered, and I was sent to learn your views." †

Before General McLaws found me, I wrote General Smith,—

---

* Smith's War Papers. † Ibid.

"Can you reinforce me? The entire enemy seems to be opposed to me. We cannot hold out unless we get help. If we can fight together, we can finish the work to-day, and Mac's time will be up. If I cannot get help, I fear that I must fall back."

General McLaws reported of his ride to my lines,—

"I went and found you with J. E. B. Stuart. You were in favor of resuming the assault, and wanted five thousand men." *

Nothing was sent in reply to McLaws's report, but we soon learned that the left wing of the army was quiet and serene in defensive positions about the New Bridge fork of the Nine Miles road.

At the first quiet of our battle, after the left wing quit the field, I ordered the brigades withdrawn to defensive position about the trenches at Seven Pines, but before the order reached the front the fight was renewed by Hooker's division upon Wilcox and Pryor, and reached out to our left near Fair Oaks. In the heat of this, General Wilcox received the order to retire, and in undue haste pulled his command out, assumed authority over Pryor, and ordered him off. Pickett, the true soldier, knowing that the order was not intended for such emergency, stood and resisted the attack. Colston was sent to his aid, and the attack was repulsed. Immediately after this repulse was a quiet advance upon Pickett's right. The commander asked, "What troops are these?" "Virginians!" "Don't fire!" he ordered; "we will capture the last one of these Virginians." Just then the Virginians rose and opened a fearful fire that drove him back to his bushy cover, which ended the battle of Seven Pines. Pickett was withdrawn to position assigned for his brigade, our line of skirmishers remaining near the enemy's during the day and night. General Wilcox reported of his battle, when

* Letter from General McLaws.

he pulled off from it, that he was doing as well as he could wish, but General Hooker reported, "Pursuit was hopeless."

The failure of the enemy to push the opportunity made by the precipitate retreat of General Wilcox, and Pickett's successful resistance, told that there was nothing in the reports of troops coming over from the east side to take part in the battle, and we were convinced that the river was not passable. I made an appeal for ten thousand men, that we might renew our battle without regard to General Smith and those about him. It received no more consideration than the appeal made through General McLaws.

Then General Lee, having been assigned to command, came upon the field after noon by the Nine Miles road, and, with General Smith, came over to the Williamsburg road. A similar proposition was made General Lee, but General Smith protested that the enemy was strongly fortified. At the time the enemy's main battle front was behind the railroad, fronting against me but exposed to easy enfilade fire of batteries to be posted on his right flank on the Nine Miles road, while his front against me was covered by the railway embankment. It is needless to add that under the fire of batteries so posted his lines would have been broken to confusion in twenty minutes. General Holmes marched down the Williamsburg road and rested in wait for General Lee. Like General Huger, he held rank over me. General Lee ordered the troops back to their former lines. Those on the Williamsburg road were drawn back during the night, the rear-guard, Pickett's brigade, passing the Casey works at sunrise on the 2d unmolested. Part of Richardson's division mistook the camp at Fair Oaks for the Casey camp, and claimed to have recovered it on the afternoon of the 1st, but it was not until the morning of the 2d that the Casey camp was abandoned.

The Confederate losses in the two days' fight were 6134; the Union losses, 5031.

It seems from Union accounts that all of our dead were not found and buried on the afternoon of the 1st. It is possible, as our battle was in the heavy forest and swamp tangles.

General Smith has written a great deal about the battle of Seven Pines during the past twenty or thirty years, in efforts to show that the failure of success was due to want of conduct on the part of the forces on the Williamsburg road. He claims that he was only out as a party of observation, to prevent reinforcement of the enemy from the east side of the river, and that he kept Sumner off of us. But he waited three hours after the enemy's ranks and lines had been broken, instead of moving with and finishing the battle, thus giving Sumner time to march from the east of the river, and strike him and beat him to disorder, and change the lost battle to success. He shows that Hill's and Longstreet's divisions could have gained the battle unaided,—which may be true enough, but it would have been a fruitless success, for the enemy got forces over to protect those of the west side; whereas, the stronger battle, ordered by the four divisions, could and would have made a complete success of it but for the balky conduct of the divisions ordered to guard the flanks. Instead of six hours' hard work to reach the enemy's third line, we could have captured it in the second hour and had the field cleaned up before Sumner crossed the river.

General Keyes, the commander of the Fourth Corps, in his "Fifty Years' Observations," says,—

> "The left of my lines were all protected by the White Oak Swamp, but the right was on ground so favorable to the approach of the enemy, and so far from the Chickahominy, that if Johnston had attacked them an hour or two earlier than he did, I could have made but a feeble defence comparatively, and every man of us would have been killed, captured, or driven into the swamp or river before assistance could have reached us."

General Smith lay in wait three hours after the enemy's positions were broken and carried, giving ample time for the march of the succoring forces. The hour of the attack was not so important as prompt and vigorous work. If the battle had opened at sunrise, Smith would have made the same wait, and Sumner's march would have been in time to beat him. All elements of success were in the plan, but balky troops will mar the strongest plans. He tries to persuade himself that he intended to join our battle on the Williamsburg road, but there was no fight in his heart after his maladroit encounter with Sedgwick's division on the afternoon of the 31st. The opportunity for enfilade fire of his artillery along the enemy's battle front, at the morning opening and all of the forenoon, was waiting him; while reports of the enemy crossing the river, reinforcing against my single contest, were demanding relief and aid.

He reported sick on the 2d and left the army. When ready for duty he was assigned about Richmond and the seaboard of North Carolina. He applied to be restored to command of his division in the field, but the authorities thought his services could be used better elsewhere. He resigned his commission in the Confederate service, went to Georgia, and joined Joe Brown's militia, where he found congenial service, better suited to his ideas of vigorous warfare.

CHAPTER IX.

ROBERT E. LEE IN COMMAND.

The Great General's Assignment not at first assuring to the Army—Able as an Engineer but limited as to Field Service—He makes the Acquaintance of his Lieutenants—Calls a Council—Gains Confidence by saying Nothing—"A Little Humor now and then"—Lee plans a Simultaneous Attack on McClellan's Front and Rear—J. E. B. Stuart's Daring Reconnoissance around the Union Army.

THE assignment of General Lee to command the army of Northern Virginia was far from reconciling the troops to the loss of our beloved chief, Joseph E. Johnston, with whom the army had been closely connected since its earliest active life. All hearts had learned to lean upon him with confidence, and to love him dearly. General Lee's experience in active field work was limited to his West Virginia campaign against General Rosecrans, which was not successful. His services on our coast defences were known as able, and those who knew him in Mexico as one of the principal engineers of General Scott's column, marching for the capture of the capital of that great republic, knew that as military engineer he was especially distinguished; but officers of the line are not apt to look to the staff in choosing leaders of soldiers, either in tactics or strategy. There were, therefore, some misgivings as to the power and skill for field service of the new commander. The change was accepted, however, as a happy relief from the existing halting policy of the late temporary commander.

During the first week of his authority he called his general officers to meet him on the Nine Miles road for a general talk. This novelty was not reassuring, as experience had told that secrecy in war was an essential element of success; that public discussion and secrecy were incompatible.

R E Lee

As he disclosed nothing, those of serious thought became hopeful, and followed his wise example. The brigadiers talked freely, but only of the parts of the line occupied by their brigades; and the meeting finally took a playful turn. General Toombs's brigade was before some formidable works under construction by General Franklin. He suggested an elevation a few hundred yards in his rear, as a better defensive line and more comfortable position for his men; a very good military point. This seemed strange in General Toombs, however, as he was known to have frequent talks with his troops, complaining of West Point men holding the army from battle, digging and throwing up lines of sand instead of showing lines of battle, where all could have fair fight.

Referring to his suggestion to retire and construct a new line, General D. H. Hill, who behind the austere presence of a major-general had a fund of dry humor, said,—

"I think it may be better to advance General Toombs's brigade, till he can bring Franklin's working parties under the fire of his short-range arms, so that the working parties may be broken up."

General Whiting, who was apprehensive of bayous and parallels, complained of sickness in his command, and asked a change of position from the unfair Fair Oaks. Though of brilliant, highly cultivated mind, the dark side of the picture was always more imposing with him. Several of the major-generals failed to join us till the conference was about to disperse. All rode back to their camps little wiser than when they went, except that they found General Lee's object was to learn of the temper of those of his officers whom he did not know, and of the condition and tone among their troops. He ordered his engineers over the line occupied by the army, to rearrange its defensive construction, and to put working parties on all points needing reinforcing. Whiting's division was broken up. Three of the brigades were ordered to A. P. Hill's division. He was permitted to choose two brigades that were to constitute his own command. Besides his own, he selected Hood's brigade. With these two he was ordered by way of Lynchburg to report to General Jackson, in the Valley district.

General Lee was seen almost daily riding over his lines, making suggestions to working parties and encouraging their efforts to put sand-banks between their persons and the enemy's batteries, and they were beginning to appreciate the value of such adjuncts. Above all, they soon began to look eagerly for his daily rides, his pleasing yet commanding presence, and the energy he displayed in speeding their labors.

The day after the conference on the Nine Miles road, availing myself of General Lee's invitation to free interchange of ideas, I rode over to his head-quarters, and renewed my suggestion of a move against General McClellan's right flank, which rested behind Beaver Dam Creek. The strength of the position was explained, and mention made that, in consequence of that strong ground, a move somewhat similar, ordered by General Johnston for the 28th of May, was abandoned. At the same time he was assured that a march of an hour could turn the head of the creek and dislodge the force behind it. He received me pleasantly and gave a patient hearing to the suggestions, without indicating approval or disapproval. A few days before he wrote General Jackson: *

"Head-quarters, near Richmond, Va.,
"June 11, 1862.

"Brigadier-General Thomas J. Jackson,
"*Commanding Valley District:*

"General,—Your recent successes have been the cause of the liveliest joy in this army as well as in the country. The admiration excited by your skill and boldness has been constantly

* Rebellion Record, vol. xii. part iii. p. 910.

mingled with solicitude for your situation. The practicability of reinforcing you has been the subject of earnest consideration. It has been determined to do so at the expense of weakening this army. Brigadier-General Lawton, with six regiments from Georgia, is on the way to you, and Brigadier-General Whiting, with eight veteran regiments, leaves here to-day. The object is to enable you to crush the forces opposed to you. Leave your enfeebled troops to watch the country and guard the passes covered by your cavalry and artillery, and with your main body, including Ewell's division and Lawton's and Whiting's commands, move rapidly to Ashland by rail or otherwise, as you may find most advantageous, and sweep down between the Chickahominy and Pamunkey, cutting up the enemy's communications, etc., while this army attacks General McClellan in front. He will thus, I think, be forced to come out of his intrenchments, where he is strongly posted on the Chickahominy, and apparently preparing to move by gradual approaches on Richmond. Keep me advised of your movements, and, if practicable, precede your troops, that we may confer and arrange for simultaneous attack.

"I am, with great respect, your obedient servant,

"R. E. LEE, *General*."

The brigades under Generals Lawton and Whiting were transported as above ordered.

As indicated in his letter to General Jackson, General Lee's plan was a simultaneous attack on General McClellan's army front and rear. Following his instructions for General Jackson, on the same day he ordered his cavalry, under General Stuart, upon a forced reconnoissance around General McClellan's army to learn if the ground behind his army was open.

These plans and the promptness with which they were conceived and put in operation ought to be a sufficient refutation of the silly report that the Confederacy had any idea of withdrawing from their capital,—a report which, notwithstanding its unreasonable nature, was given a degree of credence in some quarters.*

---

* Of interest in this connection is a letter to the author from General D. H. Hill:

Upon nearing Richmond, after leaving Yorktown, General Johnston's first thought had been to stand on the table-lands between the Pamunkey and the Chickahominy Rivers, on the flank of McClellan's march for Richmond, and force him into battle. He selected ground with that view and posted his army, where it remained some eight days, giving general and engineer officers opportunity to ride over and learn the topographical features of the surroundings. A prominent point was Beaver Dam Creek, which was so noted by the officers. When Johnston proposed to recross the Chickahominy and make battle on the 28th of May, in anticipation of McDowell's approach, the strong ground at Beaver Dam Creek again came under discussion and was common talk between the generals, so that the position and its approaches became a familiar subject. Then Stuart's famous ride had correlative relation to the same, and drew us to careful study of the grounds.

For the execution of his orders General Stuart took twelve hundred cavalry and a section of Stuart's horse artillery. The command was composed of parts of the First, Fourth, and Ninth Virginia Cavalry. The Fourth,

---

"FAYETTEVILLE, ARK., February 4, 1879.

"GENERAL JAMES LONGSTREET:

"MY DEAR GENERAL,—I never heard of the proposed abandonment of Richmond at the time General Lee took command. I had charge of one of the four divisions with which the retreat from Yorktown was effected, and was called several times into General Lee's most important councils. I never heard any officer suggest such a course in these councils or in private conversations.

"I feel sure that General Johnston always intended to fight the invading force, and so far as I know no officer of rank entertained any other view.

"I remember very well that some days before the council on the Nine Miles road (when yourself, A. P. Hill, and myself were present) that you suggested the plan of attacking McClellan's right flank, and that I expressed my preference for an attack on the other flank. This shows that there was no thought of retreat.

"Very truly yours,

"D. H. HILL."

having no field officer on duty with it, was distributed for the expedition between the First, Colonel Fitzhugh Lee, and the Ninth, Colonel W. H. F. Lee commanding; also two squadrons of the Jeff Davis Legion, Lieutenant-Colonel W. T. Martin commanding. The section of artillery was under First Lieutenant James Breathed.

On the night of the 12th of June he gathered his squadrons beyond the Chickahominy, and the next day marched by the road west of the Richmond, Fredericksburg, and Potomac Railroad towards Louisa Court-House, to produce the impression, should the march be discovered, that he was going to join General Jackson. After a march of fifteen miles, he bivouacked in the pine forests of Hanover, near the South Anna Bridge, without light or sound of bugle, and, throwing aside the cares of the day and thoughts of the morrow, sunk to repose such as the soldier knows how to enjoy. An hour before daylight he was up in readiness to move as soon as the first light of morning revealed the line of march. Up to that moment no one of the expedition, except the commander, knew the direction or the purpose of the march. He called his principal officers about him and told of the object of the ride, and impressed the necessity for secrecy, prompt and intelligent attention to orders. At the mute signal the twelve hundred men swung into their saddles and took the road leading to the right and rear of McClellan's army. At Hanover Court-House a small force of the enemy's cavalry was discovered, but they retired towards their camp, out of the line of Stuart's ride. At Hawes's Shop a picket was driven off and several vedettes captured. They proved to be of the Fifth United States Cavalry, General Lee's old regiment. Between Hawes's Shop and Old Church the advance-guard, well to the front, reported the presence of the enemy, apparently in some force. The column pressed forward, expecting a fierce encounter of Southern volunteers with United States regulars, but the latter was a single troop and retreated beyond Totopotomy Creek to Old Church, where there was a camp of four companies of the Fifth Cavalry under Captain Royal, which made a brave stand. Captain Latane led the first squadron, and Captain Royal received the first shòck, and furiously the combat went on, both leaders falling, Latane dead and Royal severely wounded. The enemy fled and scattered through the woods. A number of prisoners were taken, including several officers, and there were captured horses, arms, equipments, and four guidons. In the enemy's camp, near Old Church, several officers and privates were captured, a number of horses and arms taken, and the stores and tents were burned. Here it became a question whether to attempt to return by way of Hanover Court-House or to press on and try to make a circuit around the entire army, and take the chance of fording or swimming the Chickahominy beyond the enemy's extreme left. Stuart decided that the bolder ride "was the quintessence of prudence."*

Arriving opposite Garlick's, on the Pamunkey,—one of the enemy's supply stations,—a squadron was sent out and burned two transports with army stores and a number of wagons. Near Tunstall's Station a wagon-train was discovered guarded by five companies of cavalry, which manifested a determinatiou to stand and defend it, but they abandoned it and rode away, leaving the train in possession of Stuart, who burned it, and, night coming on, the country was brilliantly lighted up by its flames. After resting a few hours at Talleysville, the ride was resumed, and the party reached the Chickahominy at Forges Bridge at daylight. The stream was not fordable, but, by exercise of great energy and industry, a rude foot-bridge was laid. That part of the command near it dismounted and walked over, swimming their horses. In a few hours the

* Official account, Rebellion Record, vol. xi. part i. p. 1036.

bridge was made strong and the artillery and other mounts were passed safely over to the Richmond side, and resumed the march for their old camp-grounds.

This was one of the most graceful and daring rides known to military history, and revealed valuable facts concerning the situation of the Union forces, their operations, communications, etc. When congratulated upon his success, General Stuart replied, with a lurking twinkle in his eye, that he had left a general behind him. Asked as to the identity of the unfortunate person, he said, with his joyful laugh, "General Consternation."

CHAPTER X.

FIGHTING ALONG THE CHICKAHOMINY.

Retreat—Lee's Bold Initiative—Lee and his Lieutenants planning Battle—The Confederates' Loss at Mechanicsville—Gaines's Mill—A. P. Hill's Fight—Longstreet's Reserve Division put in—McClellan's Change of Base—Savage Station—Longstreet engages McClellan's Main Force at Frayser's Farm (or Glendale)—President Davis on the Field—Testimony of Federal Generals—Fierce Bayonet Charges—"Greek meets Greek"—Capture of General McCall—McClellan's Masterly Retreat.

THE day after Stuart's return I rode over to General Lee's head-quarters and suggested that General Jackson be withdrawn from the Valley to take position on our left, to march against McClellan's right, and was informed that the order for Jackson was sent when Whiting's division was detached and sent to join him.

Then it was that General Lee revealed the plan indicated in his instructions of the 11th, for General Jackson to march down and attack McClellan's rear, while he made a simultaneous attack upon his front. The suggestion was offered that the enemy had probably destroyed the bridges and ferries on the Pamunkey along the line of his rear, which might leave Jackson in perilous condition if the front attack should be delayed; that that attack must be hazardous, as the enemy was in well-fortified positions with four army corps. After deliberation, he changed the plan and accepted the suggestion in favor of combining his fighting columns on the north side of the Chickahominy in echelon march against McClellan's right flank, leaving troops in the trenches in front of McClellan to defend in case of a move towards Richmond.

At the first mention of this march before this conference a change of base was spoken of by General D. H. Hill, but with our troops to be left in the trenches, so near the flank of such a move, and our columns afield, pressing close upon its rear, it was thought impracticable. General D. H. Hill, in view of the possibility, preferred that our attack should be made against the enemy's left by crossing White Oak Swamp below the enemy's left.

Jackson was called in advance of his command to meet the Hills and myself at General Lee's head-quarters for conference on the execution. On the forenoon of the 23d of June we were advised of his approach, and called to head-quarters to meet him. He was there before us, having ridden fifty miles by relay of horses since midnight. We were together in a few minutes after his arrival, in General Lee's private office. The general explained the plan briefly : Jackson to march from Ashland by heights between the Chickahominy and Pamunkey, turning and dislodging the Federal right, thus clearing the way for the march of troops to move on his right ; A. P. Hill to cross the upper Chickahominy and march for Mechanicsville, in echelon to Jackson ; the Mechanicsville Bridge being clear, D. H. Hill's division and mine to cross, the former to reinforce Jackson's column, the latter to file to the right and march down the river in right echelon to A. P. Hill's direct march through Mechanicsville to Gaines's Mill.

General Lee then excused himself to attend to office business, asking that we talk the matter over for our better comprehension.

Turning to Jackson, I said,—

> "You have distance to overcome, and in all probability obstacles will be thrown in the way of your march by the enemy. As your move is the key of the campaign, you should appoint the hour at which the connection may be made co-operative."

He promptly responded,—

> "The morning of the 25th."

I expressed doubt of his meeting that hour, and suggested that it would be better to take a little more time, as the movements of our columns could be readily adjusted to those of his. He then appointed the morning of the 26th.

Upon his return, report was made General Lee that the officers understood, and would be prepared to execute the plans; that General Jackson had appointed the morning of the 26th, when he would lead the march. Verbal instructions were given, followed by written orders, embodying in minute detail the plan already given in general.

The topographical features of the ground about Beaver Dam Creek have been given in a former chapter. Behind it battery epaulements had been skilfully laid and constructed, as well as rifle-trenches. These were occupied by the troops of the Fifth Corps, commanded by General Fitz-John Porter. McCall's division had joined the Army of the Potomac, and was assigned as part of the Fifth Corps, with the divisions of Sykes and Morell. Two of McCall's brigades, J. F. Reynolds's and Seymour's, with thoroughly-equipped artillery, were especially charged with the defences, the Third Brigade, Meade's, in reserve, the other divisions in supporting distance. McCall's advanced brigades had guards at the bridges as far as Meadow Bridge, and a strong outpost at Mechanicsville, under orders to retire when the strength of the enemy's advance was so developed as to warrant their doing so.

Three batteries, two of six guns each and one of four, manned the epaulements at the opening of the fight.

Before sunrise on the 26th of June the division of A. P. Hill was in position at Meadow Bridge; his brigade, under General Branch, and Johnson's battery, seven miles above, at Brook Turnpike Bridge; my division and that of D. H. Hill on the heights overlooking the Mechanicsville Bridge,—all awaiting the approach of the initial column. Not anticipating delay, the divisions had no special cause to conceal their presence, nor did the lay of the ground offer good cover. Morning came, and noon passed.

A few minutes after ten A.M., General Branch received a note informing him that, at the hour of its writing, General Jackson's column was crossing the Central Railroad. He assembled his command, crossed the Chickahominy, and marched down along the route designated for his column, without sending information to the division commander. Of his march he reported,—

"Interruption by the enemy, but with no other effect than to retard without checking our march.

"Near Crenshaw's the road on which the column commanded by Major-General Ewell" (of Jackson's) "was advancing and that on which I was advancing approach within one-fourth of a mile of each other. The heads of our columns reached this point simultaneously, and, after a short personal interview between General Ewell and myself, we proceeded on our respective routes.

"After dislodging the enemy from several ambuscades with only a small loss to my command, I reached the Meadow Bridge road, when I learned from stragglers that Major-General Hill had crossed the Chickahominy, without opposition, with the remainder of the division and gone on to Mechanicsville, then distant about one and a half miles. A courier from the general soon assured me of the correctness of the information, and, closing in my skirmishers, I made all haste to join him at Mechanicsville. The brigade reached the field almost an hour before sunset." *

At three o'clock, General A. P. Hill, hearing nothing from Jackson or his brigade under Branch, decided to cross the river and make his move without reference to Jackson or Branch. He crossed and moved down against Mechanicsville, attacked by Field's brigade, Anderson and Archer on Field's left, Pender and Gregg on his right, and six field batteries (four guns each). The outpost was driven in, and Hill prepared and attacked against the front at Beaver Dam Creek. Meanwhile the Mechanicsville Bridge had been cleared, and, after a little delay re-

* Rebellion Record, vol. xi. part ii. p. 882.

pairing breaks, D. H. Hill's and Longstreet's divisions crossed.

A. P. Hill's battle soon became firm, but he waited a little for Jackson before giving it full force. Jackson came up, marched by the fight without giving attention, and went into camp at Hundley's Corner, half a mile in rear of the enemy's position of contention. A. P. Hill put his force in severe battle and was repulsed. As D. H. Hill approached, he was called into the fray by the commanding general, then by the President. He sent Ripley's brigade and five batteries, which made the battle strong and hot along the line.

The most determined efforts were against the enemy's right, where General McCall, reinforced by Kern's battery and Griffin's and Martindale's brigades (Morell's division), Edwards's battery, and the Third Regiment of Meade's brigade, beat off the repeated and formidable efforts of A. P. Hill, when he essayed a column against the crossing at Ellerson's Mill, which McCall reinforced by the Seventh Regiment of Meade's, Eastman's battery, and before night the Fourth Michigan, Twelfth New York, and Berdan's Sharp-shooters came in to reinforce the line and relieve regiments exhausted of ammunition. The battle was in close conflict till nine o'clock at night, when Hill was obliged to give over till morning. The Federal reinforcements were not all engaged, and some that were suffered but little; none very severely. McCall replenished ammunition and prepared to renew the fight the next morning.

The Federal loss in the engagement was 361 aggregate.*

No especial account of the Confederate loss was made in separate report, but it could not have been less than two thousand, and may have reached three thousand.

---

* Rebellion Record, vol. xi. part ii. p. 38.

General D. H. Hill reported of his Forty-fourth Georgia Regiment; the lieutenant-colonel, Estes (J. B.), wounded, and others, aggregating 331 killed and wounded. Of his First North Carolina Regiment, Colonel Stokes, Major Skinner, six captains, and the adjutant killed, and 133 privates killed and wounded.

During the night General McClellan ordered his troops withdrawn. They retired at daylight on the 27th, leaving a line of skirmishers to cover the march. The skirmishers were not severely pressed, the Confederates being satisfied that [illegible] he halted, and the flanking march-mo[illegible]ve. Early in the morning D. H. Hill was ordered to march to the left to turn the position, and was on the Federal right before their troops were well out of their trenches. He came up with Jackson and led the march of that column from Hundley's Corner. A. P. Hill marched by the direct route to Gaines's Mill, and Longstreet, in reserve, moved by the route near the river to Dr. Gaines's house.

D. H. Hill marched by Bethesda Church to Old Cold Harbor. He understood the plan of campaign and promptly engaged the new position along the Chickahominy Heights on the enemy's right, where he found a well-posted battery of ten guns near swamp lands commanding the only road of approach. He ordered Bondurant's battery into action, but the combat was unequal; the latter was forced to retire, and General Jackson ordered the division back to selected ground parallel to a road over which he supposed that the Federals would presently retreat.

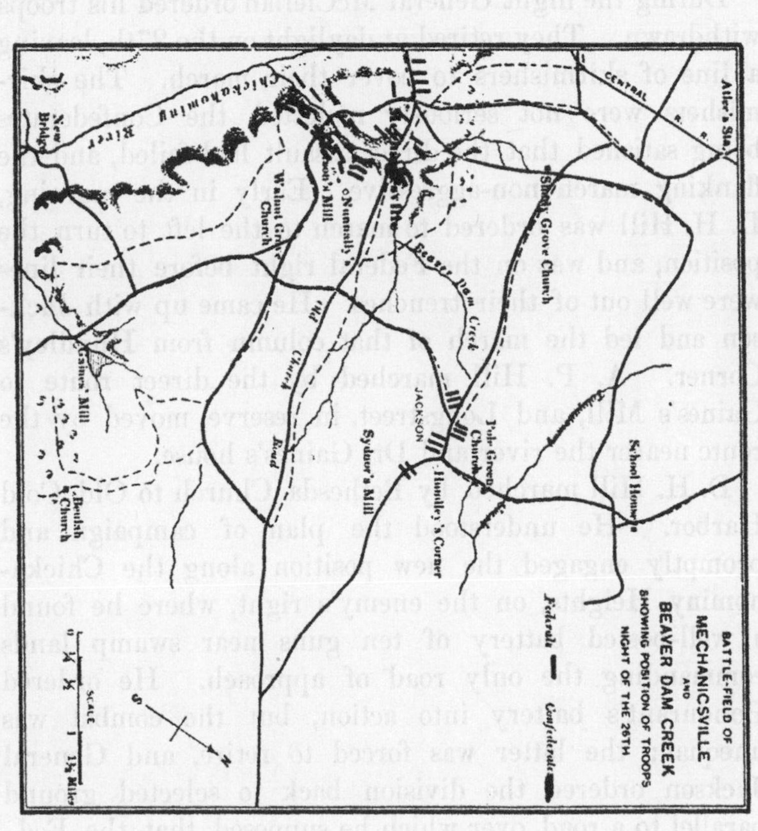

As my division was in reserve, it could only be used in the last extremity. So the driving could only be made by the division of A. P. Hill, while Jackson, with his own, Ewell's, D. H. Hill's, and Whiting's divisions, had more than half of our moving column, organized as our leading battle force, held in ambush for the enemy.

General D. H. Hill reported of his Forty-fourth Georgia Regiment, the lieutenant-colonel, Estes (J. B.), wounded, and others, aggregating 334 killed and wounded. Of his First North Carolina Regiment, Colonel Stokes, Major Skinner, six captains, and the adjutant killed, and 133 privates killed and wounded.

During the night General McClellan ordered his troops withdrawn. They retired at daylight on the 27th, leaving a line of skirmishers to cover their march. The skirmishers were not seriously molested, the Confederates being satisfied that the direct assault had failed, and the flanking march non-aggressive. Early in the morning, D. H. Hill was ordered to march to the left to turn the position, and was on the Federal right before their lines were well out of their trenches. He came up with Jackson and led the march of that column from Hundley's Corner. A. P. Hill marched by the direct route to Gaines's Mill, and Longstreet, in reserve, moved by the route nearer the river and Dr. Gaines's house.

D. H. Hill marched by Bethesda Church to Old Cold Harbor. He understood the plan of campaign and promptly engaged the new position along the Chickahominy Heights, on the enemy's right, where he found a well-posted battery of ten guns near swamp lands commanding the only road of approach. He ordered Bondurant's battery into action, but the combat was unequal; the latter was forced to retire, and General Jackson ordered the division back to selected ground parallel to a road over which he supposed that the Federals would presently retreat.

As my division was in reserve, it could only be used in the last extremity. So the driving could only be made by the division of A. P. Hill, while Jackson, with his own, Ewell's, D. H. Hill's, and Whiting's divisions, had more than half of our moving column, organized as our leading battle force, held in ambush for the enemy.

The enemy was found strongly posted upon high ground over the Grapevine Bridge, forming a semicircle, his flanks near the river. A deep and steep chasm in front of his left divided the height upon which he stood from an open plateau over which he must be attacked, if at all, on his left. The side slope leading up to that position was covered by open forest, obstructed and defended by fallen trees. On the crest were felled trees, occasional sand-bags, piles of rails, and knapsacks. Behind these lines were the divisions of Sykes and Morell, with bristling artillery for the first defence, with McCall's division of infantry and a tremendous array of artillery in reserve. Further strength was given to the position by a stream which cut in between the two heights with deep scarped banks. His right was covered to some extent by swamp lands and forest tangles almost as formidable as the approach towards his left. General Fitz-John Porter was the commander on the field.

A. P. Hill came upon a detachment at Gaines's Mill, forced his way across the creek, and followed to the enemy's strong position, where he promptly engaged about the time of D. H. Hill's withdrawal. He found himself fighting not only strong numbers, but against a very strong defensive ground. As General D. H. Hill withdrew, General Porter prepared to follow, but the fierce assaults of A. P. Hill told him that he must hold his concentration. It was a little after two P.M. when A. P. Hill put all of his force into action and pressed his battle with great zeal and courage, but he was alone. Jackson, finding the fire of the enemy steady and accumulating against A. P. Hill, ordered his troops forward into action. D. H. Hill engaged again at the swamp land, and found that he must capture the battery firing across his advance. With the aid of some of Elzey's brigade he succeeded in this, temporarily, but Sykes doubled on him, recovered it, and put it again into action. Parts of Ewell and Lawton, of Jackson's, came in on D. H. Hill's right. Meanwhile,

A. P. Hill had fought to exhaustion, and found himself obliged to put his troops down to hold his line. The enemy putting in his reserves, spliced his thinned ranks with artillery and infantry, and fought a desperate and very gallant battle, calling for troops from across the river.

My division came up near A. P. Hill's rear, being the reserve, and awaited orders. About five o'clock a messenger came from General Lee asking a diversion by part of my troops against the enemy's left to draw off troops from his right, so as to let our left in through his weakening lines. Three brigades were sent to open fire and threaten their left from the forest edge, with orders not to cross the open. These brigades engaged steadily, and parts of them essayed to pass the field in front as their blood grew hot, but were recalled, with orders repeated to engage steadily, only threatening assault. The army all the while engaged in efforts to find a point that could be forced.

Finally, a little before sunset, General Lee sent to me to say that "all other efforts had failed, and unless I could do something, the day was lost." * Pickett's brigade and part of R. H. Anderson's had been drawn up under the crest in rear of A. P. Hill's right, and Kemper's brigade was near, also under cover. Upon the receipt of the last message, Pickett and Anderson were ordered into action as assaulting columns, and Kemper called up. Just as the brigades advanced, General Whiting burst through the woods with his own and Hood's brigades, reported to me that he had lost sight of his commander, General Jackson, in the forest, and asked me to put him into battle. He was ordered to form for assault, and to follow on the left of Pickett's and Anderson's columns, then in motion, as the columns of direction. As my troops reached

*** From memory I will say that this message from General Lee was delivered by Captain A. P. Mason.**

the crest under which they had rested they came under the full blaze of the battle, but Pickett and Anderson were comparatively fresh, and dashed through the open and down the slope before the fire had time to thin their ranks. The steep descent of the hither slope from its crest soon took them below the fire of the batteries, and A. P. Hill's severe fight had so thinned the enemy's infantry lines of men and ammunition that their fire grew weaker. Whiting's brigade, sore under its recent disastrous effort in the battle of Seven Pines, drifted from my left towards the woodland, but Hood, with his Fourth Texas Regiment and Eighteenth Georgia, obliqued to the right behind that brigade and closed the interval towards Anderson's left, leaving his other regiments, the First and Fifth Texas, on Whiting's left. Hood clambered over the deep ravine with his two regiments and maintained position with the assaulting columns, while the balance of Whiting's division followed in close echelon. As the advanced lines of Pickett, Anderson, and Hood reached and crowned the stronghold of the enemy, Anderson and Pickett moved up in pursuit of the broken lines, and were almost in possession of their massed reserve artillery—had it under easy musketry range—when a dash of cavalry admonished them that their ranks, while in order for following the infantry lines, were not in proper form to receive a charge of cavalry. They concentrated well enough to pour a repelling fire into the troopers, but the delay had made time for the retreating infantry to open the field for the reserve batteries, and, night growing apace, they returned to the line of their trophies and used the captured guns against their late owners.

General Whiting asked for another brigade of Jackson's that had reported to me, and turned his forces against the enemy's line on our left. The divisions of Ewell and D. H. Hill advancing at the same time, the general break seemed almost simultaneous, and was claimed by all.

The messages from General Lee were so marked by their prompt and successful execution that, in reporting of the battle, it occurred to me that they could be better noted in his report than in mine, but he adopted the claim of a general and simultaneous break along the line.

A letter from General Porter, written since the war, assures the writer that his guns had become so foul from steady protracted fire that his men had difficulty in ramming their cartridges to the gun-chambers, and that in some instances it could only be accomplished by putting the rammers against trees and hammering them down.

The position was too strong to leave room to doubt that it was only the thinning fire, as the battle progressed, that made it assailable; besides, the repulse of A. P. Hill's repeated, desperate assaults forcibly testified to the fact. It was, nevertheless, a splendid charge, by peerless soldiers. When the cavalry came upon us our lines were just thin enough for a splendid charge upon artillery, but too thin to venture against a formidable cavalry. Five thousand prisoners were turned over to General Lee's provost-guard, a number of batteries and many thousand small-arms to the Ordnance Department, by my command. The Confederate commanders, except A. P. Hill, claimed credit for the first breach in General Porter's lines, but the solid ranks of prisoners delivered to the general provost-guard, and the several batteries captured and turned in to the Ordnance Department, show the breach to have been made by the columns of Anderson, Pickett, and Hood's two regiments. The troops of the gallant A. P. Hill, that did as much and effective fighting as any, received little of the credit properly due them. It was their long and steady fight that thinned the Federal ranks and caused them to so foul their guns that they were out of order when the final struggle came.

Early on the 28th my advance, reaching the river, found the bridges destroyed and the enemy concentrating on the other side. Under the impression that the enemy must reopen connection with his base on the Pamunkey, General Lee sent Stuart's cavalry and part of Jackson's command (Ewell's) to interpose on that line. They cut the line at Despatch Station, where Ewell's division was halted. Stuart, following down towards the depot on the Pamunkey till he approached the White House, cut off a large detachment of cavalry and horse artillery under General Stoneman that retreated down the Peninsula. At night Stuart rested his command, finding supplies of forage and provisions abandoned by the enemy. At the same time fires were seen along the line of supplies, and houses in flames. On the 29th he followed towards the depot, still in flames.

"The command was now entirely out of rations and the horses without forage. I had relied on the enemy at the White House to supply me with those essentials, and I was not disappointed, in spite of their efforts to destroy everything. Provisions and delicacies of every description lay in heaps, and men regaled themselves on fruits of the tropics as well as the substantials of the land. Large quantities of forage were left also." *

On the 28th, Major Meade and Lieutenant Johnson, engineers, were sent from my head-quarters to learn of the enemy's operations or movements. Early on the 29th they made their way across the Chickahominy, into the grounds and works of the enemy just left vacant, and sent the first account of the enemy's move on his change of base. The conflagrations of the day before told of speedy change of position in some direction, but this was the first information we had from a reliable source. Their report was sent to General Lee. While planning and ordering pursuit, he received a similar report from General Magruder, coupled with the statement that he was preparing to attack one of the enemy's forts.

* Rebellion Record, vol. xi. part ii. p. 517. Stuart.

General Jackson was ordered to follow on the enemy's rear with his column, including the division of D. H. Hill, crossing the river at Grapevine Bridge, Magruder to join pursuit along the direct line of retreat, Huger to strike at the enemy's flank; meanwhile, Ransom's brigade had joined Huger's division. My division was to cross with A. P. Hill's at New Bridge, march back near Richmond, across to and down the Darbytown road to interpose between the enemy and James River. Stuart was directed to operate against the enemy's left or rear, or front, as best he could.

All the commands, being in waiting, marched at the first moment of their orders.

Jackson was long delayed repairing Grapevine Bridge. He probably knew that the river was fordable at that season, but preferred to pass his men over dry-shod.

General D. H. Hill, of that column, reported,—

"Scouts from Hood's brigade and the Third Alabama (Rodes's brigade) succeeded in crossing, and my pioneer corps under Captain Smith, of the Engineers, repaired Grapevine Bridge on the 29th, and we crossed over at three o'clock that night." *

On the 28th the Seventh and Eighth Georgia Regiments were sent out a little before night to ascertain the probable movements of the enemy, and encountered part of W. F. Smith's division, Sixth Corps, meeting the Forty-ninth Pennsylvania and Thirty-third New York Regiments. Colonel Lamar and Lieutenant-Colonel Towers and Adjutant Harper, of the Eighth Georgia Regiment, fell into the enemy's hands, and twenty-nine others of the Seventh and Eighth Regiments were taken prisoners. Just as this affair was well begun a recall of the regiments was ordered; hence the number of casualties. About the same hour a cavalry affair at Despatch Station occurred which resulted to the credit of the Confederates.

---

* Rebellion Record, vol. xi. part ii. p. 627. D. H. Hill.

At night General McClellan called his corps commanders to head-quarters and announced his plan for change of base to the James River. The Fourth Corps had been ordered to prepare the route of crossing at White Oak Swamp, and pass over to defend it. The Fifth and Slocum's division of the Sixth were to follow at night of the 28th. The Second, Third, and Smith's division of the Sixth Corps were to defend the crossing against pursuit; the Fourth, continuing its move, was to stand at Turkey Bridge, defending the approach from Richmond by the river road; the Fifth to stand at Malvern Hill, with McCall's division across the Long Bridge road, and Slocum's across the Charles City road, defending the avenues of approach from Richmond. On the 29th, Magruder in pursuit came upon Sumner's (Second) corps at Allen's Farm, and, after a spirited affair, found Sumner too strong for him. After his success, Sumner retired to Savage Station, where he joined Franklin with his division under Smith. The Third Corps (Heintzelman's), under misconception of orders, or misleading of staff-officers, followed the marching corps across the swamp, leaving the Second and Smith's division of the Sixth as the only defending forces. At Savage Station, Magruder came upon them and again joined battle, but his force was not equal to the occasion. The commander of his left (D. R. Jones), realizing the importance of action and the necessity for additional troops, called upon General Jackson to co-operate on his left, but Jackson reported that he had other important duties to perform. The affair, therefore, against odds was too strong for Magruder, so that he was forced back without important results for the Confederates, the Federals making safe passage of the crossing and gaining position to defend against pursuit in that quarter.

On the 29th, General Holmes marched down the James River road to New Market with part of Colonel Daniel's brigade and two batteries, and General J. G. Walker's brigade and two batteries, and was there reinforced by part of General Wise's brigade and two batteries, in co-operative position to my division and that of A. P. Hill, on the Darbytown and Long Bridge roads.

On his night march along the Long Bridge road, Fitz-John Porter got on the wrong end and rubbed up against my outpost, but recognized his adversary in time to recover his route and avert a night collision. He posted McCall's division in front of Charles City cross-roads; his divisions under Morell and Sykes at Malvern Hill, and Warren's brigade, near the Fourth Corps, on the river routes from Richmond. As the divisions of the Third Corps arrived they were posted,—Kearny between the Charles City and Long Bridge roads, on McCall's right; Hooker in front of the Quaker road, on McCall's left; Sedgwick's division, Sumner's corps, behind McCall.

Before noon of the 30th, Jackson's column encountered Franklin, defending the principal crossing of White Oak Swamp by the divisions of Richardson and W. F. Smith and Naglee's brigade. About the same time my command marched down the Long Bridge road and encountered the main force of McClellan's army posted at the Charles City cross-roads (Frayser's Farm, or Glendale). My division was deployed across the Long Bridge road in front of the divisions of McCall and Kearny, holding the division of A. P. Hill at rest in the rear, except the brigade under Branch, which was posted off to my right and rear to guard against Hooker's division, standing behind the Quaker road, in threatening position on my right flank. The ground along the front of McCall and Kearny was a dark forest, with occasional heavy tangles, as was the ground in front of Hooker. The front of Slocum, along the Charles City road, was something similar, but offering some better opportunities for artillery practice and infantry tactics.

As Jackson and Franklin engaged in artillery combat, my division advanced under desultory fire of skirmishers to close position for battle, awaiting nearer approach of Jackson and signal of approach of our troops on the Charles City road. In the wait the skirmish-lines were more or less active, and an occasional shot came from one of the Federal batteries.

During the combat between Jackson and Franklin, Sedgwick's brigades under Dana and Sully were sent back to reinforce at the crossing, but upon the opening of the engagement at Frayser's Farm they were brought back on the double-quick.

After a time reports of cannon fire came from the direction of Charles City road, signalling, as we supposed, the approach of Huger's column. To this I ordered one of our batteries to return salutation. The senior brigadier of the division, R. H. Anderson, was assigned to immediate supervision of my front line, leaving his brigade under Colonel M. Jenkins. While awaiting the nearer approach of Jackson or the swelling volume of Huger's fire, the President, General Lee, and General A. P. Hill, with their staffs and followers, rode forward near my line and joined me in a little clearing of about three acres, curtained by dense pine forests. All parties engaged in pleasant talk and anticipations of the result of a combination supposed to be complete and prepared for concentrating battle,—Jackson attacking in the rear, Huger on the right flank, A. P. Hill and myself standing in front. Very soon we were disturbed by a few shells tearing and screaming through the forests over our heads, and presently one or two burst in our midst, wounding a courier and killing and wounding several horses. The little opening was speedily cleared of the distinguished group that graced its meagre soil, and it was left to more humble, active combatants.

Near the battery from which the shots came was R. H.

Anderson's brigade, in which Colonel Jenkins had a battalion of practised sharp-shooters. I sent orders for Jenkins to silence the battery, under the impression that our wait was understood, and that the sharp-shooters would be pushed forward till they could pick off the gunners, thus ridding us of that annoyance; but the gallant Jenkins, only too anxious for a dash at a battery, charged and captured it, thus precipitating battle. The troops right and left going in, in the same spirit, McCall's fire and the forest tangle thinned our ranks as the lines neared each other, and the battle staggered both sides, but, after a formidable struggle, the Confederates won the ground, and Randol's gallant battery. Sedgwick's division reinforced the front and crowded back the Confederate right, while Kearny's, reinforced by Slocum, pushed severely against my left, and then part of Hooker's division came against my right. Thus the aggressive battle became defensive, but we held most of the ground gained from McCall.

In his official account, General Heintzelman said,—

"In less than an hour General McCall's division gave way. General Hooker, being on his left, by moving to the right repulsed the rebels in the handsomest manner and with great slaughter. General Sumner, who was with General Sedgwick, in McCall's rear, also greatly aided with his artillery and infantry in driving back the enemy. They now renewed the attack with vigor on Kearny's left, and were again repulsed with heavy loss. The attack continued until some time after night.

"This attack commenced at four P.M. and was pushed by heavy masses with the utmost determination and vigor. Captain Thompson's battery, directed with great skill, firing double charges, swept them back. The whole open space, two hundred paces wide, was filled with the enemy. Each repulse brought fresh troops.

"Seeing that the enemy was giving way, I returned to the forks of the road, where I received a call from General Kearny for aid. Knowing that all of General Sedgwick's troops were unavailable, I was glad to avail myself of the kind offer of General Slocum to send the New Jersey brigade of his division to

General Kearny's aid. I rode out far enough on the Charles City road to see that we had nothing to fear from that direction." *

General McCall reported,—

"I had ridden into the regiment to endeavor to check them, but with only partial success. It was my fortune to witness one of the fiercest bayonet charges that ever occurred on this continent. Bayonet wounds, mortal and slight, were given and received. I saw skulls smashed by the butts of muskets, and every effort made by either party in this life-and-death struggle proving indeed that here Greek had met Greek. The Seventh Regiment was at this time on the right of the Fourth, and was too closely engaged with a force also of great superiority in numbers to lend any assistance to the gallant few of the Fourth who were struggling at their side. In fine, these few men, some seventy or eighty, were borne bodily off among the rebels, and when they reached a gap in the fence walked through it, while the enemy, intent on pursuing those in front of them, passed on without noticing them.

"It was at this moment, on witnessing this scene, I keenly felt the want of reinforcements. I had not a single regiment left to send to the support of those so overpowered. There was no running, but my division, reduced by the furious battles to less than six thousand, had to contend with the divisions of Longstreet and A. P. Hill (considered two of the strongest and best among many of the Confederate army, numbering that day eighteen or twenty thousand men), and it was reluctantly compelled to give way before heavier force accumulated upon them. My right was, as I say, literally forced off the ground by the weight simply of the enemy's column."

His account is incorrect in the estimate of numbers and the two divisions. Hill was not put in until a later hour, and encountered the troops of Kearny and Slocum. Hill's orders were to hold the line gained until Jackson and Huger approached, to warrant more aggressive battle.

Magruder's march had been directed to succor Holmes.

* Rebellion Record, vol. xi. part ii. p. 100. Heintzelman.

In his official account, General Holmes wrote of parts of his cavalry and artillery, "whose conduct was shameful in the extreme." He reported his casualties:

"Daniel's brigade, 2 killed, 22 wounded; Walker's brigade, 12 wounded; artillery, 15 wounded.

"The strength of the enemy's position and their imposing numbers were such that to attempt an attack upon them with my small force, unsupported, would have been perfect madness; for to have done this would have required a march of over three-quarters of a mile up a steep hill destitute of cover. I accordingly withdrew about nine P.M. to a position somewhat in advance of that occupied in the morning." *

In his account of the fight, General Kearny wrote,—

"At four P.M. the attack commenced on my line with a determination and vigor, and in such masses, as I had never witnessed. Thompson's battery, directed with great skill, literally swept the slightly falling open space with the completest execution, and, mowing them down by ranks, would cause the survivors to momentarily halt; but, almost instantly after, increased masses came up, and the wave bore on. . . .

"In concluding my report of this battle, one of the most desperate of the war, the one most fatal, if lost, I am proud to give my thanks and to include in the glory of my own division the First New Jersey Brigade, General Taylor, who held McCall's deserted ground, and General Caldwell." †

A. P. Hill's division was held at rest several hours after the battle was pitched (Branch's brigade on guard on my right retired, and Gregg's on my left). Under our plan, that Huger was to assault the Federal right and Jackson the rear, the battle joined; Hill was to be put in fresh to crown it. As night approached without indications of attack from either of those columns, Hill was advanced to relieve the pressure against my worn troops. At the first

* Rebellion Record, vol. xi. part ii. p. 107.
† Ibid., pp. 162-164.

dash he again grasped and held Randol's battery, that had been the source of contention from the first onset. Field's brigade pushed on through the enemy's line, and, supported by Pender's and Branch's, drove back reinforcements coming to their succor from one of Sedgwick's brigades; pushed Caldwell's off to Kearny's position, where, with the additional aid of part of Slocum's division, Kearny succeeded in recovering his own ground and in putting Caldwell's brigade into part of McCall's original right, leaving the Confederates holding part of McCall's first line, Field's brigade some little distance in advance of it. Archer and Branch, on Field's right, made strong that part of it. Gregg's brigade on the left made little progress beyond holding most of the ground taken by the first assault. The battle thus braced held its full and swelling volume on both sides. My right, thinned by the heavy fighting and tangled forest, found a way around the left of the contention, then gravitating towards its centre. In this effort Hooker's division came against its right flank. By change of front a clever fight was made, but Branch's brigade, ordered for service at that point, had been withdrawn by General Hill to support his centre, so that Hooker pushed us off into closed ranks along our line in rear and back; but his gallant onset was checked and failed of progress. General Hooker claimed that he threw Longstreet over on Kearny, but General McCall said that by a little stretch of the hyperbole he could have said that he threw Longstreet over the moon. To establish his centre, Hill sent in J. R. Anderson's brigade astride the Long Bridge road, which held the battle till the near approach of night, when McCall, in his last desperate effort to reinforce and recover his lost ground, was caught in the dark of twilight and invited to ride to my head-quarters. Friends near him discovered his dilemma in time to avert their own capture, and aggressive battle ceased. The artillery combat, with occasional exchanges of shots, held till an hour after the beat of tattoo.

It was the Forty-seventh Virginia Regiment that caught and invited General McCall to quarter with the Confederates. Although his gallant division had been forced from the fight, the brave head and heart of the general were not fallen till he found himself on his lonely ride. He was more tenacious of his battle than any one who came within my experience during the war, if I except D. H. Hill at Sharpsburg.

In years gone by I had known him in pleasant army service, part of the time as a brevet lieutenant of his company. When the name was announced, and as he dismounted, I approached to offer my hand and such amenities as were admissible under the circumstances, but he drew up with haughty mien, which forbade nearer approach, so that the courtesies were concluded by the offer of staff-officers to escort him to the city of Richmond.

It was during this affair that General Holmes's division advanced against the Federals at Turkey Bridge with a six-gun field battery and engaged, and was met by the fire of thirty field guns and the gunboat batteries, which drove him to confusion, abandoning two guns. Earlier in the day, Magruder's column had been ordered by a long détour to support the fight at Frayser's Farm, but the trouble encountered by Holmes's division seemed serious, and caused the Confederate commander to divert Magruder's march to support that point, through which a resolute advance might endanger our rear at Frayser's Farm. After night Magruder was called to relieve the troops on the front of my line. His march during the day was delayed by his mistaken guide.

The Confederates claimed as trophies of the battle ten pieces of artillery, some prisoners, and most of the field from which McCall's division had been dislodged. Holmes's division lost two guns in the affair at Turkey

Bridge, but other Confederates secured and afterwards made better use of them. Meanwhile, the Federals were anxiously pushing their trains to cover on the river, and before noon of July 1 all, except those of necessary ammunition, had safely passed the field selected for their Malvern Hill battle. Colonel Fairfax, who was sent to quicken the movements of General Jackson's column, describes his ride as follows:

"Potomac, Va., April 24, 1902.

"Lieutenant-General James Longstreet:

"My Dear General,—At your request, I write what I recalled to your mind not very long ago, of my awakening and ride to find Lieutenant-General Jackson after the battle of Frazier's Farm in 1862. After conducting Major-General Magruder, with his division, to your line of battle, relieving your troops under cover of darkness, I was very tired, having been in the saddle all day. I had finally fallen asleep 'mid the mournful groans of the suffering soldiers under the surgeons' saw and knife, when you came and laid down on my blanket and upon me, and whispered in my ear, 'Are you very tired?' Believing you had work for me, I quickly answered, 'No!' 'Can you find General Jackson?' was asked. I replied, 'I will try.' To the question, 'Which way will you go,' I made answer, 'Over the white-oak swamps to the left of where we fought to-day.' 'No; not that way!' you said, decisively. Then I suggested, ''Round by Seven Pines Battle-field.' 'Yes,' you agreed, 'that is the way; tell General Jackson that General Lee has a courier taken with orders from General McClellan that he will attack in the morning; bring General Jackson up as early as you can; take a courier with you.' After a long ride, I reached General Jackson at his camp on the side of the road near the swamp, about half an hour after sunrise. I delivered your order and started on return to you, when General Jackson called, 'Which way are you going?' I replied, 'Across the swamps on this road.' General Jackson said, 'You must not go that way.' 'General,' I declared, 'I believe the enemy have gone.' But General Jackson insisted that I must wait until the bridge was repaired and go with his escort. I rode to the swamp, and found his escort there. As soon as the last plank was placed, I rode over, the escort following.

"Very truly yours.

"Jno. W. Fairfax."

CHAPTER XI.

BATTLE OF MALVERN HILL.

Last Stand in the Great Retreat—Strength of McClellan's Position—The Confederates make Poor Use of their Artillery—A Mistake and Defeat for Lee's Army—The Campaign as a Whole a Great Success, but it should have been far greater—McClellan's Retreat showed him well equipped in the Science of War—Review of the Campaign—Jackson's and Magruder's Misunderstanding—Moral Effect of the Gunboats on the James River—"There should be a Gunboat in Every Family."

At Malvern Hill, hardly a league away from Frayser's, now left to silence save for the moans of the unfortunate fallen, and standing south of the line to Turkey Bridge, was Fitz-John Porter with the reserve artillery massed, supported by the divisions of Sykes and Morell on the left and Couch's on the right, from the Crew House to J. W. Binford's. The field had been carefully selected and as judiciously guarded by well-posted commands, holding the only way left which gave hope of successful passage to cover under the gunboats. During the night of the 30th of June and early morn of the 1st of July this position was reinforced by the retreating Federals,—first by the Second and Third Corps, McCall's division of the Fifth, and W. F. Smith's of the Sixth, and later by other troops. Among the trains moving for the river was one of ten siege guns under Colonel Tyler. These were dropped in Porter's rear and put in battery, giving them a sweep of the avenues of approach and extensive rake of the woodlands, and a great number of lighter batteries bristled upon the brow and down the slopes of the hill. On either flank the plateau was somewhat guarded by ravines and tangled marsh lands, while the front approach was over ascending slopes, so broken as to make advancing artillery combat slow and hazardous.

Early on the 1st, the columns under Huger, Jackson, and Magruder met at the Charles City cross-roads, but the enemy had given up that position and marched away, leaving to them the abandoned forest land. The disappointment of the Confederate commander in the failure of combination ordered for the 30th was noted by those who were near him, while the composure with which it was borne indicated the grander elements of his character, and drew those who knew his plans and purposes closer to him.

Jackson was ordered to follow on the direct line of the enemy's retreat; Huger and Magruder marched to co-operate on his right; Longstreet's and A. P. Hill's divisions were held in reserve. General Lee rode near Jackson's column to view the army on that front. Feeling unwell and much fatigued, he called me to temporary service near him. As he rode to the left, he ordered me, with the columns of Huger and Magruder, to make reconnoissance of the enemy's new position in that quarter, and to report of the feasibility of aggressive battle.

I found some difference between General Lee's maps and General Magruder's guides, but my authority was only for a reconnoissance, and posting the divisions. An elevated point was found off the enemy's left front, as high as the plateau upon which his army stood, from which a fair view was had of his position and down along his front and the open as far as Jackson's field, the latter just filing in by his batteries on much lower but open ground.

Profound silence rested upon the field. Jackson's batteries, yet a little beyond the point of range, marched to their places as quietly as if taking positions for review. Porter's field seemed as little concerned at the developments along his flank and front, indicating that there was to be no waste of ammunition on that July day. His guns could not be counted, but blocking them off by batteries there seemed to be eighty on his front, besides the

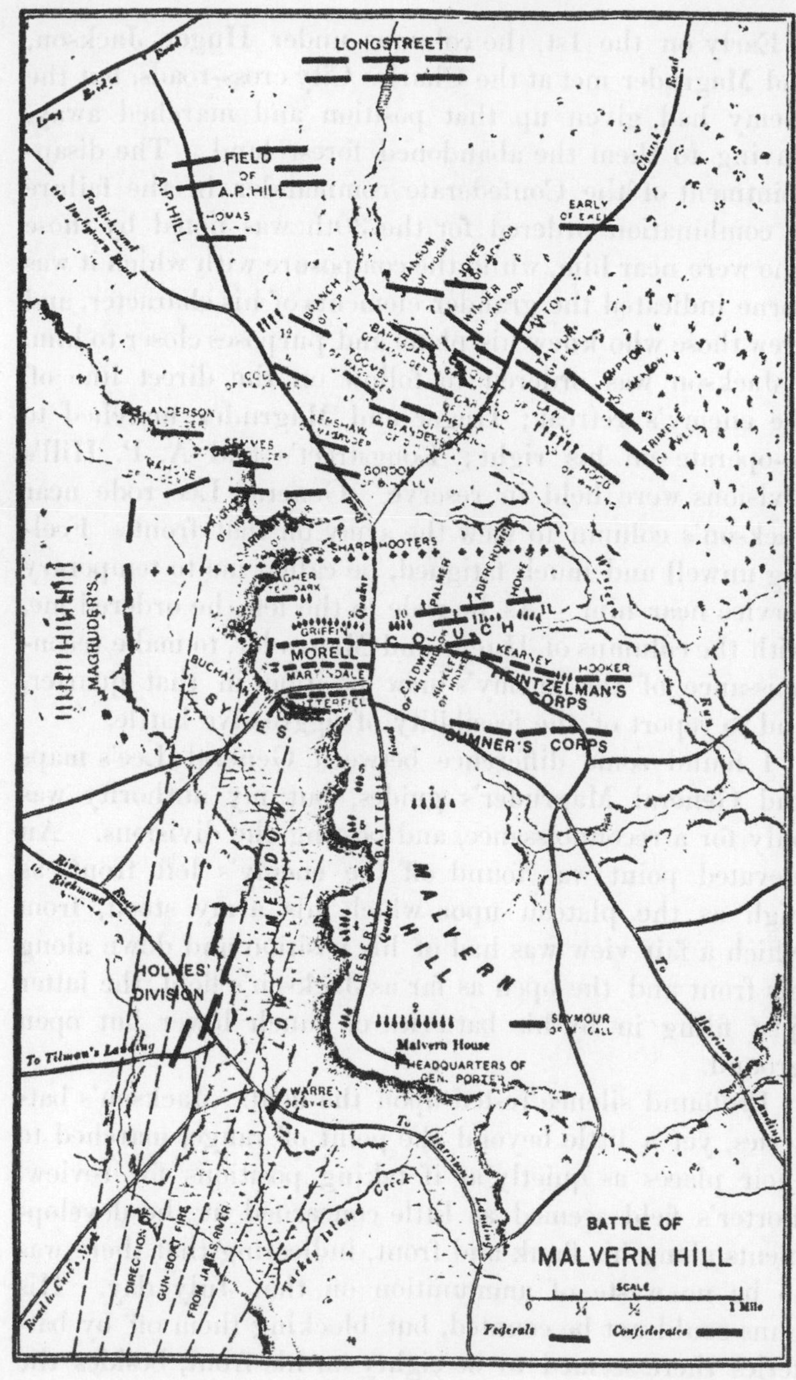
LONGSTREET
FIELD OF A.P. HILL
A.P. HILL
EARLY
BRANCH
RANSOM
JONES
WINDER
LAWTON
TAYLOR
HAMPTON
TRIMBLE
COBB
KERSHAW
G.B. ANDERSON
ANDERSON
SEMMES
GORDON
SHARPSHOOTERS
GRIFFIN
MORELL
MARTINDALE
SYKES
PALMER
ABERCROMBIE
HOWE
COUCH
KEARNEY
HOOKER
HEINTZELMAN'S CORPS
SUMNER'S CORPS
MAGRUDER'S
HOLMES' DIVISION
To Tilmen's Landing
River Road to Richmond
LOW MEADOW
MALVERN HILL
Quaker Road
SEYMOUR
Malvern House
HEADQUARTERS OF GEN. PORTER
Turkey Island Creek
DIRECTION OF GUN-BOAT FIRE FROM JAMES RIVER
BATTLE OF MALVERN HILL
SCALE
1 Mile
Federals
Confederates

siege battery in rear. His guns were all trailed to Jackson's front, thus presenting a flank towards the high point upon which I stood. From the crest at this little ridge the ground dropped off sharply some eighteen inches or two feet to a lower terrace, forming a natural parapet and terre-plein for forty or sixty guns, massed. The spacious open along Jackson's front appeared to offer a field for play of a hundred or more guns, and although his lower ground was not inviting of combat even by a hundred guns, it was yet judged that advancing combat by eighty or a hundred guns, in combination with the forty-gun battery of position, might justify assault, and the tremendous game at issue called for adventure.

I thought it probable that Porter's batteries, under the cross-fire of the Confederates thus posted on his left and front, could be thrown into disorder, and thus make way for combined assaults of the infantry. I so reported, and General Lee ordered disposition accordingly, sending the pioneer corps out to cut a road for the right batteries of position.

I suggested position to Magruder for his division, but he insisted that the Quaker road was not correctly located on General Lee's maps, so I left that part of the order to be looked after by General Lee's recognized staff. General Chilton, chief of staff, was then sent by General Lee to assist General Magruder in posting the troops, and I was ordered back to locate the batteries.

But eight guns came in proper time and were posted. These General Magruder proposed to supplement by thirty of his own under Colonel S. D. Lee, to be reinforced by the others as they came up. With this understanding I returned to head-quarters, made my report, and was permitted to go back to my command proper.

The most convenient point for observing the effect of the artillery fire was occupied by General Armistead's brigade. That officer was designated by General Lee to give notice, if the combat was successful, by advancing his brigade, under the shouts of infantry charge, as the signal for general assault.

The eight guns for the right battery were all that got into position on time, and Jackson failed to open fire by advancing all of the batteries along his front, so that the practice from those quarters was not forcibly executed. When the eight guns finally opened, Porter shifted his aim from his proper front, which Jackson failed to combat, and put in the fire of forty guns against the eight-gun battery of our right. The gunboat batteries also came into that practice, but it was found that they damaged friends almost as much as the enemy, and were ordered to discontinue. Jackson's cross-fire, feeble at best and at long range, was finally drawn off by other batteries far on the enemy's right, so that the eight guns were soon piled a heterogeneous mass of caissons, guns, limbers, and horses. Some other batteries got into action at the same point, eight or ten at a time, but suffered like disaster.

So the plan for battle and order of the day were given over by the Confederate commander, who sent for me to ride with him over to his left in search of a route by which the enemy's right might be turned. This seemed feasible under the hasty reconnoissance, and he ordered the reserves on that move. As we started on the march the noise of battle reached us and the march was arrested. Under the impression that his officers realized the failure and abandonment of his original plan, General Lee failed to issue orders specifically recalling the appointed battle.

It seems that just as the troops marched to the left under the last order, information was received by some of the officers at the front that the enemy was getting away from us.

To ascertain as to this matter, and anxious to atone for lost opportunities of the day before, part of the troops near our right moved forward, and soon encountered the enemy's infantry, as well as the formidable artillery. This impact burst into the noise of battle, and was taken as the signal for assault under the original order of the day. From the right to the left, as far as and including D. H. Hill's division, the Confederates attacked in splendid style, making repeated brave charges, but they were as firmly met by the enemy, and their dead and wounded were mingled on the same lines. The Confederate ranks thinning rapidly, Magruder called on me for reinforcements, and Jackson was sent to reinforce D. H. Hill's left, but night closed in upon us before the reinforcements could get into action.

As the order for battle had been given about noon, and had been abandoned some hours before the opening, upon receiving Magruder's call, I supposed the conflict had been brought on by the enemy to force our right back and better clear the route of his retreat. I ordered A. P. Hill direct to Magruder, and my own division for support on our extreme right. The result of the battle was a repulse of the Confederates along the entire line and the sacrifice of several thousand brave officers and men, though some of our troops held ground nearer the enemy than at the onset of the battle. During the night the enemy resumed his march for the river, leaving his dead, some of his wounded, and exhibiting other marks of the precipitate character of his retreat.

Stuart's cavalry had been recalled from north of the Chickahominy on the 30th to join us on the south side, and reached Jackson's left Tuesday night after the battle.

The morning of the 2d opened heavy and oppressive. The storm front of bursting cannon and bristling bayonets was changed to a wide sweep of heavy clouds that covered the dead that had grappled and fallen together on Malvern Hill. The enemy was gone, and reached his lodgement at Harrison's Landing on James River, the old seat of that family which has given our country two Presidents. Jackson stood on the direct route of the enemy's retreat, and was ordered to follow it; Magruder's and Huger's commands to follow Jackson. General Lee rode with them. D. H. Hill's division was left to care for the wounded and dead of Malvern Hill. To obviate pressure upon a single track, the reserve divisions were ordered by Nance's Store, but the heavy clouds soon began to let down a pelting rain that became more severe and delayed all movements.

The reports of Jackson and Stuart of the operations of the 3d are conflicting. The former claimed that he was near the landing on the morning of the 3d, and advanced his line of skirmishers. The latter reported that he found during the night of the 2d a fine position on Erlington Heights, from which the enemy could be shelled out of his new position by artillery; that he occupied and held that position by a squadron and howitzer until driven from it by the enemy at two o'clock in the afternoon of the 3d; that he reported of that position to Generals Lee and Jackson during the night of the 2d. Other accounts go with that of Stuart. It seems that the "foot cavalry" * and the reserve divisions met at the landing late in the afternoon of the 3d. The troops from the Valley district had not been engaged in the battles of the march except that of Gaines's Mill.

At daylight of the 4th I rode to the front, and ordered General Jackson to drive in the enemy's skirmishers and prepare to attack. D. R. Jones's division of Magruder's command, coming up, was ordered on Jackson's left, A. P. Hill's on his right; my own division to support Jackson's direct move for Erlington Heights. After pushing the skirmish line back, Jackson reported his troops not in condition for the work, and asked delay until the commanding general was up. As General Lee was reported near, attack was delayed, and a note was sent asking him to

* A name taken by the infantry from the Valley district on account of their swift secret marches.

ride forward as soon as convenient. He rode up in about half an hour, and, after mature deliberation, decided that the attack should not be made. He reinforced his cavalry and horse artillery by a number of his choicest field batteries, and ordered General Stuart to use them against the enemy's transports on the lower James. This expedition did some damage, but the superior batteries of the gunboats, convoys of the transports, enabled them to maintain safe-conduct along the line of supplies and reinforcements. On the 8th he withdrew his army to points more convenient to supplies, and towards the open highway to Washington City.

Passing in critical review the events of the campaign, they fail to disclose a flaw as it was projected by the Confederate chief. It even opened up grander possibilities than came within his most hopeful anticipations at the period of projection.

The Union commander left his Fifth Corps engaged at Beaver Dam Creek while Jackson's column marched by it as far as Hundley's Corner and went into camp. The object and instructions of Jackson's advanced echelon were to have him file in against any force that he might pass and attack it in flank and rear. If, instead of going into camp at Hundley's Corner on the afternoon of the 26th of June, he had filed to his right behind the Fifth Corps, he would have had it surrounded by fifty thousand men beyond the reach of succor.

He was troubled by conflicting orders. The general order for the campaign and verbal instructions were intended to supersede all others, but General Lee's letter of the 11th was not recalled, so he marched with the two orders in his pocket, which made not a little trouble.

Before Jackson's army was called from the Valley, it was reinforced and organized for our working column. On the morning of the 27th of June it was further augmented by the division under D. H. Hill and Stuart's cavalry. His line of march during the day led him around Porter's position near Gaines's Mill to the enemy's right, the most favorable point for attack. He partially engaged by D. H. Hill's division, then withdrew it, and posted his troops in a position selected to catch the Federals in their flight from A. P. Hill's division. Finally, when Porter's defence developed too much strength for A. P. Hill, he deployed into line of battle from left to right, overspreading the enemy's entire front.

On the morning of the 28th of June, General Lee thought to draw McClellan out from his works, force him to defend his base on the Pamunkey, and to so cripple him on his retreat as to warrant strong detachments from his army in the direction of Washington, and thus force him to defend his own capital.

Before marching to the opening of the campaign, he ordered a detachment of cavalry to the south side of White Oak Swamp, under careful watch for the enemy's movements by vedettes, even as far as Chickahominy River, so that on the night of the 27th he had a cordon of troops and vedettes extending completely around McClellan's army. Notwithstanding precautions so carefully laid, McClellan started to march for his new base on the night of the 27th, continued his preparations and movements through the day and night of the 28th, and the first reliable information of the move towards James River came from Major Meade and Lieutenant Johnson, engineers. The information, though coming from a source least looked for, was more than gratifying to General Lee, for he thought the enemy had essayed a move not practicable; that General McClellan's army was in his power and must be our prize, never to reach the new base.

Just as he was mapping out orders of pursuit, a staff-officer of General Magruder's came from the other side of the river to report the Federal army in retreat, and that General Magruder was preparing to assault the fort in his immediate front. General Lee said,—

"My compliments to General Magruder, and ask him not to hurt my young friends, Major Meade and Lieutenant Johnson, who are occupying that fort."

Uniformly military, but courteous in his bearing, it was very rare that he became facetious when on parade service, but anticipations that General McClellan was soon to be his prisoner excused the giving way to impulse born of this unexpected adventure.

Within an hour his troops on the east side were on the march for their crossings of the Chickahominy. He then rode across, gave orders to General Magruder, rode with him some distance, and repeated the orders before leaving him.

Following up the rear-guard, General Magruder came upon it in force at Savage Station. The Second Corps and Franklin's division under W. F. Smith of the Sixth, under General Sumner, were posted there to cover the retreat. Magruder planned battling with his own six brigades against their front, two brigades of Huger's division to come on the enemy's left down the Williamsburg road, Jackson's twelve or fifteen brigades to attack their right. But when Magruder thought his arrangements complete, he received a message from General Huger "that his brigades would be withdrawn." *

Then other information not anticipated came to him,—viz., that General Jones, commanding on Magruder's left, called for co-operation in that quarter. General Jackson sent word in reply that "he had other important duty to perform."

Referring to Jackson's orders of the 29th, General Lee wrote General Magruder:

* Rebellion Record, vol. xi. part ii. p. 664.

"HEAD-QUARTERS DEPARTMENT OF NORTHERN VIRGINIA,
"June 29, 1862.

"MAJOR-GENERAL J. B. MAGRUDER,
"*Commanding Division:*

"GENERAL,—I regret much that you have made so little progress to-day in pursuit of the enemy. In order to reap the fruits of our victory the pursuit should be most vigorous. I must urge you, then, again to press on his rear rapidly and steadily. We must lose no time, or he will escape us entirely.

"Very respectfully yours, etc.,
"R. E. LEE,
"*General.*

"P.S.—Since the order was written, I learn from Major Taylor that you are under the impression that General Jackson has been ordered not to support you. On the contrary, he has been directed to do so, and to push the pursuit vigorously." *

Sumner, besides his greater force, having some advantage from the earthworks previously constructed, repulsed Magruder's attack, and the affair of cross-purposes failed of effect.

If Jackson could have joined against the right of Sumner with his brigades, the latter could have been dislodged, the Confederates passing the swamp with him, which would have marked the beginning of the end. The occasion was especially propitious, for Heintzelman's corps, that had been designated as part of the rear-guard with Sumner and Franklin, through some misconception had marched over the swamp, to camp near Charles City cross-roads, leaving easy work for Jackson and Magruder.

When, on the forenoon of the 30th, Jackson found his way across the swamp blocked by Franklin, he had time to march to the head of and across it to the Charles City road in season for the engagement contemplated at Frayser's Farm, the distance being about four miles. General Wright, of Huger's division, marched his brigade from the head of the swamp to Jackson's line at the bridge,

* Rebellion Record, vol. xi. part ii. p. 687.

and returned, making several halts and crossings to reconnoitre.

But little remains to be said of the engagements at Frayser's Farm and Malvern Hill. The former was a halting failure of combination of forces; the latter an accident resulting from the armies standing close abreast many hours. Malvern Hill left out, the two armies would have mingled their lines between that and Westover during the 3d and 4th of July.

The failure of concert of action by the Confederates should not discount the conduct of McClellan's masterly retreat. In the emergency he showed himself well equipped in the science of war, and prepared to cross swords with his able adversary. At the opening of the campaign he had in hand one hundred and five thousand men. General Lee's returns were not accurately made, but a fair estimate puts his numbers between eighty and eighty-five thousand.

The losses of the campaign were, on the Union side, 15,249; on the Confederate side, greater; in the absence of complete returns, it is fair to say that they were from 18,000 to 19,000. Up to the time of Malvern Hill the casualties were about equally divided between the two armies, but in that battle the Confederates lost not far from 5000 men, and the Federals not more than one-third that number.

Upon reaching the gunboats, General McClellan's power was about doubled. Although fire from the gunboats was not very effective against a land battle, the moral effect of fighting batteries that could not be reached was most powerful. It was reported on the Confederate side that General McClellan, on boarding one of the boats, where he spent most of the day of battle, said, "There should be a gunboat in every family."

Some critics say that McClellan should have taken Richmond during the campaign. The great Napoleon would have done so after the disaster at Malvern Hill with his regularly organized army of veterans. They say, too, that Lee should have captured McClellan and his army. So thought General Lee, but some of his leaders were working at cross-purposes, and did not have that close attention that the times called for.

We may now consider the probable result of the plan mapped out and ordered by General Lee in his letter of June 11th to General Jackson had it been followed, —*i.e.*, Jackson to march down the right bank of the Pamunkey with his troops from the Valley district and attack McClellan's rear east of the Chickahominy, while Lee attacked from the Richmond side with his army. On the Richmond side, McClellan had four army corps, well fortified, supported by his powerful artillery. The battle of Gaines's Mill, where the troops from the Valley were reinforced by four of Lee's choice divisions and most of his cavalry,—more than doubling Jackson's column,—may be significant of the result of Jackson's attack on that side if it had been made as ordered. The battle of Malvern Hill, from an open field, may tell the result of an attack upon the four corps in their fortified position had the attack been made upon them from the Richmond front.

CHAPTER XII.

HALLECK AND POPE IN FEDERAL COMMAND.

Centres of Activity gravitate towards Orange and Culpeper Counties—Pope's Unsoldierly Preliminiary Orders—Jackson's and Pope's Encounter at Slaughter Mountaiu—Confidence in and Esteem for General Lee—The Confederate Commander's Plaus for cutting off Pope miscarry—Capture of Captain Fitzhugh with Important Orders—Longstreet puts General Toombs under Arrest—General Pope withdraws.

THE Federals had by this time organized the "Army of Virginia" from the independent forces in the State,—the First Corps under General Sigel, the Second under General Banks, the Third under General McDowell, commanded by Major-General John Pope, brought from the West for that object and appointed June 26. This army reported July 31, 46,858 strong, for field service.

On the 23d of July, General H. W. Halleck assumed command of the Federal armies as general-in-chief, by order of the President of July 11.

The quiet of General McClellan's army at Harrison's Landing assured General Lee of his opportunity for attention to the movements of the army under General Pope, working towards Richmond by the Orange and Alexandria Railway. On the 13th of July he ordered General Jackson, with his own and Ewell's division, to Gordonsville, to have a watch upon the Federal force operating in that quarter, promising reinforcements as soon as occasion should call for them. Stuart was at Hanover Court-House, in observation towards Fredericksburg, and Robertson's cavalry was ordered to Jackson, to reinforce his cavalry under Colonel Munford.

To engage attention pending these movements, General D. H. Hill, in command on the south side of the James, was ordered to have all of his artillery on that side available put in battery on the banks of the river against McClellan's camps on the north side and his transports on the water.

General Pope immediately displayed bold front as a diversion, seeking to draw General Lee away from McClellan.

So General Lee sent General A. P. Hill with his division to reinforce Jackson, with orders to the latter to strike out for the enemy in his front.

The threatening attitude of the Confederates at Gordonsville caused apprehension at Washington, and induced the authorities to consider the withdrawal of McClellan's army to reinforce the army under Pope.

Upon receipt of an intimation to that effect, General McClellan ordered a strong force under General Hooker to advance in threatening move against General Lee on the 4th of August. Hooker marched on the 5th, and occupied the ground of the battle of Malvern Hill. General Lee ordered the divisions of McLaws, D. R. Jones, that under Ripley (D. H. Hill's), and my own to march against Hooker. It was night when our troops were posted, and before daylight of the next morning Hooker had marched back to his camp at Harrison's Landing.

Just here, as a digression from following the operations of the armies of Lee and Pope, it should be remarked that the latter, by injudicious and unsoldierly attitude assumed at the outstart of his campaign, intensely incensed the people of Virginia and the South generally, the Confederate army to a man, and probably to a considerable degree discomfited the most considerate and thoughtful of his own officers and the authorities behind him. The exigencies of war did not demand some of the harsh measures that he promulgated,—such, for instance, as his notorious "General Orders No. 11" and several other of his pronunciamentos:

"HEAD-QUARTERS ARMY OF VIRGINIA,
"WASHINGTON, July 23, 1862.

"GENERAL ORDERS No. 11.*

"Commanders of army corps, divisions, brigades, and detached commands will proceed immediately to arrest all disloyal male citizens within their lines or within their reach in rear of their respective stations.

"Such as are willing to take the oath of allegiance to the United States, and will furnish sufficient security for its observance, shall be permitted to remain at their homes and pursue in good faith their accustomed avocations. Those who refuse shall be conducted south beyond the extreme pickets of this army, and be notified that if found again anywhere within our lines, or at any point in rear, they will be considered spies, and subjected to the extreme rigor of military law.

"If any person, having taken the oath of allegiance as above specified, be found to have violated it, he shall be shot, and his property seized and applied to the public use.

"All communication with any person whatever living within the lines of the enemy is positively prohibited, except through the military authorities and in the manner specified by military law; and any person concerned in writing or in carrying letters or messages in any other way will be considered and treated as a spy within the lines of the United States army.

"By command of Major-General Pope.

"GEO. D. RUGGLES,
"*Colonel, Assistant Adjutant-General, and Chief of Staff.*"

This was a measure of unnecessary severity towards non-combatants, and had an unsalutary effect. When men volunteer to fight in their country's cause they should be credited with faith in its righteousness, and with expectations of meeting soldiers worthy of their mettle. Appeals to turn their strength against women and children and non-combatants are offensive to manhood, demoralizing in influence, and more likely to aggravate and prolong war spirit than to open ways of order and amity. Besides, such orders indicate a flaw in the armor of the author.

---

* Rebellion Record, vol. xii. part ii. p. 52.

General Scott set an example worthy of eternal emulation. In his march through Mexico he was as strict in the requirement of order and protection for non-combatants as he could have been in marching through his own civil communities. The result was speedy peace, respect from all the people, admiration and affection from many.

When A. P. Hill's division joined General Jackson at Gordonsville, General Pope's army was posted,—the First Corps (Sigel's) at Sperryville, the Second (Banks's) at Culpeper Court-House, the Third (McDowell's), one division near Culpeper Court-House, and one at Fredericksburg—these two under Ricketts and King respectively; his cavalry under Buford, Bayard, and Hatch along the Rapidan from the Blue Ridge to Fredericksburg.

The point held by his left was thought essential by the Washington authorities as holding the way for reinforcements from McClellan's army on the James to join in the contemplated march by General Pope's route to Richmond.

On the 2d of August, Jackson sent part of his cavalry forward as far as Orange Court-House, under Colonel W. E. Jones, who encountered at that point a formidable cavalry guard of the enemy, when a spirited affair occurred, creditable alike to both sides. This was followed up, on the 8th, by the advance of Jackson's entire force, his own division under Winder leading, Ewell's and A. P. Hill's following.

General Pope's outpost at Cedar Run, held by cavalry and Crawford's brigade of infantry, had meantime been reinforced by the balance of the Second Corps under Banks, and Ricketts's division put in supporting position of the advance post.

On the 9th, Jackson advanced and found the enemy in strong position at Cedar Run. His division under Ewell was posted on the northeast slope of Slaughter Mountain, his own division under Winder formed to the left. The engagement was pitched and soon became severe. While yet posting his troops, Winder was mortally struck by a fragment of shell. Banks, gaining confidence in his battle, moved forward to closer and severe fight and held it an hour, at points putting Jackson's troops in disorder. Jackson, reinforced by A. P. Hill's brigades, recovered his lost ground, advanced and renewed attack, drove the enemy back, engaged against reinforcements of Ricketts's division, continued the fight till near midnight, then reorganized for battle away from the immediate front of the enemy, where he awaited next day, During the evening of the 9th, Pope received his First Corps under Sigel and called up McDowell's division, under King, from Fredericksburg. On the 10th both armies remained quiet. On the 11th a flag of truce was sent in asking for time to bury the dead, which Jackson granted, and extended to a late hour of the day. King's division coming up, Pope decided to engage again on the 12th, but Jackson, having information of the extent of reinforcements, decided to withdraw during the night.

The loss was severe on both sides,—Jackson's, 1276, including his most promising brigadier, Winder; Pope's, 2381, including three brigadiers, two wounded and one taken prisoner.

After drawing King's division to his field, General Pope had about thirty-six thousand present for service. Jackson's reports as to these forces were such that he accepted the advice of prudence and retired to stronger ground on the right bank of the Rapidan.

In the battle of the 9th the troops engaged were, according to official return of July 31,*—

Second Corps (Banks's), artillery and infantry	14,567
Ricketts's division, half of Third Corps, artillery and infantry	9,287
Total	23,854

* Rebellion Record, vol. xii. part ii. p. 53.

The absence of Lawton's brigade and one from Jackson's division reduced his force to something less than eighteen thousand. The troops engaged in battle, however, were not far from equal, Jackson probably the stronger.

That this was only a partial success—coming on the heels of the cruel orders of the Federal commander—was gratifying to the Confederates, and encouraging as well.

Inaction of the Army of the Potomac gave General Lee opportunity for movement of his troops towards Washington and the army under General Pope. On the 15th I was ordered to Gordonsville by the Central Railroad with ten brigades. Two others under Hood at Hanover Junction were ordered to join me.

Before despatching my corps, General Lee expressed his thought to advance the right column and cavalry by the lower fords of the Rapidan, the left by the fords above the railroad bridge, but left the question open, with orders to me to work on it.

The brigades that moved with me were D. R. Jones's, Kemper's, Pickett's, Pryor's, Jenkins's, Featherston's, Wilcox's, Toombs's, Evans's, and Drayton's. Hood's and Whiting's joined us near Gordonsville, Hood commanding the demi-division,—his own and Whiting's brigades.

It may be well to write just here that experience during the seven days about Richmond established between General Lee and his first lieutenant relations of confidence and esteem, official and personal, which ripened into stronger ties as the mutations of war bore heavier upon us. He always invited the views of the latter in moves of strategy and general policy, not so much for the purpose of having his own views approved and confirmed as to get new light, or channels for new thought, and was more pleased when he found something that gave him new strength than with efforts to evade his questions by compliments.

When oppressed by severe study, he sometimes sent for me to say that he had applied himself so closely to a matter that he found his ideas running around in a circle, and was in need of help to find a tangent. Our personal relations remained as sincere after the war until politics came between us in 1867.

General Pope was industriously increasing his strength. The Ninth Corps, General Burnside, had been ordered to Fredericksburg *via* Acquia Creek, and a division under General Reno of eight thousand of that corps reported to the commander at Culpeper Court-House on the 14th. Besides reinforcements called to support him from General McClellan's army, Pope was authorized to call to his aid the greater part of the army in West Virginia under General Cox.

After reaching Gordonsville and learning something of the position of the armies, and more of the features of the country, it occurred to me that a move against General Pope's right would give us vantage-ground for battle and pursuit, besides the inviting foot-hills of the Blue Ridge for strategy, and this preference was expressed to General Lee.* He joined us on the 15th, and the brigades, including those under Hood, were advanced to position for a general march. He thought it better to strike in between General Pope's left and the reinforcements that could join him from Fredericksburg than to adopt the proposition to move his army by the upper fords of the Rapidan and strike down upon the enemy's right, and decided to throw his right wing forward by the Raccoon Ford, and his left by the Somerville Ford, the latter above the railroad,—Fitzhugh Lee and Robertson's cavalry with his right, and T. T. Munford's with the left wing; General Stuart with the column on the right.

My command marched on the 16th to position for cross-

* His letter of August 14, 1862: Rebellion Record.

ing by the lower fords. Jackson was in position for the upper crossings. As all of the cavalry was not up, General Lee ordered his march for the 18th, to give time for the arrival of General Stuart and his marching troopers.

Leaving the cavalry on the march, under General Fitzhugh Lee, with instructions to camp on the plank-road opposite Raccoon Ford on the 17th, General Stuart rode on the cars to General Lee's head-quarters, received his orders, and rode out on the plank-road to join his command under Fitzhugh Lee, then due. The latter, however, "by failure to comply with instructions," as his commander expressed it subsequently, lost a day in a roundabout ride, which so jaded his horses that another day was sacrificed to give them rest. As if this were not sufficient misfortune, Captain Fitzhugh (General J. E. B. Stuart's adjutant) was captured, and, as a crowning disaster, the despatch of the Confederate commander giving instructions for the march of his army as ordered for the 18th was lost. The despatch was taken to General Pope, who, thus advised by accident, immediately set about retiring from Culpeper to the east bank of the Rappahannock. General Pope reported that

> "The cavalry expedition sent out on the 16th in the direction of Louisa Court-House captured the adjutant-general of General Stuart, and was very near capturing that officer himself. Among the papers taken was an autograph letter of General Robert E. Lee to General Stuart, dated Gordonsville, August 15, which made manifest to me the position and force of the army, and their determination to overwhelm the army under my command before it could be reinforced by any portion of the Army of the Potomac." *

Thus on that day Pope put his army in retreat by the several crossings of the Rappahannock to its strong camps of the north side, leaving his cavalry in observation.

---

* Rebellion Record, vol. xii. part ii. p. 29.

As Fitzhugh Lee's cavalry failed to get to position on my right on the 17th, I ordered two regiments of infantry to be posted as guard on the road to Raccoon Ford until the cavalry could relieve them. The detail fell upon Toombs's brigade. As we were to be in wait during the 17th, General Toombs rode off that morning to visit an old Congressional friend, and was absent when the order was received at his brigade head-quarters. The detail was filled by his next in rank, Colonel H. L. Benning, and duly posted. On his return, General Toombs rode upon his picket, claimed that his troops should not have been moved except by orders through himself, and ordered the detail back to their camps. Upon learning of General Stuart's mishap, and the ride of the Federal cavalry by Raccoon Ford, I sent to inquire how the cavalry happened to escape my picket-guard. Finding that the troops had been ordered off by General Toombs, the chief of staff was directed to put on his sword and sash and order him under arrest. Afterwards he was ordered to the rear, to confine himself to the limits of Gordonsville.

In addition to Reno's command, Stevens's division of the Ninth Corps joined General Pope on the 15th. On the 17th, Reno sent out a party of two hundred and fifty men and captured Jackson's signal-station on Clarke's Mountain; and it appears from the official report of this occurrence that the Federals were misinformed as to our position, and that up to the receipt of the captured despatch, General Pope knew nothing of the arrival of the troops of my command.

On the 18th report came from Clarke's Mountain of unusual stir in the Federal commands about Culpeper Court-House, and General Lee sent for me to ride with him to the mountain to observe the movements. From the summit we had a fair view of many points, and the camp-flags, as they opened their folds to the fitful breezes, seemed to mark places of rest. Changing our glasses to the right and left and rear, the white tops of army wagons were seen moving. Half an hour's close watch revealed that the move was for the Rappahannock River. Changing the field of view to the bivouacs, they seemed serenely quiet, under cover from the noonday August sun. As we were there to learn from personal observation, our vigilance was prolonged until the wagons rolled down the declivities of the Rappahannock. Then, turning again to view the bivouacs, a stir was seen at all points. Little clouds of dust arose which marked the tramp of soldiers, and these presently began to swell into dense columns along the rearward lines. Watching without comment till the clouds grew thinner and thinner as they approached the river and melted into the bright haze of the afternoon sun, General Lee finally put away his glasses, and with a deeply-drawn breath, expressive at once of disappointment and resignation, said, "General, we little thought that the enemy would turn his back upon us thus early in the campaign."

CHAPTER XIII.

MAKING READY FOR MANASSAS AGAIN.

General Lee modifies his Order of March—Continuous Skirmishing—Cavalry Commander Stuart gets into General Pope's Head-quarters and captures his Personal Equipment—His Uniform Coat and Hat shown along the Confederate Lines—Jackson's Superb Flank Movement—Confederates capture Trains, Supplies, Munitions, and Prisoners—Hooker and Ewell at Bristoe Station—Jackson first on the Old Field of Bull Run—Longstreet's Command joins passing Thoroughfare Gap—Pope practically throws Responsibility for Aggressive Action on McDowell—Preliminary Fighting—General Pope surprised by Jackson—Pope's Orders to Fitz-John Porter.

UNDER the retrograde of the Union army, General Lee so modified his order of march as to meet the new conditions. On the 20th of August the march was made, the right wing to the vicinity of Kelly's Ford on the Rappahannock River, the left to the railroad bridge and fords above. At Kelly's Ford it seemed possible to force a crossing. As we were preparing for it, an order came reporting the upper crossings too well defended, and calling for the right wing to march to that point, while the left marched up in search of more favorable points. As we were leaving Kelly's the enemy made a dash to cross, and engaged some of the brigades in a sharp fight, intending to delay our movements, but the main column marched on, while this affair was still in progress. By mutual consent the fight subsided, both parties joined their proper commands and proceeded on their upward march, each on its own side of the stream. At Beverley's Ford, Stuart's cavalry under Rosser crossed and made a lodgement on the east bank, but the near approach of the enemy's column threatening, before the infantry could get up in support, made necessary the abandonment of the ground, and the left wing continued to feel along higher up for a crossing. Passing up, Trimble's brigade was left at Beverley's as guard to Jackson's rear. The enemy, conceiving an opportunity, crossed at Freeman's Ford and attacked Trimble. Meanwhile, a detachment had been called for from the right wing. Hood, with his own and Whiting's brigade, was ordered, and was in time to join in Trimble's fight, which ended in repulse of the adventurous force.

The east banks of the Rappahannock lifted quite above those occupied by the Confederates, giving advantageous position to the Union artillery fire, and offering no point above Kelly's Ford to force a crossing.

When the left wing marched from Rappahannock Bridge, the enemy crossed a considerable force to the west bank, and covered it with a number of superior batteries well posted on the east side. To dislodge that force I put a number of batteries into action, including the Washington Artillery, and, later, part of the reserved battalion under Colonel S. D. Lee. The combat consumed much of the day of the 23d, when the enemy withdrew from that bank and burned some of the dwellings as he left.

Riding along the line of batteries during the combat, we passed a soldier-lad weeping over his brother, who had just been killed; just then a shell came screaming by, exploded, and dashed its fragments into the ground near enough to dust us a little. "Dad drat those Yankees!" he said; "if I had known that they were going to throw such things as that at a fellow, I would have stayed in Texas." He had travelled a thousand miles to volunteer in the same company with his brother.

Assured of the transfer of McClellan's forces from the James, General Lee called up the divisions of Generals D. H. Hill, McLaws, the half division under J. G. Walker, and Hampton's cavalry from Richmond. Anderson's division was marching from Orange Court-House as our reserve force.

On the 22d, Munford's cavalry reported the Warrenton road open as far as the vicinity of General Pope's head-quarters. General Stuart was ordered over, with parts of his brigades, to investigate and make trouble in the enemy's rear. He crossed at Waterloo and Hunt's Mill with fifteen hundred troopers and Pelham's horse artillery, and rode to Warrenton. Passing through, he directed his ride towards Catlett's Station to first burn the bridge over Cedar Creek.

Before reaching Catlett's a severe storm burst upon him, bogging the roads and flooding the streams behind him. The heavy roads delayed his artillery so that it was after night when he approached Catlett's. He caught a picket-guard and got into a camp about General Pope's head-quarters, took a number of prisoners, some camp property, and, meeting an old acquaintance and friend in a colored man, who conducted him to General Pope's tents, he found one of the general's uniform coats, a hat, a number of official despatches, a large amount of United States currency, much of the general's personal equipments, and one of the members of his staff, Major Goulding. He made several attempts to fire the bridge near Catlett's, but the heavy rains put out all fires that could be started, when he sought axes to cut it away. By this time the troops about the camps rallied and opened severe fire against him, but with little damage. The heavy rain-fall admonished him to forego further operations and return to the army while yet there was a chance to cross Cedar Creek and the Rappahannock before the tides came down. On the night of the 23d he reached Sulphur Springs, where he met General Jackson's troops trying to make comfortable lodgement on the east bank, passed over, and resumed position outside General Lee's left. The despatch-book of General Pope gave information of his troops and his anxiety for reinforcements, besides mention of those that had joined him, but General

Stuart's especial pleasure and pride were manifested over the possession of the uniform coat and hat of General Pope. Stuart rode along the line showing them, and proclaiming that he was satisfied with the exchange that made even his loss at Verdierville before the march; but the despatch lost at Verdierville was the tremendous blow that could not be overestimated.

All of the 23d was spent in severe artillery combat. General Jackson had gained the east bank at Warrenton (Sulphur Springs) crossing, and there seemed a fair prospect of making a permanent lodgement, but the tides from the severe storm of the day and night previous were coming down in torrents, threatening floods at all of the fords.

On the 22d, Pope had formed a plan of concentrating his forces to cross and attack Lee's right by the lower fords, but the freshet had shut him off in that quarter; so he turned to the detachment of Jackson, on the east side, just cut off from support. Marching up the river bank, Jackson succeeded in so reinforcing his detachment as to defend it to an upper crossing till it found safe footing on the west bank. The high water cut off all operations by direct moves on the 24th. Meanwhile, General Pope had received the divisions of Kearny and Reynolds from McClellan's army, forty-five hundred and twenty-five hundred respectively.

About this time a letter came to head-quarters of the right wing from General Toombs, expressing regret at his unfortunate mistake in relieving his troops from picket service, and asking to be released from arrest, that he might have the opportunity to show in the approaching conflicts his deep interest in the cause. The adjutant-general was instructed to say in reply that the chief of corps was pleased to know that the malefeasance was from want of experience, not intentional breach of authority, and that he would be more than welcome back by the general and the troops of his brigade.

GENERAL THOMAS J. JACKSON (STONEWALL).

On the 25th, Jackson was ordered to pull away from our main force with the left wing, march by the crossings of the upper tributaries through Thoroughfare Gap, and strike the railway in the enemy's rear at Manassas Junction, his supply depot. Stuart's cavalry was ordered to follow during the night.

By a rapid march Jackson crossed the fords of the upper streams and made his bivouac near Salem. Forcing his march on the 26th, he passed Thoroughfare Gap to Gainesville, where Stuart joined him with all of his cavalry. From Gainesville he inclined to the right for Bristoe Station, the cavalry holding the curtain between his column and Pope's. A little after sunset he reached the Orange and Alexandria Railroad, a march of thirty miles. Approaching the station, trains were heard on the rails. General Ewell divided his force and took two points on the rails, so as to cut off the trains. Munford's cavalry assisted in the job. Two trains and a number of prisoners were taken, the greater part of the detachment at the station making safe retreat. His plans against General Lee's right cut off by the high water, General Pope extended his right, under Sigel, Banks, and Reno, in search of Jackson up the river, who meanwhile had spirited himself away looking towards Pope's rear. I was left on the river bank in front, the reserve infantry, R. H. Anderson's division, and artillery near at hand.

Although the night of the 26th was very dark, and his troops were severely worn, to be sure of his opportunity, Jackson sent a detachment to Manassas Junction (seven miles). The gallant Trimble, with five hundred of his men, volunteered for the service, and set out at once on the march. Stuart was afterwards ordered to join Trimble with his cavalry, and as ranking officer to command the operations of the entire force. The infantry advanced and attacked the enemy as soon as it could be formed for work, captured three hundred prisoners, an eight-gun battery complete, and immense quantities of army supplies.

Feeling the main force of his adversary in his front awaiting opportunity, General Pope became anxious about his left and rear, and was further hampered by instructions from the Washington authorities to hold his Fredericksburg connections and "fight like the devil." (It may have been fortunate for the Confederates that he was not instructed to *fight like Jackson*.) On the 23d he was informed of strong reinforcements to reach him at Warrenton Junction on the next day, and that larger forces would be shipped him on the 24th, to join him on the 25th.

Nevertheless, he began to realize, as he felt Jackson's march to his right, that he must abandon the line of the Rappahannock and attend on the movements of that command gone astray by the mountains. He concentrated the Army of Virginia, to which Reynolds's division had been assigned, at and near Warrenton under McDowell; Reno east of Warrenton about three miles, on the turnpike; Porter's (Fifth) corps near Bealton, ordered to join Reno, and Heintzelman's (Third) corps, ten thousand strong, at Warrenton Junction. The Sixth (Franklin's) Corps, ten thousand strong, Army of the Potomac, was at Alexandria awaiting transportation, as were the divisions of Sturgis, ten thousand, and Cox, seven thousand,—the latter from West Virginia. General Pope asked to have Franklin's corps march by the Warrenton turnpike to join him, and sent instructions to different parties to see that the guards in his rear were strengthened; that at Manassas Junction by a division.

Under assurances from Washington of the prompt arrival of forces from that quarter, he looked for the approach of Franklin as far as Gainesville, marching by the Warrenton turnpike, and a division to reinforce the command at Manassas Junction, so that when Jackson cut in on his rear and captured the detachment at the Junction, he was not a little surprised. He was in position for grand tactics, however, midway between the right and left wings of his adversary's forces, that in his rear worn by severe marches and some fighting, that in his front behind a river, the crossings of which were difficult, and the lines of march to bring the distant wings to co-operation over routes that could be defended by small commands.

Communication with Washington being severed, the forces at and near Alexandria were thrown in the dark. To move by rail they were liable to run into the wrong camps, and the rapid change by water to the new position left them short of land transportation.

Pope stood on the evening of the 27th: McDowell's corps, including Reynolds's division, 15,500; Sigel's corps, 9000; Banks's, 5000; Reno's, 7000; Heintzelman's and Porter's corps, 18,000,—in all 54,500 men, with 4000 cavalry; Platt's brigade, Sturgis's division, which joined him on the 26th, not included. In his rear was Jackson, 20,000; in front on the Rappahannock was my 25,000; R. H. Anderson's reserve division, 5000; total, 50,000, with 3000 of cavalry under Stuart.

On the 26th I moved up to and crossed at Hinson's Mill Ford, leaving Anderson's division on the Warrenton Sulphur Springs route.

On the 27th, Jackson marched at daylight to Manassas Junction with his own division, under Taliaferro, and A. P. Hill's, leaving Ewell's at Bristoe Station, with orders to withdraw if severely pressed. Approaching the Junction, a cavalry regiment came in, threatening attack, and was driven off by Colonel Baylor's regiment. A field battery came from the direction of Centreville, and tried to make trouble at long range, but was driven off by superior numbers. Then a brigade of infantry under General Taylor, of New Jersey, just landed from the cars from Alexandria, advanced and made a desperate effort to recover the lost position and equipage at Manassas Junction. Field's, Archer's, Pender's, and Thomas's brigades, moving towards the railroad bridge, met Taylor's command and engaged it, at the same time moving towards its rear, threatening to cut off its retreat. It was driven back after a fierce struggle, General Taylor, commanding, mortally wounded. Part of the Kanawha division under General Scammon was ordered to its support, but was only in time to assist in its retreat. Reporting this affair, General Jackson said,—

"The advance was made with great spirit and determination, and under a leader worthy of a better cause."

The spoils were then quietly divided, such as could be consumed or hauled off, and the balance given to the torch.

I marched from the Rappahannock, following on Jackson's trail, and camped at White Plains. The march during the day was delayed about an hour by a large force of cavalry which showed itself on my right front. As I had no cavalry, a little time was spent in learning of its import and following.

General Pope ordered McDowell, with his own corps, including Reynolds's division and Sigel's corps, to march so as to be at Gainesville at nightfall; Reno's corps and Kearny's division of the Third to Greenwich to support McDowell. He rode with Hooker's division of the Third along the route by the railroad for Bristoe Station, ordered Porter's Fifth Corps to remain at Warrenton Junction till relieved by Banks's corps, then to push on towards Gainesville, Banks to follow by the railroad route.

In the afternoon, Hooker encountered Ewell at Bristoe Station, where the divisions engaged in a severe fight, which was handsomely maintained till after night. Ewell, under his orders, withdrew to join Jackson. The conduct of the affair was about equally creditable to the commands.

After this affair, General Pope so far modified his order of the day as to call Porter to him by direct route, to march at one A.M. and join him at daylight. Kearny's division was ordered for Bristoe Station, Reno's corps for Manassas Junction, and McDowell, from Gainesville, was ordered to swing around to his right and march, guided by the Manassas Gap Railroad, to Manassas Junction.

Ewell made his way along the railroad to Jackson in time to refresh his men on the good things of the captures and for several hours of sleep. Fitzhugh Lee, with three regiments of cavalry, was ordered on to Fairfax Court-House and along the railroad towards Alexandria to cut off rail connection.

General McClellan reached Alexandria, Virginia, on the 27th. On the 28th, Jackson was first to move at 12.20 A.M. He applied the torch to the stores of provisions, and marched with his division, under Taliaferro, by the New Market Sudley Springs road across the Warrenton turnpike, and pitched bivouac on a line from near Groveton, towards Sudley Mills, on the field of first Manassas, at daylight.

At one A.M., A. P. Hill marched from Manassas Junction, crossed Bull Run, and halted at Centreville. Ewell followed at daylight towards Centreville, crossed Bull Run, marched up some distance, recrossed, and joined Jackson, forming on Taliaferro's left. After the morning fires of the bivouac burned out, Jackson's position could not be seen except upon near approach. He was hid away under the cuts and embankments of an unfinished railroad.

The road upon which Porter marched was crowded during the night, so that he and his officers thought that they would make better time and be in better condition by marching at three A.M. He reached Bristoe at ten A.M., Kearny at eight, and Reno in due season. But it was late in the morning when McDowell was ready to march, and later in the day when his left swung out on the march to the Junction.

At twelve o'clock, General Pope reached Manassas Junction. Misled by the movements of A. P. Hill and Ewell, he ordered Reno's corps and Kearny's and Hooker's divisions of the Third to Centreville, in search of Jackson, while the latter was little more than a league from him, resting quietly in his hiding-place, and his detached divisions had doubled on their courses and were marching to join him. McDowell, having information of my approach, delayed his march, detaching Ricketts's division to hold me in check at Thoroughfare Gap.

The first passage at arms of the day was between part of Stuart's cavalry, supported by B. T. Johnson's infantry, and Meade's brigade of McDowell's command. As the latter swung around for his march to the Junction, the brigade approached Jackson's right. A detachment was pushed out against Meade, and some artillery practice followed. The Confederates retired, but reported no loss. Under the impression that the force encountered was some cavalry rear-guard or reconnoitring party, McDowell resumed his march "as soon as the killed and wounded were cared for."

The noise made by this affair caused Sigel to countermarch his corps, and otherwise delayed the march of McDowell's entire forces, while it gave no inconvenience to the Confederates further than a change of front of part of Jackson's command to receive battle, not intended, by his adversary. Jackson changed his front, but finding the direction of the enemy changed so as to march away from him, he took the move for a general retreat, made report of it to A. P. Hill, who was yet north of Bull Run, and ordered him to intercept the retreat by manning the lower fords of Bull Run. The order was received at ten A.M., but General Hill had intercepted despatches of General Pope giving notice of his preparation for battle at Manassas the next day, and thought it better to march on and join Jackson. He filed into line on Jackson's left about noon.

General Jackson was right. If General Hill had moved as ordered, he would have met detachments ordered by General Pope to Centreville, and held them back to the south side until Jackson could join him to hold the line. The natural sequence of Confederate operations was position to intercept General Pope's return to Washington. The scenes were shifting and inviting of adventure, and the marches should have followed them. General Hill was justified by the circumstances that influenced his march.

When General Pope reached the Junction with Heintzelman's and Reno's corps, the game was on other fields. As the last of the Confederate columns had hied away towards Centreville, he ordered thither those corps, and called up the Fifth to join him. He then changed the orders of McDowell's column, directing it towards Centreville, to mass his cavalry, and find Jackson, and presently (at two P.M.) so far modified these as to direct McDowell to use his own judgment, and give him the benefit of his views, as he knew the country better, but ordered that he should not go farther towards Manassas Junction. These instructions were urgent, with assurances that McDowell's moves should be supported by other columns. Had these been promptly executed, McDowell's entire force should have encountered Jackson before four o'clock, but McDowell did not find Jackson. As his division, under King, marched along the turnpike a little before night, Jackson saw and engaged it in battle, as we shall see.

The head of my column reached Thoroughfare Gap early in the afternoon. Reports from General Jackson were that he was resting quietly on the flank of the enemy, and between him and Washington. Parties from the Gap reported it clear, and the Confederate commander called a rest for the night, but D. R. Jones's division was ordered on to occupy the Gap.

As we approached it, officers riding to the front returned reporting the enemy coming in heavy columns on the other side. Jones was ordered to halt his division till he could advance his skirmishers. The Ninth Georgia Regiment, G. T. Anderson's brigade, was sent and followed at proper distance by the division. The skirmishers met the enemy's pickets in the Gap, drove them off, and followed till they in turn were met by a strong force and pushed back. The enemy's leading brigade reached the plateau running along the eastern side of the mountain, which, with his batteries and infantry, gave him command at that end. Anderson reinforced his Ninth by the First, then by his other regiments on the mountain-side, to the left of the Gap, and advanced till arrested by the impenetrable tangle of the mountain undergrowth.

The Gap is a pass cut through Bull Run Mountain for the flow of a streamlet, through Occoquan Creek, to the waters of the Potomac. Its mean width is eighty yards. Its faces of basaltic rock rise in vertical ascent from one hundred to three hundred feet, relieved hither and thither by wild ivy, creeping through their fissures and from the tops of boulders in picturesque drapery. It was in the midst of this bold and beautiful scenery, in this narrow gorge where the Indians had doubtless often contested ages ago, that the seasoned soldiers of our civilized armies now battled for right of way.

Finding his passage over the mountain by the left side of the Gap blocked by the mountain tangle, Jones called up Toombs's brigade, under command of Colonel Benning, and ordered it over the mountain obstacle by the south side. Drayton's brigade was held in rear. By the time the troops were so disposed, Ricketts's division was well deployed along the plateau on the east.

Benning put Major Waddell, with the Twentieth Georgia, on the mountain-side as skirmishers, and strengthened it by another under Colonel Holmes, in double time, to

BATTLE AT THOROUGHFARE GAP.

gain the crest on that side. The Twentieth gained the crest while the Federals were yet about eighty yards below on their side. The Georgians knew how to maintain their advantage, and their fire arrested farther advance of the enemy, when, after a spirited fusillade, reinforcements joined them in good season, and extended the line and held it, driving back the second assaulting force and following down the eastern slope.

As soon as the fire of the Federal batteries opened, Hood was ordered with his two brigades to cross the mountain on the north side of the Gap away by a cattle-trail, and three other brigades were despatched under General Wilcox to Hopewell Pass, about three miles north of Thoroughfare Gap.

Advancing his men, selected for their long-range rifles, Benning drove off a battery seeking position to play upon the mountain slope and eastern end of the gorge, and moved forward under cover of a ravine until he gained a flank fire upon the enemy's batteries. This, with the march of Wilcox through Hopewell Pass and the crossing of one of Hood's brigades, gave the Confederates commanding position, and Ricketts withdrew in time to escape disaster.

About six o'clock McDowell put his troops on the countermarch, Sigel's corps and Reynolds's division back by the New Market road for its crossing of the Warrenton turnpike, and King's division of his own corps down the turnpike. A. P. Hill's and Ewell's divisions, returning from the north of Bull Run, hardly had time for rest, when the march of King's division was reported. About the same time the divisions that had been ordered by Pope to Centreville reached that point, driving off some Confederate cavalry loitering along the way.

As King's division was marching by, Jackson thought to come out from his lurking-place to learn the meaning of the march. The direction of the move again impressed him that Pope was retreating, and that his escape to the north side of Bull Run would put his army in a position of safety before General Lee could join him. It was late, the sun had set, but Jackson was moved to prompt action, as the only means of arresting and holding Pope for General Lee's arrival. He was in plain view of the white smoke of the rifles of my infantry as they climbed over Bull Run Mountain, seven miles away, and in hearing of our artillery as the boom of the big guns, resounding along the rock-faced cliffs, gathered volume to offer salutations and greetings for the union of comrades and commands. He changed the front of his right division, and, noting the movement of Sigel's troops along the New Market road, called out Ewell with his brigades under Lawton and Trimble, and in addition to the artillery of these commands used the horse artillery under Pelham. As formed, this new line was broadside against the turnpike, his left a little way from Groveton.

The ground upon which the action occurred had been passed an hour before by the division commander, General Hatch, who saw no indication of the presence of a foe. As the division marched, the column was made up of the brigades of Hatch, Gibbon, Doubleday, and Patrick. The action fell against the brigade commanded by General Gibbon, who, taking it for a cavalry annoyance to cover retreat, opened against it, and essayed aggressive fight, till he found himself engaged against a formidable force of infantry and artillery. He was assisted by part of Doubleday's brigade, and asked for other assistance, which failed to reach him, till night came and ended the contest. His fight was desperate and courageous against odds, but he held it and his line till dark. His loss was seven hundred and fifty-one, including Colonel O'Connor and Major May, mortally wounded, with many other officers with lighter hurts.*

* Rebellion Record, vol. xii. part ii. p. 378.

General Doubleday joined the fight with his brigade, and reported his loss nearly half of the troops engaged. General Gibbon called it "a surprise." * And well he might, after his division commander had just passed over the route and failed to find any indication of the lurking foe.

General Jackson reported, "The conflict here was firm and sanguinary." He fails to give his number lost, but acknowledges his severe loss in the division commanders, General Ewell losing a leg, and Taliaferro severely wounded.

During the night the Federal commander reported to his subordinates that McDowell had "intercepted the retreat of Jackson, and ordered concentration of the army against him," † whereas it was, of course, Jackson who had intercepted McDowell's march. He seems to have been under the impression that he was about to capture Jackson, and inclined to lead his subordinates to the same opinion.

Of the time, Major Edward Pye reported,—

"We were sent forward towards evening to pursue the enemy, who were said to be retreating. Found the enemy, but did not see them retreat. A deadly fire from three sides welcomed and drove us back." ‡

After night Gibbon held his front by a line of skirmishers, and withdrew his command to a place of rest. At one A.M. the division was withdrawn and marched back to Manassas. Ricketts, finding himself in isolated position at Gainesville, left at daylight and marched to Bristoe. Jackson moved his forces at daylight, and re-established his line behind the unfinished railroad, his own division under General Stark, Ewell's under General Lawton, with A. P. Hill on his left.

---

* Rebellion Record, vol. xii. part ii. p. 381.
† Ibid., pp. 74, 75. ‡ Ibid., p. 371.

General Pope's orders for the night directed the march of Kearny's division from Centreville by the turnpike at one A.M., to reinforce the troops against Jackson; the other division of Heintzelman's corps (Hooker's) to march by the same route at daylight, and to be followed by the corps under Reno. These orders were urgent, and directed that the commands should move promptly, leaving fragments behind if all could not be got together in time; Kearny to attack at daylight, to be supported by Hooker.

McDowell's operations of the afternoon left Sigel's corps and Reynolds's division in the vicinity of the field of King's fight. General Pope's orders were given under the impression that King's division was still occupying the ground of the late conflict, and that Ricketts's division was not far away; but these divisions had been removed to points before mentioned, though special instructions had been sent McDowell and King to hold the position "at all hazards, to prevent the retreat of Jackson," with assurances that at daylight in the morning the entire force from Centreville and Manassas Junction should be up and in prompt co-operation.

But McDowell had probably learned that Jackson had no thought of retreating, and King had found that his ground was not tenable. The order intended for King failed to reach him.

Before he was advised of the withdrawal of King's division, General Pope sent orders to General Porter directing movements for the 29th, informing him of the orders of Kearny and Hooker, and directing Porter to move at daylight towards Centreville, for position in co-operation of the projected battle, and ordering Reno to march for the battle by the Warrenton turnpike. Under the orders, Porter marched towards Centreville, and Reno towards the field for battle. Kearny deferred his march till daylight, and was followed by Hooker's division at convenient marching distance. Reno's column followed the march of the latter.

As soon as advised of the withdrawal of King's division from the ground of the 28th, General Pope sent as substitutes for his orders of the early morning that General Porter should push forward with his corps and King's division of McDowell's command to Gainesville, to co-operate with his movements along the Warrenton turnpike.* This order was received by Porter at 9.30 A.M.,† but General McDowell joined this column, and as ranking officer objected to the transfer of his division under King to other authority, which brought out the joint order to McDowell and Porter to have their joint commands execute the move towards Gainesville.

---

* Rebellion Record, vol. xii. part ii. p. 518.
† Ibid., p. 520.

CHAPTER XIV.

SECOND BATTLE OF MANASSAS (BULL RUN).

Battle opened by the Federals on Jackson's Right, followed by Kearny —Longstreet's Reconnoissance—Stuart, the Cavalry Leader, sleeps on the Field of Battle—Pope thought at the Close of the 29th that the Confederates were retreating—Second Day—Fitz-John Porter struck in Flank—Longstreet takes a Hand in the Fight late in the Day—Lee under Fire—The Federal Retreat to Centreville—That Point turned—Pope again dislodged—"Stonewall" Jackson's Appearance and Peculiarities—Killing of "Fighting Phil" Kearny—Losses—Review of the Campaign.

GENERAL POPE at daylight sent orders to General Sigel's corps, with Reynolds's division, to attack as soon as it was light enough to see, and bring the enemy to a stand if possible. At the same time orders were sent Heintzelman and Reno for their corps to hurry along the turnpike and join on the right of Sigel. The batteries opened in an irregular combat on the left, centre, and right a little after eight o'clock, and drew from Jackson a monotonous but resolute response. And thus early upon the 29th of August was begun the second battle upon this classic and fateful field.

I marched at daylight and filed to the left at Gainesville at nine o'clock. As the head of the column approached Gainesville the fire of artillery became more lively, and its volume swelled to proportions indicating near approach to battle. The men involuntarily quickened step, filed down the turnpike, and in twenty minutes came upon the battle as it began to press upon Jackson's right, their left battery partially turning his right. His battle, as before stated, stood upon its original line of the unfinished railroad.

As my columns approached, the batteries of the leading brigades were thrown forward to ground of superior sweep. This display and the deploy of the infantry were so threatening to the enemy's left batteries that he thought prudent to change the front of that end of his line more to his left and rear. Hood's two brigades were deployed across the turnpike at right angles, supported by the brigade under Evans. A battery advanced on their right to good position and put in some clever work, which caused the enemy to rectify all that end of his line. Kemper deployed two of his brigades, supported by the third, on the right of Hood. The three brigades under Wilcox were posted in rear of Hood and Evans, and in close supporting distance. On Hood's left and near Jackson's right was open field, of commanding position. This was selected by Colonel Walton, of the Washington Artillery, for his battalion, and he brought it bounding into position as soon as called. The division under D. R. Jones was deployed in the order of the others, but was broken off to the rear, across the Manassas Gap Railroad, to guard against forces of the enemy reported in the direction of Manassas Junction and Bristoe. As formed, my line made an obtuse angle forward of Jackson's, till it approached Manassas Gap Railroad, where D. R. Jones's division was broken in echelon to the rear. At twelve o'clock we were formed for battle.

About eleven o'clock, Hooker's division filed to the right from the turnpike, to reinforce the Federal right under Kearny, who, with Sigel's corps and Reynolds's division, were engaged in a desultory affair against Jackson's left, chiefly of artillery.

R. H. Anderson's division marched at daylight along the Warrenton turnpike for Gainesville.

When I reported my troops in order for battle, General Lee was inclined to engage as soon as practicable, but did not order. All troops that he could hope to have were up except R. H. Anderson's division, which was near enough to come in when the battle was in progress. I asked him to be allowed to make a reconnoissance of the enemy's ground, and along his left. After an hour's work, mounted and afoot, under the August sun, I returned and reported adversely as to attack, especially in view of the easy approach of the troops reported at Manassas against my right in the event of severe contention. We knew of Ricketts's division in that quarter, and of a considerable force at Manassas Junction, which indicated one corps.

At two o'clock Kearny made an earnest opening against Jackson's left, but no information of battle reached us on the right. He made severe battle by his division, and with some success, but was checked by Jackson's movements to meet him. General Stevens supported his battle, but his numbers were not equal to the occasion. General Sigel joined in the affair, and part of General Hooker's division, making a gallant fight, but little progress. General Grover's brigade made a gallant charge, but a single brigade was a trifle, and it met with only partial success, and was obliged to retire with heavy loss of killed and wounded,—four hundred and eighty-four.

At one time the enemy broke through the line, cutting off the extreme left brigade, and gained position on the railroad cut; but Jackson and A. P. Hill reinforced against that attack, and were in time to push it back and recover the lost ground.

Their attacks were too much in detail to hold even the ground gained, but they held firmly to the battle and their line until after night, when they withdrew to await orders for the next day.

Though this fight opened at two o'clock, and was fiercely contested till near night, no account of it came from headquarters to my command, nor did General Jackson think to send word of it. General Lee, not entirely satisfied with the report of my reconnoissance, was thinking of sending some of the engineers for more critical survey of his right front, when his chief of cavalry sent to inform him of the approach of a formidable column of infantry and artillery threatening his right. Wilcox's division was changed to supporting position of our right, under Jones, and I rode to look at this new force, its strength, and the ground of its approach. It was the column of McDowell's and Porter's corps, marching under the joint order. Porter's corps in advance deployed Morell's division, and ordered Butterfield's brigade, preceded by a regiment of skirmishers, to advance on their right, Sykes's division to support Morell. As this was in process of execution, McDowell, whose corps was in rear, rode to the front and objected to the plan and attack so far from the main force.

A few shots were exchanged, when all became quiet again. We saw nothing of McDowell's corps, and our cavalry had not been able to get far enough towards their rear to know of its presence or force. He afterwards drew off from Porter's column and marched by the Sudley Springs road to join the main force on the turnpike. I rode back and reported to General Lee that the column was hardly strong enough to mean aggressive work from that quarter, and at the same time reported a dust along the New Market road which seemed to indicate movement of other troops from Manassas.

General Stuart rode up, making similar report, and asked for orders. As our chief was not ready with his orders at the moment, Stuart was asked to wait. The latter threw himself on the grass, put a large stone under his head, asked the general to have him called when his orders were ready for him, and went sound asleep.

Our chief now returned to his first plan of attack by his right down the turnpike. Though more than anxious to meet his wishes, and anticipating his orders, I suggested, as the day was far spent, that a reconnoissance in force be made at nightfall to the immediate front of the enemy, and if an opening was found for an entering wedge, that we have all things in readiness at daylight for a good day's work. After a moment's hesitation he assented, and orders were given for the advance at early twilight.

This gave General Stuart half an hour *siesta.* When called, he sprang to his feet, received his orders, swung into his saddle, and at a lope, singing, "If you want to have a good time, jine the cavalry," his banjo-player, Sweeny, on the jump behind him, rode to his troopers.

Wilcox was recalled and ordered to march in support of Hood and Evans when they advanced on the reconnoissance. It so happened that our advance had been anticipated by an order to move from the enemy's side against us. They attacked along the turnpike by King's division about sunset.

To the Confederates, who had been searching for an opportunity during the greater part of the day, and were about to march through the approaching darkness to find it, this was an agreeable surprise. Relieved of that irksome toil, and ready for work, they jumped at the presence, to welcome in countercharge the enemy's coming. A fierce struggle of thirty minutes gave them advantage which they followed through the dark to the base of the high ground held by bayonets and batteries innumerable as compared with their limited ranks. Their task accomplished, they were halted at nine o'clock to await the morrow. One cannon, a number of flags, and a few prisoners were taken.

Generals Wilcox and Hood were ordered to carefully examine the position of the enemy and report of the feasibility of attack at daylight. They came to corps headquarters a little before twelve o'clock, and made separate reports, both against attack, with minute items of their conclusions. Hood was ordered to have the carriage of the captured gun cut up and left, and both were ordered to withdraw their commands to their first positions.

Meanwhile, General Pope had sent orders to General Porter, dated 4.30 P.M., to attack upon my right flank, but the order was not received until it was too late for battle, and the force was not strong enough, and a fight at that hour might have been more unfortunate than the fights by detail on their right. If it had been sent to General McDowell before he left, the two corps, if he could have been induced to go in, might have given serious trouble. The field on their left was favorable for tactics, but on Porter's front it was rough, and R. H. Anderson's division was in striking distance of their left, if that effort had been made.

Anderson marched in the dark as far as Hood's front before reporting for position, and was ordered back to Gainesville.

The 4.30 order was issued under the impression that my troops, or the greater part of them, were still at Thoroughfare Gap, and General Pope said, in his official report,—

> "I believe, in fact I am positive, that at five o'clock in the afternoon of the 29th, General Porter had in his front no considerable body of the enemy. I believed then, as I am very sure now, that it was easily practicable for him to have turned the right flank of Jackson and to have fallen upon his rear; that if he had done so, we should have gained a decisive victory over the army under Jackson before he could have been joined by any of the forces of Longstreet." *

After night, Porter's column marched by its right to follow the route of McDowell.

The morning of the 30th broke fair, and for the Federal commander bright with anticipations for the day. He wired the Washington authorities of success, that "the enemy was retreating to the mountains," and told of his preparations for pursuit. It seems that he took my reconnoissance for a fight, and my withdrawal for retreat, also interpreting reports from the right as very favorable. He reported,—

> "General Hooker estimated the loss of the enemy as at least two to one, and General Kearny as at least three to one."

---

* Rebellion Record, vol. xii. part ii. p. 40. General Pope.

He construed the operations of the night of the 29th and the reports of the morning of the 30th as indications of retreat of the Confederates. Prisoners captured during the night, paroled and returning to him, so reported on the morning of the 30th, and his general officers had impressions of the Confederate left that confirmed the other accounts, and convinced him that we were in retreat.

The forces threatening our right the day before having marched around towards the turnpike, D. R. Jones's division was advanced to position near Kemper's right. Colonel S. D. Lee's artillery battalion was advanced to relieve the Washington Artillery, making our line complete, in battle front.

About one o'clock in the afternoon, General Pope ordered attack against Jackson's front by the corps under General Porter, supported by King's division, Heintzelman and Reno to move forward and attack Jackson's left, to turn it and strike down against the flank, Ricketts's division in support of it; but Ricketts was recalled and put near the turnpike, to support that part of Porter's field.

During the early part of this severe battle not a gun was fired by my troops, except occasional shots from S. D. Lee's batteries of reserve artillery, and less frequent shots from one or two of my other batteries.

Developments appearing unfavorable for a general engagement, General Lee had settled upon a move by Sudley Springs, to cross Bull Run during the night and try to again reach Pope's rear, this time with his army.

About three P.M. I rode to the front to prepare to make a diversion a little before dark, to cover the plan proposed for our night march. As I rode, batteries resting on the sides of the turnpike thought that battle was at hand, and called their officers and men to stand to their guns and horses. Passing by and beyond my lines, a message came from General Jackson reporting his lines heavily

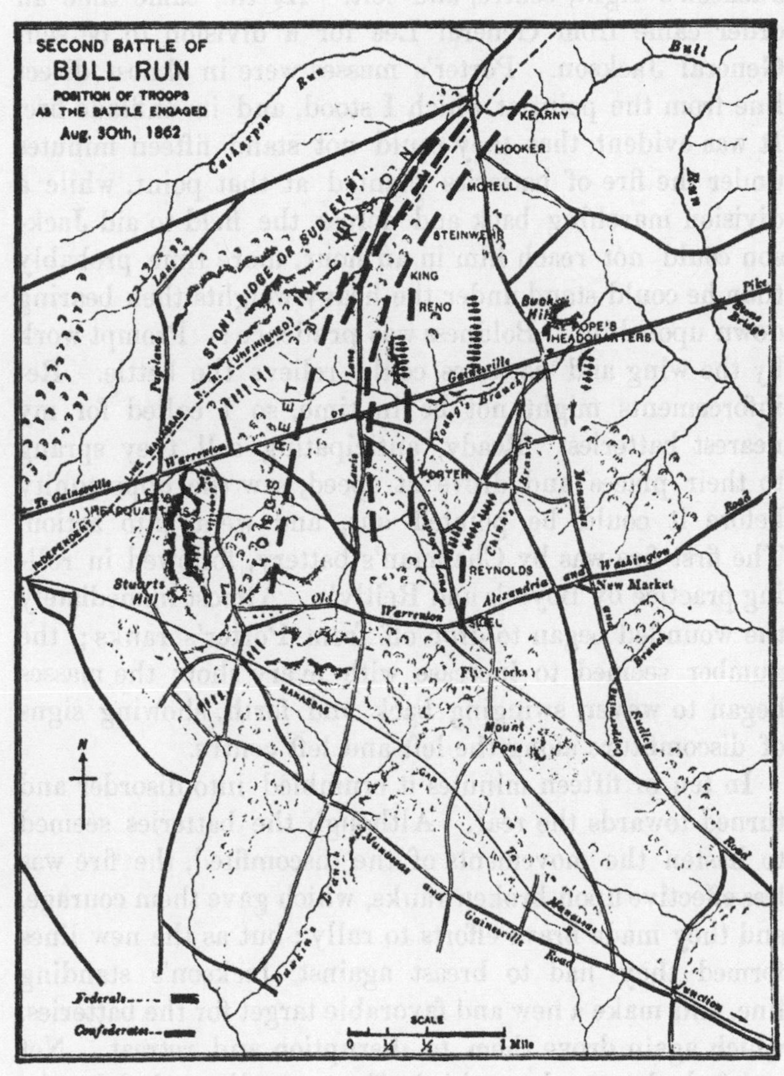
SECOND BATTLE OF
BULL RUN
POSITION OF TROOPS
AS THE BATTLE ENGAGED
Aug. 30th, 1862
Catharpen Run
Bull Run
KEARNY
HOOKER
MORELL
STEINWEHR
KING
RENO
STONY RIDGE OR SUDLEY MT.
R. R. (UNFINISHED)
Pageland Lane
Buck Hill
POPE'S HEADQUARTERS
Pike
Stone Bridge
Gainesville
Young's Branch
Warrenton
To Gainesville
PORTER
REYNOLDS
Alexandria and Washington
New Market
Stuarts Hill
Old Warrenton
SIGEL
Five Forks
Mount Pone
MANASSAS
Road
Junction
Federals
Confederates
SCALE
0 ¼ ½ 1 Mile
N

pressed, and asking to be reinforced. Riding forward a few rods to an open, which gave a view of Jackson's field, I came in sight of Porter's battle, piling up against Jackson's right, centre, and left. At the same time an order came from General Lee for a division to be sent General Jackson. Porter's masses were in almost direct line from the point at which I stood, and in enfilade fire. It was evident that they could not stand fifteen minutes under the fire of batteries planted at that point, while a division marching back and across the field to aid Jackson could not reach him in an hour, more time probably than he could stand under the heavy weights then bearing down upon him. Boldness was prudence! Prompt work by the wing and batteries could relieve the battle. Reinforcements might not be in time, so I called for my nearest batteries. Ready, anticipating call, they sprang to their places and drove at speed, saw the opportunity before it could be pointed out, and went into action. The first fire was by Chapman's battery, followed in rolling practice by Boyce's and Reilly's. Almost immediately the wounded began to drop off from Porter's ranks; the number seemed to increase with every shot; the masses began to waver, swinging back and forth, showing signs of discomfiture along the left and left centre.

In ten or fifteen minutes it crumbled into disorder and turned towards the rear. Although the batteries seemed to hasten the movements of the discomfited, the fire was less effective upon broken ranks, which gave them courage, and they made brave efforts to rally; but as the new lines formed they had to breast against Jackson's standing line, and make a new and favorable target for the batteries, which again drove them to disruption and retreat. Not satisfied, they made a third effort to rally and fight the battle through, but by that time they had fallen back far enough to open the field to the fire of S. D. Lee's artillery battalion. As the line began to take shape, this fearful fire was added to that under which they had tried so ineffectually to fight. The combination tore the line to pieces, and as it broke the third time the charge was ordered. The heavy fumes of gunpowder hanging about our ranks, as stimulating as sparkling wine, charged the atmosphere with the light and splendor of battle. Time was culminating under a flowing tide. The noble horses took the spirit of the riders sitting lightly in their saddles. As orders were given, the staff, their limbs already closed to the horses' flanks, pressed their spurs, but the electric current overleaped their speedy strides, and twenty-five thousand braves moved in line as by a single impulse. My old horse, appreciating the importance of corps headquarters, envious of the spread of his comrades as they measured the green, yet anxious to maintain his *rôle*, moved up and down his limited space in lofty bounds, resolved to cover in the air the space allotted his more fortunate comrades on the plain.

Leaving the broken ranks for Jackson, our fight was made against the lines near my front. As the plain along Hood's front was more favorable for the tread of soldiers, he was ordered, as the column of direction, to push for the plateau at the Henry House, in order to cut off retreat at the crossings by Young's Branch. Wilcox was called to support and cover Hood's left, but he lost sight of two of his brigades,—Featherston's and Pryor's,—and only gave the aid of his single brigade. Kemper and Jones were pushed on with Hood's right, Evans in Hood's direct support. The batteries were advanced as rapidly as fields were opened to them, Stribling's, J. B. Richardson's, Eshleman's, and Rogers's having fairest field for progress.

At the first sound of the charge, General Lee sent to revoke his call in favor of Jackson, asked me to push the battle, ordered R. H. Anderson's division up, and rode himself to join me.

DEFEAT OF THE FEDERAL TROOPS BY LONGSTREET'S CORPS, SECOND MANASSAS.

In the fulness of the battle, General Toombs rode up on his iron-gray under sweat and spur, his hat off, and asked for his command. He was told that a courier was about to start with an order for the division commander, and would guide him. He asked to be the bearer of the order, received it, and with the guide rode to find his post in the battle. The meeting of the brigade and its commander was more than joyful.

Jackson failed to pull up even on the left, which gave opportunity for some of the enemy's batteries to turn their fire across the right wing in enfilade, as we advanced, and the enemy strongly reinforced against us from troops drawn from Jackson's front, but we being on the jump, the fire of the batteries was not effective. It was severely threatening upon General Lee, however, who would ride under it, notwithstanding appeals to avoid it, until I thought to ride through a ravine, and thus throw a traverse between him and the fire. He sent orders to Jackson to advance and drive off or capture the batteries standing in his front and firing across our line, but it was not in season to relieve us. Hood's aggressive force was well spent when his troops approached the Chinn House, but R. H. Anderson was up and put in to reinforce and relieve his battle.

General Pope drew Ricketts's division from his right to brace his left, then Reno's command to aid in checking our march, but its progress, furiously resisted, was steady, though much delayed. Piatt's brigade was also put against us. This made time for Porter to gather his forces. His regulars of Sykes's division, particularly, made desperate resistance, that could only be overcome by our overreaching lines threatening their rear.

When the last guns were fired the thickening twilight concealed the lines of friend and foe, so that the danger of friend firing against friend became imminent. The hill of the Henry House was reached in good time, but darkness coming on earlier because of thickening clouds hovering over us, and a gentle fall of rain closely following, the plateau was shut off from view, and its ascent only found by groping through the darkening rainfall. As long as the enemy held the plateau, he covered the line of retreat by the turnpike and the bridge at Young's Branch. As he retired, heavy darkness gave safe-conduct to such of his columns as could find their way through the weird mists.

Captain William H. Powell, of the Fourth Regular Infantry, wrote of his experience,—

"As we filed from the battle-field into the turnpike leading over the stone bridge, we came upon a group of mounted officers, one of whom wore a peculiar style of hat which had been seen on the field that day, and which had been the occasion of a great deal of comment in the ranks. As we passed these officers, the one with the peculiar hat called out in a loud voice,—

"'What troops are those?'

"'The regulars,' answered somebody.

"'Second Division, Fifth Corps,' replied another.

"'God bless them! they saved the army,' added the officer.

"Subsequently we learned that he was General Irvin McDowell."

"As we neared the bridge we came upon confusion. Men singly and in detachments were mingled with sutlers' wagons, artillery caissons, supply wagons, and ambulances, each striving to get ahead of the other. Vehicles rushed through organized bodies and broke the columns into fragments. Little detachments gathered by the road-side after crossing the bridge, crying out to members of their regiments as a guide to scattered comrades. And what a night it was! Dark, gloomy, and beclouded by the volumes of smoke which had risen from the battle-field.*

At six o'clock, General Pope received report of the Sixth Corps, that had marched from Alexandria under General Franklin to the vicinity of Centreville, and ordered the several commands to concentrate about that

* Battles and Leaders of the Civil War.

hamlet during the night. The Second Corps from the Army of the Potomac under General Sumner also joined him at Centreville.

But for the dropping off of two of Wilcox's brigades from close connection with the right wing, and the deflection of Drayton's brigade, which was taken off by some unauthorized and unknown person from my right to the support of cavalry, it is possible that my working column could have gained the plateau of the Henry House before it was dark. Or if Jackson had been fresh enough to pull up even with us, he could have retained the commands under Reno and Sykes's regulars in his front, which could have given us safe sweep to the plateau, an hour before sundown, and in sight of great possibilities.

By morning of the 31st everything off the turnpike was nasty and soggy. Stuart's cavalry, followed by Pryor's brigade, were ordered across the Run at Stone Bridge as a diversion, while we were trying another move to reach the enemy's rear. The Confederates had worked all of the winter before, fortifying this new position, just taken by Pope at Centreville. Direct pursuit by the turnpike against these fortifications would therefore be fruitless.

General Jackson was called to head-quarters early in the morning. Upon receiving General Lee's orders to cross Bull Run at Sudley's and march by Little River turnpike to intercept the enemy's march, he said, "Good!" and away he went, without another word, or even a smile.

Though the suggestion of a smile always hung about his features, it was commonly said that it never fully developed, with a single exception, during his military career, though some claim there were other occasions on which it ripened, and those very near him say that he always smiled at the mention of the names of the Federal leaders whom he was accustomed to encounter over in the Valley behind the Blue Ridge. Standing, he was a graceful figure, five feet ten inches in height, with brown wavy hair, full beard, and regular features. At first glance his gentle expression repelled the idea of his severe piety, the full beard concealing the lower features, which had they been revealed would have marked the character of the man who claimed "his first duty to God, and his next to Jackson and General Lee." Mounted, his figure was not so imposing as that of the bold dragoon, Charley May, on Black Tom. He had a habit of raising his right hand, riding or sitting, which some of his followers were wont to construe into invocation for Divine aid, but they do not claim to know whether the prayers were for the slain, or for the success of other fields. The fact is, he received a shot in that hand at the First Bull Run, which left the hand under partial paralysis and the circulation through it imperfect. To relieve the pressure and assist the circulation he sometimes raised his arm.

I was ordered to look after the dead and those whose misfortune it was to be wounded, till Jackson could have time to stretch out on his new march, then to follow him, leaving the work to details and to General D. H. Hill's division, just coming in from Richmond.

After giving orders for the day, General Lee rode out towards Centreville for personal observation, halted, and dismounted at a point which seemed safe from danger or observation. Suddenly alarm was given of "The enemy's cavalry!" The group dispersed in hot haste to have the heels of their animals under them. The rush and confusion frightened the general's horse, so that he pulled him violently to the ground, severely spraining his right wrist, besides breaking some of the bones of the hand.

On reaching his head-quarters, Jackson ordered the assembly sounded, mounted his horse, and marched for the Sudley Springs crossing. He cleared the way in time for my column to reach that point at dark, the head of his own column tapping Little River turnpike. The march was over a single-track country road, bad enough on the south side of the river, much worn through a post-oak forest over quicksand subsoil on the north side. If Jackson had been followed by an enemy whose march he wished to baffle, his gun-carriages could not have made deeper cuts through the mud and quicksand.

Stuart was ordered over to the Little River turnpike, and advanced to the vicinity of Ox Hill and Fairfax Court-House. He made some interesting captures and reports of movements by the enemy. He slept near their lines, north of the turnpike, east of Chantilly.

The Little River and Warrenton turnpikes converge and join as they near Fairfax Court-House. At vulnerable points on the latter, General Pope posted parts of his command to cover his rearward march. At Ox Hill (Chantilly) were stationed Heintzelman's and Reno's corps, the divisions of Hooker, Kearny, Stevens, and Reno.

Early on the 1st of September the Confederates resumed their march. Jackson reached Ox Hill late in the afternoon, and deployed by inversion,—A. P. Hill's division on his right, Ewell's under Lawton next, his own under Stuart on his left, on the right of the road. On the left of the road were Stuart's cavalry and the artillery. Two of Hill's brigades were thrown out to find the enemy, and were soon met by his advance in search of Jackson, which made a furious attack, driving back the Confederate brigades in some disorder. Stevens, appreciating the crisis as momentous, thought it necessary to follow the opportunity by aggressive battle, in order to hold Jackson away from the Warrenton turnpike. Kearny, always ready to second any courageous move, joined in the daring battle. At the critical moment a thunder-storm burst with great violence upon the combatants, the high wind beating the rain in the faces of the Confederates. So firm was the unexpected battle that part of Jackson's line yielded to the onslaught. At one moment his artillery seemed in danger. Stevens was killed when the storm of battle, as well as that of the elements, began to quiet down. Stuart's cavalry drew near Jackson's left during the progress of the battle. As I rode up and met General Jackson, I remarked upon the number of his men going to the rear:

"General, your men don't appear to work well to-day."

"No," he replied, "but I hope it will prove a victory in the morning."

His troops were relieved as mine came up, to give them a respite till morning. While my reliefs were going around, General Philip Kearny rode to the line in search of his division. Finding himself in the presence of Confederates, he wheeled his horse and put spurs, preferring the danger of musket-balls to humiliating surrender. Several challenges called, but not heeded, were followed by the ring of half a dozen muskets, when he fell mortally hurt, and so perished one of the most gallant and dashing of the Union generals.

"September 2, 1862.

"MAJOR-GENERAL JOHN POPE,

"*United States Army*:

"SIR,—The body of General Philip Kearny was brought from the field last night, and he was reported dead. I send it forward under a flag of truce, thinking the possession of his remains may be a consolation to his family.

"I am, sir, respectfully, your obedient servant,

"R. E. LEE,

"*General*."*

The rain so concealed the fight in its last struggles that the troops escaped before we were aware that it had been abandoned.

As both Federal division commanders fell, the accounts

* Rebellion Record.

fail to do justice to their fight. Stevens in his short career gave evidence of courage, judgment, skill, and genius not far below his illustrious antagonist.

During the fight Stuart had parties out seeking information, and early on the second had his troopers in the saddle in pursuit. The army, ready to move, awaited reports of the cavalry, which came from time to time, as they followed on the line of retreat. From Fairfax Court-House came the report that the enemy's rear had passed in rapid retreat quite out of reach, approaching the fortifications of Alexandria and Washington City. Arms were ordered stacked, and a good rest was given the troops. Stuart's cavalry pursued and engaged the retreating army.

In the afternoon the First Corps started on the march *via* Dranesville for Leesburg and the Potomac River, followed on the third by the Second.

The results to the Confederates of the several engagements about Manassas Plains were seven thousand prisoners, two thousand of the enemy's wounded, thirty pieces of artillery, many thousand small-arms picked up from the field, and many colors, besides the captures made at Manassas Junction by General Jackson.*

A fair estimate of forces engaged:

Federal army, aggregate	63,000
Confederates	53,500

Losses between Rappahannock River and Washington:

Federals, aggregate	15,000
Confederates	10,000

The figures are given in round numbers, as the safest approximate estimate, but the records now accessible give

* Rebellion Record, vol. xii. part ii. p. 558. General Lee's report.

accurate details of losses in each command about the same as these.

And so it came to pass that from Cedar Run and Bull Run we had the term *All Run*. It is due to the gallant Sumner and his brave corps, however, to say that they so covered the last as to save disgraceful retreat.

A cursory review of the campaign reveals the pleasure ride of General Fitzhugh Lee by Louisa Court-House as most unseasonable. He lost the fruits of our summer's work, and lost the Southern cause. Proud Troy was laid in ashes. His orders were to meet his commander on the afternoon of the 17th, on the plank-road near Raccoon Ford, and upon this appointment was based General Lee's order of march for the 18th. If the march had been made as appointed, General Lee would have encountered the army of General Pope upon weak ground from Robertson River to near Raccoon Ford of the Rapidan, and thus our march would have been so expedited that we could have reached Alexandria and Washington before the landing of the first detachment of the Army of the Potomac at Alexandria on the 24th. The artillery and infantry were called to amend the delinquency by severe marches and battles.

It would have been possible to make good the lost time, but the despatch lost in the Stuart escapade was handed to General Pope that morning (the 18th), and gave him notice of our plans and orders. The delay thus brought about gave time for him to quit his weaker ground and retire to strong defensive heights behind the Rappahannock River, where he held us in check five days.

Referring to the solid move proposed before opening the campaign by the upper Rapidan to strike Pope's right, it may be said that it was not so dependent upon the cavalry that was marching behind us. That used by Jackson in his battle of the 9th was enough for immediate use. Jackson could have passed the upper Rapidan

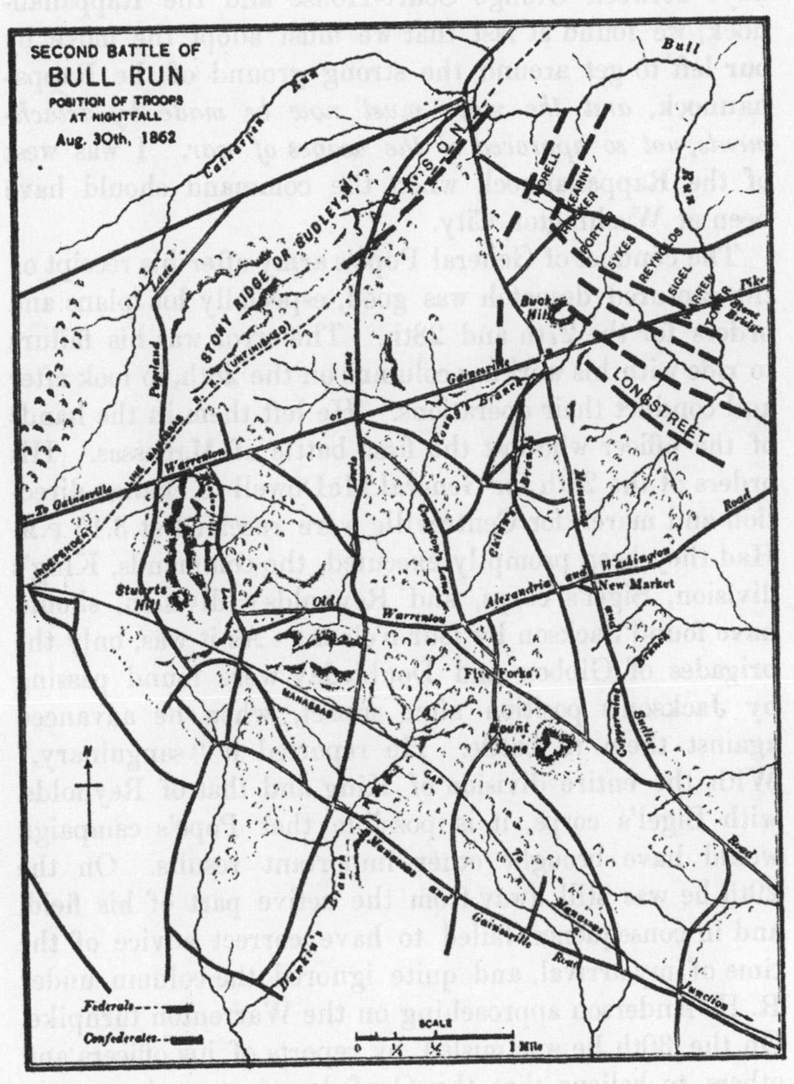
SECOND BATTLE OF
BULL RUN
POSITION OF TROOPS
AT NIGHTFALL
Aug. 30th, 1862
Bull
Run
Catharpin
STONY RIDGE OR SUDLEY MT.
(UNFINISHED)
MORELL
KEARNY
HOOKER
PORTER
SYKES
REYNOLDS
SIGEL
WARREN
LONGSTREET
Buck Hill
York Tpk.
Stone Bridge
Gainesville
Warrenton
To Gainesville
INDEPENDENT
Stuarts Hill
Old
Warrenton
Alexandria and Washington
New Market
Five Forks
Mount Pone
MANASSAS
GAP
Road
Junction
Federals
Confederates
SCALE
1 Mile

on the 16th, and followed by the right wing in time to strike Pope's right on the 17th in solid phalanx, *when time was mightier than cannon-balls.* After losing eight days between Orange Court-House and the Rappahannock, we found at last that we must adopt the move by our left to get around the strong ground of the Rappahannock, *and the move must now be made by detachments, not so approved of the usages of war.* I was west of the Rappahannock when the command should have been at Washington City.

The conduct of General Pope's army after his receipt of the captured despatch was good, especially his plans and orders for the 27th and 28th. The error was his failure to ride with his working columns on the 28th, to look after and conduct their operations. He left them in the hands of the officer who lost the first battle of Manassas. His orders of the 28th for General McDowell to change direction and march for Centreville were received at 3.15 P.M. Had they been promptly executed, the commands, King's division, Sigel's corps, and Reynolds's division, should have found Jackson by four o'clock. As it was, only the brigades of Gibbon and Doubleday were found passing by Jackson's position after sunset, when he advanced against them in battle. He reported it "sanguinary." With the entire division of King and that of Reynolds, with Sigel's corps, it is possible that Pope's campaign would have brought other important results. On the 29th he was still away from the active part of his field, and in consequence failed to have correct advice of the time of my arrival, and quite ignored the column under R. H. Anderson approaching on the Warrenton turnpike. On the 30th he was misled by reports of his officers and others to believe that the Confederates were in retreat, and planned his movements upon false premises.

Jackson's march to Bristoe and Manassas Junction was hazardous, or seemed so, but in view of his peculiar talent

for such work (the captured despatch of General Pope giving information of his affairs), and Lee's skill, it seemed the only way open for progressive manœuvre. The strength of the move lay in the time it gave us to make issue before all of the Army of the Potomac could unite with the army under General Pope. His game of hide-and-seek about Bull Run, Centreville, and Manassas Plains was grand, but marred in completeness by the failure of General A. P. Hill to meet his orders for the afternoon of the 28th. As a leader he was fine; as a wheel-horse, he was not always just to himself. He was fond of the picturesque.

CHAPTER XV.

THE MARYLAND CAMPAIGN.

General Lee continues Aggressive Work—From Foraged Fields of Virginia into a Bounteous Land—Longstreet objected to the Movement on Harper's Ferry—Lee thinks the Occasion Timely for Proposal of Peace and Independence—Confederates singing through the Streets of Fredericktown—McClellan's Movements—Cautious Marches— Lee's Lost Order handed to the Federal Chief at Frederick.

> "There is a tide in the affairs of men,
> Which, taken at the flood, leads on to fortune;
> Omitted, all the voyage of their life
> Is bound in shallows, and in miseries.
> On such a full sea are we now afloat."

As our columns approached Leesburg, "Maryland, my Maryland" was in the air, and on the lips of every man from General Lee down to the youngest drummer. Our chief could have safely ordered the ranks to break in Virginia and assemble in Fredericktown. All that they would ask was a thirty minutes' plunge in the Potomac to remove some of the surplus dust, before they encountered the smiles of the winsome lasses of Maryland. Yet he expressed doubt of trusting so far from home solely to untried and unknown resources for food-supplies. Receiving his anxious expressions really as appeals for reinforcement of his unexpressed wish, but warm to brave the venture, I related my Mexican War experiences with Worth's division, marching around the city of Monterey on two days' rations of roasting-ears and green oranges, and said that it seemed to me that we could trust the fields of Maryland, laden with ripening corn and fruit, to do as much as those of Mexico; that we could in fact subsist on the bounty of the fields until we could open communication with our organized base of supplies.

As factors in the problem, important as Lee's masterly science and Jackson's great skill, stood the fortitude and prowess of the Confederate soldiers, and their faith in the friendship and generosity of their countrymen. Hungry, sparsely clad, worn with continuous bivouac and battle since the 26th of June, proud of their record from the First to the honors of the Second Manassas, their cheery smiles and elastic step told better than words of anticipations of welcome from friends in Maryland, and of new fields of honor for their solid ranks,—of the day when they should be masters of the field and of a new-born republic.

Though a losing battle, the Union armies had made a splendid fight at Second Manassas. The stand at Ox Hill was severe; severe till the march of retreat, so that the Army of Northern Virginia should have held in profound respect its formidable adversary, seasoned by many bloody fields.

The policy of the Richmond government was defensive rather than aggressive warfare, but the situation called for action, and there was but one opening,—across the Potomac. General Lee decided to follow his success in its natural leading, and so reported to the Richmond authorities.

He was not so well equipped as an army of invasion should be, but the many friends in Maryland and the fields on the north side of the Potomac were more inviting than those of Virginia, so freely foraged. He knew from events of the past that his army was equal to the service to which he thought to call it, and ripe for the adventure; that he could march into Maryland and remain until the season for the enemy's return into Virginia for autumn or winter work had passed, improve his transportation supplies, and the clothing of his army, and do that, if not more, for relief of our Southern fields and limited means, besides giving his army and cause a moral influence of great effect at home and abroad. He decided to make his march by the most direct route from Chantilly, where he had last fought, to the Potomac, and so crossed by the fords near Leesburg. Marching by this route, he thought to cut off a formidable force of Union troops at Winchester, at Martinsburg, and a strong garrison occupying the fortified position at Harper's Ferry.

To summarize the situation, we were obliged to go into Maryland or retreat to points more convenient to supplies and the protection of Richmond.

At Leesburg Lee learned that the Union troops in the Valley had left Winchester, and sent back orders to have the crippled and feeble soldiers wending their way to the army march through the Valley to join us in Maryland. Trains of supplies were ordered to move by the same route.

On the 5th and 6th the columns crossed the Potomac by the fords near Leesburg. Stuart's cavalry, coming up from the line near Alexandria and the Long Bridge, passed to front and right flank of the army. General McLaws's division, General J. G. Walker, with two brigades of his division, and General Hampton's cavalry brigade, including Colonel Baker's North Carolina regiment, joined us on the march. On the 7th our infantry and artillery commands came together near Frederick City.

Riding together before we reached Frederick, the sound of artillery fire came from the direction of Point of Rocks and Harper's Ferry, from which General Lee inferred that the enemy was concentrating his forces from the Valley, for defence at Harper's Ferry, and proposed to me to organize forces to surround and capture the works and the garrison.

I thought it a venture not worth the game, and suggested, as we were in the enemy's country and presence, that he would be advised of any move that we made in a few hours after it was set on foot; that the Union army, though beaten, was not disorganized; that we knew a number of their officers who could put it in order and march against us, if they found us exposed, and make serious trouble before the capture could be accomplished; that our men were worn by very severe and protracted service, and in need of repose; that as long as we had them in hand we were masters of the situation, but dispersed into many fragments, our strength must be greatly reduced. As the subject was not continued, I supposed that it was a mere expression of passing thought, until, the day after we reached Frederick, upon going over to head-quarters, I found the front of the general's tent closed and tied. Upon inquiring of a member of the staff, I was told that he was inside with General Jackson. As I had not been called, I turned to go away, when General Lee, recognizing my voice, called me in. The plan had been arranged. Jackson, with his three divisions, was to recross the Potomac by the fords above Harper's Ferry, march *via* Martinsburg to Bolivar Heights; McLaws's division by Crampton's Gap to Maryland Heights; J. G. Walker's division to recross at Cheek's Ford and occupy Loudoun Heights, these heights overlooking the positions of the garrison of Harper's Ferry; D. H. Hill's division to march by the National road over South Mountain at Turner's Gap, and halt at the western base, to guard trains, intercept fugitives from Harper's Ferry, and support the cavalry, if needed; the cavalry to face the enemy and embarrass his movements. I was to march over the mountain by Turner's Gap to Hagerstown.

As their minds were settled firmly upon the enterprise, I offered no opposition further than to ask that the order be so modified as to allow me to send R. H. Anderson's division with McLaws and to halt my own column near the point designated for bivouac of General D. H.

Hill's command. These suggestions were accepted, and the order* so framed was issued.

It may be well to digress from my narrative for a moment just here to remark that General Lee's confidence in the strength of his army, the situation of affairs, and

---

* "HEAD-QUARTERS ARMY OF NORTHERN VIRGINIA,
"September 9, 1862.

"SPECIAL ORDERS, No. 191.

"The army will resume its march to-morrow, taking the Hagerstown road. General Jackson's command will form the advance, and, after passing Middletown, with such portion as he may select, take the route towards Sharpsburg, cross the Potomac at the most convenient point, and, by Friday night, take possession of the Baltimore and Ohio Railroad, capture such of the enemy as may be at Martinsburg, and intercept such as may attempt to escape from Harper's Ferry.

"General Longstreet's command will pursue the same road as far as Boonsborough, where it will halt with the reserve, supply, and baggage trains of the army.

"General McLaws, with his own division and that of General R. H. Anderson, will follow General Longstreet. On reaching Middletown he will take the route to Harper's Ferry, and by Friday morning possess himself of the Maryland Heights, and endeavor to capture the enemy at Harper's Ferry and vicinity.

"General Walker, with his division, after accomplishing the object in which he is now engaged, will cross the Potomac at Cheek's Ford, ascend its right bank to Lovettsville, take possession of Loudoun Heights, if practicable, by Friday morning, Key's Ford on his left, and the road between the end of the mountain and the Potomac on his right. He will, as far as practicable, co-operate with General McLaws and General Jackson in intercepting the retreat of the enemy.

"General D. H. Hill's division will form the rear-guard of the army, pursuing the road taken by the main body. The reserve artillery, ordnance, supply-trains, etc., will precede General Hill.

"General Stuart will detach a squadron of cavalry to accompany the commands of Generals Longstreet, Jackson, and McLaws, and with the main body of the cavalry will cover the route of the army and bring up all stragglers that may have been left behind.

"The commands of Generals Jackson, McLaws, and Walker, after accomplishing the objects for which they have been detached, will join the main body of the army at Boonsborough or Hagerstown.

"Each regiment on the march will habitually carry its axes in the regimental ordnance wagons, for use of the men at their encampments to procure wood, etc.

"By command of General R. E. Lee.

"R. H. CHILTON,
"*Assistant Adjutant-General.*

"MAJOR-GENERAL D. H. HILL,
"*Commanding Division.*"

the value of the moral effect upon the country, North and South, was made fully manifest by the nature of the campaign he had just entered upon, especially that portion of it directed against Harper's Ferry, which, as events were soon to prove, weakened the effectiveness of his army in the main issue, which happened to be Antietam.

In another and a very different way, and with even greater plainness, his high estimate of opportunity and favoring condition of circumstances existing at the time was indicated to the authorities, though of course not at that time made public. This was his deliberate and urgent advice to President Davis to join him and be prepared to make a proposal for peace and independence from the head of a conquering army. Fresh from the Second Manassas, and already entered upon the fateful Maryland campaign, he wrote the President this important letter:

"HEAD-QUARTERS NEAR FREDERICKTOWN, MD.,
"September 8, 1862.

"HIS EXCELLENCY JEFFERSON DAVIS,
"*President of the Confederate States, Richmond, Va.*:

"MR. PRESIDENT,—The present position of affairs, in my opinion, places it in the power of the government of the Confederate States to propose with propriety to that of the United States the recognition of our independence. For more than a year both sections of the country have been devastated by hostilities which have brought sorrow and suffering upon thousands of homes, without advancing the objects which our enemies proposed to themselves in beginning the contest. Such a proposition, coming from us at this time, could in no way be regarded as suing for peace; but, being made when it is in our power to inflict injury upon our adversary, would show conclusively to the world that our sole object is the establishment of our independence and the attainment of an honorable peace. The rejection of this offer would prove to the country that the responsibility of the continuance of the war does not rest upon us, but that the party in power in the United States elect to prosecute it for purposes of their own. The proposal of peace would enable the people of the United States to determine at their coming elections whether they will support those who favor a prolongation of the war, or those who wish to bring it to a termination, which can but be productive of good to both parties without affecting the honor of either.

"I have the honor to be, with great respect,

"Your obedient servant,

"R. E. LEE,

"*General.*" *

And now I return to my narrative.

General Walker's division was on detached service at the time of the order, trying to cut the canal. He marched, however, at the appointed time, found Cheek's Ford under the severe fire of the enemy's batteries, and marched on up the left bank as far as the Point of Rocks, where he crossed and rested on the 11th. On the 12th he marched to and bivouacked at Hillsboro'; on the 13th, to the foot of the Blue Ridge and occupied Loudoun Heights by a detachment under Colonel Cooke.

Not satisfied with the organization of McLaws's column, I asked and obtained permission on the 10th to strengthen it by three other brigades,—Wilcox's, under Colonel Alfred Cumming; Featherston's, and Pryor's, which were attached to R. H. Anderson's division.

The different columns from Frederick marched as ordered, except in the change authorized for Anderson's division. It was a rollicking march, the Confederates playing and singing, as they marched through the streets of Frederick, "The Girl I left behind me."

Jackson recrossed the Potomac on the 11th, at Light's Ford, ordered A. P. Hill's division by the turnpike to Martinsburg, his own and Ewell's northwest to North Mountain Depot to intercept troops that might retreat in that direction from Martinsburg. General White, commanding the Union troops, abandoned Martinsburg the night of the 11th, having timely advice of Jackson's movements, and retreated to Harper's Ferry. On the

* Rebellion Record, vol. xix. part ii. p. 600.

12th, Jackson's troops came together at Martinsburg, found some stores of bacon and bread rations, and marched on the 13th for Harper's Ferry, where he found the Union troops in battle array along Bolivar Heights.

I marched across South Mountain at Turner's Pass, and bivouacked near its western base. General Lee ordered my move continued to Hagerstown. The plans of the Confederates, as blocked out, anticipated the surrender of Harper's Ferry on Friday, the 12th, or Saturday, the 13th, at latest. The change of my position from Boonsborough to Hagerstown further misled our cavalry commander and the commanders of the divisions at Boonsborough and Harper's Ferry into a feeling of security that there could be no threatening by the army from Washington.

D. H. Hill's division crossed by Turner's Gap and halted near Boonsborough. McLaws took the left-hand road, marched through Burkittsville, and halted for the night at the east base of the mountain, near Crampton's and Brownsville Passes.

Near Crampton's Pass on the west the mountain unfolds into two parallel ridges, the eastern, the general range of South Mountain, the western, Elk Ridge, opening out Pleasant Valley, about three miles from crest to crest.

Crampton's is the northern of the two passes, and about eight miles south of Turner's. One mile south of Crampton is the Brownsville Pass, and four miles from that the river pass, which cuts in between the Blue Ridge of Virginia and South Mountain of Maryland. Through the river pass the Baltimore and Ohio Railway, the canal, and the Fredericktown turnpike reach out to the west, and at the pass is the little town of Riverton. Between Riverton and Harper's Ferry was the hamlet Sandy Hook, occupied by about fifteen hundred Federal troops. Two roads wind through Pleasant Valley, one close under

South Mountain, the other hugging the foot-hills of Elk Ridge,—the latter rugged, little used.

Harper's Ferry, against which Lee's new movement was directed, nestles at the confluence of the Potomac and Shenandoah Rivers, on the Virginia side, under the towering cliffs of Maryland or Cumberland Heights. At Harper's Ferry the river cuts in so close under Maryland Heights that they stand almost perpendicularly over it. The crowded space between the heights and the river, filled by the railway, canal, and turnpike, was made by blastings from the southern extremities of Maryland Heights. Under the precipice the railroad bridge crosses the Potomac, and a pontoon bridge was laid a few yards above it.

McLaws marched over into Pleasant Valley on the 11th, through Brownsville Pass, near which and over Elk Ridge a road passes through Solomon's Gap of Elk Ridge. From the top of this gap is a rugged way along the ridge leading down to its southern projections and limits, by which infantry only could find foothold. That southern point is called Maryland Heights. Two brigades—Kershaw's and Barksdale's—under General Kershaw were ordered to ascend Elk Ridge, march along its summit, driving off opposition, and capture the enemy's position on the heights. General Semmes was left near the pass, over which the troops had marched with his own and Mahone's brigades, the latter under Colonel Parham with orders to send a brigade to the top of Solomon's Gap to cover Kershaw's rear. General Wright, of Anderson's division, was ordered with his brigade and two pieces of artillery along the crest ridge of South Mountain to its projection over Riverton. General Cobb was ordered with his brigade along the base of Elk Ridge, to be abreast of Kershaw's column. With the balance of his command, General McLaws moved down the Valley by the South Mountain road, connecting his march, by signal, with General Kershaw's. Kershaw soon met a strong force of skirmishers, which was steadily pushed back till night. General Wright, without serious opposition, reached the end of the mountain, when R. H. Anderson sent another brigade—Pryor's—to occupy Weverton. On the 13th, Kershaw renewed his fight against very strong positions, forced his way across two abatis, along a rugged plateau, dropping off on both sides, in rocky cliffs of forty or fifty feet, encountered breastworks of logs and boulders, struggled in a severe fight, captured the position, the enemy's signal station, and at four P.M. gained possession of the entire hold. Cobb's brigade was advanced, and took possession of Sandy Hook without serious opposition. The column near South Mountain was advanced to complete the grasp against the enemy at Harper's Ferry. Up to this hour General McLaws had heard nothing direct from Generals Jackson and Walker, though from the direction of the former sounds of artillery reached him, and later a courier told that Jackson thought his leading division would approach at two o'clock that afternoon. During the day heavy cannonading was heard towards the east and northeast, and rumors reached McLaws of the advance of the enemy from Frederick, but the signal-parties and cavalry failed to discover movements, so the firing was not credited as of significance. The morning of the 14th was occupied in cutting a road for his artillery up to the point overlooking Harper's Ferry, and at two P.M. Captains Read and Carlton had their best guns in position over the town. But during these progressions the Confederates on other fields had been called to more serious work.

General McClellan, moving his columns out from the vicinity of Washington City on the 5th, made slow and very cautious marches to save fatigue of his men and at the same time cover the capital against unforeseen contingency; so slow and cautious was the march that he only covered forty or fifty miles in seven days. On the 12th his head-quarters were at Urbana, where he received the following telegram from President Lincoln:

"Governor Curtin telegraphs me, 'I have advices that Jackson is crossing the Potomac at Williamsport, and probably the whole rebel army will be drawn from Maryland.'"

The President added,—

"Receiving nothing from Harper's Ferry or Martinsburg today, and positive information from Wheeling that the line is cut, corroborates the idea that the enemy is recrossing the Potomac. Please do not let him get off without being hurt." *

Elsewhere General McClellan has written of the 12th:

"During these movements I had not imposed long marches on the columns. The absolute necessity of refitting and giving some little rest to the troops worn down by previous long-continued marches and severe fighting, together with the uncertainty as to the actual position, strength, and intentions of the enemy, rendered it incumbent upon me to move slowly and cautiously until the head-quarters reached Urbana, where I first obtained reliable information that the enemy's object was to move upon Harper's Ferry and the Cumberland Valley, and not upon Washington and Baltimore."

His army was organized: Right wing, under General Burnside: First and Ninth Corps; the Kanawha Division, under General J. D. Cox, was assigned with the Ninth Corps about the 8th instant.

Centre column: Second and Twelfth Corps, under General Sumner.

Left wing: Sixth Corps and Couch's division of the Fourth under General Franklin; Sykes's division, Fifth Corps, independent.†

Besides the despatches of the 11th and 12th, his cavalry under General Pleasonton, which was vigilant and

---

* Rebellion Record, vol. xix. part i. p. 41. McClellan's official account.

† Record, vol. xix. part i.

pushing, sent frequent reports of his steady progress. In the afternoon Pleasonton and the Ninth Corps under General Reno entered Fredericktown. This advance, by the National road, threatened to cut off two of Stuart's cavalry regiments left at the Monocacy Bridge. To detain the enemy till these were withdrawn, the outpost on that road was reinforced. Hampton retired his cavalry beyond Frederick and posted his artillery to cover the line of march, where he was soon attacked by a formidable force. To make safe the retreat of the brigade, a cavalry charge was ordered, under Colonel Butler, Lieutenant Meaghan's squadron leading. Colonel Moore, of the Twenty-eighth Ohio Infantry, and a number of other prisoners were captured. This so detained the enemy as to give safe withdrawal for the brigade to Middletown, leaving Lieutenant-Colonel Martin's cavalry and two guns on guard at the gap of the Catoctin range of mountains.

Before withdrawing from Frederick on the 12th, General Stuart sent orders for the brigade under General Fitzhugh Lee to move around the right of the Union army and ascertain the meaning and strength of its march.

Following his orders of the 12th, General Pleasonton detached a cavalry brigade on the 13th and section of artillery under Colonel McReynolds to follow Fitzhugh Lee, and Rush's Lancers were sent to Jefferson for General Franklin's column. With his main force he pursued the Confederates towards Turner's Pass of South Mountain. Midway between Frederick and South Mountain, running parallel, is a lesser range, Catoctin, where he encountered Stuart's rear-guard. After a severe affair he secured the pass, moved on, and encountered a second force near Middletown. Reinforced by Gibson's battery, he attacked and forced the way to a third stand. This in turn was forced back and into the mountain at Turner's Pass.

On that day McClellan's columns marched: Ninth Corps, to and near Middletown, eight miles; First Corps, to the Monocacy, eight miles; Twelfth Corps, to Frederick, nine miles; Second Corps, to Frederick, eight miles; Sixth Corps, to Buckeystown, seven miles; Couch's division, to Licksville, six miles; Sykes's division, to Frederick, eight miles.

At Frederick, General Lee's special order No. 191 was handed to General McClellan at his head-quarters with his centre (Sumner's) column.

How lost and how found we shall presently see, and see that by the mischance and accident the Federal commander came in possession of information that gave a spur, and great advantage, to his somewhat demoralized army.

CHAPTER XVI.

"THE LOST ORDER"—SOUTH MOUNTAIN.

How the Federals found the Despatch—With every Advantage McClellan "made haste slowly"—Lee turns back to meet him at South Mountain—Longstreet preferred that the Stand should be made at Sharpsburg—The Battle at the Pass—Many killed—General Garland of the Confederate and General Reno of the Union side—A future President among the wounded—Estimate of Forces engaged.

THE strange losing and stranger finding of Lee's "General Order No. 191," commonly referred to as "the lost despatch," which he had issued September 9 for the movement of his army, made a difference in our Maryland campaign for better or for worse.

Before this tell-tale slip of paper found its way to McClellan's head-quarters he was well advised by his cavalry, and by despatches wired him from east and west, of the movements of Lee's army, and later, on that eventful 13th day of September, he received more valuable information, even to a complete revelation of his adversary's plans and purpose, such as no other commander, in the history of war, has had at a time so momentous. So well satisfied was he that he was master of the military zodiac that he despatched the Washington authorities of Lee's "gross mistake" and exposure to severe penalties. There was not a point upon which he wanted further information nor a plea for a moment of delay. His army was moving rapidly; all that he wished for was that the plans of the enemy would not be changed. The only change that occurred in the plans was the delay of their execution, which worked to his greater advantage. By following the operations of the armies through the complications of the campaign we may form better judgment of the work of the commanders in finding ways through its intricacies:

of the efforts of one to grasp the envied crown so haplessly tendered; of the other in seeking refuge that might cover catastrophe involved in the complexity of misconceived plans.

The copy of the order that was lost was sent by General Jackson to General D. H. Hill under the impression that Hill's division was part of his command, but the division had not been so assigned, and that copy of the order was not delivered at Hill's head-quarters, but had been put to other use. The order sent to General Hill from general head-quarters was carefully preserved.

When the Federals marched into Frederick, just left by the Confederates, General Sumner's column went into camp about noon, and it was then that the despatch was found by Colonel Silas Colgrove, who took it to division head-quarters, whence it was quickly sent to the Federal commander.

General McClellan reported to General Halleck that the lost order had been handed him in the evening, but it is evident that he had it at the time of his noonday despatch to the President, from his reference to the facts it exposed.

It is possible that it was at first suspected as a *ruse de guerre*, and that a little time was necessary to convince McClellan of its genuineness, which may account for the difference between the hinted information in his despatch to General Halleck and the confident statement made at noonday to the President.

Some of the Confederates were a little surprised that a matter of such magnitude was intrusted to pen-and-ink despatches. The copy sent me was carefully read, then used as some persons use a little cut of tobacco, to be assured that others could not have the benefit of its contents.

It has been in evidence that the copy that was lost had been used as a wrapper for three fragrant Confederate cigars in the interim between its importance when issued by the Confederate chief and its greater importance when found by the Federals.

General Halleck thought the capital in imminent peril before he heard from McClellan on the 13th, as shown on that day by a despatch to General McClellan:

"The capture of this place will throw us back six months, if it should not destroy us."

But later, the "lost despatch" having turned up at head-quarters of General McClellan, that commander apprised the authorities of the true condition of affairs in the following, so pleased that he did not fail to make his bow to the ladies:

"HEAD-QUARTERS, FREDERICK, September 13, 1862, 12 M.
("Received 2.35 A.M., September 14.)

"TO THE PRESIDENT:

"I have the whole rebel force in front of me, but am confident, and no time shall be lost. I have a difficult task to perform, but with God's blessing will accomplish it. I think Lee has made a gross mistake, and that he will be severely punished for it. The army is in motion as rapidly as possible. I hope for a great success if the plans of the rebels remain unchanged. We have possession of Catoctin. I have all the plans of the rebels, and will catch them in their own trap if my men are equal to the emergency. I now feel that I can count on them as of old. All forces of Pennsylvania should be placed to co-operate at Chambersburg. My respects to Mrs. Lincoln. Received most enthusiastically by the ladies. Will send you trophies. All well, and with God's blessing will accomplish it.

"GEO. B. MCCLELLAN."

"FREDERICK CITY, MD., September 13, 1862, 11 P.M.
("Received 1 P.M., September 14.)

"MAJOR-GENERAL H. W. HALLECK,
"*General-in-Chief*:

"An order from General R. E. Lee, addressed to General D. H. Hill, which has accidentally come into my hands this evening,—the authenticity of which is unquestionable,—discloses some of the plans of the enemy, and shows most conclusively that the main rebel army is now before us, including Longstreet's, Jackson's, the two Hills's, McLaws's, Walker's, R. H. Anderson's, and Hood's commands. That army was ordered to march on the 10th, and to attack and capture our forces at Harper's Ferry and Martinsburg yesterday, by surrounding them with such a heavy force that they conceived it impossible they could escape. They were also ordered to take possession of the Baltimore and Ohio Railroad; afterwards to concentrate again at Boonsborough or Hagerstown. That this was the plan of campaign on the 9th is confirmed by the fact that heavy firing has been heard in the direction of Harper's Ferry this afternoon, and the columns took the roads specified in the order. It may, therefore, in my judgment, be regarded as certain that this rebel army, which I have good reasons for believing amounts to 120,000 men or more, and know to be commanded by Lee in person, intended to attempt penetrating Pennsylvania. The officers told their friends here that they were going to Harrisburg and Philadelphia. My advance has pushed forward to-day and overtaken the enemy on the Middletown and Harper's Ferry roads, and several slight engagements have taken place, in which our troops have driven the enemy from their position. A train of wagons, about three-quarters of a mile long, was destroyed to-day by the rebels in their flight. We took over fifty prisoners. This army marches forward early to-morrow morning, and will make forced marches, to endeavor to relieve Colonel Miles, but I fear, unless he makes a stout resistance, we may be too late.

"A report came in just this moment that Miles was attacked to-day, and repulsed the enemy, but I do not know what credit to attach to the statement. I shall do everything in my power to save Miles if he still holds out. Portions of Burnside's and Franklin's corps move forward this evening.

"I have received your despatch of ten A.M. You will perceive, from what I have stated, that there is but little probability of the enemy being in much force south of the Potomac. I do not, by any means, wish to be understood as undervaluing the importance of holding Washington. It is of great consequence, but upon the success of this army the fate of the nation depends. It was for this reason that I said everything else should be made subordinate to placing this army in proper condition to meet the large rebel force in our front. Unless General Lee has changed his plans, I expect a severe general engagement to-morrow. I feel confident that there is now no rebel force immediately threatening Washington or Baltimore, but that I have the mass of their troops to contend with, and they outnumber me when united.

"Geo. B. McClellan,

"*Major-General.*"*

With the knowledge afforded by securing Lee's "lost order" the passes of the South Mountain became important points. If he could force them, McClellan might fall on the divided columns of the Confederates and reach Harper's Ferry in time to save its garrison; but Lee received intelligence of his only moderate forward movement, and, without knowing then how it came to be made, recalled a force to make resistance, and, so supplementing or complementing by his rapid moves the Federal commander's slowness, saved his campaign from the disastrous failure that threatened it.

General McClellan claimed to have been more vigorous in pursuit after he received the "lost despatch," but events do not support the claim. He had time after the despatch was handed him to march his army to the foot of South Mountain before night, but gave no orders, except his letter to General Franklin calling for vigorous action, which was afterwards tempered by caution to wait for developments at Turner's Pass. He gave no intimation of the despatch to his cavalry leader, who should have been the first to be advised of the points in his possession. General Pleasonton had pushed the Confederate cavalry back into the mountains long before night of the 13th under his instructions of the 12th. Had he been informed of the points known by his chief in the afternoon, he would have occupied South Mountain at Turner's Pass before any of the Confederate infantry was there or apprised of his approach. General McClellan's orders for the 14th were dated,—

* Rebellion Record, vol. xix. part ii. p. 281.

"13th, 6.45 P.M., Couch to move to Jefferson with his whole division, and join Franklin.

"13th, 8.45 P.M., Sumner to move at seven A.M.

"13th, 11.30 P.M., Hooker to march at daylight to Middletown.

"13th, 11.30 P.M., Sykes to move at six A.M., after Hooker on the Middletown and Hagerstown road.

"14th, one A.M., artillery reserve to follow Sykes closely.

"14th, nine A.M., Sumner ordered to take the Shockstown road to Middletown.

"Franklin's corps at Buckeystown to march for Burkittsville." *

He wrote General Franklin at 6.20 P.M., giving the substance of information of the despatch, but not mentioning when or how he came by it, and ordered him to march for the mountain pass at Crampton's Gap, to seize the pass if it was not strongly guarded, and march for Rohrersville, to cut off the command under McLaws about Maryland Heights, capture it, and relieve the garrison at Harper's Ferry, and return to co-operate in capturing the balance of the Confederate army north of the Potomac; but, in case the gap was occupied by a strong force, to await operations against it until he heard the engagement of the army moving upon Turner's Pass. He wrote General Franklin that General Pleasonton had cleared the field east of the mountain of Confederate cavalry. After relieving Harper's Ferry, Franklin was to destroy bridges and guard against crossing of the Confederates to the north side, his idea being to cut the Confederate army in two and capture or break it up in detail. His appeal was urgent for the best work that a general could exercise. The division under General Couch was ordered to General Franklin, without waiting for all of its forces to join. This is the only order of the records that indicates unusual action on the part of the Union commander, and General Franklin's evidence before the Committee on the Conduct

* Rebellion Record, vol. xix. part i. p. 48.

of the War shows that his orders of the 13th were so modified on the 14th as to direct his wait for Couch's division to join him, and the division joined him after nightfall.

The divisions of the Ninth Corps reached Middletown on the 13th, under the orders of the 12th, issued before the lost despatch was found, one of them supporting Pleasonton's cavalry; but Rodman's, under misconception of orders, marched back towards Frederick.

South Mountain range, standing between the armies, courses across Maryland northeast and southwest. Its average height is one thousand feet; its rugged passes give it strong military features. The pass at Turner drops off about four hundred feet. About a mile south of this the old Sharpsburg road crosses at a greater elevation through rugged windings; a fork of this road, on the mountain-side, makes a second way over below Fox's Pass, while another turns to the right and leads back into the turnpike at the summit, or Mountain House.

On the north side of the turnpike a road leads off to the right, called the old Hagerstown road, which winds its course through a valley between a spur and the mountain, and courses back to the turnpike along the top. A more rugged route than this opens a way to the mountain-top by a route nearer the pike.

General Pleasonton, not advised of the lost despatch, did not push for a careful reconnoissance on the 13th. At the same time, General Stuart, forced back into the mountains, finding his cavalry unserviceable, advised General D. H. Hill of severe pressure, called for a brigade of infantry, ordered Hampton's cavalry down to Crampton's Pass to assist Robertson's brigade, Colonel Munford commanding, leaving the Jeff Davis Legion, under Colonel Martin, Colonel Rosser with another cavalry detachment, and Stuart's horse artillery to occupy the passes by the old Sharpsburg road. Colquitt's brigade of infantry reported to him under his call. After posting it near the east base of the mountain to hold the pass, he rode to join his other cavalry detachments down at Crampton's Pass. He only knew of two brigades of infantry pressing him back, and so reported. His cavalry, ordered around the Union right under General Fitzhugh Lee, for information of the force in his front, had failed to make report. General Hill ordered two brigades, Garland's and Colquitt's, into the pass to report to Stuart, and drew his other three near the foot of the mountain. Garland's brigade filed to the right after ascending the mountain, and halted near the turnpike. Colquitt's brigade took its position across the turnpike and down towards the base of the mountain, Lane's batteries at the summit.

It seems that up to the night of the 13th most of the Confederates were looking with confidence to the surrender at Harper's Ferry on the 13th, to be promptly followed by a move farther west, not thinking it possible that a great struggle at and along the range of South Mountain was impending; that even on the 14th our cavalry leader thought to continue his retrograde that day. General Hill's attention was given more to his instructions to prevent the escape of fugitives from Harper's Ferry than to trouble along his front, as the instructions covered more especially that duty, while information from the cavalry gave no indication of serious trouble from the front.

A little after dark of the 13th, General Lee received, through a scout, information of the advance of the Union forces to the foot of South Mountain in solid ranks. Later information confirmed this report, giving the estimated strength at ninety thousand. General Lee still held to the thought that he had ample time. He sent for me, and I found him over his map. He told of the reports, and asked my views. I thought it too late to march on the 14th and properly man the pass at Turner's, and expressed preference for concentrating D. H. Hill's and my own force behind the Antietam at Sharpsburg, where we could get together in season to make a strong defensive fight, and at the same time check McClellan's march towards Harper's Ferry, in case he thought to relieve the beleaguered garrison by that route, forcing him to first remove the obstacle on his flank. He preferred to make the stand at Turner's Pass, and ordered the troops to march next morning, ordering a brigade left at Hagerstown to guard the trains. No warning was sent McLaws to prepare to defend his rear, either by the commanding general or by the chief of cavalry. The hallucination that McClellan was not capable of serious work seemed to pervade our army, even to this moment of dreadful threatening.

After retiring to my couch, reflecting upon affairs, my mind was so disturbed that I could not rest. As I studied, the perils seemed to grow, till at last I made a light and wrote to tell General Lee of my troubled thoughts, and appealed again for immediate concentration at Sharpsburg. To this no answer came, but it relieved my mind and gave me some rest.

At daylight in the morning the column marched (eight brigades with the artillery), leaving Toombs's brigade. A regiment of G. T. Anderson's that had been on guard all night was not relieved in time to join the march, and remained with Toombs. The day was hot and the roads dry and beaten into impalpable powder, that rose in clouds of dust from under our feet as we marched.

Before sunrise of the 14th, General Hill rode to the top of the mountain to view the front to which his brigade had been called the day before. As he rode he received a message from General Stuart, informing him that he had sent his main cavalry force to Crampton's Pass, and was then *en route* to join it. He found Garland's brigade at the summit, near the Mountain House, on the right of the road, and Colquitt's well advanced down the east side. He withdrew the latter to the summit, and posted two regiments on the north side of the pike behind stone walls, the others on the south side under cover of a woodland. Upon learning of the approaches to his position, he ordered the brigade under G. B. Anderson and one of Ripley's regiments up, leaving Rodes's brigade and the balance of Ripley's to watch for refugees from Harper's Ferry.

While he was withdrawing and posting Colquitt's brigade, General Pleasonton was marching by the road three-fourths of a mile south, feeling his way towards Fox's Gap, with the brigade of infantry under Colonel Scammon. Co-operating with this advance, Pleasonton used his cavalry along the turnpike. His batteries were put in action near the foot of the mountain, except one section of McMullen's under Lieutenant Crome, which advanced with the infantry. The battle was thus opened by General Pleasonton and General Cox without orders, and without information of the lost despatch. The latter had the foresight to support this move with his brigade under Colonel Crook. Batteries of twenty-pound Parrott guns were posted near the foot of the mountain in fine position to open upon the Confederates at the summit.

After posting Colquitt's brigade, General Hill rode off to his right to examine the approach to Fox's Gap, near the point held by Rosser's cavalry and horse artillery. As he passed near the gap he heard noise of troops working their way towards him, and soon artillery opened fire across the gap over his head. He hurried back and sent Garland's brigade, with Bondurant's battery, to meet the approaching enemy. Garland made connection with Rosser's detachment and engaged in severe skirmish, arresting the progress of Scammon's brigade till the coming of Crook's, when Cox gave new force to his fight, and after a severe contest, in which Garland fell, the division advanced in a gallant charge, which broke the ranks of the brigade, discomfited by the loss of its gallant leader, part of it breaking in confusion down the mountain, the left withdrawing towards the turnpike. G. B. Anderson's brigade was in time to check this success and hold for reinforcements. Ripley's brigade, called up later, came, but passed to the right and beyond the fight. General Hill had posted two batteries on the summit north of the turnpike, which had a destructive cross fire on Cox as he made his fight, and part of Colquitt's right regiments were put in, in aid of G. B. Anderson's men. About two P.M., General Cox was reinforced by the division under General Wilcox, and a little after three o'clock by Sturgis's division, the corps commander, General Reno, taking command with his last division under Rodman.

As Sturgis's division came into the fight, the head of my column reached the top of the pass, where the brigades of G. T. Anderson and Drayton, under General D. R. Jones, filed to the right to meet the battle, and soon after General Hood with two brigades. The last reinforcement braced the Confederate fight to a successful stand, and held it till after night in hot contest, in which many brave soldiers and valuable officers were lost on both sides.

The fight was between eight brigades on the Union side, with a detachment of cavalry and superior artillery attachments, against two of D. H. Hill's and four of my brigades, with Rosser's detachment of cavalry and artillery. Ripley's brigade of Hill's division marched for the fight, but lost its direction and failed to engage. The Confederate batteries made handsome combat, but were of inferior metal and munitions. Numerically, the Union brigades were stronger than the Confederates, mine having lost more than half their numbers by the wayside from exhaustion under the forced march. It seems that several brigades failed to connect closely with the action. Ripley's, on the Confederate side, General Hill said, "didn't pull a trigger." G. T. Anderson claimed that some of his skirmishers pulled a few triggers, while Harland's Union brigade of Rodman's division seems to have had little use for its guns. Lieutenant Crome brought a section of McMullen's battery up in close connection with Cox's advance, put it in, and held it in gallant action till his gunners were reduced to the minimum of working force, when he took the place of cannoneer and fought till mortally wounded.

On the Union side the officers had their time to organize and place their battle, and showed skill in their work. The Confederates had to meet the battle, as it was called, after its opening, on Rosser's detachment. The lamented Garland, equal to any emergency, was quick enough to get his fine brigade in, and made excellent battle, till his men, discouraged by the loss of their chief, were overcome by the gallant assault under Cox. General Reno, on the Union side, an officer of high character and attainments, was killed about seven o'clock P.M. Among the Union wounded was Colonel Rutherford B. Hayes, afterwards President of the United States.

The pass by the lower trail, old Sharpsburg road, was opened by this fight, but the Confederates standing so close upon it made it necessary that they should be dislodged before it could be utilized.

The First Corps marched from the Monocacy at daylight and approached the mountain at one P.M. General Hooker had three divisions, under Generals Hatch, Ricketts, and Meade. General Hatch had four brigades, Generals Ricketts and Meade three each, with full artillery appointments. At two o'clock, General Hooker was ordered north of the turnpike to make a diversion in favor of the troops operating on the south side under General Reno. Meade's division was marched, followed by Hatch's and Ricketts's,—Meade's on the right, Hatch on Meade's left, Ricketts in reserve. Meade's division was deployed along the foot-hills. A cavalry regiment under

Colonel Williams, First Massachusetts, was sent to the far right in observation. Meade's advance was followed by Hatch and Ricketts.

General Hill's only available force to meet this formidable move was his brigade under General Rodes. He ordered Rodes to his left to a prominent position about a mile off which commanded that part of the field. Cutts's battalion of artillery had been posted on the left of the turnpike, to cover by its fire the route just assigned for Hooker's march. The weight of the attack fell upon Rodes's brigade, and was handsomely received. Evans's brigade, fortunately, came up, and was sent to General Hill, who ordered it out to connect with Rodes's right. Before making close connection it became engaged, and operated near Rodes's right, connecting with his fight and dropping back as the troops on his left were gradually forced from point to point.

As the brigades under Generals Kemper, Garnett, and Colonel Walker (Jenkins's brigade) approached the mountain, a report reached general head-quarters that the enemy was forcing his way down the mountain by the old Sharpsburg road. To meet this General Lee ordered those brigades to the right, and they marched a mile and more down a rugged way along the base of the mountain before the report was found to be erroneous, when the brigades were ordered back to make their way to the pike and to the top of the mountain in double time. General Rodes had five regiments, one of which he left to partially cover the wide opening between his position and the turnpike. In view of the great force approaching to attack him his fight seemed almost hopeless, but he handled his troops with skill, and delayed the enemy, with the little help that finally came, till night, breaking from time to time as he was forced nearer our centre at the turnpike.

Gibbon's brigade had been called from Hooker's corps,

and was ordered up the mountain by the direct route as the corps engaged in its fight farther off on the right.

A spur of the mountain trends towards the east, opening a valley between it and the mountain. Through this valley and over the rising ground Meade's division advanced and made successful attack as he encountered the Confederates. Cooper's battery marched, and assisted in the several attacks as they were pushed up the mountain slope. The ground was very rough, and the Confederates worked hard to make it too rough, but the divisions, with their strong lines of skirmishers, made progress. Rodes made an effort to turn the right of the advancing divisions, but Hooker put out a brigade from Hatch's division, which pushed off the feeble effort, and Rodes lost his first position.

It was near night when the brigades under Generals Kemper and Garnett and Colonel Walker returned from their march down the foot of the mountain and reached the top. They were put in as they arrived to try to cover the right of Rodes and Evans and fill the intervening space to the turnpike. As they marched, the men dropped along the road, as rapidly as if under severe skirmish. So manifest was it that nature was exhausted, that no one urged them to get up and try to keep their ranks. As the brigades were led to places along the line, the divisions of Hatch and Ricketts were advancing; the former, in range, caught the brigades under fire before their lines were formed. At the same time Meade's division was forcing Rodes and Evans from their positions, back towards the turnpike.

General McClellan claimed fifteen hundred prisoners taken by his troops, and that our loss in killed and wounded was greater than his own, which was fifteen hundred. He estimated the forces as about equal, thirty thousand each. General D. H. Hill does not admit that the Confederates had more than nine thousand.

Several efforts have been made to correctly report the numerical strength of my column, some erroneously including the brigades detached with R. H. Anderson's, and others the brigade of General Toombs and the regiment of G. T. Anderson's brigade, that were left at Hagerstown. General Hill concedes reluctantly that four thousand of my men came to his support in detachments, but does not know how to estimate the loss. Considering the severe forced march, the five brigades that made direct ascent of the mountain were in good order. The three that marched south of the turnpike, along a narrow mountain trail part of the way, through woodlands and over boulders, returning, then up the mountain, the last march at double time, were thinned to skeletons of three or four hundred men to a brigade when they reached the Mountain House. That they succeeded in covering enough of the position to conceal our retreat after night is sufficient encomium of their valorous spirit.

CHAPTER XVII.

PRELIMINARIES OF THE GREAT BATTLE.

Confederates retreat from South Mountain—Federals follow and harass them—Franklin and Cobb at Crampton's Pass—A spirited Action—Fighting around Harper's Ferry—Its Capitulation—The Confederates take Eleven Thousand Prisoners—Jackson rejoins Lee—Description of the Field of Antietam—McClellan posts his Corps—Lee's Lines advantageously placed—Hooker's Advance on the Eve of Battle should have been resisted.

At first sight of the situation, as I rode up the mountain-side, it became evident that we were not in time nor in sufficient force to secure our holding at Turner's Gap, and a note was sent General Lee to prepare his mind for disappointment, and give time for arrangements for retreat.

After nightfall General Hill and I rode down to headquarters to make report. General Lee inquired of the prospects for continuing the fight. I called upon General Hill to demonstrate the situation, positions and forces. He explained that the enemy was in great force with commanding positions on both flanks, which would give a cross-fire for his batteries, in good range on our front, making the cramped position of the Confederates at the Mountain House untenable. His explanation was too forcible to admit of further deliberation. General Lee ordered withdrawal of the commands to Keedysville, and on the march changed the order, making Sharpsburg the point of assembly. General Hill's troops were first withdrawn, and when under way, the other brigades followed and were relieved by General Fitzhugh Lee's cavalry on the mountain at three o'clock in the morning, Hood's two brigades, with G. T. Anderson's, as rearguard.

General Fitzhugh Lee's cavalry was ordered to cover our march, but Pleasonton pushed upon him so severely with part of the Eighth Illinois Cavalry and Tidball's battery that he was forced off from our line through Boonsborough and found his way to the Potomac off the rear of General Lee's left, leaving his killed and wounded and losing two pieces of artillery. Otherwise our march was not disturbed. In addition to his regular complement of artillery, General D. H. Hill had the battalion under Lieutenant-Colonel A. S. Cutts. After crossing the Antietam the batteries were assigned positions near the ridge under the crest, where they could best cover the fields on the farther side of the stream. A few minutes after our lines were manned, information came of the capitulation of Harper's Ferry, and of the withdrawal of the troops to the Virginia side of the Potomac.

General Toombs's brigade joined us early on the 15th, and was posted over the Burnside Bridge. He was subsequently ordered to detach two regiments, as guard for trains near Williamsport.

As long as the armies were linked to Harper's Ferry, the heights in front of Sharpsburg offered a formidable defensive line, and in view of possible operations from Harper's Ferry, through the river pass, east of South Mountain, formed a beautiful point of strategic diversion. But when it transpired that Harper's Ferry was surrendered and the position was not to be utilized, that the troops there were to join us by a march on the south side, its charms were changed to perplexities. The threatening attitude towards the enemy's rear vanished, his line of communication was open and free of further care, and his army, relieved of entanglements, was at liberty to cross the Antietam by the upper fords and bridges, and approach from vantage-ground General Lee's left. At the same time the Federal left was reasonably secured from aggression by cramped and rugged ground along the Confederate right. Thus the altered circumstances changed all of the features of the position in favor of the Federals.

Approaching Crampton's Gap on the morning of the 14th, Hampton's cavalry encountered the enemy's and made a dashing charge, which opened his way to Munford's, both parties losing valuable officers and men. When General Stuart rode up, he saw nothing seriously threatening, and ordered Hampton south to the river pass; thinking that there might be something more important at that point, he rode himself to Maryland Heights to see General McLaws, and to witness the operations at Harper's Ferry, posting Colonel Munford with two regiments of cavalry, two regiments of Mahone's brigade under Colonel Parham, part of the Tenth Georgia Infantry, Chew's battery of four guns, and a section of navy howitzers, to guard the pass. The infantry regiments were posted behind stone walls at the base of the mountain, the cavalry dismounted on the flanks acting as sharp-shooters.

At noon General Franklin marched through Burkittsville with his leading division under General Slocum, holding the division under General W. F. Smith in reserve. His orders were to wait until Couch's division joined him, but he judged that the wait might be more favorable to the other side. Slocum deployed his brigades, Bartlett's, Newton's, and Torbert's, from right to left, posted Wolcott's battery of six guns on his left and rear, and followed the advance of his skirmish line, the right brigade leading. When the Confederate position was well developed, the skirmishers were retired, and the order to assault followed,—the right regiments of Newton's brigade supporting Bartlett's assault, the regiments on the left supporting Torbert's. The Confederates made a bold effort to hold, but the attack was too well organized and too cleverly pushed to leave the matter long in doubt. Their flanks, being severely crowded upon, soon began to drop off, when a sweeping charge of Slocum's line gained the position. The brigades of General Brooks and Colonel Irwin of General Smith's division were advanced to Slocum's left and joined in pursuit, which was so rapid that the Confederates were not able to rally a good line; the entire mountain was abandoned to the Federals, and the pursuit ended. Some four hundred prisoners, seven hundred stand of arms, and one gun were their trophies in this affair. General Franklin's total loss was five hundred and thirty-three.*

General McLaws had ordered General Cobb's brigade and the other regiments of Mahone's to reinforce the troops at the gap, but they only came up as the Federals were making their sweeping charge, and were driven back with their discomfited comrades. General Semmes's brigade at the Brownsville Pass, a mile south, with five or six guns, attempted to relieve their comrades, but the range was too great for effective work. That McLaws was not prepared for the sudden onslaught is evident from the assurances made him by the cavalry commander. His orders for Cobb were severe enough, but Franklin was too prompt to allow Cobb to get to work. Upon hearing the noise of battle, he followed his orders, riding with General Stuart, but the game was played before he could take part in it. Night came and gave him time to organize his forces for the next day. Had the defenders been posted at the crest of the mountain it is probable they could have delayed the assaulting forces until reinforced. But cavalry commanders do not always post artillery and infantry to greatest advantage.

General Cobb made worthy effort to arrest the retreat and reorganize the forces, but was not able to fix a rallying-point till after the pass was lost and the troops were well out of fire of the pursuers. General Semmes came to his aid, with his staff, but could accomplish nothing

* Rebellion Record, vol. xix. part i. p. 183.

until he drew two of his regiments from Brownsville Pass and established them with a battery as rallying-point. General McLaws reformed his line about a mile south of the lost gap, and drew his force not necessary at Harper's Ferry to that line during the night.

After dark, Lieutenant-Colonel H. Davis rode from Harper's Ferry with the Union cavalry and escaped, capturing some fifty Confederate wagons moving south from Hagerstown. McLaws had men to guard against that escape, but was obliged to draw everything that could be taken from the Harper's Ferry entanglement to defend against the enemy let in on his rear without due notice.

We left McLaws in possession of Maryland Heights, on the 14th, with his best guns planted against the garrison at Harper's Ferry. The Potomac River was between his and Jackson's and Walker's forces, and the Shenandoah divided Jackson's and Walker's commands. Walker posted his division against the escape from Harper's Ferry, and planted three Parrott guns of Captain French's battery and two rifle pieces of Captain Branch's on Loudoun Heights, having effective fire along Bolivar Heights. General Jackson sent word to McLaws and Walker that the batteries were not to open till all were ready, but the latter, hearing the engagement along South Mountain drawing nearer, and fearing delay would prove fatal, ordered his guns to open against batteries along Bolivar Heights, and silenced those that were in range.

General Jackson ordered A. P. Hill's division along the left bank of the Shenandoah to turn the enemy's left, the division under Lawton down the turnpike in support of Hill, his own division to threaten against the enemy's right. Hill's division did its work in good style, securing eligible positions on the enemy's left and left rear of Bolivar Heights, and planted a number of batteries upon them during the night; and Jackson had some of his best guns passed over the Shenandoah to commanding points near the base of Loudoun Heights. At daylight Lawton's command moved up close to the enemy. At the same time the batteries of Hill's division opened fire, and a little later all the batteries, including those of McLaws and Walker. The signal ordered for the storming columns was to be the cessation of artillery fire. In about one hour the enemy's fire ceased, when Jackson commanded silence upon his side. Pender's brigade started, when the enemy opened again with his artillery. The batteries of Pegram and Crenshaw dashed forward and renewed rapid fire, when the signal of distress was raised.

Colonel D. H. Miles, the Federal commander at Harper's Ferry, was mortally wounded, and the actual surrender was made by General White, who gave up eleven thousand prisoners, thirteen thousand small-arms, seventy-two cannon, quantities of quartermaster's stores and of subsistence.*

General Franklin had posted his division under General Couch at Rohrersville on the morning of the 15th, and proceeded to examine McLaws's line established the night before across Pleasant Valley. He found the Confederates strongly posted covering the valley, their flanks against the mountain-side. Before he could organize for attack the firing at Harper's Ferry ceased, indicating surrender of that garrison and leaving the troops operating there free to march against him. He prepared, therefore, for that eventuality.

The "lost order" directed the commands of Generals Jackson, McLaws, and Walker, after accomplishing the objects for which they had been detached, to join the main body of the army at Boonsborough or Hagerstown. Under the order and the changed condition of affairs, they were expected, in case of early capitulation at Harper's Ferry,

* Rebellion Record, vol. xix. part i. p. 961.

to march up the Rohrersville-Boonsborough road against McClellan's left. There were in those columns twenty-six of General Lee's forty brigades, equipped with a fair apportionment of artillery and cavalry. So it seemed to be possible that Jackson would order McLaws and Walker up the Rohrersville road, and move with his own corps through the river pass east of South Mountain, against McClellan's rear, as the speedier means of relief to General Lee's forces. But prudence would have gone with the bolder move of his entire command east of the mountain against McClellan's rear, with a fair field for strategy and tactics. This move would have disturbed McClellan's plans on the afternoon of the 15th, while there seemed little hope that McClellan would delay his attack until Jackson could join us, marching by the south side.

The field, and extreme of conditions, were more encouraging of results than was Napoleon's work at Arcola.

General Jackson judged it better to join us by the south side, marched promptly with two of his divisions (leaving A. P. Hill with six brigades to receive the surrender and captured property), then ordered Walker's and McLaws's troops to follow his march. With his report of surrender of the garrison he sent advice of his march by the south side to join us.

At daylight on the 15th the head of General Lee's column reached the Antietam. General D. H. Hill, in advance, crossed and filed into position to the left of the Boonsborough turnpike, G. B. Anderson on his right, Garland's brigade under Colonel McRae, Ripley, and Colquitt, Rodes in rear near Sharpsburg, my command on his right. The two brigades under Hood were on my right, Kemper, Drayton, Jenkins (under Colonel Walker), Washington Artillery, on the ridge near the turnpike, and S. D. Lee's artillery. Pickett's brigade (under Garnett) was in a second line, G. T. Anderson's brigade in rear of the battalions, Evans's brigade on the north side of the turnpike; Toombs's brigade joined and was posted at bridge No. 3 (Burnside Bridge). As the battalions of artillery attached to the divisions were all that could find places, General Lee sent the reserve artillery under General Pendleton across the Potomac.

As soon as advised of the surrender and Jackson's march by the south side, my brigades under Hood were moved to the extreme left of the line, taking the division of General D. H. Hill within my limits, while three of S. D. Lee's batteries were sent in support of Hood's brigades. The pursuit ordered by General McClellan was the First, Second, and Twelfth Corps by the Boonsborough turnpike, the Ninth Corps and Sykes's division of the Fifth by the old Sharpsburg road;* the Ninth and Fifth to reinforce Franklin by the Rohrersville road, or move to Sharpsburg.

About two o'clock in the afternoon the advance of the Union army came in sight. General Porter had passed the Ninth Corps with his division under Sykes and joined Richardson's division of the Second. These divisions deployed on the right and left of the turnpike and posted their batteries, which drew on a desultory fire of artillery, continuing until night. The morning of the 16th opened as the evening of the previous day closed, except for the arrival of the remainder of the Union troops. The Ninth Corps took post at the lower bridge opposite the Confederate right, the First, the other divisions of the Second, and the Twelfth Corps resting nearer Keedysville. The display of their finely appointed batteries was imposing, as seen from Sharpsburg Heights.

Before maturing his plans, General McClellan had to make a careful reconnoissance, and to know of the disposition to be made of the Confederate forces from Harper's Ferry.

---

* Rebellion Record, vol. xix. part i. p. 47.

Of the latter point he was informed, if not assured, before he posted the Ninth Corps. Four batteries of twenty-pound Parrotts were planted on the height overlooking the Antietam on their right; on the crest near the Burnside Bridge, Weed's three-inch guns and Benjamin's twenty-pound Parrotts. At intervals between those were posted some ten or more batteries, and the practice became more lively as the day wore on, till, observing the unequal combat, I ordered the Confederates to hold their ammunition, and the batteries of the other side, seeming to approve the order, slackened their fire.

The Antietam, hardly worthy the name river, is a sluggish stream coming down from Pennsylvania heights in a flow a little west of south till it nears the Potomac, when it bends westward to its confluence. It is spanned by four stone bridges,—at the Williamsport turnpike, the Boonsborough-Sharpsburg turnpike, the Rohrersville turnpike, and another near its mouth. The third was afterwards known as the Burnside Bridge. From the north suburbs of Sharpsburg the Hagerstown turnpike leads north a little west two miles, when it turns east of north to the vanishing point of operations. A mile and a half from Sharpsburg on the west of this road is the Dunker chapel, near the southern border of a woodland, which spreads northward half a mile, then a quarter or more westward. East of the pike were open fields of corn and fruit, with occasional woodlands of ten or twenty acres, as far as the stream, where some heavier forests cumbered the river banks. General Lee's line stood on the Sharpsburg Heights, his right a mile southeast of the village, the line extending parallel with the Hagerstown turnpike, three miles from his right, the left curved backward towards the rear, and towards the great eastern bend of the Potomac, near which were the cavalry and horse artillery. Along the broken line were occasional ridges of limestone cropping out in such shape as to give partial cover to infantry lying under them. Single batteries were posted along the line, or under the crest of the heights, and the battalions of the Washington Artillery, Cutts's, and S. D. Lee's.

In forming his forces for the battle, General McClellan divided his right wing, posted the Ninth Corps on his left, at the Burnside Bridge, under General Cox, and assigned the First Corps, under General Hooker, for his right flank. General Burnside was retained on his left. The plan was to make the main attack against the Confederate left, or to make that a diversion in favor of the main attack, and to follow success by his reserve.

At two P.M. of the 16th, Hooker's First Corps crossed the Antietam at the bridge near Keedysville and a near-by ford, and marched against my left brigades, Generals Meade, Ricketts, and Doubleday commanding the divisions, battalions, and batteries of field artillery. The sharp skirmish that ensued was one of the marked preliminaries of the great battle; but the Federals gained nothing by it except an advanced position, which was of little benefit and disclosed their purpose.

General Jackson was up from Harper's Ferry with Ewell's division and his own, under Generals Lawton and Jones. They were ordered out to General Lee's left, and took post west of the Hagerstown turnpike, the right of his line resting on my left, under Hood, Winder's and Jones's brigades on the front, Starke's and Taliaferro's on the second line, Early's brigade of Ewell's division on the left of Jackson's division, with Hays's brigade for a second; Lawton's and Trimble's brigades were left at rest near the chapel; Poague's battery on Jackson's front; five other batteries prepared for action. Following Jackson's march to the left, General J. G. Walker came up with his two brigades, and was posted on my extreme right in the position left vacant by the change of Hood's brigades.

General Hooker was joined, as he marched that afternoon, by his chief, who rode with him some little distance conversing of pending affairs. It subsequently transpired that Hooker thought the afternoon's work ordered for his corps (thirteen thousand) so far from support extremely venturesome, and he was right. Jackson was up and in position with two divisions well on the flank of the attack to be made by Hooker. Hood with S. D. Lee's batteries received Hooker's attack, and arrested its progress for the day. If Jackson could have been put into this fight, and also the brigades under J. G. Walker, Hooker's command could have been fought out, if not crushed, before the afternoon went out. He was beyond support for the day, and the posting along the Antietam was such—we will soon see—as to prevent effective diversion in his favor. Events that followed authorize the claim for this combination, that it would have so disturbed the plans of General McClellan as to give us one or two days more for concentration, causing him more serious trouble. But Hood was left to fight alone.

Hood's skirmish line was out to be driven, or drawn in, but throughout the severe engagement his line of battle was not seriously disturbed. After night General Jackson sent the brigades of Trimble and Lawton, under General Lawton, to replace Hood's men, who were ordered to replenish ammunition, and, after getting food, to resume their places on my right. Preparing for battle, General Jackson sent the brigade under General Early to support Stuart's cavalry and horse artillery, and Lawton drew his brigade, under General Hays, to support his others on the right of Jackson's division.

General Mansfield crossed during the night with the Twelfth Corps and took position supporting General Hooker's command, with the divisions of Generals A. S. Williams and George S. Greene, and field batteries.

A light rain began to fall at nine o'clock. The troops

along either line were near enough to hear voices from the other side, and several spats occurred during the night between the pickets, increasing in one instance to exchange of many shots; but for the most part there was silence or only the soft, smothered sound of the summer rain over all that field on which was to break in the morning the storm of lead and iron.

CHAPTER XVIII.

BATTLE OF SHARPSBURG, OR ANTIETAM.

Bloodiest Single Day of the War—Comparison of Casualties—Hooker opens the Fight against Jackson's Centre—Many Officers among the Fallen early in the Day—McLaws and Walker in time to meet Sumner's Advance under Sedgwick—Around Dunker Chapel—Richardson's splendid Advance against the Confederate Centre the Signal of the bursting of another Storm—Longstreet's and D. H. Hill's Troops stood before it—Fall of General G. B. Anderson—General Richardson mortally wounded—Aggressive Spirit of his Command broken—Wonderful Cannon-shot—General D. H. Hill's Third Horse killed under him.

THE field that I have described—the field lying along the Antietam and including in its scope the little town of Sharpsburg—was destined to pass into history as the scene of the bloodiest single day of fighting of the war, and that 17th of September was to become memorable as the day of greatest carnage in the campaigns between the North and South.

Gettysburg was the greatest battle of the war, but it was for three days, and its total of casualties on either side, terrible as it was, should be one-third larger to make the average per diem equal to the losses at Sharpsburg. Viewed by the measure of losses, Antietam was the fourth battle of the war, Spottsylvania and the Wilderness, as well as Gettysburg, exceeding it in number of killed and wounded, but each of these dragged its tragedy through several days.

Taking Confederate losses in killed and wounded as the criterion of magnitude in battles, the Seven Days' Battle (following McClellan's retreat), Gettysburg, and Chickamauga exceeded Sharpsburg, but each of these occupied several days, and on no single day in any one of them was there such carnage as in this fierce struggle.

The Confederates lost in killed and wounded in the Seven Days' Battle 19,739,—more, it will be observed, than at Gettysburg (15,298), though the total loss, including 5150 captured or missing, at the latter, brought the figures up to those of the former (20,448), in which the captured or missing were only 875. Our killed and wounded at Chickamauga were 16,986, but that was in two days' battle, while at Chancellorsville in three days the killed and wounded were 10,746. It is impossible to make the comparison with absolute exactness for the Confederate side, for the reason that our losses are given for the entire campaign in Maryland, instead of separately for the single great battle and several minor engagements. Thus computed they were 12,187.* But nearly all of these are known to have been losses at Sharpsburg, and, making proper deductions for the casualties in other actions of the campaign, the Confederate loss in this single day's fighting was still in excess of that at the *three days' fight* at Chancellorsville (10,746), and for the single day far larger proportionally than in the two days at Chickamauga, three days at Gettysburg, or seven days on the bloody Chickahominy.

But the sanguinary character of this battle is most strikingly exhibited by a comparison of the accurate figures of the Federal losses, returned specifically for the day. These show a total killed and wounded of 11,657 (or, including the captured and missing, 12,410), as contrasted with 20,567 killed and wounded in *three* days at Gettysburg, 16,141 in *eight* days at Spottsylvania, and 14,283 in the *three* days at the Wilderness, while the *three* and *two* days' fighting respectively at Chancellorsville and Chickamauga were actually productive of less loss than this battle of *one* day. The exceeding losses

* Some authorities say (including a small number of "captured or missing") 12,601.

of this battle are further shown by the fact that of the 11,657 Federals stricken on the field, the great number of 2108 were actually slain,—more than two-thirds of the number killed in three days at Gettysburg (3070). And this tremendous tumult of carnage was entirely compassed in the brief hours from dawn to four o'clock in the afternoon.

At three o'clock in the morning of the 17th firing along the picket lines of the confronting and expectant armies became quite frequent, and before daylight the batteries began to plough the fields in front of them, feeling, as it were, for the ranks of men whose destruction was better suited to their ugly purpose.

As the dawn came, the fire spread along both lines from left to right, across the Antietam and back again, and the thunder of the big guns became continuous and increased to mighty volume. To this was presently added the sharper rattling of musketry, and the surge of mingling sound sweeping up and down the field was multiplied and confused by the reverberations from the rocks and hills. And in this great tumult of sound, which shook the air and seemed to shatter the cliffs and ledges above the Antietam, bodies of the facing foes were pushed forward to closer work, and soon added the clash of steel to the thunderous crash of cannon-shots.

The first impact came from Hooker's right division under Doubleday, led by the choice brigade under Gibbon. It was deployed across the turnpike and struck the centre of Jackson's division, when close engagement was strengthened by the brigades of Patrick, Phelps, and part of Hofmann's, Ricketts's division, engaged in close connection along Lawton's front. Hooker supported his battle by his division under Meade, which called into action three of D. H. Hill's brigades,—Ripley's, Colquitt's, and McRae's. Hartsuff, the leading spirit of Ricketts's division, was the first general officer to fall severely hurt, and later fell the commander of the corps, wounded also. General Starke, commanding Jackson's division, was killed. At six o'clock the Twelfth Corps came in, when General Lawton called for Hood's brigades, "and all the help he could bring." Hood's and G. T. Anderson's brigades were put in, and the brigades from my right, under J. G. Walker, marched promptly in response to this call.

The weight of Mansfield's fight forced Jackson back into the middle wood at the Dunker chapel, and D. H. Hill's brigades to closer lines. Hood was in season to brace them, and hold the line as he found it. In this fight the corps commander, General Mansfield, fell, mortally wounded, which took from that corps some of its aggressive power.

Jackson, worn down and exhausted of ammunition, withdrew his divisions at seven A.M., except Early's brigade, that was with the cavalry. This he called back to vacant ground on Hood's left. Two detachments, one under Colonel Grigsby, of Virginia, the other under Colonel Stafford, of Louisiana, remained on the wooded ground off from the left of Jackson's position. One of the regiments of Early's brigade was left with the cavalry. Stuart retired to position corresponding to the line of Jackson's broken front. The brigade under G. T. Anderson joined on Hood's right, and the brigades under J. G. Walker coming up took place on Hood's left, Walker leaving two regiments to fill a vacant place between Anderson's brigade and Hood's right. Walker, Hood, and D. H. Hill attacked against the Twelfth Corps; worn by its fight against Jackson, it was driven back as far as the post-and-rail fence in the east open, where they were checked. They were outside of the line, their left in the air and exposed to the fire of a thirty-gun battery posted at long range on the Hagerstown road by General Doubleday. Their left was withdrawn, and the line rectified, when Greene's brigade of the Twelfth resumed position in the northeast angle of the wood, which it held until Sedgwick's division came in bold march.

In these fights offensive and defensive the artillery battalions under Lieutenant-Colonel S. D. Lee and Major Frobel were in active combat, the former from the first shot made before daylight. They had been severely worked, and were nearly exhausted of ammunition. The Washington Artillery was called on for a battery to assist them, and some of the guns of the battalions were sent for ammunition. Miller's battery of four Napoleon guns came.

As Jackson withdrew, General Hooker's corps retired to a point on the Hagerstown road about three-quarters of a mile north of the battle-ground, where General Doubleday established his thirty-gun battery. Jackson's and Hooker's men had fought to exhaustion, and the battle of the Twelfth Corps, taken up and continued by Mansfield, had taken defensive relations, its chief mortally wounded.

Generals Lawton, Ripley, and J. R. Jones were severely wounded, and Colonel Douglas, commanding Lawton's brigade, killed. A third of the men of Lawton's, Hays's, and Trimble's brigades were reported killed or wounded. Four of the field officers of Colquitt's brigade were killed, five were wounded, the tenth and last contused by a shell. All of Jackson's and D. H. Hill's troops engaged suffered proportionally. Hood's, Walker's, and G. T. Anderson's, though longer engaged, did not lose so severely.

General Hooker's aggregate of loss was 2590; General Mansfield's, 1746.

The Federal batteries, of position, on the east side were more or less busy during the engagement, having occasional opportunities for a raking fire on the troops along Jackson's line and my left. The horse artillery under

Stuart was strengthening to the Confederate left, and had occasional opportunities for destructive fire across the Union right when coming into action.

Although the battle along the line of contention had become defensive, there were threatening movements on the Boonsborough pike by Sykes's division and the horse artillery under Pleasonton, and Burnside was busy at his bridge, working to find his way across.

At the close of the Walker-Hood-Hill affair, Hood found his line making a large angle with the line of the latter, which was rectified, drawing in the angle. Early's regiments were in the wood between Walker and the cavalry, and the detachments under Colonels Grigsby and Stafford in the wood some distance in advance of Early's left.

The line thus organized was thin and worn by severe attrition. The men were losing strength and the ammunition getting low. Some gathered cartridges from their fallen comrades and distributed them as far as they would go, others went for fresh supplies.

McLaws's column came up at nine o'clock. He reported at General Lee's head-quarters, where he was ordered at rest, and afterwards reported to me, with General Lee's orders for his own division, and asked the disposition to be made of R. H. Anderson's. He was ordered to send the latter to report to General D. H. Hill.

Coincident with these arrivals, heavy columns of Federal infantry and artillery were seen crossing the Antietam. Morell's division of the Fifth Corps was up and relieved Richardson's of the Second, which had been in our front since its arrival on the 15th. Richardson's following the march of the troops by the upper crossing advised us that the next engagement would be by the Second Corps, under General Sumner; Sedgwick's division was in the lead as they marched. Our left centre was almost exhausted of men and ammunition. The divisions of French and Richardson followed in left echelon to Sedgwick. Hood's brigades had retired for fresh supply of ammunition, leaving the guard to Walker's two brigades, G. T. Anderson's brigade on Walker's right, part of Early's brigade on Walker's left, and the regiments under Colonels Grigsby and Stafford off the left front. McLaws's division was called for, and on the march under conduct of Major Taylor of general head-quarters staff.

At sight of Sumner's march, General Early rode from the field in search, as he reported, of reinforcements. His regiments naturally waited on the directions of the leader.

General Sumner rode with his leading division under General Sedgwick, to find the battle. Sedgwick marched in column of brigades, Gorman, Dana, and Howard. There was no officer on the Union side in charge of the field, the other corps commanders having been killed or wounded. General Sumner testified,—

> "On going upon the field I found that General Hooker's corps had been dispersed and routed. I passed him some distance in the rear, where he had been carried wounded, but I saw nothing of his corps at all, as I was advancing with my command on the field. There were some troops lying down on the left which I took to belong to Mansfield's command. In the mean time General Mansfield had been killed, and a portion of his corps (formerly Banks's) had also been thrown into confusion." *

He passed Greene's brigade of the Twelfth, and marched through the wood, leaving the Dunker chapel on his left.

As McLaws approached, General Hood was sent to give him careful instructions of the posture, of the grounds, and the impending crisis. He marched with his brigades, —Cobb's, Kershaw's, Semmes's, and Barksdale's. The leading brigade filed to the right, before the approaching

* Report of Committee, part i. p. 368.

march. Kershaw's leading regiment filed into line as Sedgwick's column approached the south side of the Dunker chapel wood,—the latter on a diagonal march,—while Kershaw's brigade was in fair front against it.

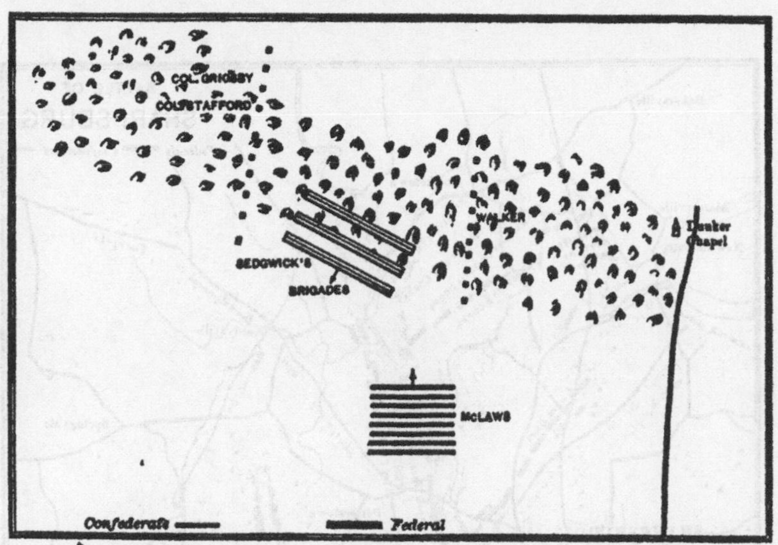

Relative positions of McLaws and other Confederates and Sedgwick at their opening.

The regiment opened prompt fire, and the other regiments came into line in double time, opening fire by company as they came to the front. The other brigades came into line by companies, and forward into line by regiments. Armistead's brigade had been drawn from R. H. Anderson's column to reinforce McLaws.

Sedgwick's diagonal march exposed his left to a scattering fire from Walker's left brigade under M. Ransom, but he kept his steady march while Walker increased his fire. McLaws increasing his fire staggered the march of Sedgwick, and presently arrested it. The regiments under Colonels Stafford and Grigsby, coming from their lurking-places, opened fire on Sedgwick's right rear. At McLaws's opening Sedgwick essayed to form line of battle; the increasing fire on his right and left

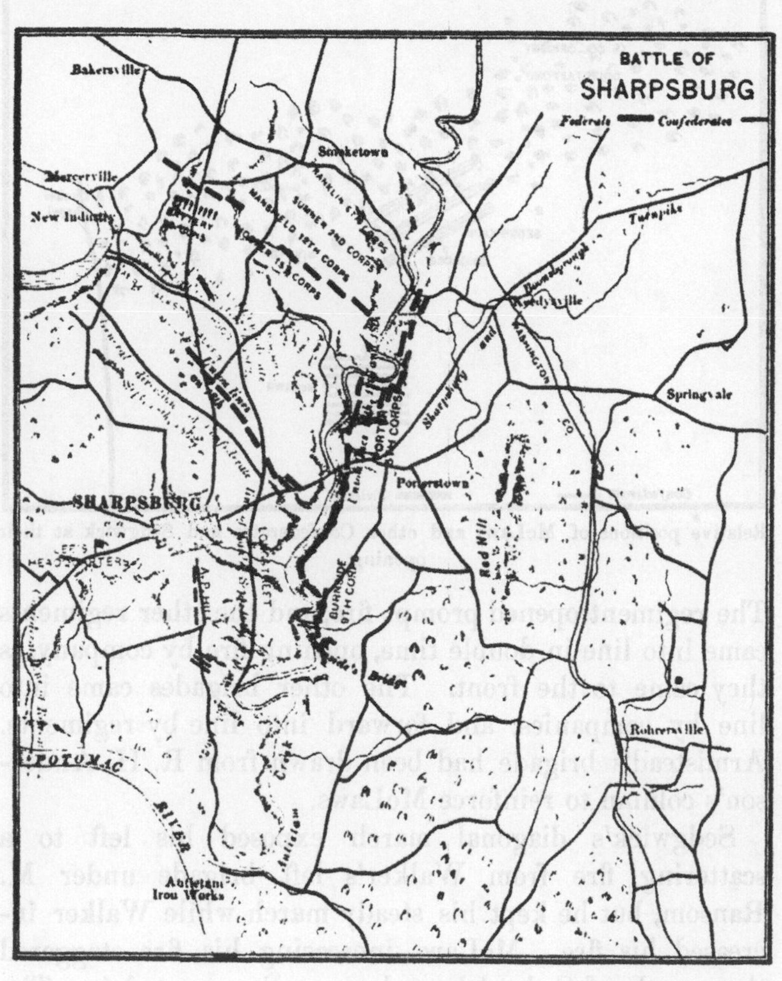
BATTLE OF
SHARPSBURG
Federals
Confederates
Bakersville
Smoketown
Mercerville
New Industry
Turnpike
Boonsborough
Keedysville
Springvale
Porterstown
SHARPSBURG
LEE'S HEADQUARTERS
Red Hill
BURNSIDE 9TH CORPS
Bridge
Rohrersville
POTOMAC
RIVER
Antietam
Antietam
Irou Works
SUMNER 2ND CORPS
MANSFIELD 12TH CORPS
HOOKER 1ST CORPS

rear, with the terrible fire in front, was confusing, but the troops were eager to return the fire they found pouring into their lines from three-quarters of a circle. To counter the rear fire of Walker, General Sumner ordered the rear brigade to face about. The troops, taking this to mean a rearward march, proceeded to execute it without awaiting further orders, which was soon followed by the other brigades.

McLaws and Walker, pushing their success, were joined by G. T. Anderson's, the brigades of D. H. Hill's left, and those of R. H. Anderson's division, making strong battle through the woodland and open to the post-and-rail fence and to the Roulette House, where they encountered Sumner's division under French, and parts of the Twelfth Corps rallied on that part of the field. This contention was firm and wasting on both sides, but held with persevering courage until Richardson's reserve, under Brooke, was put against Hill's right and broke the Confederate line back to the woodlands south of the chapel, where Early's regiments had formed a rallying line.

When Hill's right was struck and pressed so severely, Rodes's brigade, the reserve of his division, was ordered out to support his right. The brigade advanced in good strong battle, but General Rodes reported that he could not move his Sixth Alabama Regiment in time, notwithstanding his personal efforts; that with the support of that regiment the battle line of the Confederates could have waited other supports.

General Sumner was eager in riding with his leading division. He was always anxious to get in in time to use all of his power, and thought others like himself. Had he formed the corps into lines of divisions, in close echelon, and moved as a corps, he would have marched through and opened the way for Porter's command at bridge No. 2, and Pleasonton's cavalry, and for Burnside at the third bridge, and forced the battle back to the river bank.

He was criticised for his opposition to Franklin's proposed attack, but the chances are even that he was right. The stir among Franklin's troops was observed from a dead angle of our lines, and preparations were made to meet it. General Jackson was marching back to us, and it is possible that the attack might have resulted in mingling our troops with Franklin's down on the banks of the Antietam.

After this fight the artillery battalions of S. D. Lee and Frobel, quite out of ammunition, retired to replenish. The battery of Napoleons was reduced to one section, that short of ammunition and working hands.

General Hill rallied the greater part of G. B. Anderson's and Rodes's brigades in the sunken road. Some of Ripley's men came together near Miller's guns at the Hagerstown pike. General R. H. Anderson and his next in rank, General Wright, were wounded. The next officer, General Pryor, not advised of his new authority, the brigades assembled at points most suited to their convenience, in rear of D. H. Hill's brigades.

But time was up. Confederate affairs were not encouraging. Our men were all leg-weary and heavy to handle, while McClellan, with his tens of thousands, whom he had marched in healthful exercise the past two weeks, was finding and pounding us from left to right under converging fire of his batteries east and west of the Antietam.

The signal of the approaching storm was the bursting of Richardson's command, augmented by parts of French's division, through the field of corn, hardly ruffled by the affair at the Roulette House, spreading its grand march against our centre. They came in brave style, in full appreciation of the work in hand, marched better than on drill, unfolded banners making gay their gallant step.

The Fifth Corps and Pleasonton's cavalry were in active preparation to cross at the second bridge and join on Richardson's left, and Burnside at the third bridge was pressing his claim for a passage against our right.

I had posted G. T. Anderson's brigade behind a stone fence near the Hagerstown pike, about the safest spot to be found on the field of Sharpsburg,—a dead angle, so to speak. The batteries on the field north and the long-range thirty-gun battery of General Doubleday were playing their fire down the pike, taking their aim by the direction of the road, where they stood. This brought their fire into the field about one hundred yards in rear of Anderson's line. As the fire came from an enfilade direction, the troops assumed that they were under enfilade fire, and General Anderson changed position without reporting. General D. H. Hill got hold of him and moved him to the Boonsborough pike to defend against Sykes's and Pleasonton's forces, advancing in that quarter. Thus, when Richardson's march approached its objective, the Confederates had Boyce's battery, well out in the corn-field, facing the march; Miller's section of Napoleons in the centre, and a single battery at McLaws's rear, with fragments of scattered brigades along the pike, and the Twenty-seventh North Carolina Regiment to hold the left centre, besides the brigades in the sunken road, and the brigades of R. H. Anderson's division awaiting the bloody struggle. They received the severe attack in firm holding for a long half-hour, the enemy pressing closer at intervals, until an order of General Rodes's was misconstrued and part of his brigade under Lieutenant-Colonel Lightfoot, of the Sixth Alabama Regiment, was faced to the rear, and marched off, informing others that that was the order.

General G. B. Anderson fell mortally wounded. The enemy pressed in on his outer flank and called for surrender of the forces cut off and outflanked. Meagher's brigade was retired to replenish ammunition, and Barlow swung to his right and came against our fragments about

Miller's guns, standing near his flank. Miller had two guns, the others off for a supply of ammunition. Cooke's Twenty-seventh North Carolina Regiment was well organized, but short of ammunition; fragments of Ripley's brigade and some others were on the turnpike; Miller was short of hands and ammunition, even for two guns; McLaws's division and the other part of Walker's were in front of threatenings of parts of French's division and of troops rallying on their front, and the Sixth Corps was up and coming against them, so that it seemed hazardous to call them off and leave an open way. Our line was throbbing at every point, so that I dared not call on General Lee for help. Sergeant Ellis thought that he could bring up ammunition if he was authorized to order it. He was authorized, and rode for and brought it. I held the horses of some of my staff who helped to man the guns as cannoneers.

As the attacking forces drew nearer, Colonel Cooke reported his ammunition exhausted. He was ordered to hold on with the bayonet, and sent in return that he would "hold till ice forms in regions where it was never known," or words to that effect. As Richardson advanced through the corn he cut off the battery under Boyce, so that it was obliged to retire to save itself, and as Barlow came upon our centre, the battery on our left was for a time thrown out of fire lest they might injure friend as much as foe. Barlow marched in steady good ranks, and the remnants before him rose to the emergency. They seemed to forget that they had known fatigue; the guns were played with life, and the brave spirits manning them claimed that they were there to hold or to go down with the guns.

As our shots rattled against the armored ranks, Colonel Fairfax clapped his hands and ran for other charges. The mood of the gunners to a man was one of quiet but unflinching resolve to stand to the last gun. Captain

Miller charged and double-charged with spherical case and canister until his guns at the discharge leaped in the air from ten to twelve inches.

When the crest was reached, the rush that was expected to sweep us away paused,—the Confederates became hopeful. Soon the advancing ranks lay behind the crest, and presently drew nearer Richardson's part of the line, then mounting the crest over the Piper House. This latter point, once established, must cut and break the Confederate position as effectually as our centre just saved. He occupied the Piper House with two regiments under Colonel Brooke in advance of his line along the crest, and called up some of his batteries.

The Confederates meanwhile were collecting other batteries and infantry in defence, when a shot from one of our batteries brought Richardson down, mortally wounded. His taking-off broke the aggressive spirit of the division and reduced its fight to the defensive. The regiments at the Piper House found their position thus advanced too much exposed, and withdrew to the stronger line of the crest. General Meagher's brigade came up with ammunition replenished. General Hancock was despatched to take command of the division. In the midst of the tragedy, as Richardson approached the east crest, there was a moment of amusement when General Hill, with about fifty men and a battle-flag, ran to gain a vantage-point for flank fire against Richardson's left. Colonel Ross, observing the move and appreciating the opportunity, charged with two regiments for the same and secured it. General Hill claimed (and rightly) that it had effect in giving the impression that there were other forces coming to support him.

Another regiment came to the relief of the Twenty-seventh, under Cooke. The movement of troops in that quarter was construed by the enemy as a threatened flank move against Richardson, which caused some little delay in his march. Though the Confederates had but fragments here and there, the enemy were kept busy and watchful lest they should come upon another surprise move.

The Confederates were surprised but much relieved when they found this affair reduced to the defensive, and assumed that every missile they sent must have found one or more victims. But accounts of the other side make clear that the result was due to accidental artillery shots that cut down Colonel Barlow, the aggressive spirit of Richardson's right column, and General Richardson himself at his culminating moment. Barlow fell from a case- or canister-shot, as did Richardson. All the Union accounts refer to a battery on their right throwing shell, and the "two brass guns in front throwing case and canister," and this latter was the only artillery at work against them at the time of Barlow's fall. When Barlow's command drew nearer the division the brass guns were turned upon Richardson, but at the moment of his taking-off another battery was in action on his left. General D. H. Hill thought that Carter's battery was in time to divide the honor of the last shot with the section of Napoleons under Miller.

Orders were given General Pleasonton, at the second bridge, to be ready to enter the battle as soon as the attack by Richardson should open the way. To meet these orders skirmishers were advanced, and Tidball's battery, by piece, using canister, to drive back the Confederate sharp-shooters. The Fifth Corps (General Porter's) was ordered to be ready for like service.

When Richardson swung his line up along the crest at the Piper House, Pleasonton advanced troopers and batteries, crossed the bridge at a gallop by the Fifth Regular Cavalry, Farnsworth's brigade, Rush's brigade, two regiments of the Fifth Brigade under B. F. Davis, and the batteries of Tidball, Robertson, Hains, and Gibson. The batteries were put into action under the line of skirmishers, that were reinforced by Sykes's division of the Fifth and Tenth Infantry under Lieutenant Poland.

General Hill seized a musket and by example speedily collected a number of men, who joined him in reinforcing the line threatened by this heavy display. The parts of brigades under General Pryor, Colonels Cummings, Posey, and G. T. Anderson afterwards got up to help the brigade of Evans already there. By these, with the batteries of Squires, Gardner, and Richardson, this threatening demonstration was checked. Then it was reinforced by the batteries of Randol, Kusserow, and Van Reed, and the Fourth United States Infantry, Captain Dryer; the first battalion of the Twelfth, Captain Blount; second battalion of the Twelfth, Captain Anderson; first battalion of the Fourteenth, Captain Brown, and second battalion of the Fourteenth, Captain McKibbin, of Sykes's division; the batteries posted to command the field, right and left, to cover Sumner's and Burnside's fronts, as soon as they could rise to the plateau. S. D. Lee's batteries were back on the crest, replenished of ammunition, while the Union batteries were on low ground, near the river. A very clever well-organized advance was made, but their advantages of position and the tenacious hold of the Confederates, even after the attack reached the crest, enabled them to drive back the assaulting forces. The horse batteries went back to positions on the west side after replenishing with ammunition, except Gibson's, which was put in defensive attitude on the east. Pleasonton, with a comprehensive view of the opportunity, called for additional force, but two of Morell's brigades had been ordered by the upper crossing to Sumner's relief, and a detachment had been sent to assist Burnside, which reduced the Fifth Corps to the minimum of force necessary to the service to which it was assigned; not equal to the aggressive fight to which it was invited. But for the breaking up of

Richardson's aggression, this last advance could have gained the field.

The Third Brigade of the Second Division, Sixth Corps, made an erratic march across part of the field, the Seventh Maine Regiment leading, and retired like a meteor that loses its own fire.

A little after one o'clock this and other parts of the line, except at the Burnside Bridge, settled down to defensive. Burnside was still hard at work in search of a practical line of advance, Toombs standing manfully against him.

During the lull, after the rencounter of Walker's, Hill's, and Hood's divisions against Mansfield's last fight, General Lee and myself, riding together under the crest of General D. H. Hill's part of the line, were joined by the latter. We were presently called to the crest to observe movements going on in the Union lines. The two former dismounted and walked to the crest; General Hill, a little out of strength and thinking a single horseman not likely to draw the enemy's fire, rode. As we reached the crest I asked him to ride a little apart, as he would likely draw fire upon the group. While viewing the field a puff of white smoke was seen to burst from a cannon's mouth about a mile off. I remarked, "There is a shot for General Hill," and, looking towards him, saw his horse drop on his knees. Both forelegs were cut off just below the knees. The dropping forward of the poor animal so elevated his croup that it was not an easy matter for one not an expert horseman to dismount *à la militaire*. To add to the dilemma, there was a rubber coat with other wraps strapped to the cantle of the saddle. Failing in his attempt to dismount, I suggested that he throw his leg forward over the pommel. This gave him easy and graceful dismount. This was the third horse shot under him during the day, and the shot was one of the best I ever witnessed. An equally good one was made by a Confederate at Yorktown. An officer of the Topographical Engineers walked into the open, in front of our lines, fixed his plane table and seated himself to make a map of the Confederate works. A non-commissioned officer, without orders, adjusted his gun, carefully aimed it, and fired. At the report of the gun all eyes were turned to see the occasion of it, and then to observe the object, when the shell was seen to explode as if in the hands of the officer. It had been dropped squarely upon the drawing-table, and Lieutenant Wagner was mortally wounded.* Of the first shot, Major Alfred A. Woodhull, under date of June 8, 1886, wrote,—

"On the 17th of September, 1862, I was standing in Weed's battery, whose position is correctly given in the map, when a man on, I think, a gray horse, appeared about a mile in front of us, and footmen were recognized near. Captain Weed, who was a remarkable artillerist, himself sighted and fired the gun at the horse, which was struck."

---

* Of this shot, Captain A. B. More, of Richmond, Virginia, wrote, under date of June 16, 1886,—

"The Howitzers have always been proud of that shot, and, thinking it would interest you, I write to say that it was fired by Corporal Holzburton, of the Second Company, Richmond Howitzers, from a ten-pound Parrott."

CHAPTER XIX.

BATTLE OF SHARPSBURG, OR ANTIETAM (CONTINUED).

Closing Events of the Great Struggle—Burnside crosses the Bridge he made famous—Toombs made Gallant Defence, but was outnumbered and dislodged—The Confederate Brigades from Harper's Ferry under A. P. Hill in Time for the Final Crisis—Burnside's Advance arrested by them—The Battle against Burnside "appeared to spring from the Earth"—"Lee's old War Horse"—The Killing of a Kinsman at the Bridge seriously affects General D. R. Jones—The Sharp Fight at Shepherdstown—Confederates retreat—Casualties of the Battle—Confederate Losses in the Campaign—Neither McClellan's Plan nor Execution was strong.

AT one or two points near our centre were dead angles into which I rode from time to time for closer observation of the enemy when his active aggression was suspended. General Burnside was busy at his crossing, but no report of progress had been sent me. One of my rides towards the Dunker chapel revealed efforts of the enemy to renew his work on that part of the field. Our troops were ordered to be ready to receive it. Its non-aggression suggested an opportunity for the Confederates, and I ordered McLaws and Walker to prepare to assault. Hood was back in position with his brigades, and Jackson was reported on his way, all in full supply of ammunition. It seemed probable that by concealing our movements under cover of the wood from the massed batteries of Doubleday's artillery on the north, and the batteries of position on the east, we could draw our columns so near to the enemy in front before our move could be known that we would have but a few rods to march before we could mingle our ranks with those of the enemy; that our columns massed and in goodly numbers, pressing severely upon a single point, would give the enemy much trouble, and might cut him in two, and break up his battle arrangements at the lower bridge; but just then General Jackson reported, with authority from General Lee, that he with the cavalry was ordered to march around and turn the entire position of the enemy by his right flank, and strike at his rear. He found that the march would be long and extremely hazardous, and abandoned his orders. So it appears that counsels were divided on both sides, General McClellan disapproving the attack proposed by Franklin, and General Lee preferring a flank move.

Of the proposed attack from the Union side, General Franklin reported,—

"Slocum's division arrived on the field about eleven o'clock. Immediately after its arrival two of his brigades (Newton's and Torbert's) were formed in column of attack to carry the wood in the immediate vicinity of the White Church. The other brigade (Bartlett's) had been ordered by General Sumner to keep near his right. As this brigade was to form the reserve for the column of attack, I waited until it came up. About the same time General Sumner arrived on the spot and directed the attack to be postponed, and the enemy at once proceeded to fill the wood with infantry, and planted a battery there which opened a severe fire upon us. Shortly afterwards the commanding general came to the position, and decided that it would not be prudent to make the attack, our position on the right being then considerably in advance of what it had been in the morning." *

General McClellan claimed that his batteries on the east side dispersed a column marching in the afternoon to reinforce against General Sumner. This was probably Jackson's command marching to their position on the line. The fire only hurried the march of the troops to the front, where they resumed their position.

We left General Toombs defending the crossing at the Burnside Bridge, with the Second, Twentieth, and Fiftieth Georgia Regiments, and a company of Jenkins's brigade of South Carolina troops, against the Ninth Corps, com-

* Rebellion Record, vol. xix. part i. p. 377.

manded by General J. D. Cox, General Burnside, the commander of the right wing present, commanding. Toombs had in his line of infantry five hundred and fifty men part way up the swell of Sharpsburg Heights. Behind him he posted Eubank's battery, and overlooking were J. B. Richardson's and Eshleman's to rake the bridge; others near. The road on the Union side leading to the bridge runs parallel to the river about three hundred yards before it reaches the bridge, and turns up-stream after crossing. On the parallel to this line of march on the Confederate side Toombs posted his infantry, the South Carolina company in a marginal woodland above the bridge. Above and near the bridge was a fording-place for infantry; a thousand yards below was a practicable ford for infantry and artillery, by a country road. Toombs's orders were, when dislodged, to retire south so as to open the field of fire to all the troops on the heights behind him, the fire of his batteries to be concentrated upon the bridge, and his infantry arranged for a like converging fire. The ravines cutting the swells of the foot-hills gave him fair ground for retreat when he found his position no longer tenable. He was to so manœuvre as to have a flank fire on the advancing columns, and gradually encircle so as to join his division after passing the crest.

Early in the morning, General Burnside had been ordered to prepare the Ninth Corps for attack at the bridge, but to await further orders. At eight o'clock orders were sent to carry the bridge, gain possession of the heights, and to advance along their crest upon Sharpsburg and its rear. The order was repeated, and, finally, losing patience, General McClellan sent the inspector-general (Colonel Sackett)

"To deliver to General Burnside my positive order to push forward his troops without a moment's delay, and if necessary to carry the bridge at the point of the bayonet, and I ordered

Colonel Sackett to remain with General Burnside and see that the order was promptly executed." *

Upon receipt of the first order General Burnside advanced his troops, General Crook's brigade, supported by General Sturgis's division, to the bridge and ford just above it. These were preceded by the Eleventh Connecticut Regiment as skirmishers under Colonel Kingsbury, who essayed crossing by the upper ford, but after severe skirmish Colonel Kingsbury was killed and the effort failed. The division under General Rodman supported by Scammon's brigade (commanded by Colonel Ewing) moved towards the lower ford. Colonel Scammon, commanding the Kanawha division, moved with this column.

Wilcox's division was in rear of Sturgis, in reserve, and near the left of Benjamin's battery. Clark's and Durell's batteries were posted on the right. One section of Simmonds's battery was with Crook's brigade, the other with Benjamin's battery. Dahlgren's boat-howitzers covered the ford at Rodman's crossing. The last order was received at ten o'clock. The line of skirmishers advanced and engaged across the river. Crook's brigade marched for the bridge. After a severe engagement of some hours, General Crook posted two of Simmonds's guns in position to cover the bridge, and after some little time General Sturgis's division approached the bridge, led by Naglee's brigade. The Second Brigade, General Ferrero, was posted a little in reserve. The Second Maryland, Colonel Duryea, and Sixth New Hampshire Regiments were ordered forward in double time with bayonets fixed to carry the bridge. They made a gallant, dashing charge, crowding the bridge almost to its western *débouché*, but the fire concentrated a storm that stunned their ranks, thinned and cut them down until they were

* Rebellion Record, vol. i. part i. p. 63.

forced to retire. General Burnside repeated the order to force the way at all hazards. Arrangements were made, and when concluded the Fifty-first New York and Fifty-first Pennsylvania Regiments were sent. They found a route better covered from the Confederate fire than that of the first column while marching for the bridge.

By a dashing charge on double time they passed it under exulting hurrahs and most gallant work, and gained the west bank. The crossing by Rodman's division at the lower ford made our position at the bridge untenable, and General Toombs was prepared to retire the moment the west bank was gained in his rear.

Union troops were hurried over, and organized for advance over Sharpsburg Heights, but Sturgis's division had suffered, and, the ammunition getting low, it was found necessary to replace it by the division under General Wilcox, and Sturgis was ordered to hold position near the bridge in reserve. The brigades under Rodman made their crossing sooner, and waited a little for those at the bridge. As soon as the latter formed on the west bank, Rodman drew nearer. He was supported by the Scammon brigade of the Kanawha division, the brigade under General Crook to move with the troops from the bridge.

Clark's, Durell's, Cook's, Muhlenberg's, and part of Simmonds's batteries crossed with the infantry. About four o'clock the troops were over and advanced under very severe fire of artillery and infantry, increasing in force as they ascended the heights, but the march was continued in bold, admirable style, the troops engaging in steady, brave fight as they marched. Overreaching my right, they forced it back, breaking off Jones's right brigades under Drayton, Kemper, and Garnett. Toombs, working his way to the rear, managed to encircle the advancing column and join the other brigades under D. R. Jones as they were forced back. Jones used some of them in organizing a stand on the flank of the Union columns.

Toombs was joined in his rearward move by his regiments that had been sent off as train guards, by a battalion of the Eleventh Georgia under Major Little, and sent the regiments with him to replenish ammunition. Meanwhile, steady advancing battle was made by the Federals.

Batteries from all parts of our field drove to General Lee, as well as detachments of infantry, including some with fresh wounds from the morning battle, but the battle moved bravely on.

When General Lee found that General Jackson had left six of his brigades under General A. P. Hill to receive the property and garrison surrendered at Harper's Ferry, he sent orders for them to join him, and by magic spell had them on the field to meet the final crisis. He ordered two of them guided by Captain Latrobe to guard against approach of other forces that might come against him by bridge No. 4, Pender's and Brockenbrough's, and threw Branch's, Gregg's and Archer's against the fore-front of the battle, while Toombs's, Kemper's, and Garnett's engaged against its right. McIntosh's battery, sent in advance by A. P. Hill, was overrun and captured. Pegram's and Crenshaw's batteries were put in with Hill's three brigades. The Washington Artillery, S. D. Lee's, and Frobel's found places for parts of their batteries, ammunition replenished. D. H. Hill found opportunity to put in parts of his artillery under Elliott, Boyce, Carter, and Maurin. Toombs's absent regiments returned, as he made his way around to the enemy's right, and joined the right of General D. R. Jones. The strong battle concentrating against General Burnside seemed to spring from the earth as his march bore him farther from the river. Outflanked and staggered by the gallant attack of A. P. Hill's brigades, his advance was arrested.

The contention about the heights and suburbs of Sharpsburg was anxiously held. General Cox, reinforced by his reserve under General Sturgis, handled well his left against A. P. Hill; but, assailed in front and on his flank by concentrating fires that were crushing, he found it necessary to recover his lines and withdraw. A. P. Hill's brigades, Toombs and Kemper, followed. They recovered McIntosh's battery and the ground that had been lost on the right before the slow advancing night dropped her mantle upon this field of seldom equalled strife.

When the Ninth Corps dropped back under the crest they had so bravely won, the battle of Sharpsburg virtually ended, though the fire between the lines was continued till nine o'clock. The field made classic by a struggle of eighteen hours, too fearful to contemplate, was yet cumbered by the dead and wounded. After the firing ceased, parties from both sides, by mutual consent, went in search of fallen comrades.

After riding along the lines, giving instructions for the night and morning, I rode for general head-quarters to make report, but was delayed somewhat, finding wounded men hidden away under stone walls and in fence corners, not yet looked after, and afterwards in assisting a family whose home had been fired by a shell, so that all the other officers had arrived, made their reports, and were lounging about on the sod, when I rode up. General Lee walked up as I dismounted, threw his hands upon my shoulders, and hailed me with, "Here is my old war-horse at last!"

One of those peculiarly painful personal experiences which are innumerable in war, but seldom get into print (save in fiction), came under my observation in this battle. Colonel H. W. Kingsbury, who was killed while gallantly leading the Eleventh Connecticut Regiment at the ford near the Burnside Bridge, was a brother-in-law of General D. R. Jones, who commanded the Confederates immediately opposing him. His taking-off was a severe blow to Jones, and one from which he never recovered. His health had not been strong for some time. He asked

ANTIETAM. THE FIGHT AT BURNSIDE'S BRIDGE.

leave of absence shortly after this occurrence, and, gradually but hopelessly sinking, in a few months passed over to the silent majority to join his fallen kinsman.

A few shots were exchanged early on the 18th, but a kindly feeling seemed to take possession of the troops, as they were not ordered into action, and excuses were passed between the lines for looking after wounded comrades, which resulted in a *quasi* truce for the day.

The Burnside battle may be likened to that contemplated for Fitz-John Porter under his 4.30 order at the Second Manassas. The latter, however, had the smaller force, while Burnside's numbers were greater.

In the afternoon General Lee was advised of new arrivals in General McClellan's army, and, thinking the few stragglers who came up to swell his own ranks were not sufficient to justify him in renewing the battle on the 19th, ordered his trains back, and after night marched his troops across the Potomac at the ford near Shepherdstown.

General Stuart was ordered to cross ahead of the general move, recross the Potomac at Williamsport, and stand guard to the rear of the columns in case of danger to their crossing. The road being clear at nine o'clock, the army marched; the First Corps, in advance, crossed about two A.M. on the 19th, awaited to guard the crossing, and at daylight was deployed on the south side. A. P. Hill's division covered the retreat of the army, and the cavalry under Fitzhugh Lee was to follow, relieving lines of picket guards and helping the feeble footmen. The rear of the Confederate column crossed into Virginia at ten A.M., unmolested. As the pursuit was not threatening, General Lee ordered his army to continue the march to proper points of bivouac, holding the artillery reserve under General Pendleton and an infantry detail of the brigades of Armistead and Lawton, commanded by Colonels Hodges and Lamar, as guard at the ford. General

Pendleton posted some thirty guns in position for converging fire at the ford, and put a line of skirmishers near it, holding the infantry reserve and eleven guns at the rear.

About noon the Union cavalry appeared on the other bank. The batteries of Gibson, Tidball, and Robertson were put in action, but relieved about two o'clock by artillery of the Fifth Corps. After a severe combat the Fourth Michigan Regiment and parts of the One Hundred and Eighteenth Pennsylvania and Eighteenth and Twenty-second Massachusetts were ordered over under General Griffin. They forced the passage under artillery and infantry fire, scaled the heights, and got possession of five guns of different batteries and a number of small-arms, when, night approaching, the detachment was recalled.

General Pendleton reported the result to general headquarters, and General Lee ordered General Jackson to send his nearest division back to the ford early in the morning.

A. P. Hill's division was ordered. He was fortunate in approaching the ford (Boteler's) before the Federals had crossed all of their advancing column; formed his brigades in two lines and advanced to attack. General Porter, upon the report of this advance, found that his troops could not get position on the south bank in time to meet this threatening, ordered the troops withdrawn to cover about the canal and adjacent heights, and succeeded in getting most of his men safely back.

General Hill deployed the brigades of Gregg, Thomas, and Pender as his front line, under command of General Gregg. Lane's (Branch's brigade), Archer's, and Brockenbrough's brigades were of his second line, commanded by General Archer. In this order the division advanced and engaged in a severe struggle. Finding the fight on his front heavy, General Pender called to General Archer for support, and the latter, moving by his left, brought his brigade on Pender's left, when the advance was pushed to successful issue. The One Hundred and Eighteenth Pennsylvania Regiment was thrown into confusion and suffered heavy loss. One of the guns lost the day before was recovered and two hundred prisoners taken. The losses were between two hundred and fifty and three hundred on each side, the Federals losing about twenty more than the Confederates. The Confederate accounts of this affair were overdrawn, but they were reassuring after the severe experience about South Mountain and Sharpsburg.

The Army of Northern Virginia was then marched to the vicinity of Martinsburg, where it remained in repose for several days, then retired to the vicinity of Winchester. The Army of the Potomac concentrated about Harper's Ferry, refitting its supplies and transportation.

We may say of the battle of Sharpsburg that the Confederates foiled every attack that was made, and brought the Army of the Potomac to a stand at night, yet the Federal commander scored a success that was startling.

The commander of the Army of the Potomac reported his strength as 87,164. His estimate of the strength of the Army of Northern Virginia was 97,445. The Confederate commander estimated his own strength for battle at 37,000, and that of his adversary at 90,000.

The Confederates fought all of their men that were on the field, except two brigades of A. P. Hill's division and some of their field batteries.

Of the Federals, the Fifth Corps, except about one brigade of infantry, was not in action; and the Sixth Corps, except Irwin's brigade, seems to have had little serious work.

It is generally conceded that the Federals, in addition to advantage of numbers, had their organizations in hand, were better fed and clothed, and better prepared, therefore, to muster a larger portion of their number for battle.

The casualties of the First Corps, Army of Northern

Virginia, in the engagements at South Mountain, Crampton's Gap, Maryland Heights, Harper's Ferry, and Sharpsburg, as tabulated in the official report, were 7508.* Neither General Jackson's report nor General D. H. Hill's furnishes a detailed account of casualties. The former gives aggregate figures 2438, the latter 3241,—making a grand aggregate of 13,187.† None of these reports include the losses of the cavalry command, nor is there a report of them found among the Records.

The Army of Northern Virginia concentrated at and near Fredericktown on the 9th of September, 1862, numbered a trifle over 61,000, all arms. General Lee's estimate of his troops engaged at Sharpsburg was 37,000. This may not include his cavalry arm, conceding which, his force on the field should have been about 41,000. Estimating the cavalry loss at 500, our losses of battle should be 13,687, which leaves 20,000 to be accounted for as lost by severe continuous labor and marches. This, added to the losses in action, makes a grand total of 33,687 lost in the Maryland campaign. The losses from overwork were only temporary. Most of them were back in the ranks within fifteen days after the return to Virginia. But all of these large figures are trifles compared to the lamentable loss of the fruits of devoted service from the Chickahominy campaign to the Potomac.

The casualties of the Union side, reported by official count, were 12,410.

The best tactical moves at Antietam were made by Generals McLaws, A. P. Hill, Gibbon, and Patrick, and Colonels Barlow and Cross. Generals D. H. Hill and Hood were like game-cocks, fighting as long as they could stand, engaging again as soon as strong enough to rise.

---

* This includes eighty-five lost by S. D. Lee's artillery, not regularly assigned as part of the corps.

† Surgeon Lafayette Guild, medical director of the Army of Northern Virginia, in his official tabulated report, accounts for 10,291 only.

General Toombs and Colonel Benning performed very clever work at the Burnside Bridge. Of Colonel Cooke, the Twenty-seventh North Carolina Regiment, Captain Miller, Sergeant Ellis, and their men of the Washington Artillery, General Lee said, "They were heroic."

General McClellan's plan of the battle was not strong, the handling and execution were less so. Battles by the extreme right and left, divided by a river, gave us the benefit of interior lines, and it was that that saved the Confederate army, for it became manifest early in the day that his reserves were held at the bridge No. 2, which gave us freer use of our inner lines.

Following is a condensed but accurate presentation of the organization of the contending armies in the battle of Sharpsburg and the Maryland campaign: *

Army of Northern Virginia, General Robert E. Lee commanding.

Longstreet's Corps, Major-General James Longstreet.

McLaws's Division, Maj.-Gen. Lafayette McLaws:—*Kershaw's Brigade*, Brig.-Gen. J. B. Kershaw; 2d S. C., Col. John D. Kennedy; 3d S. C., Col. James D. Nance; 7th S. C., Col. D. Wyatt Aiken and Capt. John S. Hard; 8th S. C., Lieut.-Col. A. J. Hoole. *Cobb's Brigade*, Brig.-Gen. Howell Cobb, Lieut.-Col. C. C. Sanders, Lieut.-Col. William MacRae; 16th and 24th Ga., Cobb's (Ga.) Legion, 15th N. C. *Semmes's Brigade*, Brig.-Gen. Paul J. Semmes; 10th Ga., Capt. P. H. Loud; 53d Ga., Lieut.-Col. Thomas Sloan and Capt. S. W. Marshborne; 15th Va., Capts. E. M. Morrison and E. J. Willis; 32d Va., Col. E. B. Montague. *Barksdale's Brigade*, Brig.-Gen. William Barksdale; 13th Miss., Lieut.-Col. Kennon McElroy; 17th Miss., Lieut.-Col. John C. Fiser; 18th Miss., Maj. J. C. Campbell and Lieut.-Col. William H. Luse; 21st Miss., Capt. John Sims and Col. Benjamin G. Humphreys. *Artillery*, Maj. S. P. Hamilton, Col. H. C. Cabell; Manly's (N. C.) battery, Capt. B. C. Manly; Pulaski (Ga.) Art., Capt. J. P. W. Read; Richmond (Fayette) Art., Capt. M. C. Macon; Richmond Howitzers (1st Co.), Capt. E. S. McCarthy; Troup (Ga.) Art., Capt. H. H. Carlton.

Anderson's Division, Maj.-Gen. Richard H. Anderson:—*Wilcox's Brigade*, Col. Alfred Cumming; 8th, 9th, 10th, and 11th Ala. *Mahone's Brigade*, Col. William A. Parham; 6th, 12th, 16th, 41st, and 61st Va. *Featherston's Brigade*, Brig.-Gen. Winfield S. Featherston, Col. Carnot Posey; 12th Miss., 16th Miss., Capt. A. M. Feltus; 19th Miss., 2d Miss.

---

* Compiled from the official reports.

Battn. *Armistead's Brigade*, Brig.-Gen. Lewis A. Armistead, Col. J. G. Hodges; 9th, 14th, 38th, 53d, and 57th Va. *Pryor's Brigade*, Brig.-Gen. Roger A. Pryor; 14th Ala., 2d and 8th Fla., 3d Va. *Wright's Brigade*, Brig.-Gen. A. R. Wright; 44th Ala., 3d, 22d, and 48th Ga. *Artillery*, Maj. John S. Saunders; Donaldsonville (La.) Art. (Maurin's battery), Huger's (Va.) battery, Moorman's (Va.) battery, Thompson's (Grimes's) (Va.) battery.

JONES'S DIVISION, Brig.-Gen. David R. Jones:—*Toombs's Brigade*, Brig.-Gen. Robert Toombs, Col. Henry L. Benning; 2d Ga., Lieut.-Col. William R. Holmes and Major Skidmore Harris; 15th Ga., Col. W. T. Millican; 17th Ga., Capt. J. A. McGregor; 20th Ga., Col. J. B. Cumming. *Drayton's Brigade*, Brig.-Gen. Thomas F. Drayton; 50th Ga., Lieut.-Col. F. Kearse; 51st Ga., 15th S. C., Col. W. D. De Saussure. *Pickett's Brigade*, Col. Eppa Hunton, Brig.-Gen. R. B. Garnett; 8th Va., Col. Eppa Hunton; 18th Va., Maj. George C. Cabell; 19th Va., Col. J. B. Strange, Lieut. W. N. Wood, and Capt. J. L. Cochran; 28th Va., Capt. Wingfield; 56th Va., Col. William D. Stuart and Capt. McPhail. *Kemper's Brigade*, Brig.-Gen. J. L. Kemper; 1st, 7th, 11th, 17th, and 24th Va. *Jenkins's Brigade*, Col. Joseph Walker; 1st S. C. (Vols.), Lieut.-Col. D. Livingston; 2d S. C. Rifles, 5th S. C., Capt. T. C. Beckham; 6th S. C., Lieut.-Col. J. M. Steedman, Capt. E. B. Cantey; 4th S. C. (Battn.), Palmetto (S. C.) Sharp-shooters. *Anderson's Brigade*, Col. George T. Anderson; 1st Ga. (Regulars), Col. W. J. Magill; 7th, 8th, and 9th Ga.; 11th Ga., Maj. F. H. Little. *Artillery*, Fauquier (Va.) Art. (Stribling's battery),* Loudoun (Va.) Art. (Rogers's battery),* Turner (Va.) Art. (Leake's battery),* Wise (Va.) Art. (J. S. Brown's battery).

WALKER'S DIVISION, Brig.-Gen. John G. Walker:—*Walker's Brigade*, Col. Van H. Manning, Col. E. D. Hall; 3d Ark., Capt. John W. Reedy; 27th N. C., Col. J. R. Cooke; 46th N. C., Col. E. D. Hall; 48th N. C., Col. R. C. Hill; 30th Va., French's (Va.) battery, Capt. Thomas B. French. *Ransom's Brigade*, Brig.-Gen. Robert Ransom, Jr.; 24th N. C., Lieut.-Col. John L. Harris; 25th N. C., Col. H. M. Rutledge; 35th N. C., Col. M. W. Ransom; 49th N. C., Lieut.-Col. Lee M. McAfee; Branch's Field Art. (Va.), Capt. Branch.

HOOD'S DIVISION, Brig.-Gen. John B. Hood:—*Hood's Brigade*, Col. W. T. Wofford; 18th Ga., Lieut.-Col. S. Z. Ruff; Hampton (S. C.) Legion, Lieut.-Col. M. W. Gary; 1st Tex., Lieut.-Col. P. A. Work; 4th Tex., Lieut.-Col. B. F. Carter; 5th Tex., Capt. I. N. M. Turner. *Law's Brigade*, Col. E. M. Law; 4th Ala., Lieut.-Col. O. K. McLemore; 2d Miss., Col. J. M. Stone; 11th Miss., Col. P. F. Liddell; 6th N. C., Maj. Robert F. Webb. *Artillery*, Maj. B. W. Frobel; German Art. (S. C.), Capt. W. K. Bachman; Palmetto Art. (S. C.), Capt. H. R. Garden; Rowan Art. (N. C.), Capt. James Reilly.

EVANS'S BRIGADE, Brig.-Gen. Nathan G. Evans, Col. P. F. Stevens;† 17th S. C., Col. F. W. McMaster; 18th S. C., Col. W. H. Wallace; 22d S. C., Lieut.-Col. T. C. Watkins and Maj. M. Hilton; 23d S. C., Capt.

---

* Left at Leesburg.

† Commanding brigade while General Evans commanded provisional division.

S. A. Durham and Lieut. E. R. White; Holcombe (S. C.) Legion, Col. P. F. Stevens; Macbeth (S. C.) Art., Capt. R. Boyce.

ARTILLERY:— *Washington* (*La.*) *Artillery*, Col. J. B. Walton; 1st Co., Capt. C. W. Squires; 2d Co., Capt. J. B. Richardson; 3d Co., Capt. M. B. Miller; 4th Co., Capt. B. F. Eshleman. *Lee's Battalion*, Col. S. D. Lee; Ashland (Va.) Art., Capt. P. Woolfolk, Jr.; Bedford (Va.) Art., Capt. T. C. Jordan; Brooks (S. C.) Art., Lieut. William Elliott; Eubank's (Va.) battery, Capt. J. L. Eubank; Madison (La.) Light Art., Capt. G. V. Moody; Parker's (Va.) battery, Capt. W. W. Parker.

JACKSON'S CORPS, MAJOR-GENERAL THOMAS J. JACKSON.

EWELL'S DIVISION, Brig.-Gen. A. R. Lawton, Brig.-Gen. Jubal A. Early:—*Lawton's Brigade*, Col. M. Douglass, Maj. J. H. Lowe, Col. John H. Lamar; 13th and 26th Ga., 31st Ga., Lieut.-Col. J. T. Crowder; 38th, 60th, and 61st Ga. *Early's Brigade*, Brig.-Gen. Jubal A. Early, Col. William Smith; 13th Va., Capt. F. V. Winston; 25th, 31st, and 44th Va.; 49th Va., Col. William Smith; 52d Va., Col. M. G. Harman; 58th Va. *Trimble's Brigade*, Col. James A. Walker; 15th Ala., Capt. I. B. Feagin; 12th Ga., Capt. Rogers; 21st Ga., Maj. Thomas C. Glover; 21st N. C., Capt. Miller; 1st N. C. Battn.* *Hays's Brigade*, Brig.-Gen. Harry T. Hays; 5th La., 6th La., Col. H. B. Strong; 7th, 8th, and 14th La. *Artillery*,† Maj. A. R. Courtney; Charlottesville (Va.) Art. (Carrington's battery), Chesapeake (Md.) Art. (Brown's battery), Courtney (Va.) Art. (Latimer's battery), Johnson's (Va.) battery, La. Guard Art. (D'Aquin's battery), 1st Md. Batt. (Dement's battery), Staunton (Va.) Art. (Balthis's battery).

HILL'S LIGHT DIVISION, Maj.-Gen. Ambrose P. Hill:—*Branch's Brigade*, Brig.-Gen. L. O'B. Branch, Col. James H. Lane; 7th N. C., 18th N. C., Lieut.-Col. Purdie; 28th, 33d, and 37th N. C. *Gregg's Brigade*, Brig.-Gen. Maxcy Gregg; 1st S. C. (provisional army), Maj. E. McCrady, Jr., Col. D. H. Hamilton; 1st S. C. Rifles, Lieut.-Col. James M. Perrin; 12th S. C., Col. Dixon Barnes, Lieut.-Col. C. Jones, and Maj. W. H. McCorkle; 13th S. C., Col. O. E. Edwards; 14th S. C., Lieut.-Col. W. D. Simpson. *Field's Brigade*, Col. Brockenbrough; 40th, 47th, and 55th Va., 22d Va. Battn. *Archer's Brigade*, Brig.-Gen. J. J. Archer, Col. Peter Turney; 5th Ala. Battn., Captain Hooper; 19th Ga., Maj. J. H. Neal and Capt. F. M. Johnston; 1st Tenn. (provisional army), Col. Peter Turney; 7th Tenn., Maj. S. G. Shepard and Lieut. G. A. Howard; 14th Tenn., Lieut.-Col. J. W. Lockert. *Pender's Brigade*, Brig.-Gen. William D. Pender, Col. R. H. Brewer; 16th N. C., Lieut.-Col. Stowe; 22d N. C., Maj. C. C. Cole; 34th and 38th N. C. *Thomas's Brigade*, Col. Edward L. Thomas; 14th Ga., Col. R. W. Folsom; 35th Ga., 45th Ga., Maj. W. L. Grice; 49th Ga., Lieut.-Col. S. M. Manning. *Artillery*,‡ Maj. R. L. Walker; Branch (N. C.) Art. (A. C. Latham's

---

* Attached to Twenty-first North Carolina Regiment.

† John R. Johnson's and D'Aquin's batteries were the only ones present with this division at Sharpsburg.

‡ Braxton's, Crenshaw's, McIntosh's, and Pegram's batteries engaged at Sharpsburg.

battery), Crenshaw's (Va.) battery, Fredericksburg (Va.) Art. (Braxton's battery), Letcher (Va.) Art. (Davidson's battery), Middlesex (Va.) Art. (Fleet's battery), Pee Dee (S. C.) Art. (McIntosh's battery), Purcell (Va.) Art. (Pegram's battery).

Jackson's Division, Brig.-Gen. John R. Jones, Brig.-Gen. W. E. Starke, Col. A. J. Grigsby :— *Winder's Brigade*, Col. A. J. Grigsby, Lieut.-Col. R. D. Gardner (4th Va.), Maj. H. J. Williams ; 2d Va., Capt. R. T. Colston ; 4th Va., Lieut.-Col. R. D. Gardner ; 5th Va., Maj. H. J. Williams ; 27th Va., Capt. F. C. Wilson ; 33d Va., Capt. Golladay and Lieut. Walton. *Taliaferro's Brigade*, Col. E. T. H. Warren, Col. J. W. Jackson, Col. J. L. Sheffield ; 47th and 48th Ala., 10th, 23d, and 37th Va. *Jones's Brigade*, Col. B. T. Johnson, Brig.-Gen. J. R. Jones, Capt. J. E. Penn, Capt. A. C. Page, Capt. R. W. Withers ; 21st Va., Capt. A. C. Page ; 42d Va., Capt. R. W. Withers ; 48th Va., Capt. Chandler ; 1st Va. Battn., Lieut. C. A. Davidson. *Starke's Brigade*, Brig.-Gen. William E. Starke, Col. L. A. Stafford, Col. E. Pendleton ; 1st La., Lieut.-Col. M. Nolan ; 2d La., Col. J. M. Williams ; 9th La., 10th La., Capt. H. D. Monier ; 15th La., Coppens's (La.) battalion. *Artillery*, Maj. L. M. Shumaker ; Alleghany (Va.) Art. (Carpenter's battery), Brockenbrough's (Md.) battery, Danville (Va.) Art. (Wooding's battery), Hampden (Va.) Art. (Caskie's battery), Lee (Va.) Batt. (Raines's), Rockbridge (Va.) Art. (Poague's battery).

Hill's Division, Maj.-Gen. Daniel H. Hill :—*Ripley's Brigade*, Brig.-Gen. Roswell S. Ripley, Col. George Doles ; 4th Ga., Col. George Doles ; 44th Ga., Capt. Key ; 1st N. C., Lieut.-Col. H. A. Brown ; 3d N. C., Col. William L. De Rosset. *Rodes's Brigade*, Brig.-Gen. R. E. Rodes ; 3d Ala., Col. C. A. Battle ; 5th Ala., Maj. E. L. Hobson ; 6th Ala., Col. J. B. Gordon ; 12th Ala., Col. B. B. Gayle and Lieut.-Col. S. B. Pickens ; 26th Ala., Col. E. A. O'Neal. *Garland's Brigade*, Brig.-Gen. Samuel Garland, Jr., Col. D. K. McRae ; 5th N. C., Col. D. K. McRae and Capt. T. M. Garrett ; 12th N. C., Capt. S. Snow ; 13th N. C., Lieut.-Col. Thomas Ruffin, Jr. ; 20th N. C., Col. Alfred Iverson ; 23d N. C., Col. D. H. Christie. *Anderson's Brigade*, Brig.-Gen. George B. Anderson, Col. R. T. Bennett ; 2d N. C., Col. C. C. Tew and Capt. G. M. Roberts ; 4th N. C., Col. Bryan Grimes and Capts. W. T. Marsh and D. P. Latham ; 14th N. C., Col. R. T. Bennett ; 30th N. C., Col. F. M. Parker and Maj. W. W. Sillers. *Colquitt's Brigade*, Col. A. H. Colquitt ; 13th Ala., Col. B. D. Fry ; 6th Ga., Lieut.-Col. J. M. Newton ; 23d Ga., Col. W. P. Barclay ; 27th Ga., Col. L. B. Smith ; 28th Ga., Maj. T. Graybill and Capt. N. J. Garrison. *Artillery*,* Maj. Pierson ; Hardaway's (Ala.) battery, Capt. R. A. Hardaway ; Jeff Davis (Ala.) Art., Capt. J. W. Bondurant ; Jones's (Va.) battery, Capt. William B. Jones ; King William (Va.) Art., Capt. T. H. Carter.

Reserve Artillery, Brig.-Gen. William N. Pendleton :—*Brown's Battalion*,† Col. J. Thompson Brown ; Powhatan Art. (Dance's battery),

* Cutts's and Jones's battalions also under D. H. Hill's command at Sharpsburg.

† First Virginia Artillery.

Richmond Howitzers, 2d Co. (Watson's battery), Richmond Howitzers, 3d Co. (Smith's battery), Salem Art. (Hupp's battery), Williamsburg Art. (Coke's battery). *Cutts's Battalion,** Lieut.-Col. A. S. Cutts; Blackshears's (Ga.) battery, Irwin (Ga.) Art. (Lane's battery), Lloyd's (N. C.) battery, Patterson's (Ga.) battery, Ross's (Ga.) battery. *Jones's Battalion,** Maj. H. P. Jones. Morris (Va.) Art. (R. C. M. Page's battery), Orange (Va.) Art. (Peyton's battery), Turner's (Va.) battery, Wimbish's (Va.) battery. *Nelson's Battalion*, Maj. William Nelson; Amherst (Va.) Art. (Kirkpatrick's battery), Fluvanna (Va.) Art. (Ancell's battery), Huckstep's (Va.) battery, Johnson's (Va.) battery, Milledge (Ga.) Art. (Milledge's battery). *Miscellaneous*, Cutshaw's (Va.) battery, Dixie (Va.) Art. (Chapman's battery), Magruder (Va.) Art. (T. J. Page, Jr.'s, battery), Rice's (Va.) battery, Capt. W. H. Rice; Thomas's (Va.) Art. (E. J. Anderson's battery).†

CAVALRY, Maj.-Gen. James E. B. Stuart:—*Hampton's Brigade*, Brig.-Gen. Wade Hampton; 1st N. C., Col. L. S. Baker; 2d S. C., Col. M. C. Butler; 10th Va., Cobb's (Ga.) Legion, Lieut.-Col. P. M. B. Young; Jeff Davis Legion, Lieut.-Col. W. T. Martin. *Lee's Brigade*, Brig.-Gen. Fitzhugh Lee; 1st Va., Lieut.-Col. L. Tiernan Brien; 3d Va., Lieut.-Col. John T. Thornton; 4th Va., Col. William C. Wickham; 5th Va., Col. T. L. Rosser; 9th Va. *Robertson's Brigade*, Brig.-Gen. B. H. Robertson, Col. Thomas T. Munford; 2d Va., Col. T. T. Munford and Lieut.-Col. Burks; 6th Va.; 7th Va., Capt. S. B. Myers; 12th Va., Col. A. W. Harman; 17th Va. Battn.

HORSE ARTILLERY, Capt. John Pelham:—Chew's (Va.) battery, Hart's (S. C.) battery, Pelham's (Va.) battery.

ARMY OF THE POTOMAC,‡ MAJOR-GENERAL GEORGE B. MCCLELLAN, U.S. ARMY.

GENERAL HEAD-QUARTERS:—*Escort*, Capt. James B. McIntyre; Independent Company Oneida (N. Y.) Cav., Capt. Daniel P. Mann; 4th U. S. Cav., Co. A, Lieut. Thomas H. McCormick; 4th U. S. Cav., Co. E, Capt. James B. McIntyre. *Regular Engineer Battalion*, Capt. James C. Duane. *Provost Guard*, Maj. William H. Wood. 2d U. S. Cav., Cos. E, F, H, and K, Capt. George A. Gordon; 8th U. S. Inf., Cos. A, D, F, and G, Capt. Royal T. Frank; 19th U. S. Inf., Co. G, Capt. Edmund L. Smith; 19th U. S. Inf., Co. H, Capt. Henry S. Welton. *Headquarters Guard*, Maj. Granville O. Haller; 93d N. Y., Lieut.-Col. Benjamin C. Butler. *Quartermaster's Guard*, 1st U. S. Cav., Cos. B, C, H, and I, Capt. Marcus A. Reno.

---

* With D. H. Hill's division at Sharpsburg.

† Left at Leesburg.

‡ Compiled from the records of the Adjutant-General's Office. On September 14 the right wing of the army, consisting of the First and Ninth Corps, was commanded by Major-General Burnside; the centre, composed of the Second and Twelfth Corps, by Major-General Sumner, and the left wing, comprising the Sixth Corps and Couch's division (Fourth Corps), by Major-General Franklin.

FIRST ARMY CORPS,* (1) MAJOR-GENERAL JOSEPH HOOKER,† (2) BRIGADIER-GENERAL GEORGE G. MEADE. *Escort*, 2d N. Y. Cav., Cos. A, B, I, and K, Capt. John E. Naylor.

FIRST DIVISION, (1) Brig.-Gen. Rufus King,‡ (2) Brig.-Gen. John P. Hatch,§ (3) Brig.-Gen. Abner Doubleday :—*First Brigade*, Col. Walter Phelps, Jr.; 22d N. Y., Lieut.-Col. John McKie, Jr.; 24th N. Y., Capt. John D. O'Brian; 30th N. Y., Col. William M. Searing; 84th N. Y. (14th Militia), Maj. William H. de Bovoise; 2d U. S. Sharp-shooters, Col. Henry A. V. Post. *Second Brigade*, (1) Brig.-Gen. Abner Doubleday, (2) Col. William P. Wainwright, † (3) Lieut.-Col. J. William Hofmann; 7th Ind., Maj. Ira G. Grover; 76th N. Y., Col. William P. Wainwright, Capt. John W. Young; 95th N. Y., Maj. Edward Pye; 56th Pa., Lieut.-Col. J. William Hofmann, Capt. Frederick Williams. *Third Brigade*, Brig.-Gen. Marsena R. Patrick; 21st N. Y., Col. William F. Rogers; 23d N. Y., Col. Henry C. Hoffman; 35th N. Y., Col. Newton B. Lord; 80th N. Y. (20th Militia), Lieut.-Col. Theodore B. Gates. *Fourth Brigade*, Brig.-Gen. John Gibbon; 19th Ind., Col. Solomon Meredith, Lieut.-Col. Alois O. Bachman, Capt. William W. Dudley; 2d Wis., Col. Lucius Fairchild, Lieut.-Col. Thomas S. Allen; 6th Wis., Lieut.-Col. Edward S. Bragg, Maj. Rufus R. Dawes; 7th Wis., Capt. John B. Callis. *Artillery*, Capt. J. Albert Monroe; N. H. Light, First Batt., Lieut. Frederick M. Edgell; 1st R. I. Light, Batt. D., Capt. J. Albert Monroe; 1st N. Y. Light, Batt. L, Capt. John A. Reynolds; 4th U. S., Batt. B, Capt. Joseph B. Campbell, Lieut. James Stewart.

SECOND DIVISION, Brig.-Gen. James B. Ricketts :—*First Brigade*, Brig.-Gen. Abram Duryea; 97th N. Y., Maj. Charles Northrup; 104th N. Y., Maj. Lewis C. Skinner; 105th N. Y., Col. Howard Carroll; 107th Pa., Capt. James Mac Thomson. *Second Brigade*, (1) Col. William A. Christian, (2) Col. Peter Lyle; 26th N. Y., Lieut.-Col. Richard H. Richardson; 94th N. Y., Lieut.-Col. Calvin Littlefield; 88th Pa., Lieut.-Col. George W. Gile, Capt. Henry R. Myers; 90th Pa., Col. Peter Lyle, Lieut.-Col. William A. Leech. *Third Brigade*, (1) Brig.-Gen. George L. Hartsuff,† (2) Col. Richard Coulter; 16th Me.,‖ Col. Asa W. Wildes; 12th Mass., Maj. Elisha Burbank, Capt. Benjamin F. Cook; 13th Mass., Maj. J. Parker Gould; 83d N. Y. (9th Militia), Lieut.-Col. William Atterbury; 11th Pa., Col. Richard Coulter, Capt. David M. Cook. *Artillery*, 1st Pa. Light, Batt. F, Capt. Ezra W. Matthews; Pa. Light, Batt. C, Capt. James Thompson.

THIRD DIVISION, (1) Brig.-Gen. George G. Meade, (2) Brig.-Gen. Truman Seymour :—*First Brigade*, (1) Brig.-Gen. Truman Seymour, (2) Col. R. Biddle Roberts; 1st Pa. Reserves, Col. R. Biddle Roberts, Capt. William C. Talley; 2d Pa. Reserves, Capt. James N. Byrnes; 5th Pa. Re-

---

* Designation changed from Third Corps, Army of Virginia, to First Army Corps, by General Orders, No. 129, Adjutant-General's Office, September 12, 1862.

† Wounded September 17. ‡ Relieved September 14.

§ Wounded September 14.

‖ Joined September 9, and detached September 13 as railroad guard.

serves, Col. Joseph W. Fisher; 6th Pa. Reserves, Col. William Sinclair; 13th Pa. Reserves (1st Rifles), Col. Hugh W. McNeil, Capt. Dennis McGee. *Second Brigade*, Col. Albert L. Magilton; 3d Pa. Reserves, Lieut.-Col. John Clark; 4th Pa. Reserves, Maj. John Nyce; 7th Pa. Reserves, Col. Henry C. Bolinger, Major Chauncey M. Lyman; 8th Pa. Reserves, Maj. Silas M. Baily. *Third Brigade*, (1) Col. Thomas F. Gallagher,* (2) Lieut.-Col. Robert Anderson; 9th Pa. Reserves, Lieut.-Col. Robert Anderson, Capt. Samuel B. Dick; 10th Pa. Reserves, Lieut.-Col. Adoniram J. Warner, Capt. Jonathan P. Smith; 11th Pa. Reserves, Lieut.-Col. Samuel M. Jackson; 12th Pa. Reserves, Capt. Richard Gustin. *Artillery*, 1st Pa. Light, Batt. A, Lieut. John G. Simpson; 1st Pa. Light, Batt. B, Capt. James H. Cooper; 1st Pa. Light, Batt. G,† Lieut. Frank P. Amsden; 5th U. S., Batt. C, Capt. Dunbar R. Ransom.

SECOND ARMY CORPS, MAJOR-GENERAL EDWIN V. SUMNER. *Escort*, 6th N. Y. Cav., Co. D, Capt. Henry W. Lyon; 6th N. Y. Cav., Co. K, Capt. Riley Johnson.

FIRST DIVISION, (1) Maj.-Gen. Israel B. Richardson,‡ (2) Brig.-Gen. John C. Caldwell, (3) Brig.-Gen. Winfield S. Hancock; *First Brigade*, Brig.-Gen. John C. Caldwell; 5th N. H., Col. Edward E. Cross; 7th N. Y., Capt. Charles Brestel; 61st and 64th N. Y., Col. Francis C. Barlow, Lieut.-Col. Nelson A. Miles; 81st Pa., Maj. H. Boyd McKeen. *Second Brigade*, (1) Brig.-Gen. Thomas F. Meagher, (2) Col. John Burke; 29th Mass., Lieut.-Col. Joseph H. Barnes; 63d N. Y., Col. John Burke, Lieut.-Col. Henry Fowler, Maj. Richard C. Bentley, Capt. Joseph O'Neill; 69th N. Y., Lieut.-Col. James Kelly, Maj. James Cavanagh; 88th N. Y., Lieut.-Col. Patrick Kelly. *Third Brigade*, Col. John R. Brooke; 2d Del., Capt. David L. Stricker; 52d N. Y., Col. Paul Frank; 57th N. Y., Lieut.-Col. Philip J. Parisen, Maj. Alford B. Chapman; 66th N. Y., Capt. Julius Wehle, Lieut.-Col. James H. Bull; 53d Pa., Lieut.-Col. Richards McMichael. *Artillery*, 1st N. Y. Light, Batt. B, Capt. Rufus D. Pettit; 4th U. S., Batts. A and C, Lieut. Evan Thomas.

SECOND DIVISION, (1) Maj.-Gen. John Sedgwick,‡ (2) Brig.-Gen. Oliver O. Howard:—*First Brigade*, Brig.-Gen. Willis A. Gorman; 15th Mass., Lieut.-Col. John W. Kimball; 1st Minn., Col. Alfred Sully; 34th N. Y., Col. James A. Suiter; 82d N. Y. (2d Militia), Col. Henry W. Hudson; Mass. Sharp-shooters, 1st Co., Capt. John Saunders; Minn. Sharp-shooters, 2d Co., Capt. William F. Russell. *Second Brigade*, (1) Brig.-Gen. Oliver O. Howard, (2) Col. Joshua T. Owen, (3) Col. De Witt C. Baxter; 69th Pa., Col. Joshua T. Owen; 71st Pa., Col. Isaac J. Wistar, Lieut. Richard P. Smith (adjutant), Capt. Enoch E. Lewis; 72d Pa., Col. De Witt C. Baxter; 106th Pa., Col. Turner G. Morehead. *Third Brigade*, (1) Brig.-Gen. Napoleon J. T. Dana,‡ (2) Col. Norman J. Hall; 19th Mass., Col. Edward W. Hinks, Lieut.-Col. Arthur F. Devereux; 20th Mass., Col. William R. Lee; 7th Mich., Col. Norman J. Hall, Capt.

---

* Wounded September 14.

† Detached at Washington, D. C., since September 6.

‡ Wounded September 17.

Charles J. Hunt; 42d N. Y., Lieut.-Col. George N. Bomford, Maj. James E. Mallon; 59th N.Y., Col. William L. Tidball. *Artillery*, 1st R. I. Light, Batt. A, Capt. John A. Tompkins; 1st U. S., Batt. I, Lieut. George A. Woodruff.

THIRD DIVISION, Brig.-Gen. William H. French:—*First Brigade*, Brig.-Gen. Nathan Kimball; 14th Ind., Col. William Harrow; 8th Ohio, Lieut.-Col. Franklin Sawyer; 132d Pa., Col. Richard A. Oakford, Lieut.-Col. Vincent M. Wilcox; 7th W. Va., Col. Joseph Snider. *Second Brigade*, Col. Dwight Morris; 14th Conn., Lieut.-Col. Sanford H. Perkins; 108th N. Y., Col. Oliver H. Palmer; 130th Pa., Col. Henry I. Zinn. *Third Brigade*, (1) Brig.-Gen. Max Weber,* (2) Col. John W. Andrews; 1st Del., Col. John W. Andrews, Lieut.-Col. Oliver H. Hopkinson; 5th Md., Maj. Leopold Blumenberg, Capt. E. F. M. Faehtz; 4th N. Y., Lieut.-Col. John D. McGregor. *Unattached Artillery*, 1st N. Y. Light, Batt. G, Capt. John D. Frank; 1st R. I. Light, Batt. B, Capt. John G. Hazard; 1st R. I. Light, Batt. G, Capt. Charles D. Owen.

FOURTH ARMY CORPS.

FIRST DIVISION,† Maj.-Gen. Darius N. Couch:—*First Brigade*, Brig.-Gen. Charles Devens, Jr.; 7th Mass., Col. David A. Russell; 10th Mass., Col. Henry L. Eustis; 36th N. Y., Col. William H. Browne; 2d R. I., Col. Frank Wheaton. *Second Brigade*, Brig.-Gen. Albion P. Howe; 62d N. Y., Col. David J. Nevin; 93d Pa., Col. James M. McCarter; 98th Pa., Col. John F. Ballier; 102d Pa., Col. Thomas A. Rowley; 139th Pa.,‡ Col. Frank H. Collier. *Third Brigade*, Brig.-Gen. John Cochrane; 65th N. Y., Col. Alexander Shaler; 67th N. Y., Col. Julius W. Adams; 122d N. Y., Col. Silas Titus; 23d Pa., Col. Thomas H. Neill; 61st Pa., Col. George C. Spear; 82d Pa., Col. David H. Williams. *Artillery*, N. Y. Light, 3d Batt.,§ Capt. William Stuart; 1st Pa. Light, Batt. C, Capt. Jeremiah McCarthy; 1st Pa. Light, Batt. D, Capt. Michael Hall, 2d U. S., Batt. G, Lieut. John H. Butler.

FIFTH ARMY CORPS, MAJOR-GENERAL FITZ-JOHN PORTER. *Escort*, 1st Maine Cavalry (detachment), Capt. George J. Summat.

FIRST DIVISION, Maj.-Gen. George W. Morell:—*First Brigade*, Col. James Barnes; 2d Me., Col. Charles W. Roberts; 18th Mass., Lieut.-Col. Joseph Hayes; 22d Mass., Lieut.-Col. William S. Tilton; 1st Mich., Capt. Emory W. Belton; 13th N. Y., Col. Elisha G. Marshall; 25th N. Y., Col. Charles A. Johnson; 118th Pa., Col. Charles M. Prevost; Mass. Sharpshooters, 2d Co., Capt. Lewis E. Wentworth. *Second Brigade*, Brig.-Gen. Charles Griffin; 2d D. of C., Col. Charles M. Alexander; 9th Mass., Col. Patrick R. Guiney; 32d Mass., Col. Francis J. Parker; 4th Mich., Col. Jonathan W. Childs; 14th N. Y., Col. James McQuade; 62d Pa., Col. Jacob B. Sweitzer. *Third Brigade*, Col. T. B. W. Stockton; 20th

* Wounded September 17.

† Assigned to the Sixth Corps as the Third Division, September 26, 1862.

‡ Joined September 17. § Joined September 15.

Me., Col. Adelbert Ames; 16th Mich., Lieut.-Col. Norval E. Welch; 12th N. Y., Capt. William Huson; 17th N. Y., Lieut.-Col. Nelson B. Bartram; 44th N. Y., Maj. Freeman Conner; 83d Pa., Capt. Orpheus S. Woodward; Mich. Sharp-shooters, Brady's co., Lieut. Jonas H. Titus, Jr. *Artillery*, Mass. Light, Batt. C, Capt. Augustus P. Martin; 1st R. I. Light, Batt. C, Capt. Richard Waterman; 5th U. S., Batt. D, Lieut. Charles E. Hazlett. *Sharp-shooters*, 1st U. S., Capt. John B. Isler.

SECOND DIVISION, Brig.-Gen. George Sykes:—*First Brigade*, Lieut.-Col. Robert C. Buchanan; 3d U. S., Capt. John D. Wilkins; 4th U. S., Capt. Hiram Dryer; 12th U. S., 1st Battn., Capt. Matthew M. Blunt; 12th U. S., 2d Battn., Capt. Thomas M. Anderson; 14th U. S., 1st Battn., Capt. W. Harvey Brown; 14th U. S., 2d Battn., Capt. David B. McKibbin. *Second Brigade*, Maj. Charles S. Lovell; 1st and 6th U. S., Capt. Levi C. Bootes; 2d and 10th U. S., Capt. John S. Poland; 11th U. S., Capt. DeL. Floyd-Jones; 17th U. S., Maj. George L. Andrews. *Third Brigade*, Col. Gouverneur K. Warren; 5th N. Y., Capt. Cleveland Winslow; 19th N. Y., Lieut.-Col. John W. Marshall. *Artillery*, 1st U. S., Batts. E and G, Lieut. Alanson M. Randol; 5th U. S., Batt. I, Capt. Stephen H. Weed; 5th U. S., Batt. K, Lieut. William E. Van Reed.

THIRD DIVISION,* Brig.-Gen. Andrew A. Humphreys:—*First Brigade*, Brig.-Gen. Erastus B. Tyler; 91st Pa., Col. Edgar M. Gregory; 126th Pa., Col. James G. Elder; 129th Pa., Col. Jacob G. Frick; 134th Pa., Col. Matthew S. Quay. *Second Brigade*, Col. Peter H. Allabach; 123d Pa., Col. John B. Clark; 131st Pa., Lieut.-Col. William B. Shaut; 133d Pa., Col. Franklin B. Speakman; 155th Pa., Col. Edward J. Allen. *Artillery*, Capt. Lucius N. Robinson; 1st N. Y. Light, Batt. C, Capt. Almont Barnes; 1st Ohio Light, Batt. L, Capt. Lucius N. Robinson. *Artillery Reserve*, Lieut.-Col. William Hays; 1st Battn. N. Y. Light, Batt. A, Lieut. Bernhard Wever; 1st Battn. N. Y. Light, Batt. B, Lieut. Alfred von Kleiser; 1st Battn. N. Y. Light, Batt. C, Capt. Robert Langner; 1st Battn. N. Y. Light, Batt. D, Capt. Charles Kusserow; N. Y. Light, 5th Batt., Capt. Elijah D. Taft; 1st U. S., Batt. K, Capt. William M. Graham; 4th U. S., Batt. G, Lieut. Marcus P. Miller.

SIXTH ARMY CORPS, MAJOR-GENERAL WILLIAM B. FRANKLIN.
Escort, 6th Pa. Cav., Cos. B and G, Capt. Henry P. Muirheid.

FIRST DIVISION, Maj.-Gen. Henry W. Slocum:—*First Brigade*, Col. Alfred T. A. Torbert; 1st N. J., Lieut.-Col. Mark W. Collet; 2d N. J., Col. Samuel L. Buck; 3d N. J., Col. Henry W. Brown; 4th N. J., Col. William B. Hatch. *Second Brigade*, Col. Joseph J. Bartlett; 5th Me., Col. Nathaniel J. Jackson; 16th N. Y., Lieut.-Col. Joel J. Seaver; 27th N. Y., Lieut.-Col. Alexander D. Adams; 96th Pa., Col. Henry L. Cake. *Third Brigade*, Brig.-Gen. John Newton; 18th N. Y., Lieut.-Col. George R. Myers; 31st N. Y., Lieut.-Col. Francis E. Pinto; 32d N. Y., Col. Roderick Matheson; Maj. George F. Lemon; 95th Pa., Col. Gustavus W. Town. *Artillery*, Capt. Emory Upton; Md. Light, Batt. A, Capt. John

---

* This division was organized September 12, and reached the battlefield of Antietam September 18.

W. Wolcott; Mass. Light, Batt. A, Capt. Josiah Porter; N. J. Light, Batt. A, Capt. William Hexamer; 2d U. S., Batt. D, Lieut. Edward B. Williston.

SECOND DIVISION, Maj.-Gen. William F. Smith:—*First Brigade*, (1) Brig.-Gen. Winfield S. Hancock,* (2) Col. Amasa Cobb; 6th Me., Col. Hiram Burnham; 43d N. Y., Maj. John Wilson; 49th Pa., Lieut.-Col. William Brisbane; 137th Pa., Col. Henry M. Bossert; 5th Wis., Col. Amasa Cobb. *Second Brigade*, Brig.-Gen. W. T. H. Brooks; 2d Vt., Maj. James H. Walbridge; 3d Vt., Col. Breed N. Hyde; 4th Vt., Lieut.-Col. Charles B. Stoughton; 5th Vt., Col. Lewis A. Grant; 6th Vt., Maj. Oscar L. Tuttle. *Third Brigade*, Col. William H. Irwin; 7th Me., Maj. Thomas W. Hyde; 20th N. Y., Col. Ernest von Vegesack; 33d N. Y., Lieut.-Col. Joseph W. Corning; 49th N. Y., Lieut.-Col. William C. Alberger, Maj. George W. Johnson; 77th N. Y., Capt. Nathan S. Babcock. *Artillery*, Capt. Romeyn B. Ayres; Md. Light, Batt. B, Lieut. Theodore J. Vanneman; N. Y. Light, 1st Batt., Capt. Andrew Cowan; 5th U. S., Batt. F, Lieut. Leonard Martin.

NINTH ARMY CORPS, MAJOR-GENERAL AMBROSE E. BURNSIDE,† MAJOR-GENERAL JESSE L. RENO,‡ BRIGADIER-GENERAL JACOB D. COX. *Escort*, 1st Me. Cav., Co. G, Capt. Zebulon B. Blethen.

FIRST DIVISION, Brig.-Gen. Orlando B. Willcox:—*First Brigade*, Col. Benjamin C. Christ; 28th Mass., Capt. Andrew P. Carraher; 17th Mich., Col. William H. Withington; 79th N. Y., Lieut.-Col. David Morrison; 50th Pa., Maj. Edward Overton, Capt. William H. Diehl. *Second Brigade*, Col. Thomas Welsh; 8th Mich., Lieut.-Col. Frank Graves, Maj. Ralph Ely; 46th N. Y., Lieut.-Col. Joseph Gerhart; 45th Pa., Lieut.-Col. John I. Curtin; 100th Pa., Col. David A. Leckey. *Artillery*, Mass. Light, 8th Batt., Capt. Asa M. Cook; 2d U. S., Batt. E, Lieut. Samuel N. Benjamin.

SECOND DIVISION, Brig.-Gen. Samuel D. Sturgis:—*First Brigade*, Brig.-Gen. James Naglee; 2d Md., Lieut.-Col. J. Eugene Duryea; 6th N. H., Col. Simon G. Griffin; 9th N. H., Col. Enoch Q. Fellows; 48th Pa., Lieut.-Col. Joshua K. Sigfried. *Second Brigade*, Brig.-Gen. Edward Ferrero; 21st Mass., Col. William S. Clark; 35th Mass., Col. Edward A. Wild, Lieut.-Col. Sumner Carruth; 51st N. Y., Col. Robert B. Potter; 51st Pa., Col. John F. Hartranft. *Artillery*, Pa. Light, Batt. D, Capt. John W. Durell; 4th U. S., Batt. E, Capt. Joseph C. Clark, Jr.

THIRD DIVISION, Brig.-Gen. Isaac P. Rodman: §—*First Brigade*, Col. Harrison S. Fairchild; 9th N. Y., Lieut.-Col. Edgar A. Kimball; 89th N. Y., Maj. Edward Jardine; 103d N. Y., Maj. Benjamin Ringold. *Second Brigade*, Col. Edward Harland; 8th Conn., Lieut.-Col. Hiram Ap-

---

* Assigned to First Division, Second Army Corps, September 17.

† On the 16th and 17th, Major General Burnside exercised general command on the left, and Brigadier-General Cox was in immediate command of the corps.

‡ Killed September 14.

§ Wounded September 17.

pelman, Maj. John E. Ward; 11th Conn., Col. Henry W. Kingsbury; 16th Conn., Col. Francis Beach; 4th R. I., Col. William H. P. Steere, Lieut.-Col. Joseph B. Curtis. *Artillery*, 5th U. S., Batt. A, Lieut. Charles P. Muhlenberg.

KANAWHA DIVISION, (1) Brig.-Gen. Jacob D. Cox, (2) Col. Eliakim P. Scammon. *First Brigade*, (1) Col. Eliakim P. Scammon, (2) Col. Hugh Ewing; 12th Ohio, Col. Carr B. White; 23d Ohio, Lieut.-Col. Rutherford B. Hayes, Maj. James M. Comly; 30th Ohio, Col. Hugh Ewing, Lieut.-Col. Theodore Jones, Maj. George H. Hildt; Ohio Light Art., 1st Batt., Capt. James R. McMullin; Gilmore's co. W. Va. Cav., Lieut. James Abraham; Harrison's co. W. Va. Cav., Lieut. Dennis Delaney. *Second Brigade*, Col. George Crook; 11th Ohio, Lieut.-Col. Augustus H. Coleman, Maj. Lyman J. Jackson; 28th Ohio, Lieut.-Col. Gottfried Becker; 36th Ohio, Lieut.-Col. Melvin Clarke; Schambeck's co. Chicago Dragoons, Capt. Frederick Schambeck; Ky. Light Art., Simmonds's battery, Capt. Seth J. Simmonds. *Unattached*, 6th N. Y. Cav. (8 cos.), Col. Thomas C. Devin; Ohio Cav., 3d Ind. Co., Lieut. Jonas Seamen; 3d U. S. Art., Batts. L and M, Capt. John Edwards, Jr.

TWELFTH ARMY CORPS,* (1) MAJOR-GENERAL JOSEPH K. F. MANSFIELD,† (2) BRIGADIER-GENERAL ALPHEUS S. WILLIAMS. *Escort*, 1st Mich. Cav., Co. L, Capt. Melvin Brewer.

FIRST DIVISION, (1) Brig.-Gen. Alpheus S. Williams, (2) Brig.-Gen. Samuel W. Crawford,‡ (3) Brig.-Gen. George H. Gordon. *First Brigade*, (1) Brig.-Gen. Samuel W. Crawford, (2) Col. Joseph F. Knipe; 5th Conn., Capt. Henry W. Daboll; 10th Me., Col. George L. Beal; 28th N.Y., Capt. William H. H. Mapes; 46th Pa., Col. Joseph F. Knipe, Lieut.-Col. James L. Selfridge; 124th Pa., Col. Joseph W. Hawley, Maj. Isaac L. Haldeman; 125th Pa., Col. Jacob Higgins; 128th Pa., Col. Samuel Croasdale, Lieut.-Col. William W. Hamersly, Maj. Joel B. Wanner. *Third Brigade*, (1) Brig.-Gen. George H. Gordon, (2) Col. Thomas H. Ruger; 27th Ind., Col. Silas Colgrove; 2d Mass., Col. George L. Andrews; 13th N. J., Col. Ezra A. Carman; 107th N. Y., Col. R. B. Van Valkenburgh; Zouaves d'Afrique,§ Pa.; 3d Wis., Col. Thomas H. Ruger.

SECOND DIVISION, Brig.-Gen. George S. Greene:—*First Brigade*, (1) Lieut.-Col. Hector Tyndale,‡ (2) Maj. Orrin J. Crane; 5th Ohio, Maj. John Collins; 7th Ohio, Maj. Orrin J. Crane, Capt. Frederick A. Seymour; 29th Ohio,‖ Lieut. Theron S. Winship; 66th Ohio, Lieut.-Col. Eugene Powell; 28th Pa., Maj. Ario Pardee, Jr. *Second Brigade*, Col. Henry J. Stainrook; 3d Md., Lieut.-Col. Joseph M. Sudsburg; 102d N.Y.,

---

* Designation changed from Second Corps, Army of Virginia, to Twelfth Army Corps, by General Orders, No. 129, Adjutant-General's Office, September 12, 1862.

† Mortally wounded September 17.

‡ Wounded September 17.

§ No officers present; enlisted men of company attached to Second Massachusetts.

‖ Detached September 9.

Lieut.-Col. James C. Lane; 109th Pa.,* Capt. George E. Seymour; 111th Pa., Maj. Thomas M. Walker. *Third Brigade*, (1) Col. William B. Goodrich,† (2) Lieut.-Col. Jonathan Austin; 3d Del., Maj. Arthur Maginnis; Purnell Legion, Md., Lieut.-Col. Benjamin L. Simpson; 60th N. Y., Lieut.-Col. Charles R. Brundage; 78th N. Y., Lieut.-Col. Jonathan Austin, Capt. Henry R. Stagg. *Artillery*, Capt. Clermont L. Best; Me. Light, 4th Batt., Capt. O'Neil W. Robinson; Me. Light, 6th Batt., Capt. Freeman McGilvery; 1st N. Y. Light, Batt. M., Capt. George W. Cothran; N. Y. Light, 10th Batt., Capt. John T. Bruen; Pa. Light, Batt. E, Capt. Joseph M. Knap; Pa. Light, Batt. F, Capt. Robert B. Hampton; 4th U. S., Batt. F, Lieut. Edward D. Muhlenberg.

CAVALRY DIVISION, Brig.-Gen. Alfred Pleasonton:—*First Brigade*, Maj. Charles J. Whiting; 5th U. S., Capt. Joseph H. McArthur; 6th U. S., Capt. William P. Sanders. *Second Brigade*, Col. John F. Farnsworth; 8th Ill., Maj. William H. Medill; 3d Ind., Maj. George H. Chapman; 1st Mass., Capt. Casper Crowninshield; 8th Pa., Capt. Peter Keenan. *Third Brigade*, Col. Richard H. Rush; 4th Pa., Col. James H. Childs, Lieut.-Col. James K. Kerr; 6th Pa., Lieut.-Col. C. Ross Smith. *Fourth Brigade*, Col. Andrew T. McReynolds; 1st N. Y., Maj. Alonzo W. Adams; 12th Pa., Major James A. Congdon. *Fifth Brigade*, Col. Benj. F. Davis; 8th N. Y., Col. Benjamin F. Davis; 3d Pa., Lieut.-Col. Samuel W. Owen. *Artillery*, 2d U. S., Batt. A, Capt. John C. Tidball; 2d U. S., Batts. B and L, Capt. James M. Robertson; 2d U. S., Batt. M, Lieut. Peter C. Hains; 3d U. S., Batts. C and G, Capt. Horatio G. Gibson. *Unattached*, 1st Me. Cav.,‡ Col. Samuel H. Allen; 15th Pa. Cav. (detachment), Col. William J. Palmer.

---

* Detached September 13.
† Killed September 17.
‡ Detached at Frederick, Md.

CHAPTER XX.

REVIEW OF THE MARYLAND CAMPAIGN.

Confederate Expectations—General Lee's Salutatory to the People of Maryland—The "Lost Despatch"—McClellan's Movements—Turn in the Tide of War—A Miracle great as the throwing down of the Walls of Jericho—In Contempt of the Enemy the Confederate Army was dispersed—Harper's Ferry a "Man-Trap"—It diverted the Army from the Main Issue—Lee and McClellan compared and contrasted—Tribute to the Confederate Private Soldier.

FOR conveying to the reader a comprehensive view of the military zodiac at the time we crossed the quiet Potomac, the 5th day of September, 1862, and an understanding of the logical sequence of the events following, something should be added here to the plain narrative of occurrences, and so I undertake a review of the Maryland campaign.

The Army of Northern Virginia was afield without a foe. Its once grand adversary, discomfited under two commanders, had crept into cover of the bulwarks about the national capital. The commercial, social, and blood ties of Maryland inclined her people to the Southern cause. A little way north of the Potomac were inviting fields of food and supplies more plentiful than on the southern side; and the fields for march and manœuvre, strategy and tactics, were even more inviting than the broad fields of grain and comfortable pasture-lands. Propitious also was the prospect of swelling our ranks by Maryland recruits.

At the head of the army of sixty thousand men encouraged, matured, and disciplined by victory stood the Confederate chief, challenging on its own soil the army that had marched to conquer the Southern capital. On the 7th he pitched his bivouac about Frederick City. On the 8th he made his salutatory to the people in these words:

"HEAD-QUARTERS ARMY OF NORTHERN VIRGINIA,
"NEAR FREDERICKTOWN, MD., September 8, 1862.

"TO THE PEOPLE OF MARYLAND:

"It is right that you should know the purpose that brought the army under my command within the limits of your State, so far as that purpose concerns yourselves. The people of the Confederate States have long watched with the deepest sympathy the wrongs and outrages that have been inflicted upon the citizens of a commonwealth allied to the States of the South by the strongest social, political, and commercial ties. They have seen with profound indignation their sister State deprived of every right and reduced to the condition of a conquered province. Under the pretence of supporting the Constitution, but in violation of its most valuable provisions, your citizens have been arrested and imprisoned upon no charge and contrary to all forms of law. The faithful and manly protest against this outrage made by the venerable and illustrious Marylander, to whom in better days no citizen appealed for right in vain, was treated with scorn and contempt; the government of your chief city has been usurped by armed strangers; your legislature has been dissolved by the unlawful arrest of its members; freedom of the press and of speech has been suppressed; words have been declared offences by an arbitrary decree of the Federal Executive, and citizens ordered to be tried by a military commission for what they may dare to speak. Believing that the people of Maryland possessed a spirit too lofty to submit to such a government, the people of the South have long wished to aid you in throwing off this foreign yoke, to enable you again to enjoy the inalienable rights of freemen, and to restore independence and sovereignty to your State. In obedience to this wish, our army has come among you, and is prepared to assist you with the power of its arms in regaining the rights of which you have been despoiled.

"This, citizens of Maryland, is our mission, so far as you are concerned. No constraint upon your free will is intended; no intimidation will be allowed within the limits of this army, at least. Marylanders shall once more enjoy their ancient freedom of thought and speech. We know no enemies among you, and will protect all, of every opinion. It is for you to decide your destiny freely and without constraint. This army will respect your choice, whatever it may be; and while the Southern people will rejoice to welcome you to your natural position among them, they will only welcome you when you come of your own free will.

"R. E. Lee,
"*General, Commanding.*"

At this very time the recently displaced commander, General McClellan, reinstated in command, was marching for an opportunity to recover his good name, and the Union cavalry was active and aggressive in work against the Confederates at Poolesville.

On the 9th the Confederate commander organized his plans for the surrounding and capture of Harper's Ferry, and put his army in motion on the 10th. Close upon the heels of the march followed the Army of the Potomac, only twenty-five miles behind the rear of the Confederate army, with the cavalry of the armies in contact. The march of the former was as cautious as that of the latter was venturesome. On the 10th the Union commander was informed of the march of J. G. Walker's brigades up the river from Cheek's Ford. On the 11th his signal service reported the camp across the river at Point of Rocks. On the 12th, at Urbana, he was informed of the combination against Harper's Ferry, and the march towards the Cumberland Valley, and ordered pressing pursuit to force the Confederates to a stand. Under that order General Pleasonton, the Federal cavalry leader, hurried his troops and cleared the way to South Mountain on the 13th. From day to day the Confederates marched their diverging columns, from day to day the Union columns converged in easy, cautious marches. At noon of the 13th, General Lee's order distributing his forces and a despatch from the Governor of Pennsylvania were handed General McClellan,—the former the celebrated "lost despatch," given on a previous page,—the latter reading as follows:

"HARRISBURG, PA., September 13, 1862.

"MAJOR-GENERAL GEORGE B. McCLELLAN:

"When may we expect General Reynolds here? Services needed immediately. Longstreet's division is said to have reached Hagerstown last night. Jackson crossed the Potomac at Williamsport to capture Martinsburg and Harper's Ferry. We are assembling militia rapidly at Chambersburg. Can we do anything to aid your movements?

"A. G. CURTIN,
"*Governor of Pennsylvania.*"

This told of the change of march of my brigades from Turner's Pass to Hagerstown, and, with the "lost despatch," revealed that Hill's five brigades were the only troops at the former place.

The same afternoon General McClellan's signal service despatched him that the Union signal station on Maryland Heights had gone down. General Lee's signals failed to connect, so that General McClellan was better informed of the progress of the Confederate movements than was the Confederate commander. That afternoon the Union army was in hand for battle. The Confederates were dispersed and divided by rivers, and drifting thirty and forty and fifty miles apart. Under similar circumstances General Scott, or General Taylor, or General Worth would have put the columns at the base of South Mountain before night, and would have passed the unguarded gaps before the sun's rays of next morning could have lighted their western slopes.

The Union commander claims to have ordered more vigorous pursuit after the "lost despatch" was handed him, but there is nothing to support the claim except his call on General Franklin, and in that he only ordered preparation at Crampton's to await events at Turner's Pass.

General Pleasonton was at Turner's Pass on the afternoon of the 13th, and made a reconnoissance of the ways leading up the east side of the mountain. He was not informed of the despatches received by his chief, nor had he any information of Confederate movements except such as he had gleaned in closely following their rear. At daylight of the 14th he led General Cox and the Ninth Corps to attack, and in this manner the battle was opened.

His orders to call the Confederates to a stand did not anticipate the opening of a general engagement, but a wait for his chief, who rode up about one o'clock. The latter thought that he was battling against seventeen brigades, while there were but five; and, had the battle been held in wait for McClellan, his well-known habit of careful reconnoissance would have consumed the balance of the day. His last orders for General Franklin directed a wait for Couch's division, which joined him at eight o'clock in the evening. It is difficult to find that a quicker move was given the Union army in consequence of the "lost despatch;" but one may rather concede General Hill's claim, that in consequence of that despatch the Union army was so delayed as to give the Confederates time to make their way back to the soil of "Old Virginia." Without it, the main column of the Union forces could have marched through Crampton's Pass, and relieved Harper's Ferry on the 14th, but, guided by it, their commander found it important to first guard against the seventeen brigades that should be at Turner's Pass, on the right rear of a column, moving against Crampton's.

The razing of the walls of Jericho by encircling marches of priests and soldiers, at the signal of long-drawn blasts of sacred horns and shouts of the multitude, was scarcely a greater miracle than the transformation of the conquering army of the South into a horde of disordered fugitives before an army that two weeks earlier was flying to cover under its homeward ramparts.

Providence helps those who can avail themselves of

His tender care, but permits those who will to turn from Him to their own arrogance. That His gracious hand was with the Confederates in their struggles on the Chickahominy, and even through the errors of the Bull Run campaign, cannot be questioned. When, however, in self-confidence, they lost sight of His helping hand, and in contempt of the enemy dispersed the army, they were given up to the reward of vainglory. That the disaster was not overwhelming they have to thank the plodding methods of the Union commander. With as much faith as Captain Joshua, his success would have been as complete.

But for the proper solution of the campaign we must turn again to the condition of the Confederate army when it crossed into Maryland. It was then all that its leaders could ask, and its claim as master of the field was established, but it was worn by severe marches and battles, and in need of rest. Its record before and after shows that, held in hand and refreshed by easy marchings and comfortable supplies, it would have been prepared to maintain its supremacy. The first necessity was a little time to refresh, while the grand object was to draw the enemy from his intrenched lines to free and open battle. These facts carefully observed, the Confederate army would have been assured of its claim and prestige.

In the confusion about Washington incident to the Bull Run campaign, General McClellan was ordered to receive the retreating columns and post them to defend and hold their fortified lines. He had not emerged from the clouds that hung about his untoward campaign in Virginia, but, familiar with the provisions that had been made for defence, he was most available for the service. He had hardly posted the troops and arranged the garrison when he found that the Confederates, instead of moving against his fortifications, had turned the head of their columns north, and were marching to invade Union territory. He was quick to discover that it was his opportunity, and, after hastily posting guards for the works about the capital, assumed command of the army and took the field, lest another commander should be assigned. His clouded fame and assumption of authority committed him to early aggressive work. He had nothing to lose, and the world to gain, but only on the battle-field.

All that the Confederates had to do was to hold the army in hand and draw the enemy to a good field. When made, his battle was halting and balky, though thrown into his hands under most favorable circumstances, which goes to show that the Confederates, if held in hand and refreshed a little, could have made their grandest success.

It had been arranged that the Southern President should join the troops, and from the head of his victorious army call for recognition. Maryland would have put out some of her resources, and her gallant youth would have helped swell the Southern ranks,—the twenty thousand soldiers who had dropped from the Confederate ranks during the severe marches of the summer would have been with us. Volunteers from all parts of the South would have come, swimming the Potomac to find their President and his field-marshal, while Union troops would have been called from Kentucky and Tennessee, and would have left easy march for the Confederate armies of the West to the Ohio River.

Even though the Confederates were not successful, the fall elections were against the Federal administration. With the Southern armies victorious, the results of the contest at the polls would have been so pronounced as to have called for recognition of the Confederacy.

General McClellan wrote General Halleck of the effect, in case of defeat of his army,—

"But if we should be so unfortunate as to meet with defeat, our country is at their mercy."

So much has been said and written about Harper's Ferry and the surrender of the garrison, that it seems difficult to pass it without notice. In more than one report General McClellan mentioned it as a "shameful" surrender. He had disapproved the position as false, and asked if it could not be given up. Colonel Miles, the commander, who gave his life in its defence, was acting under the following order from the department commander,—viz.:

"BALTIMORE, September 5, 1862.

"COLONEL MILES, HARPER'S FERRY:

"The position on the heights ought to enable you to punish the enemy passing up the road in the direction of Harper's Ferry. Have your wits about you, and do all you can to annoy the rebels should they advance on you. Activity, energy, and decision must be used. You will not abandon Harper's Ferry without defending it to the last extremity.

"JOHN E. WOOL,
"*Major-General.*" *

The simple truth is, it was defended to the last extremity. The nearer the approach of the succoring army, the more imperative would have been the demand for action on the part of the Confederate columns, and had battle been forced it could not possibly have resulted in any save one way,—Confederate victory, and an overwhelming one at that.

The position was denounced as a "man-trap," and so it proved to Colonel Miles and his eleven thousand troops, but it was in fact a far more formidable trap for the Confederates, who to seize it sacrificed the fruits of heavy war,—victory in the main battle of the campaign,—and were forced to draw their crippled ranks to homeward defence. General Jackson wanted it till he got possession; then gave it up. General McClellan wanted to give it up before it was taken. After it had been taken

* Rebellion Record, vol. xix. part i. p. 520.

and given up, he reoccupied it. It was left severely alone in the Gettysburg campaign,—an admission by both sides of its uselessness as a *point d'appui.*

A word in closing about the chiefs opposed in this great campaign. General Lee and General McClellan were both graduates of the United States Military Academy at West Point. The former took the second honor of the class of 1829, the latter the second honor of the class of 1846. Their service in the United States army was as military engineers. In 1854 they were both selected by Secretary of War Jefferson Davis for promotion to the new cavalry regiments as lieutenant-colonel and captain respectively. Their early opportunities, social and educational, were superior. They studiously improved them in youth, and applied them with diligence in after-life. Aspirations leading to the higher walks of social and professional life seem to have been alike controlling forces in the character and career of each. They were not unmindful that physical development was important in support of mental improvement. In moral tone and habits they may be called exemplars. In his service, General Lee's pride was duty to his government and to the army under his command. He loved admiration of the outside world, but these duties better. General McClellan's ambition was not so limited.

In stature General Lee stood five feet ten inches, was of well-developed muscular figure, as trim as a youth, and weighed one hundred and seventy pounds. In features he was a model of manly beauty. His teeth were of ivory whiteness; his mouth handsome and expressive of frankness, kindness, and generosity. His nose and chin were full, regular, strong, and gave his face force and character. 'Twas seldom that he allowed his mind to wander to the days of his childhood, and talk of his father and his early associates, but when he did, he was far more charming than he thought. As a commander he was much of the

Wellington "Up-and-at-'em" style. He found it hard, the enemy in sight, to withhold his blows. With McClellan it was more difficult to strike than to march for the enemy.

General McClellan was of short, stout figure, but was of soldierly presence, graceful, and handsome-featured.

In their mounts neither of the great commanders lost anything of his admirable presence. Both were masters of the science but not of the art of war. Lee was successful in Virginia; McClellan in Maryland.

Unjust criticism has been passed upon the Confederate soldiers in the Maryland campaign, based principally upon the great number of absentees. To those who have spent their lives near the ranks of soldiers and learned from experience that there is a limit to physical endurance, explanation is not called for; to those who look upon the soldier as a machine, not even needing oil to facilitate motive power, I will say, try to put yourselves in the soldiers' places. Another point to be noted was, that in the Confederate ranks there were thousands of soldiers who had been wounded once, twice, and in some instances three times, who in any other service would have been on the pension-rolls at their comfortable homes.

Sickness and weakness that creep into an army from irregular food, collected in the stress of march, were no trifling impediments to the maintenance of our ranks in vigorous form.

When, in mature judgment, the historian builds monuments of words for the leaders of the campaign in Maryland, there will be flowers left for the private soldiers, and for the private soldiers' graves.

The full significance of Sharpsburg to the Federal authorities lay in the fact that they needed a victory on which to issue the Emancipation Proclamation, which President Lincoln had prepared two months before and had held in abeyance under advice of members of his

Cabinet until the Union arms should win a success. Although this battle was by no means so complete a victory as the President wished, and he was sorely vexed with General McClellan for not pushing it to completion, it was made the most of as a victory, and his Emancipation Proclamation was issued on the 22d of September, five days after the battle. This was one of the decisive political events of the war, and at once put the great struggle outwardly and openly upon the basis where it had before only rested by tacit and covert understanding. If the Southern army had been carefully held in hand, refreshed by easy marches and comfortable supplies, the proclamation could not have found its place in history. On the other hand, the Southern President would have been in Maryland at the head of his army with his manifesto for peace and independence.

CHAPTER XXI.

REORGANIZATION AND REST FOR BOTH ARMIES.

The Confederates appoint Seven Lieutenant-Generals—The Army of Northern Virginia organized in Corps—General McClellan relieved, and General Burnside appointed Commander of the Army of the Potomac—A Lift for the South—McClellan was growing—Burnside's "Three Grand Divisions"—The Campaign of the Rappahannock—Getting Ready for Fredericksburg—Longstreet occupies Fredericksburg—The Town called to surrender by General Sumner—Exodus of the Inhabitants under a Threat to shell the Town.

UNDER an act not long before passed by the Confederate Congress authorizing the appointment of seven lieutenant-generals, the authorities at Richmond about this time sent commissions to Lieutenant-Generals Longstreet, Polk, Holmes, Hardee, E. K. Smith, Jackson, and Pemberton, and made appointments of a number of major-generals. Under these appointments General Lee organized the Army of Northern Virginia into corps substantially as it subsequently fought the battle of Fredericksburg.*

The Confederate army rested along the lines between the Potomac and Winchester till late in October. On the 8th, General Stuart was ordered across to ride around the Union army, then resting about Sharpsburg and Harper's Ferry. His ride caused some excitement among the Union troops, and he got safely to the south side with the loss of a few men slightly wounded, on the 12th. On the 26th, General McClellan marched south and crossed the Potomac east of the Blue Ridge. Jackson was assigned the duty of guarding the passes. I marched south, corresponding with the march of the Army of the Potomac.

---

* See organization of the army appended to account of the battle of Fredericksburg.

A division crossed at Ashby's Gap to Upperville to look for the head of McClellan's army. He bore farther eastward and marched for Warrenton, where he halted on the 5th of November. The division was withdrawn from Upperville and marched for Culpeper Court-House, arriving at that point at the same time as McClellan's at Warrenton,—W. H. F. Lee's cavalry the day before me. Soon after the return to Culpeper Court-House, Evans's brigade was relieved of duty with the First Corps and ordered south. Hood had a brush with a cavalry force at Manassas Gap, and part of McLaws's division a similar experience at the east end of Chester Gap.

I reached Culpeper Court-House with the divisions of McLaws, R. H. Anderson, and Pickett. Hood's division was ordered behind Robertson River, and Ransom to Madison Court-House, General Jackson with the Second Corps remaining in the Shenandoah Valley, except one division at Chester Gap of the Blue Ridge.

The Washington authorities issued orders on the 5th of November relieving General McClellan of, and assigning General Burnside to, command of the Army of the Potomac. On the 9th the army was put under General Burnside, in due form.

When informed of the change, General Lee expressed regret, as he thought that McClellan could be relied upon to conform to the strictest rules of science in the conduct of war. He had been McClellan's preceptor, they had served together in the engineer corps, and our chief thought that he thoroughly understood the displaced commander. The change was a good lift for the South, however; McClellan was growing, was likely to exhibit far greater powers than he had yet shown, and could not have given us opportunity to recover the morale lost at Sharpsburg, as did Burnside and Hooker.

General Burnside, soon after assuming command, and while waiting at Warrenton, made a radical change in the organization of the army by consolidating the corps into three "Grand Divisions" as follows:

THE RIGHT GRAND DIVISION, GENERAL SUMNER COMMANDING.—Second Army Corps, General D. N. Couch; Ninth Army Corps, General O. B. Wilcox.

CENTRE GRAND DIVISION, GENERAL JOSEPH HOOKER COMMANDING.—Third Army Corps, General George Stoneman; Fifth Army Corps, General Daniel Butterfield.

LEFT GRAND DIVISION, GENERAL W. B. FRANKLIN COMMANDING.—First Army Corps, General J. F. Reynolds; Sixth Army Corps, General W. F. Smith.

CAVALRY DIVISION.—General Alfred Pleasonton.

Artillery, siege, and field batteries, 370 guns, General Henry J. Hunt, Chief.

At the time of the change of commanders the Confederates were looking for a Federal move north of Culpeper Court-House, and were surveying the ground behind Robertson River for a point of concentration of the two wings to meet that move.

General Burnside, however, promptly planned operations on other lines. He submitted to President Lincoln his proposition to display some force in the direction of Gordonsville as a diversion, while with his main army he would march south, cross the Rappahannock at Fredericksburg, and reach by a surprise march ground nearer Richmond than the holdings of the Confederates. This was approved by the President with the suggestion that its success depended upon prompt execution.

On the 15th light began to break upon the Confederates, revealing a move south from Warrenton, but it was not regarded as a radical change from the Orange and Alexandria Railroad line of advance. A battery of artillery was sent with a regiment of infantry to reinforce the Confederate outpost at Fredericksburg under Colonel Ball.

On the 17th information came that the Right Grand Division under General Sumner had marched south, leaving the railroad, and General W. H. F. Lee's cavalry was ordered to Fredericksburg.

The next morning I marched with two divisions, McLaws's and Ransom's, the former for Fredericksburg, the latter towards the North Anna. The same day, General Lee ordered a forced reconnoissance by his cavalry to Warrenton, found that the Union army was all on the march towards Fredericksburg, and ordered my other divisions to follow on the 19th.

At the first disclosure he was inclined to move for a position behind the North Anna, as at that time the position behind Fredericksburg appeared a little awkward for the Confederates, but, taking into careful consideration the position of the Union army on the Stafford side, the former appeared the less faulty of the two. Defence behind the Anna would have been stronger, but the advantage of the enemy's attack would also have been enhanced there. Then, too, anticipation of the effect of surprising the enemy in their intended surprise had some influence in favor of Fredericksburg.

The Burnside march was somewhat of the Horace Greeley "On-to-Richmond" *nolens-volens* style, which, if allowed to run on long enough, sometimes gains headway that is troublesome.

General Sumner reached Falmouth on the 17th, and proposed to cross, but his advance was met and forced back by Colonel Ball's command.

I rode with the leading division for Fredericksburg, and was on the heights on the 19th. My head-quarters were there when General Sumner called upon the civil authorities to surrender the city by the following communication:

"Head-Quarters Army of the Potomac,
"November 21, 1862.

"Mayor and Common Council of Fredericksburg:

"Gentlemen,—Under cover of the houses of your city shots have been fired upon the troops of my command. Your mills and manufactories are furnishing provisions and the material for clothing for armed bodies in rebellion against the government of the United States. Your railroads and other means of transportation are removing supplies to the depots of such troops. This condition of things must terminate, and, by direction of General Burnside, I accordingly demand the surrender of the city into my hands, as the representative of the government of the United States, at or before five o'clock this afternoon.

"Failing an affirmative reply to this demand by the hour indicated, sixteen hours will be permitted to elapse for the removal from the city of women and children, the sick and wounded and aged, etc., which period having expired, I shall proceed to shell the town. Upon obtaining possession of the city, every necessary means will be taken to preserve order and secure the protective operation of the laws and policy of the United States government.

"I am, very respectfully, your obedient servant,

"E. V. Sumner,

"*Bvt. Maj.-Gen. U. S. Army, commanding Right Grand Division.*" *

The officers who received the call, by consent of General Patrick, who delivered it, referred the paper to my head-quarters. I asked the civil authorities to reply that the city would not be used for the purposes complained of, but that neither the town nor the south side of the river could be occupied by the Union army except by force of arms.

General Sumner ordered two batteries into position commanding the town, but in a few hours received the following reply from the mayor:

"Mayor's Office,

"Fredericksburg, November 21, 1862.

"Brevet Major-General E. V. Sumner,

"*Commanding U. S. Army:*

"Sir,—I have received, at 4.40 o'clock this afternoon, your communication of this date. In it you state that, under cover of the houses of this town, shots have been fired upon the troops of your command; that our mills and manufactories are furnishing provisions and the material for clothing for armed bodies in

* Rebellion Record, vol. xxi. part i. p. 783.

rebellion against the government of the United States; that our railroads and other means of transportation are removing supplies to the depots of such troops; that this condition of things must terminate; that, by command of Major-General Burnside, you demand the surrender of this town into your hands, as the representative of the government of the United States, at or before five o'clock this afternoon; that, failing an affirmative reply to this demand by the time indicated, sixteen hours will be permitted to elapse for the removal from the town of the women and children, the sick, wounded, and aged, which period having elapsed, you will proceed to shell the town.

"In reply I have to say that this communication did not reach me in time to convene the Council for its consideration, and to furnish a reply by the hour indicated (five P.M.). It was sent to me through the hands of the commanding officer of the Confederate States near this town, to whom it was first delivered, by consent of General Patrick, who bore it from you, as I am informed, and I am authorized by the commander of the Confederate army to say that there was no delay in passing it through his hands to me.

"In regard to the matters complained of by you, the firing of shot upon your troops occurred upon the northern suburbs of the town, and was the act of the military officer commanding the Confederate forces near here, for which matter (neither) the citizens nor civil authorities of this town are responsible. In regard to the other matters of complaint, I am authorized by the latter officer to say that the condition of things therein complained of shall no longer exist; that your troops shall not be fired on from this town; that the mills and manufactories here will not furnish any further supplies of provisions or material for clothing for the Confederate troops, nor will the railroads or other means of transportation here convey supplies from the town to the depots of said troops.

"Outside of the town the civil authorities of Fredericksburg have no control, but I am assured by the military authorities of the Confederate army near here that nothing will be done by them to infringe the conditions herein named as to matters within the town. But the latter authorities inform us that, while their troops will not occupy the town, they will not permit yours to do so.

"You must be aware that there will not be more than three or four hours of daylight within the sixteen hours given by you for the removal of the sick and wounded, the women and children, the aged and infirm, from this place; and I have to inform you that, while there is no railroad transportation accessible to the town, because of the interruption thereof by your batteries, all other means of transportation within the town are so limited as to render the removal of the classes of persons spoken of within the time indicated as an utter impossibility.

"I have convened the Council, which will remain in session awaiting any further communications you may have to make.

"Very respectfully, your obedient servant,

"M. SLAUGHTER,

"*Mayor.*"

To this General Sumner responded the same day,—

"MAYOR AND COMMON COUNCIL OF FREDERICKSBURG, VA.:

"Your letter of this afternoon is at hand, and, in consideration of your pledges that the acts complained of shall cease, and that your town shall not be occupied by any of the enemy's forces, and your assertion that a lack of transportation renders it impossible to remove the women, children, sick, wounded, and aged, I am authorized to say to you that our batteries will not open upon your town at the hour designated.

"General Patrick will meet a committee or representative from your town to-morrow morning, at nine o'clock, at the Lacy House.

"Very respectfully, your obedient servant,

"E. V. SUMNER,

"*Brevet Major-General, U. S. Army, Commanding Division.*"

As the inference from the correspondence was that the shelling was only postponed, the people were advised to move with their valuables to some place of safety as soon as possible. Without complaint, those who could, packed their precious effects and moved beyond reach of the threatened storm, but many preferred to remain and encounter the dangers rather than to leave their homes and valuables. The fortitude with which they bore their trials quickened the minds of the soldiers who were there to defend them. One train leaving with women and children was fired upon, making some confusion and dismay among them, but the two or three shells did no other mischief, and the firing ceased.

CHAPTER XXII.

BATTLE OF FREDERICKSBURG.

Description of the Field—Marye's Heights—Position of the Troops of Longstreet's Command—General Jackson called down from Orange Court-House, and Preparations made for a Determined Stand—Signal Guns at Three o'Clock in the Morning announce the Long-Expected Battle—Burnside's Bridge-Builders thrice driven back from their Work—The Crossing finally made by Boats—Federals under Hot Fire enter Fredericksburg—How they obtained their Foothold on the West Bank of the Rappahannock—Gallant Officers and Men—Ninety-seven killed or wounded in the Space of Fifty Yards—General Burnside's Plan of Battle—Strength of the Contending Forces.

McLaws's division of the First Corps was posted on the heights in rear of the city, one brigade in the sunken road in front of the Marye mansion, the others extending across the Telegraph road through the wood of Lee's Hill. As the other divisions of the corps came up they were posted, R. H. Anderson on Taylor's Hill; Ransom in reserve, near corps head-quarters; Pickett in the wood, in rear of McLaws's right; Hood at Hamilton's Crossing.

The Federal Grand Divisions under Franklin and Hooker marched on the 18th of November, and on the 19th pitched their camps, the former at Stafford Court-House, and the latter at Hartwood, each about ten miles from Falmouth. A mile and a half above Fredericksburg the Rappahannock cuts through a range of hills, which courses on the north side in a southeasterly direction, nearly parallel, and close to its margin. This range (Stafford Heights) was occupied by the enemy for his batteries of position, one hundred and forty-seven siege guns and long-range field batteries. These heights not only command those of the west, but the entire field and flats opened by the spreading out of the range on the west side. At points, however, they stand so close beside the river that the guns on their crest could not be so depressed as to plunge their fire to the water. The heights are cut at points by streamlets and ravines leading into the river, and level up gradually as they approach nearer to the Potomac on its west slope, and towards the sea on the south. The city of Fredericksburg nestles under those heights on the opposite bank. McLaws had a brigade on picket service, extending its guard up and down the banks of the river, in connection with details from R. H. Anderson's division above and Hood's below, the latter meeting Stuart's cavalry vedettes lower down.

At the west end of the ridge where the river cuts through is Taylor's Hill (the Confederate left), which stands at its highest on a level with Stafford Heights. From that point the heights on the south side spread, unfolding a valley about a mile in width, affording a fine view of the city, of the arable fields, and the heights as they recede to the vanishing limits of sight. Next below Taylor's is Marye's Hill, rising to half the elevation of the neighboring heights and dropping back, leaving a plateau of half a mile, and then swelling to the usual altitude of the range. On the plateau is the Marye mansion. Along its base is a sunken road, with retaining walls on either side. That on the east is just breast-high for a man, and just the height convenient for infantry defence and fire. From the top of the breast-work the ground recedes gradually till near the canal, when it drops off three or four feet, leaving space near the canal of a rod or two of level ground. The north end of the sunken road cuts into the plank or Gordonsville road, which is an extension of Hanover Street from near the heart of the town. At the south end it enters the Telegraph road, extending out from the town limits and up over the third, or Telegraph Hill, called, in its bloody baptismal, "Lee's Hill." An unfinished railroad lies along the Telegraph road as far as the highlands. The Fredericksburg and

Potomac Railroad lies nearly parallel with the river four miles, and then turns south through the highlands. The old stage road from the city runs about half-way between the river and the railroad four miles, when it turns southwest and crosses the railroad at Hamilton's Crossing. The hamlet of Falmouth, on the north side of the river, was in front of the right centre of the Federal position, half a mile from Fredericksburg.

General Jackson, advised of General Burnside's move to Fredericksburg, drew his corps east of the Blue Ridge as far as Orange Court-House.

Before the end of November it became evident that Fredericksburg was to be our winter station and the scene of a severe battle before it could be relieved. General Lee advised the citizens who still remained in the place (and some who had returned) to remove their effects. Those who had friends found comfortable places of rest, but many took the little that they could get away with, and made their homes in the deep forest till the storm could pass. Still, none complained of the severe ordeal which they were called upon to endure.

Towards the latter part of the month General Jackson was called down and assigned position on the right near Hamilton's Crossing and the Massaponax. He objected to the position, preferring the North Anna, but General Lee had already weighed the matter, and had decided in favor of Fredericksburg. Hood's division, relieved at Hamilton's Crossing, was drawn to my right and stretched across the valley of Deep Run, a little to the rear of Jackson's left and McLaws's right.

Batteries of position were assigned from the reserve artillery along the heights, with orders to cover the guns, by epaulements or pitting them. The work was progressing while the guns were held under cover remote from the enemy's better appointed artillery until the positions were covered by solid banks or good pits. The small field pieces were removed for safety to convenient points for field service in case opportunity called for them. The Confederates had three hundred and six guns, including two thirty-pound Parrotts of Richmond make. These were covered by epaulements on Lee's Hill.

On the 1st of December the batteries of reserve artillery were relieved from the First Corps by those of the Washington and Alexander's artillery. Orders were given to examine all lines of approach, and to measure particularly the distance of the crossings of the canal on the Plank and Telegraph roads; to inspect and improve the parapets and pits along the front, and to traverse all batteries not securely covered against the batteries opposite Taylor's Hill, and others within range of our lines, and McLaws was directed to open signal line with his brigade and guards along the river bank.

The day after Jackson joined us several gun-boats were reported in the lower river at Port Royal. D. H. Hill's division was detached with several select batteries to watch and guard at that point against a crossing, should it be attempted, and to engage and try the metal of the gun-boats. After some little practice the boats drew off and dropped down-stream; but Hill's division was left near the point in observation with W. H. F. Lee's cavalry. The brigade of cavalry under General Hampton kept careful watch of the fords of the upper Rappahannock. To guard against further encroachments of the gun-boats, a battery was intrenched on the river bank under direction of Major T. M. R. Talcot, of the general staff. At the river, sharp-shooters, by concealing themselves in the ravines and pits, could escape artillery fire and lie in secure readiness to attack parties engaged in laying bridges. After driving off working parties they were to seek cover till again needed. By such practice they were to delay the bridge-builders till the commands had time to assemble at their points of rendezvous. The narrow, deep bed of the stream, a mile away from any point of the Confederate lines where batteries could be planted, and covered as it was by the guns of Stafford Heights, prevented the thought of successful resistance to laying bridges at any point from Falmouth to the extreme left of the Federal line; but the strong ground upon which the Confederates were to accept battle offset the uncomfortable feeling in regard to the crossing of the river.

General Burnside made some show of disposition to cross fourteen miles below, at Skinker's Neck, but that was under guard of D. H. Hill's division, and he saw that his purpose could not be effected. The plan which he finally adopted was to span the river by bridges near the centre and lower limits of the city, and two others a mile below the latter, and just below the mouth of Deep Run, the Right Grand Division to cross by the upper and second bridges, the Left Grand Division by the lower bridges, and the Centre Grand Division to be in position near the others to reinforce their battle.

The stir and excitement about the enemy's camps on the 10th of December, as well as the reports of scouts, gave notice that important movements were pending. Notice was given the commands, and the batteries were ordered to have their animals in harness an hour before daylight of the next morning, and to continue to hitch up daily at that hour until further orders.

At three o'clock on the morning of the 11th the deep boom of a cannon aroused both armies, and a second gun was recognized as the signal for battle. In a few minutes the commands were on the march for their positions. Orders were sent to call D. H. Hill's division and all of the Second Corps to their ground along the woodland over Hamilton's Crossing.

Barksdale's brigade of Mississippians was on picket duty in Fredericksburg at the time; the Seventeenth and Eighteenth Regiments, with the Eighth Florida, of R. H. Anderson's division, were on the river line; the other regiments of the brigade and the Third Georgia, of R. H. Anderson's, in reserve.

The first noise made by the enemy's bridge-builders was understood by the picket guards, as was all of their early work of construction, but a heavy mist along the water concealed them from view until their work upon the bridge was well advanced. As soon as the forms of the workmen could be discerned the skirmishers opened fire, which was speedily answered from the other side in efforts to draw the fire from the bridge-builders, but the Confederates limited their attention to the builders till they were driven off, when they ceased firing. Another effort to lay the bridge met a like result. Then a third received the same stormy repulse, when it seemed that all the cannon within a mile of the town turned their concentrating fire of shot and shell upon the buildings of the devoted city, tearing, crushing, bursting, burning their walls with angry desperation that must have been gratifying to spirits deep down below.

Under the failures to lay the bridge, General Hunt suggested that the pontoon-boats be filled with infantrymen, rushed across and landed on the other bank until a sufficient force was in position to protect the bridge-builders. Barksdale had been notified before noon that the army was in position, and that he could withdraw his troops at any moment, but he preferred his little fight in Fredericksburg. At four o'clock, when the landing was made by the boats, he thought the city safe against artillery practice, and was pleased to hold till night could cover his withdrawal.

Colonel Norman J. Hall, of the Seventh Michigan Regiment, commanded the troops working for a foothold on the west bank. After the several attempts to have the bridge built, he accepted General Hunt's proposition to load the boats and have the men push across. Lieutenant-

Colonel Baxter, commanding the regiment, volunteered to lead the party. Captain Weymouth, of the Nineteenth Massachusetts, proposed to support the move. Under signal for artillery fire to cease, the command of Lieutenant-Colonel Baxter pushed across. Under the best fire the pickets could bring to bear only one man was killed and Lieutenant-Colonel Baxter and several men were wounded. The party of seventy were rushed up the bank, gained position, captured some prisoners, and were soon reinforced. The enemy's fire over the west bank was so sweeping that Barksdale could not reinforce at the point of landing. The Nineteenth Massachusetts was deployed to the right, and the Seventh Michigan to the left. The Twenty-eighth Massachusetts reinforced them. The Twelfth and Fifty-ninth New York and One Hundred and Twenty-seventh Pennsylvania Regiments joined the command in the city. Colonel Hall found that he must prepare for some fighting, and speedily, as night was coming on. He sent to the rear to ask for time to prepare and make his fight to suit him, but was hurried on by the division pushing forward to get across the bridge, with orders to secure the streets at all hazards. The Seventh Michigan and Nineteenth Massachusetts had been brought to a stand, when the Twenty-eighth Massachusetts was rushed forward in gallant style. Colonel Hall reported, "Platoon after platoon were swept away, but the head of the column did not falter. Ninety-seven officers and men were killed or wounded in the space of about fifty yards." The eastern part of the town was occupied, and at a late hour of the night the Confederates retired.

As Barksdale's brigade withdrew, he was relieved at the sunken road by the Eighteenth and Twenty-fourth Georgia Regiments and Cobb's Georgia Legion, General T. R. R. Cobb in command.

The Third Grand Division had no severe work in laying the bridges below Deep Run, and were ready for co-operation some hours in advance of the right.

The Federals occupied the 12th in moving the Right Grand Division into the city by the upper bridges, and the Left Grand Division by the bridges below Deep Creek. One hundred and four guns crossed with the right, one hundred and twenty with the left. The Centre Grand Division was held in reserve. Two divisions of the Third Corps were sent to the lower bridges during the night to support the battle of the left, and were ordered over on the 13th.

The plan of battle by the Federal commander, in brief, was to drive the Confederate right back into the highlands and follow that success by attacking the Confederate left by his Right Grand Division.

The *beginning* only of this plan was carried out. The Left Grand Division having duly crossed the river at the lower bridges on the 12th,—the Sixth Corps and Bayard's brigade of cavalry, then the First Corps,—the Sixth deployed two divisions, supported by the third, parallel to the old Richmond road; the First formed at right angles to the Sixth, its right on the left of the Sixth, its left on the river, two divisions on the front line, one in support. The cavalry was sent out to reconnoitre. The entire field of the command was an open plain between the highlands and the river, traversed by the old Richmond road, which had well-formed embankments and ditches on both sides.

The Federal troops of their left divisions were in full view of the heights (Lee's Hill) occupied by the Confederates; those of the right were concealed by the buildings of Fredericksburg and under the river banks, and their bridges were under the steep also. The two brigades on the right of the Sixth Corps were to the right of Deep Run; the others, of the First and Sixth Corps, on the left. The batteries of the corps were under authority of corps commanders. There were but few shots exchanged during the 12th, and these not of great damage.

On the Confederate side the First Corps (Longstreet's) was in position from Taylor's Hill across Deep Run Bottom. The Second Corps was in mass about the wooded heights at Hamilton's Crossing. His cavalry and horse artillery were on his right in the Massaponax Valley. General R. Ransom's division was posted in rear of the left of Marye's Hill; his Twenty-fourth North Carolina Regiment was advanced to the left of Cobb's line in the sunken road. His brigade under Colonel Cooke was deployed as sharp-shooters on the crest of the hill. He was especially charged with looking after the left of Cobb's line. In front of this line and about six hundred yards from it was a canal, or large wet ditch, about four hundred yards out from the city limits. The crossings at the Plank and Telegraph roads had been bridged, and the bridges were ordered wrecked, but were only partially destroyed, the string-pieces being left in place. The corps in position, the Confederate commander prepared to stand and receive battle.

In concluding this account of the confronting armies on the eve of battle, let us glance at their relative strength as expressed in numbers.

The Army of the Potomac, as reported by General Burnside, had on December 10 an "aggregate present for duty" of 132,017 * officers and men (not including cavalry). The Army of Northern Virginia was reported by General Lee on the same date to have had an aggregate of 69,391 † (not including cavalry).

* Rebellion Record, vol. xxi. part i. p. 1121.
† Ibid., p. 1057.

CHAPTER XXIII.

BATTLE OF FREDERICKSBURG (CONTINUED).

The Battle-field veiled by a Heavy Fog—Terrific Fighting of the 13th of December—Forlorn Hope of the Federals—General Meade's Division of Franklin's Command makes the First Advance—General French leads against the Confederate Left—Hancock follows—General Cobb killed—The Sunken Road and Stone Wall below Marye's Hill—Desperate Advances and Determined Repulses—Humphreys's Heroic Assault—The Stone Wall "a Sheet of Flame"—General Jackson loses his Opportunity to advance—The Charge of Meade's Divisions compared with that of Pickett, Pettigrew, and Trimble's Columns at Gettysburg—Forty Per Cent. killed in charging Lines here, and Sixty Per Cent. at Gettysburg—Total Losses—Peace to be declared because Gold had gone to 200—Organization of the Army of Northern Virginia.

On the morning of the 13th of December the confronting armies, which were destined that day to clash in one of the bloodiest conflicts of the war, stood completely veiled from each other's sight by an impenetrable mist. The entire Confederate army was now for the first time upon the field, for General Jackson had during the night brought up his scattered divisions from down the river.

Before daylight I rode to view my line and troops from right to left. Hood's division on the right was found on the alert, as was the enemy near that point. The voices of the Union officers as they gave their commands were carried to us with almost startling clearness by the heavy fog that covered the field and surroundings. So heavy was this fog that nothing could be seen at a distance of ten or twelve rods, and yet so distinctly were the voices of the officers brought to us that they seemed quite near at hand, and General Hood was looking for assaulting columns against his front. He was told that such move would put the enemy's column in a *cul-de-sac*, and therefore his position was in no danger of attack; that the attack would be aimed against Jackson's front; that in case it broke through there he should swing around to his right and take the attacking forces in reverse; that Pickett's division would be ordered to a corresponding move on his left, with the batteries of the two divisions in the plain off the left; that my front would be attacked, but it was safely posted, and not likely to need other than the troops on that ground. Pickett's command was under arms, expecting orders. They were given instructions similar to those just mentioned for Hood. The divisions of McLaws, Ransom, and R. H. Anderson were in readiness, as were all the batteries. But the fog, nothing abated, hung so heavy that not a sight for a cannon-shot was open till a late hour of the morning.

The front of the Second Corps was occupied by A. P. Hill's division, the brigades of Archer, Lane, and Pender on the first line; those of Thomas, Gregg, and Brockenbrough on the second. A third line was occupied by Taliaferro's and Early's divisions. D. H. Hill's division was off to the rear of the right. Lieutenant-Colonel Walker posted a fourteen-gun battery of the division artillery on A. P. Hill's right, and two other field batteries on the plain on his left. Stuart's horse artillery and cavalry were on the plain on the right, in the valley of the Massaponax, supporting the Second Corps.

About 7.45 in the morning General Hardie, of Burnside's staff, reported to General Franklin that his orders would reach him in a few minutes by the hands of an aide-de-camp. Hardie was ordered to remain near General Franklin's head-quarters. At eight o'clock the order came, and at 8.30 Meade's division moved towards the general direction of Jackson's position.

At ten o'clock the fog lifted and revealed Meade's lines, six batteries on his left and four on his right, Gibbon's division supporting the right and Doubleday's covering the left. The order for the commander of the Left Grand

Division was to make the advance by at least one division. The divisions of the First Corps were thought to fully meet the terms of the order.

Meade's lines advanced in handsome, solid ranks, leaving heavy reserves of the Sixth Corps and two divisions of the Third that had been called over from the Centre Grand Division. The fire of Stuart's horse artillery against their left caused delay until some of the batteries of the left engaged and drove off the fire. After half an hour's delay the advance was resumed, the batteries thrown to the front to shell the field in search of the Confederate batteries. The latter had been ordered, for the most part, to reserve their fire for infantry. After an hour's heavy artillery practice Meade's march was resumed, and with great vigor, the batteries ploughing the way for the infantry columns. At the same time the fourteen-gun battery of A. P. Hill's right and his left batteries replied with equal spirit and practice, though with unequal metal.

The view of the battle of the enemy's left burst upon us at Lee's Hill, as the mist rolled away under the bright noonday sun. We noted the thin, pale smoke of infantry fire fading in the far away of their left, the heavy clouds rising from the batteries on both sides of the river, the bright armored ranks and banners, and our elevation seemed to draw them so close to us, on their right, that we thought to turn our best guns upon that part of the line, and General Lee authorized the test of their range. Only a few shots were sent when the troops that had been lying concealed in the streets of the city came flying out by both roads in swarms at double time and rushed towards us. Every gun that we had in range opened upon the advancing columns and ploughed their ranks by a fire that would test the nerves of the bravest soldiers. But the battle of the Federal left had the first opening, and calls for first notice.

THE BATTLE OF FREDERICKSBURG, FROM THE BATTERY ON LEE'S HILL.

Under a strong artillery combat Meade marched forward, with Gibbon's division in close support on his right, and Doubleday's farther off on his left. The line encountered Lane's brigade front in a steady, hard fight, and, developing against Archer's left, broke through, forcing the brigades back, encountered Thomas's and Gregg's brigades, threw the latter into confusion, and killed General Gregg. Brockenbrough's and Pender's brigades turned against the penetrating columns and were forced back. Under skilful handling the brigades finally brought the battle to steady work, but Meade's impetuous onward march was bravely made and pressed until three brigades of Early's division were advanced and thrown into action, commanded by Colonels Atkinson, Walker, and Hoke. These, with the combined fire of Hill's broken lines, forced Meade back. Two regiments of Berry's brigade of the Third Corps came to the relief of Meade and were driven back, when Gibbon's division which followed was met, and after severe battle was repulsed. The Confederates made a partial following of the success, beyond the railroad, and until they encountered the fire of the relieving divisions under Birney and Sickles and the reserve batteries. Doubleday's division protected Meade's left as Jackson's right under Taliaferro partially engaged against them; both encountered loss. Hood got one of his brigades in in time to follow the troops as they retired towards their reserve line. At the first moment of the break on Jackson's lines Pickett rode to Hood and urged that the opportunity anticipated was at hand, but Hood failed to see it in time for effective work. About two P.M. the battle quieted into defensive practice of artillery and sharp-shooters.

The opening against the Confederate left, before referred to, was led by French's division of the Second Corps, about 10.30. The Eighteenth and Twenty-fourth Georgia Regiments, Cobb's Georgia Legion, and the

Twenty-fourth North Carolina Regiment were in the sunken road, the salient point. On Marye's Hill, back and above, was the Washington Artillery, with nine guns, Ransom's and Cooke's North Carolina brigade in open field, the guns under partial cover, pitted. Other batteries on Taylor's and Lee's Hills posted to this defence as many as twenty guns, holding under range by direct and cross fire the avenues of approach and the open field along Cobb's front.

French's division came in gallant style, but somewhat hurried. He gathered his ranks behind the swell of ground near the canal and moved to the assault. An intervening plank fence gave the troops some trouble in crossing under fire, so that his ranks were not firm after passing it to the attack. Hancock, coming speedily with his division, was better organized and in time to take up the fight as French was obliged to retire. This advance was handsomely maintained, but the galling fire they encountered forced them to open fire. Under this delay their ranks were cut up as rapidly as they had collected at the canal, and when within a hundred yards of the stone wall they were so thinned that they could do nothing but surrender, even if they could leap to the road-bed. But they turned, and the fire naturally slackened, as their hurried steps took them away to their partial cover. The troops behind the stone wall were reinforced during this engagement by two of Cooke's regiments from the hill-top, ordered by General Ransom, and General McLaws ordered part of Kershaw's brigade in on their right.

After Hancock's engagement some minutes passed before arrangements were made for the next. Howard's division had been feeling for a way to get by Cobb's left, when he was called to the front attack, and ordered over the same ground. He arranged his forces with care, and advanced in desperate fight. Under the severe fire of the Confederates his troops were provoked to return fire, and during the delay thus caused his ranks were so speedily decimated that they in turn were obliged to return to cover. The Confederate commander, General Cobb, was killed. General Kershaw, with the other regiments of his brigade, was ordered to the front. The Washington Artillery, exhausted of ammunition, was relieved by guns of Alexander's battalion. The change of batteries seemed to give new hope to the assaulting forces. They cheered and put in their best practice of sharp-shooters and artillery. The greater part of Alexander's loss occurred while galloping up to his position. General Ransom advanced the other regiments of his brigade to the crest of the hill. At the suggestion of General Lee the brigades of Jenkins and Kemper of Pickett's division were called up and assigned, the former to General McLaws and the latter to General Ransom. A supply of ammunition was sent down to the troops in the road in time to meet the next attack, by Sturgis's division of the Ninth Corps, which made the usual brave fight, and encountered the same damaging results. Getty's division of the Ninth Corps came to his support on the left, but did not engage fiercely, losing less than eight hundred men. Carroll's brigade of Whipple's division, Third Corps, came in on Sturgis's left, but only to brace that part of the fight.

As the troops hurried forward from the streets of the city for the Telegraph road, they came at once under the fire of the long-range guns on Lee's Hill. The thirty-pound Parrotts were particularly effective in having the range and dropping their shells in the midst of the columns as they dashed forward. Frequently commands were broken up by this fire and that of other long-range guns, and sought shelter, as they thought, in the railroad cut, but that point was well marked, and the shots were dropped in, in enfilade fire, with precision, often making wide gaps in their ranks. The siege guns of Stafford Heights gave their especial attention to our heavy guns and put their shots over the parapets very often.

One shell buried itself close under the parapet at General Lee's side, as he sat among the officers of his staff, but it failed to explode. Soon after this our big Parrott gun burst into many fragments. It was closely surrounded by General Lee and staff, officers of the First Corps head-quarters, and officers and gunners of the battery, but the explosion caused no other damage than the loss of the gun.

Griffin's division was next ordered to attack, and made the usual desperate struggle. The Confederates meanwhile had accumulated such force in the road that a single division, had it reached that point, would have found its equal in numbers, and of greater vigor, with Ransom at the top of the hill prepared to rush down and join in the mêlée. At that hour we could have safely invited one division into our midst, if assured it was to be the last.

The next attack was made by Humphreys's division. Its commander was a man of superior attainments and accomplishments in the walks of civil as well as military life. He measured justly the situation, and arranged his battle in the only order by which success could have been made possible, but he had only two brigades with which to take a position not assailable and held by more than three brigades of superior troops. His troops were new, so that he felt called to personal example as well as skilful handling. He ordered the attack with empty muskets, and led with his brigade commanders, but half-way up towards the goal his men stopped to load and open fire, which neither he nor his officers could prevent, so they were driven back. Then he made a like effort with his other brigade, under special orders from Generals Burnside and Hooker that the point must be carried before night,—and the dew was then falling. (Just then our second big

Parrott gun went into fragments, but without damage to the men.) The troops that had been driven back from previous attacks joined in trying to persuade Humphreys's men not to go forward. Notwithstanding the discouraging surroundings, he led his men on, encountered the same terrific and death-dealing opposition, and his men retired in greater confusion, going beyond his control to the vicinity of the city before he could get them again in ranks. His account of the last effort is interesting:

"The stone wall was a sheet of flame that enveloped the head and flanks of the column. Officers and men were falling rapidly, and the head of the column was at length brought to a stand when close up to the wall. Up to this time not a shot had been fired by the column, but now some firing began. It lasted but a minute, when, in spite of all our efforts, the column turned and began to retire slowly. I attempted to rally the brigade behind the natural embankment so often mentioned, but the united efforts of General Tyler, myself, our staff, and other officers could not arrest the retiring mass." *

At that time there were three brigades behind the stone wall and one regiment of Ransom's brigade. The ranks were four or five deep,—the rear files loading and passing their guns to the front ranks, so that the volleys by brigade were almost incessant pourings of solid sheets of lead.

Two brigades of Sykes's division, First and Second Regulars, were sent to the front to guard the line. It was some time after nightfall, so that their line could only be distinguished by the blaze of their fire. Some of the batteries and infantry engaged against their fire till night was well advanced.

General Jackson thought to advance against the enemy's left late in the afternoon, but found it so well posted and guarded that he concluded the venture would be too hazardous. He lost his opportunity, failing to follow close upon the repulse of Meade's and Gibbon's divisions. His

* Rebellion Record, vol. xxi. part i. p. 432.

command was massed and well in hand, with an open field for infantry and artillery. He had, including the divisions of Hood and Pickett,—ordered to work with him,—about fifty thousand men. Franklin had, including troops of the Centre Grand Division, about equal force.

The charge of Meade's division has been compared with that of Pickett's, Pettigrew's, and Trimble's at Gettysburg, giving credit of better conduct to the former. The circumstances do not justify the comparison.

When the fog lifted over Meade's advance he was within musket-range of A. P. Hill's division, closely supported on his right by Gibbon's, and guarded on his left by Doubleday's division. On Hill's right was a fourteen-gun battery, on his left eight guns. Meade broke through Hill's division, and with the support of Gibbon forced his way till he encountered part of Ewell's division, when he was forced back in some confusion. Two fresh divisions of the Third Corps came to their relief, and there were as many as fifty thousand men at hand who could have been thrown into the fight. Meade's march to meet his adversary was half a mile,—the troops of both sides fresh and vigorous.

Of the assaulting columns of Pickett, Pettigrew, and Trimble, only four thousand seven hundred under Pickett were fresh; the entire force of these divisions was only fifteen thousand strong. They had a mile to march over open field before reaching the enemy's line, strengthened by field-works and manned by thrice their numbers. The Confederates at Gettysburg had been fought to exhaustion of men and munitions. They lost about sixty per cent. of the assaulting forces,—Meade about forty. The latter had fresh troops behind him, and more than two hundred guns to cover his rallying lines. The Confederates had nothing behind them but field batteries almost exhausted of ammunition. That Meade made a brave, good fight is beyond question, but he had superior numbers and appointments. At Gettysburg the Confederate assault was made against intrenched lines of artillery and infantry, where stood fifty thousand men.

A series of braver, more desperate charges than those hurled against the troops in the sunken road was never known, and the piles and cross-piles of dead marked a field such as I never saw before or since.

Between 1.30 and 2.30 of the afternoon several orders and messages were sent by General Burnside calling on General Franklin to renew the battle of the left. Before 2.30 he received from General Burnside, through his aide-de-camp, Captain Goddard, this despatch:

"Tell General Franklin, with my compliments, that I wish him to make a vigorous attack with his whole force. Our right is hard pressed."

Under ordinary circumstances this would be regarded as a strong order, but Franklin had gone far enough in his first battle to be convinced that an attack by his "whole force," the other end of the army "hard pressed," would be extremely hazardous. If undertaken and proved disastrous, he could have been made to shoulder the whole responsibility, for a "wish" implies discretion. It is not just to the subordinate to use such language if orders are intended to be imperative. Men bred as soldiers have no fancy for orders that carry want of faith on their face.

The losses at Fredericksburg were as follows: *

UNION ARMY.

Organization.	Killed.	Wounded.	Captured or Missing.	Total.
Right Grand Division (Sumner) . .	523	4281	640	5,444
Centre Grand Division (Hooker) .	352	2501	502	3,355
Left Grand Division (Franklin) .	401	2761	625	3,787
Engineers	8	49	2	59
Artillery Reserve	. .	8	. .	8
Aggregate	1284	9600	1769	12,653

* Vol. xxi. of the Official Records.

CONFEDERATE ARMY.

Organization.	Killed.	Wounded.	Captured or Missing.	Total.
First Army Corps (Longstreet)	251	1516	127	1894
Second Army Corps (Jackson) . . .	344	2545	526	3415
Stuart's Cavalry	. .	13	. .	13
Aggregate	595	4074	653	5322

During the night, before twelve o'clock, a despatch-bearer lost his way and was captured. He had on his person a memorandum of the purpose of General Burnside for renewing the battle against Marye's Hill in the morning. The information was sent up to general headquarters, and orders were sent General Ransom to intrench his brigade along the crest of the hill. Orders were sent other parts of the line to improve defences and prepare for the next day in ammunition, water, and rations, under conviction that the battle of next day, if made as ordered, would be the last of the Army of the Potomac.

Morning came and passed without serious demonstrations on the part of the enemy. Orders were sent out, however, for renewed efforts to strengthen the position. Colonel Alexander found a point at which he could pit a gun in enfilade position to the swell of ground behind which the enemy assembled his forces before advancing to the charge, and Lieutenant-Colonel Latrobe sunk a gun in similar position for fire across the field of their charges. We were so well prepared that we became anxious before the night of the 14th lest General Burnside would not come again. In the night he drew back to the river, and during the night of the 15th recrossed and sent his troops to their camps.

The stone wall was not thought before the battle a very important element. We assumed that the formidable advance would be made against the troops of McLaws's division at Lee's Hill, to turn the position at the sunken road, dislodge my force stationed there, then to occupy the sunken road, and afterwards ascend to the plateau upon which the Marye mansion stands; that this would bring their forces under cross and direct fire of all of our batteries—short- and long-range guns—in such concentration as to beat them back in bad disorder.

General Hood's failure to meet his orders to make counter to the anticipated attack upon Jackson was reported in the official accounts. As he was high in favor with the authorities, it did not seem prudent to attempt to push the matter, as called for under the ordinary usages of war. "*Bis peccare in bello non licet.*"

General Lee went down to Richmond soon after the battle to propose active operations, and returned with information that gold had advanced to 200 in New York; that the war was over and peace would be announced in sixty days; that it was useless to harass the troops by winter service. As gold had gone well up on the Southern side without bringing peace, it was difficult for soldiers to see the bearing that it could have on the other side; still, we had some trust and hope in the judgment of superiors.

The forces available for battle at Fredericksburg were: Federal (according to General Burnside's report), 116,683; Confederate, 78,000. About fifty thousand of the Union troops were put into battle, and less than twenty thousand of the Confederates were engaged.

The organization of the Confederate army at this time was as follows:

ARMY OF NORTHERN VIRGINIA.

FIRST CORPS, LIEUTENANT-GENERAL JAMES LONGSTREET.

MCLAWS'S DIVISION, Maj.-Gen. Lafayette McLaws:—*Kershaw's Brigade*, Brig.-Gen. Joseph B. Kershaw; 2d S. C., Col. John D. Kennedy; 3d S. C., Col. James D. Nance, Lieut.-Col. William D. Rutherford, Maj. Robert C. Maffett, Capt. William W. Hance, Capt. John C. Summer, Capt. John K. G. Nance; 7th S. C., Lieut.-Col. Elbert Bland; 8th S. C.,

Capt. E. T. Stackhouse ; 5th S. C., Col. W. D. DeSaussure ; 3d S. C. Battn., Lieut.-Col. W. G. Rice. *Barksdale's Brigade*, Brig.-Gen. William Barksdale ; 13th Miss., Col. J. W. Carter ; 17th Miss., Col. John C. Fiser ; 18th Miss., Lieut.-Col. W. H. Luse ; 21st Miss., Col. Benjamin G. Humphreys. *Cobb's Brigade*, (1) Brig.-Gen. T. R. R. Cobb, (2) Col. Robert McMillan ; 16th Ga., Col. Goode Bryan ; 18th Ga., Lieut.-Col. S. Z. Ruff; 24th Ga., Col. Robert McMillan ; Cobb Legion ; Phillips's Legion, Col. B. F. Cook. *Semmes's Brigade*, Brig.-Gen. Paul J. Semmes ; 10th, 50th, 51st, and 53d Ga. *Artillery*, Col. H. C. Cabell ; Manly's (N. C.) battery, Read's (Ga.) battery, Richmond Howitzers (1st), McCarthy's battery ; Troup (Ga.) Art. (Carlton's battery).

ANDERSON'S DIVISION, Maj.-Gen. Richard H. Anderson :—*Wilcox's Brigade*, Brig.-Gen. Cadmus M. Wilcox ; 8th, 9th, 10th, 11th, and 14th Ala. *Mahone's Brigade*, Brig.-Gen. William Mahone ; 6th, 12th, 16th, 41st, and 61st Va. *Featherston's Brigade*, Brig.-Gen. W. S. Featherston ; 12th, 16th, 19th, and 48th Miss. (5 cos.). *Wright's Brigade*, Brig.-Gen. A. R. Wright ; 3d (Col. Edward J. Walker), 22d, 48th (Capt. M. R. Hall), and 2d Ga. Battn. (Capt. C. J. Moffett). *Perry's Brigade*, Brig.-Gen. E. A. Perry ; 2d, 5th, and 8th Fla., Capt. David Lang, Capt. Thomas R. Love. *Artillery*, Donaldsonville (La.) Art., Capt. V. Maurin ; Huger's (Va.) battery, Capt. Frank Huger ; Lewis's (Va.) battery, Capt. John W. Lewis ; Norfolk (Va.) Light Art. Blues, Lieut. William T. Peet.

PICKETT'S DIVISION, Maj.-Gen. George E. Pickett :—*Garnett's Brigade*, Brig.-Gen. Richard B. Garnett ; 8th, 18th, 19th, 28th, and 56th Va. *Armistead's Brigade*, Brig.-Gen. Lewis A. Armistead ; 9th, 14th, 38th, 53d, and 57th Va. *Kemper's Brigade*, Brig.-Gen. James L. Kemper ; 1st, 3d, 7th, 11th, and 24th Va. *Jenkins's Brigade*, Brig.-Gen. M. Jenkins ; 1st (Hagood's), 2d (Rifles), 5th, and 6th S. C. ; Hampton Legion ; Palmetto Sharp-shooters. *Corse's Brigade*, Brig.-Gen. Montgomery D. Corse ; 15th, 17th, 30th, and 32d Va. *Artillery*, Dearing's (Va.) battery, Fauquier (Va.) Art. (Stribling's battery), Richmond (Fayette) Art. (Macon's battery).

HOOD'S DIVISION, Maj.-Gen. John B. Hood :—*Law's Brigade*, Brig.-Gen. E. M. Law ; 4th and 44th Ala. ; 6th and 54th N. C. (Col. J. C. S. McDowell) ; 57th N. C., Col. A. C. Goodwin. *Robertson's Brigade*, Brig.-Gen. J. B. Robertson ; 3d Ark. ; 1st, 4th, and 5th Tex. *Anderson's Brigade*, Brig.-Gen. George T. Anderson ; 1st (Regulars), 7th, 8th, 9th, and 11th Ga. *Toombs's Brigade*, Col. H. L. Benning ; 2d, 15th, 17th, and 20th Ga. *Artillery*, German (S. C.) Art. (Bachman's battery), Palmetto (S. C.) Light Art. (Garden's battery), Rowan (N. C.) Art. (Reilly's battery).

RANSOM'S DIVISION, Brig.-Gen. Robert Ransom, Jr. :—*Ransom's Brigade*, Brig.-Gen. Robert Ransom, Jr. ; 24th, 25th (Lieut.-Col. Samuel C. Bryson), 35th, and 49th N. C. ; Branch's (Va.) battery. *Cooke's Brigade*, (1) Brig.-Gen. J. R. Cooke, (2) Col. E. D. Hall ; 15th N. C. ; 27th N. C., Col. John A. Gilmer, Jr. ; 46th N. C., Col. E. D. Hall ; 48th N. C., Lieut.-Col. Samuel H. Walkup ; Cooper's (Va.) battery.

FIRST CORPS ARTILLERY :*— *Washington (La.) Artillery*, Col. J. B.

* Not assigned to divisions.

Walton ; 1st Co., Capt. C. W. Squires ; 2d Co., Capt. J. B. Richardson ; 3d Co., Capt. M. B. Miller ; 4th Co., Capt. B. F. Eshleman. *Alexander's Battalion*, Lieut.-Col. E. Porter Alexander ; Bedford (Va.) Art., Capt. Tyler C. Jordan ; Eubank's (Va.) battery, Capt. J. L. Eubank ; Madison Light Art. (La.), Capt. Geo. V. Moody ; Parker's (Va.) battery, Capt. William W. Parker ; Rhett's (S. C.) battery, Capt. A. B. Rhett ; Woolfolk's (Va.) battery, Capt. P. Woolfolk, Jr.

SECOND CORPS, LIEUTENANT-GENERAL THOMAS J. JACKSON.

D. H. HILL'S DIVISION, Maj.-Gen. Daniel H. Hill :—*First Brigade*, Brig.-Gen. R. E. Rodes ; 3d, 5th, 6th, 12th, and 26th Ala. *Second (Ripley's) Brigade*, Brig.-Gen. George Doles ; 4th Ga. ; 44th Ga., Col. John B. Estes ; 1st and 3d N. C. *Third Brigade*, Brig.-Gen. A. H. Colquitt ; 13th Ala. ; 6th, 23d, 27th, and 28th Ga. *Fourth Brigade*, Brig.-Gen. Alfred Iverson ; 5th, 12th, 20th, and 23d N. C. *Fifth (Ramseur's) Brigade*, Col. Bryan Grimes ; 2d, 4th, 14th, and 30th N. C. *Artillery*, Maj. H. P. Jones ; Hardaway's (Ala.) battery, Jeff Davis (Ala.) Art. (Bondurant's battery), King William (Va.) Art. (Carter's battery), Morris (Va.) Art. (Page's battery), Orange (Va.) Art. (Fry's battery).

A. P. HILL'S DIVISION, Maj.-Gen. Ambrose P. Hill :—*First (Field's) Brigade*, Col. J. M. Brockenbrough ; 40th, 47th (Col. Robert M. Mayo), 55th, and 22d Va. Battn., Lieut.-Col. E. P. Tayloe. *Second Brigade*, (1). Brig.-Gen. Maxcy Gregg, (2) Col. D. H. Hamilton ; 1st S. C. (P. A.), Col. D. H. Hamilton ; 1st S. C. Rifles ; 12th, 13th, and 14th S. C. (Col. Samuel McGowan). *Third Brigade*, Brig.-Gen. E. L. Thomas ; 14th, 35th, 45th, and 49th Ga. *Fourth Brigade*, Brig.-Gen. J. H. Lane ; 7th N. C., Lieut.-Col. J. L. Hill ; 18th N. C., Col. Thomas J. Purdie ; 28th N. C., Col. S. D. Lowe ; 33d N. C., Col. Clark M. Avery ; 37th N. C., Col. W. M. Barbour. *Fifth Brigade*, Brig.-Gen. J. J. Archer ; 5th Ala. Battn., Maj. A. S. Van de Graaff, Capt. S. D. Stewart ; 19th Ga., Lieut.-Col. A. J. Hutchins ; 1st Tenn. (Pro. Army), Col. Peter Turney, Lieut.-Col. N. J. George, Capt. M. Turney, Capt. H. J. Hawkins ; 7th Tenn., Col. John F. Goodner ; 14th Tenn., Lieut.-Col. J. W. Lockert. *Sixth Brigade*, (1) Brig.-Gen. William D. Pender, (2) Col. A. M. Scales ; 13th N. C., Col. A. M. Scales ; 16th N. C., Col. John S. McElroy ; 22d N. C., Maj. Christopher C. Cole ; 34th and 38th N. C. *Artillery*, Lieut.-Col. R. L. Walker ; Branch (N. C.) Art., Lieut. J. R. Potts ; Crenshaw (Va.) Batt., Lieut. J. Ellett ; Fredericksburg (Va.) Art., Lieut. E. A. Marye ; Johnson's (Va.) battery, Lieut. V. J. Clutter ; Letcher (Va.) Art., Capt. G. Davidson ; Pee Dee (S. C.) Art., Capt. D. G. McIntosh ; Purcell (Va.) Art., Capt. W. J. Pegram.

EWELL'S DIVISION, Brig.-Gen. Jubal A. Early :—*Lawton's Brigade*, (1) Col. E. N. Atkinson, (2) Col. C. A. Evans ; 13th Ga., Col. J. M. Smith ; 26th Ga., Capt. B. F. Grace ; 31st Ga., Col. C. A. Evans ; 38th Ga., Capt. William L. McLeod ; 60th Ga., Col. W. H. Stiles ; 61st Ga., Col. J. H. Lamar, Maj. C. W. McArthur. *Trimble's Brigade*, Col. R. F. Hoke ; 15th Ala. ; 12th Ga. ; 21st Ga., Lieut.-Col. Thomas W. Hooper ; 21st N. C. and 1st N. C. Battn. *Early's Brigade*, Col. J. A. Walker ; 13th Va., Lieut.-Col. J. B. Terrill ; 25th, 31st, 44th, 49th, 52d, and 58th Va. *Hays's (1st La.) Brigade*, Gen. Harry T. Hays ; 5th, 6th, 7th, 8th, and 9th La. *Artillery*, Capt. J. W. Latimer ; Charlottesville (Va.) Art., Capt.

J. McD. Carrington; Chesapeake (Md.) Art., Lieut. John E. Plater; Courtney (Va.) Art., Lieut. W. A. Tanner; 1st Md. Batt., Capt. William F. Dement; La. Guard Art., Capt. Louis E. D'Aquin; Staunton (Va.) Art., Lieut. Asher W. Garber.

JACKSON'S DIVISION, Brig.-Gen. William B. Taliaferro:—*First Brigade*, Brig.-Gen. E. F. Paxton; 2d Va., Capt. J. Q. A. Nadenbousch; 4th Va., Lieut.-Col. R. D. Gardner, Maj. William Terry; 5th Va., Lieut.-Col. H. J. Williams; 27th Va., Lieut.-Col. J. K. Edmondson; 33d Va., Col. Edwin G. Lee. *Second Brigade*, Brig.-Gen. J. R. Jones; 21st, 42d, and 48th Va.; 1st Va. Battn. *Third (Taliaferro's) Brigade*, Col. E. T. H. Warren; 47th Ala., Capt. James M. Campbell; 48th Ala., Capt. C. B. St. John; 10th Va., Capt. W. B. Yancey; 23d Va., Capt. A. J. Richardson; 37th Va., Col. T. V. Williams. *Fourth (Starke's) Brigade*, Col. Edmund Pendleton; 1st La. (Vols.), Lieut.-Col. M. Nolan; 2d La., Maj. M. A. Grogan; 10th La., Maj. John M. Legett; 14th La., Capt. H. M. Verlander; 15th La., Lieut.-Col. McG. Goodwyn; Coppens's (La.) Battn. *Artillery*, Capt. J. B. Brockenbrough; Carpenter's (Va.) battery, Lieut. George McKendree; Danville (Va.) Art., Capt. G. W. Wooding; Hampden (Va.) Art., Capt. W. H. Caskie; Lee (Va.) Art., Lieut. C. W. Statham; Lusk's (Va.) battery.

RESERVE ARTILLERY,* Brig.-Gen. W. N. Pendleton:—*Brown's Battalion*, Col. J. Thompson Brown; Brooke's (Va.) battery, Dance's battery, Powhatan Art., Hupp's battery, Salem Art., Poague's (Va.) battery, Rockbridge Art., Smith's battery, 3d Howitzers; Watson's battery, 2d Howitzers. *Cutts's (Ga.) Battalion*, Lane's battery, Patterson's battery, Ross's battery, Capt. H. M. Ross. *Nelson's Battalion*, Maj. William Nelson; Kirkpatrick's (Va.) battery, Amherst Art.; Massie's (Va.) battery, Fluvanna Art.; Milledge's (Ga.) battery. *Miscellaneous Batteries*, Ells's (Ga.) battery; Nelson's (Va.) battery, Hanover Art., Capt. G. W. Nelson; Breathed (Va.) battery, J. Breathed; Chew's (Va.) battery, R. P. Chew; Hart's (S. C.) battery, J. F. Hart; Henry's (Va.) battery, M. W. Henry; Moorman's (Va.) battery, M. N. Moorman.

CAVALRY,† Maj.-Gen. James E. B. Stuart:—*First Brigade*,‡ Brig.-Gen. Wade Hampton; 1st N. C., Col. L. S. Baker; 1st S. C., Col. J. L. Black; 2d S. C., Col. M. C. Butler; Cobb (Ga.) Legion, Lieut.-Col. P. M. B. Young; Phillips's (Ga.) Legion, Lieut.-Col. William W. Rich. *Second Brigade*, Brig.-Gen. Fitzhugh Lee; 1st Va., Col. James H. Drake; 2d Va., Col. Thomas T. Munford; 3d Va., Col. T. H. Owen; 4th Va., Col. William C. Wickham; 5th Va. *Third Brigade*, Brig.-Gen. W. H. F.

---

* Majors Garnett, Hamilton, and T. J. Page, Jr., are mentioned in the reports as commanding artillery battalions, but their composition is not stated.

† Organization of brigades as established November 10, 1862. On roster for December 16, 1862, Hart's, Breathed's, Moorman's, and Chew's batteries appear as attached, respectively, to the First, Second, Third, and Fourth Brigades. Commanders are given as reported December 16, 1862.

‡ Detachment on raid to Dumfries.

Lee ; 2d N. C., Col. S. Williams ; 9th Va., Col. R. L. T. Beale ; 10th Va., Col. J. Lucius Davis ; 13th Va., Col. J. R. Chambliss, Jr. ; 15th Va., Col. William B. Ball. *Fourth Brigade*,* Brig.-Gen. W. E. Jones ; 6th Va., Col. John S. Green ; 7th Va., Col. R. H. Dulany ; 12th Va., Col. A. W. Harman ; 17th (Va.) Battn., Lieut.-Col. O. R. Funsten ; White's (Va.) Battn., Maj. E. V. White.

For the organization of the Union Army at the battle of Fredericksburg, see Appendix, p. 660.

*** In the Shenandoah Valley.**

CHAPTER XXIV.

PREPARING FOR THE SPRING OF '63.

Burnside's Abortive Moves—The "Mud March"—General Hooker supersedes Burnside—The Confederates strengthen their Position for the Winter—Longstreet ordered to Petersburg—Secretary of War Seddon and the Author talk of General Grant and the Confederate Situation on the Mississippi and in the West—Longstreet makes a Radical Proposition for Confederate Concentration in Tennessee, thus to compel Grant to abandon Vicksburg—The Skilful Use of Interior Lines the Only Way of equalizing the Contest—Battle of Chancellorsville, Lee's Brilliant Achievement—Criticism—Death of "Stonewall" Jackson—The Resolve to march Northward—The Army reorganized in Three Corps—Ewell and A. P. Hill appointed Lieutenant-Generals.

BEFORE we were fully settled in our winter quarters, and when just beginning to enjoy our camp theatricals, we heard that General Burnside was looking for another crossing by the lower Rappahannock. We were not greatly concerned about that, however, as we thought the quicksands along the flats, made especially protective by the winter rains, would so delay his march as to allow us ample time to prepare for him. But the Washington authorities having received reports of it through some of the superior officers of the Army of the Potomac, the march was arrested by orders of the War Department.

Another move was set on foot a few weeks later, at a time when General Lee happened to be in Richmond. The information was forwarded to him and the army ordered under arms, prepared to take the field. A few weeks before, General Burnside had ordered material to be hauled to the point below, which he had chosen when preparing for his crossing that had been arrested by the War Department. When we found that his army was in motion, General Jackson insisted that the crossing would be made below, and proposed to march his corps down to meet it. He was told that the neck of land between the Potomac and the Rappahannock was so interlaced with wet-weather streams and ravines that the route leading below was not practicable at that season; that the quicksands on the flats of the west side were formidable obstacles to the march of an army; that the only possible route for crossing the river was by the fords of the highlands, and that he must hold his troops ready to move accordingly. He was not satisfied with the refusal to accept his construction of the enemy's purpose, and demurred against authority less than General Lee's, but found that the order must be obeyed.

Not many hours after the report came, the noise of the army working through the mud was distinctly heard by my picket guards along the upper river. Some of the guards called out derisively, offering help to get the batteries through the mud if they could only be assured that the army would cross. The bottomless roads and severe weather broke up the campaign, and the move back to camp was reported to me before the Confederates marched from their camps. This effort, called by Burnside's soldiers "The Mud March," was followed by the assignment of General Hooker to command of the Army of the Potomac.

Long and close study of the field from the Potomac to the James River, and the experiences of former campaigns, made it clear that the Army of the Potomac had been drawn into a false position, and it became manifest that there were but two moves left open for its spring campaign,—first, by crossing the upper fords of the Rappahannock; secondly, by detaching forces to the south side of the James, and by that route moving against Richmond.

To guard against the former I laid out lines for field-works and rifle-pits covering all approaches by the upper fords as far as the road leading from United States Ford. From that point the line broke to the rear, crossing the Plank road and extending back half a mile to command the road from Chancellorsville to Spottsylvania Court-House. When the lines for these works were well marked, I was ordered, with the divisions of Hood and Pickett and Dearing's and Henry's artillery battalions, to the south side near Petersburg, to be in position to meet the latter move, leaving the divisions of McLaws and R. H. Anderson to finish the work on the lines of defence.

After passing to the south side of James River, assigning the troops to points of observation near Blackwater River, and establishing head-quarters at Petersburg, I learned that there was a goodly supply of produce along the east coast of Virginia and North Carolina, inside the military lines of the Federal forces. To collect and transport this to accessible points for the Confederates, it was necessary to advance our divisions so as to cover the country, and to hold the Federal forces in and about their fortified positions while our trains were at work. To that end I moved with the troops in Virginia across the Blackwater to close lines about the forts around Suffolk, and ordered the troops along our line in North Carolina to a like advance. The movements were executed without serious trouble, and the work was prosecuted up to the time of my recall by General Lee.

While lying near Suffolk a couple of young men dressed as citizens entered my tent one night with letters from Secretary of War Seddon, recommending them as trustworthy and efficient scouts. They were sent off through the swamp to find their way to Norfolk and southward to report of roads or routes for our troops in case we should wish to make a détour for the capture of Suffolk. One of them, Harrison, proved to be an active, intelligent, enterprising scout, and was retained in service.

The accounts that we gained indicated that Suffolk

could be turned and captured with little loss, but as we had given it up the year before as untenable, and were liable to be called upon at any moment to give it up again, it appeared that the "cost of the whistle" would be too high.

The only occurrence of serious moment while we had our forces about Suffolk was the loss of Captain Stribling's battery, which had been inadvertently posted by the officer in charge of the artillery on a neck running out into a bend of the Nansemond River. The Federal gun-boats, seeing the opportunity, came into the river and took positions commanding the neck in rear of the battery so as to sweep the field against all succoring parties, and cut off retreat while direct attack was made upon our battery, resulting in its capture.

About this time the soldiers on both sides had considerable amusement over a Federal signal station that was inside our lines as we had laid them. The Union troops had some time previously trimmed up a tall pine-tree and built near the top a platform for use as a signal station, and, coming upon this, to gratify his curiosity a Confederate soldier climbed to the staging and seated himself for a leisurely view of the Federal forces inside their works. An artillerist of the other side, after allowing sufficient time to satisfy a reasonable curiosity, trained one of his rifle guns upon the platform, and sent a shell screaming and bursting too near for the comfort of the "man up a tree." As he did not care to be seen in precipitate retreat, he thought to wait a little, but a second shot admonished him that hurry, if less graceful, might be more wise than deliberate retreat. Acting under pressure of the situation, his legs, to the amusement of the men on both sides, soon brought him to safe cover. When night closed in over the belligerents this soldier went to work on a scheme by which he hoped to get even with the Yankees. He carefully constructed and equipped a full-sized man, dressed in a new suit of improved "butternut"* dry-goods, and, in due form christening him "Julius Cæsar," took him to the platform, adjusted him to graceful position, and made him secure to the framework by strong cords. A little after sunrise "Julius Cæsar" was discovered by some of the Federal battery officers, who prepared for the target,—so inviting to skilful practice. The new soldier sat under the hot fire with irritating indifference until the Confederates, not able to restrain their hilarity, exposed the joke by calling for "three cheers for Julius Cæsar." The other side quickly recognized the situation, and good-naturedly added to ours their cheers for the old hero.

About the 28th day of April the Army of the Potomac, under General Hooker, took up its march for the fords of the upper Rappahannock to cross against General Lee at Fredericksburg. At the same time General Grant crossed the Mississippi below Vicksburg, marched against General Pemberton's army in Mississippi, and was driving it back upon its fortifications about Vicksburg.

When General Hooker's movements were so developed as to make sure of his purpose, repeated calls came to me over the wires to pull away from Suffolk and return to General Lee with all speed. These came from General Lee, and also from the Richmond authorities. In reply I despatched that our trains were at the front along the coast collecting supplies; that they would be hurried to our rear, and as soon as safe we would march. The calls became so frequent and urgent, however, that I inquired if we should abandon our trains. To this no answer came; and I was left to the exercise of my own judgment.

As soon as the trains were safely back, we drew off, marched back to the Blackwater, and thence *en route* for

* The Confederate dry-goods factories, for want of other dye-stuffs, had long before this resorted to the use of the butternut coloring.

Richmond and Fredericksburg. Before we reached the former place a telegram came announcing the great battle and victory of Chancellorsville.

Passing through Richmond, I called to report to Secretary of War Seddon, who referred to affairs in Mississippi, stating that the department was trying to collect an army at Jackson, under General Joseph E. Johnston, sufficient to push Grant away from his circling lines about Vicksburg. He spoke of the difficulty of feeding as well as collecting an army of that magnitude in Mississippi, and asked my views.

The Union army under General Rosecrans was then facing the Confederate army under General Bragg in Tennessee, at Murfreesboro' and Shelbyville.

I thought that General Grant had better facilities for collecting supplies and reinforcements on his new lines, and suggested that the only prospect of relieving Vicksburg that occurred to me was to send General Johnston and his troops about Jackson to reinforce General Bragg's army; at the same time the two divisions of my command, then marching to join General Lee, to the same point; that the commands moving on converging lines could have rapid transit and be thrown in overwhelming numbers on Rosecrans before he could have help, break up his army, and march for Cincinnati and the Ohio River; that Grant's was the only army that could be drawn to meet this move, and that the move must, therefore, relieve Vicksburg.

It was manifest before the war was accepted that the only way to equalize the contest was by skilful use of our interior lines, and this was so impressed by two years' experience that it seemed time to force it upon the Richmond authorities. But foreign intervention was the ruling idea with the President, and he preferred that as the easiest solution of all problems.

The only objection offered by the Secretary was that

Grant was such an obstinate fellow that he could only be induced to quit Vicksburg by terribly hard knocks.

On the contrary, I claimed that *he was a soldier*, and would obey the calls of his government, but was not lightly to be driven from his purpose.

My march was continued, and we joined General Lee at Fredericksburg, where I found him in sadness, notwithstanding that he was contemplating his great achievement and brilliant victory of Chancellorsville, for he had met with great loss as well as great gains. The battle had cost heavily of his army, but his grief was over the severe wounding of his great lieutenant, General Thomas Jonathan Jackson, the head of the Second Corps of the Army of Northern Virginia; cut off, too, at a moment so much needed to finish his work in the battle so handsomely begun. With a brave heart, however, General Lee was getting his ranks together, and putting them in condition for other useful work.

At the time of the battle of Chancellorsville the Army of the Potomac, according to its return of a few days before, consisted of officers and men actually available for line of battle, 113,838, with 404 pieces of artillery.* The return of casualties showed the enormous loss of 17,287. Returns of the Army of Northern Virginia for March, 1863, showed an effective aggregate of 59,681; † batteries in action, about 160 guns. To this may possibly be added one thousand of troops returning during April in time for the battle. The casualties reported by the medical director numbered 10,281, but reports of the commanders showed over 12,000, not including artillery or cavalry, or slightly wounded and missing, which would probably add another thousand.

Chancellorsville is usually accepted as General Lee's most brilliant achievement, and, considered as an indepen-

* Rebellion Record, vol. xxv. part ii. p. 320.
† Ibid., p. 696.

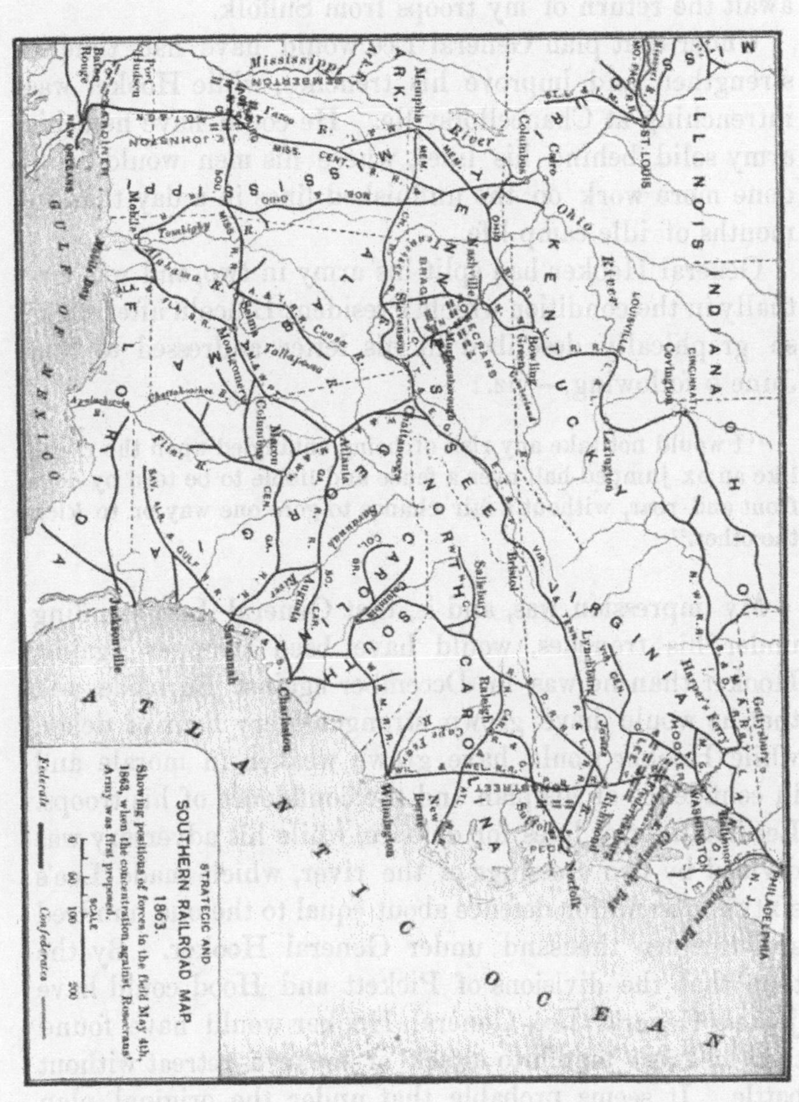

STRATEGIC AND SOUTHERN RAILROAD MAP, 1863.
Showing positions of forces in the field May 4th, 1863, when the concentration against Rosecrans' Army was first proposed.
SCALE 0 50 100 200
Federals —— Confederates ——

dent affair, it was certainly grand. As I had no part in its active conduct, it is only apropos to this writing to consider the plan of battle as projected some four months previous,—*i.e.*, to stand behind our intrenched lines and await the return of my troops from Suffolk.

Under that plan General Lee would have had time to strengthen and improve his trenches, while Hooker was intrenching at Chancellorsville. He could have held his army solid behind his lines, where his men would have done more work on the unfinished lines in a day than in months of idle camp life.

General Hooker had split his army in two, and was virtually in the condition which President Lincoln afterwards so graphically described in his letter addressed to him June 5 following,—viz.:

> "I would not take any risk of being entangled upon the river, like an ox jumped half over a fence and liable to be torn by dogs front and rear, without a fair chance to gore one way or to kick the other."

My impression was, and is, that General Lee, standing under his trenches, would have been stronger against Hooker than he was in December against Burnside, and that he would have grown stronger every hour of delay, while Hooker would have grown weaker in morale and in confidence of his plan and the confidence of his troops. Lee had interior lines for defence, while his adversary was divided by two crossings of the river, which made Lee's sixty thousand for defence about equal to the one hundred and thirteen thousand under General Hooker. By the time that the divisions of Pickett and Hood could have joined General Lee, General Hooker would have found that he must march to attack or make a retreat without battle. It seems probable that under the original plan the battle would have given fruits worthy of a general engagement. The Confederates would then have had opportunity, and have been in condition to so follow Hooker as to have compelled his retirement to Washington, and that advantage might have drawn Grant from Vicksburg; whereas General Lee was actually so crippled by his victory that he was a full month restoring his army to condition to take the field. In defensive warfare Lee was perfect. When the hunt was up, his combativeness was overruling.

It was probably a mistake to draw McLaws away from his position at Marye's Hill, where he and Ransom had successfully held against six or seven severe attacks of the Burnside battle, with three brigades, two of his own and one of Ransom's. General Early was assigned to that position with five brigades. He was attacked by about one-fourth the number of McLaws's assailants, the position was carried, and Early was driven off in confusion, losing, besides large numbers as prisoners, many pieces of artillery. His especial assignment was to defend the Plank road against the enemy's march to attack General Lee's rear. Instead, he retreated by the Telegraph road, leaving the Plank road free for the enemy. After driving Early off, the enemy marched by the Plank road, and Early marched back to his late position at Marye's Hill. So General Lee was obliged to take McLaws and Anderson from his battle at Chancellorsville to drive back the force threatening his rear.

The battle as pitched and as an independent affair was brilliant, and if the war was for glory could be called successful, but, besides putting the cause upon the hazard of a die, it was crippling in resources and of future progress, while the wait of a few days would have given time for concentration and opportunities against Hooker more effective than we experienced with Burnside at Fredericksburg. This was one of the occasions where success was not a just criterion.

After reporting to General Lee, I offered the suggestions made to Secretary Seddon, in regard to the means that should be adopted for the relief of Vicksburg. I thought that honor, interest, duty, and humanity called us to that service, and asked the aid of his counsels with the War Department, and reinforcements from his army for the West, to that end. I suggested that General Johnston, instead of trying to collect an army against General Grant, should be sent to reinforce General Bragg, then standing against the Union forces under General Rosecrans in Middle Tennessee; that at the same time he should send my divisions, just up from Suffolk, to join Johnston's reinforcements to Bragg's army; that the combination once made should strike immediately in overwhelming force upon Rosecrans, and march for the Ohio River and Cincinnati.

He recognized the suggestion as of good combination, and giving strong assurance of success, but he was averse to having a part of his army so far beyond his reach. He reflected over the matter one or two days, and then fell upon the plan of invading the Northern soil, and so threatening Washington as to bring about the same hoped-for result. To that end he bent his energies.

His plan or wishes announced, it became useless and improper to offer suggestions leading to a different course. All that I could ask was that the policy of the campaign should be one of defensive tactics; that we should work so as to force the enemy to attack us, in such good position as we might find in his own country, so well adapted to that purpose,—which might assure us of a grand triumph. To this he readily assented as an important and material adjunct to his general plan. His confidence in making moves threatening Washington and the invasion of Maryland and Pennsylvania grew out of the known anxiety of the Washington authorities as to the safety of their capital and of quiet within the Union lines.

In the midst of his work of preparation came the announcement that General Jackson's trouble had taken an unfortunate turn, that he was thought to be sinking, and not many hours after that the news came that he had gone to rest. But the full realization of all that this meant was delayed until, at the railroad station, the train that was to bear his remains to their final resting-place started upon its sad journey. Then officers and soldiers gathered to do last honors to their dead comrade and chieftain seemed suddenly to realize that they were to see "Stonewall" Jackson no more forever, and fully to measure the great misfortune that had come upon them. And as we turned away, we seemed to face a future bereft of much of its hopefulness.

General Jackson's death suggested to General Lee a reorganization of his army into three corps, and R. S. Ewell and A. P. Hill, appointed lieutenant-generals, were assigned to the Second and Third respectively.

As the senior major-general of the army, and by reason of distinguished services and ability, General Ewell was entitled to the command of the Second Corps, but there were other major-generals of rank next below Ewell whose services were such as to give them claims next after Ewell's, so that when they found themselves neglected there was no little discontent, and the fact that both the new lieutenant-generals were Virginians made the trouble more grievous.* Afterwards, when Early, noted as the weakest general officer of the Army of Northern Virginia, was appointed lieutenant-general over those who held higher rank than he, there was a more serious feeling of "too much Virginia." Longstreet and Jackson had been assigned by General Johnston.

In our anxious hours and hopeful anticipations the little

---

* General D. H. Hill was next in rank to General Ewell. He was the hero of Bethel, Seven Pines, South Mountain, and the hardest fighter at Sharpsburg. His record was as good as that of "Stonewall" Jackson, but, not being a Virginian, he was not so well advertised.

quarrel was soon lost sight of,—displaced by affairs of greater moment. Reaction began to show the effect of General Lee's strong hand and hard work. Hope and confidence impaired by the failure of the Maryland campaign were restored, and we prepared to abandon all uncomfortable thoughts with the graves of our fallen comrades.

As soon as affairs took such shape as to assure me that the advance northward was inevitable, I sent a requisition down to Richmond for gold coin for my scout Harrison, gave him what he thought he would need to get along in Washington, and sent him off with secret orders, telling him that I did not care to see him till he could bring information of importance,—that he should be the judge of that. He wanted to know where he would find us, and was told that the head-quarters of the First Corps were large enough for any intelligent man to find. With these orders he left us, and after about three weeks was arrested in Pennsylvania and brought under guard to my head-quarters.

CHAPTER XXV.

INVASION OF PENNSYLVANIA.

Plan of the Confederate March North—General Lee hoped to draw Troops from the South and develop Important Results North of the Potomac—He wanted Beauregard sent to support the Movement—The Authorities in Richmond failed to comprehend—The Value of the "Interior Lines" not appreciated—Spirited Cavalry Fight at Brandy Station between Stuart's and Pleasonton's Commands—Engagement of Ewell and Milroy at Winchester—The Question of Authority for the Cavalry Movements—Lieutenant-Colonel Fremantle of the Coldstream Guards, British Army, as a Guest and Observer—The Confederate Advance reaches Pennsylvania Soil—General Lee issues Orders for a March on Harrisburg—Municipal Authorities of York and Gettysburg surrender to General John B. Gordon.

THE absorbing study now was the projected campaign into Maryland and Pennsylvania,—the invasion of the enemy's country. The plan of defensive tactics gave some hope of success, and, in fact, I assured General Lee that the First Corps would receive and defend the battle if he would guard its flanks, leaving his other corps to gather the fruits of success. The First Corps was as solid as a rock—a great rock. It was not to be broken of good position by direct assault, and was steady enough to work and wait for its chosen battle.

The Valley of the Shenandoah gave us firm, broad roads for the march north, curtained by the solid range of the Blue Ridge and South Mountains. There were some Federal troops occupying points in the Valley of Virginia, but not more than enough to give healthful employment to our leading columns as they advanced. The army as reorganized in three corps had three divisions of each corps, with four brigades to the division, except R. H. Anderson's, Pickett's, and Rodes's, each of which had five. J. E. B. Stuart's cavalry consisted of the brigades of Wade Hampton, Fitzhugh Lee, W. H. F. Lee, Beverly Robertson, and W. E. Jones. The cavalry of Jenkins and Imboden, operating in the Valley and West Virginia near our route, was to move, the former with Ewell, the latter on his left. Six batteries of horse artillery under Major R. F. Beckham were of Stuart's command, and to each army corps were attached five battalions of artillery of four guns to a battery, and four batteries to a battalion, making of the whole artillery organization, including batteries of reserve and the thirty guns of horse artillery, two hundred and eighty-seven guns. In the three army corps there were thirty-nine brigades, proper, of infantry.

In the Army of the Potomac were fifty-one brigades of infantry, eight brigades of cavalry, and three hundred and seventy guns of artillery. The artillery appointments were so superior that our officers sometimes felt humiliated when posted to unequal combat with their better metal and munitions. In small-arms also the Union troops had the most improved styles.

Notwithstanding, we were prepared to march forward and cheerfully accept the gage, hoping to overbalance these advantages through the morale afforded by brave hearts, and by strategic skill to throw the onus of battle upon the enemy.

The plan of campaign as projected was by the march of the Second Corps through the Valley of the Shenandoah to drive off or capture the Federal forces stationed along the Valley, and continue the march to Pennsylvania until further orders, meanwhile collecting supplies for the advance and for those who were to follow, Jenkins's brigade of cavalry working with the advance, and Imboden's on its left; the First Corps and main force of cavalry to march near the east base of the Blue Ridge, threatening towards the rear line of the Army of the Potomac, and occupy the Blue Ridge, while the trains and other troops passed behind the mountains to follow the advance march. Stuart's cavalry brigades were to observe between the First Corps and the Union army. When the Third Corps had passed behind the First, the latter and the cavalry were to withdraw and follow the general march. Stuart, whose movements were to correspond to those of the First Corps, was to follow its withdrawal and cross the Potomac on our right flank at Shepherdstown. The brigades of Generals M. Jenkins and M. D. Corse of Pickett's division, left in Virginia near Petersburg and Hanover Junction, were to follow and join their division, as will soon appear.

General Beauregard was to be called from his post, in the South, with such brigades as could be pulled away temporarily from their Southern service, and thrown forward, with the two brigades of Pickett's division (Jenkins's and Corse's) and such others as could be got together, along the Orange and Alexandria Railroad in threatening attitude towards Washington City, and he was to suddenly forward Pickett's brigades through the Valley to the division, and at his pleasure march on, or back towards Richmond.

As the season of fevers along the coast of the Carolinas was approaching, General Lee thought that active operations in the far South, especially along the seaboard, would be suspended, that his move northward might draw most of them towards him, and possibly troops operating in the Southwest, the latter being really the prominent feature and object of his northern march. He thought that Beauregard's appearance in Northern Virginia would increase the known anxiety of the Washington authorities and cause them to draw troops from the South, when in the progress of events other similar movements might follow on both sides until important results could be developed north of the Potomac.

His early experience with the Richmond authorities

taught him to deal cautiously with them in disclosing his views, and to leave for them the privilege and credit of approving, step by step, his apparently hesitant policy, so that his plans were disclosed little at a time; and, finding them slow in approving them, still slower in advancing the brigades of Pickett's division, and utterly oblivious of the effect of a grand swing north on our interior lines, he did not mention the part left open for Beauregard until he had their approval of the march of the part of his command as he held it in hand. The part assigned for Beauregard became the subject for correspondence between the authorities and the officers who knew nothing of the general ideas and plans. The latter failed to see any benefit to accrue by taking troops from their commands, and naturally offered objections to their going. The authorities, not comprehending the vast strength to be gathered by utilizing our interior lines, failed to bring about their execution, and the great possibility was not fully tested.

In pursuance of the plan for the northern campaign our march was taken up on Wednesday, the 3d of June, McLaws's division of the First Corps marching on that date from Fredericksburg, and Hood's from near Orange Court-House on the 4th; Rodes's division of the Second Corps followed, and on the 5th Johnson's and Early's of the Second. Pickett of the First, with three of his brigades, followed the course of Hood's division. All were to assemble at Culpeper Court-House, near our cavalry head-quarters. The Third Corps, General A. P. Hill, was left in observation of the enemy at Fredericksburg.

When General Hooker discovered the thinning of our camps in rear of Fredericksburg, he put a bridge across the Rappahannock at Deep Run, crossed a considerable force of artillery and infantry, and constructed a line of rifle-pits along the river bank. At the report of these movements, General Lee thought to delay the movements of the Second Corps, though he hurried those of the First to draw off the Federals from action against Hill, but holding the Second ready to go back to him should there be need. Hill made a similar demonstration against Hooker, threatening on the river below, though not so far as to cross it, which caused the Federals to draw their troops from the south side. The Second Corps was then hurried on to Culpeper Court-House.

The First and Second Corps waited at the court-house to know if indications about Fredericksburg were such as to warrant the onward march. General Hooker, not convinced that General Lee had left him, ordered his cavalry under General Pleasonton, supported by two brigades of infantry, to cross the Rappahannock in search of Stuart's cavalry, and to secure information of the Confederate plans. Pleasonton's force, including infantry, was eleven thousand. He divided his command, sending one half by Beverley's, the other by Kelly's Ford, to march on converging roads to Brandy Station, near Fleetwood, the latter point the head-quarters of our cavalry chief, five miles west of Rappahannock Bridge.

Happily for the Confederates, the cavalry brigades had been drawn together on the 8th for review by General Lee, and rested that night not remote from cavalry headquarters. On the 9th, Pleasonton's columns made an unlooked-for advance and engaged the Confederates, before notice could be sent to the columns at their camps. The march resulted in a very severe and strongly disputed cavalry fight, ending in heavy losses on both sides. General Stuart called for infantry supports before the close of the conflict, but succeeded in recovering his position before the infantry reached him,—not, however, until some important despatches were taken by the enemy, which gave the information they were seeking. Stuart reported 485 officers and men lost; Pleasonton, 907, and three pieces of artillery. On the 10th, Ewell took up his march for the Valley by Chester Gap. Now, General Milroy had a division of nine thousand Federals at Winchester, and sought to hold it contrary to his orders to retire to the command at Harper's Ferry. He had a brigade on outpost at Berryville under McReynolds. General Kelly had ten thousand men at Harper's Ferry, with a strong detachment of infantry and a battery at Martinsburg, under Colonel B. F. Smith.

Upon entering the Valley, General Ewell detached Rodes's division and Jenkins's cavalry to cut off and capture the force at Berryville, but McReynolds withdrew in time to join the forces at Winchester. This Confederate column then marched for Martinsburg, and got possession there on the 14th, the garrison marching out and joining the troops on Maryland Heights. The artillery trying to escape north towards Williamsport was followed so closely that they lost some three or four guns. With his divisions under Johnson and Early, General Ewell marched to Winchester and attacked and carried the outworks of Milroy's fortified position, when the latter, after calling a council, decided to retreat, leaving his artillery and wagon-trains. Ewell had anticipated this, and sent a part of Johnson's division, one brigade, to intercept him on the Martinsburg road. The commands met about daylight, and there ensued a severe engagement, successful to the Federals till reinforcements came to the Confederates, when Milroy's command was broken up, part of his troops escaping to Harper's Ferry and part getting over the Potomac at Hancock. The Federals at Harper's Ferry abandoned their position in Virginia, seeking shelter on the heights on the Maryland side.

On his march through the Valley, General Ewell took 4000 prisoners and small-arms, 25 cannon, 11 standards, 250 wagons, 400 horses, and large quantities of subsistence and quartermaster's stores, with a loss of 269 of all arms. He crossed the Potomac on the 15th, occupying Hagerstown and Sharpsburg, on the Maryland side, and sent the cavalry brigade, under Jenkins, north towards Chambersburg.

By the plan of march from the Valley of Virginia the leading corps (Second) was to divide and cross the Potomac River at Williamsport and Shepherdstown, the column through Williamsport to march through Hagerstown and Chambersburg towards Harrisburg, collecting produce and supplies for the army, Imboden's cavalry on its left flank. The eastern column was to march through Sharpsburg, Emmitsburg, and Gettysburg towards the bridge over the Susquehanna River at Wrightsville, Jenkins's cavalry brigade working with the two columns. The Third Corps, passing behind the Blue Ridge, was to cross at Shepherdstown and follow the line of the intended march of the eastern column. The First Corps was to draw back from the Blue Ridge and cross the Potomac at Williamsport, to be followed by the cavalry, which was to cross at Shepherdstown and ride severely towards Baltimore, to call the enemy to eastern concentration.

The object of the march of the eastern columns, besides opening a wide field for foraging, was to draw the enemy from the route of travel of our supply trains, and to press him off east to give opportunity for the western columns to file in between him and Washington.

Nevertheless, circumstances in novel ways, or by some freak of favor, or most likely by the interposition of kind Providence, brought us face to face, save our absent body of cavalry, to the goal so ardently sought in our deep work at Fredericksburg. These doubtless disturbed the mind of our great leader even to discomfiture, which, with the success of the first day's fight, may have moved him to make precipitate battle as his safest means of escape. But the situation which led us into Pennsylvania was unchanged; when we marched we were virtually entered upon our last campaign. Our cause was plainly at its climax and the enemy still in power. With that sense upon us we had resolved upon the desperate move and should have nerved ourselves to all of its leadings, especially that which we marched out upon as the most desirable. The cavalry could easily take care of itself. If this was not so, why was it so far away and alone? Besides, we could better help it by keeping the enemy in an attitude of active defense. It was before us to strike the blow we had sought, desperate as it was, but not more so than the march of our army for Northern soil. In fact, this was, indeed, the happy result that could not have been anticipated when the cavalry raid was set on foot, and should have been cheerfully accepted as a precious gift.

We now know from dispatches from the Union commander that the march of the Confederates around his left would have broken up his stronghold, and thrown him off to his supplies at Westminster, and quite cut off his guard of Washington; and so far nothing but strong battles could recover defensive ground. But the question remained: Was that possible? The Union troops under an untried leader, himself seeking the most effectual defensive position that might be available, badly worsted in two previous battles, and in desperate fight for life on his own soil. Was it possible for him by aggressive work to have recovered his lost morale, even to successful aggressive battle over the enemy so swollen by victory and morale?

The Army of the Potomac in the entanglements on the heights of Gettysburg was standing for defensive battle, along its front and sides surrounded by the Army of Northern Virginia, except its eastern side, leaving the only open way leading to Westminster. The commander of the Army of the Potomac wired the authorities on the afternoon of the 3d, about three o'clock, that he would fall back on his supplies at Westminster in the event of the enemy turning his left. But the question may be asked, Was such a move possible? The circumstances certainly did not favor it. A formidable army was pressing in close observation, but ready to fall upon him at all points; a strong column was marching alongside his right flank, ready to attack at the first good opportunity. It seems hardly possible, therefore, in view of such an array of circumstances, that the whole army could have got away in safety. General Lee thought that we would have destroyed it. McMahon, of the Franco-German War, in a similar effort to escape lost his entire army, and Lee, attempting to get away from Grant at Petersburg, lost his army.

The reconnoissance and cavalry fight made against Stuart at Fleetwood gave General Hooker conclusive evidence of the march of the Army of Northern Virginia, and he drew off from Stafford Heights on the 13th, and marched towards the Orange and Alexandria Railroad and the Potomac River. The First Corps was ordered north along the east base of the Blue Ridge to guard our line of march and cover, in a measure, the Confederate plans, Stuart's cavalry to ride between the First Corps and the Union army. On the 19th the divisions of the First Corps were posted along the Blue Ridge from Ashby's Gap on the right to Snicker's Gap on the left, McLaws at the former, Hood at the latter, Pickett's three brigades between the others. Under the impression that the cavalry was to operate with the First Corps, in the general plan, the commander was ordered to follow its withdrawal west of the Blue Ridge and cross the Potomac on its right at Shepherdstown, and make his ride towards Baltimore. He claimed that General Lee had given him authority to cross east of the Blue Ridge.

After the First Corps was in position on the Blue Ridge, and while the Third was passing our rear down the Valley, it seems that General Lee so far modified the plan of march north as to authorize his cavalry chief to cross the Potomac with part of his command east of the Blue Ridge, and to change the march of the Third Corps by Hagerstown and Chambersburg. The point at which the cavalry force should cross the river was not determined between the Confederate commander and his chief of cavalry, there being doubt whether the crossing could better be made at Point of Rocks, between the Union army and the Blue Ridge, or between that army and Washington City. That question was left open, and I was ordered to choose between the two points named at the moment that my command took up its line of march.

The First Corps was withdrawn from the Blue Ridge on the 20th, forded the Shenandoah, and camped on its left bank. On the 21st, Pleasonton came, in full force, supported by infantry, against Stuart's cavalry brigades. The severe part of the fight came from Upperville, and succeeded in driving Stuart back into Ashby's Gap. Part of McLaws's division was sent back in time to support Stuart, and in the morning McLaws ordered Wofford's brigade down upon the plain, but Pleasonton had withdrawn. The infantry was recalled after an exchange of a few shots at great range.

Connected with the cavalry raid and orders authorizing it are matters of more than usual interest. On the 22d the Confederate commander sent unsealed instructions to his cavalry chief, through head-quarters of the First Corps, to be forwarded, provided the cavalry could be spared from my front and could make the ride without disclosing our plans, expressing his preference for the ride through Hopewell Gap east of the Union army. As previously stated, I was to decide at the last moment between the two points that had been named. As my front was changed to the rear for the march north, the cavalry could be of no service there. The extent of authority with me, therefore, was to decide whether the crossing should be made at the Point of Rocks or around through Hopewell Gap east of the Union army. The crossing at Point of Rocks was not only hazardous, but more likely to indicate our plans than any move that could be made, leaving the ride through Hopewell Gap the only route for the raiding party. In my note to General Stuart enclosing General Lee's instructions was this item:

"P. S.—I think your passage of the Potomac by our rear at the present moment will, in a measure, disclose our plans. You had better not leave us, therefore, unless you can take the route in rear of the enemy."

This has been put in italics and published as evidence that the raid was made by my orders, as well as by General Lee's. In the postscript three points are indicated:

First, the move along my rear to the crossing at Point of Rocks.

Second, my preferred march on my flank to the Shepherdstown crossing.

Third, the route indicated by General Lee.

All of which General Stuart understood as well as I. Especially did he know that *my orders to him were that he should ride on the right of my column, as originally designed*, to the Shepherdstown crossing. In the body of my note were orders that he should report to me of affairs along the cavalry line before leaving; that he should assign General Hampton to command of the cavalry to be left with us, with orders to report at my head-quarters. These orders, emanating properly from the commander of the rear column of the army, should not have been questioned, but they were treated with contumely. He assigned General Robertson to command the cavalry on the mountain, without orders to report at my head-quarters, left him there to guard the passes of the Blue Ridge, and rode with his other troopers. The raid and the absence of the cavalry at the critical moment were severely criticised throughout the army and the country. If General Stuart could have claimed the authority of my orders for his action, he would not have failed to do so in his official account. He offered no such excuse, but asserted that he had acted under the authority of his chief, claiming only, however, that General Lee had given consent to his proposition. So our plans, adopted after deep study, were suddenly given over to gratify the youthful cavalryman's wish for a nomadic ride.

About this time a distinguished visitor joined us. An officer of the British service, Lieutenant-Colonel Arthur J. L. Fremantle, of the Coldstream Guards, brought letters from the Secretary of War to General Lee and myself. He was seeking opportunity to observe the campaign as a non-combatant; he travelled with us, divided his time between general head-quarters and head-quarters of the First Corps, cheerfully adapted his tastes to the rough ways of Confederate soldiers, and proved to be an interesting companion. To avoid the blockade he came to the Confederacy through Mexico. He gave a graphic account of his experience in Texas and travel after crossing the Rio Grande to the interior in a two-horse hack. The drivers of his conveyance were Mr. Sargeant and Judge Hyde, two characters whom I had met years before while in army service on the Texas frontier. They called their team Grant and Sherman, and enjoyed their glorious rides down the smooth slopes of the prairie roads, as they rattled their heels upon the box of the hack and plied their team, Grant and Sherman, with whips and oaths. But the great novelty to him was the position of the judge. In England there are few judges comparatively, and those of high estate. To find an American judge playing assistant to a hack-driver was refreshing, and Colonel Fremantle thoroughly enjoyed it. I now have the pleasure to salute our genial war-time visitor as governor at Malta and Lieutenant-General Sir Arthur James Lyon Fremantle, K.C.M., G.C.B., and to offer congratulations to Her Most Noble Majesty upon her worthy subject.

On the 23d of June the divisions of the Third Corps passed on towards the Potomac, followed by those of the First, the former crossing at Shepherdstown, the latter at Williamsport. The corps came together at Hagerstown, in Maryland, continued their march till the 27th, and rested two days at Chambersburg, in Pennsylvania. The cavalry under General Imboden, ordered on General Ewell's left, was due as far north as McConnellsburg, but had halted at Hancock.

On the 28th, General Lee issued orders for the march upon Harrisburg.* General Ewell had marched his main column through Chambersburg to Carlisle. His column, ordered to move east of the mountains through Emmitsburg and Gettysburg, had marched parallel to the main column as far as Greenwood, when orders were renewed for it to march east through Gettysburg. General Early, commanding, ordered Gordon's brigade and a detachment of cavalry through Gettysburg; but his other troops marched north through Mummasburg. The failure of the Imboden cavalry on his left caused General Ewell to send General George H. Steuart through McConnellsburg as guard of that flank. Steuart's command rejoined him at Carlisle. As General Ewell marched he sent us three thousand head of beef cattle and information of five thousand barrels of flour. He halted at Carlisle on the 27th. The municipal authorities of Gettysburg and York surrendered to General Gordon, who took some prisoners

---

* *Vide* Appendix to Chapter XXV.

of the State militia, and marched to the bridge over the Susquehanna at Wrightsville, where he had other prisoners; but the bridge was burned before him. His brigade returned to the vicinity of York, where the division had marched and bivouacked on the night of the 28th.

CHAPTER XXVI.

GETTYSBURG—FIRST DAY.

Information of Federal Force and Positions brought by the Scout Harrison—General Lee declines to credit it—General Longstreet suggests a Change of Direction in Conformance with the Revelation—General Meade had succeeded Hooker in Command Five Days before Battle—Positions on the Eve of the First Day—Confederate Cavalry "not in sight"—"The Eyes of the Army" sadly needed—A Description of the Famous Battle-field—Generals Ewell and A. P. Hill engage the Federals—Death of General John F. Reynolds—The Fight on Seminary Ridge—General Hancock in Federal Command on the Field—Concerning the Absent Cavalry and Information given by the Scout—Conditions at the Close of the First Day's Fight.

THE eve of the great battle was crowded with events. Movements for the concentration of the two vast armies went on in mighty force, but with a silence in strong contrast to the swift-coming commotion of their shock in conflict. It was the pent quiet of the gathering storm whose bursting was to shake the continent and suddenly command the startled attention of the world.

After due preparation for our march of the 29th, all hands turned in early for a good night's rest. My mind had hardly turned away from the cares and labors of the day, when I was aroused by some one beating on the pole of my tent. It proved to be Assistant Inspector-General Fairfax. A young man had been arrested by our outlying pickets under suspicious circumstances. He was looking for General Longstreet's head-quarters, but his comfortable apparel and well-to-do, though travel-stained, appearance caused doubt in the minds of the guards of his being a genuine Confederate who could be trusted about head-quarters. So he was sent up under a file of men to be identified. He proved to be Harrison, the valued scout. He had walked through the lines of the

Union army during the night of the 27th and the 28th, secured a mount at dark of the latter day to get in as soon as possible, and brought information of the location of two corps of Federals at night of the 27th, and approximate positions of others. General Hooker had crossed the Potomac on the 25th and 26th of June. On the 27th he had posted two army corps at Frederick, and the scout reported another near them, and two others near South Mountain, as he escaped their lines a little after dark of the 28th. He was sent under care of Colonel Fairfax to make report of his information at general head-quarters. General Lee declined, however, to see him, though he asked Colonel Fairfax as to the information that he brought, and, on hearing it, expressed want of faith in reports of scouts, in which Fairfax generally agreed, but suggested that in this case the information was so near General Longstreet's ideas of the probable movements of the enemy that he gave credit to it. I also sent up a note suggesting a change of direction of the head of our column east. This I thought to be the first and necessary step towards bringing the two armies to such concentration east as would enable us to find a way to draw the enemy into battle, in keeping with the general plan of campaign, and at the same time draw him off from the travel of our trains.

There were seven corps of the Army of the Potomac afield. We were informed on the 28th of the approximate positions of five of them,—three near Frederick and two near the base of South Mountain. The others, of which we had no definite information, we now know were the Sixth (Sedgwick's), south of Frederick and east of the Monocacy, and the Twelfth, towards Harper's Ferry.

On the 26th, General Hooker thought to use the Twelfth Corps and the garrison of Harper's Ferry to strike the line of our communication, but General Halleck forbade the use of the troops of that post, when General Hooker asked to be relieved of the responsibility of command, and was succeeded by General Meade on the night of the 27th.

If General Hooker had been granted the authority for which he applied, he would have struck our trains, exposed from Chambersburg to the Potomac without a cavalryman to ride and report the trouble. General Stuart was riding around Hooker's army, General Robertson was in Virginia, General Imboden at Hancock, and Jenkins's cavalry was at our front with General Ewell.

By the report of the scout we found that the march of Ewell's east wing had failed of execution and of the effect designed, and that heavy columns of the enemy were hovering along the east base of the mountain. To remove this pressure towards our rear, General Lee concluded to make a more serious demonstration and force the enemy to look eastward. With this view he changed direction of the proposed march north, by counter-orders on the night of the 28th, calling concentration east of the mountains at Cashtown, and his troops began their march under the last orders on the 29th.

It seems that General Hill misconstrued the orders of the day, or was confused by the change of orders, and was under the impression that he was to march by York and cross the Susquehanna towards Philadelphia or Harrisburg. He ordered his leading division under Heth to Cashtown, however, and followed with Pender's division on the 30th, leaving orders for the division of R. H. Anderson to follow on the 1st. The purpose of General Lee's march east was only preliminary,—a concentration about Cashtown.

General Ewell was ready to march for Harrisburg on the 29th, when orders reached him of the intended concentration at Cashtown. He was at Carlisle with Rodes's and E. Johnson's divisions and the reserve artillery; his other division under Early was at York. On the 30th, Rodes was at Heidlersburg, Early near by, and Johnson, with the reserve artillery, near Green Village.

Pettigrew's brigade of Heth's division, advancing towards Gettysburg on the 30th, encountered Buford's cavalry and returned to Cashtown.

On the 29th, General Meade wired General Halleck,—

"If Lee is moving for Baltimore, I expect to get between his main army and that place. If he is crossing the Susquehanna, I shall rely upon General Couch, with his force, holding him, until I can fall upon his rear and give him battle, which I shall endeavor to do. . . . My endeavor will be, in my movements, to hold my force well together, with the hope of falling upon some portion of Lee's army in detail.*

As the change of orders made Gettysburg prominent as the point of impact, the positions of the commands relative thereto and their distances therefrom are items of importance in considering the culmination of events.

POSITIONS OF ARMY OF NORTHERN VIRGINIA, NIGHT OF JUNE 30.

General Lee's head-quarters, Greenwood, sixteen miles.

First Corps, Chambersburg, twenty-four miles to Gettysburg; part at Greenwood, sixteen miles.

Second Corps and Jenkins's cavalry, Heidlersburg, ten miles; part near Green Village, twenty-three miles (Johnson's division and trains).

Third Corps, near Greenwood, sixteen miles, and Cashtown, eight miles.

Stuart's cavalry, circling between York and Carlisle, out of sight.

Robertson's cavalry, in Virginia, beyond reach.

Imboden's cavalry, at Hancock, out of sight.

The Confederates not intending to precipitate battle.

POSITIONS OF ARMY OF THE POTOMAC.

General Meade's head-quarters, Taneytown, fourteen miles.

General Hunt, artillery reserve, Taneytown.

First Corps, Marsh Run, six miles.

* Report Committee, vol. i. p. 480.

Second Corps, Uniontown, twenty-two miles.
Third Corps, Bridgeport, twelve miles.
Fifth Corps, Union Mills, fifteen miles.
Sixth Corps, Manchester, twenty-two miles.
Eleventh Corps, Emmitsburg, twelve miles.
Twelfth Corps, Littletown, nine miles.
Kilpatrick's cavalry, Hanover, thirteen miles.
Gregg's cavalry, Manchester, twenty-two miles.
Buford's cavalry, Gettysburg.

It should be borne in mind that the field of contention was south and east of Gettysburg, so that the Union troops were from two to four miles nearer their field of battle than were the Confederates, who had to march from two to four miles *beyond the town.*

Referring to the map, it may be seen that the Confederate corps had two routes by which to march for concentration,—viz., from Heidlersburg to Cashtown, part of the Second Corps; on the road from Chambersburg, the First, Third, and part of the Second Corps (with all of the trains of the latter), with but a single track, the Chambersburg-Gettysburg turnpike. Some of their distances were greater than any of the columns of the enemy, while the Army of the Potomac had almost as many routes of march as commands, and was marching from day to day anticipating a general engagement, which they were especially cautioned on the 30th was imminent.

General Hill decided to go beyond Cashtown on the 1st to ascertain as to the enemy reported at Gettysburg. He gave notice of his intentions to General Ewell, and sent back to the commanding general to have Anderson's division sent forward. He was at Cashtown with Heth's and Pender's divisions and their batteries; his reserve artillery with Anderson's division at Fayetteville.

The armies on the night of June 30 stood thus:

The Confederate: First Corps, two divisions at Greenwood (except one brigade detached under orders from head-quarters at New Guilford); Pickett's three brigades at Chambersburg, left under orders from head-quarters to guard trains; the Second Corps, two divisions near Heidlersburg, one near and north of Chambersburg; the Third Corps at Cashtown and Fayetteville; cavalry not in sight or hearing, except Jenkins's brigade and a small detachment.

The Union army: the First Corps on Marsh Run, the Second at Uniontown, the Third at Bridgeport, the Fifth at Union Mills, the Sixth at Manchester, the Eleventh at Emmitsburg, the Twelfth at Littlestown, Fitzpatrick's cavalry at Hanover, Buford's at Gettysburg (except one brigade, detached, guarding his trains). General Meade's head-quarters and reserve artillery were at Taneytown. His army, including cavalry, in hand.

General Lee's orders called his troops on converging lines towards Cashtown, but he found that part of his infantry must be left at Chambersburg to await the Imboden cavalry, not up, and one of Hood's brigades must be detached on his right at New Guilford to guard on that side in place of Robertson's cavalry (in Virginia). So that as he advanced towards his adversary, the eyes and ears of his army were turned afar off, looking towards the homes of non-combatants. It is bootless to this writing to restate whence came this mishap. There is no doubt it greatly disturbed General Lee's mind, and he would have called a halt under ordinary circumstances, but his orders did not contemplate immediate movements beyond Cashtown. In that he felt safe, depending upon his cavalry coming up in time to meet him there.

He was in his usual cheerful spirits on the morning of the 1st, and called me to ride with him. My column was not well stretched on the road before it encountered the division of E. Johnson (Second Corps) cutting in on our front, with all of Ewell's reserve and supply trains. He ordered the First Corps halted, and directed that Johnson's division and train should pass on to its corps, the

First to wait. During the wait I dismounted to give Hero a little respite. (The Irish groom had christened my favorite horse "*Haro.*")

After a little time General Lee proposed that we should ride on, and soon we heard reports of cannon. The fire seemed to be beyond Cashtown, and as it increased he left me and rode faster for the front.

The brigades of Gamble and Devin of Buford's cavalry were the force that met Pettigrew's brigade on the afternoon of the 30th, when the latter retired to the post of the divisions at Cashtown.

From Gettysburg roads diverge to the passes of the mountains, the borders of the Potomac and Susquehanna, and the cities of Baltimore and Washington; so that it was something of a strategic point. From the west side two broad roads run, one northwest to Chambersburg *via* Cashtown, the other southwest through Fairfield to Hagerstown. They cross an elevated ridge, a mile out north, and south of the Lutheran Seminary, known to the Confederates as Seminary Ridge, covered by open forests. At the northward, about two miles from the town, the ridge divides, a lesser ridge putting out west, and presently taking a parallel course with the greater. This was known as McPherson's Ridge, and was about five hundred yards from the first, where the road crosses it. Nearly parallel with the Chambersburg pike and about two hundred yards distant was the cut of an unfinished railroad. Willoughby's Run flows south in a course nearly parallel to and west of the ridge, and is bordered by timbered lands. North of Gettysburg the grounds are open and in fair fields. Directly south of it a bold ridge rises with rough and steep slopes. The prominent point of the south ridge is Cemetery Hill, and east of this is Culp's Hill, from which the ridge turns sharply south half a mile, and drops off into low grounds. It was well wooded and its eastern ascent steep. East of it and flowing south is Rock Creek. From Cemetery Hill the ground is elevated, the ridge sloping south to the cropping out of Little Round Top, Devil's Den, and the bolder Round Top, the latter about three miles south of the town. Cemetery Ridge is nearly parallel to Seminary Ridge, and is more elevated.

At five o'clock on the morning of July 1, General A. P. Hill marched towards Gettysburg with the divisions of Heth and Pender, and the battalions of artillery under Pegram and McIntosh, Heth's division and Pegram's artillery in advance. R. H. Anderson's division, with the reserve artillery left at Fayetteville, was ordered to march and halt at Cashtown. About ten o'clock Heth encountered Buford's cavalry. Archer's brigade, leading, engaged, and Davis's brigade came up on his left with part of Pegram's artillery. The cavalry was forced back till it passed Willoughby's Run.

On the 30th of June, General John F. Reynolds had been directed to resume command of the right wing of the Union army,—First, Third, and Eleventh Corps. He was advised that day of the threatening movements of the Confederates on the Cashtown and Mummasburg roads. At the same time the indications from General Meade's head-quarters pointed to Pipe Creek as the probable line in case of battle. Reynolds, however, prepared to support Buford's line of cavalry, and marched at eight o'clock on the 1st of July with Wadsworth's division and Hall's battery, leaving the other divisions of Doubleday and Robinson with the artillery to follow under General Doubleday, who became commander of the corps upon the assignment of Reynolds to command of the wing.

As Reynolds approached Gettysburg, in hearing of the cavalry fight, he turned the head of his column to the left and marched through the fields towards the engagement. As the cavalry skirmish line retired and passed Willoughby's Run, he approached with his reinforcements,

Brigadier-General Cutler in advance, and was put in on the north of the Cashtown road, followed by Hall's battery. Brigadier-General Meredith following, his brigade was put into line on the left. As fast as the troops got into line they became severely engaged. Doubleday, in advance of the divisions under him, put Meredith's brigade in favorable position in a strip of woodland on the left.

As the Confederate left advanced through the railroad cut they came upon Hill's battery, and were about to get it, when it was saved by speedy withdrawal, which caused the Union right to retire, while Archer's brigade of the Confederate right, in pushing to the front, came into an open space before Meredith's brigade, which in turn made a gallant advance, drove Archer back, followed across the run, and captured General Archer and one thousand of Heth's men. Two brigades of Heth's division, Pettigrew's and Brockenbrough's, were put in on the right of Archer's men. During the severe engagement on his right the advance of the Confederate infantry got in so close along the railroad cut that General Reynolds, in efforts to extricate his right, was shot, when the right, still under severe pressure, was forced to retire towards Seminary Ridge. Hall's battery, severely crippled, succeeded in getting away as the right retired.

Doubleday's other divisions came up about the moment General Reynolds was killed. The Second (Robinson's) and Third (Rowley's) Divisions deployed on the right and left. Cooper's battery of four three-inch guns followed the left division. At the same time Hill reinforced by his division under Pender, Thomas's brigade on his left, Lane, Scales, and Perrin to the right. These restored the Confederate right, overlapping the Federal left; at the same time Thomas's brigade made successful battle on the left, pushing off Wadsworth's right and Hall's battery, when the two brigades of the

Second Division (Robinson's) were sent to their support, but were, in turn, forced back towards Seminary Ridge. The Confederate sharp-shooters cut down the horses of one of Hall's guns and forced him to drop it. Hill advanced Pegram's and McIntosh's artillery to McPherson's Ridge, forcing the entire Union line back to Seminary Ridge. General Doubleday, anticipating such contingency, had ordered trenches made about Seminary Ridge, and sent his three other batteries under Colonel Wainwright to that point. He formed his line along the ridge and occupied the trenches by part of his infantry. At this period Ewell's divisions under Rodes approached against Doubleday's right.

General Howard, upon his first approach to the battle, marched the Eleventh Corps to Cemetery Hill, and there posted it until called upon by General Doubleday for assistance. To meet the call he ordered his divisions under Generals Barlow and Schurz to Doubleday's right, to occupy a prominent point at the north end of Seminary Ridge, reserving his division under Steinwehr and part of his artillery on Cemetery Hill.

As the divisions of the Eleventh Corps approached the Confederate left, Rodes's division of Ewell's corps advanced. The Federals then stood across the Cashtown road, their left in advance of the Seminary, their right thrown or standing more to the rear. Rodes was in season to sweep the field of approach to the high point intended to be occupied by the divisions sent by Howard, and came in good position to enfilade Robinson's division of the First Corps. As Rodes approached he was threatened by Buford's cavalry, but, finding cover under woodland, he made advance by three brigades in line till he came to the point of view which gave him command of that end of the field in elevated position, and in plunging fire down Robinson's line and in advance of the divisions sent by General Howard to occupy that point. While posting his infantry, Rodes ordered Carter's battery of artillery into action against Robinson's lines stretched out and engaged against Hill's corps. At that moment the divisions of the Eleventh Corps were not in full front of Rodes, so that his fire upon Robinson's line was something of a surprise, as well as most discomfiting. The divisions and artillery of the Eleventh came to the front, however, almost simultaneously with Robinson's necessitated change of right front rearward towards Rodes.

These changes and dispositions gave Hill opportunity to press on by his front, when Doubleday was obliged to call for help, and Schurz called for support on his right. Coster's brigade was sent from Steinwehr's reserve, and Buford's cavalry was ordered to brace as far as practicable the centre of the First Corps, and another battery was sent to Schurz's division. At 2.45 another call for help by the First Corps was received, and General Schurz was asked to answer it if he could by a regiment or more. Calls were sent to hurry Slocum's (Twelfth) corps, some miles away, but then Ewell was swinging his division under Early into line nearer to Gettysburg, Gordon's brigade and Jones's battery coming in in good time to make strong Rodes's left, and Hill's corps had overlapped the left of the First Corps, so that General Howard found himself forced to command a steady, orderly retreat to Cemetery Hill.

The Confederates pushed rapidly on, particularly the fresher troops of Ewell, cleared the field, and followed on through the streets of Gettysburg at four o'clock. The retreat began and continued in good order till they passed Gettysburg, when the ranks became so scattered that the final march was little better than "*Sauve qui peut.*"

As the troops retreated through Gettysburg, General Hancock rode upon the field, and under special assignment assumed command at three o'clock. As the retreating troops arrived, Wadsworth's division on the right, the

Eleventh Corps across the Baltimore pike, the balance of the First under Doubleday on the left of the Eleventh, General Howard and others assisted in forming the new line.

The total effectives of the First and Eleventh Corps, according to the consolidated morning report of June 30, was 19,982. From the latest returns of General Lee's army, an average estimate of his four divisions gave his total as 25,252. Part of the reserve division of the Eleventh Corps was not engaged, but Buford had two brigades of cavalry, and so the foregoing may be a fair estimate of the forces engaged on the first day at Gettysburg.

At Cashtown, General Lee found that General Hill had halted his division under R. H. Anderson and his reserve artillery. He had General Anderson called, who subsequently wrote me of the interview as follows:

"About twelve o'clock I received a message notifying me that General Lee desired to see me. I found General Lee intently listening to the fire of the guns, and very much disturbed and depressed. At length he said, more to himself than to me, 'I cannot think what has become of Stuart. I ought to have heard from him long before now. He may have met with disaster, but I hope not. In the absence of reports from him, I am in ignorance as to what we have in front of us here. It may be the whole Federal army, or it may be only a detachment. If it is the whole Federal force, we must fight a battle here. If we do not gain a victory, those defiles and gorges which we passed this morning will shelter us from disaster.'"

He ordered Anderson forward, and rode on to Seminary Ridge in time to view the closing operations of the engagement. The Union troops were in disorder, climbing Cemetery Heights, the Confederates following through the streets of Gettysburg. Two other divisions of Confederates were up soon after, E. Johnson's of the Second and R. H. Anderson's of the Third Corps.

After a long wait I left orders for the troops to follow

the trains of the Second Corps, and rode to find General Lee. His head-quarters were on Seminary Ridge at the crossing of the Cashtown road. Anderson's division was then filed off along the ridge, resting. Johnson's had marched to report to the corps commander. Dismounting and passing the usual salutation, I drew my glasses and made a studied view of the position upon which the enemy was rallying his forces, and of the lay of the land surrounding. General Lee was engaged at the moment. He had announced beforehand that he would not make aggressive battle in the enemy's country. After the survey and in consideration of his plans,—noting movements of detachments of the enemy on the Emmitsburg road, the relative positions for manœuvre, the lofty perch of the enemy, the rocky slopes from it, all marking the position clearly defensive,—I said, "We could not call the enemy to position better suited to our plans. All that we have to do is to file around his left and secure good ground between him and his capital." This, when said, was thought to be the opinion of my commander as much as my own. I was not a little surprised, therefore, at his impatience, as, striking the air with his closed hand, he said, "If he is there to-morrow I will attack him."

In his official account, General Lee reported,—

"It had not been intended to deliver a general battle so far from our base unless attacked. But coming unexpectedly upon the whole Federal army, to withdraw through the mountains with our extensive trains would have been difficult and dangerous."

When he rode away from me in the forenoon he made no mention of his absent cavalry, nor did he indicate that it was not within call. So I was at a loss to understand his nervous condition, and supported the suggestion so far as to say, "If he is there to-morrow it will be because he wants you to attack," and queried, "If that height has become the objective, why not take it at once?

We have forty thousand men, less the casualties of the day; he cannot have more than twenty thousand." Then it was that I heard of the wanderings of the cavalry and the cause of his uneven temper. So vexed was he at the halt of the Imboden cavalry at Hancock, *in the opening of the campaign*, that he was losing sight of Pickett's brigades as a known quantity for battle. His manner suggested to me that a little reflection would be better than further discussion, and right soon he suggested to the commander of the Second Corps to take Cemetery Hill if he thought it practicable, but the subordinate did not care to take upon himself a fight that his chief would not venture to order.*

The following circular orders were sent the commanders of columns of the First Corps:

"HEAD-QUARTERS FIRST ARMY CORPS,
"NEAR GETTYSBURG, July 1, 5.30 P.M.

"COLONEL,—The commanding general desires you to come on to-night as fast as you can without distressing your men and animals. Hill and Ewell have sharply engaged the enemy, and you will be needed for to-morrow's battle. Let us know where you will stop to-night.

"Respectfully,
"G. M. SORREL,
"*A. A. General.*

"COLONEL WALTON,
"*Chief of Artillery.*"

* From General Lee's official report: ". . . It was ascertained from the prisoners that we had been engaged with two corps of the army formerly commanded by General Hooker, and that the remainder of that army, under General Meade, was approaching Gettysburg. Without information as to its proximity, the strong position which the enemy had assumed could not be attacked without danger of exposing the four divisions present, already weakened and exhausted by a long and bloody struggle, to overwhelming numbers of fresh troops. General Ewell was, therefore, instructed to carry the hill occupied by the enemy, if he found it practicable, but to avoid a general engagement until the arrival of the other divisions of the army, which were ordered to hasten forward. He decided to await Johnson's division, which had marched from Carlisle by the road west of the mountains to guard the trains of his corps, and consequently did not reach Gettysburg until a late hour. . . ."

At 12.15 of the afternoon of the 1st, General Halleck sent a cipher despatch to General Meade approving his tactics, but asking, as to his strategy, "Are you not too far east, and may not Lee attempt to turn your left and cut you off from Frederick ?"

In this connection may be noted the plan that General Meade had mapped in his own mind and given to some of his generals for battle to be formed behind Pipe Creek, a position that would have met the views of General Halleck, as well as his own, covering Washington and Baltimore under close lines that could not be turned. At Gettysburg the Confederates had comparatively an open field.

Reports coming in to head-quarters about six o'clock that the enemy was in some force off our right towards Fairfield, General Lee ordered General Anderson to put one of his brigades out on the right as picket-guard. Wilcox's brigade and Ross's battery were marched and posted near Black Horse Tavern.

Nothing coming from the *centre troops* about Cemetery Hill, General Lee ordered the Second Corps, *after night, from his left to his right*, for work in that direction, but General Ewell rode over and reported that another point—Culp's Hill—had been found on his left, which had commanding elevation over Cemetery Hill, from which the troops on the latter could be dislodged, by artillery, and was under the impression that his troops were in possession there. That was accredited as reported and approved, and the corps commander returned, and ordered the hill occupied if it had not been done. But the officer in charge had waited for specific orders, and when they were received he had made another reconnoissance. It was then twelve o'clock. By the reconnoissance it was found that the enemy was there, and it was thought that this should be reported, and further orders waited.

General Ewell's troops and trains passed the junction

of the roads at four o'clock. The train was fourteen miles long. It was followed by the troops of the First Corps that had been waiting all day. After night the Washington Artillery and McLaws's division camped at Marsh Run, four miles from Gettysburg. Here is Hood's account of his march:

"While lying in camp near Chambersburg information was received that Hill and Ewell were about to come into contact with the enemy near Gettysburg. My troops, together with McLaws's division, were at once put in motion upon the most direct road to that point, which we reached after a hard march at or before sunrise on July 2. So imperative had been our orders to hasten forward with all possible speed that on the march my troops were allowed to halt and rest only about two hours during the night from the 1st to the 2d of July."

When I left General Lee, about seven o'clock in the evening, he had formed no plans beyond that of seizing Culp's Hill as his point from which to engage, nor given any orders for the next day, though his desperate mood was painfully evident, and gave rise to serious apprehensions. He had heard nothing of the movements of the enemy since his crossing the Potomac, except the report of the scout. His own force on the field was the Second Corps, Rodes's, Early's, and E. Johnson's divisions from right to left through the streets of Gettysburg around towards Culp's Hill; on Rodes's right, Pender's division of the Third; on Seminary Ridge, R. H. Anderson's division of the Third (except Wilcox's brigade at Black Horse Tavern); behind Seminary Ridge, Heth's division of the Third; on the march between Cashtown and Greenwood, part of the First Corps, and parts at Chambersburg and New Guilford.

CHAPTER XXVII.

GETTYSBURG—SECOND DAY.

The Confederate Commander reviews the Field and decides on Plan of Battle—Positions on the Morning of July 2—Night March of the Federal Sixth Corps—It was excelled by Law's Brigade of Confederates—The Battle was opened after Mid-day—General Hood appeals for Permission to turn the Federal Left—Failure to make the Flanking Movement by the Confederate Right was a Serious Mistake—Hood, in his usual Gallant Style, led his Troops forward among the Rocks—Desperate Charges against an Earnest Adversary—Hood wounded—General Law succeeds him in command of the Division—"Little Round Top" an Important Point—"The Citadel of the Field"—It was a Fight of Seventeen Thousand Confederates against twice their Number—Quiet along the Lines of other Confederate Commands—"A Man on the Left who didn't care to make the Battle win"—Evidence against the Alleged Order for "Battle at Sunrise"—The "Order" to Ewell was Discretionary—Lee had lost his Balance.

THE stars were shining brightly on the morning of the 2d when I reported at General Lee's head-quarters and asked for orders. After a time Generals McLaws and Hood, with their staffs, rode up. After sunrise their commands filed off the road to the right and rested. The Washington Artillery was with them, and about nine o'clock, after an all-night march, Alexander's batteries were up as far as Willoughby's Run, where he parked and fed, and rode to head-quarters to report.

As indicated by these movements, General Lee was not ready with his plans. He had not heard from his cavalry, nor of the movements of the enemy further than the information from a despatch captured during the night, that the Fifth Corps was in camp about five miles from Gettysburg, and the Twelfth Corps was reported near Culp's Hill. As soon as it was light enough to see, however, the enemy was found in position on his formidable heights awaiting us.

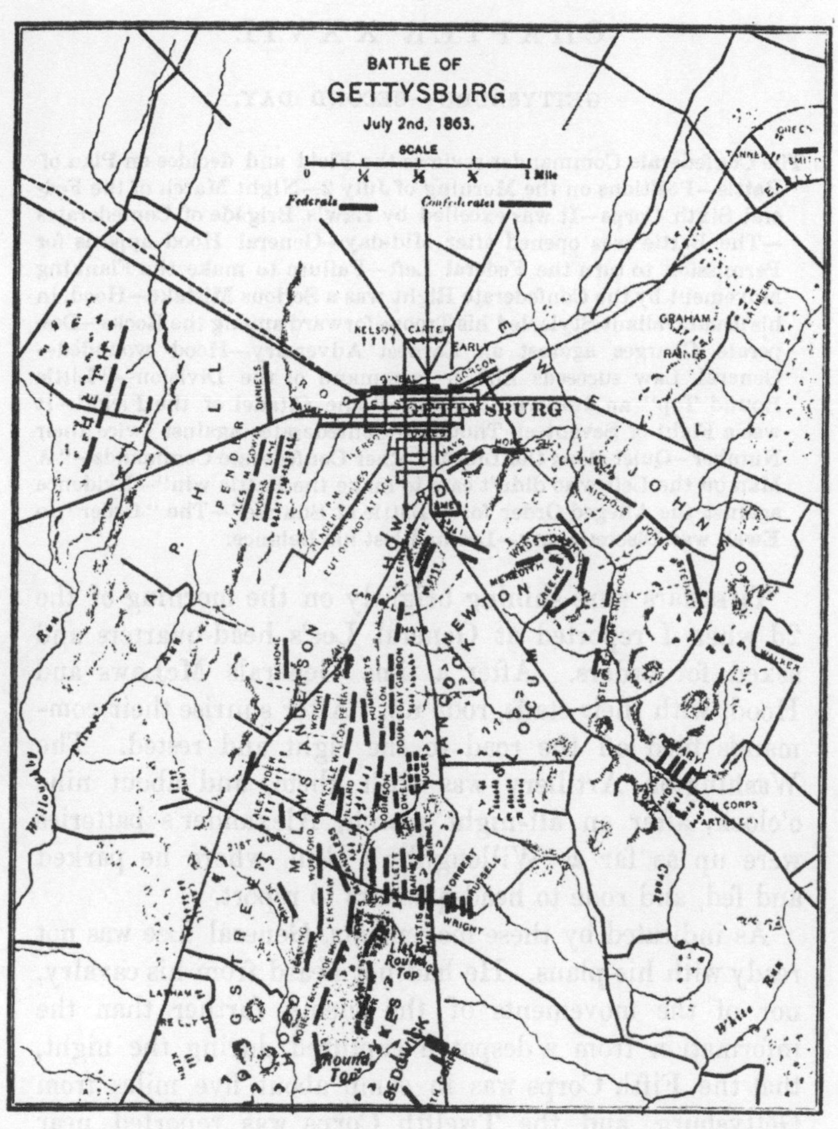
BATTLE OF
GETTYSBURG
July 2nd, 1863.
SCALE
0 ¼ ½ ¾ 1 Mile
Federals
Confederates
GETTYSBURG
NELSON
CARTER
EARLY
GORDON
HAYS
HOKE
GRAHAM
RAINES
NICHOLS
GREENE
WALKER
PENDER
HETH
ANDERSON
HOWARD
NEWTON
SLOCUM
McLAWS
HOOD
SYKES
SEDGWICK
WRIGHT
TORBERT
RUSSELL
LATHAM
Little Round Top
Round Top
Willoughby Run
White Run

The result of efforts during the night and early morning to secure Culp's Hill had not been reported, and General Lee sent Colonel Venable of his staff to confer with the commander of the Second Corps as to opportunity to make the battle by his left. He was still in doubt whether it would be better to move to his far-off right. About nine o'clock he rode to his left to be assured of the position there, and of the general temper of affairs in that quarter. After viewing the field, he held conference with the corps and division commanders. They preferred to accept his judgment and orders, except General Early, who claimed to have learned of the topographical features of the country during his march towards York, and recommended the right of the line as the point at which strong battle should be made. About ten o'clock General Lee returned to his head-quarters, but his engineer who had been sent to reconnoitre on his right had not come back. To be at hand for orders, I remained with the troops at his head-quarters. The infantry had arms stacked; the artillery was at rest.

The enemy occupied the commanding heights of the city cemetery, from which point, in irregular grade, the ridge slopes southward two miles and a half to a bold outcropping height of three hundred feet called Little Round Top, and farther south half a mile ends in the greater elevation called Round Top. The former is covered from base to top by formidable boulders. From the cemetery to Little Round Top was the long main front of General Meade's position. At the cemetery his line turned to the northeast and east and southeast in an elliptical curve, with his right on Culp's Hill.

At an early hour of the 2d the Union army was posted: the Twelfth Corps at Culp's Hill, extending its left to Wadsworth's division of the First; on Wadsworth's left the Eleventh Corps; on the left of the Eleventh the other troops of the First; on their left the Second, and left of that to Little Round Top the Third Corps; the Fifth Corps stood in reserve across the bend from the right of the Twelfth to the left of the Second Corps. Thus there was formed a field of tremendous power upon a convex curve, which gave the benefit of rapid concentration at any point or points. The natural defences had been improved during the night and early morning. The Sixth Corps was marching from Manchester, twenty-two miles from Gettysburg. Its first order, received near Manchester before night of the 1st, was to march for Taneytown, but after passing the Baltimore pike the orders were changed, directing a prompt march to Gettysburg. The march has been variously estimated from thirty to thirty-five miles, but the distance from Manchester *via* Taneytown to Gettysburg is only twenty-nine miles, and as the ground for which the corps marched was three miles east of Gettysburg, the march would have been only twenty-six miles *via* Taneytown; as the corps marched back and took the Baltimore pike, some distance must have been saved. It was on the field at three o'clock of the afternoon, —the Union cavalry under General Pleasonton in reach.

The Confederate left was covering the north and east curve of the enemy's line, Johnson's division near Culp's Hill, Early's and Rodes's extending the line to the right through Gettysburg; Pender's division on the right of Rodes's; the other divisions of the Third Corps resting on Seminary Ridge, with McLaws's division and Hood's three brigades near general head-quarters; Pickett's brigades and Law's of Hood's division at Chambersburg and New Guilford, twenty-two and twenty-four miles away. Law had received orders to join his division, and was on the march. The cavalry was not yet heard from. The line so extended and twisted about the rough ground that concentration at any point was not possible.

It was some little time after General Lee's return from his ride to the left before he received the reports of the reconnoissance ordered from his centre to his right. His mind, previously settled to the purpose to fight where the enemy stood, now accepted the explicit plan of making the opening on his right, and to have the engagement general. He ordered the commander of the Third Corps to extend the centre by Anderson's division, McLaws's and Hood's divisions to extend the deployment to his right. Heth's division of the Third was drawn nearer the front, and notice of his plans was sent the commander of the Second Corps.

At the intimation that the battle would be opened on the right by part of the First Corps, Colonel Alexander was asked to act as director of artillery, and sent to view the field in time to assign the batteries as they were up. It was eleven o'clock when General Lee's order was issued, but he had ordered Law's brigade to its division, and a wait of thirty minutes was necessary for it to get up. Law had received his orders at three in the morning, and had marched twenty-three miles. The battle-ground was still five miles off by the route of march, but Law completed his march of twenty-eight miles in eleven hours,—the best marching done in either army to reach the field of Gettysburg.

The battle was to be opened on the right by two divisions of the First Corps, supported on their left by four of the brigades of Anderson's division; the opening to be promptly followed on Lee's left by the Second Corps, and continued to real attack if the opportunity occurred; the Third (centre) Corps to move to severe threatening and take advantage of opportunity to attack; the movements of the Second and Third Corps to be prompt, and in close, severe co-operation, so as to prevent concentration against the battle of the right. The little cavalry that was with the army was kept on the extreme left. Not so much as one trooper was sent us.

General Lee ordered his reconnoitring officer to lead

the troops of the First Corps and conduct them by a route concealed from view of the enemy. As I was relieved for the time from the march, I rode near the middle of the line. General Lee rode with me a mile or more. General Anderson marched by a route nearer the enemy's line, and was discovered by General Sickles, who commanded the Third Corps, the left of the Union line. A little uncomfortable at his retired position, and seeing that the battle was forming against him, General Sickles thought to put the Third Maine Regiment and the Berdan Sharpshooters on outpost in a bold woodland cover, to develop somewhat of the approaching battle, and presently threw his corps forward as far as the Peach Orchard, half a mile forward of the position assigned to it in the general line. The Tenth Alabama Regiment was sent against the outpost guard, and, reinforced by the Eleventh Regiment, drove it back, and Anderson's division found its place in proper line.

General Birney's account of the affair at the outpost puts it at twelve o'clock, and the signal accounts, the only papers dated on the field, reported,—

"The enemy's skirmishers advancing from the west one mile from here—11.45."

And presently,—

"The rebels are in force; our skirmishers give way—12.55."

There is no room for doubt of the accuracy of these reports, which go to show that it was one o'clock in the afternoon when the Third Corps, upon which the First Corps was to form, was in position.

Under the conduct of the reconnoitring officer, our march seemed slow,—there were some halts and countermarches. To save time, I ordered the rear division to double on the front, and we were near the affair of Anderson's regiments with the outpost guard of Sickles. Anderson's division deployed,—Wilcox's, Perry's, Wright's, Posey's, and Mahone's brigades from right to left.

General Hood was ordered to send his select scouts in advance, to go through the woodlands and act as vedettes, in the absence of cavalry, and give information of the enemy, if there. The double line marched up the slope and deployed,—McLaws on the right of Anderson, Hood's division on his right, McLaws near the crest of the plateau in front of the Peach Orchard, Hood spreading and enveloping Sickles's left. The former was readily adjusted to ground from which to advance or defend. Hood's front was very rugged, with no field for artillery, and very rough for advance of infantry. As soon as he passed the Emmitsburg road, he sent to report of the great advantage of moving on by his right around to the enemy's rear. His scouting parties reported that there was nothing between them and the enemy's trains. He was told that the move to the right had been proposed the day before and rejected; that General Lee's orders were to guide my left by the Emmitsburg road.

In our immediate front were the divisions of the Third Corps under Generals Humphreys and Birney, from right to left, with orders for supports of the flanks by divisions of the Second and Fifth Corps. The ground on the left of Birney's division was so broken and obstructed by boulders that his left was dropped off to the rear, forming a broken line. In rear of the enemy, and between his lines and Little Round Top, was a very rough elevation of eighty feet formed by upheavals that left open passage deep down Devil's Den. Smith's battery was on Birney's left, Winslow's between the right and next brigade. Other batteries in position were Clark's, Ames's, Randolph's, Seeley's, and Turnbull's.

As McLaws's division came up on line, Barksdale's brigade was in front of a battery about six hundred yards off. He appealed for permission to charge and capture it, but was told to wait. On his right was Kershaw's brigade, the brigades of Semmes and Wofford on the second line. Hood's division was in two lines,—Law's and Robertson's brigades in front, G. T. Anderson's and Benning's in the second line. The batteries were with the divisions,—four to the division. One of G. T. Anderson's regiments was put on picket down the Emmitsburg road.

General Hood appealed again and again for the move to the right, but, to give more confidence to his attack, he was reminded that the move to the right had been carefully considered by our chief and rejected in favor of his present orders.

The opportunity for our right was in the air. General Halleck saw it from Washington. General Meade saw and was apprehensive of it. Even General Pendleton refers to it in favorable mention in his official report. Failing to adopt it, General Lee should have gone with us to his right. He had seen and carefully examined the left of his line, and only gave us a guide to show the way to the right, leaving the battle to be adjusted to formidable and difficult grounds without his assistance. If he had been with us, General Hood's messengers could have been referred to general head-quarters, but to delay and send messengers five miles in favor of a move that he had rejected would have been contumacious. The opportunity was with the Confederates from the assembling on Cemetery Hill. It was inviting of their preconceived plans. It was the object of and excuse for the invasion as a substitute for more direct efforts for the relief of Vicksburg. Confederate writers and talkers claim that General Meade could have escaped without making aggressive battle, but that is equivalent to confession of the inertia that failed to grasp the opportunity.

Beaten in the battle of the 1st, dislodged of position, and outgeneralled, the Union army would have felt the want of spirit and confidence important to aggressive battle; but the call was with the Confederates, and these circumstances would have made their work facile, while the Union commander would have found the call to save his capital imperative. Even as events passed it was thought helpful to the Union side to give out the report on the night of the 2d that General McClellan was at hand and would command the army.

Four of the brigades of Anderson's division were ordered to advance in echelon in support of my left.

At three o'clock the artillery was ordered to open practice. General Meade was then with General Sickles discussing the feasibility of withdrawing his corps to the position to which it was originally assigned, but the opening admonished him that it was too late. He had just sent a cipher telegram to inform General Halleck, commander-in-chief, that in the event of his having no opportunity to attack, and should he find the Confederates moving to interpose between him and Washington, he would fall back on his supplies at Westminster.* But my right division was then nearer to Westminster, and our scouting parties of infantry were within rifle range of the road leading to that point and to Washington. So it would have been convenient, after holding our threatening attitude till night, to march across his line at dark, in time to draw other troops to close connection before the next morning.

Prompt to the order the combat opened, followed by artillery of the other corps, and our artillerists measured up to the better metal of the enemy by vigilant work. Hood's lines were not yet ready. After a little practice by the artillery, he was properly adjusted and ordered to bear down upon the enemy's left, but he was not prompt, and the order was repeated before he would strike down.†

In his usual gallant style he led his troops through the rocky fastnesses against the strong lines of his earnest

---

* Report of Committee, vol. i. p. 488.

† His account.

adversary, and encountered battle that called for all of his power and skill. The enemy was tenacious of his strong ground; his skilfully-handled batteries swept through the passes between the rocks; the more deadly fire of infantry concentrated as our men bore upon the angle of the enemy's line and stemmed the fiercest onset, until it became necessary to shorten their work by a desperate charge. This pressing struggle and the cross-fire of our batteries broke in the salient angle, but the thickening fire, as the angle was pressed back, hurt Hood's left and held him in steady fight. His right brigade was drawn towards Round Top by the heavy fire pouring from that quarter, Benning's brigade was pressed to the thickening line at the angle, and G. T. Anderson's was put in support of the battle growing against Hood's right.

I rode to McLaws, found him ready for his opportunity, and Barksdale chafing in his wait for the order to seize the battery in his front. Kershaw's brigade of his right first advanced and struck near the angle of the enemy's line where his forces were gathering strength. After additional caution to hold his ranks closed, McLaws ordered Barksdale in. With glorious bearing he sprang to his work, overriding obstacles and dangers. Without a pause to deliver a shot, he had the battery. Kershaw, joined by Semmes's brigade, responded, and Hood's men, feeling the impulsion of relief, resumed their bold fight, and presently the enemy's line was broken through its length. But his well-seasoned troops knew how to utilize the advantage of their grounds and put back their dreadful fires from rocks, depressions, and stone fences, as they went for shelter about Little Round Top.

That point had not been occupied by the enemy, nor marked as an important feature of the field. The broken ranks sought shelter under its rocks and defiles as birds fly to cover. General Hood fell seriously hurt, and General Law succeeded to command of the division, but the well-seasoned troops were not in need of a close guiding hand. The battle was on, and they knew how to press its hottest contention.

General Warren, chief engineer of the Federal army, was sent at the critical moment to Little Round Top, and found that it was the citadel of the field. He called for troops to occupy it. The Fifth Corps (Sykes's) was hurried to him, and General Hancock sent him Caldwell's division of the Second Corps. At the Brick House, away from his right, General Sickles had a detachment that had been reinforced by General Hancock. This fire drew Anderson's brigade of direction (Wilcox) a little off from support of Barksdale's left. General Humphreys, seeing the opportunity, rallied such of his troops as he could, and, reinforced by Hays's division (Willard's brigade) of Hancock's corps, came against Barksdale's flank, but the latter moved bravely on, the guiding spirit of the battle. Wright's Georgia and Perry's Florida brigades were drawn in behind Wilcox and thrown against Humphreys, pushing him off and breaking him up.

The fighting had by this time become tremendous, and brave men and officers were stricken by hundreds. Posey and Wilcox dislodged the forces about the Brick House.

General Sickles was desperately wounded!

General Willard was dead!

General Semmes, of McLaws's division, was mortally wounded!

Our left relieved, the brigades of Anderson's division moved on with Barksdale's, passed the swale, and moved up the slope. Caldwell's division, and presently those of Ayres and Barnes of the Fifth Corps, met and held our strongest battle. While thus engaged, General Sykes succeeded in putting Vincent's and Weed's brigades and Hazlett's battery on the summit of Little Round Top, but presently we overreached Caldwell's division, broke it off, and pushed it from the field. Of his brigade commanders,

Zook was killed, and Brooke and Cross were wounded, the latter mortally. General Hancock reported sixty per cent. of his men lost. On our side, Barksdale was down dying, and G. T. Anderson wounded.

We had carried Devil's Den, were at the Round Tops and the Wheat-Field, but Ayres's division of regulars and Barnes's division were holding us in equal battle. The struggle throughout the field seemed at its tension. The brigades of R. H. Anderson's division could hold off other troops of Hancock's, but were not strong enough to step to the enemy's lines. When Caldwell's division was pushed away, Ayres's flank and the gorge at Little Round Top were only covered by a sharp line of picket men behind the boulders. If we could drive in the sharp-shooters and strike Ayres's flank to advantage, we could dislodge his and Barnes's divisions, occupy the gorge behind Sykes's brigades on Round Top, force them to retreat, and lift our desperate fighters to the summit. I had one brigade —Wofford's—that had not been engaged in the hottest battle. To urge the troops to their reserve power in the precious moments, I rode with Wofford. The rugged field, the rough plunge of artillery fire, and the piercing musket-shots delayed somewhat the march, but Alexander dashed up with his batteries and gave new spirit to the worn infantry ranks. By a fortunate strike upon Ayres's flank we broke his line and pushed him and Barnes so closely that they were obliged to use most strenuous efforts to get away without losing in prisoners as well as their killed and wounded. We gained the Wheat-Field, and were so close upon the gorge that our artillery could no longer venture their fire into it. We were on Little Round Top grappling for the crowning point. The brigade commanders there, Vincent and Weed, were killed, also the battery commander, Hazlett, and others, but their troops were holding to their work as firmly as the mighty boulders that helped them. General Meade thought that the Confederate army was working on my part of the field. He led some regiments of the Twelfth Corps and posted them against us, called a division of Newton's corps (First) from beyond Hancock's, and sent Crawford's division, the last of the Fifth Corps, splitting through the gorge, forming solid lines, in places behind stone fences, and making steady battle, as veterans fresh in action know so well how to make. While Meade's lines were growing my men were dropping; we had no others to call to their aid, and the weight against us was too heavy to carry. The extreme left of our lines was only about a mile from us across the enemy's concentric position, which brought us within hearing of that battle, if engaged, and near enough to feel its swell, but nothing was heard or felt but the clear ring of the enemy's fresh metal as he came against us. No other part of our army had engaged! My seventeen thousand against the Army of the Potomac! The sun was down, and with it went down the severe battle. I ordered recall of the troops to the line of Plum Run and Devil's Den, leaving picket lines near the foot of the Round Tops. My loss was about six thousand, Meade's between twelve and fourteen thousand; but his loss in general and field officers was frightful. When General Humphreys, who succeeded to Barksdale's brigade, was called back to the new line, he thought there was some mistake in the orders, and only withdrew as far as a captured battery, and when the order was repeated, retired under protest.

General Stuart came down from Carlisle with his column of cavalry late in the afternoon of the 2d. As he approached he met a cavalry force of the enemy moving towards the Confederate left rear, and was successful in arresting it. He was posted with Jenkins's three thousand cavalry * on the Confederate left.

* In his official report he puts Jenkins's force at the opening campaign at three thousand eight hundred.

Notwithstanding the supreme order of the day for general battle, and the reinforcement of the cavalry on our left, the Second and Third Corps remained idle during all of the severe battle of the Confederate right, except the artillery, and the part of that on the extreme left was only in practice long enough to feel the superior metal of the enemy, when it retired, leaving a battery of four guns in position. General Early failed to even form his division in battle order, leaving a brigade in position remote from the line, and sending, later, another to be near Stuart's cavalry. The latter returned, however, before night.

At eight o'clock in the evening the division on our extreme left, E. Johnson's, advanced. The brigades were J. M. Jones's, Nicholls's, Steuart's, and Walker's. Walker's was detached, as they moved, to look for a detachment of the enemy reported threatening the far away left. When the three brigades crossed Rock Creek it was night. The enemy's line to be assaulted was occupied by Greene's brigade of the Twelfth Corps. It was reinforced by three regiments of Wadsworth's division and three from the Eleventh Corps. After brave attack and defence, part of the line was carried, when the fight, after a severe fusillade between the infantry lines, quieted, and Walker's brigade returned to the division. Part of the enemy's trenches, east of the point attacked (across a swale), vacated when the corps moved over to the left, General Johnson failed to occupy.

Before this, General Rodes discovered that the enemy, in front of his division, was drawing off his artillery and infantry to my battle of the right, and suggested to General Early that the moment had come for the divisions to attack, and drew his forces from entanglements about the streets to be ready. After E. Johnson's fight on our extreme left, General Early ordered two brigades under General Harry T. Hays to attack. Hays had with

SECOND DAY'S BATTLE, GETTYSBURG.

his Louisiana brigade Hoke's North Carolina brigade under Colonel Avery. He made as gallant a fight as was ever made. Mounting to the top of the hill, he captured a battery, and pushed on in brave order, taking some prisoners and colors, until he discovered that his two brigades were advancing in a night affair against a grand army, when he found that he was fortunate in having night to cover his weakness, and withdrew. The gallant Colonel Avery, mortally wounded and dying, wrote on a slip of paper, "*Tell father that I died with my face to the enemy.*" When Rodes was prepared, Hays had retired, and the former did not see that it was part of the order for general engagement to put his division in night attack that could not be supported.

Thus the general engagement of the day was dwarfed into the battle of the right at three o'clock, that on the left at eight by a single division, and that nearer the centre at nine o'clock by two brigades.

There was a man on the left of the line who did not care to make the battle win. He knew where it was, had viewed it from its earliest formation, had orders for his part in it, but so withheld part of his command from it as to make co-operative concert of action impracticable. He had a pruriency for the honors of the field of Mars, was eloquent, before the fires of the bivouac and his chief, of the glory of war's gory shield; but when its envied laurels were dipping to the grasp, when the heavy field called for bloody work, he found the placid horizon, far and away beyond the cavalry, more lovely and inviting. He wanted command of the Second Corps, and, succeeding to it, held the honored position until General Lee found, at last, that he must dismiss him from field service.

General Lee ordered Johnson's division of his left, occupying part of the enemy's trenches about Culp's Hill, to be reinforced during the night of the 2d by two brigades of Rodes's division and one of Early's division. Why the other brigades of those divisions were not sent does not appear, but it does appear that there was a place for them on Johnson's left, in the trenches that were vacated by the Federal Twelfth Corps when called over to reinforce the battle of Meade's left. Culp's Hill bore the same relations to the enemy's right as Little Round Top did to his left. General Fitzhugh Lee quotes evidence from General Meade that had Culp's Hill been occupied, in force, by Confederates, it would have compelled the withdrawal of the Federal troops.*

General Meade, after the battle of his left, ordered the divisions of his Twelfth Corps back to their trenches, to recover the parts occupied by the Confederate left. It was night when the First Division approached. General Ruger, commanding, thought to feel his way through the dark by a line of skirmishers. He found the east end of his trenches, across the swale, unoccupied, and took possession. Pressing his adventure, he found the main line of his works occupied by the Confederates in force, and disposed his command to wait for daylight. The Second Division came during the night, when General Williams, commanding the corps, posted it on the left of the First, and the division commanders ordered batteries in proper positions.

During the night, General Meade held a council, which decided to fight it out. So it began to look as if the vicissitudes of the day had so worked as to call General Meade from defensive to aggressive battle for Culp's Hill. But the Confederates failed to see the opportunity and force the issue as it was presented.

In General Meade's evidence before the Committee on the Conduct of the War, he puts his losses of the first and second days at twenty thousand, and assigns two-thirds of these to the battle of the 2d. As the fighting

* General Lee, by Fitzhugh Lee (note), p. 299.

against the three brigades of our left after night, and two brigades, later in the night, from our centre, could not have been very severe,* I claim that his loss in the battle of his left was from twelve to fourteen thousand.

As events of the battle of the 2d passed, it seems fair to claim that with Pickett's brigades present at the moment of Wofford's advance for the gorge at Little Round Top, we could have had it before Crawford was there.

Under ordinary circumstances this account of the second day, made from the records, would be conclusive; but the battle of Gettysburg, which may be called the epitome of the war, has been the subject of many contentions of words. Knights of the quill have consumed many of their peaceful hours in publishing their plans for the battle, endeavoring to forestall the records and to find a scapegoat, and their representations may be given, though they do not deserve it, a word of reply.

General W. N. Pendleton led off when making a lecturing tour through the South for a memorial church for General Lee. He claims that he made a reconnoissance on the afternoon of the 1st of July, and that upon his reporting it, General Lee ordered General Longstreet to attack at sunrise the next day. He did not venture to charge that the Second and Third Corps, that were on the field and had had a good night's rest, were part of the command ordered for the early battle, for the commanders, both Virginians, and not under the political ban, could have brought confusing evidence against him; nor did he intend to put General Lee in the anomalous position, inferentially, of ordering part of the First Corps—that should march through the night and all night—to make the battle alone. The point of battle was east of the Emmitsburg road; to find it, it was necessary to cross that road, but General Sickles was moving part of his

* Loss less than three thousand during the three days.

corps over the road during that afternoon, and rested there the latter part of the day and during the night. So, to make the reconnoissance, General Pendleton passed the Union troops in Confederate uniform—he was military in his dress—and found the point of battle. Giving him credit, for the moment, for this delicate work and the mythical order, let us find the end to which it would lead.

The only troops that could come under the order were McLaws's division, part of Hood's, and the artillery,—about ten thousand men. These, after a hurried all-night's march, reached General Lee's head-quarters about sunrise of the 2d, and by continued forced march could have reached the point of battle, about five miles away, by seven o'clock, where they would have encountered a division of the Third Corps (Birney's); presently the Second and Fifth Corps under Hancock and Sykes; then the First, Eleventh, and Twelfth under Newton, Howard, and Slocum; then the balance of the Third coming in on our rear along the Emmitsburg road,—making sixty thousand men and more. There was reason to be proud of the prowess of the troops of the First Corps, but to credit a part of it with success under the circumstances was not reasonable.

That the Confederate Second Corps did not have orders for the alleged sunrise battle is evidenced by the report of its commander, who, accounting for his work about Culp's Hill during the night of the 1st and morning of the 2d, reported of the morning, "It was now daylight, and too late," meaning that it was too late for him to attack and carry that hill, as General Lee had authorized and expected him to do during the night before. If he had been ordered to take part in the sunrise battle, he would have been in the nick of time. That the Third Corps was not to be in it is evidenced by the position of the greater part of it on Seminary Ridge until near noon of the 2d. So General Lee must have ordered a position carried, at sunrise, by ten thousand men, after it had gathered strength all night,—a position that he would not assault on the afternoon of the 1st with forty thousand men, lest they should encounter "overwhelming numbers."*

As the other corps, after receiving their orders for the general battle of the 2d, failed to engage until after nightfall, it is not probable that they would have found the sunrise battle without orders.

General Pendleton's official report is in conflict with his memorial lecture. In the former he makes no reference to the sunrise-battle order, but mentions the route by which the left of the enemy could be turned.

Letters from the active members of General Lee's staff and from his military secretary, General A. L. Long, show that the sunrise battle was not ordered, and a letter from Colonel Fairfax shows that the claim that it was so ordered was set up after General Lee's death.†

---

* His official report.

† Following are the essential portions of the letters referred to, affording unquestionable and overwhelming testimony against the claim that General Longstreet was ordered to give battle "at sunrise":

"NORFOLK, VA., April 28, 1875.

"DEAR GENERAL,— . . . I can only say that I never before heard of the 'sunrise attack' you were to have made, as charged by General Pendleton. If such an order was given you I never knew of it, or it has strangely escaped my memory. I think it more than probable that if General Lee had had your troops available the evening previous to the day of which you speak, he would have ordered an early attack, but this does not touch the point at issue. I regard it as a great mistake on the part of those who, perhaps because of political differences, now undertake to criticise and attack your war record. Such conduct is most ungenerous, and I am sure meets the disapprobation of all good Confederates with whom I have had the pleasure of associating in the daily walks of life.

"Yours, very respectfully,

"W. H. TAYLOR."

"UNIVERSITY OF VIRGINIA, May 11, 1875.

"GENERAL JAMES LONGSTREET:

"DEAR GENERAL,— . . . I did not know of any order for an attack on the enemy at sunrise on the 2d, nor can I believe any such order was issued by General Lee. About sunrise on the 2d of July I was sent by

In a published account, General Long mentions my suggestion on the afternoon of the 1st for the turning

---

General Lee to General Ewell to ask him what he thought of the advantages of an attack on the enemy from his position. (Colonel Marshall had been sent with a similar order on the night of the 1st.) General Ewell made me ride with him from point to point of his lines, so as to see with him the exact position of things. Before he got through the examination of the enemy's position, General Lee came himself to General Ewell's lines. In sending the message to General Ewell, General Lee was explicit in saying that the question was whether he should move all the troops around on the right and attack on that side. I do not think that the errand on which I was sent by the commanding general is consistent with the idea of an attack at sunrise by any portion of the army.

" Yours, very truly,

" CHARLES S. VENABLE."

" BALTIMORE, MD., May 7, 1875.

" DEAR GENERAL,— . . . I have no personal recollection of the order to which you refer. It certainly was not conveyed by me, nor is there anything in General Lee's official report to show the attack on the 2d was expected by him to begin earlier, except that he notices that there was not proper concert of action on that day. . . .

" Respectfully,

" CHARLES MARSHALL."

" BIG ISLAND, BEDFORD, VA., May 31, 1875.

" DEAR GENERAL,— . . . I do not recollect of hearing of an order to attack at sunrise, or at any other designated hour, pending the operations at Gettysburg during the first three days of July, 1863. . . .

" Yours truly,

" A. L. LONG."

" FREESTONE P. O., PRINCE WILLIAM COUNTY, VA.,

" November 12, 1877.

" MY DEAR GENERAL LONGSTREET,— . . . The winter after the death of General Lee I was in Lexington, visiting my sons at the V. M. I. General Pendleton called to see me at the hotel. General Custis Lee was in my room when he came in. After General Lee left, General Pendleton asked me if General Longstreet was not ordered to attack on the 2d of July at Gettysburg at six o'clock in the morning, and did not attack until four o'clock in the evening. I told him it was not possible. When he left me I was under the impression I had convinced him of his mistaken idea. I told General Pendleton that you and General Lee were together the greater part of the day up to about three o'clock or later; that you separated at the mouth of a lane not long thereafter. You said to me, 'Those troops will be in position by the time you get there; tell General Hood to attack.' When I gave the order to General Hood he was standing within a step or two of his line of battle. I asked him

march around the enemy's left, which he says, "after consideration, was rejected."

Colonel Taylor claims that the attack by the Confederate right should have been sooner, and should have met the enemy back on his first or original line, and before Little Round Top was occupied. But Little Round Top was not occupied in force until after my battle opened, and General Sickles's advance to his forward lines was made in consequence of the Confederate threatening, and would have been sooner or later according as that threatening was made. He calls the message of General Lee to General Ewell on the afternoon of the 1st an order. General Lee says,—

"The strong position which the enemy had assumed could not be attacked without danger of exposing the four divisions present, exhausted by a long and bloody struggle, to overwhelming numbers of fresh troops. General Ewell was thereupon instructed to carry the hill occupied by the enemy if he found it practicable."

It is the custom of military service to accept instructions of a commander as orders, but when they are coupled with conditions that transfer the responsibility of battle and defeat to the subordinate, they are not orders, and General Ewell was justifiable in not making attack that his commander would not order, and the censure of his failure is unjust and *very ungenerous.*

---

to please delay his attack until I could communicate to General Longstreet that he can turn the enemy,—pointing to a gorge in the mountain, where we would be sheltered from his view and attack by his cavalry. General Hood slapped me on the knee and said, 'I agree with you,—bring General Longstreet to see for himself.' When I reported to you, your answer was, 'It is General Lee's order; the time is up,—attack at once.' I lost no time in repeating the same to General Hood, and remained with him to see the attack, which was made instantly. We had a beautiful view of the enemy's left from Hood's position, which was close up to him. He gave way quickly. General Hood charged, and I spurred to report to you; found you with hat in hand cheering on General McLaws's division. . . .

"Truly your friend,

"JOHN W. FAIRFAX."

The Virginia writers have been so eager in their search for a flaw in the conduct of the battle of the First Corps that they overlook the only point into which they could have thrust their pens.

At the opening of the fight, General Meade was with General Sickles discussing the feasibility of moving the Third Corps back to the line originally assigned for it, but the discussion was cut short by the opening of the Confederate battle. If that opening had been delayed thirty or forty minutes the corps would have been drawn back to the general line, and my first deployment would have enveloped Little Round Top and carried it before it could have been strongly manned, and General Meade would have drawn off to his line selected behind Pipe Creek. The point should have been that the battle was opened too soon.

Another point from which they seek comfort is that Sedgwick's corps (Sixth) was not up until a late hour of the 2d, and would not have been on the field for an earlier battle. But Sedgwick was not engaged in the late battle, and could have been back at Manchester, so far as the afternoon battle was concerned. And they harp a little on the delay of thirty minutes for Law's brigade to join its division. But General Lee called for the two divisions, and had called for Law's brigade to join his division. It was therefore his order for the division that delayed the march. To have gone without it would have justified censure. As we were not strong enough for the work with that brigade, it is not probable that we could have accomplished more without it.

Colonel Taylor says that General Lee urged that the march of my troops should be hastened, and was chafed at their non-appearance. Not one word did he utter to me of their march until he gave his orders at eleven o'clock for the move to his right. Orders for the troops to hasten their march of the 1st were sent without even a suggestion from him, but upon his announcement that he intended to fight the next day, if the enemy was there.*

* Upon the various matters of this momentous day, which have been subject of controversy, the following testimony from J. S. D. Cullen is interesting and important:

"RICHMOND, VA., May 18, 1875.

"GENERAL JAMES LONGSTREET:

"DEAR GENERAL,— . . . It was an astounding announcement to the survivors of the First Army Corps that the disaster and failure at Gettysburg was alone and solely due to its commander, and that had he obeyed the orders of the commander-in-chief Meade's army would have been beaten before its entire force had assembled, and its final discomfiture thereby made certain. It is a little strange that these charges were not made while General Lee was alive to substantiate or disprove them, and that seven years or more were permitted to pass by in silence regarding them. You are fortunate in being able to call upon the adjutant-general and the two confidential officers of General Lee's staff for their testimony in the case, and I do not think that you will have any reason to fear their evidence. They knew every order that was issued for that battle, when and where attacks were to be made, who were slow in attacking, and who did not make attacks that were expected to be made. I hope, for the sake of history and for your brave military record, that a quietus will at once be put on this subject. I distinctly remember the appearance in our head-quarters camp of the scout who brought from Frederick the first account that General Lee had of the definite whereabouts of the enemy; of the excitement at General Lee's head-quarters among couriers, quartermasters, commissaries, etc., all betokening some early movement of the commands dependent upon the news brought by the scout. That afternoon General Lee was walking with some of us in the road in front of his head-quarters, and said, 'To-morrow, gentlemen, we will not move to Harrisburg as we expected, but will go over to Gettysburg and see what General Meade is after.' Orders had then been issued to the corps to move at sunrise on the morning of the next day, and promptly at that time the corps was put on the road. The troops moved slowly a short distance when they were stopped by Ewell's wagon-trains and Johnson's division turning into the road in front of them, making their way from some point north to Cashtown or Gettysburg. How many hours we were detained I am unable to say, but it must have been many, for I remember eating a lunch or dinner before moving again. Being anxious to see you, I rode rapidly by the troops (who, as soon as they could get into the road, pushed hurriedly by us also), and overtook you about dark at the hill this side of Gettysburg, about half a mile from the town. You had been at the front with General Lee, and were returning to your camp, a mile or two back. I spoke very exultingly of the victory we were thought to have obtained that day, but was surprised to find that you did not take the same cheerful view of it that I did, and presently you remarked that it would have been better had we not fought than to

That he was excited and off his balance was evident on the afternoon of the 1st, and he labored under that oppression until enough blood was shed to appease him.

---

have left undone what we did. You said that the enemy were left occupying a position that it would take the whole army to drive them from and then at a great sacrifice. We soon reached the camp, three miles, perhaps, from Gettysburg, and found the column near by. Orders were issued to be ready to march at 'daybreak,' or some earlier hour, next morning. About three o'clock in the morning, while the stars were shining, you left your head-quarters and rode to General Lee's, where I found you sitting with him *after sunrise* looking at the enemy on Cemetery Hill. . . ."

"I am yours, very truly,
"J. S. D. Cullen."

CHAPTER XXVIII.

GETTYSBURG—THIRD DAY.

The Stroke of Arms that shook the Continent—Longstreet opposed the Attack as planned and made—The Confederate Column of Assault—It was weak in Numbers but strong in Spirit—Tremendous Artillery Combat begins the Day's Fighting—Charge of Generals Pickett, Trimble, and Pettigrew—Armistead falls by the Side of the Federal Guns—The Federal Cavalry Charge of General Farnsworth—The Commander falls with Five Mortal Wounds—Could the Assaulting Column have been safely augmented from Longstreet's Right?—Testimony as to that Point—Where rested the Responsibility for Disaster?—Criticism of the Battle as a whole—Cemetery Hill stronger than Marye's Hill at Fredericksburg—Controverted Points—Casualties of the Three Days' Fight—Organization of the Forces engaged.

General Lee reported of arrangements for the day,—

"The general plan was unchanged. Longstreet, reinforced by Pickett's three brigades, which arrived near the battle-field during the afternoon of the 2d, was ordered to attack the next morning, and General Ewell was ordered to attack the enemy's right at the same time. The latter during the night reinforced General Johnson with two brigades from Rodes's and one from Early's division." *

This is disingenuous. He did not give or send me orders for the morning of the third day, nor did he reinforce me by Pickett's brigades for morning attack. As his head-quarters were about four miles from the command, I did not ride over, but sent, to report the work of the second day. In the absence of orders, I had scouting parties out during the night in search of a way by which we might strike the enemy's left, and push it down towards his centre. I found a way that gave some promise of results, and was about to move the command, when he rode

---

* Rebellion Record.

over after sunrise and gave his orders. His plan was to assault the enemy's left centre by a column to be composed of McLaws's and Hood's divisions reinforced by Pickett's brigades.* I thought that it would not do; that the point had been fully tested the day before, by more men, when all were fresh; that the enemy was there looking for us, as we heard him during the night putting up his defences; that the divisions of McLaws and Hood were holding a mile along the right of my line against twenty thousand men, who would follow their withdrawal, strike the flank of the assaulting column, crush it, and get on our rear towards the Potomac River; that thirty thousand men was the minimum of force necessary for the work; that even such force would need close co-operation on other parts of the line; that the column as he proposed to organize it would have only about thirteen thousand men (the divisions having lost a third of their numbers the day before); that the column would have to march a mile under concentrating battery fire, and a thousand yards under long-range musketry; that the conditions were different from those in the days of Napoleon, when field batteries had a range of six hundred yards and musketry about sixty yards.

He said the distance was not more than fourteen hundred yards. General Meade's estimate was a mile or a mile and a half (Captain Long, the guide of the field of Gettysburg in 1888, stated that it was a trifle over a mile). He then concluded that the divisions of McLaws and Hood could remain on the defensive line; that he would reinforce by divisions of the Third Corps and Pickett's brigades, and stated the point to which the march should be directed. I asked the strength of the column. He stated fifteen thousand. Opinion was then expressed that the fifteen thousand men who could make successful as-

* "Four Years with General Lee," W. H. Taylor, page 103.

sault over that field had never been arrayed for battle; but he was impatient of listening, and tired of talking, and nothing was left but to proceed. General Alexander was ordered to arrange the batteries of the front of the First and Third Corps, those of the Second were supposed to be in position; Colonel Walton was ordered to see that the batteries of the First were supplied with ammunition, and to prepare to give the signal-guns for the opening combat. The infantry of the Third Corps to be assigned were Heth's and Pettigrew's divisions and Wilcox's brigade.

At the time of the conversation and arrangement of the assault by the Confederate right, artillery fire was heard on our extreme left. It seems that General Lee had sent orders to General Ewell to renew his battle in the morning, which was intended, and directed, as a co-operation of the attack he intended to order on his right, but General Ruger, anticipating, opened his batteries against Ewell at daylight. The Union divisions—Ruger's and Geary's—were on broken lines, open towards the trenches held by the Confederates, so that assault by our line would expose the force to fire from the enemy's other line. Ruger had occupied the trenches left vacant on his right, and Geary reached to his left under Greene, who held his line against the attack of the day before. It seems that the Confederates failed to bring artillery up to their trenches, and must make their fight with infantry, while on the Union side there were some fifteen or twenty guns playing, and many more at hand if needed.

As the Union batteries opened, Johnson advanced and assaulted the enemy's works on his right towards the centre and the adjacent front of the new line, and held to that attack with resolution, putting in fresh troops to help it from time to time. Ruger put two regiments forward to feel the way towards Johnson's left. They got into hot engagement and were repulsed; Johnson tried to follow, but was in turn forced back. He renewed his main attack again, but unsuccessfully, and finally drew back to the trenches. Ruger threw a regiment forward from his left which gained the stone wall; his division was then advanced, and it recovered the entire line of trenches.

While this contention was in progress the troops ordered for the column of assault were marching and finding positions under the crest of the ridge, where they could be covered during the artillery combat. Alexander put a battery of nine guns under the ridge and out of the enemy's fire to be used with the assaulting column.

General Lee said that the attack of his right was not made as early as expected,—which he should not have said. He knew that I did not believe that success was possible; that care and time should be taken to give the troops the benefit of positions and the grounds; and he should have put an officer in charge who had more confidence in his plan. Two-thirds of the troops were of other commands, and there was no reason for putting the assaulting forces under my charge. He had confidence in General Early, who advised in favor of that end of the line for battle. Knowing my want of confidence, he should have given the benefit of his presence and his assistance in getting the troops up, posting them, and arranging the batteries; but he gave no orders or suggestions after his early designation of the point for which the column should march. Fitzhugh Lee claims evidence that General Lee did not even appear on that part of the field while the troops were being assigned to position, a singular indifference.

As the commands reported, Pickett was assigned on the right, Kemper's and Garnett's brigades to be supported by Armistead's; Wilcox's brigade of the Third Corps in echelon and guarding Pickett's right; Pettigrew's division on Pickett's left, supported by the brigades of Scales and Lane, under command of General Trimble. The brigades of Pettigrew's division were Archer's, Pettigrew's, Brockenbrough's, and Davis's. (General Archer having been taken prisoner on the 1st, his brigade was under command of Colonel Fry; General Scales being wounded on the same day, his brigade was commanded by Colonel Lowrance.) The ridge upon which the commands were formed was not parallel to that upon which the enemy stood, but bending west towards our left, while the enemy's line bore northwest towards his right, so that the left of the assaulting column formed some little distance farther from the enemy's line than the right. To put the troops under the best cover during the artillery combat they were thus posted for the march, but directed to spread their steps as soon as the march opened the field, and to gain places of correct alignment.

Meanwhile, the enemy's artillery on his extreme right was in practice more or less active, but its meaning was not known or reported, and the sharp-shooters of the command on the right had a lively fusillade about eleven o'clock, in which some of the artillery took part. The order was that the right was to make the signal of battle. General Lee reported that his left attacked before due notice to wait for the opening could be given, which was a mistake, inasmuch as the attack on his left was begun by the Federals, which called his left to their work. General Meade was not apprehensive of that part of the field, and only used the two divisions of the Twelfth Corps, Shaler's brigade of the Sixth, and six regiments of the First and Eleventh Corps in recovering the trenches of his right, holding the other six corps for the battle of his centre and left. He knew by the Confederate troops on his right just where the strong battle was to be.

The director of artillery was asked to select a position on his line from which he could note the effect of his practice, and to advise General Pickett when the enemy's fire was so disturbed as to call for the assault. General Pickett's was the division of direction, and he was ordered to have a staff-officer or courier with the artillery director to bear notice of the moment to advance.

The little affair between the skirmish lines quieted in a short time, and also the noise on our extreme left. The quiet filing of one or two of our batteries into position emphasized the profound silence that prevailed during our wait for final orders. Strong battle was in the air, and the veterans of both sides swelled their breasts to gather nerve and strength to meet it. Division commanders were asked to go to the crest of the ridge and take a careful view of the field, and to have their officers there to tell their men of it, and to prepare them for the sight that was to burst upon them as they mounted the crest.

Just then a squadron of Union cavalry rode through detachments of infantry posted at intervals in rear of my right division. It was called a charge, but was probably a reconnoissance.

Colonel Black had reported with a hundred of the First South Carolina Cavalry, not all mounted, and a battery of horse artillery, and was put across the Emmitsburg road, supported by infantry, in front of Merritt's brigade of cavalry.

When satisfied that the work of preparation was all that it could be with the means at hand, I wrote Colonel Walton, of the Washington Artillery,—

"HEAD-QUARTERS, July 3, 1863.

"COLONEL,—Let the batteries open. Order great care and precision in firing. When the batteries at the Peach Orchard cannot be used against the point we intend to attack, let them open on the enemy's on the rocky hill.

"Most respectfully,

"JAMES LONGSTREET,

"*Lieutenant-General, Commanding.*"

At the same time a note to Alexander directed that Pickett should not be called until the artillery practice indicated fair opportunity. Then I rode to a woodland hard by, to lie down and study for some new thought that might aid the assaulting column. In a few minutes report came from Alexander that he would only be able to judge of the effect of his fire by the return of that of the enemy, as his infantry was not exposed to view, and the smoke of the batteries would soon cover the field. He asked, if there was an alternative, that it be carefully considered before the batteries opened, as there was not enough artillery ammunition for this and another trial if this should not prove favorable.

He was informed that there was no alternative; that I could find no way out of it; that General Lee had considered and would listen to nothing else; that orders had gone for the guns to give signal for the batteries; that he should call the troops at the first opportunity or lull in the enemy's fire.

The signal-guns broke the silence, the blaze of the second gun mingling in the smoke of the first, and salvoes rolled to the left and repeated themselves, the enemy's fine metal spreading its fire to the converging lines, ploughing the trembling ground, plunging through the line of batteries, and clouding the heavy air. The two or three hundred guns seemed proud of their undivided honors and organized confusion. The Confederates had the benefit of converging fire into the enemy's massed position, but the superior metal of the enemy neutralized the advantage of position. The brave and steady work progressed.

Before this the Confederates of the left were driven from their captured trenches, and hope of their effective co-operation with the battle of the right was lost, but no notice of it was sent to the right of the battle. They made some further demonstrations, but they were of little effect. Merritt's cavalry brigade was in rear of my right, threatening on the Emmitsburg road. Farnsworth's brigade took position near Merritt's and close on my right rear.

Infantry regiments and batteries were broken off from my front line and posted to guard on that flank and rear.

Not informed of the failure of the Confederates on the left and the loss of their vantage-ground, we looked with confidence for them to follow the orders of battle.

General Pickett rode to confer with Alexander, then to the ground upon which I was resting, where he was soon handed a slip of paper. After reading it he handed it to me. It read:

> "If you are coming at all, come at once, or I cannot give you proper support, but the enemy's fire has not slackened at all. At least eighteen guns are still firing from the cemetery itself.
>
> "Alexander."

Pickett said, "General, shall I advance?"

The effort to speak the order failed, and I could only indicate it by an affirmative bow.* He accepted the duty with seeming confidence of success, leaped on his horse, and rode gayly to his command. I mounted and spurred for Alexander's post. He reported that the batteries he had reserved for the charge with the infantry had been spirited away by General Lee's chief of artillery; that the ammunition of the batteries of position was so reduced that he could not use them in proper support of the infantry. He was ordered to stop the march at once and fill up his ammunition-chests. But, alas! there was no more ammunition to be had.

The order was imperative. The Confederate commander had fixed his heart upon the work. Just then a number of the enemy's batteries hitched up and hauled off, which gave a glimpse of unexpected hope. Encouraging messages were sent for the columns to hurry on,

---

* A *sobriquet* of my boyhood was "Peter." General Pickett had written to the lady who afterwards became his wife, but had not mailed his letter. After receiving his orders, he wrote on the envelope, "If old Peter's nod means death, then good-by, and God bless you, little one!"

—and they were then on elastic springing step. General Pickett, a graceful horseman, sat lightly in the saddle, his brown locks flowing quite over his shoulders. Pettigrew's division spread their steps and quickly rectified the alignment, and the grand march moved bravely on. General Trimble mounted, adjusting his seat and reins as if setting out on a pleasant afternoon ride. When aligned to their places solid march was made down the slope and past our batteries of position.

Confederate batteries put their fire over the heads of the men as they moved down the slope, and continued to draw the fire of the enemy until the smoke lifted and drifted to the rear, when every gun was turned upon the infantry columns. The batteries that had been drawn off were replaced by others that were fresh. Soldiers and officers began to fall, some to rise no more, others to find their way to the hospital tents. Single files were cut here and there, then the gaps increased, and an occasional shot tore wider openings, but, closing the gaps as quickly as made, the march moved on. The divisions of McLaws and Hood were ordered to move to closer lines for the enemy on their front, to spring to the charge as soon as the breach at the centre could be made. The enemy's right overreached my left and gave serious trouble. Brockenbrough's brigade went down and Davis's in impetuous charge. The general order required further assistance from the Third Corps if needed, but no support appeared. General Lee and the corps commander were there, but failed to order help.

Colonel Latrobe was sent to General Trimble to have his men fill the line of the broken brigades, and bravely they repaired the damage. The enemy moved out against the supporting brigade in Pickett's rear. Colonel Sorrel was sent to have that move guarded, and Pickett was drawn back to that contention. McLaws was ordered to press his left forward, but the direct fire of infantry and cross-fire of artillery was telling fearfully on the front. Colonel Fremantle ran up to offer congratulations on the apparent success, but the big gaps in the ranks grew until the lines were reduced to half their length. I called his attention to the broken, struggling ranks. Trimble mended the battle of the left in handsome style, but on the right the massing of the enemy grew stronger and stronger. Brigadier Garnett was killed, Kemper and Trimble were desperately wounded; Generals Hancock and Gibbon were wounded. General Lane succeeded Trimble, and with Pettigrew held the battle of the left in steady ranks.

Pickett's lines being nearer, the impact was heaviest upon them. Most of the field officers were killed or wounded. Colonel Whittle, of Armistead's brigade, who had been shot through the right leg at Williamsburg and lost his left arm at Malvern Hill, was shot through the right arm, then brought down by a shot through his left leg.

General Armistead, of the second line, spread his steps to supply the places of fallen comrades. His colors cut down, with a volley against the bristling line of bayonets, he put his cap on his sword to guide the storm. The enemy's massing, enveloping numbers held the struggle until the noble Armistead fell beside the wheels of the enemy's battery. Pettigrew was wounded, but held his command.

General Pickett, finding the battle broken, while the enemy was still reinforcing, called the troops off. There was no indication of panic. The broken files marched back in steady step. The effort was nobly made, and failed from blows that could not be fended. Some of the files were cut off from retreat by fire that swept the field in their rear. Officers of my staff, sent forward with orders, came back with their saddles and bridles in their arms. Latrobe's horse was twice shot.

Looking confidently for advance of the enemy through our open field, I rode to the line of batteries, resolved to hold it until the last gun was lost. As I rode, the shells screaming over my head and ploughing the ground under my horse, an involuntary appeal went up that one of them might take me from scenes of such awful responsibility; but the storm to be met left no time to think of one's self. The battery officers were prepared to meet the crisis,—no move had been made for leaving the field. My old acquaintance of Sharpsburg experience, Captain Miller, was walking up and down behind his guns, smoking his pipe, directing his fire over the heads of our men as fast as they were inside of the danger-line; the other officers equally firm and ready to defend to the last. A body of skirmishers put out from the enemy's lines and advanced some distance, but the batteries opened severe fire and drove it back. Our men passed the batteries in quiet walk, and would rally, I knew, when they reached the ridge from which they started.

General Lee was soon with us, and with staff-officers and others assisted in encouraging the men and getting them together.

As the attack failed, General Kilpatrick put his cavalry brigade under General Farnsworth on the charge through the infantry detachment in rear of my right division. The regiments of G. T. Anderson's brigade had been posted at points in rear as guards against cavalry, and the First Texas, Fourth and Fifteenth Alabama, and Bachman's and Reilly's batteries were looking for that adventure. Farnsworth had a rough ride over rocks and stone fences, but bore on in spite of all, cutting and slashing when he could get at the skirmishers or detachments. He made a gallant ride along the rear of our right, but was obliged to come under the infantry and artillery fire at several points. He fell, pierced, it is said, by five mortal wounds. Calls for him to surrender were made, but the cavalry were not riding for that. The command lost heavily, but claimed captives equal to their loss.

Kilpatrick's mistake was in not putting Farnsworth in on Merritt's left, where he would have had an open ride, and made more trouble than was ever made by a cavalry brigade. Had the ride been followed by prompt advance of the enemy's infantry in line beyond our right and pushed with vigor, they could have reached our line of retreat. General Meade ordered his left, but delay in getting the orders and preparing to get through the rough grounds consumed time, and the move was abandoned. The Fifth and Sixth Corps were in convenient position, and would have had good ground for marching after getting out of the rocky fastnesses of Round Top.

As we had no cavalry on our right, the Union cavalry was held on their right to observe the Confederates under Stuart, except Kilpatrick's division (and Custer's brigade of that division was retained on their right). A little while after the repulse of our infantry column, Stuart's cavalry advanced and was met by Gregg's, and made one of the severest and most stubborn fights of cavalry on record. General Wade Hampton was severely wounded. The Union forces held the field.

When affairs had quieted a little, and apprehension of immediate counter-attack had passed, orders were sent the divisions of McLaws and Hood to draw back and occupy the lines from which they had advanced to engage the battle of the second. Orders sent Benning's brigade by the division staff were not understood, and Benning, under the impression that he was to relieve part of McLaws's division, which he thought was to be sent on other service, ordered the Fifteenth Georgia Regiment to occupy that position. When he received the second order he sent for his detached regiment. Meanwhile, the enemy was feeling the way to his front, and before Colonel DuBose received his second order, the enemy was on his front and had passed his right and left flanks. The moment he received the final order, Colonel DuBose made a running fight and escaped with something more than half his men.

In regard to this, as to other battles in which the First Corps was concerned, the knights of peaceful later days have been busy in search of points on which to lay charges or make innuendoes of want of conduct of that corps. General Early has been a picturesque figure in the combination, ready to champion any reports that could throw a shadow over its record, but the charge most pleasing to him was that of *treason* on the part of its commander. The subject was lasting, piquant, and so consoling that one is almost inclined to envy the comfort it gave him in his latter days.

Colonel Taylor and members of the staff claim that General Lee ordered that the divisions of McLaws and Hood should be a part of the assaulting column. Of this General Lee says,—

"General Longstreet was delayed by a force occupying the high, rocky hill on the enemy's extreme left, from which his troops could be attacked from reverse as they advanced. His operations had been embarrassed the day previously from the same cause, and he now deemed it necessary to defend his flank and rear with the divisions of Hood and McLaws. He was therefore reinforced by Heth's division and two brigades of Pender's, to the command of which Major-General Trimble was assigned. General Hill was directed to hold his line with the rest of the command, to afford General Longstreet further assistance if required, and to avail himself of any success that might be gained."

Colonel Taylor says,—

"As our extreme right was comparatively safe, being well posted, and not at all threatened, one of the divisions of Hood and McLaws, and a greater part of the other, could be moved out of the lines and be made to take part in the attack."

On this point I offer the evidence of General Warren before the Committee of Investigation:

"General Meade had so arranged his troops on our left during the third day that nearly one-half of our army was in reserve in that position. It was a good, sheltered position, and a convenient one from which to reinforce other points of the line, and when the repulse of the enemy took place on that day, General Meade intended to move forward all the forces he could get in hand and assault the enemy in line. He ordered the advance of the Fifth Corps, but it was carried so slowly that it did not amount to much, if anything."

General Hancock's evidence on that point is:

"General Meade told me before the fight that if the enemy attacked me, he intended to put the Fifth and Sixth Corps on the enemy's flank."

From which it is evident that the withdrawal of the divisions of my right, to be put in the column of assault, would have been followed by those corps swinging around and enveloping the assaulting columns and gaining Lee's line of retreat.

Colonel Venable thinks it a mistake to have put Heth's division in the assaulting column. He says,—

"They were terribly mistaken about Heth's division in this planning. It had not recuperated, having suffered more than was reported on the first day."

But to accept for the moment Colonel Taylor's premises, the two divisions referred to would have swelled the columns of assault to twenty-three thousand men. We were alone in the battle as on the day before. The enemy had seventy-five thousand men on strong ground, with well-constructed defences. The Confederates would have had to march a mile through the blaze of direct and cross fire and break up an army of seventy-five thousand well-seasoned troops, well defended by field-works!

A rough sketch of the positions of the forces about my right and rear will help to show if it "was comparatively safe, and not at all threatened."

General Gibbon's testimony in regard to the assaulting columns of the 3d:

"I was wounded about the time I suppose the enemy's second line got into our batteries,—probably a little before that. As described to me afterwards, the result, I think, will carry out my idea in regard to it, because the enemy broke through, forced back my weakest brigade under General Webb, got into our batteries, and the men were so close that the officers on each side were using their pistols on each other, and the men frequently clubbed their muskets, and the clothes of men on both sides were burned by the powder of exploding cartridges. An officer of my staff, Lieutenant Haskell, had been sent by me, just previously to the attack, to General Meade with a message that the enemy were coming. He got back on the top of the hill hunting for me, and was there when this brigade was forced back, and, without waiting orders from me, he rode off to the left and ordered all the troops of the division there to the right. As they came up helter-skelter, everybody for himself, with their officers among them, they commenced firing upon these rebels as they were coming into our lines."

Had the column been augmented by the divisions of my right, its brave men might have penetrated far enough to reach Johnson's Island as prisoners; their return to General Lee by any other route is unlikely.

When engaged collecting the broken files after the repulse, General Lee said to an officer who was assisting, "It is all my fault."

A letter from Colonel W. M. Owen assures me that

General Lee repeated this remark at a roadside fire of the Washington Artillery on the 5th of July. A letter from General Lee during the winter of 1863–64 repeated it in substance.*

Colonel T. J. Goree, of Texas, says upon the subject:

"I was present, however, just after Pickett's repulse, when General Lee so magnanimously took all the blame of the disaster upon himself. Another important circumstance, which I distinctly remember, was in the winter of 1863–64, when you sent me from East Tennessee to Orange Court-House with some despatches to General Lee. Upon my arrival there, General Lee asked me into his tent, where he was alone, with two or three Northern papers on the table. He remarked that he had just been reading the Northern reports of the battle of Gettysburg; that he had become satisfied from reading those reports *that if he had permitted you to carry out your plan, instead of making the attack on Cemetery Hill, he would have been successful.*"

Further testimony comes from another source:

"In East Tennessee, during the winter of 1863–64, you called me into your quarters, and asked me to read a letter just received from General Lee in which he used the following words: 'Oh, general, *had I but followed your advice, instead of pursuing the course that I did, how different all would have been!*' You wished me to bear this language in mind as your correspondence might be lost.

"ERASMUS TAYLOR.

"ORANGE COUNTY, VA."

A contributor to *Blackwood's Magazine* reported,—

"But Lee's inaction after Fredericksburg was, as we have called it, an unhappy or negative blunder. Undoubtedly the greatest positive blunder of which he was ever guilty was the unnecessary onslaught which he gratuitously made against the strong position into which, by accident, General Meade fell back at Gettysburg. We have good reason for saying that during the five years of calm reflection which General Lee passed at Lexington, after the conclusion of the American war, his maladroit manipu-

* So satisfied was General Lee on this point that he wrote to the Richmond authorities, on his return to Culpeper Court-House with his army, asking to be relieved from command by some younger officer.

lation of the Confederate army during the Gettysburg campaign was to him a matter of ceaseless self reproach.

"'If,' said he, on many occasions, 'I had taken General Longstreet's advice on the eve of the second day of the battle of Gettysburg, and filed off the left corps of my army behind the right corps, in the direction of Washington and Baltimore, along the Emmitsburg road, the Confederates would to-day be a free people.'" *

It is difficult to reconcile these facts with the reports put out after his death by members of his family and of his staff, and *post-bellum* champions, that indicate his later efforts to find points by which to so work up public opinion as to shift the disaster to my shoulders.

It does not appear, even at this late day, that Cemetery Ridge, if the Confederates had carried it, could have been as favorable for future military operations as was the position they occupied about Seminary Ridge.

Some of the statements of the members of the staff have been referred to. General Fitzhugh Lee claims evidence that General Lee said that he would have gained the battle if he had had General Jackson with him. But he had Jackson in the Sharpsburg campaign, which was more awkward than that of Gettysburg.† In another account Fitzhugh Lee wrote of General Lee,—

"He told the father of the writer, his brother, that he was controlled too far by the great confidence he felt in the fighting qualities of his people, and by assurances of most of his higher officers."

---

* *Eclectic Magazine*, May, 1872.

† At Sharpsburg, General Jackson left the field at seven o'clock in the morning and did not return until four o'clock in the afternoon, when he was ordered with his command and the cavalry to turn and strike down against the Union right. He started to execute the order, then gave it up without even asking permission. He made a brave and gallant fight in the morning, losing 1601 officers and men. But D. H. Hill was there from the first to the last gun, losing from his division 1872 officers and men. Jackson had the greater part of two divisions. But Hill was not a Virginian, and it would not do to leave the field for refreshments. The figures include Jackson's losses at Harper's Ferry and Sharpsburg; Hill's at South Mountain and Sharpsburg.

No assurances were made from officers of the First Corps, but rather objections. The only assurances that have come to light, to be identified, are those of General Early, who advised the battle, but *from the other end of the line from his command,* which should have given warning that it did not come from the heart of a true soldier.

And this is the epitome of the Confederate battle. The army when it set out on the campaign was all that could be desired, (except that the arms were not all of the most approved pattern), but it was despoiled of two of its finest brigades, Jenkins's and Corse's of Pickett's division, and was fought out by detail. The greatest number engaged at any one time was on the first day, when twenty-six thousand engaged twenty thousand of the First and part of the Eleventh Corps. On the afternoon of the second day about seventeen thousand were engaged on the right, and at night about seven thousand on the left; then later at night about three thousand near the centre. On the third day about twelve thousand were engaged at daylight and until near noon, and in the afternoon fifteen thousand,—all of the work of the second and third days against an army of seventy thousand and more of veteran troops in strong position defended by field-works.

General Lee was on the field from about three o'clock of the afternoon of the first day. Every order given the troops of the First Corps on that field up to its march on the forenoon of the 2d was issued in his presence. If the movements were not satisfactory in time and speed of moving, it was his power, duty, and privilege to apply the remedy, but it was not a part of a commander's duty or privilege to witness things that did not suit him, fail to apply the remedy, and go off and grumble with his staff-officers about it. In their efforts to show culpable delay in the movements of the First Corps on the 2d, some of the Virginia writers endeavor to show that General Lee did not even give me a guide to lead the way to the field from which his battle was to be opened. He certainly failed to go and look at it, and assist in selecting the ground and preparing for action.

Fitzhugh Lee says of the second day, "Longstreet was attacking the Marye's Hill of the position." * At Fredericksburg, General Burnside attacked at Marye's Hill in six or more successive assaults with some twenty or thirty thousand against three brigades under McLaws and Ransom and the artillery; he had about four hundred yards to march from his covered ways about Fredericksburg to Marye's Hill. When his last attack was repulsed in the evening, he arranged and gave his orders for the attack to be renewed in the morning, giving notice that he would lead it with the Ninth Corps, but upon reports of his officers abandoned it. General Lee's assaulting columns of fifteen or twenty thousand had a march of three-fourths of a mile to attack twice their number, better defended than the three Confederate brigades at Marye's Hill who drove back Burnside. The enemy on Cemetery Hill was in a stronger position than the Confederates at Marye's Hill.

Fitzhugh Lee writes in the volume already quoted,—

> "Over the splendid scene of human courage and human sacrifice at Gettysburg there arises in the South an apparition, like Banquo's ghost at Macbeth's banquet, which says the battle was lost to the Confederates because some one blundered."

Call them Banquo, but their name is Legion. Weird spirits keep midnight watch about the great boulders, while unknown comrades stalk in ghostly ranks through the black fastnesses of Devil's Den, wailing the lament, "Some one blundered at Gettysburg! Woe is me, whose duty was to die!"

---

* "General Lee," by Fitzhugh Lee. Marye's Hill was the stronghold at Fredericksburg, held by six thousand and attacked by thirty thousand; at Gettysburg the figures were reversed.

Fitzhugh Lee makes his plans, orders, and movements to suit his purpose, and claims that they would have given Gettysburg to the Confederates, but he is not likely to convince any one outside of his coterie that over the heights of Gettysburg was to be found honor for the South.

General Meade said that the suggestion to work towards his line of communication was sound "military sense." That utterance has been approved by subsequent fair judgment, and it is that potent fact that draws the spiteful fire of latter-day knights.

Forty thousand men, unsupported as we were, could not have carried the position at Gettysburg. The enemy was there. Officers and men knew their advantage, and were resolved to stay until the hills came down over them. It is simply out of the question for a lesser force to march over broad, open fields and carry a fortified front occupied by a greater force of seasoned troops.

Referring to the proposed move around the Union left to cut the line of communication, a parallel in the Franco-German war is appropriate. When the manœuvres of the campaign had pushed Marshal MacMahon's army back to the road between Paris and Metz, the latter fortified and occupied by the army under Marshal Bazaine, MacMahon hesitated between Paris and Metz, and was manœuvred out of position to a point north of the line. Von Moltke seized the opportunity and took position on the line, which gave him shorter routes east and west. So that MacMahon, to reach either point, must pass the German forces under Von Moltke. He made a brave effort to reach Metz, and Von Moltke, to maintain his advantage, was called to skilful manœuvre and several gallant affairs, but succeeded in holding his advantage that must call MacMahon to general engagement or surrender. Outgeneralled, and with a demoralized army, he thought the latter his proper alternative.

The relative conditions of the armies were similar. The Union army, beaten at Fredericksburg and Chancellorsville, and drawn from its aggressive campaign to defensive work in Pennsylvania, had met disaster in its battle of the 1st. If it had been outgeneralled, and dislodged of position without further attack, it would have been in poor condition to come in aggressive battle against its adversary in well-chosen defensive grounds.

Again, in our own war, when the Union army carried the Confederate works west of Petersburg on the 2d of April, 1865, General Meade got his army together and was about to march east to finish his work by the capture of Petersburg. General Grant objected,—that the Confederates would retreat during the night; at Petersburg he would be behind them; in his then position he would be alongside of them, and have an even start, with better prospect to strike across their march and force them to general battle or surrender; and he ordered arrangements for the march west at daylight.

Even Napoleon Bonaparte, the first in the science and greatest in the execution of the art of war, finally lost grasp of his grandest thought:

"In war men are nothing; a man is everything."*

The Confederate chief at Gettysburg looked something like Napoleon at Waterloo.

Fitzhugh Lee quotes evidence of Governor Carroll, of Maryland, that General Lee said, "Longstreet is the hardest man to move in my army."

It does not look like generalship to lose a battle and a cause and then lay the responsibility upon others. He held command and was supported by his government. If his army did not suit him, his word could have changed it in a minute. If he failed to apply the remedy, it was his

* *Vide* "The French under the First and Last Bonaparte;" the Second Corps of the Army of Northern Virginia under Stonewall Jackson in 1862, in the Valley of Virginia, and J. A. Early in 1864.

fault. Some claim that his only fault as a general was his tender, generous heart. But a heart in the right place looks more to the cause intrusted to its care than for hidden ways by which to shift its responsibility to the shoulders of those whose lives hang upon his word.

When he set out on his first campaign (Chickahominy) with the army, the key of the campaign was intrusted to General Jackson, who named the hour for the opening and failed to meet his own appointment. At the time he appointed, A. P. Hill's, D. H. Hill's, and Longstreet's commands were in position waiting. About eight hours after his time he was up, but deliberately marched past the engagement and went into camp, half a mile or more behind the hot battle. He remained in his camp next morning, and permitted the enemy, dislodged of his position of the day before, to march by him to a strong position at Gaines's Mill. When his column reached that position, his leading division (D. H. Hill's) engaged the enemy's right without orders. He called the division off and put his command in position to intercept the enemy's retreat towards the Pamunkey, from which he was afterwards called to his part in the general engagement. The next day he had the cavalry and part of his infantry in search of the enemy's next move. At my head-quarters were two clever young engineers who were sent to find what the enemy was about. They were the first to report the enemy's retreat towards James River. Orders were given for Jackson to follow on the direct line of retreat, also Magruder and Huger. My command was ordered around through the outskirts of Richmond by the Darbytown road to interpose between McClellan's army and the James River, about twenty miles; the other troops marching by routes of about nine miles. We were in position on the evening of the 29th of June, and stood in front of the enemy all of the 30th, fighting a severe battle in the afternoon. Magruder and Huger got up after night, and Jackson on the morning of the 1st. After the battle of the 1st, Jackson, Magruder, and Huger were ordered in direct pursuit along the route of retreat, my command by the longer route of Nance's Store. Jackson's column and mine met on the evening of the 3d near Westover, the enemy's new position.

At the Second Manassas my command relieved the pressure against Jackson. He called on me for relief by a route that would have taken an hour or an hour and a half. A way was found by which he was relieved in about thirty minutes. When relieved, he left the battle on my hands. I was at Sharpsburg all day; Jackson only about two and a half hours. At Fredericksburg, anticipating the move against him, half of my command was ordered to swing off from my right and join in his battle.

But General Lee's assertion seems to refer to the operations at Gettysburg, after Jackson had found his Happy Home. Let us see how far this assertion is supported by events. General Lee reported,—

"The advance of the enemy to the latter place (Gettysburg) was unknown, and, the weather being inclement, the march was conducted with a view to the comfort of the troops."

When, on the forenoon of the 2d, he decided upon his plan, the Second Corps was deployed in the immediate front of the enemy's line on our left, except two brigades sent off by General Early. One division of the Third was close on the right of the Second, all within thirty minutes' march of the enemy's lines. Two divisions of the Third Corps and two of the First were on Seminary Ridge. When the order was announced the divisions on Seminary Ridge had to find their positions and deploy to the right. By the route ordered for the march it was five or six miles to the point at which the battle was to be opened. The troops of the Third had a shorter route. The march of the First was made in time for prompt deployment on the right of the Third.

We were left to our own resources in finding ground upon which to organize for battle. The enemy had changed position somewhat after the march was ordered, but as we were not informed of his position before the march, we could not know of the change. The Confederate commander did not care to ride near us, to give information of a change, to assist in preparing for attack, nor to inquire if new and better combinations might be made.

Four brigades of the right of the Third Corps were assigned as part of my command. The engagement was to be general. My artillery combat was opened at three P.M., followed in half an hour by the infantry, and I made progressive battle until sundown. A division of the Second Corps attacked on our left at nightfall, and later two brigades. Other parts of the Second and Third Corps did not move to the battle.

On the 3d I was ordered to organize the column of assault, the other corps to co-operate and assist the battle. There was an affair on the Confederate left before the assaulting columns were organized, brought on by attack of the enemy. The assaulting force marched at one P.M. Its work has been described, but it is important to note that neither of the other corps took part in the battle while the Southern chief stood in view of the attack and near the rear of those corps. So it looks as if the commander of the First Corps was easier to move than any one in his army, rather than harder, and his chief left him to fight the battles alone.

After the retreat, and when resting on the south banks of the Rapidan, reading of the progress of the march of General Rosecrans's army towards Georgia, it seemed sinful to lie there idle while our comrades in the West were so in need of assistance, and I wrote the Secretary of War suggesting that a detachment should be sent West from the idle army. General Lee objected, but the suggestion was ordered to be executed. In this instance the subordinate was easier to move than his chief, though the interests of the cause depended largely on the movement of the latter.

The forces engaged at Gettysburg were:

CONFEDERATE.—According to the latest official accounts, the Army of Northern Virginia, on the 31st of May, numbered 74,468. The detachments that joined numbered 6400, making 80,868. Deducting the detachments left in Virginia,—Jenkins's brigade, Pickett's division, 2300; Corse's brigade, Pickett's division, 1700; detachments from Second Corps and of cavalry, 1300, in all 5300,—leaves the actual aggregate 75,568.

UNION.—According to the reports of the 30th of June, and making allowance for detachments that joined in the interim in time to take part in the battle, the grand aggregate was 100,000 * officers and men.

The Confederates lost many men after the battle, and before they recrossed the Potomac, from the toils of the march and the continuous and severe harassment of the enemy's cavalry, which followed closely and in great force. The casualties were:

CONFEDERATE.†

First Corps	7,539
Second Corps	5,937
Third Corps	6,735
Cavalry	1,426
Aggregate	21,637

* General Meade's monthly return for June 30 shows 99,131 "present for duty, equipped." The Comte de Paris estimates the force actually on the field, including the Sixth Corps, which was in reserve, at 82,000.

† Rebellion Record, vol. xxvii.

UNION.*

First Corps	6,059
Second Corps	4,369
Third Corps	4,211
Fifth Corps	2,187
Sixth Corps	242
Eleventh Corps	3,801
Twelfth Corps	1,082
Cavalry	1,094
Staff	4
Aggregate	23,049

The organization of the contending armies at Gettysburg was as follows:

ARMY OF NORTHERN VIRGINIA, GENERAL ROBERT E. LEE, COMMANDING.

FIRST ARMY CORPS, LIEUTENANT-GENERAL JAMES LONGSTREET.

MCLAWS'S DIVISION, Maj.-Gen. Lafayette McLaws:—*Kershaw's Brigade*, Brig.-Gen. J. B. Kershaw; 2d S. C., Col. J. D. Kennedy, Lieut.-Col. F. Gaillard; 3d S. C., Maj. R. C. Maffett, Col. J. D. Nance; 7th S. C., Col. D. Wyatt Aiken; 8th S. C., Col. J. W. Henagan; 15th S. C., Col. W. D. De Saussure, Maj. William M. Gist; 3d S. C. Battn., Lieut.-Col. W. G. Rice. *Barksdale's Brigade*, Brig.-Gen. William Barksdale, Col. B. G. Humphreys; 13th Miss., Col. J. W. Carter; 17th Miss., Col. W. D. Holder, Lieut.-Col. John C. Fiser; 18th Miss., Col. T. M. Griffin, Lieut.-Col. W. H. Luse; 21st Miss., Col. B. G. Humphreys. *Semmes's Brigade*,† Brig.-Gen. P. J. Semmes, Col. Goode Bryan; 10th Ga., Col. John B. Weems; 50th Ga., Col. W. R. Manning; 51st Ga., Col. E. Ball; 53d Ga., Col. James P. Simms. *Wofford's Brigade*, Brig.-Gen. W. T. Wofford; 16th Ga., Col. Goode Bryan; 18th Ga., Lieut.-Col. S. Z. Ruff; 24th Ga., Col. Robert McMillan; Cobb's (Ga.) Legion, Lieut.-Col. Luther J. Glenn; Phillips (Ga.) Legion, Lieut.-Col. E. S. Barclay. *Artillery*, Col. H. C. Cabell; 1st N. C. Art., Batt. A, Capt. B. C. Manly; Pulaski (Ga.) Art., Capt. J. C. Fraser, Lieut. W. J. Furlong; 1st Richmond Howitzers, Capt. E. S. McCarthy; Troup (Ga.) Art., Capt. H. H. Carlton, Lieut. C. W. Motes.

PICKETT'S DIVISION, Maj.-Gen. George E. Pickett:—*Garnett's Brigade*, Brig.-Gen. R. B. Garnett, Maj. C. S. Peyton; 8th Va., Col. Eppa Hunton; 18th Va., Lieut.-Col. H. A. Carrington; 19th Va., Col. Henry

---

* Rebellion Record, vol. xxxvii. part i. p. 187.

† No reports on file for this brigade. Bryan was in command July 7, and was probably Semmes's immediate successor. The commanders of the Tenth, Fifty-first, and Fifty-third Georgia are given as reported for June 22 and July 31. Manning reported in command of Fiftieth Georgia, June 22. No commander reported on return for July 31.

Gantt, Lieut.-Col. John T. Ellis; 28th Va., Col. R. C. Allen, Lieut.-Col. William Watts; 56th Va., Col. W. D. Stuart, Lieut.-Col. P. P. Slaughter. *Kemper's Brigade*, Brig.-Gen. J. L. Kemper, Col. Joseph Mayo, Jr.; 1st Va., Col. Lewis B. Williams, Lieut.-Col. F. G. Skinner; 3d Va., Col. Joseph Mayo, Jr., Lieut.-Col. A. D. Callcote; 7th Va., Col. W. T. Patton, Lieut.-Col. C. C. Flowerree; 11th Va., Maj. Kirkwood Otey; 24th Va., Col. William R. Terry. *Armistead's Brigade*, Brig.-Gen. L. A. Armistead, Col. W. R. Aylett; 9th Va., Maj. John C. Owens; 14th Va., Col. James G. Hodges, Lieut.-Col. William White; 38th Va., Col. E. C. Edmonds, Lieut.-Col. P. B. Whittle; 53d Va., Col. W. R. Aylett; 57th Va., Col. John Bowie Magruder. *Artillery*, Maj. James Dearing; Fauquier (Va.) Art., Capt. R. M. Stribling; Hampden (Va.) Art., Capt. W. H. Caskie; Richmond Fayette Art., Capt. M. C. Macon; Virginia Batt., Capt. Joseph G. Blount.

HOOD'S DIVISION, Maj.-Gen. John B. Hood, Brig.-Gen. E. M. Law:—*Law's Brigade*, Brig.-Gen. E. M. Law, Col. James L. Sheffield; 4th Ala., Lieut.-Col. L. H. Scruggs; 15th Ala., Col. William C. Oates, Capt. B. A. Hill; 44th Ala., Col. William F. Perry; 47th Ala., Col. James W. Jackson, Lieut.-Col. M. J. Bulger, Maj. J. M. Campbell; 48th Ala., Col. James L. Sheffield, Capt. T. J. Eubanks. *Robertson's Brigade*, Brig.-Gen. J. B. Robertson; 3d Ark., Col. Van H. Manning, Lieut.-Col. R. S. Taylor; 1st Tex., Lieut.-Col. P. A. Work; 4th Tex., Col. J. C. G. Key, Maj. J. P. Bane; 5th Tex., Col. R. M. Powell, Lieut.-Col. K. Bryan, Maj. J. C. Rogers. *Anderson's Brigade*, Brig.-Gen. George T. Anderson, Lieut.-Col. William Luffman; 7th Ga., Col. W. W. White; 8th Ga., Col. John R. Towers; 9th Ga., Lieut.-Col. John C. Mounger, Maj. W. M. Jones, Capt. George Hillyer; 11th Ga., Col. F. H. Little, Lieut.-Col. William Luffman, Maj. Henry D. McDaniel, Capt. William H. Mitchell; 59th Ga., Col. Jack Brown, Capt. M. G. Bass. *Benning's Brigade*. Brig.-Gen. Henry L. Benning; 2d Ga., Lieut.-Col. William T. Harris, Maj. W. S. Shepherd; 15th Ga., Col. D. M. DuBose; 17th Ga., Col. W. C. Hodges; 20th Ga., Col. John A. Jones, Lieut.-Col. J. D. Waddell. *Artillery*, Maj. M. W. Henry; Branch (N. C.) Art., Capt. A. C. Latham; German (S.C.) Art., Capt. William K. Bachman; Palmetto (S. C.) Light Art., Capt. Hugh R. Garden; Rowan (N. C.) Art., Capt. James Reilly.

ARTILLERY RESERVE, Col. J. B. Walton:—*Alexander's Battalion*, Col. E. P. Alexander; Ashland (Va.) Art., Capt. P. Woolfolk, Jr., Lieut. James Woolfolk; Bedford (Va.) Art., Capt. T. C. Jordan; Brooks (S. C.) Art., Lieut. S. C. Gilbert; Madison (La.) Light Art., Capt. George V. Moody; Va. Batt., Capt. W. W. Parker; Va. Batt., Capt. O. B. Taylor. *Washington (La.) Artillery*, Maj. B. F. Eshleman; First Co., Capt. C. W. Squires; Second Co., Capt. J. B. Richardson; Third Co., Capt. M. B. Miller; Fourth Co., Capt. Joe Norcom, Lieut. H. A. Battles.

SECOND ARMY CORPS, LIEUTENANT-GENERAL RICHARD S. EWELL. *Escort*, Randolph's Company Virginia Cavalry, Capt. William F. Randolph.

EARLY'S DIVISION, Maj.-Gen. Jubal A. Early:—*Hays's Brigade*, Brig.-Gen. Harry T. Hays; 5th La., Maj. Alexander Hart, Capt. T. H. Biscoe; 6th La., Lieut.-Col. Joseph Hanlon; 7th La., Col. D. B. Penn;

8th La., Col. T. D. Lewis, Lieut.-Col. A. de Blanc, Maj. G. A. Lester ; 9th La., Col. Leroy A. Stafford. *Smith's Brigade*, Brig.-Gen. William Smith ; 31st Va., Col. John S. Hoffman ; 49th Va., Lieut.-Col. J. Catlett Gibson ; 52d Va., Lieut.-Col. James H. Skinner. *Hoke's Brigade*, Col. Isaac E. Avery, Col. A. C. Godwin ; 6th N. C., Maj. S. McD. Tate ; 21st N. C., Col. W. W. Kirkland ; 57th N. C., Col. A. C. Godwin. *Gordon's Brigade*, Brig.-Gen. J. B. Gordon ; 13th Ga., Col. James M. Smith ; 26th Ga., Col. E. N. Atkinson ; 31st Ga., Col. Clement A. Evans ; 38th Ga., Capt. William L. McLeod ; 60th Ga., Capt. W. B. Jones ; 61st Ga., Col. John H. Lamar. *Artillery*, Lieut.-Col. H. P. Jones ; Charlottesville (Va.) Art., Capt. James McD. Carrington ; Courtney (Va.) Art., Capt. W. A. Tanner ; Louisiana Guard Art., Capt. C. A. Green ; Staunton (Va.) Art., Capt. A. W. Garber.

JOHNSON'S DIVISION, Maj.-Gen. Edward Johnson :—*Steuart's Brigade*, Brig.-Gen. George H. Steuart ; 1st Md. Battn. Inf., Lieut.-Col. J. R. Herbert, Maj. W. W. Goldsborough, Capt. J. P. Crane ; 1st N. C., Lieut. Col. H. A. Brown ; 3d N. C., Maj. W. M. Parsley ; 10th Va., Col. E. T. H. Warren ; 23d Va., Lieut.-Col. S. T. Walton ; 37th Va., Maj. H. C. Wood. *Stonewall Brigade*, Brig.-Gen. James A. Walker ; 2d Va., Col. J. Q. A. Nadenbousch ; 4th Va., Maj. William Terry ; 5th Va., Col. J. H. S. Funk ; 27th Va., Lieut.-Col. D. M. Shriver ; 33d Va., Capt. J. B. Golladay. *Nicholls's Brigade*,* Col. J. M. Williams ; 1st La., Capt. E. D. Willett ; 2d La., Lieut.-Col. R. E. Burke ; 10th La., Maj. T. N. Powell ; 14th La., Lieut.-Col. David Zable ; 15th La., Maj. Andrew Brady. *Jones's Brigade*, Brig.-Gen. John M. Jones, Lieut.-Col. R. H. Dungan ; 21st Va., Capt. W. P. Moseley ; 25th Va., Col. J. C. Higginbotham, Lieut.-Col. J. A Robinson ; 42d Va., Lieut.-Col. R. W. Withers, Capt. S. H. Saunders ; 44th Va., Maj. N. Cobb, Capt. T. R. Buckner ; 48th Va., Lieut.-Col. R. H. Dungan, Maj. Oscar White ; 50th Va., Lieut.-Col. L. H. N. Salyer. *Artillery*, Maj. J. W. Latimer, Capt. C. I. Raine ; 1st Md. Batt., Capt William F. Dement ; Alleghany (Va.) Art., Capt. J. C. Carpenter ; Chesapeake (Md.) Art., Capt. William D. Brown ; Lee (Va.) Batt., Capt. C. I. Raine, Lieut. William W. Hardwicke.

RODES'S DIVISION, Maj.-Gen. R. E. Rodes :—*Daniel's Brigade*, Brig.-Gen. Junius Daniel ; 32d N. C., Col. E. C. Brabble ; 43d N. C., Col. T. S. Kenan, Lieut.-Col. W. G. Lewis ; 45th N. C., Lieut.-Col. S. H. Boyd, Maj. John R. Winston, Capt. A. H. Gallaway, Capt. J. A. Hopkins ; 53d N. C., Col. W. A. Owens ; 2d N. C. Battn., Lieut.-Col. H. L. Andrews, Capt. Van Brown. *Doles's Brigade*, Brig.-Gen. George Doles ; 4th Ga., Lieut.-Col. D. R. E. Winn, Maj. W. H. Willis ; 12th Ga., Col. Edward Willis ; 21st Ga., Col. John T. Mercer ; 44th Ga., Col. S. P. Lumpkin, Maj. W. H. Peebles. *Iverson's Brigade*, Brig.-Gen. Alfred Iverson ; 5th N. C.,† Capt. Speight B. West, Capt. Benjamin Robinson ; 12th N. C.,

---

* The regimental commanders are given as reported for June 14.

† The four captains present (West, Robinson, James M. Taylor, Thomas N. Jordan) were reported as wounded July 1 ; Robinson and Taylor as having rejoined July 2, but it does not appear who commanded during Robinson's absence.

Lieut.-Col. W. S. Davis; 20th N. C.,* Lieut.-Col. Nelson Slough, Capt. Lewis T. Hicks; 23d N. C.,† Col. D. H. Christie, Capt. William H. Johnston. *Ramseur's Brigade*, Brig.-Gen. S. D. Ramseur; 2d N. C., Maj. D. W. Hurtt, Capt. James T. Scales; 4th N. C., Col. Bryan Grimes; 14th N. C., Col. R. Tyler Bennett, Maj. Joseph H. Lambeth; 30th N. C., Col. Francis M. Parker, Maj. W. W. Sillers. *O'Neal's Brigade*, Col. E. A. O'Neal; 3d Ala., Col. C. A. Battle; 5th Ala., Col. J. M. Hall; 6th Ala., Col. J. N. Lightfoot, Capt. M. L. Bowie; 12th Ala., Col. S. B. Pickens; 26th Ala., Lieut.-Col. John C. Goodgame. *Artillery*, Lieut.-Col. Thomas H. Carter; Jeff Davis (Ala.) Art., Capt. W. J. Reese; King William (Va.) Art., Capt. W. P. Carter; Morris (Va.) Art., Capt. R. C. M. Page; Orange (Va.) Art., Capt. C. W. Fry. *Artillery Reserve*, Col. J. Thompson Brown; 1st Va. Art., Capt. Willis J. Dance; 2d Richmond (Va.) Howitzers, Capt. David Watson; 3d Richmond (Va.) Howitzers, Capt. B. H. Smith, Jr.; Powhatan (Va.) Art., Lieut. John M. Cunningham; Rockbridge (Va.) Art., Capt. A. Graham; Salem (Va.) Art., Lieut. C. B. Griffin; Nelson's Battn., Lieut.-Col. William Nelson; Amherst (Va.) Art., Capt. T. J. Kirkpatrick; Fluvanna (Va.) Art., Capt. J. L. Massie; Ga. Batt., Capt. John Milledge, Jr.

THIRD ARMY CORPS, LIEUTENANT-GENERAL AMBROSE P. HILL.

ANDERSON'S DIVISION, Maj.-Gen. R. H. Anderson:—*Wilcox's Brigade*, Brig.-Gen. Cadmus M. Wilcox; 8th Ala., Lieut.-Col. Hilary A. Herbert; 9th Ala., Capt. J. H. King; 10th Ala., Col. William H. Forney, Lieut.-Col. James E. Shelley; 11th Ala., Col. J. C. C. Sanders, Lieut.-Col. George E. Tayloe; 14th Ala., Col. L. Pinckard, Lieut.-Col. James A. Broome. *Mahone's Brigade*, Brig.-Gen. William Mahone; 6th Va., Col. George T. Rogers; 12th Va., Col. D. A. Weisiger; 16th Va., Col. Joseph H. Ham; 41st Va., Col. William A. Parham; 61st Va., Col. V. D. Groner. *Wright's Brigade*, Brig.-Gen. A. R. Wright, Col. William Gibson; 3d Ga., Col. E. J. Walker; 22d Ga., Col. Joseph Wasden, Capt. B. C. McCurry; 48th Ga., Col. William Gibson, Capt. M. R. Hall; 2d Ga. Battn., Maj. George W. Ross, Capt. Charles J. Moffett. *Perry's Brigade*, Col. David Lang; 2d Fla., Maj. W. R. Moore; 5th Fla., Capt. R. N. Gardner; 8th Fla., Col. David Lang. *Posey's Brigade*, Brig.-Gen. Carnot Posey; 12th Miss., Col. W. H. Taylor; 16th Miss., Col. Samuel E. Baker; 19th Miss., Col. N. H. Harris; 48th Miss., Col. Joseph M. Jayne. *Artillery (Sumter Battalion)*, Maj. John Lane; Co. A, Capt. Hugh M. Ross; Co. B, Capt. George M. Patterson; Co. C, Capt. John T. Wingfield.

HETH'S DIVISION, Maj.-Gen. Henry Heth, Brig.-Gen. J. J. Pettigrew:—*First Brigade*, Brig.-Gen. J. J. Pettigrew, Col. J. K. Marshall; 11th N. C., Col. Collett Leventhorpe; 26th N. C., Col. Henry K. Burgwyn, Jr., Capt. H. C. Albright; 47th N. C., Col. G. H. Faribault; 52d N. C., Col. J. K. Marshall, Lieut.-Col. Marcus A. Parks. *Second Brigade*, Col.

* Lieutenant-Colonel Slough and Major John S. Brooks reported as wounded at four P.M., July 1.

† Colonel Christie, Lieutenant-Colonel R. D. Johnston, Major C. C. Blacknall, and the senior captain (Abner D. Pearce) reported as wounded early in the fight, July 1.

J. M. Brockenbrough ; 40th Va., Capt. T. E. Betts, Capt. R. B. Davis ; 47th Va., Col. Robert M. Mayo ; 55th Va., Col. W. S. Christian ; 22d Va. Battn., Maj. John S. Bowles. *Third Brigade*, Brig.-Gen. James J. Archer, Col. B. D. Fry, Lieut.-Col. S. G. Shepard ; 13th Ala., Col. B. D. Fry ; 5th Ala. Battn., Maj. A. S. Van de Graaff ; 1st Tenn. (provisional army), Maj. Felix G. Buchanan ; 7th Tenn., Lieut.-Col. S. G. Shepard ; 14th Tenn., Capt. B. L. Phillips. *Fourth Brigade*, Brig.-Gen. Joseph R. Davis ; 2d Miss., Col. J. M. Stone ; 11th Miss., Col. F. M. Green ; 42d Miss., Col. H. R. Miller ; 55th N. C., Col. J. K. Connally. *Artillery*, Lieut.-Col. John J. Garnett ; Donaldsonville (La.) Art., Capt. V. Maurin ; Huger (Va.) Art., Capt. Joseph D. Moore ; Lewis (Va.) Art., Capt. John W. Lewis ; Norfolk Light Art. Blues, Capt. C. R. Grandy.

PENDER'S DIVISION, Maj.-Gen. William D. Pender, Maj.-Gen. I. R. Trimble, Brig.-Gen. James H. Lane :—*First Brigade*, Col. Abner Perrin ; 1st S. C. (provisional army), Maj. C. W. McCreary ; 1st S. C. Rifles, Capt. William M. Hadden ; 12th S. C., Col. John L. Miller ; 13th S. C., Lieut.-Col. B. T. Brockman ; 14th S. C., Lieut.-Col. Joseph N. Brown. *Second Brigade*, Brig.-Gen. James H. Lane, Col. C. M. Avery ; 7th N. C., Capt. J. McLeod Turner, Capt. James G. Harris ; 18th N. C., Col. John D. Barry ; 28th N. C., Col. S. D. Lowe, Lieut.-Col. W. H. A. Speer ; 33d N. C., Col. C. M. Avery ; 37th N. C., Col. W. M. Barbour. *Third Brigade*, Brig.-Gen. Edward L. Thomas ; 14th, 35th, 45th, and 49th Ga., Col. S. T. Player. *Fourth Brigade*, Brig.-Gen. A. M. Scales, Lieut.-Col. G. T. Gordon, Col. W. Lee J. Lowrance ; 13th N. C., Col. J. H. Hyman, Lieut.-Col. H. A. Rogers ; 16th N. C., Capt. L. W. Stowe ; 22d N. C., Col. James Conner ; 34th N. C., Col. William Lee J. Lowrance, Lieut.-Col. G. T. Gordon ; 38th N. C., Col. W. J. Hoke, Lieut.-Col. John Ashford. *Artillery*, Maj. William T. Poague ; Albemarle (Va.) Art., Capt. James W. Wyatt ; Charlotte (N. C.) Art., Capt. Joseph Graham ; Madison (Miss.) Light Art., Capt. George Ward ; Virginia Batt., Capt. J. V. Brooke.

ARTILLERY RESERVE, Col. R. Lindsay Walker :—*McIntosh's Battalion*, Maj. D. G. McIntosh ; Danville (Va.) Art., Capt. R. S. Rice ; Hardaway (Ala.) Art., Capt. W. B. Hurt ; 2d Rockbridge (Va.) Art., Lieut. Samuel Wallace ; Virginia Batt., Capt. M. Johnson. *Pegram's Battalion*, Maj. W. J. Pegram, Capt. E. B. Brunson ; Crenshaw (Va.) Batt. ; Fredericksburg (Va.) Art., Capt. E. A. Marye ; Letcher (Va.) Art., Capt. T. A. Brander ; Pee Dee (S. C.) Art., Lieut. William E. Zimmerman ; Purcell (Va.) Art., Capt. Joseph McGraw.

CAVALRY.

STUART'S DIVISION, Maj.-Gen. J. E. B. Stuart :—*Hampton's Brigade*, Brig.-Gen. Wade Hampton, Col. L. S. Baker ; 1st N. C., Col. L. S. Baker ; 1st and 2d S. C. ; Cobb's (Ga.) Legion, Jeff. Davis Legion, Phillips (Ga.) Legion. *Robertson's Brigade*, Brig.-Gen. Beverly H. Robertson ;* 4th N. C., Col. D. D. Ferebee ; 5th N. C. *Fitzhugh Lee's Brigade*, Brig.-Gen. Fitzhugh Lee ; 1st Md. Battn.,† Maj. Harry Gilmor, Maj. Ridgely Brown ;

---

* Commanded his own and W. E. Jones's brigade.

† Serving with Ewell's corps.

1st Va., Col. James H. Drake; 2d Va., Col. T. T. Munford; 3d Va., Col. Thomas H. Owen; 4th Va., Col. William C. Wickham; 5th Va., Col. T. L. Rosser. *Jenkins's Brigade*, Brig.-Gen. A. G. Jenkins, Col. M. J. Ferguson; 14th, 16th, and 17th Va.; 34th Va. Battn., Lieut.-Col. V. A. Witcher; 36th Va. Battn.; Jackson's (Va.) Batt., Capt. Thomas E. Jackson. *Jones's Brigade*, Brig.-Gen. William E. Jones; 6th Va., Maj. C. E. Flournoy; 7th Va., Lieut.-Col. Thomas Marshall; 11th Va., Col. L. L. Lomax. *W. H. F. Lee's Brigade*, Col. J. R. Chambliss, Jr.; 2d N. C.; 9th Va., Col. R. L. T. Beale; 10th Va., Col. J. Lucius Davis; 13th Va. *Stuart's Horse Artillery*, Maj. R. F. Beckham; Breathed's (Va.) Batt., Capt. James Breathed; Chew's (Va.) Batt., Capt. R. P. Chew; Griffin's (Md.) Batt., Capt. W. H. Griffin; Hart's (S. C.) Batt., Capt. J. F. Hart; McGregor's (Va.) Batt., Capt. W. M. McGregor; Moorman's (Va.) Batt., Capt. M. N. Moorman.

IMBODEN'S COMMAND,* Brig.-Gen. J. D. Imboden; 18th Va. Cav., Col. George W. Imboden; 62d Va. Inf. (mounted), Col. George H. Smith; Virginia Partisan Rangers, Capt. John H. McNeill; Virginia Batt., Capt. J. H. McClanahan.

ARTILLERY,† Brig.-Gen. W. N. Pendleton.

ARMY OF THE POTOMAC, MAJOR-GENERAL GEORGE G. MEADE, U. S. ARMY, COMMANDING.

GENERAL HEAD-QUARTERS:—*Command of the Provost-Marshal-General*, Brig.-General Marsena R. Patrick; 93d N. Y.,‡ Col. John S. Crocker; 8th U. S. (8 cos.),‡ Capt. Edwin W. H. Reed; 2d Pa. Cav., Col. R. Butler Price; 6th Pa. Cav., Cos. E and I, Capt. James Starr; Regular Cav. (detachments from 1st, 2d, 5th, and 6th Regiments).

SIGNAL CORPS, Capt. Lemuel B. Norton.

GUARDS AND ORDERLIES, Oneida (N. Y.) Cav., Capt. Daniel P. Mann.

ARTILLERY,§ Brig.-Gen. Henry J. Hunt.

ENGINEER BRIGADE,‖ Brig.-Gen. Henry W. Benham:—15th N. Y. (3 cos.), Maj. Walter L. Cassin; 50th N. Y., Col. William H. Pettes; U. S. Battn., Capt. George H. Mendell.

FIRST ARMY CORPS,¶ MAJOR-GENERAL ABNER DOUBLEDAY, MAJOR-GENERAL JOHN NEWTON. *General Head-quarters*, 1st Me. Cav., Co. L, Capt. Constantine Taylor.

FIRST DIVISION, Brig.-Gen. James S. Wadsworth:—*First Brigade*, Brig.-Gen. Solomon Meredith, Col. William W. Robinson; 19th Ind.,

---

* Mounted.

† See battalions attached to corps and cavalry. ‡ Not engaged.

§ See artillery brigades attached to army corps and the reserves.

‖ Not engaged. With exception of the regular battalion, it was, July 1, and while at Beaver Dam Creek, Md., ordered to Washington, D. C., where it arrived July 3.

¶ Major-General John F. Reynolds, of this corps, was killed July 1, while in command of the left wing of the army; General Doubleday commanded the corps July 1, and General Newton, who was assigned to that command on the 1st, superseded him July 2.

Col. Samuel J. Williams; 24th Mich., Col. Henry A. Morrow, Capt. Albert M. Edwards; 2d Wis., Col. Lucius Fairchild, Maj. John Mansfield, Capt. George H. Otis; 6th Wis., Lieut.-Col. Rufus R. Dawes; 7th Wis., Col. William W. Robinson, Maj. Mark Finnicum. *Second Brigade*, Brig.-Gen. Lysander Cutler; 7th Ind., Col. Ira G. Grover; 76th N. Y., Maj. Andrew J. Grover, Capt. John E. Cook; 84th N. Y. (14th Militia), Col. Edward B. Fowler; 95th N. Y., Col. George H. Biddle, Maj. Edward Pye; 147th N. Y., Lieut.-Col. Francis C. Miller, Maj. George Harney; 56th Pa. (9 cos.), Col. J. William Hofmann.

SECOND DIVISION, Brig.-Gen. John C. Robinson:—*First Brigade*, Brig.-Gen. Gabriel R. Paul, Col. Samuel H. Leonard, Col. Adrian R. Root, Col. Richard Coulter, Col. Peter Lyle; 16th Me., Col. Charles W. Tilden, Maj. Archibald D. Leavitt; 13th Mass., Col. Samuel H. Leonard, Lieut.-Col. N. Walter Batchelder; 94th N. Y., Col. Adrian R. Root, Maj. Samuel A. Moffett; 104th N. Y., Col. Gilbert G. Prey; 107th Pa., Lieut.-Col. James MacThomson, Capt. Emanuel D. Roath. *Second Brigade*, Brig.-Gen. Henry Baxter; 12th Mass., Col. James L. Bates, Lieut.-Col. David Allen, Jr.; 83d N. Y. (9th Militia), Lieut.-Col. Joseph A. Moesch; 97th N. Y., Col. Charles Wheelock, Maj. Charles Northrup; 11th Pa.,* Col. Richard Coulter, Capt. Benjamin F. Haines, Capt. John V. Overmyer, 88th Pa., Maj. Benezet F. Foust, Capt. Henry Whiteside; 90th Pa., Col. Peter Lyle, Maj. Alfred J. Sellers.

THIRD DIVISION, Brig.-Gen. Thomas A. Rowley, Maj.-Gen. Abner Doubleday:—*First Brigade*, Brig.-Gen. Thomas A. Rowley, Col. Chapman Biddle; 80th N. Y. (20th Militia), Col. Theodore B. Gates; 121st Pa., Maj. Alexander Biddle, Col. Chapman Biddle; 142d Pa., Col. Robert P. Cummins, Lieut.-Col. A. B. McCalmont; 151st Pa., Lieut.-Col. George F. McFarland, Capt. Walter L. Owens, Col. Harrison Allen. *Second Brigade*, Col. Roy Stone, Col. Langhorne Wister, Col. Edmund L. Dana; 143d Pa., Col. Edmund L. Dana, Lieut.-Col. John D. Musser; 149th Pa., Lieut.-Col. Walton Dwight, Capt. James Glenn; 150th Pa., Col. Langhorne Wister, Lieut.-Col. H. S. Huidekoper, Capt. Cornelius C. Widdis. *Third Brigade*, Brig.-Gen. George J. Stannard, Col. Francis V. Randall; 12th Vt.,† Col. Asa P. Blunt; 13th Vt., Col. Francis V. Randall, Maj. Joseph J. Boynton, Lieut.-Col. William D. Munson; 14th Vt., Col. William T. Nichols; 15th Vt.,† Col. Redfield Proctor; 16th Vt., Col. Wheelock G. Veazey. *Artillery Brigade*, Col. Charles S. Wainwright; Me. Light, 2d Batt. B, Capt. James A. Hall; Me. Light, 5th Batt. E, Capt. Greenleaf T. Stevens, Lieut. Edward N. Whittier; 1st N. Y. Light, Batt. L,‡ Capt. Gilbert H. Reynolds, Lieut. George Breck; 1st Pa. Light, Batt. B, Capt. James H. Cooper; 4th U. S., Batt. B, Lieut. James Stewart.

---

* Transferred, in the afternoon of July 1, to the First Brigade.

† Guarding trains, and not engaged in the battle.

‡ Battery E, First New York Light Artillery, attached.

SECOND ARMY CORPS,* MAJOR-GENERAL WINFIELD S. HANCOCK, BRIGADIER-GENERAL JOHN GIBBON. *General Head-quarters*, 6th N. Y. Cav., Cos. D and K, Capt. Riley Johnson.

FIRST DIVISION, Brig.-Gen. John C. Caldwell:—*First Brigade*, Col. Edward E. Cross, Col. H. Boyd McKeen; 5th N. H., Lieut.-Col. Charles E. Hapgood; 61st N. Y., Lieut.-Col. K. Oscar Broady; 81st Pa., Col. H. Boyd McKeen, Lieut.-Col. Amos Stroh; 148th Pa., Lieut.-Col. Robert McFarlane. *Second Brigade*, Col. Patrick Kelly; 28th Mass., Col. R. Byrnes; 63d N. Y. (2 cos.), Lieut.-Col. Richard C. Bentley, Capt. Thomas Touhy; 69th N. Y. (2 cos.), Capt. Richard Moroney, Lieut. James J. Smith; 88th N. Y. (2 cos.), Capt. Denis F. Burke; 116th Pa. (4 cos.), Maj. St. Clair A. Mulholland. *Third Brigade*, Brig.-Gen. Samuel K. Zook, Lieut.-Col. John Fraser; 52d N. Y., Lieut.-Col. C. G. Freudenberg, Capt. William Scherrer; 57th N. Y., Lieut.-Col. Alford B. Chapman; 66th N. Y., Col. Orlando H. Morris, Lieut.-Col. John S. Hammell, Maj. Peter Nelson; 140th Pa., Col. Richard P. Roberts, Lieut.-Col. John Fraser. *Fourth Brigade*, Col. John R. Brooke; 27th Conn. (2 cos.), Lieut.-Col. Henry C. Merwin, Maj. James H. Coburn; 2d Del., Col. William P. Baily, Capt. Charles H. Christman; 64th N. Y., Col. Daniel G. Bingham, Maj. Leman W. Bradley; 53d Pa., Lieut.-Col. Richards McMichael; 145th Pa. (7 cos.), Col. Hiram L. Brown, Capt. John W. Reynolds, Capt. Moses W. Oliver.

SECOND DIVISION, Brig.-Gen. John Gibbon, Brig.-Gen. William Harrow:—*First Brigade*, Brig.-Gen. William Harrow, Col. Francis E. Heath; 19th Me., Col. Francis E. Heath, Lieut.-Col. Henry W. Cunningham; 15th Mass., Col. George H. Ward, Lieut.-Col. George C. Joslin; 1st Minn.,† Col. William Colvill, Jr., Capt. Nathan S. Messick, Capt. Henry C. Coates; 82d N. Y. (2d Militia), Lieut.-Col. James Huston, Capt. John Darrow. *Second Brigade*, Brig.-Gen. Alexander S. Webb; 69th Pa., Col. Dennis O'Kane, Capt. William Davis; 71st Pa., Col. Richard Penn Smith; 72d Pa., Col. DeWitt C. Baxter, Lieut.-Col. Theodore Hesser; 106th Pa., Lieut.-Col. William L. Curry. *Third Brigade*, Col. Norman J. Hall; 19th Mass., Col. Arthur F. Devereux; 20th Mass., Col. Paul J. Revere, Lieut.-Col. George N. Macy, Capt. Henry L. Abbott; 7th Mich., Lieut.-Col. Amos E. Steele, Jr., Maj. Sylvanus W. Curtis; 42d N. Y., Col. James E. Mallon; 59th N. Y. (4 cos.), Lieut.-Col. Max A. Thoman, Capt. William McFadden. *Unattached*, Mass. Sharpshooters, 1st Co., Capt. William Plumer, Lieut. Emerson L. Bicknall.

---

* After the death of General Reynolds, General Hancock was assigned to the command of all the troops on the field of battle, relieving General Howard, who had succeeded General Reynolds. General Gibbon, of the Second Division, assumed command of the corps. These assignments terminated on the evening of July 1. Similar changes in commanders occurred during the battle of the 2d, when General Hancock was put in command of the Third Corps, in addition to that of his own. He was wounded on the 3d, and Brigadier-General William Hays was assigned to the command of the corps.

† 2d Company Minnesota Sharp-shooters attached.

THIRD DIVISION, Brig.-Gen. Alexander Hays:—*First Brigade*, Col. Samuel S. Carroll; 14th Ind., Col. John Coons; 4th Ohio, Lieut.-Col. Leonard W. Carpenter; 8th Ohio, Lieut.-Col. Franklin Sawyer; 7th W. Va., Lieut. Col. Jonathan H. Lockwood. *Second Brigade*, Col. Thomas A. Smyth, Lieut.-Col. Francis E. Pierce; 14th Conn., Maj. Theodore G. Ellis; 1st Del., Lieut.-Col. Edward P. Harris, Capt. Thomas P. Hizar, Lieut. William Smith, Lieut. John T. Dent; 12th N. J., Maj. John T. Hill; 10th N. Y. (Battn.), Maj. George F. Hopper; 108th N. Y., Lieut.-Col. Francis E. Pierce. *Third Brigade*, Col. George L. Willard, Col. Eliakim Sherrill, Lieut.-Col. James M. Bull; 39th N. Y. (4 cos.), Maj. Hugo Hildebrandt; 111th N. Y., Col. Clinton D. McDougall, Lieut.-Col. Isaac M. Lusk, Capt. Aaron P. Seeley; 125th N. Y., Lieut.-Col. Levin Crandell; 126th N. Y., Col. Eliakim Sherrill, Lieut.-Col. James M. Bull. *Artillery Brigade*, Capt. John G. Hazard; 1st N. Y. Light, Batt. B,* Lieut. Albert S. Sheldon, Capt. James McKay Rorty, Lieut. Robert E. Rogers; 1st R. I. Light, Batt. A, Capt. William A. Arnold; 1st R. I. Light, Batt. B, Lieut. T. Fred. Brown, Lieut. Walter S. Perrin; 1st U. S., Batt. I, Lieut. George A. Woodruff, Lieut. Tully McCrea; 4th U. S., Batt. A, Lieut. Alonzo H. Cushing, Sergt. Frederick Fuger.

THIRD ARMY CORPS, MAJOR-GENERAL DANIEL E. SICKLES, MAJOR-GENERAL DAVID B. BIRNEY.

FIRST DIVISION, Maj.-Gen. David B. Birney, Brig.-Gen. J. H. Hobart Ward:—*First Brigade*, Brig.-Gen. Charles K. Graham, Col. Andrew H. Tippin; 57th Pa. (8 cos.), Col. Peter Sides, Capt. Alanson H. Nelson; 63d Pa., Maj. John A. Danks; 68th Pa., Col. Andrew H. Tippin, Capt. Milton S. Davis(?), 105th Pa., Col. Calvin A. Craig; 114th Pa., Lieut.-Col. Frederick F. Cavada, Capt. Edward R. Bowen; 141st Pa., Col. Henry J. Madill. *Second Brigade*, Brig.-Gen. J. H. Hobart Ward, Col. Hiram Berdan; 20th Ind., Col. John Wheeler, Lieut.-Col. William C. L. Taylor; 3d Me., Col. Moses B. Lakeman; 4th Me., Col. Elijah Walker, Capt. Edwin Libby; 86th N. Y., Lieut.-Col. Benjamin L. Higgins; 124th N. Y., Col. A. Van Horne Ellis, Lieut.-Col. Francis M. Cummins; 99th Pa., Maj. John W. Moore; 1st U. S. Sharp-shooters, Col. Hiram Berdan, Lieut.-Col. Caspar Trepp; 2d U. S. Sharp-shooters (8 cos.), Maj. Homer R. Stoughton. *Third Brigade*, Col. P. Regis de Trobriand; 17th Me., Lieut.-Col. Charles B. Merrill; 3d Mich., Col. Byron R. Pierce, Lieut.-Col. Edwin S. Pierce; 5th Mich., Lieut.-Col. John Pulford; 40th N. Y., Col. Thomas W. Egan; 110th Pa. (6 cos.), Lieut.-Col. David M. Jones, Maj. Isaac Rogers.

SECOND DIVISION, Brig.-Gen. Andrew A. Humphreys:—*First Brigade*, Brig.-Gen. Joseph B. Carr; 1st Mass., Lieut.-Col. Clark B. Baldwin; 11th Mass., Lieut.-Col. Porter D. Tripp; 16th Mass., Lieut.-Col. Waldo Merriam, Capt. Matthew Donovan; 12th Mass., Capt. John F. Langley; 11th N. J., Col. Robert McAllister, Capt. Luther Martin,

* Transferred from Artillery Reserve, July 1; Fourteenth New York Battery attached.

Lieut. John Schoonover, Capt. William H. Lloyd, Capt. Samuel T. Sleeper; 26th Pa., Maj. Robert L. Bodine; 84th Pa.,* Lieut.-Col. Milton Opp. *Second Brigade*, Col. William R. Brewster; 70th N. Y., Col. J. Egbert Farnum; 71st N. Y., Col. Henry L. Potter; 72d N. Y., Col. John S. Austin, Lieut.-Col. John Leonard; 73d N. Y., Maj. Michael W. Burns; 74th N. Y., Lieut.-Col. Thomas Holt; 120th N. Y., Lieut.-Col. Cornelius D. Westbrook, Maj. John R. Tappen. *Third Brigade*, Col. George C. Burling; 2d N. H., Col. Edward L. Bailey; 5th N. J., Col. William J. Sewell, Capt. Thomas C. Godfrey, Capt. Henry H. Woolsey; 6th N. J., Lieut.-Col. Stephen R. Gilkyson; 7th N. J., Col. Louis R. Francine, Maj. Frederick Cooper; 8th N. J., Col. John Ramsey, Capt. John G. Langston; 115th Pa., Maj. John P. Dunne. *Artillery Brigade*, Capt. George E. Randolph, Capt. A. Judson Clark; N. J. Light, 2d Batt., Capt. A. Judson Clark, Lieut. Robert Sims; 1st N. Y. Light, Batt. D, Capt. George B. Winslow; N. Y. Light, 4th Batt., Capt. James E. Smith; 1st R. I. Light, Batt. E, Lieut. John K. Bucklyn, Lieut. Benjamin Freeborn; 4th U. S., Batt. K, Lieut. Francis W. Seeley, Lieut. Robert James.

FIFTH ARMY CORPS, MAJOR-GENERAL GEORGE SYKES. *General Head-quarters*, 12th N. Y. Inf., Cos. D and E, Capt. Henry W. Rider; 17th Pa. Cav., Cos. D and H, Capt. William Thompson.

FIRST DIVISION, Brig.-Gen. James Barnes:—*First Brigade*, Col. William S. Tilton; 18th Mass., Col. Joseph Hayes; 22d Mass., Lieut.-Col. Thomas Sherwin, Jr.; 1st Mich., Col. Ira C. Abbott, Lieut.-Col. William A. Throop; 118th Pa., Lieut.-Col. James Gwyn. *Second Brigade*, Col. Jacob B. Sweitzer; 9th Mass., Col. Patrick R. Guiney; 32d Mass., Col. G. L. Prescott; 4th Mich., Col. Harrison H. Jeffords, Lieut.-Col. George W. Lumbard; 62d Pa., Lieut.-Col. James C. Hull. *Third Brigade*, Col. Strong Vincent, Col. James C. Rice; 20th Me., Col. Joshua L. Chamberlain; 16th Mich., Col. Norval E. Welch; 44th N. Y., Col. James C. Rice, Lieut.-Col. Freeman Conner; 83d Pa., Capt. Orpheus S. Woodward.

SECOND DIVISION, Brig.-Gen. Romeyn B. Ayres:—*First Brigade*, Col. Hannibal Day; 3d U. S. (6 cos.), Capt. Henry W. Freedley, Capt. Richard G. Lay; 4th U. S. (4 cos.), Capt. Julius W. Adams, Jr.; 6th U. S. (5 cos.), Capt. Levi C. Bootes; 12th U. S. (8 cos.), Capt. Thomas S. Dunn; 14th U. S. (8 cos.), Maj. Grotius R. Giddings. *Second Brigade*, Col. Sidney Burbank; 2d U. S. (6 cos.), Maj. Arthur T. Lee, Capt. Samuel A. McKee; 7th U. S. (4 cos.), Capt. David P. Hancock; 10th U. S. (3 cos.), Capt. William Clinton; 11th U. S. (6 cos.), Maj. De Lancey Floyd-Jones; 17th U. S. (7 cos.), Lieut.-Col. J. Durell Greene. *Third Brigade*, Brig.-Gen. Stephen H. Weed, Col. Kenner Garrard; 140th N. Y., Col. Patrick H. O'Rorke, Lieut.-Col. Louis Ernst; 146th N. Y., Col. Kenner Garrard, Lieut.-Col. David T. Jenkins; 91st Pa., Lieut.-Col. Joseph H. Sinex; 155th Pa., Lieut.-Col. John H. Cain.

THIRD DIVISION,† Brig.-Gen. Samuel W. Crawford:—*First Brigade*,

* Guarding corps trains, and not engaged in the battle.

† Joined corps June 28. The Second Brigade left in the Department of Washington.

Col. William McCandless; 1st Pa. Reserves (9 cos.), Col. William C. Talley; 2d Pa. Reserves, Lieut.-Col. George A. Woodward; 6th Pa. Reserves, Lieut.-Col. Wellington H. Ent; 13th Pa. Reserves, Col. Charles F. Taylor, Maj. William R. Hartshorne. *Third Brigade*, Col. Joseph W. Fisher; 5th Pa. Reserves, Lieut.-Col. George Dare; 9th Pa. Reserves, Lieut.-Col. James McK. Snodgrass; 10th Pa. Reserves, Col. Adoniram J. Warner; 11th Pa. Reserves, Col. Samuel M. Jackson; 12th Pa. Reserves (9 cos.), Col. Martin D. Hardin. *Artillery Brigade*, Capt. Augustus P. Martin; Mass. Light, 3d Batt. C, Lieut. Aaron F. Walcott; 1st N. Y. Light, Batt. C, Capt. Almont Barnes; 1st Ohio Light, Batt. L, Capt. Frank C. Gibbs; 5th U. S., Batt. D, Lieut. Charles E. Hazlett, Lieut. Benjamin F. Rittenhouse; 5th U. S., Batt. I, Lieut. Malbone F. Watson, Lieut. Charles C. MacConnell.

SIXTH ARMY CORPS, MAJOR-GENERAL JOHN SEDGWICK. *General Head-quarters*, 1st N. J. Cav., Co. L, 1st Pa. Cav., Co. H, Capt. William S. Craft.

FIRST DIVISION, Brig.-Gen. Horatio G. Wright:—*Provost Guard*, 4th N. J. (3 cos.), Capt. William R. Maxwell. *First Brigade*, Brig.-Gen. A. T. A. Torbert; 1st N. J., Lieut.-Col. William Henry, Jr.; 2d N. J., Lieut.-Col. Charles Wiebecke; 3d N. J., Col. Edward L. Campbell; 15th N. J., Col. William H. Penrose, *Second Brigade*, Brig.-Gen. Joseph J. Bartlett;* 5th Me., Col. Clark S. Edwards; 121st N. Y., Col. Emory Upton; 95th Pa., Lieut.-Col. Edward Carroll; 96th Pa., Maj. William H. Lessig. *Third Brigade*, Brig.-Gen. David A. Russell; 6th Me., Col. Hiram Burnham; 49th Pa. (4 cos.), Lieut.-Col. Thomas M. Hulings; 119th Pa., Col. Peter C. Ellmaker; 5th Wis., Col. Thomas S. Allen.

SECOND DIVISION,† Brig.-Gen. Albion P. Howe:—*Second Brigade*, Col. Lewis A. Grant; 2d Vt., Col. James H. Walbridge; 3d Vt., Col. Thomas O. Seaver; 4th Vt., Col. Charles B. Stoughton; 5th Vt., Lieut.-Col. John R. Lewis; 6th Vt., Col. Elisha L. Barney. *Third Brigade*, Brig.-Gen. Thomas H. Neill; 7th Me. (6 cos.), Lieut.-Col. Selden Connor; 33d N. Y. (detachment), Capt. Henry J. Gifford; 43d N. Y., Lieut.-Col. John Wilson; 49th N. Y., Col. Daniel D. Bidwell; 77th N. Y., Lieut.-Col. Winsor B. French; 61st Pa., Lieut.-Col. George F. Smith.

THIRD DIVISION, Maj.-Gen. John Newton,‡ Brig.-Gen. Frank Wheaton:—*First Brigade*, Brig.-Gen. Alexander Shaler; 65th N. Y., Col. Joseph E. Hamblin; 67th N. Y., Col. Nelson Cross; 122d N. Y., Col. Silas Titus; 23d Pa., Lieut.-Col. John F. Glenn; 82d Pa., Col. Isaac C. Bassett. *Second Brigade*, Col. Henry L. Eustis; 7th Mass., Lieut.-Col. Franklin P. Harlow; Tenth Mass., Lieut.-Col. Joseph B. Parsons; 37th Mass., Col. Oliver Edwards; 2d R. I., Col. Horatio Rogers, Jr. *Third Brigade*, Brig.-Gen. Frank Wheaton, Col. David J. Nevin; 62d N. Y., Col. David J. Nevin, Lieut.-Col. Theodore B. Hamilton; 93d Pa., Maj. John I. Nevin; 98th Pa., Maj. John B. Kohler; 102d Pa.,§ Col. John W. Pat-

---

* Also in command of the Third Brigade, Third Division, on July 3.

† No First Brigade in division. ‡ See foot-note (¶), p. 415.

§ Guarding wagon-train at Westminster, and not engaged in the battle.

terson; 139th Pa., Col. Frederick H. Collier, Lieut.-Col. William H. Moody. *Artillery Brigade*, Col. Charles H. Tompkins; Mass. Light, 1st Batt. (A), Capt. William H. McCartney; N. Y. Light, 1st Batt., Capt. Andrew Cowan; N. Y. Light, 3d Batt., Capt. William A. Harn; 1st R. I. Light, Batt. C, Capt. Richard Waterman; 1st R. I. Light, Batt. G, Capt. George W. Adams; 2d U. S., Batt. D, Lieut. Edward B. Williston; 2d U. S., Batt. G, Lieut. John H. Butler; 5th U. S., Batt. F, Lieut. Leonard Martin.

ELEVENTH ARMY CORPS,* MAJOR-GENERAL OLIVER O. HOWARD. *General Head-quarters*, 1st Ind. Cav., Cos. I and K, Capt. Abram Sharra; 8th N. Y. Inf. (1 co.), Lieut. Herman Foerster.

FIRST DIVISION, Brig.-Gen. Francis C. Barlow, Brig.-Gen. Adelbert Ames:—*First Brigade*, Col. Leopold von Gilsa; 41st N. Y. (9 cos.), Lieut.-Col. Detleo von Einsiedel; 54th N. Y., Maj. Stephen Kovacs, Lieut. Ernst Poth(?); 68th N. Y., Col. Gotthilf Bourry; 153d Pa., Maj. John F. Frueauff. *Second Brigade*, Brig.-Gen. Adelbert Ames, Col. Andrew L. Harris; 17th Conn., Lieut.-Col. Douglas Fowler, Maj. Allen G. Brady; 25th Ohio, Lieut.-Col. Jeremiah Williams; Capt. Nathaniel J. Manning, Lieut. William Maloney, Lieut. Israel White; 75th Ohio, Col. Andrew L. Harris, Capt. George B. Fox; 107th Ohio, Col. Seraphim Meyer, Capt. John M. Lutz.

SECOND DIVISION, Brig.-Gen. Adolph von Steinwehr:—*First Brigade*, Col. Charles R. Coster; 134th N. Y., Lieut.-Col. Allan H. Jackson; 154th N. Y., Lieut.-Col. D. B. Allen; 27th Pa., Lieut.-Col. Lorenz Cantador; 73d Pa., Capt. D. F. Kelley. *Second Brigade*, Col. Orland Smith; 33d Mass., Col. Adin B. Underwood; 136th N. Y., Col. James Wood, Jr.; 55th Ohio, Col. Charles B. Gambee; 73d Ohio, Lieut.-Col. Richard Long.

THIRD DIVISION, Maj.-Gen. Carl Schurz:—*First Brigade*, Brig.-Gen. Alex. Schimmelfennig, Col. George von Amsberg; 82d Ill., Lieut.-Col. Edward S. Salomon; 45th N. Y., Col. George von Amsberg; Lieut.-Col. Adolphus Dobke; 157th N. Y., Col. Philip P. Brown, Jr.; 61st Ohio, Col. Stephen J. McGroarty; 74th Pa., Col. Adolph von Hartung; Lieut.-Col. Alexander von Mitzel, Capt. Gustav Schleiter, Capt. Henry Krauseneck. *Second Brigade*, Col. W. Krzyzanowski; 58th N. Y., Lieut.-Col. August Otto, Capt. Emil Koenig; 119th N. Y., Col. John T. Lockman, Lieut.-Col. Edward F. Lloyd; 82d Ohio, Col. James S. Robinson, Lieut.-Col. David Thomson; 75th Pa., Col. Francis Mahler, Maj. August Ledig; 26th Wis., Lieut.-Col. Hans Boebel, Capt. John W. Fuchs. *Artillery Brigade*, Maj. Thomas W. Osborn; 1st N. Y. Light, Batt. I, Capt. Michael Wiedrich; N. Y. Light, 13th Batt., Lieut. William Wheeler; 1st Ohio Light, Batt. I., Capt. Hubert Dilger; 1st Ohio Light, Batt. K,

* During the interval between the death of General Reynolds and the arrival of General Hancock, on the afternoon of July 1, all the troops on the field of battle were commanded by General Howard, General Schurz taking command of the Eleventh Corps, and General Schimmelfennig of the Third Division.

Capt. Lewis Heckman; 4th U. S., Batt. G, Lieut. Bayard Wilkeson, Lieut. Eugene A. Bancroft.

TWELFTH ARMY CORPS, MAJOR-GENERAL HENRY W. SLOCUM,* BRIGADIER-GENERAL ALPHEUS S. WILLIAMS. *Provost Guard*, 10th Me. (4 cos.), Capt. John D. Beardsley.

FIRST DIVISION, Brig.-Gen. Alpheus S. Williams, Brig.-Gen. Thomas H. Ruger:—*First Brigade*, Col. Archibald L. McDougall; 5th Conn., Col. W. W. Packer; 20th Conn., Lieut.-Col. William B. Wooster; 3d Md., Col. Jos. M. Sudsburg; 123d N. Y., Lieut.-Col. James C. Rogers, Capt. Adolphus H. Tanner; 145th N. Y., Col. E. L. Price; 46th Pa., Col. James L. Selfridge. *Second Brigade*,† Brig.-Gen. Henry H. Lockwood; 1st Md., Potomac Home Brigade, Col. William P. Maulsby; 1st Md., Eastern Shore, Col. James Wallace; 150th N. Y., Col. John H. Ketcham. *Third Brigade*, Brig.-Gen. Thomas H. Ruger, Col. Silas Colgrove; 27th Ind., Col. Silas Colgrove, Lieut.-Col. John R. Fesler; 2d Mass., Lieut. Col. Charles R. Mudge, Maj. Charles F. Morse; 13th N. J., Col. Ezra A. Carman; 107th N. Y., Col. Nirom M. Crane; 3d Wis., Col. William Hawley.

SECOND DIVISION, Brig.-Gen. John W. Geary:—*First Brigade*, Col. Charles Candy; 5th Ohio, Col. John H. Patrick; 7th Ohio, Col. William R. Creighton; 29th Ohio, Capt. Wilbur F. Stevens, Capt. Edward Hayes; 66th Ohio, Lieut.-Col. Eugene Powell; 28th Pa., Capt. John Flynn; 147th Pa. (8 cos.), Lieut.-Col. Ario Pardee, Jr. *Second Brigade*, Brig.-Gen. Thomas L. Kane, Col. George A. Cobham, Jr.; 29th Pa., Col. William Rickards, Jr.; 109th Pa., Capt. F. L. Gimber; 111th Pa., Lieut.-Col. Thomas M. Walker, Col. George A. Cobham, Jr. *Third Brigade*, Brig.-Gen. George S. Greene; 60th N. Y., Col. Abel Godard; 78th N. Y., Lieut.-Col. Herbert von Hammerstein; 102d N. Y., Col. James C. Lane, Capt. Lewis R. Stegman; 137th N. Y., Col. David Ireland; 149th N. Y., Col. Henry A. Barnum, Lieut.-Col. Charles B. Randall. *Artillery Brigade*, Lieut. Edward D. Muhlenberg; 1st N. Y. Light, Batt. M, Lieut. Charles E. Winegar; Pa. Light, Batt. E, Lieut. Charles A. Atwell; 4th U. S., Batt. F, Lieut. Sylvanus T. Rugg; 5th U. S., Batt. K, Lieut. David H. Kinzie.

CAVALRY CORPS, MAJOR-GENERAL ALFRED PLEASONTON.

FIRST DIVISION, Brig.-Gen. John Buford:—*First Brigade*, Col. William Gamble; 8th Ill., Maj. John L. Beveridge; 12th Ill. (4 cos.), 3d Ind. (6 cos.), Col. George H. Chapman; 8th N. Y., Lieut.-Col. William L. Markell. *Second Brigade*, Col. Thomas C. Devin; 6th N. Y., Maj. William E. Beardsley; 9th N. Y., Col. William Sackett; 17th Pa., Col. J. H. Kellogg; 3d W. Va. (2 cos.), Capt. Seymour B. Conger. *Reserve Brigade*, Brig.-Gen. Wesley Merritt; 6th Pa., Maj. James H. Haseltine;

---

* Exercised command of the right wing of the army during a part of the battle.

† Unassigned during progress of battle; afterwards attached to First Division, as Second Brigade.

1st U. S., Capt. Richard S. C. Lord; 2d U. S., Capt. T. F. Rodenbough; 5th U. S., Capt. Julius W. Mason; 6th U. S., Maj. Samuel H. Starr, Lieut. Louis H. Carpenter, Lieut. Nicholas Nolan, Capt. Ira W. Claflin.

SECOND DIVISION, Brig.-Gen. David McM. Gregg:—*Head-quarters Guard*, 1st Ohio, Co. A, Capt. Noah Jones. *First Brigade*, Col. John B. McIntosh; 1st Md. (11 cos.), Lieut.-Col. James M. Deems; Purnell (Md.) Legion, Co. A, Capt. Robert E. Duvall; 1st Mass.,* Lieut.-Col. Greely S. Curtis; 1st N. J., Maj. M. H. Beaumont; 1st Pa., Col. John P. Taylor, 3d Pa., Lieut.-Col. E. S. Jones; 3d Pa. Heavy Art., Section Batt. H,† Capt. W. D. Rank. *Second Brigade*,‡ Col. Pennock Huey; 2d N. Y., Lieut.-Col. Otto Harhaus; 4th N. Y., Lieut.-Col. Augustus Pruyn; 6th Ohio (10 cos.), Maj. William Stedman; 8th Pa., Capt. William A. Corrie. *Third Brigade*, Col. J. Irvin Gregg; 1st Me. (10 cos.), Lieut.-Col. Charles H. Smith; 10th N. Y., Maj. M. Henry Avery; 4th Pa., Lieut.-Col. William E. Doster; 16th Pa., Lieut.-Col. John K. Robison.

THIRD DIVISION, Brig.-Gen. Judson Kilpatrick:—*Head-quarters Guard*, 1st Ohio, Co. C, Capt. Samuel N. Stanford. *First Brigade*, Brig.-Gen. Elon J. Farnsworth, Col. Nathaniel P. Richmond; 5th N.Y., Maj. John Hammond; 18th Pa., Lieut.-Col. William P. Brinton; 1st Vt., Lieut.-Col. Addison W. Preston; 1st W. Va. (10 cos.), Col. Nathaniel P. Richmond, Maj. Charles E. Capehart. *Second Brigade*, Brig.-Gen. George A. Custer; 1st Mich., Col. George H. Town; 5th Mich., Col. Russell A. Alger; 6th Mich., Col. George Gray; 7th Mich. (10 cos.), Col. William D. Mann.

HORSE ARTILLERY:—*First Brigade*, Capt. James M. Robertson; 9th Mich. Batt., Capt. Jabez J. Daniels; 6th N. Y. Batt., Capt. Joseph W. Martin; 2d U. S., Batts. B and L, Lieut. Edward Heaton; 2d U. S., Batt. M, Lieut. A. C. M. Pennington, Jr.; 4th U. S., Batt. E, Lieut. Samuel S. Elder. *Second Brigade*, Capt. John C. Tidball; 1st U. S., Batts. E and G, Capt. Alanson M. Randol; 1st U. S., Batt. K, Capt. William M. Graham; 2d U. S., Batt. A, Lieut. John H. Calef; 3d U. S., Batt. C., Lieut. William D. Fuller.§

ARTILLERY RESERVE, Brig.-Gen. Robert O. Tyler, Capt. James M. Robertson. *Head-quarters Guard*, 32d Mass. Inf., Co. C, Capt. Josiah C. Fuller. *First Regular Brigade*, Capt. Dunbar R. Ransom; 1st U. S., Batt. H, Lieut. Chandler P. Eakin, Lieut. Philip D. Mason; 3d U. S., Batts. F and K, Lieut. John G. Turnbull; 4th U. S., Batt. C, Lieut. Evan Thomas; 5th U. S., Batt. C, Lieut. Gulian V. Weir. *First Volunteer Brigade*, Lieut.-Col. Freeman McGilvery; Mass. Light, 5th Batt. (E),‖ Capt. Charles A. Phillips; Mass. Light, 9th Batt., Capt. John Bigelow, Lieut. Richard S. Milton; N. Y. Light, 15th Batt., Capt. Patrick Hart; Pa. Light, Batts. C and F, Capt. James Thompson. *Second Volunteer Brigade*, Capt. Elijah D. Taft; 1st Conn. Heavy, Batt. B,¶ Capt. Albert F. Brooker; 1st Conn. Heavy, Batt. M,¶ Capt. Franklin A. Pratt;

* Served with the Sixth Army Corps, and on the right flank.

† Serving as light artillery.

‡ At Westminster, etc., and not engaged in the battle.

§ With Huey's Cavalry Brigade, and not engaged in the battle.

‖ Tenth New York Battery attached.

¶ Not engaged.

Conn. Light, 2d Batt., Capt. John W. Sterling; N. Y. Light, 5th Batt., Capt. Elijah D. Taft. *Third Volunteer Brigade*, Capt. James F. Huntington; N. H. Light, 1st Batt., Capt. Frederick M. Edgell; 1st Ohio Light, Batt. H, Lieut. George W. Norton; 1st Pa. Light, Batts. F and G, Capt. R. Bruce Ricketts; W. Va. Light, Batt. C, Capt. Wallace Hill. *Fourth Volunteer Brigade*, Capt. Robert H. Fitzhugh; Me. Light, 6th Batt. (F), Lieut. Edwin B. Dow; Md. Light, Batt. A, Capt. James H. Rigby; N. J. Light, 1st Batt., Lieut. Augustus N. Parsons; 1st N.Y. Light, Batt. G, Capt. Nelson Ames; 1st N.Y. Light, Batt. K,* Capt. Robert H. Fitzhugh. *Train Guard*, 4th N. J. Inf. (7 cos.), Maj. Charles Ewing.

PENNSYLVANIA VOLUNTEERS AND MILITIA.

Called into Service during the Gettysburg Campaign.†

Emergency Militia.—Ind. Co. Cav. (Murray Troop), Capt. Frank A. Murray; Ind. Co. Cav. (First Philadelphia City Troop), Capt. Samuel J. Randall; Ind. Co. Cav. (Luzerne Rangers), Capt. Henry H. Brown; Ind. Co. Cav. (Wissahickon Cav.), Capt. Samuel W. Comly; Ind. Co. Cav. (Continental Troop), Capt. Alban H. Myers; Ind. Co. Cav. (Curtin Horse Guards), Capt. John W. Jones; Ind. Batt., Capt. E. Spencer Miller; Ind. Batt., Capt. Henry D. Landis; 20th Inf., Col. William B. Thomas; 26th Inf., Col. William W. Jennings; 27th Inf., Col. Jacob G. Frick; 28th Inf., Col. James Chamberlin; 29th Inf., Col. Joseph W. Hawley; 30th Inf., Col. William N. Monies; 31st Inf., Col. John Newkumet; 33d Inf. (Blue Reserves), Col. William W. Taylor; Ind. Battn. Inf., Lieut.-Col. Robert Litzinger; Ind. Co. Inf., Capt. John Spear; Ind. Co. Inf., Capt. William B. Mann; Ind. Co. Inf., Capt. James B. German.

Ninety-Days' Militia.—1st Battn. Cav., Lieut.-Col. Richard F. Mason; Ind. Co. Cav., Capt. James M. Bell; Ind. Co. Cav., Capt. William B. Dick; Ind. Co. Cav. (Dana Troop), Capt. R. W. Hammell; Ind. Batt., Capt. Joseph M. Knap; Ind. Batt., Capt. Benoni Frishmuth; Ind. Batt. Capt. W. C. Ermentrout; Ind. Batt. (2d Keystone Batt.), Capt. Edward Fitzki; Ind. Batt. (Chester Co. Art.), Capt. George R. Guss; 32d Inf. (Gray Reserves), Col. Charles S. Smith; 34th Inf., Col. Charles Albright; 35th Inf., Col. Henry B. McKean; 36th Inf., Col. Henry C. Alleman; 37th Inf., Col. John Trout; 38th Inf., Col. Melchior H. Horn; 39th Inf., Col. James Nagle; 40th Inf. (1st Coal Regt.), Col. Alfred Day; 41st Inf., Col. Edward R. Mayer; 42d Inf., Col. Charles H. Hunter; 43d Inf., Col. William W. Stott; 44th Inf. (Merchants' Regt.), Col. Enos Woodward; 45th Inf., Col. James T. Clancy; 46th Inf., Col. John J. Lawrence; 47th Inf., Col. James P. Wickersham; 48th Inf., Col. John B. Embich; 49th Inf. (2d Corn Exchange), Col. Alexander Murphy;

---

* Eleventh New York Battery attached.

† The emergency militia and the six months' volunteers were mustered into the United States service, and the ninety-days' militia into the State service. Under act of Congress approved April 12, 1866, the State was reimbursed by the United States for money expended in payment of the latter troops.

50th Inf., Col. Emlen Franklin; 51st Inf. (2d Coal Regt.), Col. Oliver Hopkinson; 52d Inf. (2d Union League), Col. William A. Gray; 53d Inf., Col. Henry Royer; 54th Inf., Col. Thomas F. Gallagher; 55th Inf., Col. Robert B. McComb; 56th Inf., Col. Samuel B. Dick; 57th Inf., Col. James R. Porter; 58th Inf., Col. George H. Bemus; 59th Inf. (3d Union League), Col. George P. McLean; 60th Inf., Col. William F. Small; Ind. Battn. Inf., Lieut.-Col. John McKeage; Ind. Co. Inf., Capt. Joseph K. Helmbold; Ind. Co. Inf., Capt. Horace A. Beale; Ind. Co. Inf., Capt. Benjamin T. Green; Ind. Co. Inf., Capt. David Mitchel; Ind. Co. Inf., Capt. Osborn E. Stephens; Ind. Co. Inf., Capt. William F. Rich.

Six Months' Volunteers.—20th Cav., Col. John E. Wynkoop; 21st Cav., Col. William H. Boyd; 22d Cav. (Battn.), Maj. B. Mortimer Morrow; 1st Battn. Cav., Lieut.-Col. Richard C. Dale; Ind. Batt. (Park Batt.), Capt. Horatio K. Tyler; Ind. Batt., Capt. W. H. Woodward; Ind. Batt., Capt. Robert J. Nevin; 1st Battn. Inf., Lieut.-Col. Joseph F. Ramsey; 2d Battn. Inf., Lieut.-Col. John C. Lininger: 3d Battn. Inf., Lieut.-Col. T. Ellwood Zell; Ind. Co. Inf., Capt. Samuel T. Griffith; Ind. Co. Inf., Capt. William M. Schrock.

CHAPTER XXIX.

THE WAVE ROLLS BACK.

Confederates retreat from Gettysburg—The Federals pursue—Crossing the Potomac under Difficulties—Kilpatrick's Cavalry Dash on Pettigrew's Command—General Lee thought to rest his Army in the Valley of Virginia, but Meade followed too fast—Engagements that harassed the Retreat—General Lee wished to be relieved of Command, but President Davis would not consent to the Appointment of Joseph E. Johnston or General Beauregard.

THE armies rested on the "Fourth,"—one under the bright laurels secured by the brave work of the day before, but in profound sorrow over the silent forms of the host of comrades who had fallen during those three fateful days, whose blood bathed the thirsty fields of Gettysburg, made classic by the most stupendous clash of conflict of that long and sanguinary war; while gentle rain came to mellow the sod that marked the honored rest of friend and foe; the other, with broken spirits, turned from fallen comrades to find safety away from the fields that had been so promising of ennobling fruits. The enemy had cast his lines on grounds too strong for lead and steel, and, exhausted alike of aggressive force and means of protracted defence, there was nothing left for the vanquished but to march for distant homeward lines.

The cavalry left on the Blue Ridge joined the Confederate left late on the afternoon of the 3d. Orders for retreat were issued before noon of the 4th, and trains of wounded and other impedimenta were put in motion by the Chambersburg and Fairfield routes, the army to march after night by the latter,—the Second Corps as rear-guard, the First to follow the Third and push on to secure the crossings of the Potomac at Williamsport and Falling Waters. It was daylight of the 5th when the road was open for the march of the First, and a later hour of the morning before the Second could follow.

Pursuit was made by the enemy, led by cavalry and the Sixth Corps, and the rear-guard had to deploy near Fairfield to check it. Rain was helping us. Before the enemy could get through the mud and push his batteries over the boggy fields, our trains had reached the mountain gorge, and the rear-guard was on the march following. Direct pursuit of the solid ranks was changed to march down the east of the mountains, but the firmer broad road gave the Confederates easier march. Kilpatrick got his cavalry in on the wagon-trains and destroyed a number, but did not delay the march of the column.

On this retreat the army, already crippled of its pride, was met by the dispiriting news of another defeat at Vicksburg, which meant that the Mississippi was free to the Federals from its source to the Gulf. Diverting incidents occurred, but we were in poor mood for them. As we approached Hagerstown, two grotesque figures stepped into the road about a hundred yards in front of us,—one a negro of six feet and a hundred and eighty pounds, the other a white man of about five feet seven. The negro was dressed in full uniform of the Union infantry, the white man in travel-stained butternut dry-goods. The negro had a musket on his shoulder. Riding up to them, it was observed that the musket was at the cock-notch. The negro was reminded that it was unsoldier-like to have the gun at a cock, but said that he wanted to be ready to save and deliver his prisoner to the guard; it was his proudest capture during the march, and he wanted credit for it. The man was a recruit lately from abroad, and did not seem to care whether or not he was with his comrades. However, there were doubts if he understood a word that was said. The uniform was a tight fit, and the shoes were evidently painful, but the black man said that he could exchange them. He was probably the only man of the army who had a proud story to take home.

The Union cavalry came severely upon our left flank at Hagerstown, forcing Stuart to call for infantry support. Parts of Semmes's and G. T. Anderson's brigades were sent, crossed the Antietam, and had uncomfortable experience with the horse artillery near Funkstown. They had dire complaints to make of the way cavalrymen put them in columns of fours against batteries, when they could have advanced more rapidly and effectively in line of battle and saved half of their men lost.

Halting for rest near Falling Waters, a sudden alarm was brought down the road by a cavalryman riding at speed, who reported all of the enemy's cavalry on a sweeping ride against us. The troops were thrown together to wait, but the cavalry charge proved to be a carriage-load of lady refugees. Some of the cavalry did get over upon the trains parked at Williamsport, but there were many wounded near there who could handle their muskets, many infantry up from Winchester, and some of Imboden's cavalry, besides some batteries who held the ground, and Stuart eventually got up, when the enemy drew off.

On the 6th and 7th the commands were up, and deployed their lines from Falling Waters to cover the bridge and ford at Williamsport. But the river was full, past fording at Williamsport, and a raiding party from Harper's Ferry had partially destroyed the bridge at Falling Waters. Infantry trenches were made along the lines, batteries were put in position, and we were ready in a day or two to receive our successful adversary. He found some mud along his route, and was not up until the 12th, when he appeared and spread his lines along the Confederate front, but positions were changed,—he had the longer outer curve, while the Confederates were on the concentrating inner lines. He made his field-works and other arrangements, had some reinforcements since his battle, and was well organized.

On the forenoon of the 13th, General Lee sent for me, and announced that the river was fordable and the bridge repaired, that the trains would be started at once, and the troops would follow when night could conceal the move. The First and Third Corps were to cross by the bridge, the Second by the ford. As the lines were comfortable, the roads heavy, it occurred to me that the hurried move during a single night would be troublesome; suggestion was offered that the trains and wounded should move over during the night, and give us easy march the next night, but the waters on the other side were high, and only enough mills running to supply food from day to day, and the weather treacherous, so the general thought it better to hurry on. The march by the Williamsport crossing over the firm, broad turnpike was made without trouble. The route to the bridge was over a new road; at the ends of the bridge were green willow polés to prevent the wheels cutting through the mud, but the soil underneath was wet and soggy under the long season of rain, and before night rain again began to fall.

General Lee, worn by the strain of the past two weeks, asked me to remain at the bridge and look to the work of the night. And such a night is seldom experienced even in the rough life of the soldier. The rain fell in showers, sometimes in blinding sheets, during the entire night; the wagons cut deep in the mud during the early hours, and began to "stall" going down the hill, and one or two of the batteries were "stalled" before they reached the bridge. The best standing points were ankle-deep in mud, and the roads half-way to the knee, puddling and getting worse. We could only keep three or four torches alight, and those were dimmed at times when heavy rains came. Then, to crown our troubles, a load of the wounded came down, missed the end of the bridge, and plunged the wagon into the raging torrent. Right at the end of the bridge the water was three feet deep, and the current swift and surging. It did not seem possible that a man could be saved, but every one who could get through the mud and water rushed to their relief, and Providence was there to bring tears of joy to the sufferers. The wagon was righted and on the bridge and rolled off to Virginia's banks. The ground under the poles became so puddled before daylight that they would bend under the wheels and feet of the animals until they could bend no farther, and then would occasionally slip to one side far enough to spring up and catch a horse's foot and throw him broadside in the puddled mud. Under the trials and vexations every one was exhausted of patience, the general and staff were ready for a family quarrel as the only relief for their pent-up trouble, when daylight came, and with it General Lee to relieve and give us opportunity for a little repose.

The division of the Third Corps under General Heth formed the rear of the infantry line, which was to be covered by Fitzhugh Lee's cavalry. But the cavalry brigadier rode off and crossed the river, leaving, it is said, a squadron for the duty, and the squadron followed the example of the brigadier. The consequence was that when Kilpatrick's cavalry rode up it was taken to be the Confederates ordered for their rear-guard. Instead of friends, however, General Heth found a foe. He was surprised by a dashing cavalry charge, General Pettigrew was wounded, and died after a few days. Some artillery, three standards (of the Virginia infantry), and a large number of prisoners were taken. General Meade claimed two thousand.

General Lee thought to occupy the gaps of the Blue Ridge by his cavalry, and rest his army in the Valley of Virginia, in threatening lines against Washington City, but found the Shenandoah River full and past fording, and before the tide began to recede General Meade crossed the

RETREAT FROM GETTYSBURG. ACCIDENT DURING THE NIGHT-CROSSING OF THE POTOMAC ON A PONTOON BRIDGE.

Potomac east of the Blue Ridge and began to occupy the gaps, which called for a southern march of the Confederates. On the 19th my command was ordered to Millwood to secure, if possible, Ashby's Gap, but as the enemy's cavalry was on the opposite bank, and the waters were too high for us to get over, we marched on to Manassas, then for Chester Gap. As high up as Front Royal the river was found past fording, but part of a pontoon bridge was at hand. General Corse, who had joined us, hurried and succeeded in getting his brigade over in time to occupy Chester Gap, and putting his regiment under Colonel Arthur Herbert in the west end of Manassas Gap. The balance of Pickett's men crossed by putting the arms and ammunition in the boats, the men swimming, and sent reinforcements to General Corse and Colonel Herbert, when the enemy's cavalry withdrew. Our bridge was laid and spliced, and the march southward was resumed.

The next day another demonstration was made by the enemy's cavalry at Manassas Gap, but Hood's division was there and McLaws's was at the Chester Gap, where another heavy body of cavalry approached. An effort was made to get behind the latter by hidden lines of march, but the plan of catching cavalry with infantry was not successful, though General Wofford thought for a time that his trap was well laid. The march was continued, and the head of the column reached Culpeper Court-House on the 24th. Benning's brigade, left on guard at Gaines's Cross-Roads till the Third Corps could relieve him, was attacked by a strong cavalry force. On the approach of the Third Corps he thought to organize, with General A. P. Hill, another plan to entrap the cavalry in a thick wood, but the riders found little difficulty in getting away. General Ewell was detained a little, and found, upon approaching Front Royal, that General Wright's brigade, left there to hold the gaps for him, was engaged in skirmishing with the enemy's infantry. He reinforced the brigade, held the enemy back, then changed his march west, crossed the Blue Ridge at Thornton's Gap, and ordered Early's division, that was not yet up, through the Valley by Strasburg. He reached Madison Court-House on the 29th.

General Meade got his army together near Warrenton on the 31st of July, and ordered a detachment of artillery, cavalry, and infantry across the Rappahannock at Kelly's Ford and the railroad bridge. The command drove our cavalry back till it was reinforced by infantry, when the enemy was pushed back beyond Brandy Station.

General Ewell was called down from Madison Court-House, behind the Rapidan, and the First and Third Corps were marched into position behind the river on the 3d of August, leaving the cavalry at Culpeper Court-House.

General Lee suffered during the campaign from his old trouble, sciatica, and as soon as he found rest for his army applied to the authorities for a change of commanders. The President refused, pleading that he had no one to take his place. At the time he had two generals who were not in authority adequate to their rank,—Joseph E. Johnston, the foremost soldier of the South, who commanded the army until he was wounded at Seven Pines, and G. T. Beauregard, the hero of Sumter and the first Bull Run, well equipped for high command. But the President was jealous of Johnston, and nourished prejudice against Beauregard; though he found at last, when too late, that he must call them to the field.

CHAPTER XXX.

LONGSTREET MOVES TO GEORGIA.

The Author reverts to the Perils and Opportunities in the West—Proposes to the Secretary of War to reinforce against Rosecrans from the Army of Northern Virginia—Makes Plan known to General Lee—The Move finally effected—Difficulties of Transportation—A Roundabout Route—General Longstreet narrowly escapes capture when seeking Bragg's Head-quarters—General Bragg assigns Longstreet to Command of the Left—Instructions for the Battle of Chickamauga—The Armies in Position—Federals in Command of Generals Rosecrans, Crittenden, McCook, and George H. Thomas.

WHILE the army was lying idle on the south bank of the Rapidan my mind reverted to affairs in the West, and especially to the progressive work of the Union army in Tennessee towards the northern borders of Georgia. Other armies of the South were, apparently, spectators, viewing those tremendous threatenings without thought of turning minds or forces to arrest the march of Rosecrans.

To me the emergency seemed so grave that I decided to write the Honorable Secretary of War (excusing the informality under the privilege given in his request in May) expressing my opinion of affairs in that military zone. I said that the successful march of General Rosecrans's army through Georgia would virtually be the finishing stroke of the war; that in the fall of Vicksburg and the free flow of the Mississippi River the lungs of the Confederacy were lost; that the impending march would cut through the heart of the South, and leave but little time for the dissolution; that to my mind the remedy was to order the Army of Northern Virginia to defensive work, and send detachments to reinforce the army in Tennessee; to call detachments of other commands to the same service, and strike a crushing blow against General Rosecrans before he could receive reinforcing help; that our interior lines gave the opportunity, and it was only by the skilful use of them that we could reasonably hope to equalize our power to that of the better-equipped adversary; that the subject had not been mentioned to my commander, because like all others he was opposed to having important detachments of his army so far beyond his reach; that all must realize that our affairs were languishing, and that the only hope of reviving the waning cause was through the advantage of interior lines.

A few days after the letter was despatched the subject happened up while discussing affairs with General Lee, when I felt warranted in expressing my views and relieving my mind of the serious apprehensions that haunted me. He inquired if I was willing to go West and take charge there. To that I consented, provided the change could be so arranged as to give me an opportunity, by careful handling of the troops before accepting battle, to gain their confidence; providing, at the same time, that means could be arranged for further aggressive march in case of success.

At that time the railway passing our camps on the Rapidan through Virginia and East Tennessee to Chattanooga was open and in good working order. General Bragg's army was near Chattanooga, General Buckner's in East Tennessee, near Knoxville, General Samuel Jones's army, or parts of an army, in Southwest Virginia. There was but one railway,—from Cincinnati *via* Louisville and Nashville to Chattanooga. On that road General Rosecrans was marching against General Bragg. On the direct route to East Tennessee over the Cumberland Mountains General Burnside was marching over dirt roads into East Tennessee against General Buckner's forces.

A few days after the conversation with General Lee, he was called down to Richmond. In the course of a week he wrote, viz.:

"[Confidential.]

"RICHMOND, August 31, 1863.

"LIEUTENANT-GENERAL J. LONGSTREET,

"*Head-quarters Army of Northern Virginia:*

"GENERAL,—I have wished for several days past to return to the army, but have been detained by the President. He will not listen to my proposition to leave to-morrow. I hope you will use every exertion to prepare the army for offensive operations, and improve the condition of our men and animals. I can see nothing better to be done than to endeavor to bring General Meade out and use our efforts to crush his army while in its present condition.

* * * * * * * * *

"Very respectfully and truly yours,

"R. E. LEE,

"*General.*"

REPLY.

"HEAD-QUARTERS, September 2, 1863.

"GENERAL R. E. LEE,

"*Commanding:*

"GENERAL,—Your letter of the 31st is received. I have expressed to Generals Ewell and Hill your wishes, and am doing all that can be done to be well prepared with my own command. Our greatest difficulty will be in preparing our animals. I do not see that we can reasonably hope to accomplish much by offensive operations, unless you are strong enough to cross the Potomac. If we advance to meet the enemy on this side he will in all probability go into one of his many fortified positions. These we cannot afford to attack.

"I know but little of the condition of our affairs in the West, but am inclined to the opinion that our best opportunity for great results is in Tennessee. If we could hold the defensive here with two corps and send the other to operate in Tennessee with that army, I think that we could accomplish more than by an advance from here.

* * * * * * * * *

"I remain, general, very respectfully,

"Your obedient servant,

"JAMES LONGSTREET,

"*Lieutenant-General.*"

General Lee next wrote to inquire as to the time necessary for the movement of my corps into Tennessee. As there were but two divisions, McLaws's and Hood's, and Alexander's batteries, two days was supposed to be ample time. The transportation was ordered by the quartermaster's department at Richmond, and the divisions were made ready to board the trains as soon as they could reach us.

The success of the plan was thought from the first to depend upon its prompt and vigorous execution, and it was under those conditions that General Lee agreed to reinforce the army in Tennessee, together with the assurance that vigorous pursuit, even to the Ohio River, should follow success. The onward march was repeatedly urged, not only in return for the use of part of the army, but to relieve General Lee of apprehension from the army in front of him; but it was not until the 9th of September that the first train came to Orange Court-House to start with its load of troops. Meanwhile, General Buckner had left his post in East Tennessee and marched south to draw nearer the army under General Bragg about Chattanooga, leaving nothing of his command in East Tennessee except two thousand men at Cumberland Gap, under General Frazer, partially fortified. General Burnside had crossed the mountains, and was not only in East Tennessee, but on that very day General Frazer surrendered to him his command at Cumberland Gap without a fight.

These facts were known to the Richmond authorities at the time of our movements, but not to General Lee or myself until the move was so far advanced as to prevent recall. So that we were obliged to make the circuit through the Carolinas to Augusta, Georgia, and up by the railroad, thence through Atlanta to Dalton and Ringgold. It was the only route of transit left us. There were two routes between Richmond and Augusta, one *via* Wilmington, the other through Charlotte, North Carolina, but only a single track from Augusta to Chattanooga. The gauges of the roads were not uniform, nor did the roads connect at the cities (except by drays and other such conveyances). The roads had not been heavily worked before the war, so that their rolling stock was light and limited.

Instead of two days of moving, it was not until the 25th that our artillery joined us near Chattanooga. Hood's division was first shipped, and three brigades, or the greater part of three, were landed at the railroad station, and joined General Bragg's army on the 18th and 19th of September, but that army had been manœuvred and flanked out of Chattanooga, Buckner's out of East Tennessee, and both were together down below the borders of Georgia.

As I left General Lee's tent, after bidding him good-by, he walked out with me to my horse. As my foot was in the stirrup he said again, "Now, general, you must beat those people out in the West." Withdrawing my foot to respectful position I promised, "If I live; but I would not give a single man of my command for a fruitless victory." He promised again that it should not be so; said that arrangements had been made that any success we had should be followed; that orders to that effect had been given; that transportation was also ordered to be prepared, and the orders would be repeated.

While the troops were in transit, Jenkins's South Carolina brigade was transferred to Hood's division, so that we had two South Carolina and four Georgia brigades of the two divisions, which gave us some little trouble in keeping our men on the cars passing by their homes. The people crowded every station to give us their all in most acceptable rations, and to cheer us with wishes for a happy issue.

The train upon which I rode reached Catoosa about two o'clock of the afternoon of the 19th of September. That upon which our horses were came up at four o'clock. Only part of the staff of the corps was with me, and General Alexander was with his batteries far away in South Carolina. As soon as our horses could be saddled we started, Lieutenant-Colonels Sorrel and Manning and myself, to find the head-quarters of the commanding general. We were told to follow the main road, and did so, though there were many men coming into that road from our right bearing the wounded of the day's battle; the firing was still heard off to the right, and wagons were going and coming, indicating our nearness to the field. Nothing else occurring to suggest a change of the directions given us, we followed the main road.

It was a bright moonlight night, and the woodlands on the sides of the broad highway were quite open, so that we could see and be seen. After a time we were challenged by an outlying guard, "Who comes there?" We answered, "Friends." The answer was not altogether satisfying to the guard, and after a very short parley we asked what troops they were, when the answer gave the number of the brigade and of the division. As Southern brigades were called for their commanders more than by their numbers, we concluded that these friends were the enemy. There were, too, some suspicious obstructions across the road in front of us, and altogether the situation did not look inviting. The moon was so bright that it did not seem prudent to turn and ride back under the fire that we knew would be opened on us, so I said, loudly, so that the guard could hear, "Let us ride down a little way to find a better crossing." Riding a few rods brought us under cover and protection of large trees, sufficiently shading our retreat to enable us to ride quietly to the rear and take the road over which we had seen so many men and vehicles passing while on our first ride.

We reached General Bragg's head-quarters at eleven o'clock, reported, and received orders, which he had previously given other commanders, for attack early in the morning. Our bivouac was made near the general head-quarters, and we rode at daylight to find the troops. Hood's brigades that had arrived before us had been at work with the left of the army, which was assigned as my command. Lieutenant-General Polk was commanding the right wing.

Two brigades of McLaws's division, Kershaw's and Humphreys's, came in the afternoon, and marched during the night and across the Chickamauga River.

The army had forced its way across the Chickamauga under severe skirmishes, little less than a battle, during the greater part of the 19th, and some of the commands had been engaged on the 18th working on the same plan.

The written order giving the plan was issued on the 18th. In general terms, it was to cross the Chickamauga, strike the enemy's left, and roll it back on his right by a wheel to the left so as to come in between the enemy and Chattanooga. The work had been so persistent and assiduous during part of the 18th and all of the 19th, that General Rosecrans came to understand the plan as well as his adversary, and to arrange accordingly.

With my instructions for the 20th the commanding general gave me a map showing prominent topographical features of the grounds from the Chickamauga River to Mission Ridge, and beyond to the Lookout Mountain range.

At early dawn I found the left wing. It was composed of Buckner's corps (Stewart's and Preston's divisions), a new division under General Bushrod R. Johnson, the division of General T. C. Hindman, and three of Hood's brigades. Buckner's corps had been cut in two. His division on the right of the left wing was under General Stewart, while Preston's division, on the extreme left, on the bank of the Chickamauga, was assigned, by the order for battle, as the pivot upon which the battle should wheel. The commands stood . Stewart's, Johnson's, Hindman's, and Preston's divisions; Hood's brigades in rear of Johnson's line. General Buckner reported his artillery as amounting to about thirty guns. Three batteries were reported, of four guns each, with Hindman's division, Johnson's and Hood's commands being without artillery. The brigades of Kershaw and Humphreys were ordered, with Hood's, to be used as a column of assault, by brigades, at a hundred paces interval.

As the battle was ordered for daylight, it seemed too late to draw Buckner's divisions into reciprocal relations, and we had yet to find the right wing. As it was not in touch or sight, General Stewart was ordered to find it. He marched about half a mile to his right and found that he was nearly half a mile in advance of the right wing. His move made place for Hood's column, which was called to the line, and General Stewart broke his right to rear to guard that flank until the right wing could get to the front. The divisions were formed in two lines, two brigades on the front line, others of the second line in support, except Hood's five brigades in column. General McLaws and two of his brigades, two of Hood's, and Alexander's artillery were on the rails, speeding for the battle as fast as steam could carry them, but failed to reach it. When organized for battle the left wing stood about three hundred yards east of the Lafayette-Chattanooga dirt road. As the battle was ordered for wheel to the left on Preston's division as pivot, his (Trigg's) brigade was echeloned on the left of Hindman's division. The purpose of the commander in ordering the wheel on the left as pivot was to push in, from the start, between the enemy and his new base at Chattanooga.

No chief of artillery for the command reported, and a brief search failed to find one. The field, so far as it could be surveyed, however, was not a field, proper, but a heavy woodland, not adapted to the practice of artillery. The hour of battle was at hand, but the right wing was not yet organized. Some of the troops were without rations, their wagons, having lost the lines of march through the woodlands, failing to reach them until after daylight, when they were further delayed cooking their food.

The right wing was formed of D. H. Hill's corps, Breckenridge's and Cleburne's divisions, W. H. T. Walker's corps of Walker's and Liddell's divisions, Cheatham's division of Polk's corps, artillery battalions of Majors Melancthon Smith, T. R. Hotchkiss, and R. E. Graves, and batteries of Lieutenant R. T. Beauregard, Captain E. P. Howell, Captain W. H. Fowler, and Lieutenant Shannon.

As it formed it stood with D. H. Hill's corps on the right, Breckenridge's and Cleburne's divisions from right to left, Cheatham's division on the left of Cleburne's rear, and Walker's reserve corps behind Hill's corps; but when arranged for battle it was about half a mile in rear of the line upon which the left wing was established. The Confederate commander rode early in the morning to hear the opening of the battle. As the sounds failed to reach him, he became anxious, sent orders of inquiry for the cause of delay, repeated his orders for attack, and finally rode to his right wing and gave peremptory orders.

Marching through the woods to line up on the left wing, the left of the right wing was found to overlap my division on the right, yet our extreme right was found to overreach the left of the enemy's field-works by two brigades, and reconnoissance found the road between the enemy and Chattanooga open and free of obstructions or troops to defend it. On the right of Breckenridge's division was Armstrong's division of cavalry dismounted, and beyond his right was Forrest's other division of cavalry, Pegram's. Some miles off from our left was Wheeler's division of cavalry, under Wharton and Martin.

The Union army from left to right was: first the Fourteenth Corps, General George H. Thomas commanding, four divisions,—Baird's division on the left, then Reynolds's and Brannan's, the latter retired to position of reserve, and Negley's. (The last named had been left, on the night of the 19th, on guard near the Glen House, but was ordered early on the 20th to join General Thomas, and one of the brigades did move promptly under the order; the other brigades (two) failed to receive the order.) Then the Twentieth Corps, three divisions,—Jefferson C. Davis's, R. W. Johnson's, and P. H. Sheridan's,—on the right, General A. McD. McCook commanding the corps. Next was the Twenty-first Corps, three divisions,—T. J. Wood's, J. M. Palmer's, and H. P. Van Cleve's,—General T. L. Crittenden commanding the corps. It was in position on the east slope of Mission Ridge, ordered to be prepared to support the corps of the right or left, or both; one of its brigades had been left to occupy Chattanooga. Wilder's mounted infantry, on the right of the Twentieth Corps, was ordered to report to the commander of that corps for the day's work. A reserve corps under General Gordon Granger was off the left of the Union army to cover the gap in Mission Ridge at Rossville and the road from the Union left to that gap. Minty's cavalry was with this corps, and posted at Mission Mills. General Granger had Steedman's division of two brigades and a brigade under Colonel D. McCook. General R. B. Mitchell, commanding Union cavalry, was on their right at Crawfish Springs, with orders to hold the crossings of the Chickamauga against the Confederate cavalry.

It seems that parts of the Twentieth and Twenty-first Corps, Johnson's and Van Cleve's divisions, were under General Thomas in the fight of his left on the 19th, and remained with him on the 20th. The purpose of the posting of the Union army was to hold open its routes for Chattanooga by the Rossville and Dry Valley roads. As before stated, the Confederate commander's design was to push in between the Union army and Chattanooga, recover his lost ground, and cut the enemy's line of supplies.

The commanders of the armies were on the field early on the 20th. The failure of the opening of the Confederates at daylight gave opportunity for a reconnoissance by light of day, by which it was learned that the road from the Union left was open, not guarded nor under close observation; but the commander ordered direct assault under the original plan,—his back to the river, the Union army backing on Mission Ridge. The Chickamauga River, rising from the mountains south, flows in its general course a little east of north to conflux with the Tennessee River. The Ridge runs nearly parallel with the river, and opens up a valley a mile wide. It is a bold outcropping of limestone about one hundred feet above the valley, with occasional passes, or gaps, that are strong points of guard for defence. Four miles northwest from the Union left was the gap at Rossville, called for the old Cherokee chief. Behind its right was the pass of the Dry Valley road, and immediately in its rear was the McFarland Gap. The line of the Lafayette road lies about parallel with the Ridge a mile beyond the Union left, whence it bends westward and leads to the Rossville Gap. The Dry Valley road crosses the Chickamauga at Glass's Mills, courses along the east slope of the Ridge, crosses it, and joins on the west the road that crosses at the McFarland Gap.

The Union line towards its left was east of the Chattanooga-Rossville road, but the flank crossed the road to the west and formed in broken front. The left and right of Thomas's line was retired or broken to the rear. The Union commander rode over his lines on the afternoon of the 19th and ordered his front covered by such field-works as could be constructed during the night.

General Thomas covered his lines by log and rail obstructions. The corps of Rosecrans's right formed two lines of rail defences for infantry. The batteries had the ascending slopes of the Ridge for positions, and their field was more favorable otherwise for artillery practice than was that of the Confederates advancing from the valley and more densely timbered forests. They had two hundred and forty-six guns. The records do not give satisfactory accounts of the number of Confederate guns, but they probably numbered not less than two hundred.

CHAPTER XXXI.

BATTLE OF CHICKAMAUGA.

Tactical Features—The Battle opened by Direct Attack on the Federals in the Early Morning of September 20—Repeated and Determined Front Assaults—Brigadiers Helm killed and Adams wounded—The Union Commands lay behind Defences—Hood's Brigades surged through the Forest against the Covered Infantry and Artillery—Hood wounded—Longstreet suggests a Plan for Progressive Action—Halting Tactics at High Tide of Success—The Confederate Left fought a Separate Battle—General Thomas retreats—First Confederate Victory in the West, and one of the Bloodiest Battles of the War—Forces engaged—Losses.

SATISFIED that the opening of the battle was to be the attack against his left, the Union commander ordered Negley's division out from its position near the Glen House to report to General Thomas and assist in meeting the attack, but only Beattie's brigade was in time for that service, the other brigades waiting to be relieved from their positions in line. Meanwhile, Baird's left had been extended by Dodge's brigade of Johnson's division of the Twentieth Corps.

Before the Confederate commander engaged his battle he found the road between the enemy's left and Chattanooga open, which gave him opportunity to interpose or force the enemy from his works to open battle to save his line. But he preferred his plan of direct attack as the armies stood, and opened his battle by attack of the right wing at 9.30 A.M. of the 20th. He was there, and put the corps under Lieutenant-General D. H. Hill to the work. Breckenridge's and Cleburne's divisions, Breckenridge on the right, overreached the enemy's left by two brigades, Stovall's and Adams's, but the other brigade, Helm's, was marched through the wood into front assault of the enemy behind his field-works. This brigade made desperate repeated and gallant battle until the commander, Benjamin H. Helm, one of the most promising brigadiers, was killed, when its aggressive work was suspended.

The other brigades crossed the Chattanooga road, changed front, and bore down against the enemy's left. This gave them favorable ground and position. They made resolute attack against Baird's left, threatening his rear, but he had troops at hand to meet them. They had a four-gun battery of Slocum's of the Washington Artillery,* and encountered Dodge's brigade and parts of Willick's, Berry's, and Stanley's, and superior artillery. In the severe contention General Adams fell seriously hurt, and the brigades were eventually forced back to and across the road, leaving General Adams on the field.

A separate attack was then made by Cleburne's division, the brigades of Polk and Wood assaulting the breast-works held by the divisions of Johnson and Palmer. These brigades, after severe fight, were repulsed, and their positions were covered by Deshler's brigade. General Deshler received a mortal wound from a fragment of shell, leaving the brigade in the hands of the gallant Colonel Roger Q. Mills (our afterwards distinguished statesman). General Thomas called repeatedly for reinforcements, and received assurances that they were coming, even to include the army if necessary to hold the left.

Johnson's brigade of Cheatham's division was ordered to support the brigade under Colonel Mills, and the reserve corps under General W. H. T. Walker (Gist's and Liddell's divisions) was ordered into the Breckenridge battle, Gist's brigade against the left angle of the breast-works, and Walthall's to the place of Cleburne's division. The other brigade of Gist's division supported the battle of his own brigade, and General Liddell was ordered with Govan's brigade to advance, passing beyond the enemy's

---

* That company did not go with the battalion to Virginia.

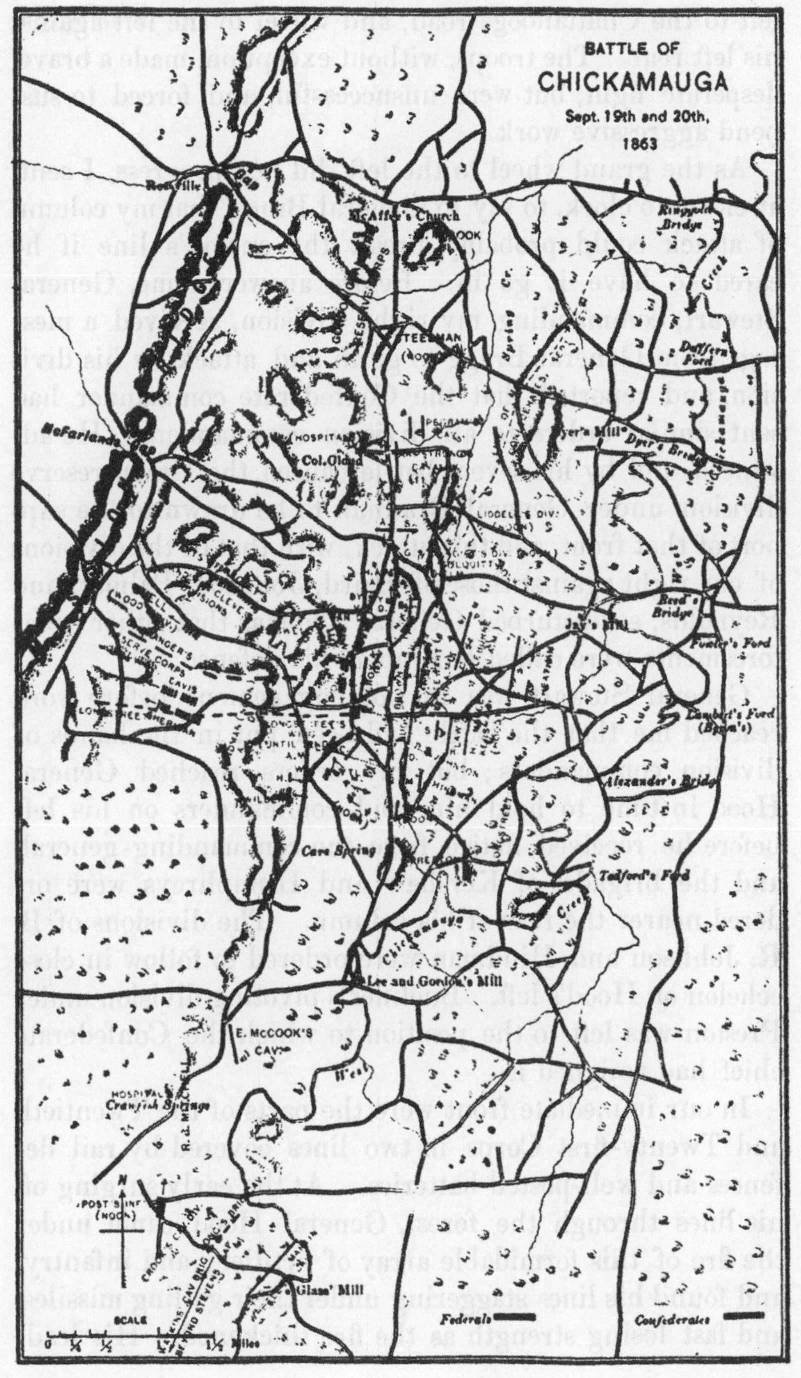
BATTLE OF
CHICKAMAUGA
Sept. 19th and 20th,
1863
Rossville
McAfee's Church
Ringgold Bridge
Dyer's Mill
Dyer's Bridge
Reed's Bridge
Fowler's Ford
Lambert's Ford
(Byram's)
Alexander's Bridge
Telford's Ford
McFarlands Gap
Col. Glenn
HOSPITAL
Cave Spring
Lee and Gordon's Mill
E. McCOOK'S CAV.
HOSPITAL
Crawfish Springs
POST'S INF.
(NOON)
Glass' Mill
SCALE
Miles
Federals
Confederates

left to the Chattanooga road, and wheel to the left against his left rear. The troops, without exception, made a brave, desperate fight, but were unsuccessful, and forced to suspend aggressive work.

As the grand wheel to the left did not progress, I sent, at eleven o'clock, to say to General Bragg that my column of attack could probably break the enemy's line if he cared to have it go in. Before answer came, General Stewart, commanding my right division, received a message from General Bragg to go in and attack by his division, and reported that the Confederate commander had sent similar orders to all division commanders. He advanced, and by his severe battle caused the Union reserve division under General Brannan to be drawn to the support of that front, and this attack, with that of the divisions of our right against those of Baird, Johnson, Palmer, and Reynolds, so disturbed General Thomas that other reinforcements were called to support his defence.

General Stewart was in hot engagement before word reached me that the battle had been put in the hands of division commanders; but my orders reached General Hood in time to hold him and commanders on his left before he received notice from the commanding general, and the brigades of Kershaw and Humphreys were ordered nearer the rear of his column. The divisions of B. R. Johnson and Hindman were ordered to follow in close echelon on Hood's left. Buckner's pivoting division under Preston was left to the position to which the Confederate chief had assigned it.

In our immediate front were the parts of the Twentieth and Twenty-first Corps in two lines covered by rail defences and well-posted batteries. At the early surging of his lines through the forest, General Hood came under the fire of this formidable array of artillery and infantry, and found his lines staggering under their galling missiles, and fast losing strength as the fire thickened. His leading brigade was decimated, but his others pushed to the front to take and pursue the assault. The divisions of B. R. Johnson and Hindman were pressed hard on Hood's left, and the brigades of Kershaw and Humphreys closed to his support, when a bold push gave us the first line of the enemy and a large number of his guns; but General Hood was fearfully wounded, supposed to be fatally; General Benning, of his "Rock Brigade," lost his horse, and thought General Hood was killed. He cut a horse loose from a captured gun, mounted, and using part of a rope trace as his riding whip, rode to meet me and report disaster. He had lost his hat in the mêlée, and the brigade disappeared under the steady crushing fire so quickly that he was a little surprised. He reported, "General Hood killed, my horse killed, my brigade torn to pieces, and I haven't a man left." I asked if he didn't think he could find one man. The question or the manner seemed to quiet somewhat his apprehensions and brought affirmative answer, when he was told to collect his men and join us at the front; that we had broken and carried the first line; that Johnson's division, on his left, was then in the breach and pushing on, with Hindman on his left, spreading battle to the enemy's limits; that Stewart's division would hold it on our right, and the brigades of Kershaw and Humphreys then on the quick step would be with us in a minute and help restore the battle to good organization. Just then these two brigades burst through the brush in cheerful, gallant march, and brought him back to his usual courageous, hopeful confidence.

As we approached a second line, Johnson's division happened to strike it while in the act of changing position of some of the troops, charged upon and carried it, capturing some artillery, Hood's and Hindman's troops pressing in close connection. This attack forced the parts of the Twentieth and Twenty-first Corps from that part of the field, back over Missionary Ridge, in disordered retreat, and part of Negley's division of the Fourteenth Corps by the same impulsion. As our right wing had failed of the progress anticipated, and had become fixed by the firm holding of the enemy's left, we could find no practicable field for our work except by a change of the order of battle from wheel to the left, to a swing to the right on my division under General Stewart. The fire of the enemy off my right readily drew Hood's brigades to that bearing. Johnson's and Hindman's divisions were called to a similar move, and Buckner's pivotal division under General Preston, but General Buckner objected to having his left "in the air."

Presently a discouraging account came from General Hindman, that in the progress of his battle his left and rear had been struck by a formidable force of cavalry; that Manigault's brigade was forced back in disorder, and his other brigades exposed on their open left could not be handled. I wrote him a note commending the brave work of his division, and encouraging renewed efforts; urged him to have his brigades in hand, and bring them around to close connection on Johnson's left.

On the most open parts of the Confederate side of the field one's vision could not reach farther than the length of a brigade. Trigg's brigade was ordered to the relief of Manigault's, which had been forced back to the Lafayette road, and the balance of Preston's division was ordered to follow, if necessary, to support that part of the field, and our cavalry far away from my left was called to clean it up and pursue the retreating columns. It seems that Wilder's brigade of mounted infantry had struck Manigault's left and put it back in disorder, and a brigade, or part of a brigade, of cavalry coming against the rear, increased the confusion and drove it back to the Lafayette road, when Trigg's brigade advanced to its relief. The two put the attacking forces back until they found it necessary to retire beyond the ridge and cover the withdrawal of trains left exposed by the retreat of troops of the Twentieth and Twenty-first Corps. General Hindman gathered his forces and marched for the left of Johnson's division, and Preston's brigade under General Trigg was returned to the point of its first holding.

Our front, cleared of opposing forces, was soon changed forward, and formed at right angle to its first line to seek the enemy's line standing against our right wing. Calls were repeated for the cavalry to ride in pursuit of the retreating forces, and guard the gaps of the ridge behind the enemy standing in front of our right wing. In the new position of the left wing its extreme left encountered the enemy rallying in strong position that was heavily manned by field batteries. At the same time my left was approaching the line of fire of one of our batteries of the right wing.

General Johnson thought that he had the key of the battle near Snodgrass Hill. It was a key, but a rough one. He was ordered to reorganize his own brigades and those of Hindman's division for renewed work; to advance a line of skirmishers, and give time to the troops for refreshment, while I rode along the line to observe the enemy and find relations with our right wing.

It was after one o'clock, and the hot and dry and dusty day made work fatiguing. My lunch was called up and ordered spread at some convenient point while I rode with General Buckner and the staffs to view the changed conditions of the battle. I could see but little of the enemy's line, and only knew of it by the occasional exchange of fire between the lines of skirmishers, until we approached the angle of the lines. I passed the right of our skirmishers, and, thinking I had passed the enemy's, rode forward to be accurately assured, when I suddenly found myself under near fire of his sharpshooters concealed behind the trees and under the brush. I saw enough, however, to mark the ground line of his field-works as they were spread along the front of the right wing, and found that I was very fortunate in having the forest to cover the ride back until out of reach of their fire. In the absence of a chief of artillery, General Buckner was asked to establish a twelve-gun battery on my right to enfilade the enemy's works and line standing before our right wing, and then I rode away to enjoy my spread of Nassau bacon and Georgia sweet potatoes. We were not accustomed to potatoes of any kind in Virginia, and thought we had a luxury, but it was very dry, as the river was a mile and more from us, and other liquids were over the border. Then, before we had half finished, our pleasures were interrupted by a fragment of shell that came tearing through the woods, passed through a book in the hands of a courier who sat on his horse hard by reading, and struck down our chief of ordnance, Colonel P. T. Manning, gasping, as was supposed, in the struggles of death. Friends sprang forward to look for the wound and to give some aid and relief. In his hurry to enjoy and finish his lunch he had just taken a large bite of sweet potato, which seemed to be suffocating him. I suggested that it would be well to first relieve him of the potato and give him a chance to breathe. This done, he revived, his breath came freer, and he was soon on his feet ready to be conveyed to the hospital. In a few days he was again on duty.

After caring for and sending him off, and before we were through with our lunch, General Bragg sent for me. He was some little distance in rear of our new position. The change of the order of battle was explained, and the necessity under which it came to be made. We had taken some forty or more field-pieces and a large number of small-arms, and thought that we had cut off and put to disorder the Twentieth and Twenty-first Corps that had retreated through the pass of the Ridge by the Dry Valley road. He was informed of orders given General

Johnson for my left, and General Buckner for a battery on the right. I then offered as suggestion of the way to finish our work that he abandon the plan for battle by our right wing, or hold it to defence, draw off a force from that front that had rested since the left wing took up the battle, join them with the left wing, move swiftly down the Dry Valley road, pursue the retreating forces, occupy the gaps of the Ridge behind the enemy standing before our right, and call that force to its own relief.

He was disturbed by the failure of his plan and the severe repulse of his right wing, and was little prepared to hear suggestions from subordinates for other moves or progressive work. His words, as I recall them, were: "There is not a man in the right wing who has any fight in him." From accounts of his former operations I was prepared for halting work, but this, when the battle was at its tide and in partial success, was a little surprising. His humor, however, was such that his subordinate was at a loss for a reopening of the discussion. He did not wait, nor did he express approval or disapproval of the operations of the left wing, but rode for his head-quarters at Reed's Bridge.

There was nothing for the left wing to do but work along as best it could. The right wing ceased its active battle as the left forced the enemy's right centre, and the account of the commanding general was such as to give little hope of his active use of it in supporting us. After his lunch, General Johnson was ordered to make ready his own and Hindman's brigades, to see that those of Hood's were in just connection with his right, and await the opening of our battery. Preston's division was pulled away from its mooring on the river bank to reinforce our worn battle.* The battery not opening as promptly as expected, General Johnson was finally ordered into *strong*,

* This was my first meeting with the genial, gallant, lovable William Preston.

steady battle. He pushed through part of the woodland, drove back an array of artillery and the supporting infantry, and gained other elevated ground. The sound of battle in his rear, its fire drawing nearer, had attracted the attention of General Granger of the reserve corps, and warned him that it was the opportunity for his command. He marched, without orders, towards the noise, and passed by the front of Forrest's cavalry and the front of our right wing, but no report of his march was sent us. Day was on the wane. Night was advancing. The sun dipped to the palisades of Lookout Mountain, when Lieutenant-Colonel Claiborne reported that the cavalry was not riding in response to my calls. He was asked to repeat the order *in writing*, and despatched as follows:

"BATTLE-FIELD, September 20, 1863, 5.09 P.M.

"GENERAL WHEELER:

"Lieutenant-General Longstreet orders you to proceed down the road towards the enemy's right, and with your artillery endeavor to enfilade his line, with celerity.

"By order of Lieutenant-General Longstreet.

"THOMAS CLAIBORNE,
"*Lieutenant-Colonel Cavalry.*"

Then our foot-scouts reported that there was nothing on the road taken by the enemy's retreating columns but squads of footmen. Another written order for the cavalry was despatched at 5.30.*

General Preston reinforced us by his brigade under Gracie, pushed beyond our battle, and gained a height and intervening dell before Snodgrass Hill, but the enemy's reserve was on the hill, and full of fight, even to the aggressive. We were pushed back through the valley and up the slope, until General Preston succeeded in getting part of his brigade under Trigg to the support. Our battery got up at last under Major Williams

* Rebellion Record.

and opened its destructive fire from eleven guns, which presently convinced General Thomas that his position was no longer tenable. He drew Reynolds's division from its trenches near the angle, for assignment as rear-guard. Lieutenant-Colonel Sorrel, of the staff, reported this move, and was sent with orders to General Stewart to strike down against the enemy's moving forces. It seems that at the same time Liddell's division of the extreme right of our right wing was ordered against the march of the reserves. Stewart got into part of Reynolds's line and took several hundred prisoners. Meanwhile, Reynolds was used in meeting the attack and driving back the division of General Liddell. That accomplished, he was ordered to position to cover the retreat. As no reports came to the left from the commanding general or from the right wing, the repulse of Liddell's division was thought to indicate the strong holding of the enemy along his intrenched front line, and I thought that we should wait to finish the battle on the morrow.

The direct road to Chattanooga was thought to be closed by our right wing. McFarland's Gap, the only *débouché*, was supposed to be occupied by the cavalry. Another blind road was at the base of the mountain on its east side. During the artillery practice the fire of some of the guns of our battery was turned to the contest at Snodgrass Hill, which disturbed part of our infantry fiercely struggling for that ground, and they complained, but the fire was effective. As the woods were full of the enemy, a shot would find a mark.

The intrenched line was crumbling faster than we supposed, and their reserve was engaged in hot defensive battle to hold secure the Gap while yet there were two hours of daylight. Had the four brigades of Cheatham's division that had not been in action gone in at the same time as Liddell's division, it is hardly possible that the Con-

BATTLE OF CHICKAMAUGA. CONFEDERATES FLANKING THE UNION FORCES.

federate commander could have failed to find the enemy's empty lines along the front of his right wing, and called both wings into a grand final sweep of the field to capture Thomas's command; but he was not present, and the condition of affairs was embarrassing to the subordinate commanders whose efforts had not been approved.

A reconnoissance made just before the first strokes of the morning engagement discovered an open way around the enemy's left by turning his intrenched line in reverse, which General Hill thought to utilize by change of tactics, but General Bragg present, and advised of the opportunity, preferred his tactics, and urged prompt execution. At the later hour when Liddell's division was passed beyond the enemy's intrenchments to strike at his reinforcing march under General Granger, the subordinate of the right wing could not see how he was to be justified in using a greater force in that direction, affairs of the wing being similar to those of the opening, while the relations of the right and left were in reverse of tactical orders; but a vigilant chief present and caring for the weaker part of his battle, advised that the enemy was on his last legs, with his reserves could well have sprung the right wing into the opening beyond his right, securing crushing results. Earlier in the afternoon he did send an order for renewed efforts of the right wing under his plan of parallel assault, but the troops had tested the lines in their first battle, and were not in condition for a third effort, at parallel battle.

The contention by our left wing was maintained as a separate and independent battle. The last of the reserve, Trigg's brigade, gave us new strength, and Preston gained Snodgrass Hill. The trampled ground and bushy woods were left to those who were too much worn to escape the rapid strides of the heroic Confederates. The left wing swept forward, and the right sprang to the broad Chattanooga highway. Like magic the Union army had melted away in our presence. A few hundred prisoners were picked up by both wings as they met, to burst their throats in loud huzzas. The Army of Tennessee knew how to enjoy its first grand victory. The dews of twilight hung heavy about the trees as if to hold down the voice of victory; but the two lines nearing as they advanced joined their continuous shouts in increasing volume, not as the burstings from the cannon's mouth, but in a tremendous swell of heroic harmony that seemed almost to lift from their roots the great trees of the forest.

Before greetings and congratulations upon the success had passed it was night, and the mild beams of the quartering moon were more suggestive of Venus than of Mars. The haversacks and ammunition supplies were ordered replenished, and the Confederate army made its bivouac on the ground it had gained in the first pronounced victory in the West, and one of the most stubbornly contested battles of the war.

Our cavalry had failed to close McFarland Gap, and through that General Thomas made his march for the stand at Rossville Gap.

It has been stated that this retreat was made under the orders of the Union commander. General Thomas did, in fact, receive a message from his chief a little after four o'clock, saying that he was riding to Chattanooga to view the position there; that he, General Thomas, was left in command of all of the organized forces, and should seek strong and threatening position at Rossville, and send the other men back to Chattanooga to be reorganized. This was a suggestion more than an order, given under the conviction that the Confederates, having the Dry Valley road, would pass the ridge to the west side, cut General Thomas off, and strike his rear at pleasure. The order to command of the troops in action, and the conditions referring to duties at Chattanooga, carried inferential discretion. That General Thomas so construed it was evidenced by his decision to hold "until nightfall if possible." But directly, under the practice of our enfilading battery, he became convinced that it was not possible, changed his purpose, and at 5.30 gave orders for his commanders to prepare to retire, and called Reynolds's division from its trenches to be posted as rear-guard to cover the retreat.

General Granger was then engaged in severe contention against my left at Snodgrass Hill. His march along the front of our cavalry and right wing suggested the advance of Liddell's division to the Chattanooga road to try to check it. The withdrawal of Reynolds's division was in season to aid in driving Liddell's division back to its former ground. Reynolds was posted on eminent ground as rear-guard, and organized retreat followed. It was not until after sunset that Rosecrans's *order* for retreat was issued, as appears from the letter written from Rossville by General James A. Garfield, chief of staff, dated 8.40, three hours and more after the move was taken up, viz.:

"Your order to retire to this place was received a little after sunset and communicated to Generals Thomas and Granger. The troops are now moving back, and will be here in good shape and strong position before morning." *

So events and the evidence seem conclusive that it was our artillery practice that made the confusion of Chickamauga forests unbearable, and enforced retreat before Rosecrans order was issued.

The Union army and reserve had been fought, and by united efforts we held the position at Snodgrass Hill, which covered McFarland Gap and the retreat. There were yet five brigades of Confederates that had not been in active battle. The Confederate commander was not present, and his next in rank thought night pursuit without authority a heavy, unprofitable labor, while a flank move,

* Rebellion Record, vol. xxx. part i. p. 144.

after a night's rest, seemed promising of more important results. The Confederate chief did not even know of his victory until the morning of the 21st, when, upon riding to his extreme right, he found his commander at that point seeking the enemy in his immediate front, and commended the officer upon his vigilance,—twelve hours after the retreat of the enemy's forces.

The forces engaged and their respective casualties follow:

General Bragg's returns of the 20th of August—the last of record—reported his aggregate of all arms	43,866
Reinforced from J. E. Johnston's army in August	9,000
Reinforced from J. E. Johnston's army in September (Gregg and McNair)	2,500
Reinforced from General Lee's army, September 18 and 19 (a large estimate)	5,000
Total	60,366
Losses on the 18th and 19th	1,124
Aggregate for battle on the 20th	59,242
General Rosecrans's return of September 20, 1863, showed: Aggregate of infantry, equipped	46,561
Aggregate of cavalry, equipped	10,114
Aggregate of artillery, equipped	4,192
Total	60,867
Confederate losses (estimated; returns imperfect)	17,800
Union losses by returns (infantry, artillery, and cavalry)	16,550

The exceeding heaviness of these losses will be better understood, and the desperate and bloody character of the Chickamauga battle more fully appreciated, upon a little analysis. The battle, viewed from the stand-point of the Union losses, was the fifth greatest of the war, Gettysburg, Spottsylvania, the Wilderness, and Chancellorsville alone exceeding it, but each of these battles were of much longer time. Viewed by comparison of Confederate losses, Chickamauga occupies similar place—fifth—in the scale of magnitude among the battles of the war.

But the sanguinary nature of the contention is best

illustrated by a simple suggestion of proportions. Official reports show that on both sides the casualties—killed, wounded, and missing—embraced the enormous proportion of thirty-three per cent. of the troops actually engaged.

On the Union side there were over a score of regiments in which the losses in this single fight exceeded 49.4 per cent., which was the heaviest loss sustained by a German regiment at any time during the Franco-German war. The "charge of the Light Brigade" at Balaklava has been made famous in song and history, yet there were thirty Union regiments that each lost ten per cent. more men at Chickamauga, and many Confederate regiments whose mortality exceeded this.

Longstreet's command in less than two hours lost nearly forty-four per cent. of its strength, and of the troops opposed to a portion of their splendid assaults, Steedman's and Brannan's commands lost respectively forty-nine and thirty-eight in less than four hours, and single regiments a far heavier percentage.

Of the Confederate regiments sustaining the heaviest percentages of loss (in killed, wounded, and missing,—the last a scarcely appreciable fraction) the leading ones were:

Regiment.	Per cent.
Tenth Tennessee	68.0
Fifth Georgia	61.1
Second Tennessee	60.2
Fifteenth and Thirty-seventh Tennessee	59.9
Sixteenth Alabama	58.6
Sixth and Ninth Tennessee	57.9
Eighteenth Alabama	56.3
Twenty-second Alabama	55.2
Twenty-third Tennessee	54.1
Twenty-ninth Mississippi	52.7
Fifty-eighth Alabama	51.7
Thirty-seventh Georgia	50.1
Sixty-third Tennessee	49.7
Forty-first Alabama	48.6
Thirty-second Tennessee	48.3
Twentieth Tennessee	48.0
First Arkansas	45.1
Ninth Kentucky	44.3

These are only a few of the cases in which it was possible to compute percentages of casualties, the number of effectives taken into battle not having been mentioned, but they serve to illustrate the sanguinary severity of the fight and the heroism of the troops.

CHAPTER XXXII.

FAILURE TO FOLLOW SUCCESS.

Longstreet differs with General Bragg as to Movements of Pursuit—The Confederates on Lookout Mountain—Federals gain Comfortable Positions around it—Superior Officers of Bragg's Command call for his Removal—Bragg seeks Scapegoats—President Davis visits the Army—Tests the Temper of the Officers towards Bragg—He offers the Command to Longstreet—He declines—His Reasons—General Bragg ignores Signal-Service Reports and is surprised—General Joe Hooker's Advance—Night Attack beyond Lookout Mountain—Colonel Bratton's Clever Work—Review of the Western Movement and Combination—It should have been effected in May instead of September—Inference as to Results had the First Proposition been promptly acted upon.

About sunrise of the next morning, General Bragg rode to my bivouac, when report was made to him of orders of the night before, to replenish supplies and prepare to take up pursuit at daylight. He asked my views of the next step to be taken, explaining that there were some defensive works about Chattanooga to cover the enemy in that position.

I knew nothing of the country except of its general geographical features, but the hunt was up and on the go, when any move towards his rear was safe, and a speedy one encouraging of great results. I suggested that we cross the Tennessee River north of Chattanooga and march against the line of the enemy's rear; that if, after so threatening as to throw General Rosecrans to full retreat, we found it inconvenient to pursue him, we turn back with part of the army and capture or disperse the Union army in East Tennessee under General Burnside. He stated that he would follow that course, ordered the right wing to march,* and the left wing to follow as soon as the way was clear,—the left to care for the dead and wounded during the wait. As it was night when the rear of the right wing stretched out on the road, my march was not taken up until the morning of the 22d. General McLaws joined me on the 21st with his other brigades, and General Jenkins joined Hood's division. Afterwards G. T. Anderson's brigade joined the latter. When our march reached General Bragg's head-quarters and reported on the 22d, he gave me orders to direct a division from the line of march to follow the enemy towards Chattanooga.

When asked if he had abandoned the course upon which his march was ordered, he said the people would be greatly gratified to know that his army was marching through the streets of Chattanooga with bands of music and salutations of the soldiers. I thought, and did not fail to say, that it would give them greater pleasure to know that he had passed the Tennessee River, turned the enemy out of Chattanooga in eager flight, to save his rearward lines, whilst we marched hammering against the broken flanks of his columns. But the cavalry had reported that the enemy was in hurried and confused retreat, his trains crossing the river and passing over the nose of Lookout Mountain in disorder.

The praise of the inhabitants of a city so recently abandoned to the enemy, and a parade through its streets with bands of music and flaunting banners, were more alluring to a spirit eager for applause than was the tedious march for fruition of our heavy labors.

General Rosecrans prepared, no doubt, to continue his retreat, anticipating our march towards his rear, but finding

* In his official report of the battle, General Bragg denies that his march of the 21st was for the crossing of the Tennessee River; refers to the proposition as visionary, and says of the country, "Affording no subsistence for men or animals."—Rebellion Record

that we preferred to lay our lines in front of him, concluded that it would be more comfortable to rest at Chattanooga, reinforce, repair damages, and come to meet us when ready for a new trial.

When General Bragg found that the enemy had changed his mind, and was not inclined to continue his rearward march, he stretched his army in a semicircle of six miles along the southeast front of Chattanooga, from the base of Lookout Mountain on his left, to his right resting on the Tennessee River, and [illegible] batteries on the top of the mountain, [illegible] McLaws's, Hood's and Walker's divisions occupying the left of his line of investment. His plan was to shell the enemy from his works by field batteries, but the works were strengthened from day to day [illegible]. Our infantry were posted along the lines as supports for the batteries, with orders not to [illegible] unless especially ordered.

The [illegible] Lookout Mountain [illegible] which A[illegible] were [illegible] upon the Tennessee [illegible] the abutment and [illegible] the mountain [illegible] [illegible] from its [illegible] the mountain [illegible] [illegible] Alexander managed to drop an occasional shot not about the enemy's lines by lifting the trails of his guns, but the [illegible] of other batteries was not effective.

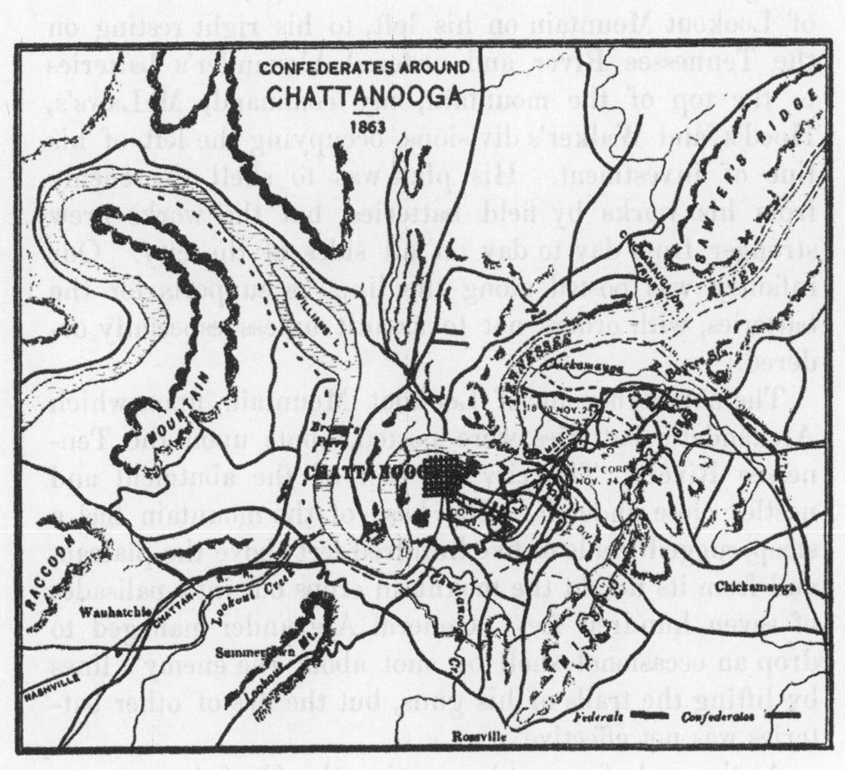

At the end of a week's practice the Confederate commander found the enemy getting more comfortable in his works, and thought to break him up by a grand cavalry raid. On the 30th he ordered General Wheeler to organize a force of his effective mounts, cross the river, and ride against the railway and such depots and supply-trains as he could reach. The cavalry destroyed some wagon-trains and supplies, and gave the enemy more that we preferred to lay our lines in front of him, concluded that it would be more comfortable to rest at Chattanooga, reinforce, repair damages, and come to meet us when ready for a new trial.

When General Bragg found that the enemy had changed his mind, and was not inclined to continue his rearward march, he stretched his army in a semicircle of six miles along the southeast front of Chattanooga, from the base of Lookout Mountain on his left, to his right resting on the Tennessee River, and ordered Alexander's batteries to the top of the mountain, my command, McLaws's, Hood's, and Walker's divisions, occupying the left of his line of investment. His plan was to shell the enemy from his works by field batteries, but the works grew stronger from day to day on all sides of the city. Our infantry was posted along the line, as supports for the batteries, with orders not to assault unless especially ordered.

The northern point of Lookout Mountain, upon which Alexander's batteries were posted, abuts upon the Tennessee River. The city lies east of the abutment and nestles close under it. The base of the mountain has a steep, rugged grade of five hundred feet above the plateau, and from its height the mountain crops out into palisades of seven hundred feet. General Alexander managed to drop an occasional shell or shot about the enemy's lines by lifting the trails of his guns, but the fire of other batteries was not effective.

At the end of a week's practice the Confederate commander found the enemy getting more comfortable in his works, and thought to break him up by a grand cavalry raid. On the 30th he ordered General Wheeler to organize a force of his effective mounts, cross the river, and ride against the railway and such depots and supply-trains as he could reach. The cavalry destroyed some wagon-trains and supplies, and gave the enemy more trouble than the artillery practice, yet failed to convince him that it was time to abandon his position, but, on the contrary, satisfied him that he was safe from further serious trouble.

At that time the shortest line of the enemy's haul of provisions from the depot at Stevenson was along the road on the north bank of the river. The Confederate chief conceived, as our cavalry ride had failed of effect, that a line of sharp-shooters along the river on our side could break up that line of travel, and ordered, on the 8th of October, a detail from my command for that purpose. As the line was over the mountain about seven miles beyond support, by a rugged road not practicable for artillery, I ordered a brigade of infantry detailed to go over and protect the sharp-shooters from surprise or capture. The detail fell upon Law's brigade. The line for this practice extended from the east side of Lookout Creek some ten miles down the river. The effect of the fire was about like that of the cavalry raid. It simply put the enemy on shorter rations until he could open another route for his trains.

But more to be deplored than these novel modes of investment was the condition of the Confederate army. After moving from Virginia to try to relieve our comrades of the Army of Tennessee, we thought that we had cause to complain that the fruits of our labor had been lost, but it soon became manifest that the superior officers of that army themselves felt as much aggrieved as we at the halting policy of their chief, and were calling in letters and petitions for his removal. A number of them came to have me write the President for them. As he had not called for my opinion on military affairs since the Johnston conference of 1862, I could not take that liberty, but promised to write to the Secretary of War and to General Lee, who I thought could excuse me under the strained condition of affairs. About the same time they framed and forwarded to the President a petition praying for relief.* It was written by General D. H. Hill (as he informed me since the war).

While the superior officers were asking for relief, the Confederate commander was busy looking along his lines for victims. Lieutenant-General Polk was put under charges for failing to open the battle of the 20th at daylight; Major-General Hindman was relieved under charges for conduct before the battle, when his conduct of the battle with other commanders would have relieved him of any previous misconduct, according to the customs of war, and pursuit of others was getting warm.

On the Union side the Washington authorities thought vindication important, and Major-Generals McCook and Crittenden, of the Twentieth and Twenty-first Corps, were relieved and went before a Court of Inquiry; also one of the generals of division of the Fourteenth Corps.

The President came to us on the 9th of October and called the commanders of the army to meet him at General Bragg's office. After some talk, in the presence of General Bragg, he made known the object of the call, and asked the generals, in turn, their opinion of their commanding officer, beginning with myself. It seemed rather a stretch of authority, even with a President, and I gave an evasive answer and made an effort to turn the channel of thought, but he would not be satisfied, and got back to his question. The condition of the army was briefly referred to, and the failure to make an effort to get the fruits of our success, when the opinion was given, in substance, that our commander could be of greater service elsewhere than at the head of the Army of Tennessee. Major-General Buckner was called, and gave opinion somewhat similar. So did Major-General Cheatham, who was then commanding the corps recently com-

* Rebellion Record.

manded by Lieutenant-General Polk, and General D. H. Hill, who was called last, agreed with emphasis to the views expressed by others.

The next morning the President called me to private conference, and had an all day talk. He thought to assign me to command, but the time had passed for handling that army as an independent force. Regarding this question, as considered in Virginia, it was understood that the assignment would be made at once, and in time for opportunity to handle the army sufficiently to gain the confidence of the officers and soldiers before offering or accepting battle. The action was not taken, a battle had been made and won, the army was then seriously entangled in a *quasi* siege, the officers and soldiers were disappointed, and disaffected in *morale.* General Grant was moving his army to reinforce against us, and an important part of the Union army of Virginia was moving to the same purpose.

In my judgment our last opportunity was lost when we failed to follow the success at Chickamauga, and capture or disperse the Union army, and it could not be just to the service or myself to call me to a position of such responsibility. The army was part of General Joseph E. Johnston's department, and could only be used in strong organization by him in combining its operations with his other forces in Alabama and Mississippi. I said that under him I could cheerfully work in any position.* The suggestion of that name only served to increase his displeasure, and his severe rebuke.

I recognized the authority of his high position, but called to his mind that neither his words nor his manner were so impressive as the dissolving scenes that foreshadowed the dreadful end. He referred to his worry and troubles with politicians and non-combatants. In that

* Later on he offered the command to Lieutenant-General Hardee, who declined it.

connection, I suggested that all that the people asked for was success; with that the talk of politicians would be as spiders' webs before him. And when restored to his usual gracious calm I asked to have my resignation accepted, to make place for some one who could better meet his ideas of the important service. He objected that my troops would not be satisfied with the change. I suggested a leave of absence, as winter was near, when I would go to the Trans-Mississippi Department, and after the troops were accustomed to their new commander, send in my written resignation, from Texas, but he was not minded to accept that solution of the premises.

Finally, I asked his aid in putting the divisions that were with me in more efficient working order, by assigning a major-general to command Hood's division. He had been so seriously crippled that he could not be in condition to take the field again even if he recovered, and a commander for the division was essential to its proper service. As he had no one, or failed to name any one, for the place, I suggested the promotion of the senior brigadier then in command of it, General M. Jenkins, who was a bright, gallant, and efficient officer of more than two years' experience in active warfare, loved by his troops, and all acquaintances as well. He had been transferred, recently, by the War Department to the division, upon application of General Hood, and in consequence there was some feeling of rivalry between him and Brigadier-General Law, the next in rank, who had served with the division since its organization, and had commanded it at Gettysburg after General Hood was wounded, and after his taking off in the battle of Chickamauga. The President referred to the services of General Law with the division, but failed to indicate a preference. I thought it unwise and not military to choose a junior for assignment to command over his senior officers, and prejudicial to the *esprit de corps* and *morale* of any army, except under most eminent services, and in this instance where service, high military character, and equipment were on the side of the senior it was more objectionable, but consented that it would be better to have General Law promoted, and the feeling of rivalry put at rest, than to leave the question open; General Jenkins's heart was in the service, and he could submit to anything that seemed best for its interests; but the President failed to assign a commander.

The interview was exciting, at times warm, but continued until Lookout Mountain lifted above the sun to excuse my taking leave. The President walked as far as the gate, gave his hand in his usual warm grasp, and dismissed me with his gracious smile; but a bitter look lurking about its margin, and the ground-swell, admonished me that clouds were gathering about head-quarters of the First Corps even faster than those that told the doom of the Southern cause.

A day or two after this interview the President called the commanders to meet him again at General Bragg's head-quarters. He expressed desire to have the army pulled away from the lines around Chattanooga and put to active work in the field, and called for suggestions and plans by which that could be done, directing his appeal, apparently, to me as first to reply.

I suggested a change of base to Rome, Georgia, a march of the army to the railway bridge of the Tennessee River at Bridgeport, and the crossing of the river as an easy move,—one that would cut the enemy's rearward line, interrupt his supply train, put us between his army at Chattanooga and the reinforcements moving to join him, and force him to precipitate battle or retreat.

General Bragg proposed that we march up and cross the river and swing around towards the enemy's rear and force him out by that means. No other plans were offered, nor did other officers express preference for either of the plans that were submitted.

Maps were called for and demonstrations given of the two plans, when the President ordered the move to be made by the change of base to Rome, and in a day or two took leave of us. He had brought General Pemberton with him to assign to the corps left by General Polk, but changed his mind. General D. H. Hill was relieved of duty; after a time General Buckner took a leave of absence, and General Hardee relieved General Cheatham of command of the corps left to him by General Polk.

About this time General Lee wrote me, alluding to the presence of the President, the questions under consideration, my proposition for him to leave the army in Virginia in other hands and come West to grander, more important fields, to his purpose in sending me West to be assigned to command there, and expressing anticipation of my return to Virginia.*

---

* "Camp Rappahannock, October 26, 1863.

"My dear General,—I have received your three letters, September 26, October 6, and October 11. The first was received just as I was about to make a move upon General Meade, to prevent his detaching reinforcements to Rosecrans. The second when I had gone as far as I thought I could advantageously go; and the third since my return to this place. I have read them all with interest and pleasure, but have not had time to reply till now.

"I rejoice at your great victory deeply. It seemed to me to have been complete. I wish it could have been followed up by the destruction of the Federal army. As regards your proposition as to myself, I wish that I could feel that it was prompted by other reasons than kind feelings to myself. I think that you could do better than I could. It was with that view I urged your going. The President, being on the ground, I hope will do all that can be done. He has to take a broad view of the whole ground, and must order as he deems best. I will cheerfully do anything in my power.

"In addition to other infirmities, I have been suffering so much from rheumatism in my back that I could scarcely get about. The first two days of our march I had to be hauled in a wagon, and subsequently every motion of my horse, and indeed of my body, gave much pain. I am rather better now, though I still suffer. We could not come up with Meade. We had to take circuitous and by-roads, while he had broad and passable routes on either side of the railroad. We struck his rear-guards three times,—the last at Bristoe, where Hill with his advance of two brigades fell too precipitately on one of his corps,—suffered a repulse and loss. He was finally driven beyond Bull Run. I

The President left the army more despondent than he found it. General Pemberton's misfortune at Vicksburg gave rise to severe prejudice of the people and the army, and when the troops heard of the purpose of the President to assign him to command of Polk's corps, parts of the army were so near to mutiny that he concluded to call General Hardee to that command. A few days after he left us a severe season of rain set in, and our commander used the muddy roads to excuse his failure to execute the campaign that the President had ordered.

Late on the 20th of September and during the 21st, General Rosecrans reported his condition deplorable, and expressed doubt of his holding at Chattanooga, and called to General Burnside in East Tennessee, to whom he looked for aid; but finding only feeble efforts to follow our success he recovered hope, prepared defensive works, and was looking to renewal of his aggressive work when he was relieved.

From accounts made public since the war it appears that his animals were so reduced from want of forage at

---

saw he could easily get behind his intrenchments in front of Alexandria. Our men were dreadfully off for shoes, blankets, and clothes. One division alone had over a thousand barefooted men. We had failed to take any, and I fear had failed to manage as well as we might. The country was a perfect waste. A northeast storm broke upon us. There was neither shelter nor food for man or beast. I saw no real good I could accomplish by manœuvring. The enemy had destroyed the bridge over the Rappahannock and blown up one of the piers. The freshet after we left the Rapidan carried away the railroad bridge over that river. I therefore withdrew to the Rappahannock, destroying the railroad from Cub Run (this side Manassas Junction) to the Rappahannock River.

"We inflicted some punishment upon the enemy,—captured upward of two thousand four hundred prisoners.

"But I missed you dreadfully, and your brave corps. Your cheerful face and strong arms would have been invaluable. I hope you will soon return to me. I trust we may soon be together again. May God preserve you and all with you.

"Very truly yours,

"R. E. LEE.

"GENERAL LONGSTREET."

the time of the October rains that General Rosecrans could not move his artillery over the muddy roads, which suggests mention that the campaign ordered by the President from the change of base could have forced him from his works in his crippled condition, and given us comfortable operations between him and his reinforcements coming from Virginia and Mississippi.

In his official account, General Bragg said that the road on the south side was left under my command, which is misleading. My command—three divisions—was on his line of investment, east of the city and of the mountain; the road was west of the mountain from six to twenty miles from the command. We were in support of his batteries, to be ready for action at the moment his artillery practice called for it. We held nearly as much of his line as the other eight divisions. None of the commanders had authority to move a man from the lines until the 8th of October, when he gave orders for posting the sharp-shooters west of the mountain. The exposure of this detachment was so serious that I took the liberty to send a brigade as a rallying force for it, and the exposure of these led me to inquire as to the assistance they could have from our cavalry force operating on the line from the mountain to Bridgeport, some eight or ten miles behind them. The cavalry was not found as watchful as the eyes of an army should be, and I reported them to the general, but he thought otherwise, assured me that his reports were regular, daily and sometimes oftener.

Nevertheless, prudence suggested more careful guard, and I ordered Captain Manning, who brought from Virginia part of my signal force, to establish a station in observation of Bridgeport and open its communication with my head-quarters. General Bragg denied all reports sent him of the enemy from my signal party, treated them with contempt, then reported that the road was under my command.

His report is remarkable in that he failed to notice the conduct of his officers, except of the killed and wounded and one division commander whom he found at daylight of the 21st advancing his line of skirmishers in careful search of the enemy who had retreated at early twilight the evening before under shouts from the Confederate army that made the heavy wood reverberate with resounding shouts of victory. That officer he commended as the "ever vigilant." He gave due credit to his brave soldiers for their gallant execution of his orders to charge and continue to charge against the enemy's strongholds, as he knew that they would under his orders until their efforts were successful, but the conduct of the battle in all of its phases discredits this claim. When the right wing of his army stepped into the Lafayette-Rossville road the enemy's forces were in full retreat through McFarland Gap, and all fighting and charging had ceased, except the parting blows of Preston's division with Granger's reserve corps. A peculiar feature of the battle was the early ride of both commanders from the field, leaving the battle to their troops. General Rosecrans was generous enough to acknowledge that he left his battle in other hands. General Bragg claimed everything for himself, failing to mention that other hands were there.

While General Rosecrans was opening a route beyond reach of our sharp-shooters, his chief engineer, General W. F. Smith, was busy upon a plan for opening the line of railway on the south side, and his first step was to break up the line of sharp-shooters. On the 19th he made a survey of the river below Chattanooga. On the same day General Rosecrans was superseded in command by General George H. Thomas. A day or two after that my signal party reported some stir about the enemy's camps near Bridgeport, and the cavalry reported a working force at Nicojack Cave.

The cavalry was put under my orders for a reconnoissance, and I was ordered to send a brigade of infantry scouting for the working party. Nothing was found at the Cave or by the reconnoissance, and the cavalry objected to my authority. On the 25th orders came to me to hold the mountain by a brigade of infantry. After ordering the brigade, I reported a division necessary to make possession secure, suggesting that the enemy's best move was from Bridgeport and along the mountain crest; that we should assume that he would be wise enough to adopt it, unless we prepared against it. But our commander was disturbed by suggestions from subordinates, and thought them presumptuous when they ventured to report of the probable movements of the enemy.

On the night of the 27th of October, General Smith moved to the execution of his plan against our line of sharp-shooters. He put fifty pontoon-boats and two flat-boats in the river at Chattanooga, the former to take twenty-five men each, the latter from forty to seventy-five,—the boats to float quietly down the river eight miles to Brown's Ferry, cross and land the troops. At the same time a sufficient force was to march by the highway to the same point, to be in readiness for the boats to carry them over to their comrades. The sharp-shooters had been posted for the sole purpose of breaking up the haul along the other bank, and not with a view of defending the line, nor was it defensible, while the enemy had every convenience for making a forced crossing and lodgement.

The vigilant foe knew his opportunity, and only waited for its timely execution. It is needless to say that General Smith had little trouble in establishing his point. He manned his boats, floated them down to the crossing, landed his men, and soon had the boats cross back for his other men, pushed them over, and put them at work intrenching the strong ground selected for their holding. By daylight he was comfortably intrenched, and had his artillery on the other side in position to sweep along the front.

The Confederate commander did not think well enough of his line when he had it to prepare to hold it, but when he found that the enemy proposed to use it, he thought to order his infantry down to recover the ground just demonstrated as indefensible, and ordered me to meet him on the mountain next morning to learn his plans and receive his instructions for the work.

That afternoon the signal party reported the enemy advancing from Bridgeport in force,—artillery and infantry. This despatch was forwarded to head-quarters, but was discredited. It was repeated about dark, and again forwarded and denied.

On the morning of the 28th I reported as ordered. The general complained of my party sending up false alarms. The only answer that I could make was that they had been about two years in that service, and had not made such mistakes before.

While laying his plans, sitting on the point of Lookout rock, the enemy threw some shells at us, and succeeded in bursting one about two hundred feet below us. That angered the general a little, and he ordered Alexander to drop some of his shells about their heads. As this little practice went on, a despatch messenger came bursting through the brushwood, asking for General Longstreet, and reported the enemy marching from Bridgeport along the base of the mountain,—artillery and infantry. General Bragg denied the report, and rebuked the soldier for sensational alarms, but the soldier said, "General, if you will ride to a point on the west side of the mountain I will show them to you." We rode and saw the Eleventh and Twelfth Corps under General Hooker, from the Army of the Potomac, marching quietly along the valley towards Brown's Ferry. The general was surprised. So was I. But my surprise was that he did not march along the mountain top, instead of the valley. It could have been occupied with as little loss as he afterwards had and less danger. He had marched by our line of cavalry without their knowing, and General Bragg had but a brigade of infantry to meet him if he had chosen to march down along the top of the mountain, and that was posted twenty miles from support.

My estimate of the force was five thousand. General Bragg thought it not so strong, and appearance from the elevation seemed to justify his estimate. Presently the rear-guard came in sight and made its bivouac immediately in front of the point upon which we stood. The latter force was estimated at fifteen hundred, and halted about three miles in rear of the main body.

A plan was laid to capture the rear-guard by night attack. He proposed to send me McLaws's and Jenkins's divisions for the work, and ordered that it should be done in time for the divisions to withdraw to the point of the mountain before daylight, left me to arrange details for attack, and rode to give orders for the divisions, but changed his mind without giving me notice, and only ordered Jenkins's division. After marching his command, General Jenkins rode to the top of the mountain and reported.

The route over which the enemy had marched was along the western base of a series of lesser heights, offering strong points for our troops to find positions of defence between his main force and his rear-guard. After giving instructions to General Jenkins, he was asked to explain the plan of operations to General McLaws in case the latter was not in time to view the position from the mountain before night. A point had been selected and ordered to be held by one of Jenkins's brigades supported by McLaws's division, while General Jenkins was to use his other brigades against the rear-guard, which rested in the edge of a woodland of fair field of approach. The point at which Law's brigade rested after being forced from its guard of the line of sharp-shooters was near the northern base of the mountain about a mile east of the route of the enemy's line of march. As General Law's detached service had given him opportunity to learn something of the country, his brigade was chosen as the brigade of position between the parts of the enemy's forces. General Law was to move first, get into position by crossing the bridge over Lookout Creek, to be followed by Jenkins's other brigades, when McLaws's division was to advance to position in support of Law's brigade.

I waited on the mountain, the only point from which the operations could be seen, until near midnight, when, seeing no indications of the movements, I rode to the point that had been assigned for their assembly, found the officers in wait discussing the movements, and, upon inquiry, learned that McLaws's division had not been ordered. Under the impression that the other division commander understood that the move had miscarried, I rode back to my head-quarters, failing to give countermanding orders.

The gallant Jenkins, however, decided that the plan should not be abandoned, and went to work in its execution by his single division. To quiet the apprehensions of General Law he gave him Robertson's brigade to be posted with his own, and Benning's brigade as their support, and ordered his own brigade under Colonel Bratton to move cautiously against the rear-guard, and make the attack if the opportunity was encouraging.

As soon as Colonel Bratton engaged, the alarm spread, the enemy hastened to the relief of his rear, encountered the troops posted to receive them, and made swift, severe battle. General Law claimed that he drove off their fight, and, under the impression that Colonel Bratton had finished his work and recrossed the bridge, withdrew his command, leaving Colonel Bratton at the tide of his engagement. General Jenkins and Colonel Bratton were left to their own cool and gallant skill to extricate the brigade from the swoop of numbers accumulating against them, and, with the assistance of brave Benning's Rock brigade, brought the command safely over, Benning's brigade crossing as Bratton reached the bridge.

The conduct of Bratton's forces was one of the cleverest pieces of work of the war, and the skill of its handling softened the blow that took so many of our gallant officers and soldiers.

Colonel Bratton made clever disposition of his regiments, and handled them well. He met gallant resistance, and in one instance had part of his command forced back, but renewed the attack, making his line stronger, and forced the enemy into crowded ranks and had him under converging circular fire, with fair prospects, when recalled under orders to hasten to the bridge. So urgent was the order that he left the dead and some of the wounded on the field.

General Law lost of his own brigade (aggregate) . . .	43
General Robertson (1 wounded and 8 missing) . . .	9
Colonel Bratton lost (aggregate)	356
Confederate loss	408
Union loss (aggregate)	420

It was an oversight of mine not to give definite orders for the troops to return to their camps before leaving them.

General Jenkins was ordered to inquire into the conduct of the brigades of position, and reported evidence that General Law had said that he did not care to win General Jenkins's spurs as a major-general. He was ordered to prepare charges, but presently when we were ordered into active campaign in East Tennessee he asked to have the matter put off to more convenient time.

We may pause here to reflect upon the result of the combination against Rosecrans's army in September, after our lines of transit were seriously disturbed, and after the severe losses in Pennsylvania, Mississippi, and Tennessee; and to consider in contrast the probable result of the combination if effected in the early days of May, when it was first proposed (see strategic map).

At that time General Grant was marching to lay siege upon Vicksburg. The campaign in Virginia had been settled, for the time, by the battle of Chancellorsville. Our railways were open and free from Virginia through East Tennessee, Georgia, Alabama, to Central Mississippi. The armies of Rosecrans and Bragg were standing near Murfreesboro' and Shelbyville, Tennessee. The Richmond authorities were trying to collect a force at Jackson, Mississippi, to drive Grant's army from the siege. Two divisions of the First Corps of the Army of Northern Virginia were marching from Suffolk to join General Lee at Fredericksburg. Under these circumstances, positions, and conditions, I proposed to Secretary Seddon, and afterwards to General Lee, as the only means of relief for Vicksburg, that Johnston should be ordered with his troops to join Bragg's army; that the divisions marching for Fredericksburg should be ordered to meet Johnston's, the transit over converging lines would give speedy combination, and Johnston should be ordered to strike Rosecrans in overwhelming numbers and march on to the Ohio River.

As the combination of September and battle of Chickamauga drew General Grant's army from its work in Mississippi to protect the line through Tennessee and Kentucky, and two Federal corps from the Army of the Potomac, the inference is fair that the earlier, more powerful combination would have opened ways for grand results for the South, saved the eight thousand lost in defending the march for Vicksburg, the thirty-one thousand surrendered there, Port Hudson and its garrison of six thousand, and the splendid Army of Northern Virginia the twenty thousand lost at Gettysburg. And

who can say that with these sixty-five thousand soldiers saved, and in the ranks, the Southern cause would not have been on a grand ascending grade with its bayonets and batteries bristling on the banks of the Ohio River on the 4th day of July, 1863!

The elections of 1862 were not in support of the Emancipation Proclamation. With the Mississippi River still closed, and the Southern army along the banks of the Ohio, the elections of 1864 would have been still more pronounced against the Federal policy, and a new administration could have found a solution of the political imbroglio. "Blood is thicker than water."

CHAPTER XXXIII.

THE EAST TENNESSEE CAMPAIGN.

General Bragg's Infatuation—General Grant in Command of the Federal Forces—Longstreet ordered into East Tennessee—His Plans for the Campaign—Poorly supported by his Superior—Foraging for Daily Rations—General Burnside's Forces—Advance upon Knoxville—Affairs at Lenoir's and Campbell's Stations—Engagement near Knoxville an Artillery Combat—Reprehensible Conduct of Officers—Allegement that One was actuated by Jealousy—Federals retire behind their Works—Laying the Confederate Lines about Knoxville.

ABOUT the 1st of November it was rumored about camp that I was to be ordered into East Tennessee against General Burnside's army. At the moment it seemed impossible that our commander, after rejecting a proposition for a similar move made just after his battle, when flushed with victory and the enemy discomfited, could now think of sending an important detachment so far, when he knew that, in addition to the reinforcements that had joined the Union army, another strong column was marching from Memphis under General Sherman, and must reach Chattanooga in fifteen or twenty days. But on second thoughts it occurred to me that it might, after all, be in keeping with his peculiarities, and then it occurred to me that there are many ways to compass a measure when the spirit leads. So I set to work to try to help his plans in case the report proved true.

After a little reflection it seemed feasible that by withdrawing his army from its lines about Chattanooga to strong concentration behind the Chickamauga River, and recalling his detachment in East Tennessee (the latter to give the impression of a westward move), and at the moment of concentration sending a strong force for swift march against General Burnside.—strong enough to crush him,—and returning to Chattanooga before the army under General Sherman could reach there (or, if he thought better, let the detachment strike into Kentucky against the enemy's communications), something worth while could be effected.

Presently I was called, with Lieutenant-General Hardee and Major-General Breckenridge, the other corps commanders, to learn his plans and receive his orders. He announced his purpose in general terms to send me into East Tennessee, then paused as if inviting the opinions of others, when I stated that the move could be made, but it would be hazardous to make a detachment strong enough for rapid work while his army was spread along a semicircle of six miles, with the enemy concentrated at the centre, whence he could move in two or three threatening columns, to hold his line to its extension, and give his real attack such power that it must break through by its weight. Then I suggested the operations herein just mentioned.

He ordered the move to be made by my two divisions, Alexander's and Leydon's artillery, and Wheeler's cavalry and horse artillery. We had the promise of a force, estimated from three to five thousand, that was to come from Southwest Virginia and meet us, but that command was to start from a point two hundred miles from our starting, march south as we marched north, and meet us at Knoxville. General Bragg estimated General Burnside's force south of Knoxville at fifteen thousand. I repeated the warning that the move as ordered was not such as to give assurances of rapid work, saying that my march and campaign against the enemy's well-guarded positions must be made with care, and that would consume so much time that General Grant's army would be up, when he would organize attack that must break through the line before I could return to him. His sardonic smile seemed to say that I knew little of his army or of himself in assuming such a possibility. So confident was he of his position that I ventured to ask that my column should be increased to twenty thousand infantry and artillery, but he intimated that further talk was out of order.

General Grant had in the mean time joined the army and assumed command on the 22d of October, and it was known that General Sherman was marching to join him.

On the 20th of October General Burnside reported by letter * to General Grant an army of twenty-two thousand three hundred men, with ninety-odd guns, but his returns for November show a force of twenty-five thousand two hundred and ninety and over one hundred guns. Eight thousand of his men were on service north of Knoxville and about Cumberland Gap.

To march, and capture or disperse this formidable force, fortified at points, I had McLaws's and Hood's divisions of infantry, Colonel Alexander's and Major Leydon's artillery, and four brigades of General Wheeler's cavalry. Kershaw's, Humphreys's, Wofford's, and Bryan's brigades constituted McLaws's division. Hood's division, which was commanded during the campaign by Brigadier-General M. Jenkins, was made up of Jenkins's, Anderson's, Benning's, Law's, and Robertson's brigades. General Wheeler's cavalry was organized into two divisions of two brigades each,—General John T. Morgan's Alabama and Colonel Cruse's Georgia brigades, under Major-General W. T. Martin; Colonels G. G. Dibbrell's Tennessee and Thomas Harrison's Texas brigades, under Brigadier-General Frank Armstrong. This made about fifteen thousand men, after deducting camp guards and foraging parties. The remote contingent that was to come from Southwest Virginia was an unknown quantity, not to be considered until it could report for service.

As soon as the conference at head-quarters adjourned

* Rebellion Record, vol. xxxi. part i. p. 680.

orders were issued for Alexander's artillery to be withdrawn from Lookout Mountain, and General McLaws was ordered to withdraw his division from the general line after night. Both commands were ordered to Tyner's Station to take the cars for Sweetwater on the 4th.

Control of the trains was under General Bragg's quartermaster, who had orders for the cars to be ready to transport the troops on their arrival, but the trains were not ready until the 5th. The brigades arrived at Sweetwater on the 6th, 7th, and 8th. Alexander's batteries were shipped as soon as cars were ready. To expedite matters, his horses and wagons were ordered forward by the dirt road; the batteries found cars, the last battery getting to Sweetwater on the 10th. Jenkins's division and Leydon's batteries were drawn from the lines on the 5th and ordered to meet the cars at the tunnel through Missionary Ridge. They reached the station in due season, but the cars were not there. After waiting some days, the battery horses and horses of mounted officers were ordered by the wagon road. Tired of the wait, I advised the troops to march along the road and find the cars where they might have the good fortune to meet them, the officers, whose horses had been sent forward, marching with the soldiers.

General Bragg heard of the delay and its cause, but began to urge the importance of more rapid movements. His effort to make his paper record at my expense was not pleasing, but I tried to endure it with patience. He knew that trains and conductors were under his exclusive control, but *he wanted papers that would throw the responsibility of delay upon other shoulders.*

On the 8th and 9th the infantry marched as far as Cleveland, about thirty miles, where the train-masters gave notice that the trains could meet them, but it was not until the 12th that the last of the brigades reached Sweetwater.

While waiting for transportation, I wrote some of my friends to excuse my failure to stop and say good-by. The letter written to General Buckner was returned to me some months after, endorsed by him as having important bearing upon events as they transpired,—viz.:

"WEDNESDAY, November 5, 1863.

"MY DEAR GENERAL,—I start to-day for Tyner's Station, and expect to get transportation to-morrow for Sweetwater. The weather is so bad, and I find myself so much occupied, that I shall not be able to see you to say good-by.

"When I heard the report around camp that I was to go into East Tennessee, I set to work at once to try and plan the means for making the move with security and the hope of great results. As every other move had been proposed to the general and rejected or put off until time had made them inconvenient, I came to the conclusion, as soon as the report reached me, that it was to be the fate of our army to wait until all good opportunities had passed, and then, in desperation, seize upon the least favorable movement.

"As no one had proposed this East Tennessee campaign to the general, I thought it possible that we might accomplish something by encouraging his own move, and proposed the following plan,—viz.: to withdraw from our present lines and our forces in East Tennessee (the latter to be done in order to give the impression to the enemy that we were retiring from East Tennessee and concentrating near him for battle or for some other movement) and place our army in a strong concentrated position behind Chickamauga River. The moment the army was together, to make a detachment of twenty thousand to move rapidly against Burnside and destroy him; and by continued rapid movements to threaten the enemy's rear and his communications to the extent that might be necessary to draw him out from his present position. This, at best, is but a tedious process, but I thought it gave promise of some results, and was, therefore, better than being here destroying ourselves. The move, as I proposed it, would have left this army in a strong position and safe, and would have made sure the capture of Burnside,—that is, the army could spare twenty thousand, if it were in the position that I proposed, better than it can spare twelve, occupying the lines that it now does. Twenty thousand men, well handled, could surely have captured Burnside and his forces. Under

present arraugements, however, the lines are to be held as they now are and the detachment is to be of twelve thousand. We thus expose both to failure, and really take no chance to ourselves of great results. The only notice my plan received was a remark that General Hardee was pleased to make, 'I don't think that that is a bad idea of Longstreet's.' I undertook to explain the danger of having such a long line under fire of the enemy's batteries, and he coucentrated, as it were, right in our midst, and within twenty minutes' march of any portion of our line. But I was assured that he would not disturb us. I repeated my ideas, but they did not even receive notice. It was not till I had repeated them, however, that General Hardee noticed me. Have you any maps that you can give or lend me? I shall need everything of the kind. Do you know any reliable people, living near and east of Knoxville, from whom I might get information of the condition, strength, etc., of the enemy? I have written in such hurry and confusion of packing and striking camp (in the rain and on the head of an empty flour barrel) that I doubt if I have made myself understood. I remain

"Sincerely your friend,

"J. LONGSTREET,

"*Lieutenant-General.*

"TO MAJOR-GENERAL S. B. BUCKNER,

"*Commanding Division.*"

Three months thereafter General Buckner returned the letter with the following:

(Endorsement.)

"MORRISTOWN, TENN., February 1, 1864.

"GENERAL,—It seems to me, after reading this letter again, that its predictions are so full a vindication of your judgment of the movements then ordered, that it should remain in your possession, with a view that at some future day it may serve to 'vindicate the truth of history.' I place it at your disposal with that view.

"Truly your friend,

"S. B. BUCKNER,

"*Major-General.*

"TO LIEUTENANT-GENERAL J. LONGSTREET."

I asked at general head-quarters for maps and information of the country through which I was to operate, for a quartermaster and commissary of subsistence who knew of the resources of the country, and for an engineer officer who had served with General Buckner when in command of that department. Neither of the staff-officers was sent, nor a map, except one of the topographical outlines of the country between the Hiawassee and Tennessee Rivers, which was much in rear of the field of our proposed operations. General Buckner was good enough to send me a plot of the roads and streams between Loudon and Knoxville.

We were again disappointed at Sweetwater. We were started from Chattanooga on short rations, but comforted by the assurance that produce was abundant at that point, and so it proved to be; but General Stevenson, commanding the outpost, reported his orders from the commanding general were to ship all of his supplies to his army, and to retire with his own command and join him upon our arrival. In this connection it should be borne in mind that we were recently from Virginia,—coming at the heated season,—where we left most of our clothing and blankets and all of our wagon transportation; and by this time, too, it was understood through the command that the Richmond authorities were holding thunder-clouds over the head of the commander, and that General Bragg was disposed to make them more portentous by his pressing calls for urgency.

Thus we found ourselves in a strange country, not as much as a day's rations on hand, with hardly enough land transportation for ordinary camp equipage, the enemy in front to be captured, and our friends in rear putting in their paper bullets. This sounds more like romance than war, but I appeal to the records for the facts, including reports of my chiefs of quartermaster and subsistence departments and General Alexander's account of the condition of some of the battery horses and ammunition.

Our foraging parties were lively, and we lost but a day

and part of another in gathering in rations for a start. Anticipating proper land transportation, plans were laid for march across the Little Tennessee above its confluence with the greater river, through Marysville to the heights above Knoxville on the east bank, by forced march. This would have brought the city close under fire of our field batteries and forced the enemy into open grounds. A guide had been secured who claimed to be familiar with the country, and was useful in laying our plans. But when our pontoon bridge came up it was without a train for hauling. So our plan must be changed.

Fortunately, we found a point in a bend of the river near the railroad at which we could force a crossing. At dark the cars were rolled up to that point by hand, and we learned that the Little Tennessee River above us was fordable for cavalry. General Wheeler had been ordered to have vedettes along the river from Loudon to some distance below Kingston, where a considerable body of Union troops occupied the north bank. He was ordered with his other troops to prepare for orders to cross the Little Tennessee at its fords, ride to Marysville, capture the enemy's cavalry outpost at that point, ride up the east side of the river to Knoxville, and seize the heights overlooking the city; or, finding that not feasible, to endeavor to so threaten as to hold the enemy's forces there to their works, while we marched against the troops of the west side; but when he found his service on that side ceased to be effective or co-operative with our movements, to cross the river and join the main column.

As just now explained, the failure of wagons for our pontoon bridge forced us to cross at Loudon, and to make direct march upon Knoxville by that route.

Weary of the continual calls of General Bragg for hurried movements, it seemed well to make cause for him to assign another commander or to move him to discontinue his work at a paper record; so I wired to remind him that he assured me before sending me away that he was safe in his position, and that he was told before my leaving that the command was not strong enough to excuse any but a careful, proper campaign; that he had since been informed that all delays of our movements were due to his inefficient staff corps, and that we were dependent upon foraging for our daily rations for men and animals. It began to look more like a campaign against Longstreet than against Burnside.

As General Burnside's orders were to hold Knoxville, he decided to act on the defensive. Leaving the troops in the northern district of his department in observation of that field, he withdrew his division on the south side of Tennessee River as we marched for Loudon, took up his pontoon bridge, and broke up the railroad bridge.

Orders were issued on the 12th for the general move of my cavalry by Marysville, the infantry and artillery along the railroad route. Pains were taken to have the bridge equipments carried by hand to the river, and skirmishing parties put in the boats and drifted to the opposite bank. The troops in rear were marched during the night to the vicinity of Loudon and held in readiness in case the enemy came to oppose our crossing. The bridge was laid under the supervision of General Alexander and Major Clark, our chief engineer, at Huff's Ferry, without serious resistance.

A few miles east of Loudon the Holston * and Little Tennessee Rivers come together, making the Tennessee River, which flows from the confluence west to Kingston, where it resumes its general flow southwest. The Holston rises in the mountains north and flows south to the junction. The Little Tennessee rises in the mountains east and flows west to the junction. The railroad crosses the main river at Loudon, thirty miles from Knoxville, and runs about

* Since those days the name of Holston has been changed to the Tennessee.

parallel to the Holston River, and near its west bank. West of the railroad and parallel is a broken spur of the Clinch Mountain range, with occasional gaps or passes for vehicles, and some other blind wagon-roads and cattle-trails. West of this spur, and near its base, is the main wagon-road to Knoxville, as far as Campbell Station, about seventeen miles, where it joins the Kingston road, passes a gap, and unites with the wagon-road that runs with the railroad east of the mountain spur at Campbell Station. South of this gap, about eleven miles, is another pass at Lenoir's Mill, and three miles south of that another pass, not used.

A detail of sharp-shooters under Captain Foster, of Jenkins's brigade, manned the first boats and made a successful lodging, after an exchange of a few shots with the enemy's picket-guard on the north bank. They intended to surprise and capture the picket and thus secure quick and quiet passage, but in that they were not successful. The north bank was secured, however, without loss, and troops were passed rapidly over to hold it, putting out a good skirmish line in advance of the bridge-head. As we advanced towards Loudon, the part of General White's Union division that had been on the opposite bank of the river was withdrawn to Lenoir's Station.

During the 13th and 14th the command was engaged in making substantial fastenings for the bridge and constructing its defences. General Vaughn's regiments and a battery of Major Leydon's (with broken-down horses) were assigned to guard the bridge.

On the afternoon of the 14th the enemy appeared on our front in strong force, drove our skirmish line back, and seemed prepared to give battle. As we were then waiting the return of our foraging wagons, we could only prepare to receive him. Some of the provisions looked for came in during the night, and we advanced on the 15th, finding that the enemy had retired. The force that came back to meet us on the 15th was part of White's division (Chapin's brigade) sent by General Burnside, and General Potter, commanding the Ninth Corps, sent General Ferrero with his division. The move was intended probably to delay our march. It was Chapin's brigade that made the advance against our skirmishers, and it probably suffered some in the affair. We lost not a single man.

General Wheeler crossed the Little Tennessee River at Motley's Ford at nightfall on the 13th, and marched to cut off the force at Marysville. He came upon the command, only one regiment, the Eleventh Kentucky Cavalry, that was advised in time to prepare for him. He attacked as soon as they came under fire, dispersed them into small parties that made good their escape, except one hundred and fifty taken by Dibbrell's brigade. Colonel Wolford brought up the balance of his brigade and made strong efforts to support his broken regiment, but was eventually forced back, and was followed by the Eighth and Eleventh Texas and Third Arkansas Cavalry and General John T. Morgan's brigade. The next day he encountered Sanders's division of cavalry and a battery, and, after a clean cavalry engagement of skilful manœuvres on both sides, succeeded in reaching the vicinity of the city of Knoxville, but found it too well guarded to admit of any very advantageous work.

On the 15th our advance was cautiously made by Hood's division and Alexander's artillery leading; McLaws's division and Leydon's artillery following. All along the route of the railroad the valley between the mountain and the river is so narrow and rough that a few thousand men can find many points at which they can make successful stands against great odds. Our course was taken to turn all of those points by marching up the road on the west side of the mountain. A few miles out from our bridge we encountered a skirmishing party near the lower gap of the mountain, which, when pressed back, passed through the gap. General Jenkins continued his march—leaving a guard at the gap till it could be relieved by General McLaws—to Lenoir's Station.

The enemy was looking for us to follow through the lower gaps and attack his strong front, and was a little surprised to find us close on his right flank. He was well guarded there, however, against precipitate battle by the mountain range and narrow pass and the heavy, muddy roads through which our men and animals had to pull. Arrangements were made for a good day's work from early morning.

Our guide promised to lead part of our men through a blind route during the night by which we could cut off the enemy's retreat, so that they would be securely hemmed in. Generals Jenkins and McLaws came up during the night. The former was ordered to advance part of his command to eligible points at midnight and hold them ready for use at daylight. The guide was sent with a brigade to the point which was to intercept the enemy's retreat. McLaws was held on the road, ready for use east or west of the ridge. Jenkins was ordered to have parties out during the night to watch that the enemy did not move, and report. As no report came from them, all things were thought to be properly adjusted, when we advanced before daylight. In feeling our way through the weird gray of the morning, stumps seen on the roadside were taken to be sharp-shooters, but we were surprised that no one shot at us, when, behold! before it was yet quite light, we came upon a park of eighty wagons, well loaded with food, camp equipage, and ammunition, with the ground well strewn with spades, picks, and axes.* The ani-

* Writing of these operations since the war, General E. M. Law, in an article in the Philadelphia *Weekly Press* of July 18, 1888, said,—

"During the night the sounds of retreat continued, and when daylight came the valley about Lenoir presented the scene of an encampment deserted with ignominious haste."

But he did not take the trouble to report the retreat until nearly

mals had been taken from the wagons to double their teams through the mud. General Potter had sent the division under General Hartranft back to the Campbell Station Pass to occupy the junction of his line of retreat with the Kingston road and the road upon which we were marching, and was well on the march with the balance of the Ninth Corps, Ferrero's division and his cavalry, before we knew that there was an opening by which he could escape.

Our guide, who promised to post the brigade so as to command the road in rear of the enemy, so far missed his route as to lead the brigade out of hearing of the enemy's march during the night.

Hart's cavalry brigade that was left in observation near Kingston had been called up, and with McLaws's division advanced on the roads to Campbell Station, while General Jenkins followed the direct line of retreat on double time, and right royally did his skirmishers move. He brought the rear to an occasional stand, but only leaving enough to require him to form line for advance, when the enemy again sped away on their rearward march at double time. General Jenkins made the march before noon, but the enemy had passed the gap and the junction of the roads, and was well posted in battle array in rear of them. General McLaws was not up. He was not ordered on double time, as it was thought to first bring the enemy to bay on the east road, when some of his infantry could be called over the mountain on the enemy's flank. General Ferrero, who covered the retreat, reported that it was necessary to attach from sixteen to twenty animals to a piece to make the haul through the mud.

The retreat was very cleverly conducted, and was in time to cover the roads into Campbell's Station, forming into line of battle to meet us. Jenkins's division, being in advance, was deployed on the right with Alexander's

---

tweny-five years after the war. Had he done so at the proper time the work at Campbell's Station would have been in better season.

battalion. As soon as the line was organized the batteries opened practice in deliberate, well-timed combat, but General Alexander had the sympathy of his audience. His shells often exploded before they reached the game, and at times as they passed from the muzzles of his guns, and no remedy could be applied that improved their fire.

As General McLaws came up his division was put upon our left with the other batteries, and Hart's brigade of cavalry was assigned in that part to observe the enemy's, farther off. It was not yet past meridian. We had ample time to make a battle with confident hope of success, by direct advance and the pressing in on the enemy's right by McLaws's left, but our severe travel and labor after leaving Virginia were not to find an opportunity to make a simply successful battle. As the rear of the enemy was open and could be covered, success would have been a simple victory, and the enemy could have escaped to his trenches at Knoxville, leaving us crippled and delayed; whereas as he stood he was ours. How we failed to make good our claim we shall presently see.

McLaws was ordered to use one of his brigades well out on his left as a diversion threatening the enemy's right, and to use Hart's cavalry for the same purpose, while General Jenkins was ordered to send two of his brigades through a well-covered way off our right to march out well past the enemy's left and strike down against that flank and rear. General Law, being his officer next in rank, was ordered in charge of his own and Anderson's brigades. General Jenkins rode with the command, and put it in such position that the left of this line would strike the left of the enemy's, thus throwing the weight of the two brigades past the enemy's rear. I rode near the brigades, to see that there could be no mismove or misconception of orders. After adjusting the line of the brigades, and giving their march the points of direction, General Jenkins rode to his brigades on the front to handle them in direct attack. I remained near the front of the flanking brigades for complete assurance of the adjustment of their march, and waited until they were so near that it was necessary to ride at speed, close under the enemy's line, to reach our main front, to time its advance with the flanking move. The ride was made alone, as less likely to draw the enemy's fire, the staff riding around.

As I approached the front, the men sprang forward without orders to open the charge, but were called to await the appearance of the flanking move of our right. But General Law had so changed direction as to bring his entire force in front instead of in the rear of the enemy's left. This gave him opportunity to change position to strong ground in rear, which made other movements necessary in view of the objective of the battle. There was yet time for successful battle, but it would have been a fruitless victory. Before other combinations suited to our purpose could be made it was night, and the enemy was away on his march to the fortified grounds about Knoxville.

The demonstration of our left under General McLaws was successful in drawing the enemy's attention, and in causing him to change front of part of his command to meet the threatening.

In his official account General Jenkins reported,—

"In a few minutes, greatly to my surprise, I received a message from General Law that in advancing his brigades he had obliqued so much to the left as to have gotten out of its line of attack. This careless and inexcusable movement lost us the few moments in which success from this point could be attained." *

Apropos of this the following memorandum of a staff-officer is interesting and informative:

* Rebellion Record, vol. xxxi. part i. p. 526.

"I know at the time it was currently reported that General Law said he might have made the attack successfully, but that Jenkins would have reaped the credit of it, and hence he delayed until the enemy got out of the way."

This has been called a battle, by the other side, but it was only an artillery combat, little, very little, musket ammunition being burnt. The next day the enemy was safely behind his works about Knoxville, except his cavalry under General Sanders and his horse artillery left to delay our march. McLaws's division reached the suburbs of the city a little after noon, and was deployed from near the mouth of Third Creek as his right, the enemy holding a line of dismounted cavalry skirmishers about a thousand yards in advance of his line of works. Alexander's artillery was disposed near McLaws's deployment. Jenkins got up before night and was ordered to deploy on McLaws's left as far as the Tazewell road, preceded by Hart's cavalry, which was to extend the line north to the Holston River. General Wheeler came up later and was assigned to line with Colonel Hart.

The city stands on the right bank of the Holston River, on a plateau about one and a half miles in width and extending some miles down south. At Knoxville the plateau is one hundred and twenty feet above the river, and there are little streams called First, Second, and Third Creeks, from the upper to the lower suburbs of the city,—First Creek between the city and East Knoxville, or Temperance Hill; Second Creek between the city and College Hill; Third Creek below and outside the enemy's lines of defence. The plateau slopes down to the valley through which the railway passes, and west of the valley it rises to the usual elevation. The Confederates were posted on the second plateau, with their batteries of position. The line of the enemy's works, starting at its lower point on the west bank of the river, was just above the mouth of Second

Creek, lying at right angles to the river. It ran to a fort constructed by the Confederates, when occupied by them years before, called Fort Loudon, above the Kingston road, and about a thousand yards in front of the college. East from that point it was about parallel with the river, reaching to Temperance Hill, to Mabry's Hill, and to the Holston, below the glass-works. An interior line extended from Temperance Hill to Flint Hill on the east, and another on the west, between the outer line and Second Creek. Dams were built across First and Second Creeks, flooding and forming formidable wet ditches over extensive parts of the line. Abatis, chevaux-de-frise, and wire entanglements were placed where thought to be advantageous for the defenders.

The heights on the northeast across the river are much more elevated than the plateaux of the city side, and command all points of the west bank. These were defended at some points by earthworks well manned. From the lower point of the enemy's line the Confederates extended to his right at the river, conforming to his defensive lines. The part of our line occupied by the cavalry was a mere watch-guard.

Our move was hurried, and our transportation so limited that we had only a few tools in the hands of small pioneer parties, and our wagons were so engaged in collecting daily rations that we found it necessary to send our cavalry down to Lenoir's for the tools captured there for use in making rifle-pits for our sharp-shooters.

When General Burnside rode to the front to meet us at Lenoir's he left General Parke in command at Knoxville, and he and Captain Poe, of the engineers, gave attention to his partially-constructed works.

Upon laying our lines about Knoxville, the enemy's forces in the northeast of his department were withdrawn towards Cumberland Gap, but we had no information of the troops ordered to meet us from Southwest Virginia.

CHAPTER XXXIV.

BESIEGING KNOXVILLE.

Closing on the Enemy's Lines—A Gallant Dash—The Federal Positions—Fort Loudon, later called Fort Sanders—Assault of the Fort carefully planned—General McLaws advises Delay—The Order reiterated and emphasized—Gallant Effort by the Brigades of Generals Wofford, Humphreys, and Bryan at the Appointed Time—A Recall ordered, because carrying the Works was reported impossible—General Longstreet is ordered by the President to General Bragg's Relief—Losses during the Assault and the Campaign.

THE enemy's line of sharp-shooters and Fort Sanders stood in our direct line of advance,—the fort manned by the heaviest and best field guns. Benjamin's battery, an old familiar acquaintance who had given us many hard knocks in our Eastern service, opened upon us as soon as we were in its reach. It was not until night of the 17th that our line was well established, and then only so as to enclose the enemy's front, leaving the country across the river to be covered when the troops from Virginia should join us.

When General McLaws advanced on the morning of the 18th he found the enemy's line of skirmishers—cavalry dismounted—behind a line of heavy rail defences. General Alexander was ordered to knock the rails about them and drive them out, and was partially successful, but the enemy got back before our infantry could reach them, so we had to carry the line by assault. Part of our line drove up in fine style, and was measurably successful, but other parts, smarting under the stiff musket fire, hesitated and lay down under such slight shelter as they could find, but close under fire,—so close that to remain inactive would endanger repulse. Captain Winthrop, of Alexander's staff, appreciating the crisis, dashed forward on his horse and led the halting lines successfully over the works. In his gallant ride he received a very severe hurt. Neither our numbers nor our condition were such as to warrant further aggressive action at the moment, nor, in fact, until the column from Virginia joined us. Our sharp-shooters were advanced from night to night and pitted before daylight, each line being held by new forces as the advance was made. The first line occupied was a little inside of the rail piles.

It seemed probable, upon first examination of the line along the northwest, that we might break through, and preparations were made for that effort, but, upon closer investigation, it was found to be too hazardous, and that the better plan was to await the approach of the other forces.

When within six hundred yards of the enemy's works, our lines well pitted, it seemed safe to establish a battery on an elevated plateau on the east (or south) side of the river. Some of our troops were sent over in flat-boats, and the reconnoissance revealed an excellent point commanding the city and the enemy's lines of works, though parts of his lines were beyond our range. Some of our best guns were put in position, and our captured pontoon bridges down at Lenoir's were sent for, to be hauled up along the river, but impassable rapids were found, and we were obliged to take part of our supply-train to haul them. They were brought up, and communication between the detachment and main force was made easy. The brigades of Law and Robertson were left on the east (or south) side as guard for that battery.

The Union forces were posted from left to right,—the Ninth Corps, General R. D. Potter commanding. General Ferrero's division extended from the river to Second Creek; General Hartranft's along part of the line between Second and First Creeks; Chapin's and Reilly's brigades over Temperance Hill to near Bell's house, and the brigades of Hoskins and Casement to the river. The

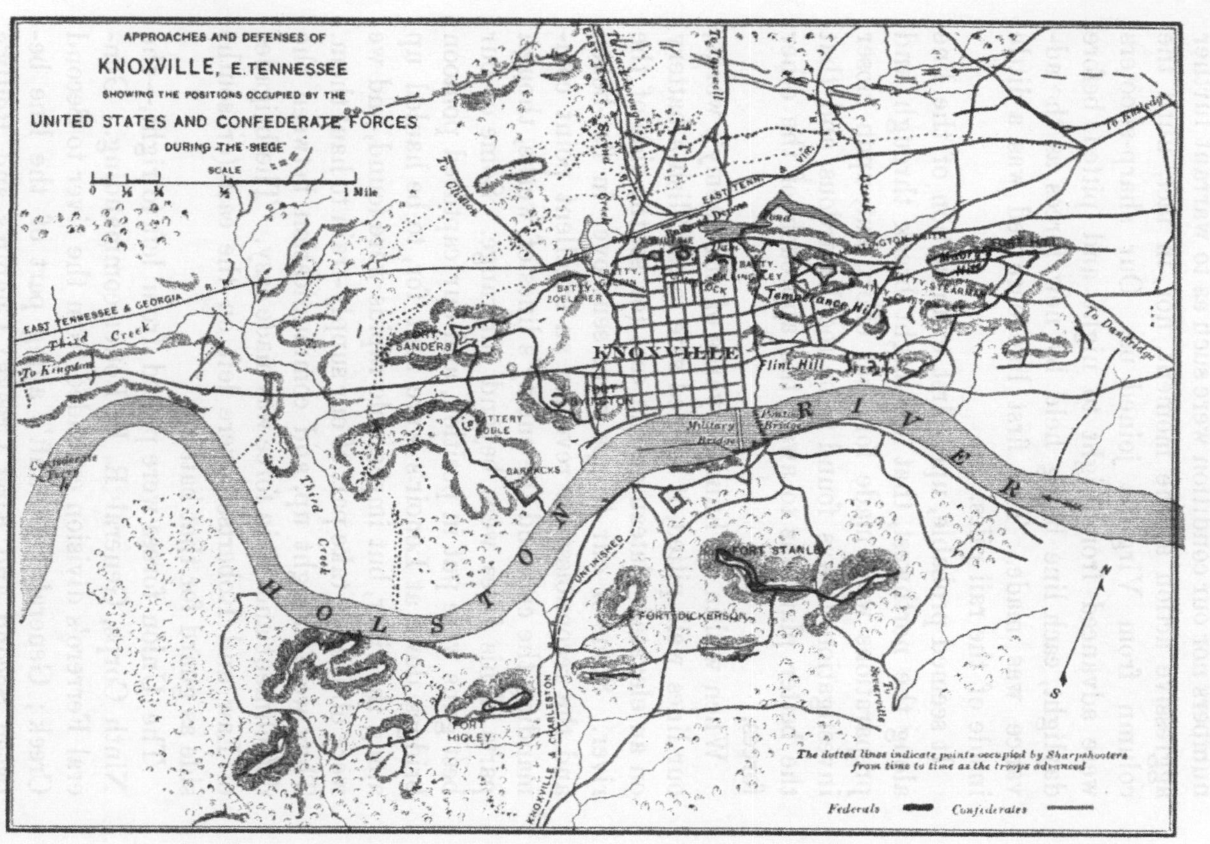
APPROACHES AND DEFENSES OF
KNOXVILLE, E. TENNESSEE
SHOWING THE POSITIONS OCCUPIED BY THE
UNITED STATES AND CONFEDERATE FORCES
DURING THE SIEGE
SCALE
0 ¼ ½ ¾ 1 Mile
The dotted lines indicate points occupied by Sharpshooters from time to time as the troops advanced
Federals
Confederates
HOLSTON RIVER
KNOXVILLE
To Rutledge
To Dandridge
To Sevierville
To Tazewell
To Jacksborough
To Clinton
To Kingston
KNOXVILLE & CHARLESTON
EAST TENNESSEE & GEORGIA R. R.
Military Bridge
Pontoon Bridge
Temperance Hill
Flint Hill
Mabry's Hill
FORT HILL
Second Creek
Third Creek
Pond
FORT STANLEY
FORT DICKERSON
FORT HIGLEY
UNFINISHED
FORT SANDERS
BATTERY NOBLE
BARRACKS
BATTY. ZOELLNER
BATTY. STEARMAN
Confederate Ferry
N
S

interior line was held by regiments of loyal Tennesseeans recently recruited. The positions on the south (or east) side of the river were occupied by Cameron's brigade of Hascall's division and Shackelford's cavalry (dismounted), Reilly's brigade in reserve,—two sections of Wilder's battery and Konkle's battery of four three-inch rifle guns.

The batteries of the enemy's front before the city were Romer's four three-inch rifles at the university, Benjamin's four twenty-pound Parrotts and Beecher's six twelve-pound Napoleons (at the fort), Gittings's four ten-pound Parrotts, Fifteenth Indiana Battery of six rifle guns (three-inch), James's (Indiana) Battery of six rifle guns, Henshaw's battery of two (James's) rifle guns and four six-pounders, Shields's battery of six twelve-pound Napoleons, and one section of Wilder's three-inch rifle guns, extending the line from the fort to the river on the north.

In his official account, General Burnside reported "about twelve thousand effective men, exclusive of the recruits and loyal Tennesseeans." He had fifty-one guns of position, including eight on the southeast side.

Fort Loudon, afterwards called for the gallant Sanders, who fell defending it, was a bastion earthwork, built upon an irregular quadrilateral. The sides were, south front, one hundred and fourteen yards; west front, ninety-five yards; north front, one hundred and twenty-five yards; east front, eighty-five yards. The eastern front was open, intended to be closed by a stockade. The south front was about half finished; the western front finished, except cutting the embrasures, and the north front nearly finished. The bastion attacked was the only one that was finished. The ditch was twelve feet wide, and generally seven to eight feet deep. From the fort the ground sloped in a heavy grade, from which the trees had been cut and used as abatis, and wire net-work was stretched between the stumps.

General Burnside reported,—

"Many citizens and persons who had been driven in by the enemy volunteered to work on the trenches and did good service, while those who were not inclined from disloyalty to volunteer were pressed into service. The negroes were particularly efficient in their labors during the siege. On the 20th of November our line was in such condition as to inspire the entire command with confidence."

General Poe reported,—

"The citizens of the town and all contrabands within reach were pressed into service and relieved the almost exhausted soldiers, who had no rest for more than a hundred hours. Many of the citizens were Confederates and worked with a very poor grace, which blistered hands did not tend to improve."

On the 22d, General McLaws thought his advance near enough the works to warrant assault. He was ordered to it with assaulting columns supported by the division. General Jenkins was also ordered up, and General Wheeler was ordered to push his troops and his horse artillery forward as McLaws's attack opened, so that the entire line would engage and hold to steady work till all the works were carried. After consulting his officers, General McLaws reported that they preferred to have daylight for their work. On the 23d reports came of a large force of the enemy at Kingston advancing. General Wheeler was sent with his main force of cavalry to look after them. He engaged the enemy on the 24th, and after a skirmish withdrew. Soon afterwards, receiving orders from General Bragg to join him, leaving his cavalry under command of Major-General Martin, he rode to find his commander. General Martin brought the brigades back and resumed position on our left. Colonel Hart, who was left at Kingston with his brigade, reported that there were but three regiments of cavalry and a field battery, that engaged General Wheeler on the 24th.

On the night of the 24th the enemy made a sortie against a point of General Wofford's line which broke through, but was speedily driven back with a loss of some prisoners and a number of killed and wounded. General Wofford's loss was five wounded, two mortally.

Our cavalry, except a brigade left at Kingston, resumed its position on the left of our line on the 26th. On the 23d a telegram came from General Bragg to say that the enemy had moved out and attacked his troops at Chattanooga. Later in the day he announced the enemy still in front of him, but not engaging his forces.

On the 25th I had a telegram from General Bushrod R. Johnson at Loudon, who was marching with two brigades to reinforce us, saying that the enemy was throwing his cavalry forward towards Charleston. This, in connection with the advance of the enemy towards General Bragg, reported by his despatch of the 23d, I took to be an effort to prevent reinforcements coming to us, or to cut in and delay their march.

That night General Leadbetter, chief engineer of General Bragg's army, reported at head-quarters with orders from General Bragg that we should attack at Knoxville, and very promptly. I asked him to make the reconnoissance and designate the assailable points. At the same time he was asked to consider that the troops from Virginia were on the march and would join us in eight or ten days, when our investment could be made complete; that the enemy was then on half rations, and would be obliged to surrender in two weeks; also whether we should assault fortifications and have the chance of repulse, rather than wait for a surrender. From his first reconnoissance he pronounced Fort Sanders the assailable point, but, after riding around the lines with General Jenkins and General Alexander, he pronounced in favor of assault from our left at Mabry's Hill. On the 27th, after more thorough reconnoissance in company with my officers, he came back to his conclusion in favor of assault at Fort Sanders. I agreed with him that the field at Mabry's Hill was too wide, and the march under fire too long, to warrant attack at that point. He admitted that the true policy was to wait and reduce the place by complete investment, but claimed that the crisis was on, the time imperative, and that the assault must be tried.

Meanwhile, rumors reached us, through the telegraph operator, of a battle at Chattanooga, but nothing official, though outside indications were corroborative. In the afternoon Colonel Giltner, of the command from Virginia, reported with his cavalry, and next day (28th) General W. E. Jones, of that command, reported with his cavalry. The brigades from Chattanooga under General B. R. Johnson were at hand, but not yet up. The artillery and infantry coming from Virginia were five or six days' march from us; but General Leadbetter was impatient.

General McLaws was ordered to double his force of sharp-shooters and their reserve, advance during the night and occupy the line of the enemy's pickets, and arrange for assault. The artillery was to open on the fort as soon as the weather cleared the view. After ten minutes' practice the assaulting column was to march, but the practice was to hold until the near approach of the storming party to the Fort. The assault was to be made by three of McLaws's brigades, his fourth, advancing on his right, to carry the line of works in its front as soon as the fort was taken. Three brigades of Jenkins's division were to follow in echelon on the left of McLaws's column, G. T. Anderson's, of his right, leading at two hundred yards' interval from McLaws's, Anderson to assault the line in his front, and upon entering to wheel to his left and sweep up that line, followed by Jenkins's and Benning's brigades; but, in case of delay in McLaws's assault, Anderson was to wheel to his right and take the fort through its rear opening, leaving the brigades of Jenkins and Benning to follow the other move to their left.

The ditch and parapets about the fort were objects of careful observation from the moment of placing our lines, and opinions coincided with those of reconnoitring officers that the former could be passed without ladders. General Alexander and I made frequent examinations of them within four hundred yards.

After careful conference, General McLaws ordered,—

"*First.* Wofford's Georgia and Humphreys's Mississippi brigades to make the assault, the first on the left, the second on the right, this latter followed closely by three regiments of Bryan's brigade; the Sixteenth Georgia Regiment to lead the first and the Thirteenth Mississippi the second assaulting column.

"*Second.* The brigades to be formed for the attack in columns of regiments.

"*Third.* The assault to be made with fixed bayonets, and without firing a gun.

"*Fourth.* Should be made against the northwest angle of Fort Loudon or Sanders.

"*Fifth.* The men should be urged to the work with a determination to succeed, and should rush to it without hallooing.

"*Sixth.* The sharp-shooters to keep up a continuous fire into the embrasures of the enemy's works and along the fort, so as to prevent the use of the cannon, and distract, if not prevent, the fire of all arms."

General B. R. Johnson was in time to follow the main attack by General McLaws with his own and Gracie's brigades (two thousand six hundred and twenty-five effectives).

The order was given for the 28th, but the weather became so heavy and murky as to hide the fort from view of our artillery, so operations were put off until the 29th.

On the 28th reports were brought of an advance of Union troops from the direction of Cumberland Gap. The cavalry under General W. E. Jones was sent to arrest their march pending operations ordered for the 29th, and he was authorized to call the artillery and infantry marching from Virginia to his assistance if the force proved formidable.

After arranging his command, General McLaws wrote me as follows:

"HEAD-QUARTERS DIVISION,
"November 28, 1863.

"GENERAL,—It seems to be a conceded fact that there has been a serious engagement between General Bragg's forces and those of the enemy; with what result is not known so far as I have heard. General Bragg may have maintained his position, may have repulsed the enemy, or may have been driven back. If the enemy has been beaten at Chattanooga, do we not gain by delay at this point? If we have been defeated at Chattanooga, do we not risk our entire force by an assault here? If we have been defeated at Chattanooga, our communications must be made with Virginia. We cannot combine again with General Bragg, even if we should be successful in our assault on Knoxville. If we should be defeated or unsuccessful here, and at the same time General Bragg should have been forced to retire, would we be in condition to force our way to the army in Virginia? I present these considerations, and with the force they have on my mind I beg leave to say that I think we had better delay the assault until we hear the result of the battle of Chattanooga. The enemy may have cut our communication to prevent this army reinforcing General Bragg, as well as for the opposite reason,—viz., to prevent General Bragg from reinforcing us, and the attack at Chattanooga favors the first proposition.*

"Very respectfully,
"L. MCLAWS,
"*Major-General.*"

In reply I wrote,—

"HEAD-QUARTERS, November 28, 1863.

"MAJOR-GENERAL MCLAWS:

"GENERAL,—Your letter is received. I am not at all confident that General Bragg has had a serious battle at Chattanooga, but there is a report that he has, and that he has fallen back to Tunnel Hill. Under this report I am entirely convinced that our only safety is in making the assault upon the enemy's position to-morrow at daylight, and it is the more important that I should

* Rebellion Record, vol. xxxi. part i. p. 491.

have the entire support and co-operation of the officers in this connection; and I do hope and trust that I may have your entire support and all the force you may be possessed of in the execution of my views. It is a great mistake to suppose that there is any safety for us in going to Virginia if General Bragg has been defeated, for we leave him at the mercy of his victors, and with his army destroyed our own had better be, for we will be not only destroyed, but disgraced. There is neither safety nor honor in any other course than the one I have chosen and ordered.

"Very respectfully, your obedient servant,

"JAMES LONGSTREET,

"Lieutenant-General Commanding.

"P.S.—The assault must be made at the time appointed, and must be made with a determination which will insure success."

After writing the letter it occurred to me to show it to General Leadbetter, who was stopping at our head-quarters, when he suggested the postscript which was added.

The assault was made by the brigades of Generals Wofford, Humphreys, and Bryan at the appointed time and in admirable style. The orders were, that not a musket should be discharged except by the sharp-shooters, who should be vigilant and pick off every head that might appear above the parapets until the fort was carried. The troops marched steadily and formed regularly along the outside of the works around the ditch. I rode after them with the brigades under General B. R. Johnson until within five hundred yards of the fort, whence we could see our advance through the gray of the morning. A few men were coming back wounded. Major Goggin, of General McLaws's staff, who had been at the fort, rode back, met me, and reported that it would be useless for us to go on; that the enemy had so surrounded the fort with net-work of wire that it was impossible for the men to get in without axes, and that there was not an axe in the command. Without a second thought I ordered the recall, and ordered General Johnson to march his brigades back to their camps. He begged to be allowed to go on, but, giving full faith to the report, I forbade him. I had known Major Goggin many years. He was a classmate at West Point, and had served with us in the field in practical experience, so that I had confidence in his judgment.

Recall was promptly sent General Jenkins and his advance brigade under General Anderson, but the latter, seeing the delay at the fort, changed his direction outside the enemy's works and marched along their front to the ditch, and was there some little time before he received the order. In his march and countermarch in front of the enemy's line he lost four killed and thirty-three wounded.

As a diversion in favor of the assaulting columns, our troops on the south side were ordered to a simultaneous attack, and to get in on that side if the opportunity occurred. They were reinforced by Russell's brigade of Morgan's division of cavalry, and Harrison's brigade of Armstrong's division, dismounted, General Morgan commanding. This demonstration had the effect anticipated in detaining troops to hold on that side that were intended as reserve for the fort.

Just after the troops were ordered back it occurred to me that there must be some mistake about the wire network, for some of our men had been seen mounting and passing over the parapets, but it was too late to reorganize and renew the attack, and I conceived that some of the regimental pioneers should have been at hand prepared to cut the wires, but all had been armed to help swell our ranks.

Since reading the accounts of General Poe, the engineer in charge of the works, I am convinced that the wires were far from being the serious obstacle reported, and that we could have gone in without the use of axes; and from other accounts it appears that most of the troops had retired from the fort, leaving about a hundred and fifty

THE ASSAULT ON FORT SANDERS, KNOXVILLE.

infantry with Benjamin's battery. Our muskets from the outside of the parapet could have kept the infantry down, and the artillery practice, except the few hand-grenades, prepared at the time by the artillerists. Johnson's brigades would have been at the ditch with me in ten minutes, when we would have passed over the works. Hence it seems conclusive that the failure was due to the order of recall. It is not a part of my nature to listen to reports that always come when stunning blows are felt, but hope in the conduct of the war was lost, and the tone and spirit for battle were stolen away by the efforts of those in authority to damage, if not prevent, the success of work ordered in their own vital interest: a poor excuse for want of golden equipoise in one who presumes to hold the lives of his soldiers, but better than to look for ways to shift the responsibility of a weakening spirit that creeps upon us unawares.

After the repulse, General Burnside was so considerate as to offer a "flag of truce" for time to remove our killed and wounded about his lines.

About half an hour after the repulse, and while yet on the slope leading up to the fort, Major Branch, of Major-General Ransom's staff, came with a telegram from the President informing me that General Bragg had been forced back by superior numbers, and ordering me to proceed to co-operate with his army.

Orders were issued at once for our trains to move south, and preparations were begun for a move of the troops after nightfall. In the afternoon word came from General Wheeler, authorized by General Bragg, that I should join him, if practicable, at Ringgold. But our first step was to be relieved of the threatening from the direction of Cumberland Gap. General Martin was sent to reinforce General Jones, with orders to hurry his operations, and return in time to cover anticipated movements. His brigades which had done their clever work on the south side were withdrawn to go with him. When he came up with Jones, the latter was severely engaged, but it was then night, too late for other operations.

Their arrangements were made during the night and battle renewed at early dawn and severely contested, the Union troops giving from point to point until they crossed the ford at Walker's and were beyond further threatening. They lost some fifty killed and wounded and one company captured at Colonel Graham's camp.

Generals Martin and Jones joined us in good season after their affair of the morning. Their loss was slight, but not detailed in separate reports.

Confederate loss in the assault	822
Union loss in the assault	673
Confederate losses during the campaign	1296
Union losses during the campaign	1481

CHAPTER XXXV.

CUT OFF FROM EAST AND WEST.

Impracticability of joining General Bragg—Wintering in East Tennessee—General Longstreet given Discretionary Authority over the Department by President Davis—Short Rations—Minor Movements of Hide-and-Seek in the Mountains—Longstreet's Position was of Strategic Importance—That Fact fully appreciated by President Lincoln, Secretary Stanton, and Generals Halleck and Grant—"Drive Longstreet out of East Tennessee and keep him out"—Generals Robertson and McLaws—The Charges against them and Action taken—Honorable Mention for Courage and Endurance—The Army finally fares sumptuously on the Fat Lands of the French Broad.

As General Wheeler's note indicated doubt of the feasibility of the move towards General Bragg, it occurred to me that our better course was to hold our lines about Knoxville, and in that way cause General Grant to send to its relief, and thus so reduce his force as to stop, for a time, pursuit of General Bragg.

Under this impression, I ordered our trains back, and continued to hold our lines. The superior officers were called together and advised of affairs, and asked for suggestions. The impression seemed to be that it would not be prudent to undertake to join General Bragg. At the same time reports came from him to inform me that he had retired as far as Dalton, and that I must depend upon my own resources.

We were cut off from communication with the army at Dalton, except by an impracticable mountain route, and the railway to the north was broken up by the removal of bridges and rails for a distance of a hundred miles and more.

Deciding to remain at Knoxville, I called on General Ransom to join us with his main force, to aid in reinvesting it, or to hold it while we could march against a succoring force if the numbers should warrant. On the 1st of December, Colonel Giltner, commanding one of General Ransom's cavalry brigades, reported that he had orders to join General Ransom with his brigade. On the same day a courier going from General Grant to General Burnside was captured, bearing an autograph letter for the latter, stating that three columns were advancing for his relief,—one by the south side under General Sherman, one by Decherd under General Elliott, the third by Cumberland Gap under General Foster.

When General Leadbetter left us on the 29th of November, he was asked to look after affairs at Loudon, and to order General Vaughn to destroy such property as he could not haul off, and retire through the mountains to General Bragg's army. Finding that General Vaughn had not been moved, he was ordered on the 1st of December to cross the river to our side with everything that he could move, and to be ready to destroy property that he must leave, and march to join us as soon as the pressure from General Sherman's force became serious. At the same time an order came from General Bragg that his cavalry be ordered back to his army. As I had relieved the pressure against him in his critical emergency, and affairs were getting a little complicated about my position, I felt warranted in retaining the cavalry for the time.

Reports coming at the same time of reinforcements for the enemy at Kingston, pressing towards General Vaughn at Loudon, he was ordered to join us. As he had no horses for the battery, he tumbled it from the bridge into the middle of the Tennessee River, burned the bridge, and marched.

Under the circumstances there seemed but one move left for us,—to march around Knoxville to the north side, up the Holston, and try to find the column reported to be marching down from Cumberland Gap, the mountain ranges and valleys of that part of the State offering beautiful fields for the manœuvre of small armies. The order was issued December 2. Trains were put in motion on the 3d, and ordered up the railroad route under escort of Law's and Robertson's brigades and one of Alexander's batteries. On the night of the 4th the troops were marched from the southwest to the north side of the city, and took up the march along the west bank of the Holston. General Martin, with his own and General W. E. Jones's cavalry, was left to guard the rear of our march and pick up weak men or stragglers. He was ordered to cross part of his cavalry to the east bank at Strawberry Plains and march up on that side, and General W. E. Jones to follow on our rear with his and the balance of Martin's corps. As we were not disturbed, we reached Blain's Cross-roads on the afternoon of the 5th, where we met General Ransom with his infantry and the balance of his artillery. On the 6th we marched to Rutledge, halting two days to get food and look for the succoring column by Cumberland Gap, which failed to appear. However, it was time for us to be looking for better fields of food for men and animals, who had not had comfortable rations for weeks. It seemed, too, that General Bragg's call for his cavalry could not be longer left in abeyance. To get away from convenient march of the enemy we went up the river as far as Rogersville, where we might hope to forage under reduced cavalry force. We marched on the 8th, ordering our cavalry, except Giltner's brigade, across the Holston near Bean's Station, General Ransom's command to cover our march, General Bragg's cavalry to go by an eastern route through the mountains to Georgia. We halted at Rogersville on the 9th, where we were encouraged to hope for full rations for a few days, at least; but to be sure of accumulating a few days' extra supply (the mills being only able to grind a full day's rations for us), every man and animal was put on short rations until we could get as much as three days' supply on hand.

On the 7th of December the Union army, under Major-General John G. Parke, took the field along the rear of our march, and reached Rutledge on the 9th, the enemy's cavalry advancing as far as Bean's Station. The object was supposed to be the securing of the forage and subsistence stores of the country; but of these movements we were not fully advised until the 11th. On the 10th of December, General Morgan's brigade of cavalry was attacked at Russellville while engaged in foraging, but got force enough, and in time, to drive the enemy away.

On the 10th a telegram from the President gave me discretionary authority over the movements of the troops of the department, and I ordered the recall of General Martin, and put his command between us and the enemy. On the 12th we had information that General Sherman had taken up his march for return to General Grant's army with the greater part of his troops. At the same time we had information of the force that had followed our march as far as Rutledge and Blain's Cross-roads, under General Parke, who had posted a large part of the force of artillery, cavalry, and infantry at Bean's Station, a point between the Clinch Mountain and the Holston River. The mountain there is very rugged, and was reported to be inaccessible, except at very rough passes. The valley between it and the river is about two miles wide, at some places less.

I thought to cut off the advance force at Bean's Station by putting our main cavalry force east of the river, the other part west of the mountain (except Giltner's), so as to close the mountain pass on the west, and bar the enemy's retreat by my cavalry in his rear,—which was to cross the Holston behind him,—then by marching the main column down the valley to capture this advance part of the command. My column, though complaining a little of short rations and very muddy roads, made its march in good season. So also did Jones on the west of the mountain, and Martin on the other side of the Holston; but the latter encountered a brigade at May's Ford, which delayed him and gave time for the enemy to change to a position some four miles to his rear.

As we approached the position in front of the Gap, Giltner's cavalry in advance, General B. R. Johnson met and engaged the enemy in a severe fight, but forced him back steadily. As we were looking for large capture more than fight, delay was unfortunate. I called Kershaw's brigade up to force contention till we could close the west end of the Gap. The movements were nicely executed by Johnson and Kershaw, but General Martin had not succeeded in gaining his position, so the rear was not closed, and the enemy retired. At night I thought the army was in position to get the benefit of the small force cut off at the Gap, as some reward for our very hard work. We received reports from General Jones, west of the mountain, that he was in position at his end of the Gap, and had captured several wagon-loads of good things. As his orders included the capture of the train, he had failed of full comprehension of them, and after nightfall had withdrawn to comfortable watering-places to enjoy his large catch of sugar and coffee, and other things seldom seen in Confederate camps in those days. Thus the troops at the Gap got out during the night, some running over the huge rocks and heavy wood tangles along the crest, by torch-light, to their comrades, some going west by easier ways. So when I sent up in the morning, looking for their doleful surrender, my men found only empty camp-kettles, mess-pans, tents, and a few abandoned guns, and twelve prisoners, while the Yankees were, no doubt, sitting around their camp-fires enjoying the joke with the comrades they had rejoined.

During our march and wait at Rogersville, General Foster passed down to Knoxville by a more southern route and relieved General Burnside of command of the department on the 12th.

General Jenkins was ordered to follow down the valley to the new position of the enemy. His brigades under Generals Law and Robertson had been detached guarding trains. General Law, commanding them, had been ordered to report to the division commander on the 13th, but at night of the 14th he was eight miles behind. Orders were sent him to join the division at the earliest practicable moment on the 15th. He reported to the division commander between two and three o'clock in the afternoon. If he started at the hour he should have marched, six A.M. at the latest, he was about eight hours making as many miles.

Meanwhile, the enemy had been reinforced by a considerable body of infantry, and later it appeared that he was advancing to offer battle. General McLaws was ordered to reinforce our front by a brigade. He sent word that his men had not yet received their bread rations. He sent Kershaw's brigade, however, that had captured rations the day before, but then it was night, and the appearance of General Martin's cavalry on or near the enemy's flank caused a change of his plans. During the night he retreated, and we occupied his trenches. I could have precipitated an affair of some moment, both at this point and at Bean's Station Gap, but my purpose was, when I fought, to fight for all that was on the field. The time was then for full and glorious victory; a fruitless one we did not want.

The enemy retired to Blain's Cross-roads, where General Foster, after reinforcing by the Fourth Corps, decided to accept battle. He reported his force as twenty-six thousand, and credited the Confederates with equal numbers, but twenty thousand would have been an over-estimate for us. He assigned the true cause of our failure to follow up and find him:

"General Longstreet, however, did not attack, in consequence, probably, of the very inclement weather, which then set in with such severity as to paralyze for a time the efforts of both armies."

And now the weather grew very heavy, and the roads, already bad, became soft and impracticable for trains and artillery. The men were brave, steady, patient. Occasionally they called pretty loudly for *parched corn*, but always in a bright, merry mood. There was never a time when we did not have enough of corn, and plenty of wood with which to keep us warm and parch our corn. At this distance it seems almost incredible that we got along as we did, but all were then so healthy and strong that we did not feel severely our really great hardships. Our serious trouble was in the matter of clothing and shoes. As winter had broken upon us in good earnest, it seemed necessary for us to give up the game of war for the time, seek some good place for shelter, and repair railroads and bridges, to open our way back towards Richmond.

General Bragg had been relieved from command of the army at Dalton by Lieutenant-General W. J. Hardee, who declined, however, the part of permanent commander, to which, after a time, General Joseph E. Johnston was assigned.

On his return from Knoxville, General Sherman proposed to General Grant to strike at General Hardee and gain Rome and the line of the Oostenaula. He wrote,—

"Of course we must fight if Hardee gives us battle, but he will not. Longstreet is off and cannot do harm for a month. Lee, in Virginia, is occupied, and Hardee is alone."

But General Halleck was much concerned about the Confederate army in East Tennessee, the only strategic field then held by Southern troops. It was inconveniently near Kentucky and the Ohio River, and President Lincoln and his War Secretary were as anxious as Halleck on account of its politico-strategic bearing. General Halleck impressed his views upon General Grant, and despatched General Foster that it was of first importance to "drive Longstreet out of East Tennessee and keep him out." General Grant ordered, "Drive Longstreet to the farthest point east that you can." And he reported to the authorities,—

"If Longstreet is not driven out of the valley entirely and the road destroyed east of Abingdon, I do not think it unlikely that the last great battle of the war will be fought in East Tennessee. Reports of deserters and citizens show the army of Bragg to be too much demoralized and reduced by desertions to do anything this winter. I will get everything in order here in a few days and go to Nashville and Louisville, and, if there is still a chance of doing anything against Longstreet, to the scene of operations there. I am deeply interested in moving the enemy beyond Saltville this winter, so as to be able to select my own campaign in the spring, instead of having the enemy dictate it to me."

Referring to his orders, General Foster reported his plan to intrench a line of infantry along Bull's Gap and Mulberry Gap, and have his cavalry ready for the ride against Saltville, but the Confederates turned upon him, and he despatched General Grant on the 11th,—

"Longstreet has taken the offensive against General Parke, who has fallen back to Blain's Cross-roads, where Granger is now concentrating his corps. I intend to fight them if Longstreet comes."

The failure to follow has been explained.

The summing up of the plans laid for General Hardee and Saltville is brief. Hardee was not disturbed. The ride towards Saltville, made about the last of the month, was followed by General W. E. Jones and came to grief, as will be elsewhere explained.

Upon relinquishing command of his army, General Bragg was called to Richmond as commander-in-chief near the President.

Before General Hood was so seriously hurt at the battle of Chickamauga, he made repeated complaints of want of conduct on the part of Brigadier-General J. B. Robertson. After the *fiasco* in Lookout Valley on the night of the 28th of October, I reported to General Bragg of the representations made by General Hood, and of want of conduct on the part of General Robertson in that night attack, when General Bragg ordered me to ask for a board of officers to examine into the merits of the case. The board was ordered, and General Robertson was relieved from duty by orders from General Bragg's head-quarters, "while the proceedings and actions of the examining board in his case were pending."

On the 8th, without notice to my head-quarters, General Bragg ordered, "Brigadier-General Robertson will rejoin his command until the board can renew its session." *

On the 18th of December the division commander preferred "charges and specifications" against Brigadier-General Robertson, in which he accused him of calling the commanders of his Texas regiments to him and saying there were but

> "Three days' rations on hand, and God knows where more are to come from; that he had no confidence in the campaign; that whether we whipped the enemy in the immediate battle or not, we would be compelled to retreat, the enemy being believed by citizens and others to be moving around us, and that we were in danger of losing a considerable part of our army; that our men were in no condition for campaigning; that General Longstreet had promised shoes, but how could they be furnished? that we only had communication with Richmond, and could only get a mail from there in three weeks; that he was opposed to the movement; would require written orders, and would obey under protest."

General Robertson was ordered to Bristol to await the action of the Richmond authorities, who were asked for a court-martial to try the case.

---

* Rebellion Record.

On the 17th the following orders concerning General McLaws were issued:

"HEAD-QUARTERS NEAR BEAN'S STATION,
"December 17, 1863.

"SPECIAL ORDERS NO. 27.

"Major-General L. McLaws is relieved from further duty with this army, and will proceed to Augusta, Georgia, from which place he will report by letter to the adjutant- and inspector-general. He will turn over the command of the division to the senior brigadier present.

"By command of Lieutenant-General Longstreet.

"G. MOXLEY SORREL,
"*Lieutenant-Colonel and Assistant Adjutant-General.*

"MAJOR-GENERAL MCLAWS,
"*Confederate States Army.*"

On the same day he wrote,—

"CAMP ON BEAN'S STATION GAP ROAD,
"December 17, 1863.

"LIEUTENANT-COLONEL SORREL,
"*Assistant Adjutant-General:*

"I have the honor to acknowledge the receipt of Special Orders No. 27, from your head-quarters, of this date, relieving me from further duty with this army. If there is no impropriety in making inquiry, and I cannot imagine there is, I respectfully request to be informed of the particular reason for the order.

"Very respectfully,
"L. MCLAWS,
"*Major-General.*"

In reply the following was sent:

"HEAD-QUARTERS NEAR BEAN'S STATION,
"December 17, 1863.

"MAJOR-GENERAL MCLAWS,
"*Confederate States Army:*

"GENERAL,—I have the honor to acknowledge the receipt of your note of to-day, asking for the particular reason for the issue of the order relieving you from duty with this army. In reply I am directed to say that throughout the campaign on which we are engaged you have exhibited a want of confidence in the efforts and plans which the commanding general has thought proper to adopt, and he is apprehensive that this feeling will extend more or less to the troops under your command. Under these circumstances the commanding general has felt that the interest of the public service would be advanced by your separation from him, and as he could not himself leave, he decided upon the issue of the order which you have received.

"I have the honor to be, general, with great respect,

"G. MOXLEY SORREL,

"*Lieutenant-Colonel and Assistant Adjutaut-General.*"

On the 19th, General Law handed in his resignation at head-quarters, and asked leave of absence on it. This was cheerfully granted. Then he asked the privilege of taking the resignation with him to the adjutant-general at Richmond. This was a very unusual request, but the favor he was doing the service gave him some claim to unusual consideration, and his request was granted.

The Law disaffection was having effect, or seemed to be, among some of the officers, but most of them and all of the soldiers were true and brave, even through all of the hardships of the severest winter of the four years of war. Marching and fighting had been almost daily occupation from the middle of January, 1863, when we left Fredericksburg to move down to Suffolk, Virginia, until the 16th of December, when we found bleak winter again breaking upon us, away from our friends, and dependent upon our own efforts for food and clothing. It is difficult for a soldier to find words that can express his high appreciation of conduct in officers and men who endured so bravely the severe trials they were called to encounter.

Orders were given to cross the Holston River and march for the railroad, only a few miles away. Before quitting the fields of our arduous labors mention should be made of General Bushrod R. Johnson's clever march of sixteen miles, through deep mud, to Bean's Station on the 13th, when he and General Kershaw attacked and pushed the enemy back from his front at the Gap before he could get out of it. Honorable mention is also due General Jenkins for his equally clever pursuit of the enemy at Lenoir's Station; Brigadier-General Humphreys and Bryan for their conduct at the storming assault; Colonel Ruff, who led Wofford's brigade, and died in the ditch; Colonel McElroy, of the Thirteenth Mississippi Regiment, and Colonel Thomas, of the Sixteenth Georgia, who also died in the ditch; Lieutenant Cumming, adjutant of the Sixteenth Georgia Regiment, who overcame all obstacles, crowned the parapet with ten or a dozen men, and, entering the fort through one of the embrasures, was taken prisoner; and Colonel Fiser, of the Eighteenth Mississippi, who lost an arm while on the parapet. Not the least of the gallant acts of the campaign was the dash of Captain Winthrop, who led our once halting lines over the rail defences at Knoxville.

The transfer of the army to the east bank of the river was executed by diligent work and the use of such flat-boats and other means of crossing as we could collect and construct. We were over by the 20th, and before Christmas were in our camps along the railroad, near Morristown. Blankets and clothes were very scarce, shoes more so, but all knew how to enjoy the beautiful country in which we found ourselves. The French Broad River and the Holston are confluent at Knoxville. The country between and beyond them contains as fine farming lands and has as delightful a climate as can be found. Stock and grain were on all farms. Wheat and oats had been hidden away by our Union friends, but the fields were full of maize, still standing. The country about the French Broad had hardly been touched by the hands of foragers. Our wagons immediately on entering the fields were loaded to overflowing. Pumpkins were on the ground in places like apples under a tree. Cattle, sheep, and swine, poultry, vegetables, maple-sugar, honey, were all abundant for immediate wants of the troops.

When the enemy found we had moved to the east bank, his cavalry followed to that side. They were almost as much in want of the beautiful foraging lands as we, but we were in advance of them, and left little for them. With all the plenitude of provisions and many things which seemed at the time luxuries, we were not quite happy. Tattered blankets, garments, and shoes (the latter going—many gone) opened ways, on all sides, for piercing winter blasts. There were some hand-looms in the country from which we occasionally picked up a piece of cloth, and here and there we received other comforts, some from kind and some from unwilling hands, which nevertheless could spare them. For shoes we were obliged to resort to the raw hides of beef cattle as temporary protection from the frozen ground. Then we began to find soldiers who could tan the hides of our beeves, some who could make shoes, some who could make shoe-pegs, some who could make shoe-lasts, so that it came about that the hides passed rapidly from the beeves to the feet of the soldiers in the form of comfortable shoes. Then came the opening of the railroad, and lo and behold! a shipment of three thousand shoes from General Lawton, quartermaster-general! Thus the most urgent needs were supplied, and the soldier's life seemed passably pleasant,—that is, in the infantry and artillery. Our cavalry were looking at the enemy all of this while, and the enemy was looking at them, both frequently burning powder between their lines.

General Sturgis had been assigned to the cavalry of the other side to relieve General Shackelford, and he seemed to think that the dead of winter was the time for cavalry work; and our General Martin's orders were to have the enemy under his eye at all hours. Both were vigilant, active, and persevering.

About the 20th of December a raid was made by General Averill from West Virginia upon a supply depot of General Sam Jones's department, at Salem, which was partially successful, when General Grant, under the impression that the stores were for troops of East Tennessee, wired General Foster, December 25, "This will give you great advantage," and General Foster despatched General Parke, commanding his troops in the field, December 26, "Longstreet will feel a little timid now, and will bear a little pushing."

Under the fierce operations of General Sturgis's cavalry against General Martin's during the latter days of December, General W. E. Jones's cavalry was on guard for my right and rear towards Cumberland Gap. While Sturgis busied himself against our front and left, a raiding party rode from Cumberland Gap against the outposts of our far-off right, under Colonel Pridemore. As W. E. Jones was too far to support Martin's cavalry, he was called to closer threatenings against Cumberland Gap, that he might thus draw some of Sturgis's cavalry from our front to strengthen the forces at the Gap. Upon receipt of orders, General Jones crossed Clinch River in time to find the warm trail of the raiders who were following Pridemore. He sent around to advise him of his ride in pursuit of his pursuers, and ordered Pridemore, upon hearing his guns, to turn and join in the attack upon them.

The very cold season and severe march through the mountain fastnesses stretched Jones's line so that he was in poor condition for immediate attack when he found the enemy's camp at daylight on the 3d of January; but he found a surprise: not even a picket guard out in their rear. He dashed in with his leading forces and got the enemy's battery, but the enemy quickly rallied and made battle, which recovered the artillery, and got into strong position about some farm-houses and defended with desperate resolution. Finding the position too strong, Jones thought to so engage as to make the enemy use his battery until his ammunition was exhausted, and then put in

all of his forces in assault. Towards night the enemy found himself reduced to desperate straits and tried to secure cover of the mountains, but as quick as he got away from the farm-houses Jones put all of his forces in, capturing three pieces of artillery, three hundred and eighty prisoners, and twenty-seven wagons and teams of the Sixteenth Illinois Cavalry and Twenty-second Ohio Light Artillery. A number of the men got away through the mountains.

CHAPTER XXXVI.

STRATEGIC IMPORTANCE OF THE FIELD.

Longstreet again considers Relief from Service—General Grant at Knoxville—Shoeless Soldiers leave Bloody Trails on Frozen Roads—A Confederate Advance—Affair at Dandridge—Federals retreat—Succession of Small Engagements—General Grant urges General Foster's Army to the Offensive—General Foster relieved—General Schofield in Command of Federals—General Grant's Orders—General Halleck's Estimate of East Tennessee as a Strategic Field—Affair of Cavalry—Advance towards Knoxville—Longstreet's Command called back to Defensive for Want of Cavalry.

DURING the last few days of the year 1863 the cold of the severest winter of the war came on, and constantly increased until the thermometer approached zero, and on New Year's dropped below, hanging near that figure for about two weeks. The severe season gave rest to every one. Even the cavalry had a little quiet, but it was cold comfort, for their orders were to keep the enemy in sight.

The season seemed an appropriate one for making another effort to be relieved from service,—that service in which the authorities would not support my plans or labors,—for now during the lull in war they would have ample time to assign some one to whom they could give their confidence and aid. But this did not suit them, and the course of affairs prejudicial to order and discipline was continued. It was difficult under the circumstances to find apology for remaining in service.

The President asked Congress to provide for another general officer when he had five on his rolls,—one of whom was not in command appropriate to his rank,—and appointed Lieutenant-General Smith, of the Trans-Mississippi Department, of lower rank than mine, to hold rank above me. A soldier's honor is his all, and of that they would rob him and degrade him in the eyes of his troops. The cause had passed beyond hope, except from miraculous interposition. The occasion seemed to demand enforced resignation, but that would have been unsoldierly conduct. Dispassionate judgment suggested, as the proper rounding of the soldier's life, to stay and go down with faithful comrades of long and arduous service.

On the other side of the picture affairs were bright and encouraging. The disaffected were away, and with them disappeared their influence. The little army was cheerful and ready for any work to which it could be called.

General Grant made his visit to Knoxville about New Year's, and remained until the 7th. He found General Foster in the condition of the Confederates,—not properly supplied with clothing, especially in want of shoes. So he authorized a wait for the clothing, then in transit and looked for in a week; and that little delay was a great lift for the Confederates. We were not timid, but began to think ourselves comfortable, and were expectant of even better condition. Our quartermaster was furnishing a hundred pairs of shoes a day of our own make, the hand-looms of the farmers were giving help towards clothing our men, promises from Richmond were encouraging, and we were prepared to enjoy rest that we had not known for a twelvemonth. The medical inspector of the Cis-Mississippi District came to see us, and after careful inspection told us that the army was in better health and better heart than the other armies of the district.

Before leaving General Foster, General Grant ordered him on the receipt of the clothing to advance and drive us "at least beyond Bull's Gap and Red Bridge." And to prepare for that advance he ordered the Ninth and Twenty-third Corps to Mossy Creek, the Fourth Corps to Strawberry Plains, and the cavalry to Dandridge.

The Union army—equipped—marched on the 14th and 15th of January.

The Confederate departments were not so prompt in

filling our requisitions, but we had hopes. The bitter freeze of two weeks had made the rough angles of mud as firm and sharp as so many freshly-quarried rocks, and the partially protected feet of our soldiers sometimes left bloody marks along the roads.

General Sturgis rode in advance of the army, and occupied Dandridge by Elliott's, Wolford's, and Garrard's divisions of cavalry and Mott's brigade of infantry. The Fourth and Twenty-third Corps followed the cavalry, leaving the Ninth Corps to guard at Strawberry Plains.

General Martin gave us prompt notice that the march was at Dandridge, and in force. The move was construed as a flanking proceeding, but it was more convenient to adopt the short march and meet it at Dandridge than to leave our shoe factory and winter huts and take up the tedious rearward move. The army was ordered under arms, the cavalry was ordered concentrated in front of General Sturgis, and the divisions of Jenkins and B. R. Johnson and Alexander's batteries were marched to join General Martin. McLaws's division under General Wofford, and Ransom's under General Carr, with such batteries as they could haul, were assigned to positions on the Morristown (Strawberry Plains) road, to strike forward or reinforce at Dandridge as plans developed. The men without shoes were ordered to remain as camp guards, but many preferred to march with their comrades.

I rode in advance to be assured that our cavalry had not mistaken a strong cavalry move for one by the enemy in force. We found General Martin on the Bull's Gap road sharply engaged with the enemy, both sides on strong defensive grounds and using their horse batteries, but no infantry was in sight. General Martin was ordered to push on, gain the opposing plateau, and force the enemy to show his infantry.

He met the enemy in strong fight, but got the plateau, when the enemy deployed to his rear in stronger force;

but his infantry did not appear. When asked to take the next hill, he thought it could not be done without infantry, but my idea was to save the infantry the trying march, if possible, and to that end it was necessary to push with the cavalry. He was called to send me a detachment of his troopers, and about six hundred came,—Harrison's brigade, as I remember.

We rode away from the enemy's left, concealing our march under traverse of an elevated woodland, while General Martin engaged their front attention. At a secluded spot, a little beyond the enemy's left, the men dismounted, leaving their animals under guards, moved under cover to good position, deployed into single line, and marched for the second plateau. Part of the march was over a small opening, near a farm-house. The exposure brought us under fire of some sharp-shooters, but we hadn't time to stop and shoot. As our line marched, a chicken, dazed by the formidable appearance, crouched in the grass until it was kicked up, when it flew and tried to clear the line, but one of the troopers jumped up, knocked it down with the end of his gun, stooped, picked it up, put it in his haversack, and marched on without losing his place or step and without looking to his right or left, as though it was as proper and as much an every-day part of the exercise of war as shooting at the enemy. Presently we got up the hill, and General Martin advanced his mounts to meet us. We lost but two men,—wounded,—an officer and a soldier. The officer was at my side, and, hearing the thud of the blow, I turned and asked if he was much hurt. He said it was only a flesh-wound, and remained with his command until night. From that point we saw enough to tell that a formidable part of the army was before us, and orders were sent for the command to speed their march as much as they could without severe trial.

When General Martin made his bold advance General Sturgis thought to ride around by a considerable détour and strike at his rear, but in his ride was surprised to encounter our marching columns of infantry, and still more surprised when he saw a thousand muskets levelled and sending whistling bullets about his men, and our batteries preparing something worse for him. His troopers got back faster than they came. In trying by a rapid ride to find position for handling his men he lost a member of his staff, captured, and narrowly escaped himself.

It was near night when the command got up skirmishers from the advance division, reinforced the cavalry, and pushed the enemy back nearer the town.

Dandridge is on the right bank of the French Broad River, about thirty miles from Knoxville. Its topographical features are bold and inviting of military work. Its other striking characteristic is the interesting character of its citizens. The Confederates—a unit in heart and spirit—were prepared to do their share towards making an effective battle, and our plans were so laid.

At the time ordered for his advance, General Foster was suffering from an old wound, and General Parke became commander of the troops in the field. The latter delayed at Strawberry Plains in arranging that part of his command, and General Sheridan, marching with the advance, became commander, until superseded by the corps commander, General Gordon Granger.

Our plans were laid before the army was all up. Our skirmish line was made stronger and relieved the cavalry of their dismounted service. A narrow unused road, practicable for artillery, was found, that opened a way for us to reach the enemy's rearward line of march. Sharpshooters were organized and ordered forward by it, to be followed by our infantry columns. It was thought better to move the infantry alone, as the ringing of the iron axles of the guns might give notice of our purpose; the artillery to be called as our sharp-shooters approached the junction of the roads. The head of the turning force encountered a picket-guard, some of whom escaped without firing, but speedily gave notice of our feeling towards their rear. General Granger decided to retire, and was in time to leave our cross-road behind him, his rear-guard passing the point of intersection before my advance party reached it about midnight.

The weather moderated before night, and after dark a mild, gentle rain began to fall.

When I rode into Dandridge in the gray of the morning the ground was thawing and hardly firm enough to bear the weight of a horse. When the cavalry came at sunrise the last crust of ice had melted, letting the animals down to their fetlocks in heavy limestone soil. The mud and want of a bridge to cross the Holston made pursuit by our heavy columns useless. The cavalry was ordered on, and the troops at Morristown, on the Strawberry Plains road, were ordered to try that route, but the latter proved to be too heavy for progress with artillery.

While yet on the streets of Dandridge, giving directions for such pursuit as we could make, a lady came out upon the sidewalk and invited us into her parlors. When the orders for pursuit were given, I dismounted, and with some members of my staff walked in. After the compliments of the season were passed, we were asked to be seated, and she told us something of General Granger during the night before. She had never heard a person swear about another as General Granger did about me. Some of the officers proposed to stop and make a battle, but General Granger swore and said it "was no use to stop and fight Longstreet. You can't whip him. It don't make any difference whether he has one man or a hundred thousand." Presently she brought out a flask that General Granger had forgotten, and thought that I should have it. It had about two horizontal fingers left in it. Though not left with compliments, it was accepted. Although the weather had moderated, it was very wet and nasty, and as we had taken our coffee at three o'clock, it was resolved to call it noon and divide the spoils. Colonel Fairfax, who knew how to enjoy good things, thought the occasion called for a sentiment, and offered, "General Granger—may his shadow never grow less."

The cavalry found the road and its side-ways so cut up that their pursuit was reduced to labored walk. The previous hard service and exposure had so reduced the animals that they were not in trim for real effective cavalry service. They found some crippled battery forges and a little of other plunder, but the enemy passed the Holston and broke his bridges behind him. Our army returned to their huts and winter homes.

Part of our cavalry was ordered to the south side of the French Broad, and General Martin was ordered to press close on the enemy's rear with the balance of his force. General Armstrong followed the line of retreat, and by the use of flat-boats passed his cavalry over the Holston and rode to the vicinity of Knoxville. He caught up with some stragglers, equipments, ammunition, and remains of some caissons, and at last made a grand haul of a herd of eight hundred beef cattle and thirty-one wagons.

Upon getting his cavalry back to Knoxville, General Foster crossed them over the bridge at the city below the French Broad to foraging grounds about Louisville, and called his Dandridge march a foraging excursion, saying that he was building a bridge to cross to the south side when we bore down against him. But the strategy of his tedious march by our front to find a crossing point at Dandridge and build a bridge in our presence, when he could have crossed to the south side of the French Broad by his bridge at Knoxville and reached those foraging grounds unmolested, was not like Napoleon. He claimed that he recovered two hundred of the lost herd of beef cattle. In that our reports do not agree. It is possible that his officers may have confounded that adventure with another. My explanation of the discrepancy—from memory—is that another of our parties undertook to get in a herd of swine, with which there was a smaller herd of beef cattle; that all of the latter herd were recovered, and the reports of the two adventures were confounded.

On the 14th, General Vance came down from the mountains of North Carolina on a raid towards Sevierville. He captured a number of wagons, but was promptly pursued by the enemy, his prize recovered, and he and a number of his staff were taken prisoners, with the loss of a hundred or more horses and equipments. They were not a part of my command, and failed to give us notice of their ride. The first intimation we had of them was of their unfortunate adventure.

On the 21st orders came from Richmond to send Corse's brigade back to Petersburg, in Virginia. It was so ordered, and Hodges's brigade was ordered to us from the department of West Virginia, in place of Corse's.

To seek some of the fruits of our advantage at Dandridge, the roads being a little firmer, our leading division, under General Jenkins, was ordered on the 21st to prepare to march towards Strawberry Plains, and the Richmond authorities were asked to send us a pontoon bridge, tools of construction, and to hurry forward such shoes as they could send.

On the 24th, as the Official Records show, General Grant sent word to General Halleck of our return towards Knoxville, that he had ordered General Foster to give battle, if necessary, and that he would send General Thomas with additional troops to insure that we would be driven from the State. He also directed General Thomas to go in person and take command, and said, "I want Longstreet routed and pursued beyond the limits of the State of Tennessee." And he ordered General Foster to put his cavalry on a raid from Cumberland Gap to cut in upon our rear.

On the 26th we were advised of the advance of the enemy's cavalry up the south side of the French Broad to some of the fords above Dandridge. General Martin was ordered to cross in force below it, get in rear of the enemy, and endeavor to put him to confusion. He crossed with Morgan's division, and called Armstrong's to follow, but the enemy, finding opportunity to put his force against the division, advanced and made a severe battle on the 27th, which became desperate as developed until, in their successive gallant charges, our ranks were broken to confusion, when the enemy made a dash and got two of our guns and two hundred prisoners, driving us towards the river.

General Armstrong crossed pending these operations and received the enemy's attack on the 28th. General B. R. Johnson's infantry division had been ordered near Dandridge, and crossed while Armstrong's command held the enemy. The latter was caught in battle from which there was no escape but to fight it out. Johnson's infantry crossed in time to march towards the enemy's rear before he could dislodge Armstrong. I rode a little in advance of Johnson's command. The enemy, advised of the approach of infantry, made his final charge and retired south towards Marysville. In his last effort one of his most reckless troopers rode in upon head-quarters, but Colonel Fairfax put spurs into his horse, dashed up against him, had his pistol at his head, and called "surrender" before the man could level his gun. The trooper was agreeably surprised to find it no worse. The enemy's move to Marysville left us in possession of the foraging grounds.

On the 30th, General Grant urged General Foster's army to the offensive, and called for the cavalry raid through the Powell River Valley and Cumberland Gap towards our rear, and General Foster called on General Thomas for a force of ten thousand infantry and working details to repair the railroad and bridges between Knoxville and Chattanooga. General Thomas was willing to respond to the call for troops, but asked timely notice so that he could call Sherman's forces from Mississippi to replace those to be sent and make a co-operative move against General Johnston at Dalton. At the same time General Foster called for a pontoon bridge to make his crossing of the Holston at Strawberry Plains, which was ordered.

General Sturgis could not approve the ride through Powell River Valley, and expressed preference for a route through the mountains of North Carolina towards Asheville, to find our rear. General Grant had suggested raids from both these points on the 24th of January, but General Foster decided against the raid from Cumberland Gap, explaining that General Jones was at Little War Gap to intercept a column that might ride from that point. He found, too, upon counting his effectives for the raid, that he could only mount fifteen hundred men, and that our guards at weak points had been doubled.

Our railroad was in working order on the 26th of January, and the part of the pontoon bridge ordered for us was on the road. General Jenkins was ordered with the leading division down towards Strawberry Plains to collect such material as he could, and be prepared to throw the bridge across the Holston as soon as it was up and ready for us. Notice was given General A. E. Jackson of indications of raids; to Captain Osborn, commanding scouts; to General Wharton; to Rucker's Cavalry Legion and Jones's cavalry; and General Vaughn was ordered to collect his command at Rogersville, to be prepared to threaten Cumberland Gap if the forces there should be reduced.

Due notice was sent our outlying parties and scouts to be on the watch for the reported raiding parties, and the guards of bridges in our rear were reinforced.

On the 6th of February, General Grant reported from Nashville,—

"**Major-General H. W. Halleck,**

"*General-in-Chief:*

"**I am making every effort to get supplies to Knoxville for the support of a large force—large enough to drive Longstreet out. The enemy have evidently fallen back with most of their force from General Thomas's front, some going to Mobile. Has there been any movement in that direction by our troops?**

"**U. S. Grant,**

"*Major-General, Commanding.*"

"**Major-General Thomas:**

"**Reports of scouts make it evident that Joe Johnston has removed most of his force from your front, two divisions going to Longstreet. Longstreet has been reinforced by troops from the East. This makes it evident the enemy intends to secure East Tennessee if they can, and I intend to drive them out or get whipped this month. For this purpose you will have to detach at least ten thousand men besides Stanley's division (more will be better). I can partly relieve the vacuum at Chattanooga by troops from Logan's command. It will not be necessary to take artillery or wagons to Knoxville, but all the serviceable artillery horses should be taken to use on artillery there. Six mules to each two hundred men should also be taken, if you have them to spare. Let me know how soon you can start.**

"**Grant,**

"*Major-General.*"

On the 9th, Major-General J. M. Schofield arrived at Knoxville, and assumed command of the Army of the Ohio.

General Grant reported on the 11th,—

"**Major-General H. W. Halleck,**

"*General-in-Chief:*

"**I expect to get off from Chattanooga by Monday next a force to drive Longstreet out of East Tennessee. It has been impossible heretofore to subsist the troops necessary for this work.**

"**U. S. Grant,**

"*Major-General.*"

"Major-General J. M. Schofield,
"*Knoxville, Tenn.*:

"I deem it of the utmost importance to drive Longstreet out immediately, so as to furlough the balance of our veterans, and to prepare for a spring campaign of our own choosing, instead of permitting the enemy to dictate it for us. Thomas is ordered to start ten thousand men, besides the remainder of Granger's corps, at once. He will take no artillery, but will take his artillery horses, and three mules to one hundred men. He will probably start next Monday.

"U. S. Grant,
"*Major-General.*"

General Schofield ordered preparations for the eastern raid continued, but to await further orders of execution, and reported that its execution would require all of his effective mounts, break his animals down, and leave him without cavalry.

General Grant wired these several despatches from Nashville on February 12:

"Major-General Thomas:

"Conversation with Major-General Foster has undecided me as to the propriety of the contemplated move against Longstreet. Schofield telegraphs the same views. I will take the matter into consideration during the day, after further talk with Foster, and give you the conclusion arrived at. If decided that you do not go I will instruct Schofield to let Granger send off his veterans at once.

"Should you not be required to go into East Tennessee, could you not make a formidable reconnoissance towards Dalton, and, if successful in driving the enemy out, occupy that place and complete the railroad up to it this winter?

"Grant,
"*Major-General.*"

"Major-General Thomas:

"Logan's troops started yesterday morning. If I decide not to make the move at present into East Tennessee, I will send them back, unless you require them to aid in advance on Dalton. (See my telegram of this morning.)

"Grant,
"*Major-General.*"

"MAJOR-GENERAL J. M. SCHOFIELD:

"No movement will be made against Longstreet at present. Give your men and animals all the rest you can preparatory to early operations in the spring. Furlough all the veterans you deem it prudent to let go.

"U. S. GRANT,
"Major-General."

"MAJOR-GENERAL J. M. SCHOFIELD,
"Knoxville, Tenn.:

"You need not attempt the raid with the cavalry you now have. If that in Kentucky can recruit up it may do hereafter to send it on such an expedition. I have asked so often for a co-operative movement from the troops in West Virginia that I hardly expect to see anything to help us from there. General Halleck says they have not got men enough. Crook, however, has gone there, and may undertake to strike the road about New River.

"U. S. GRANT,
"Major-General."

"MAJOR-GENERAL HALLECK,
"General-in-Chief, Washington:

"GENERAL,—I have got General Thomas ready to move a force of about fourteen thousand infantry into East Tennessee to aid the force there in expelling Longstreet from the State. He would have started on Monday night if I had not revoked the order. My reasons for doing this are these: General Foster, who is now here (or left this morning), says that our possession of the portion of East Tennessee is perfectly secure against all danger. The condition of the people within the rebel lines cannot be improved now after losing all they had. Longstreet, where he is, makes more secure other parts of our possessions. Our men, from scanty clothing and short rations, are not in good condition for an advance. There are but very few animals in East Tennessee in condition to move artillery or other stores. If we move against Longstreet with an overwhelming force he will simply fall back towards Virginia until he can be reinforced or take up an impregnable position. The country being exhausted, all our supplies will have to be carried from Knoxville the whole distance advanced. We would be obliged to advance rapidly and return soon whether the object of the expedition was accomplished or not. Longstreet could return with impunity on the heels of our returning column, at least as far down the valley as he can supply

himself from the road in his rear. Schofield telegraphs to the same effect. All these seem to be good reasons for abandoning the movement, and I have therefore suspended it. Now that our men are ready for an advance, however, I have directed it to be made on Dalton, and hope to get possession of that place and hold it as a step towards a spring campaign. Our troops in East Tennessee are now clothed; rations are also accumulating. When Foster left most of the troops had ten days' supplies, with five hundred barrels of flour and forty days' meat in store, and the quantity increasing daily.

"I am, general, very respectfully, your obedient servant,

"U. S. GRANT,

"*Major-General.*"

Later despatches from General Grant and Commander-in-Chief Halleck were as follows:

"NASHVILLE, TENN., February 13, 1864.

"MAJOR-GENERAL H. W. HALLECK,

"*General-in-Chief:*

"Despatches just received from General Schofield and conversation with General Foster, who is now here, have determined me against moving immediately against Longstreet. I will write more fully. No danger whatever to be apprehended in East Tennessee.

"U. S. GRANT,

"*Major-General.*"

"KNOXVILLE, February 15, 1864, 6.30 P.M.

"MAJOR-GENERAL THOMAS:

"In consequence of Longstreet's movement in this direction I have ordered one division of Granger's corps to this place. I think Stanley should move up as far as Athens and Sweet Water so as to protect the railroad. Longstreet has not advanced farther than Strawberry Plains. No further news from him to-day.

"J. M. SCHOFIELD,

"*Major-General.*"

"[Confidential.]

"WASHINGTON, D. C., February 17, 1864.

"MAJOR-GENERAL GRANT,

"*Nashville, Tenn.:*

"GENERAL,—Your letter of the 12th instant is just received. I fully concur with you in regard to the present condition of

affairs in East Tennessee. It certainly is very much to be regretted that the fatal mistake of General Burnside has permitted Longstreet's army to winter in Tennessee. It is due to yourself that a full report of this matter should be placed on file, so that the responsibility may rest where it properly belongs.

"H. W. HALLECK,
"General-in-Chief."

The raids ordered north and south of us were now given over. General Thomas made his advance towards Dalton, and retired, unsuccessful.

General Halleck was right in his estimate of East Tennessee as a strategic field essential to the Union service, the gate-way to Kentucky, to the Union line of communication, and the Ohio River; but General Grant found it so far from his lines of active operations that it could not be worked without interrupting plans of campaigns for the summer, and giving his adversary opportunity to dictate the work of the year. He thought it better to depend upon the conservative spirit that controlled at the South, to draw the army in East Tennessee off to meet threatenings in Virginia and Georgia, when he had prepared for them in the spring of the year.

On the 10th of February, General Jenkins was ordered with his division at Strawberry Plains to use the pontoon and flat-boats in bridging the Holston River. Other columns were ordered to approximate concentration, including Wharton's brigade from Bull's Gap, and Hodges's brigade coming from the Department of West Virginia. Rucker's cavalry was ordered to Blain's Cross-roads on the west bank, and outlying forces were advised of the advance. General Jenkins was ordered to put some of the cavalry over to be in observation towards Knoxville, and a brigade of infantry as supporting force; batteries on the hither bank to cover the troops and the bridge in case the enemy was disposed to dispute our crossing, and await my arrival and further orders. The army being ready for the crossing and move for Knoxville, inquiry was made of General Johnston as to the condition of affairs with the enemy at Chattanooga. In answer he said,—

"Our scouts report that troops have been sent from Chattanooga to Loudon. They could not learn the number."

On the 17th I asked the Richmond authorities for ten thousand additional men, and General Lee, approving our work, asked to have Pickett's division sent, and other detachments to make up the number.

On the 19th I was informed from General Johnston's head-quarters that "eight trains loaded with troops went up from Chattanooga on the night of the 17th." A telegram came on the 19th from Richmond to say that the additional troops called for could not be sent, and on the same day a telegram from the President ordered me to send General Martin with his cavalry to General Johnston. In reply I reported that the order depriving me of the cavalry would force me to abandon the move, then in progress, against Knoxville, and draw the troops back towards Bristol. Then came other despatches from General Johnston that the enemy was still drawing forces from Chattanooga, but no authority came from Richmond authorizing me to retain the cavalry, so we were obliged to draw back to fields that could be guarded by smaller commands.

Referring to the proposed advance, General Grant said, "Longstreet cannot afford to place his force between Knoxville and the Tennessee." It was not so intended, but to put the army alongside of Knoxville to hold the enemy to his intrenched lines, while the troops asked for would be employed in breaking the railroad and bridges between that point and Chattanooga. It was thought that the army at Chattanooga could not afford sufficient detachments to drive me from that work without exposing that position to danger from General Johnston at Dalton, but upon inquiry of General Johnston if he could avail himself of such opportunity, he replied that he was ordered to reinforce General Polk, who was operating in Mississippi in front of General Sherman. Instead of reinforcing General Polk, the latter should have been ordered to General Johnston. That would have drawn General Sherman to General Thomas, but Polk, having interior lines of transit, could have been in time for Johnston to strike and break up the road and bridge behind Thomas before Sherman could reach him. The break could have forced Thomas to care for his own position, and the want of the bridge behind him might have forced him to abandon it, in search of safe communication with his supplies. But the authorities could not be induced to abandon the policy of placing detachments to defend points to which the enemy chose to call us. We had troops enough in Tennessee, Georgia, Alabama, and Mississippi, if allowed to use them in co-operative combination, to break the entire front of the Federal forces and force them back into Kentucky before the opening of the spring campaign, when we might have found opportunity to "dictate" their campaign. The enemy was in no condition for backward move at the time of my advance upon Knoxville, so simultaneous advance of our many columns could have given him serious trouble, if not confusion.

The order for the return of Martin's cavalry to Georgia, and the notice that other troops could not be sent me, called for the withdrawal of the command east, where we could find safer lines of defence and good foraging. The order to retire was issued, and the march was taken up on the 22d of February, Jenkins's division and the cavalry to cover the march. He was ordered to reship the pontoon-boats, destroy trestlings, flat-boats, the railroad bridge, and march in advance of the cavalry. He inquired if he should cut the wires and crossings of small streams, but was ordered to leave them undisturbed, as the enemy would not be so likely to trouble us when he found we were disposed to be accommodating.

The march was not seriously disturbed. The enemy's cavalry, reduced by severe winter service, was in poor condition to follow, and the roads we left behind us were too heavy for artillery. A good position was found behind Bull's Gap, and the army was deployed to comfortable camps from the Holston River on the right to the Nolachucky on the left.

The prime object of the second advance upon Knoxville was to show the strategic strength of the field, and persuade the authorities that an army of twenty thousand in that zone could be of greater service than double that force on the enemy's front or elsewhere, but they could not or would not hear of plans that proposed to take them from the settled policy of meeting the enemy where he was prepared for us.

CHAPTER XXXVII.

LAST DAYS IN TENNESSEE.

Longstreet's Army at Bull's Gap—U. S. Grant made Lieutenant-General—Richmond Authorities awake to the Gravity of the Situation—Longstreet's Proposition for Campaign—Approved by General Lee—Richmond Authorities fail to adopt it—General Bragg's Plan—A Memorable and Unpleasant Council at the Capital—Orders from President Davis—The Case of General Law—Longstreet ordered to the Army of Northern Virginia—Resolutions of Thanks from Confederate Congress.

It would be difficult to find a country more inviting in agriculture and horticulture than East Tennessee, and its mineral resources are as interesting, but for those whose mission was strategic, its geographical and topographical features were more striking. Our position at Bull's Gap was covered by a spur of the mountains which shoots out from the south side of the Holston River towards the north bend of the Nolachucky, opening gaps that could be improved by the pick and shovel until the line became unassailable. In a few days our line was strong enough, and we looked for the enemy to come and try our metal, until we learned that he was as badly crippled of the cavalry arm as we. General Martin was ordered with his division to General Johnston in Georgia, and Colonel Gary with his legion was ordered to South Carolina to be mounted for cavalry service.

The armies under General Lee in Virginia and General Johnston in Georgia were in defensive positions, with little prospect of striking by their right or left flanks in search of a way to break their bounds, and the army in East Tennessee had been called back to the defensive for want of cavalry, but the latter still covered gate-ways through the mountains that offered routes to Kentucky for strategic manœuvres. The Trans-Mississippi Department was an open field of vast opportunities, but was lying fallow.

An officer of the Union service had worked his way during three years of severe field service from obscure position with a regiment, to command of armies, and had borne his banners in triumph through battle and siege, over the prejudice of higher officers, until President Lincoln's good judgment told him that Grant was the man for the times. Congress provided the place, and the President sent his commission as lieutenant-general to the United States Senate, where it was promptly confirmed, and the lieutenant-general was presently assigned as commander over half a million of men, to the surprise of many, more than all to the bureau general-in-chief. He was soon at work arranging his combination for the campaign of the coming year. He was a West Point boy, and we had been together during three years of academic service, then two years in the United States Fourth Regiment of Infantry, and later in Worth's division in Mexico.

Forced to extremities, the Richmond authorities began to realize the importance of finding a way out of our pent-up borders before the Union commander could complete his extensive arrangements to press on with his columns. They called upon General Lee, General Johnston, and myself for plans or suggestions that could anticipate the movements of the enemy, disconcert his plans, and move him to new combinations. In front of General Lee and on his right and left the country had been so often foraged by both Union and Confederate armies that it was denuded of supplies. Besides, a forced advance of Lee's army could only put the enemy back a few miles to his works about Washington. General Johnston's opportunities were no better, and in addition to other difficulties, he was working under the avowed displeasure of the authorities, more trying than his trouble with the enemy.

I was under the impression that we could collect an army of twenty thousand men in South Carolina by stripping our forts and positions of all men not essential for defence; that that army could be quietly moved north by rail through Greenville to the borders of North Carolina, and promptly marched by Abingdon, Virginia, through the mountain passes, while my command covered the move by its position in East Tennessee. That army passing the mountains, my command could drop off by the left to its rear and follow into Kentucky,—the whole to march against the enemy's only line of railway from Louisville, and force him to loose his hold against General Johnston's front, and give the latter opportunity to advance his army and call all of his troops in Alabama and Mississippi to like advance, the grand junction of all of the columns to be made on or near the Ohio River,—General Beauregard to command the leading column, with orders not to make or accept battle until the grand junction was made. That General Johnston should have like orders against battle until he became satisfied of fruitful issues. The supplies and transportation for Beauregard to be collected at the head of the railroad, in advance of the movement of troops, under the ostensible purpose of hauling for my command. The arrangements perfected, the commander of the leading column to put his troops on the rail at or near Charleston and march with them as they arrived at the head of the road.

With this proposition I went to Virginia and submitted it to General Lee. He approved, and asked me to take it to the Richmond authorities. I objected that the mere fact of its coming from me would be enough to cause its rejection, and asked, if he approved, that he would take it and submit it as his own. He took me with him to Richmond, but went alone next morning to see the President. He met, besides the President, the Secretary of War and General Bragg. Conference was held during the forenoon, but was not conclusive. In the afternoon he called me with him for further deliberation.

At the opening of the afternoon council it appeared that General Bragg had offered a plan for early spring campaign, and that it had received the approval of the President,—viz.:

"General Johnston to march his army through the mountains of Georgia and East Tennessee to the head-waters of Little Tennessee River; my command to march through the mountains east of Knoxville to join General Johnston. The commands united, to march west, cross the river into Middle Tennessee, and march for the enemy's line of supplies about Nashville."

When asked an opinion of this, I inquired as to General Johnston's attitude towards it, and was told that he objected; that he thought the sparsely-settled country of the mountains through which he would move could not supply his army; that he would consume all that he could haul before turning westward for the middle country, and would be forced to active foraging from his first step between the two armies of the enemy.

General Lee inquired if General Johnston had maturely considered the matter. I thought that he had, and that the objections of the officer who was to conduct the campaign were, of themselves, reasons for overruling it; but its advocates were not ready to accept a summary disposal of their plans, and it began to transpire that the President had serious objections to General Beauregard as a commander for the field.

But General Lee called us to business, asking if anything more could be said in extenuation of General Johnston's objections. I called attention to General Bragg's official account of the battle of Chickamauga, in which he reported that a similar move had been proposed for him through Middle Tennessee towards the enemy's line of communication at Nashville early on the morning after the battle; that he rejected it, reported it "visionary"; said that it would leave his rear open to the enemy, and alluded to the country through which the march was proposed as "affording no subsistence to men or animals." This at harvest season, too! the enemy demoralized by the late battle, and the Confederates in the vigor of success! Now, after a winter of foraging by the Union armies, the country could not be so plethoric of supplies as to support us, while an active army was on each flank, better prepared to dispute our march.

General Lee wore his beard full, but neatly trimmed. He pulled at it nervously, and more vigorously as time and silence grew, until at last his suppressed emotion was conquered. The profound quiet of a minute or more seemed an hour. When he spoke, it was of other matters, but the air was troubled by his efforts to surrender hopeful anticipations to the caprice of empirics. He rose to take leave of the august presence, gave his hand to the President, and bowed himself out of the council chamber. His assistant went through the same forms, and no one approached the door to offer parting courtesy.

I had seen the general under severe trial before, especially on his Pennsylvania campaign when he found the cavalry under General Imboden had halted for rest at Hancock, at the opening of an aggressive movement. My similar experience with the President in the all-day talk, on Missionary Ridge, six months before, had better prepared me for the ordeal, and I drew some comfort from the reflection that others had their trials. General Lee took the next train for his army on the Rapidan, and I that by the direct route to my command by the Southside Railway.

When ordered from Virginia in September my wife remained in Petersburg with her good friend Mrs. Dunn. On the 20th of October following a son was born, and christened Robert Lee. After continuous field service since the 1st of July, 1861, I thought to avail myself of the privilege as department commander to take a two days' leave of absence to see the precious woman and her infant boy. While there it occurred to me to write to the President, and try to soften the asperities of the Richmond council; also to find a way to overcome the objections to General Beauregard. So I suggested that General Lee be sent to Tennessee and assigned to command. In reply the President sent a rebuke of my delay.

On my return to head-quarters at Greenville the other division of General Johnston's cavalry was ordered to him through the mountains. Just then a severe snow-storm came upon us and blocked all roads. Meanwhile, the enemy had mended his ways, secured munitions, and thought to march out from Mossy Creek as far as Morristown. Orders were given for a march to meet him, but we found ourselves in need of forage, so we rested in position, and presently learned that the enemy had retired towards his works.

Our reduced cavalry force made necessary a change of position behind the Holston River, where a small force could at least observe our flanks, and give notice of threatenings on either side.

A letter from the President under date of the 25th ordered that we be prepared to march to meet General Johnston for the campaign through Middle Tennessee. He was informed that we were ready, only needing supplies for the march and his orders; that I had cared for the bridges in that direction, so that there was no reason with us for delay.

On the 7th of April I was ordered, with the part of my command that had originally served with the Army of Northern Virginia, back to service with General Lee on the Rapidan. The move was made as soon as cars could be had to haul the troops, halting under orders at Charlottesville to meet a grand flanking move then anticipated. On the 22d we were ordered down as far as Mechanicsville, five miles west of Gordonsville, watching there for a lesser flank move. On the 29th, General Lee came out and reviewed the command.

Referring to the general officers who had been put under charges while in East Tennessee, General Robertson had been sentenced to suspension, and an excellent officer, General Gregg, had been sent to report, and was assigned to the Texas brigade. In the case of General McLaws, the court-martial ordered official reprimand, but the President disapproved the proceedings, passing reprimand upon the court and the commanding general, and ordered the officer to be restored to duty, which was very gratifying to me, who could have taken several reprimands to relieve a personal friend of embarrassing position. General McLaws was a classmate, and had been a warm personal friend from childhood. I had no desire to put charges against him, and should have failed to do so even under the directions of the authorities. I am happy to say that our personal relations are as close and interesting as they have ever been, and that his heart was big enough to separate official duties and personal relations.

Charges had been preferred against Brigadier-General E. M. Law for surreptitiously disposing of an official communication to the War Department that had been intrusted to his care, in which was enclosed his pretended resignation from the Confederate army. The President refused to entertain the charges, and ordered the officer released from arrest and restored to his command.

Of the paper that was improperly disposed of, General Cooper, adjutant and inspector-general of the army, reported,—

"The resignation within referred to never came to the office. It appears from inquiry at the War Department that it was presented by a friend of General Law, unofficially, to the Secretary of War, and never came through the regular channels as an official paper." *

General Lee wrote to the Department of the charges,—

"I examined the charges against General Law and find them of a very grave character. I think it due to General Law, as well as to the interest of the service, that they should be investigated and his innocence or guilt should be declared by a court-martial. There have been instances of officers obtaining indulgences on not true grounds, which I think discreditable and prejudicial to military discipline, and should be stopped." †

The indorsement of General Cooper shows that the paper was fraudulently handled. The letter of General Lee shows the offence a high crime and misdemeanor.

General Lee wrote to inform me that the authorities at Richmond had ordered General Law to be restored to duty with his command. The limit of endurance had thus been reached and passed. I ordered the rearrest of General Law upon his appearance within the limits of the command. To hold me at the head of the command while encouraging mutinous conduct in its ranks was beyond all laws and customs of war, and I wrote General Lee that my orders were out to have General Law again put under arrest, and that the case should be brought before a military tribunal, or I must be relieved of duty in the Confederate States service. The authorities then thought to find their way by transferring me to another command, but on that point General Lee became impatient, and inclined to serious thought and action. The commander of the army was involved as well as the commander of the First Corps, and both or neither must be relieved. The authorities halted, and that was the last that I heard of General Law until his newspaper articles began to appear, years after the surrender.

The following vote of thanks given by the Congress at

* Rebellion Record. † Ibid.

this juncture affords a remarkable commentary upon the conduct of the authorities, as well as constituting a compliment most heartily appreciated by the recipients:

"THANKS OF THE CONFEDERATE CONGRESS TO LIEUTENANT-GENERAL JAMES LONGSTREET AND HIS COMMAND.*

"No. 42.—JOINT RESOLUTIONS of thanks to Lieutenant-General Longstreet and the officers and men of his command.

"*Resolved by the Congress of the Confederate States of America*, That the thanks of Congress are due, and hereby cordially tendered, to Lieutenant-General James Longstreet and the officers and men of his command, for their patriotic services and brilliant achievements in the present war, sharing as they have the arduous fatigues and privations of many campaigns in Virginia, Maryland, Pennsylvania, Georgia, and Tennessee, and participating in nearly every great battle fought in those States, the commanding general ever displaying great ability, skill, and prudence in command, and the officers and men the most heroic bravery, fortitude, and energy, in every duty they have been called upon to perform.

"*Resolved*, That the President be requested to transmit a copy of the foregoing resolution to Lieutenant-General Longstreet for publication to his command.

"Approved February 17, 1864."

---

* Rebellion Record, vol. xxxi. part i. p. 549.

CHAPTER XXXVIII.

BATTLE OF THE WILDERNESS.

Campaign of 1864—General Grant in the Field—Strength of the Armies—Their Positions—Description of the Wilderness—The Battle opened—A Brisk Day's Fighting—Longstreet's Command faces Hancock's on the Morning of the Second Day—An Effective Flank Movement—General Wadsworth mortally wounded—General Jenkins falls under Fire of Friends, and Longstreet is seriously wounded—Carried from the Field on a Litter—Tribute to General Jenkins—Criticism and Controversy.

After reporting the return of my command to service with the Army of Northern Virginia, I took the earliest opportunity to suggest that the preliminaries of the campaign should be carefully confined to strategic manœuvre until we could show better generalship. That accomplished, I argued, the enemy's forces would lose confidence in the superiority of their leader's skill and prowess; that both armies were composed of intelligent, experienced veterans, who were as quick to discover the better handling of their ranks as trained generals; that by such successful manœuvres the Confederates would gain confidence and power as the enemy began to lose prestige; that then we could begin to look for a favorable opportunity to call the enemy to aggressive work, while immediate aggression from us against his greater numbers must make our labors heavy and more or less doubtful; that we should first show that the power of battle is in generalship more than in the number of soldiers, which, properly illustrated, would make the weaker numbers of the contention the stronger force.

In this connection I refer to the policy of *attrition* which became a prominent feature during part of the campaign, and showed that the enemy put his faith in numbers more than in superior skill and generalship.

General Grant made his head-quarters near the Army of the Potomac, in Culpeper County, Virginia, commanded by Major-General George G. Meade. It had been organized into three corps, Second, Fifth, and Sixth, commanded respectively by Major-General W. S. Hancock, Major-General G. K. Warren, and Major-General John Sedgwick, all in cantonment near Culpeper Court-House. The Ninth Corps was a distinct body reorganized under Major-General A. E. Burnside, and posted in co-operative position near the railroad bridge over the Rappahannock River. The aggregate of the two commands was about one hundred and thirty thousand men, classified as follows:

Army of the Potomac:	
Infantry present for duty, equipped (aggregate)	73,390
Cavalry (aggregate)	12,424
Artillery and engineers	2,764
Quartermaster's, subsistence, and medical departments, extra-duty men, and engineer brigade	19,183
Ninth Corps, present for duty, equipped	19,486
Total	127,247
But deducting extra-duty men, claimed as non-combatants	19,183
Leaves	108,064

These figures are from Major-General A. A. Humphreys, chief of staff of the Army of the Potomac. But General Badeau, in his "Military History of U. S. Grant," p. 94, gives as the exact numbers put into battle (after deducting a division of colored troops, not then used for battle service) the following:

Army of the Potomac	97,273
Ninth Corps	22,708
Total	119,981
From which he deducts the division of colored troops	3,095
Leaving	116,886

The Army of Northern Virginia stood on the west side of Rapidan River, Mine Run on its right, extending north, the left division, R. H. Anderson's, looking towards Madison Court-House; the Second and Third Corps, commanded by Lieutenant-Generals R. S. Ewell and A. P. Hill; two divisions and Alexander's artillery of Longstreet's (First) corps being held at Mechanicsville.

Colonel Taylor, chief of staff with the Army of Northern Virginia, gives the strength of the army at the opening of the campaign, from the returns of April 20, the latest up to date, as follows: *

Second Corps	17,093
Third Corps	22,199
Unattached commands, Maryland Line, etc.	1,125
"A liberal estimate," as he calls it, of my command	10,000
Total	50,417
Cavalry	8,727
Artillery corps	4,854
Making a total of	63,998

But General Badeau objects, on authority of a letter from General Bragg to General Joseph E. Johnston, stating that I had fourteen thousand men in my command. If General Bragg's letter referred to my command in East Tennessee it was accurate enough. But Buckner's division of that command, the cavalry, and other detachments were left in East Tennessee. General Badeau claims, besides, six thousand furloughed men and conscripts as joining the army between the 20th of April and the 4th of May. Of this there is no official record, and it is more than probable that new cases of sick and furloughed men of that interval were as many at least as the fragmentary parties that joined us. General Humphreys reported me as having fifteen thousand men. If he intended those figures as the strength of the First Corps, he is accurate enough, but Pickett's division of that corps was not with it, nor did it return to the Army of Northern Virginia until late in the campaign. So I find no

* "Four Years with General Lee."

good reason for changing the figures of Colonel Taylor, except so far as to add Johnson's brigade of Rodes's division, which is reported to have joined the Second Corps on the 6th of May,—estimated at 1500, which, added to 63,998, would make the total 65,498. But General Ewell's official account of numbers on the morning of the 6th of May puts his force at 15,500, which is better authority than Colonel Taylor's from the return of April 20, or General Badeau's computation. To these figures should be added Johnson's brigade, that reported later of the day, estimated by General Badeau at 1500, which makes the aggregate of the Second Corps 17,000, and brings that of the Army of Northern Virginia back to 65,405.

However, the numerical strength of armies should not be considered as of exclusive bearing upon the merits of the campaign. The commanders had chosen their battle after mature deliberation. They knew of each other's numbers and resources before they laid their plans, and they had even known each other personally for more than twenty years. Each had the undivided support and confidence of his government and his army, and it was time now to leave the past and give attention to the future.

General Lee had acquired fame as a strategist in his two years' service in the Army of Northern Virginia, and General Grant, by his three years' service in the West, had come to be known as an all-round soldier, seldom if ever surpassed; but the biggest part of him was his heart. They were equally pugnacious and plucky,—Grant the more deliberate.

Six months before the opening of the impending campaign, in November, 1863, General Meade, essaying a blow at the Army of Northern Virginia, crossed the Rapidan below General Lee's right, and deployed along the south side of Mine Run, but found Lee's line so strong and so improved by field-works that he felt constrained to withdraw without making battle.

As the purpose of this writing is to convey ideas of personal observations and experience, it will be confined, as far as practicable, to campaigns or parts of them with which I was directly or indirectly connected. So, when participants and partisans have passed away, I shall have contributed my share towards putting the historian in possession of evidence which he can weigh with that of other actors in the great drama.

At midnight of the 3d of May, 1864, the Army of the Potomac took its line of march for the lower crossings of the Rapidan River at Germania and Ely's Fords, the Fifth and Sixth Corps for the former, the Second for the latter, Wilson's division of cavalry leading the first, Gregg's the second column. The cavalry was to secure the crossings and lay bridges for the columns as they came up. Wilson's cavalry crossed at Germania ford, drove off the Confederate outpost, and began the construction of a bridge at daylight. Gregg also was successful, and the bridges were ready when the solid columns came. Warren's (Fifth Corps) crossed after Wilson's cavalry, marching westward as far as Wilderness Tavern. Sedgwick's corps followed and pitched camp near the crossing. Hancock's corps followed Gregg's cavalry, and made camp at Chancellorsville. Generals Grant and Meade went over after Warren's column and established head-quarters near the crossing. General Grant despatched for Burnside's corps to come and join him by night march. Sheridan was expected to engage Stuart's cavalry at Hamilton's Crossing near Fredericksburg.

General Grant had no fixed plan of campaign beyond the general idea to avoid the strong defensive line occupied by General Lee behind Mine Run, and find a way to draw him out to open battle.

The Wilderness is a forest land of about fifteen miles square, lying between and equidistant from Orange Court-House and Fredericksburg. It is broken occasionally by small farms and abandoned clearings, and two roads,—the Orange Plank road and the turnpike, which are cut at right angles by the Germania road,—in general course nearly parallel, open ways through it between Fredericksburg and the Court-House. The Germania Ford road joins the Brock road, the strategic line of the military zone, and crosses the turnpike at Wilderness Tavern and the Plank road about two miles south of that point.

Though the march was set on foot at midnight it was soon made known to General Lee, and its full purport was revealed by noon of the 4th, and orders were sent the different commanders for their march to meet the enemy,—the Second Corps (Ewell's) consisting of Rodes's, Johnson's, and Early's divisions, by the Orange Turnpike; the Third (A. P. Hill's)—R. H. Anderson's, Heth's, and Wilcox's divisions—by the Orange Plank road.

General Lee's signals were interpreted and sent to General Grant, who so far modified his plans as to prepare for immediate battle. The commands of the First Corps, Field's and Kershaw's divisions and Alexander's batteries, were stationed, Field's north of Gordonsville, where he had been posted on the 1st of May in anticipation of a move around our left, the other commands near Mechanicsville. We were ordered forward by the Plank road to Parker's Store; the order was received after one o'clock, and sent out for information of the commanders, who were ordered to prepare and march. But I asked for and received authority to march by a shorter route that would at the same time relieve the Plank road of pressure of troops and trains (for we had been crowded off the road once before by putting too many troops upon a single track). By the same despatch I asked and subsequently obtained leave to go on to the Brock road, where we could look for and hope to intercept the enemy's march, and cause him to develop plans before he could

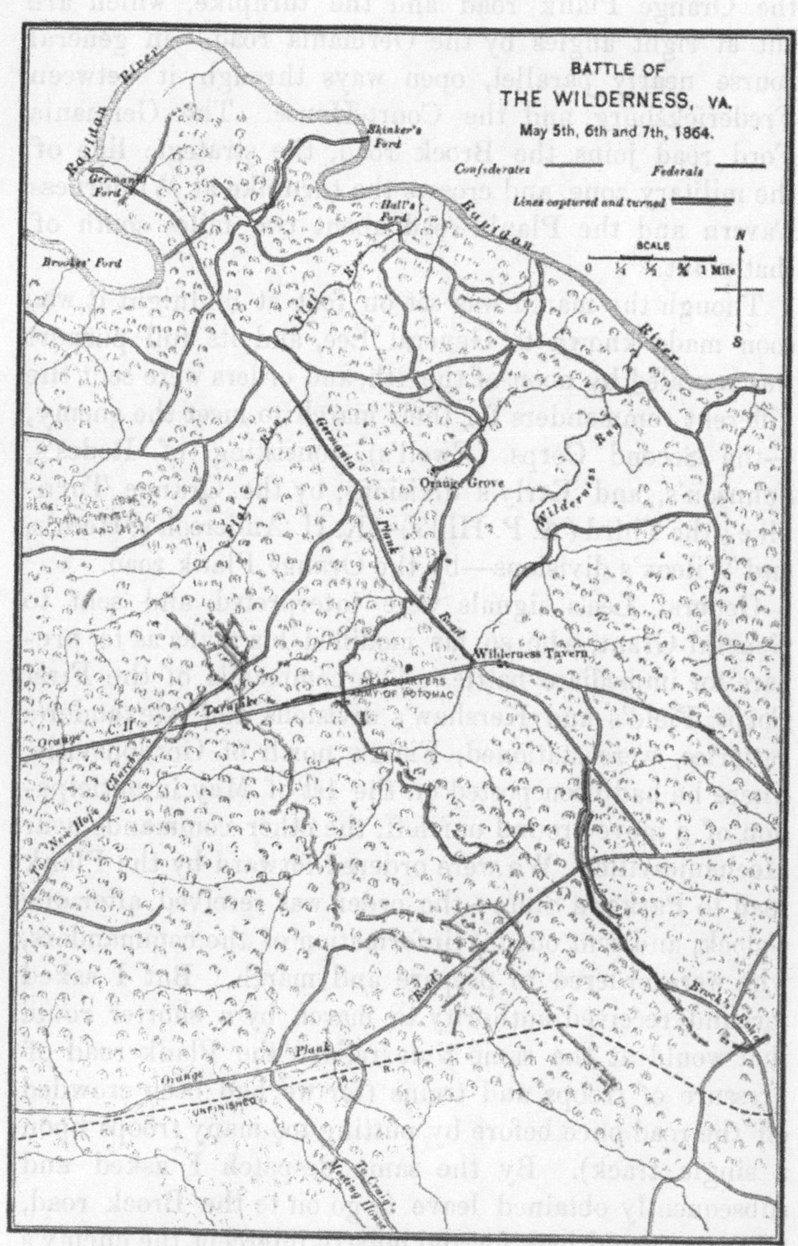

BATTLE OF
THE WILDERNESS, VA.
May 5th, 6th and 7th, 1864.
Confederates
Federals
Lines captured and turned
SCALE
0 ¼ ½ ¾ 1 Mile
N
S
Rapidan River
Rapidan River
Germanna Ford
Skinker's Ford
Hull's Ford
Brookes' Ford
Flat Run
Germanna Plank Road
Orange Grove
Wilderness Run
Wilderness Tavern
HEADQUARTERS ARMY OF POTOMAC
Turnpike
Orange C. H.
To New Hope Church
Brock's Road
Plank
Orange
Road
UNFINISHED
To Craig Meeting House

get out of the Wilderness. We marched at four o'clock by the Lawyer's road. Our chief quartermaster, Colonel Taylor, whose home was between Orange Court-House and the Wilderness, had been ordered to secure the services of the most competent guide to be found. We halted at Brock's Bridge for rest, and there Colonel Taylor brought up our guide, James Robinson, who had been for several years the sheriff of the county, and whose whole life had been spent in the Wilderness. The march was resumed, and continued with swinging step, with occasional rests, until we reached Richard's Shops, at five P.M. of the 5th. There we overtook Rosser's cavalry, engaged in severe encounter with part of Sheridan's. The enemy abandoned the contest and rode away, leaving his dead with some of ours on the field.

The distance of march was twenty-eight miles. Soon after my arrival at the shops, Colonel Venable, of general head-quarters staff, came with orders for a change of direction of the column through the wood to unite with the troops of the Third Corps on the Plank road. The rear of my column closed up at dark, and orders were sent to prepare to resume march at twelve o'clock. The accounts we had of the day's work were favorable to the Confederates; but the change of direction of our march was not reassuring.

In accordance with the general plan of turning the Confederate right without touching our intrenched line along Mine Run, the Army of the Potomac had been put in motion early on the 5th, the Second Corps towards Shady Grove Church by the Todd's Tavern road, the Fifth by the dirt road towards Parker's Store on the Plank road, the Sixth on the right, to follow the Fifth as movements developed. General Warren moved with three divisions, leaving Griffin's on the turnpike. Presently, after taking up his march towards Parker's Store, the Confederates were discovered on the Plank road, and

General Meade ordered the corps made ready for battle. The Sixth, except Getty's division, was ordered to make connection on the right of the Fifth by wood roads, and prepare for the battle. Getty's division was ordered to the Plank road at the Brock road crossing, to hold that point at all hazards until the Second Corps could join it, the latter being recalled from Todd's Tavern for that holding and developments there indicated.

At noon General Warren was prepared on the turnpike and attacked with Griffin's and Wadsworth's divisions.

General Lee's orders were against a general engagement until his forces were in hand, but the troops had met and action could not wait. Warren's attack had some success, as by his orders General Ewell felt called upon to delay battle, but a sudden dash of the enemy broke into disorder his brigade under J. M. Jones, also Battle's brigade; but other of his troops joined them, recovered his ground, drove off the attacking forces, taking two guns, and called Warren's corps to better concentration. The Sixth was to be with Warren, but was delayed by the narrow, tangled roads till night. General Ewell prepared for the next day by intrenching his front.

Meanwhile, General Hill had pushed the divisions under Heth and Wilcox along the Plank road until they were near the Brock road crossing, occupied by Getty's division of the Sixth Corps.

General Getty was in time to drive back a few of our men who had reached the Brock road in observation, and Hancock's corps joined him at two P.M., fronting his divisions—Birney's, Mott's, Gibbon's, and Barlow's—along the Brock road, on the left of Getty's. His artillery was massed on his left, near Barlow, except a battery nearer the Plank road, and one section at the crossing. He ordered his line intrenched.

As soon as he found his troops in hand at the cross-roads, General Meade ordered them into action. Getty's division, supported by the Second Corps, was to drive Hill back, occupy Parker's Store, and connect with Warren's line. He afterwards learned of the repulse of Warren on the turnpike, but repeated his orders for the advance on the Plank road. At 4.15 Getty's division advanced, and met the divisions of Heth and Wilcox a few hundred yards in advance of their trenches.

In the fierce engagement that followed, Birney's and Mott's divisions were engaged on Getty's left, and later the brigades of Carroll and Owen, of Gibbon's division. Wadsworth's division and Baxter's brigade of the Fifth Corps were put in to aid Getty's right. The combination forced Heth and Wilcox back about half a mile, when the battle rested for the night. Hancock reinforced his front by Webb's brigade of Gibbon's division, and was diligently employed at his lines during the night putting up field-works.

About eleven o'clock in the night the guide reported from General Lee to conduct my command through the wood across to the Plank road, and at one o'clock the march was resumed. The road was overgrown by the bushes, except the side-tracks made by the draft animals and the ruts of wheels which marked occasional lines in its course. After a time the wood became less dense, and the unused road was more difficult to follow, and presently the guide found that there was no road under him; but no time was lost, as, by ordering the lines of the divisions doubled, they were ready when the trail was found, and the march continued in double line. At daylight we entered the Plank road, and filed down towards the field of strife of the afternoon of the 5th and daylight of the 6th.

R. H. Anderson's division of the Third Corps, marching on the Plank road, had rested at Verdierville during the night, and was called to the front in the morning.

The divisions of Heth and Wilcox rested during the night of the 5th where the battle of that day ceased, but did not prepare ammunition nor strengthen their lines for defence, because informed that they were to be relieved from the front. Both the division commanders claim that they were to be relieved, and that they were ordered not to intrench or replenish supplies. So it seems that they were all night within hearing of the voices of Hancock's men, not even reorganizing their lines so as to offer a front of battle! General Heth has stated that he proposed to arrange for battle, but was ordered to give his men rest. While Hancock was sending men to his advanced line during the night and intrenching there and on his second line, the Confederates were all night idle.

Hancock advanced and struck the divisions before sunrise, just as my command reported to General Lee. My line was formed on the right and left of the Plank road, Kershaw on the right, Field on the left. As the line deployed, the divisions of Heth and Wilcox came back upon us in disorder, more and more confused as their steps hurried under Hancock's musketry. As my ranks formed the men broke files to give free passage for their comrades to the rear. The advancing fire was getting brisk, but not a shot was fired in return by my troops until the divisions were ready. Three of Field's brigades, the Texas, Alabama, and Benning's Georgia, were formed in line on the left of the road, and three of Kershaw's on the right. General Lee, appalled at the condition of affairs, thought to lead the Texas brigade alone into desperate charge, before my lines were well formed. The ordeal was trying, but the steady troops, seeing him off his balance, refused to follow, begged him to retire, and presently Colonel Venable, of his staff, reported to me General Lee's efforts to lead the brigade, and suggested that I should try to call him from it. I asked that he would say, with my compliments, that his line would be recovered in an hour if he would permit me to handle the troops, but if my services were not needed, I would like to ride to some place of safety, as it was not quite comfortable where we were.

As full lines of battle could not be handled through the thick wood, I ordered the advance of the six brigades by heavy skirmish lines, to be followed by stronger supporting lines. Hancock's lines, thinned by their push through the wood, and somewhat by the fire of the disordered divisions, weaker than my line of fresh and more lively skirmishers, were checked by our first steady, rolling fire, and after a brisk fusillade were pushed back to their intrenched line, when the fight became steady and very firm, occasionally swinging parts of my line back and compelling the reserves to move forward and recover it.

General Lee sent General M. L. Smith, of the engineers, to report to me. He was ordered through the wood on my right to the unfinished railroad to find a way around the left of the enemy's line, while we engaged his front. R. H. Anderson's division of the Third Corps came up about eight o'clock and was ordered to report to me.

Hancock's early advance was under a general order including the Army of the Potomac. The Ninth Corps that had been called up reported to General Grant, and was ordered in between the Plank and Turnpike roads. At eight o'clock Hancock was reinforced by Stevenson's division of the Ninth, and Wadsworth of the Fifth was put under his orders. At nine o'clock he attacked with Wadsworth's, Birney's, Stevenson's, and Mott's divisions, and the brigades of Webb, Carroll, and Owen, of Gibbon's division, making as formidable battle as could be organized in the wood, but the tangle thinned his lines and our fire held him in desperate engagement.

Two divisions of the Ninth Corps, at the same time marching for Parker's Store, were encountered between the Plank and Turnpike roads by our Second Corps (Ewell's). Under this combination the forces struggled an hour at the extreme tension of skill and valor.

About ten o'clock General Smith returned and reported favorably of his reconnoissance: that the heavy woodland concealed the route of the proposed flank march, and that there was no force of the enemy in observation. Hancock's left on the Brock road was in strong, well-guarded position, but there was room along its front for our troops to march near the unfinished railroad beyond view of that left on the Brock road.

General Smith was then asked to take a small party and pass beyond the Brock road and find a way for turning the extreme Union left on that road. There were two brigades of Field's division and one of Kershaw's not on the line of battle, but on flank march as supports, and R. H. Anderson's division of the Third Corps. Colonel Sorrel, chief of staff, was ordered to conduct three brigades, G. T. Anderson's of Field's, Mahone's of R. H. Anderson's, and Wofford's of Kershaw's division, by the route recommended by General Smith, have them faced to the left, and marched down against Hancock's left. Davis's brigade of the Third Corps also got into this command.

As soon as the troops struck Hancock his line began to break, first slowly, then rapidly. Somehow, as they retreated, a fire was accidentally started in the dry leaves, and began to spread as the Confederates advanced. Mahone's brigade approached the burning leaves and part of it broke off a little to get around, but the Twelfth Virginia was not obstructed by the blaze and moved directly on. At the Plank road Colonel Sorrel rode back to join us. All of the enemy's battle on the right of the Plank road was broken up, and General Field was fighting severely with his three brigades on the left against Wadsworth and Stevenson, pushing them a little.

The Twelfth Virginia Regiment got to the Plank road some little time before the other regiments of the brigade, and, viewing the contention on the farther side between Field's and Wadsworth's divisions, dashed across and struck the left of Wadsworth's line. This relieved Field a little, and, under this concentrating push and fire, Wadsworth fell mortally wounded. In a little while followed the general break of the Union battle. The break of his left had relieved Kershaw's troops, and he was waiting for the time to advance, and Jenkins's brigade that had been held in reserve and that part of R. H. Anderson's division not in use were ready and anxious for opportunity to engage, and followed as our battle line pushed forward.

General Smith then came and reported a way across the Brock road that would turn Hancock's extreme left. He was asked to conduct the flanking brigades and handle them as the ranking officer. He was a splendid tactician as well as skilful engineer, and gallant withal. He started, and, not to lose time or distance, moved by inversion, Wofford's left leading, Wofford's favorite manœuvre. As Wofford's left stepped out, the other troops moved down the Plank road, Jenkins's brigade by the road, Kershaw's division alongside. I rode at the head of the column, Jenkins, Kershaw, and the staff with me. After discussing the dispositions of their troops for reopening battle, Jenkins rode closer to offer congratulations, saying, "I am happy; I have felt despair of the cause for some months, but am relieved, and feel assured that we will put the enemy back across the Rapidan before night." Little did he or I think these sanguine words were the last he would utter.

When Wadsworth fell the Union battle broke up in hasty retreat. Field's brigades closed to fresh ranks, the flanking brigades drew into line near the Plank road, and with them the other regiments of Mahone's brigade; but the Twelfth Regiment, some distance in advance of the others, had crossed the road to strike at Wadsworth's left before the other regiments were in sight, and was returning to find its place in line. The order for the flanking brigades to resume march by their left had not moved those brigades of the right. As the Twelfth Regiment marched back to find its place on the other side of the Plank road, it was mistaken, in the wood, for an advance of the enemy, and fire was opened on it from the other regiments of the brigade. The men threw themselves to the ground to let the fire pass. Just then our party of officers was up and rode under the fire. General Jenkins had not finished the expressions of joyful congratulations which I have quoted when he fell mortally wounded.

Captain Doby and the orderly, Bowen, of Kershaw's staff, were killed. General Kershaw turned to quiet the troops, when Jenkins's brigade with levelled guns were in the act of returning the fire of the supposed enemy concealed in the wood, but as Kershaw's clear voice called out "*F-r-i-e-n-d-s!*" the arms were recovered, without a shot in return, and the men threw themselves down upon their faces.

At the moment that Jenkins fell I received a severe shock from a minie ball passing through my throat and right shoulder. The blow lifted me from the saddle, and my right arm dropped to my side, but I settled back to my seat, and started to ride on, when in a minute the flow of blood admonished me that my work for the day was done. As I turned to ride back, members of the staff, seeing me about to fall, dismounted and lifted me to the ground.

Orders were given General Field, the senior officer present, to push on before the enemy could have time to rally. The two lines marching along the Plank road, southward, in pursuit, and the flanking brigades to move in the other direction, were, for the moment, a little perplexing, as he was not accurately advised of the combina-

THE WOUNDING OF GENERAL LONGSTREET AT THE WILDERNESS, MAY 6, 1864.

tions, but he grasped the situation. Before he was prepared, however, General R. H. Anderson came into command as senior, and then General Lee came up. The plans, orders, and opportunity were explained to him, but the woods concealed everything except the lines of troops alongside the road. General Lee did not care to handle the troops in broken lines, and ordered formation in a general line for parallel battle. The change in the forest tangle consumed several hours of precious time, and gave General Hancock time to collect his men into battle order, post his heavy reinforcements, and improve his intrenchments.

After several hours of work our new line was finally adjusted and ordered forward. It approached the enemy's stronghold (in ranks a little thinned by the march through the wood and the enemy's fire), made desperate and repeated charges, and Jenkins's gallant brigade mounted their breastworks, but the solid ranks behind them threw it off, with the lines that essayed to give it support, and the whole were forced back from their fight. Thus the battle, lost and won three times during the day, wore itself out.

General Ewell found opportunity before night to push some of his brigades around the enemy's right, and did clever work in taking a number of prisoners,—Generals Seymour and Shaler among them,—but it was too late in the day to follow his work with a strong fight. He handled his troops with skill and care, putting defensive works before them whenever they halted.

Like attention by General Hancock may be noted; while in marked contrast was the conduct of the Third Corps after their affair on the afternoon of the 5th. The commanders of the leading divisions of the Third had proposed to prepare their troops for the next day, but were ordered to give their men rest,* and told that they

* General Heth's personal account.

were to be relieved and withdrawn from the battle. Not even a line of battle was formed, so that they were in disorder when they were struck in the morning, and speedily fell into confusion.

My command, less than ten thousand, had found the battle on the Plank road in retreat, little less than a panic. In a few hours we changed defeat to victory, the broken divisions of the Third Corps rallying in their rear.

As my litter was borne to the rear my hat was placed over my face, and soldiers by the road-side said, "He is dead, and they are telling us he is only wounded." Hearing this repeated from time to time, I raised my hat with my left hand, when the burst of voices and the flying of hats in the air eased my pains somewhat.

But Micah Jenkins, who fell by the same fire, was no more. He was one of the most estimable characters of the army. His taste and talent were for military service. He was intelligent, quick, untiring, attentive, zealous in discharge of duty, truly faithful to official obligations, abreast with the foremost in battle, and withal a humble, noble Christian. In a moment of highest earthly hope he was transported to serenest heavenly joy; to that life beyond that knows no bugle call, beat of drum, or clash of steel. May his beautiful spirit, through the mercy of God, rest in peace! Amen!

"*L'audace, l'audace, toujours l'audace.*" An Americanism which seems an appropriate substitute is, *A level head, a level head, always a level head.* With patience to wait ten minutes to see my flanking brigades stretched out on their march to retrieve my *aplomb*, we could have found a good battle against Hancock's strong left, while we broke over his confused front. Fearing another change of plan, I hurried on to execute before it could be ordered.

There were twenty-two thousand men in the Third Corps. It is not claiming too much, therefore, to say that

that corps, carefully prepared during the night of the 5th, could have held Hancock's battle on the morning of the 6th.

Under these conditions events support the claim that the Third Corps, intrenched in their advanced position, with fresh supplies and orders to hold their ground, could have received and held against Hancock's early battle until my command could have come in on his left rear and completed a strongly organized battle by which we could have carried the Wilderness, even down and into the classic Rapidan.

General Field says, in his account of the day,—

"I was at Longstreet's side in a moment, and in answer to my anxious inquiry as to his condition, he replied that he would be looked after by others, and directed me to take command of the corps and push ahead. Though at this moment he could not have known the extent or character of his wounds (that they were severe was apparent), he seemed to forget himself in the absorbing interest of the movement he was making.

"Had our advance not been suspended by this disaster, I have always believed that Grant would have been driven across the Rapidan before night; but General Lee was present, and ordered that our line, which was nearly a right angle (my division being the base, and Kershaw's and the other flanking force the perpendicular), should first be straightened out. The difficulty of manœuvring through the brush made this a tedious operation, so that when we did advance with large reinforcements from Ewell's corps placed under my orders, the enemy was found awaiting us behind new breastworks, thoroughly prepared."

Colonel Fairfax says,—

"On reaching the line of troops you were taken off the horse and propped against a tree. You blew the bloody foam from your mouth and said, 'Tell General Field to take command, and move forward with the whole force and gain the Brock road,' but hours were lost." *

---

* Letter to the writer.

A Northern historian says,—

"It seemed, indeed, that irretrievable disaster was upon us; but in the very torrent and tempest of the attack it suddenly ceased and all was still. What could cause this surcease of effort at the very height of success was then wholly unknown to us." *

Some years after the affair on the Plank road, General Hancock said to me,—

"You rolled me up like a wet blanket, and it was some hours before I could reorganize for battle."

He explained that reinforcements crowding up through the wood, the retreating troops, and confusion caused by mixing in with wagon-trains and horses, made a troublesome tangle, but it was unravelled and his troops at rest when the final attack was made. He had sixty thousand men in hand.

Bad as was being shot by some of our own troops in the battle of the Wilderness,—that was an honest mistake, one of the accidents of war,—being shot at, since the war, by many officers, was worse. Fitzhugh Lee wrote of me in the Southern Historical Society papers, vol. v., No. 4, April, 1878, saying, among other things, "He lost his way and reached the Wilderness twenty-four hours behind time."

Now, from Mechanicsville to Parker's Store by our line of march was thirty-four miles,—by the Plank road, thirty-five; from Parker's Store to the battle, three miles. From the time of our march to going into battle was thirty-six hours, including all of two nights. Deducting twenty-four hours alleged as lost leaves twelve hours, including all night of the 4th, for the march of thirty-seven miles!

His logic and method of injury remind one of the French teacher who, when out of patience with the boys, used to say, "I will give you zero and mark you absent."

---

* Decisive Battles of the War, Swinton, p. 378.

Another report started by Fitzhugh Lee as coming from his cousin, G. W. C. Lee, was that General Lee said that he "sent an officer to Longstreet to stay with and show him the roads."

This, like all other reported sayings of General Lee in regard to me, was not published until after General Lee's death. When it was first published I wrote General G. W. C. Lee for the name of the officer sent. He referred me to the members of General Lee's staff. Not one of them knew of the circumstance or the officer, but referred me to General Lee's engineers. After long search I found the engineers and applied for information, but not one of them knew anything of the alleged fact. I had the letters published as an advertisement for the officer who was claimed as my guide. No response came. I inquired of the members of the staff, First Corps; not one had seen or heard of such a person. The quartermaster, Colonel Taylor, who was ordered to secure a competent guide at the first moment of receipt of orders to march, reported of the matter thus:

"MEADOW FARM, ORANGE COURT-HOUSE,
"July 1, 1879.

"GENERAL JAMES LONGSTREET:

"DEAR GENERAL,—Your favor of the 30th ultimo is this moment to hand, and I reply at once. I think General Fitzhugh Lee entirely in error as to any engineer or other officer being sent to guide you in the spring of 1864 from your camp near Gordonsville to the Wilderness. I well remember your sending for me, and directing me to procure a guide for you, which I did after some difficulty in the person of Mr. James Robinson, the then sheriff of the county. I saw no such person, nor can I think that any such was at any time at our quarters before we broke camp.

"Sincerely yours,
"ERASMUS TAYLOR."

These efforts to secure one witness in support of the allegation, or rather to prove a negation, were all that occurred to me at the time, and now I can think of but one more chance, which is for Fitzhugh Lee to offer a liberal reward. It is not probable that he would fail to find a false witness who could answer for a time to support the false charges.

It may be added that the accounts of the march by other officers agree with mine, as already given. I present here a letter from General Alexander and an extract from one written me by Colonel Venable. The former says,—

"AUGUSTA, GA., June 12, 1879.

"MY DEAR GENERAL,—Absence prevented an earlier response to your favor of the 5th. My recollection of the events is as follows: My command, the artillery, got orders to move about noon on May 4, 1864, being in camp near Mechanicsville, some four or five miles west of Gordonsville. We marched about four P.M., and with only short rests all night and all next day till about five P.M., when we halted to rest and bivouac at a point which I cannot remember; but our cavalry had had a skirmish there with the enemy's cavalry just before our arrival, and I remember seeing some killed and wounded of each side. Your whole corps, Hood's and McLaws's, and the artillery, I think, was concentrated at that point, and my recollection is that we had orders to move on during the night, or before daylight the next morning, to get on the enemy's left flank on the Brock road.

"But whatever the orders were, I remember distinctly that during the night news of the fight on the Plank road came, and with it a change of orders, and that we marched at one A.M., or earlier, and turned to the left and struck the Plank road at Parker's Store, and pushed rapidly down it to where the battle had already begun. I remember, too, that the march was so hurried that at one point, the head of the leading division (I forget which it was, however) having lost a little distance by taking the wrong road, the rear division was not allowed to halt, but pushed right on, so that it got abreast of the leading division, and the two came down the road side by side, filling the whole road and crowding the retreating men of the divisions which were being driven back into the woods on each side.

"These are facts as I recollect them, and while I don't know what your orders were, I remember that there was a change in them during the night, according to my understanding, and that the change was as promptly and vigorously and successfully carried out as time and distance could possibly permit. There was certainly *no loss of time* from the moment we received orders to the moment we went under fire in the Wilderness, as the distance covered will show.

"Very truly yours,

"E. P. ALEXANDER.

"GENERAL LONGSTREET."

Colonel Venable writes,—

"July 25, 1879.

"DEAR GENERAL,— . . . Well, the morning came. The enemy attacked Wilcox and Heth before your arrival. Disaster seemed imminent. I was sent to meet you and hasten your march. I met your two divisions within less than half a mile of the battle-field coming up in parallel columns very rapidly (I was going to say in double-quick) on the Plank road, side by side, and that they came in grandly, forming line of battle, Kershaw on the right and Field on the left, restoring the battle. It was superb, and my heart beats quicker to think about it even at this distance of time. . . .

"Yours, very truly,

"CHARLES S. VENABLE.

"GENERAL LONGSTREET."

CHAPTER XXXIX.

AGAIN IN FRONT OF RICHMOND.

Longstreet absent on Leave, nursing his Wounds—Hears of the Death of Cavalry Leader J. E. B. Stuart—Returns to Virginia—Assigned to Command on the North Side of James River—Affair on the Williamsburg Road—Lee's Apprehension of Grant's March into Richmond—Closing Scenes of the Campaign of 1864 about the Confederate Capital—General Benjamin F. Butler's Move against Fort Fisher—Remote Effects on the Situation in Virginia.

FROM the Wilderness I was taken to the Meadow Farm home of my friend Erasmus Taylor, and carefully nursed by his charming wife until put on board of a train for Lynchburg and taken to my good kinswoman, Mrs. Caroline Garland, who had lost her only son and child, General Samuel Garland, killed two years before at South Mountain. From her hospitable home, when strong enough for a ride in the fresh air, I was taken to the home of a cherished friend, Colonel John D. Alexander, at Campbell Court-House. But a raiding party rode through the village early one morning, which suggested a change, and I was taken to my kinsfolk, the Sibleys, at Augusta, Georgia, and after a time to other good friends, the Harts and Daniels, at and near Union Point, on the Georgia Railroad.

Before I was strong enough to sit more than a few minutes news came of the change of commanders in the Army of Georgia,—the superseding of General Joseph E. Johnston by assignment of General J. B. Hood, and I was asked to take command of the corps left vacant by assignment of General Hood. Answer was made that when able for duty I would be prepared to obey orders.

Later came sadder news from Virginia announcing the fall of our Cavalier J. E. B. Stuart. The most famous

American rider fell mortally wounded on the 18th of May, 1864, near Yellow Tavern, in a cavalry engagement with General Sheridan, just then budding into fame. Stuart, endowed by nature with the gifts that go to make a perfect cavalryman, improved and cultivated through years of active warfare, experience, and discipline, was the embodiment of all that goes to make up the ideal soldierly character,—the bold, dashing dragoon. His death was possibly a greater loss to the Confederate army even than that of the swift-moving General "Stonewall" Jackson. Through all the vicissitudes of war he held his troopers beside him peerless in prowess and discipline. After his fall their decline came swifter than their upbuilding had been accomplished by his magic hand.

In society he was gay, bright, and genial, abstemious to a degree. In idle hours of week-days he was fond of his banjo-player, Sweeny, but he was devout withal, and to him the grandest, sweetest music was "Rock of Ages." To this day that sublime air never fails to bring before my mind's vision his noble figure. May his great spirit rest near "The Rock of Ages" always! Amen!

About the 1st of October I was strong enough to ride horseback, and after a little practice, and having become weary of idle hours, took leave of wife and children, and travelled back to Richmond to find our great commander and his noble followers.

The general seemed worn by past labor, besides suffering at seasons from severe sciatica, while his work was accumulating and his troubles multiplying to proportions that should have employed half a dozen able men. The military staff of his head-quarters was made up of excellent, intelligent, active, zealous young men, more than anxious to anticipate his wants and to meet their official obligations, and it is a source of gratification to write that they were efficient, affectionate, admirable, and polite. But facts will not justify like commendation of the purveying department. Complaints had been made early in the war and continued of our inefficient subsistence department at Richmond. The diminishing resources of the country called for exceptionally earnest, methodical business faculties in that department, but, unfortunately, as our resources became more circumscribed, the officers, instead of putting forth stronger efforts in their business, seemed to lose the energy of their former service, and General Lee found himself called upon to feed as well as fight his army. Although anxious to assist in his severe trials, and relieve him of part of his work, I feared that he might think a cripple an additional incumbrance, and wrote the chief of staff,—

"RANDOLPH'S HOUSE,
"NEAR RICHMOND, VA., October 18, 1864.

"COLONEL W. H. TAYLOR,
"*Assistant Adjutant-General*:

"SIR,—I have not reported formally for duty, because I doubted the propriety of being assigned, in my crippled condition, to position now filled by officers of vigorous health. If I can be of service in any position, I prefer to go to duty. If there is nothing to which I can be assigned on this side of the Mississippi River, without displacing an efficient officer, I will cheerfully accept service in the Trans-Mississippi Department.

"The doctors give me little reason to hope to recover the use of my arm even within a year; hence my desire to be assigned for duty, or to have an extended leave of absence.

"Very respectfully, your obedient servant,
"J. LONGSTREET,
"*Lieutenant-General*."

An order came assigning me to command on the north side of James River and Drury's Bluff, and Pickett's division on the south side, along Bermuda Hundred front as far as Swift Creek. On the north side were the local defence troops under Lieutenant-General Ewell, and Hoke's and Field's divisions and Gary's brigade of one thousand cavalry.

There had been severe fighting on that side a few days previous, in an attack of the Federals upon Fort Harrison of our line, which resulted in the capture of the fort; then a more desperate fight of the Confederates to recover it, which was not successful. The loss of Fort Harrison broke our line off a little near the river, and caused a new line to be taken from that point to our left, where it joined the line occupied in 1862, when General McClellan was against us. The line of the north side extended from Chapin's Bluff on the James River, by Fort Gilmer, across north of White Oak Swamp to the vicinity of the Chickahominy at New Bridge. Hoke's and Field's divisions occupied the line from Fort Gilmer, covering Charles City road on the left, and Gary's cavalry had a strong picket force on the Nine Miles road, with vedettes, to guard and patrol the west side of the swamp and the south side of the Chickahominy. The crossings of the swamp were heavily obstructed by fallen timber. The batteries at Chapin's and Drury's Bluffs were manned by officers of the navy and sailors, and other organized artillery and infantry, and the local defence contingent lined out towards Fort Gilmer. My men had become experts in fortifying, so that parapets and dams along the front grew apace. Our officers during their experience in East Tennessee had become skilled as foragers, and soon began to find in nooks and corners of Northern Virginia food and forage which relieved General Lee of the trouble of supplying the men on the north side, and my troops were beginning to feel comfortable. But there were more serious embarrassments on the south side, and desertions were becoming more numerous from day to day.

Towards the latter part of October, General Grant conceived a plan by which he proposed to extend and advance his left, so as to get the Southside Railroad and connect this new point with his line of intrenchments. At the same time he thought to have General Butler on his extreme right break through the lines on the north side into Richmond. For his left attack he ordered the Second Corps, under Hancock, to be supported by parts of the Fifth and Ninth Corps. General Lee had his Third Corps (A. P. Hill's), Heth's and Wilcox's divisions and Mahone's in reserve. Hancock's advance was met by Mahone's division, and the entire march of the different commands was arrested after a severe rencounter, in which Mahone got a number of prisoners and some pieces of artillery,—the latter not brought off, as the enemy held the bridge.

According to the reports of the Adjutant-General's Office the Federal losses were 1284. The Confederate losses were not accurately accounted for, but the Federal accounts claimed two hundred prisoners taken at one time, and other losses equal to their own.

I was informed of troops crossing the bridge to the north side on the 25th, and that the crossings continued at intervals till after the night of the 26th. The plan of operations contemplated that General Butler should have "twenty thousand men north of the James where Longstreet was now in command."* These were parts of the Tenth and Eighteenth Corps, commanded by Generals Terry and Weitzel. General Terry was to make a fierce demonstration against our front along the Darby and Charles City roads with the Tenth, while General Weitzel was to march the Eighteenth across White Oak Swamp and get in the unoccupied lines on the Williamsburg road, or between that and Gary's cavalry on the Nine Miles road.

Early on the 27th, General Terry moved out with the Tenth Corps and made demonstration for formidable attack, putting his infantry in sharp practice along the outer edge of our abatis, and his artillery in practice near

---

* Military History of U. S. Grant. Badeau.

the roads. Our sharp-shooters opened in reply from behind their breastworks and held a lively rattle of musketry for quite a time. The delay in making more serious work told me that some other was the point of danger, which must mean the unoccupied lines beyond White Oak Swamp. Field was ordered to pull his division out of the works and march for the Williamsburg road, Hoke to cover the line of Field by extending and doubling his sharp-shooters.

When the head of General Field's column got to the Williamsburg road the enemy's skirmishers were deployed and half-way across the field approaching our line. Just behind the trenches was a growth of pines which concealed our troops until a line of sharp-shooters stepped into the works. Their fire surprised the enemy somewhat, as they had seen nothing but part of Gary's cavalry, and their skirmish line gave up the field for their heavy infantry.

The open in front of the breastworks was about six hundred yards wide and twelve hundred in length, extending from the York River Railroad on the north to a ditch draining towards the head of White Oak Swamp on the south. About midway of the field is a slight depression or swale of five or six feet.

Quickly following the repulse of the skirmish line, and just as Field had adjusted the infantry and artillery to their trenches, came the Eighteenth Corps bursting into the open and deploying on both sides of the road in solid ranks. They were at once in fair canister range, and soon under the terrific fire of a solid line of infantry,—infantry so experienced that they were not likely to throw as much as one bullet without well-directed aim. At the first fire they began to drop, and they fell more rapidly until they reached the swale, when the entire line dropped to the ground. They had just enough cover there for their bodies as they spread themselves closely to the ground, but not enough to permit them to load or rise to deliver fire without exposing their persons to our fire. To attempt to retreat would have been as disastrous as to advance; so they were entrapped.

General Gary reported that the field of the Nine Miles road was clear, and was ordered to come in on the flank of the entrapped infantry and order surrender; but before he was there another report reached him of a formidable force advancing against his squadron on the Nine Miles road. He was sent on a gallop to meet this. Meanwhile, the troops hiding under the swell of ground found ways to drop off on their right under the railroad cut, and many others got away down the dry ditch on their left, until Captain Lyle, of the Fifth South Carolina Regiment, got a force out on the flank and secured the surrender of the remainder. He picked up about six hundred prisoners.

General Gary's guard on the Nine Miles road held an open work by a section of artillery and a squadron of cavalry. The advance against it was so well executed, and our cavalry so interested in the operations on the Williamsburg road, that the guard was taken by surprise and pushed away from its post by the first attack, losing its field-works and a piece of artillery. Gary soon made amends for the careless watch by dismounting his brigade and marching in line of battle at right angles to the line of the enemy, striking him in flank, recovering the lost cannon, and driving him back the way he came. Under cover of the night the Federals returned to their fortified lines, where they were as strong as were the lines held by the Confederates in their front.

The Confederates lost: Field's division, 45; Gary's cavalry, 8; artillery, 11; total, 64. Federal "losses, killed, wounded, and missing, 1103." *

*** Virginia Campaigns, 1864-65, by General A. A. Humphreys, Army of the Potomac.**

General Grant sent orders to have the positions gained by his left held and intrenched, but they were abandoned because they were weak in the too extended line.

After the loss of Fort Harrison, General Lee became more anxious for his line on the north side, and rode out to witness the operations on that front, under the threatening of Butler's forces; and as our cavalry had made no report of the enemy crossing the swamp, he was not quite satisfied to have the troops moved over to the Williamsburg road, but did not order them retained. His idea was that the north side was the easier route of Grant's triumphal march into Richmond, and that sooner or later he would make his effort there in great force.

These were the closing scenes between the armies about Richmond and Petersburg for the year 1864. The defeat of General Early in the Valley of Virginia on the 19th of October concluded active work in that quarter. Most of Sheridan's infantry was sent back to the Army of the Potomac, and the greater part of Early's to the Army of Northern Virginia.

Kershaw's division of the First Corps had been left with General Early for his battle of the 19th of October. In his account of the battle, General Early alludes to its outcome and finality as a causeless panic started by the break of his left division under General Gordon, followed by Kershaw's and other troops. It is sufficient for this writing to say that the general called the rout "thorough and disgraceful, mortifying beyond measure: we had within our grasp a great and glorious victory, and lost it by the uncontrollable propensity of our men for plunder." *

Kershaw's division was restored to duty with the First Corps in November.

Late in December I was informed of a move of the

---

* General Early's official account.

enemy's land and naval forces for Fort Fisher about Wilmington harbor. The information was despatched to General Lee at Petersburg, and brought a midnight order for me to send Hoke's division to Wilmington. Hoke was relieved and on the move before daylight. General Bragg was relieved of duty at Richmond and ordered to Wilmington.

General Butler was in command of the land forces and Admiral Porter of the navy. Between them, or under the direction of one or the other, was the steamer "Louisiana," freighted with about two hundred and fifty tons of gunpowder intended to blow up Fort Fisher. But its only tangible effect was to relieve the commander of the land forces from further service in the field.

In Georgia, General Hood led his army off from the front of General Sherman at Atlanta, and marched west and north, and the latter took up his line of march south for Savannah on the 16th of November.

These moves brought Sherman's army into remote bearing upon our army at Richmond, and as a matter of course it began to receive more careful attention from General Lee. In order to better guard our position on the north side, I ordered, in addition to the timber obstructions over White Oak Swamp, the roads leading around towards our left to be broken up by subsoil ploughs, so as to make greater delay of any movements in that direction during the winter rains, and wrote to ask General Lee if he could not order the roads upon which General Grant would probably march against the Southside Railroad broken in the same way; also suggesting that the roads in Georgia upon which General Sherman was marching could be obstructed in this and other ways so as to delay and annoy his march, with the possibility that it might eventually be broken up.

The pickets along our lines were in more or less practice shooting at each other from their rifle-pits until I ordered it stopped on the north end of the line, as an annoyance, and not a legitimate part of war to carry on the shooting of sentinels on guard duty. The example was soon followed by the army on our front, so that the men on the picket lines became friendly, and afterwards came to mutual agreements to give the other side notice, in case of battle, in time for the pickets to get to their pits before the batteries could open on them. Before the winter was half gone the pickets established quite a bartering trade, giving tobacco for sugar and coffee.

Our foraging parties of the north side were fortunate in collecting supplies, and at times were in condition to aid our comrades of the south side. But the officers found that they could only get a small portion of the produce by impressment or tax in kind. They were ordered to locate all supplies that they could not collect.

The chief of staff of the First Corps, Colonel Sorrel, was appointed brigadier-general, and relieved of his duties by Colonel Osmun Latrobe.

The Army of Tennessee, under General Hood, pursuing its march northward late in November and early in December, came upon the Federal forces under General Schofield at Franklin, and General Thomas at Nashville, Tennessee, where desperate battles were fought, until Hood's army was reduced to skeleton commands and forced to retreat. And thus with Sherman's progressive movements in the extreme South, our own ill success in Virginia, and an apparent general strengthening of the Federal cause, the year 1864 drew to a close with little of happy omen for the Confederacy.

CHAPTER XL.

TALK OF PEACE.

Second Federal Move against Fort Fisher and Wilmington Harbor—Confederate Disaffection—Act of Congress appointing a Supreme Commander of the Armies—Montgomery Blair's Peace Conference—Longstreet has a Meeting with General Ord, Commander of the Army of the James—Military Convention proposed—Correspondence between General Grant and General Lee—Longstreet's Suggestions for Measures in the Critical Juncture near the Close of the War.

THE second expedition against Wilmington was sent in January, 1865, General Terry commanding the land and Rear-Admiral Porter the naval forces. After very desperate work the fort and outworks were carried, the commander, General Whiting, being mortally and Colonel Lamb severely wounded. All points of the harbor were captured by the enemy, the Confederates losing, besides most of the armaments of the forts, about two thousand five hundred officers and men in killed, wounded, and prisoners. General Terry's loss was about five hundred. A remarkable success,—the storming of a position fortified during months and years of labor and by most approved engineering.*

As the first months of 1865 passed, the Confederate Congress realized the extreme tension of affairs, and provided, among other expedients, for the enrollment of negroes as Confederate soldiers. Other measures for giving confidence and strength to the cause were adopted.

On the 21st of January the Confederate President was informed of disaffection in the Virginia Legislature, and,

* One of our weeklies announced, upon learning that General Bragg was ordered there, "We understand that General Bragg is ordered to Wilmington. Good-by, Wilmington!"

what was more significant, in the Confederate Congress, where a resolution expressive of want of confidence in the Chief Executive was under informal consideration, and would undoubtedly pass by a large vote if introduced. At this critical juncture it seems that a compromise was effected. It was agreed that Congress should enact a law providing a supreme commander of the Confederate armies, this law to be approved by the President, who should then call General Lee to the exercise of the functions of that office. The intention was to invest him with dictatorial power.

During the early days of February, Hon. Montgomery Blair visited Richmond upon a mission of peace, and brought about a meeting at Hampton Roads between President Lincoln and Secretary Seward and the Confederate Vice-President, Alexander H. Stephens, and the Hon. R. M. T. Hunter and Judge J. A. Campbell. President Lincoln was firm for the surrender of the Confederate armies and the abolition of slavery, which the Confederate President did not care to consider.

About the 15th of February, Major-General J. C. Breckenridge was appointed Secretary of War, and Brigadier-General F. M. St. John was appointed commissary-general of subsistence.

General Ord, commanding the Army of the James, sent me a note on the 20th of February to say that the bartering between our troops on the picket lines was irregular; that he would be pleased to meet me and arrange to put a stop to such intimate intercourse. As a soldier he knew his orders would stop the business; it was evident, therefore, that there was other matter he would introduce when the meeting could be had. I wrote in reply, appointing a time and place between our lines.

We met the next day, and presently he asked for a side interview. When he spoke of the purpose of the meeting, I mentioned a simple manner of correcting the matter, which he accepted without objection or amendment. Then he spoke of affairs military and political.

Referring to the recent conference of the Confederates with President Lincoln at Hampton Roads, he said that the politicians of the North were afraid to touch the question of peace, and there was no way to open the subject except through officers of the armies. On his side they thought the war had gone on long enough; that we should come together as former comrades and friends and talk a little. He suggested that the work as belligerents should be suspended; that General Grant and General Lee should meet and have a talk; that my wife, who was an old acquaintance and friend of Mrs. Grant in their girlhood days, should go into the Union lines and visit Mrs. Grant with as many Confederate officers as might choose to be with her. Then Mrs. Grant would return the call under escort of Union officers and visit Richmond; that while General Lee and General Grant were arranging for better feeling between the armies, they could be aided by intercourse between the ladies and officers until terms honorable to both sides could be found.

I told General Ord that I was not authorized to speak on the subject, but could report upon it to General Lee and the Confederate authorities, and would give notice in case a reply could be made.

General Lee was called over to Richmond, and we met at night at the President's mansion. Secretary-of-War Breckenridge was there. The report was made, several hours were passed in discussing the matter, and finally it was agreed that favorable report should be made as soon as another meeting could be arranged with General Ord. Secretary Breckenridge expressed especial approval of the part assigned for the ladies.

As we separated, I suggested to General Lee that he should name some irrelevant matter as the occasion of his call for the interview with General Grant, and that once they were together they could talk as they pleased. A telegram was sent my wife that night at Lynchburg calling her to Richmond, and the next day a note was sent General Ord asking him to appoint a time for another meeting.

The meeting was appointed for the day following, and the result of the conference was reported. General Ord asked to have General Lee write General Grant for an interview, stating that General Grant was prepared to receive the letter, and thought that a way could be found for a military convention, while old friends of the military service could get together and seek out ways to stop the flow of blood. He indicated a desire on the part of President Lincoln to devise some means or excuse for paying for the liberated slaves, which might be arranged as a condition and part of the terms of the convention, and relieve the matter of political bearing; but those details were in the form of remote probabilities to be discussed when the parties became advanced in their search for ways of settlement.

On the 1st of March I wrote General Lee giving a report of the second interview, and on the 2d he wrote General Grant as follows:

"HEAD-QUARTERS CONFEDERATE STATES ARMIES,
"March 2, 1865.

"LIEUTENANT-GENERAL U. S. GRANT,
"*Commanding United States Armies:*

"GENERAL,—Lieutenant-General Longstreet has informed me that, in a recent conversation between himself and Major-General Ord as to the possibility of arriving at a satisfactory adjustment of the present unhappy difficulties by means of a military convention, General Ord states that if I desired to have an interview with you on the subject you would not decline, provided I had authority to act. Sincerely desiring to leave nothing untried which may put an end to the calamities of war, I propose to meet you at such convenient time and place as you may designate, with the hope that upon an interchange of views it may be found practicable to submit the subjects of controversy between the belligerents to a convention of the kind mentioned. In such event I am authorized to do whatever the result of the proposed interview may render necessary or advisable. Should you accede to this proposition, I would suggest that, if agreeable to you, we meet at the place selected by Generals Ord and Longstreet for their interview, at eleven A.M. on Monday next.

"Very respectfully, your obedient servant,

"R. E. LEE,

"*General.*"

The letter was sent to me open, with instructions to read, seal, and forward. I rode into Richmond to ask that some other business should be named as the cause of the call for the interview, but he was not disposed to approach his purpose by diplomacy, and ordered the letter to be delivered.

He sent another letter, however:

"HEAD-QUARTERS CONFEDERATE STATES ARMIES,

"March 2, 1865.

"LIEUTENANT-GENERAL U. S. GRANT,

"*Commanding United States Armies:*

"GENERAL,—Lieutenant-General Longstreet has informed me that in an interview with Major-General Ord, that officer expressed some apprehension lest the general terms used by you with reference to the exchange of political prisoners should be construed to include those charged with capital offences.

"General Ord further stated that you did not intend to embrace that class of cases in the agreement to exchange. I regret to learn that such is your interpretation, as I had hoped that by exchanging those held under charges by each party it would be possible to diminish, to some extent, the sufferings of both without detriment to their interests. Should you see proper to assent to the interview proposed in my letter of this date, I hope it may be found practicable to arrive at a more satisfactory understanding on this subject.

"Very respectfully, your obedient servant,

"R. E. LEE,

"*General.*"

To which General Grant replied,—

"CITY POINT, VIRGINIA,
"March 4, 1865.

"GENERAL R. E. LEE,
"*Commanding Confederate States Armies:*

"Your two letters of the 2d instant were received yesterday. In regard to any apprehended misunderstanding in reference to the exchange of political prisoners, I think there need be none. General Ord and General Longstreet have probably misunderstood what I said to the former on the subject, or I may have failed to make myself understood possibly. A few days before the interview between Generals Longstreet and Ord I had received a despatch from General Hoffman, Commissary-General of Prisoners, stating in substance that all prisoners of war who were or had been in close confinement or irons, whether under charges or sentence, had been ordered to City Point for exchange. I forwarded the substance of that despatch to Lieutenant-Colonel Mulford, Assistant Agent of Exchange, and presumed it probable that he had communicated it to Colonel Robert Ould. A day or two after, an officer who was neither a prisoner of war nor a political prisoner, was executed, after a fair and impartial trial, and in accordance with the laws of war and the usage of civilized nations. It was in explanation of this class of cases I told General Ord to speak to General Longstreet. Reference to my letter of February 16 will show my understanding on the subject of releasing political or citizen prisoners.

"In regard to meeting you on the 6th instant, I would state that I have no authority to accede to your proposition for a conference on the subject proposed. Such authority is vested in the President of the United States alone. General Ord could only have meant that I would not refuse an interview on any subject on which I have a right to act, which, of course, would be such as are purely of a military character, and on the subject of exchanges which has been intrusted to me.

(Signed) "U. S. GRANT,
"*Lieutenant-General.*"

Under the impression that General Lee would construe the act of Congress in its broad sense and proceed to handle the Confederate armies and affairs under his own good judgment, I wrote, begging that he would call General Joseph E. Johnston back to service and command, and presently suggested and then wrote that I was credibly informed that there was plenty of produce in the country which the farmers would cheerfully deliver at Richmond or Petersburg if liberal prices *in gold* could be paid them; that the authority given to impress bread and meat stuffs should be applied as including gold; that right or wrong the emergency called for it, and that I would undertake to secure the gold upon his authority. I suggested that as Grant's combinations were looking to concentration against the Army of Northern Virginia and Richmond, we should use the railways for collecting and drawing detachments from southern points, calling cavalry by the dirt roads, while the farmers were bringing their produce by private conveyance. Furthermore, I cited the fact that there were eight or ten thousand non-combatants in Richmond who could be put in my trenches as conscripts, and officered by the officers of the department on duty there, and twelve hundred in Lynchburg that could be made similarly available; and argued that using them in the trenches would enable him to draw the First Corps out for a movable force to meet flanking efforts of his adversary, and keep open his lines of communication. In that way, I continued, he could collect a hundred thousand men at Richmond, with a good supply of rations, while General Grant was drawing his two hundred thousand together to attack us; that when concentrated Grant would find himself obliged to give speedy battle, as he could not long supply his large force; that our interior lines would enable us to repel and break up the attack and relieve Richmond.

The times were heavy of events, Executive authority intended to be suspended, and it seemed possible that the use of a little gold would so manifest its power as to induce our people to let cotton and tobacco go for foreign exchange which might put us on a gold basis for a twelvemonth. This was the expedient that offered light and hope for the future, and the times called either for heroic methods or the giving over of the forms of war.

General Lee agreed that the provisions were in the country and would be delivered for gold, but did not think the gold could be found. He made his orders assuming command of the armies, but instead of exercising authority on a scale commensurate with the views of Congress and the call of the crisis, applied to the Richmond authorities for instructions under the new assignment, and wrote that he would assign General Johnston to command if he could be ordered to report to him for duty.

General Johnston was so ordered, and was assigned to command of such fragments of troops as he could collect in the Carolinas. General Wade Hampton was relieved of duty as chief of cavalry in the Army of Northern Virginia and ordered to join General Johnston. After collecting such detachments as he could gather, General Johnston threw them from time to time along the flank of Sherman's march from Georgia for Virginia, and had some spirited affairs with that army, which was gathering strength along the seaboard as it marched.

General Lee was ready to accept the services of non-combatants about Richmond and Lynchburg, but was not prepared to exercise authority as dictator and put them under enrolment, nor to authorize the seizure of gold.

CHAPTER XLI.

BATTLE OF FIVE FORKS.

Various Affairs of the Closing Campaign—The Massing of Grant's Forces—Sortie against Fort Steadman—Captured but quickly retaken—General Grant's Move around the Confederate Right—General Lee anticipates with Aggressive Work—Sheridan makes Battle with his Whole Force at Five Forks—Desperate Situation of the Confederates—Disparity of Numbers—Splendid Stand and Battle of Generals Pickett and Ransom—Colonel Pegram mortally wounded—W. H. F. Lee, the "Noble Son of a Noble Sire"—Corse's Division—Pickett's Generalship—Casualties.

MEANWHILE General Grant was drawing forces from the North and West to further strengthen his already overwhelming combinations against Richmond. General Schofield was called from Tennessee to North Carolina to guard and join on, if necessary, the flank of Sherman's column. The cavalry and infantry of the Valley of Virginia were brought down to the Union army about Richmond and Petersburg,—the latter by transports.

General Sheridan marched his cavalry, ten thousand strong, from the Valley to ride across James River, through Lynchburg, to join the northward march of Sherman's column. His divisions were under Generals Custer and Devens; General Wesley Merritt was his chief of cavalry. He was to destroy railroads, canals, bridges, and other works of value as he marched. At Staunton he decided to take in the balance of General Early's command near his route at Waynesboro'. He found that command posted behind field-works, but the line did not cover the left of the position near the river. After some preliminary dashes, General Custer found his way around General Early's left, and, with part of the cavalry dismounted, made a bold, simultaneous charge on the front and flank, breaking up the line and capturing most of the troops.

Some of the Union commanders claimed that the Confederates cheered them as they surrendered. This, however, the Confederates deny. The affair is mentioned in the diary of Major J. Hoskiss, the engineer of the Confederate army of the Valley, in not more creditable terms than General Early gave of his battle of Cedar Run.

Pickett's division, Fitzhugh Lee's cavalry, and other detachments were sent to Lynchburg to defend against Sheridan's ride; but the high waters of James River and other obstacles turned Sheridan from his southern course to a sweep down the north side.

Generals Pickett and Fitzhugh Lee were recalled and ordered to the north side to join me at Richmond for a march to intercept Sheridan's forces. General Pickett reported on the 13th, and we marched for Hanover on the 14th. I made requisition for a pontoon bridge, and was delayed a day waiting for it and for the cavalry. The bridge was not sent. As we marched towards the Pamunkey River, General Sheridan heard of the move and crossed to the north bank with his main force, leaving a brigade to watch our march, but presently drew the brigade after him.

General Rosser reported to me with five hundred cavalry, one of the remnants of General Early's army not captured, and was ordered across the Pamunkey River to follow Sheridan's ride. Our artillery and infantry were delayed part of a day and night building a bridge from the timbers of an old barn that stood near the bank of the river, and part of the command crossed early in the morning to find a cold cavalry trail, growing colder. As the prospect of overhauling the march was not encouraging, we retraced our steps, returning to Richmond on the 18th, where Pickett's men rested until the 24th.

As Sherman's army drew towards Richmond, General Grant gave up the thought of taking the city by attack of his strong columns on the north side, lest he should leave open the way of escape of the Confederate army, and give time for it to combine with Johnston's forces before he could overhaul it. He found, too, that the "attrition" policy could not be made effective, even with his superior numbers, unless he could so manœuvre as to call his adversary from his fortified grounds to make the work of attrition mutual.

On the 14th of March he gave instructions of preparation for a general move by his left, and on the 24th gave definite orders for the move to be made on the 29th.

On the 24th, General Lee gave consent to the making of a sortie from his line at Hare's Hill, in front of Petersburg, against Fort Steadman of the enemy's works. The distance between the lines at that point was one hundred and fifty yards, the distance between the picket lines fifty yards. Union officers had given out that deserters from the Confederate army were permitted to march into the Union lines with their arms.

Under the circumstances it was conceived to be practicable to gain Fort Steadman by surprise, and the Confederate chief was led to believe that there were other forts to the rear of Steadman that could be carried and held until General Grant could be forced to make a longer line to reach our southern communications, and give us time to find dry roads for our march away, or for reinforcements to join us. It was a hazardous adventure at best, but his brave heart usually went with a proposition for a bold fight.

The Second Corps, under Major-General Gordon, was assigned for the sortie, to be reinforced by other troops to be called. Pickett's division of the First Corps, that had been resting on the north side since the 18th, was called to report to General Lee at Petersburg, without intimation of the service proposed, but all calls and orders of the times were looked upon as urgent. The quartermaster was despatched to Richmond to have the transportation at the station as soon as the troops could reach the depot, and the division was ordered to march in anticipation of due preparation for their transit. But the quartermaster found that the railroad company could furnish transportation for three brigades only. General Lee was informed of the fact, and I suggested that his only way to be assured of the service of a division was to draw Mahone's from Bermuda Hundred and have Pickett's march to replace it. He preferred part of Pickett's division,—finding it could not be used as a division, as Pickett, the ranking officer, would be called to command the work during the early morning, for which he had no opportunity to prepare.

General Lee collected about eighteen thousand men near the sallying field, ordered men selected to cut away the fraise and abatis for the storming column that should advance with empty guns (to avoid premature alarms), and ordered a squadron of cavalry ready to dash across the lines to cut the wires about General Grant's lines.

The Army of the Potomac, General Meade commanding, was posted,—the Ninth Corps on the right from James River to Fort Howard, including Fort Steadman, General Parke commanding; next, on Parke's left, was the Sixth Corps, under General Wright; then General Humphreys with the Second Corps, General Warren with the Fifth; General Sheridan's cavalry, armed with repeating rifles, on the extreme left; General Ord, commanding the Army of the James, on the north side, Generals Gibbon and Weitzel commanding corps,—all officers of the highest attainments and veterans in service. The armies of the Potomac and the James and Sheridan's cavalry, constituting General Grant's immediate command, numbered one hundred and eleven thousand soldiers.* Colonel W. H. Taylor, chief of staff with General Lee, reports, "Lee had at that time only

* General Badeau's "Military History of U. S. Grant."

thirty-nine thousand eight hundred and ninety-seven available muskets for the defence of Richmond and Petersburg."*

The stormers advanced before daylight, gained quiet possession of the enemy's picket line, carried his works between Batteries 9 and 10, moved to the right and left, captured Fort Steadman and its garrison, and turned the guns there and at Battery 10 against the enemy. But the alarm spread and the enemy was afield, feeling his way towards the assailants, for it was not yet light enough to see and direct his artillery fire over his own men. Batteries 11 and 12 were taken, and guides sent to conduct the Confederate columns to forts reported to be in rear of Steadman were in search, but there were no forts there. Redoubts constructed on the main line had commanding positions over Fort Steadman, and a sweeping fire along its lines, in anticipation of a surprise attack, but their fire was withheld for daylight to direct it.

Light broke and the fire opened. General Parke called his field artillery under Tidball into practice from high ground over the Confederates, put the divisions of Hartranft and Wilcox against the Confederate flanks, and held them back near the troops crowding in along the breach, and called for a division from the Second Corps.

The Confederate columns were strong enough to repel the attack of two divisions,—were put there for that purpose,—but so far from breaking up and pushing back the ninety thousand men in front of them, they were not so handled as to check two divisions long enough for the forces to get back to their lines.

The artillery fire not only tore the Confederate ranks, but crossed fire in their rear, cutting off reinforcements and retreat. Our side was without artillery, except captured guns, which were handled by infantry. As the

* Four Years with General Lee.

sortie was noised along the line, General Humphreys and General Wright advanced the Second and Sixth Corps against the Confederate lines along their fields to learn if troops had been drawn from their fronts to join the attack. Batteries 11 and 12 were recovered before eight o'clock, and General Parke ordered Hartranft's division to regain Fort Steadman and Battery 10, which was done with slight loss before nine o'clock.

Many Confederates got back to their lines in disordered flight, but 1949 prisoners and nine stands of colors were taken by the Ninth Corps.

The aggregate of Union losses was reported as 2107. Confederate losses are not reported in detail or in numbers. General Meade's estimate of our loss was 5000.

General Humphreys captured the intrenched picket line in front of him, but found the Confederate works in front well manned. General Wright got well in on the front of his line to favorable position, from which he assaulted and carried the Confederate works on the 2d of April.

Corse's and Terry's brigades of Pickett's division remained in wait under arms until a late hour of the 25th, but were not called to take part in the sortie.*

The result calls for little comment upon the adventure. For an army of forty thousand veterans, without field batteries, to dislodge from their well-chosen and strongly-fortified lines an army of ninety thousand well-armed and thoroughly-appointed veterans was impossible.

Pursuant to previous orders, General Grant started on his move around the Confederate right on the 27th. General Ord was called to the south side with fourteen thousand men of the Army of the James, leaving General Weitzel with twenty thousand on the north side.† In front of that force we had ten thousand men of Field's

* Diary of a member of Corse's brigade.

† Estimated from returns.

and Kershaw's divisions and G. W. C. Lee's division of local defence troops (not including Gary's cavalry, the sailors and marines) holding the forts at Drury's and Chapin's farms. General Grant's orders were that his troops at all points should be ready to receive orders for assault.

Duly informed of the enemy's movements, and understanding his purpose, General Lee marched to his right on the 29th. Fitzhugh Lee's cavalry was called in advance to march for Five Forks. General Lee marched with fifteen thousand infantry, three thousand cavalry (including Fitzhugh Lee's division), and a quota of artillery, along the White Oak road to his right.

The purpose of the enemy was to overreach the fortified grounds and call the Confederates to field work, and General Lee thought to anticipate him by aggressive work as soon as he was in the open field, and ordered battle for the 31st.

General Pickett, with three brigades of his division, two of B. R. Johnson's division (Ransom's and Wallace's), with the cavalry, was ordered to engage Sheridan's cavalry at Five Forks, while General Lee attacked, with McGowan's, Gracie's, Hunton's, and Wise's brigades, the Fifth Army Corps, that was between Pickett and our line of fortifications. The opening of this part of the battle was in favor of the Confederates. General Lee drove back the advance division of the Fifth Corps to the next, and pushed the two back to concentration upon the third, where that part of the battle rested.

General Pickett made his part of the battle by putting W. H. F. Lee's and Rosser's divisions of cavalry on his right, and following that leading by his infantry and artillery, leaving Fitzhugh Lee's cavalry division, under General T. T. Munford, along the right front of Sheridan's cavalry. He pressed his separate battle by his right advance until night, forcing Sheridan back to Dinwiddie

Court-House, where the latter reported to General Grant that the force in front of him was too strong, and asked for reinforcements. Pickett prepared to follow his success by early morning battle and rested for the night, but Miles's division of the Second Corps was put against the other end of the battle, and the Fifth Corps rallied and advanced against the brigades that were with General Lee. They were forced back to the White Oak road, then into their fortified lines, leaving an interval of five miles behind Pickett's left.

Responding to General Sheridan's call, General Grant ordered the Fifth Corps, under General Warren, fifteen thousand * strong, and Mackenzie's cavalry division (sixteen hundred). The design was that the Fifth Corps should come in on Pickett's left rear and cut off his retreat, but heavy rains of the 30th and morning of the 31st had so flooded the streams and roads that the night march was slow and fatiguing, and Pickett, receiving notice during the night of the projected move against his rear, changed his orders for battle, and directed the troops withdrawn for Five Forks before daylight. His retrograde was made in time to escape the Fifth Corps, and was followed by Sheridan's cavalry, but no serious effort was made to delay his movements. He made his march of five miles to Five Forks, put his troops in order of battle by nine o'clock of the morning of the 1st of April, and ordered his well-chosen line examined and put under construction of field-works. Corse's, Terry's, and Steuart's brigades of Pickett's division, and Ransom's and Wallace's brigades of B. R. Johnson's division, were posted from right to left. Of Pegram's artillery, three guns were planted at the Forks, and three more near his right; W. H. F. Lee's division of cavalry on his right; Fitzhugh Lee's division on his left,—General T. T. Munford

* Estimated from general return for March.

commanding the latter; Rosser's division in rear guarding trains. General Fitzhugh Lee was chief of cavalry.

As soon as the infantry line was formed, the troops set to work intrenching the position. The line of battle was parallel to and lay along the White Oak road, the left broken smartly to the rear, the retired end in traverse and flanking defence. The extreme right of the infantry line was also refused, but not so much. Four miles east from Pickett's left was the right of the fortified lines of General Lee's army. On the right and outside of those lines was a detachment of cavalry under General Roberts. The division of Fitzhugh Lee's cavalry was ordered to cover the ground between Roberts's cavalry and Pickett's left by a line of vedettes, and his division was posted on that part of the field.

W. H. F. Lee's cavalry held strong guard on the right, and had the benefit of some swamp lands. His lines formed and field-works under construction, General Pickett rode to the rear for his noon lunch, and was soon followed by the cavalry chief.

Sheridan's cavalry followed close on Pickett's march, but did not attempt to seriously delay it. He made a dash about ten o'clock to measure the strength of the works under construction, and found them too strong to warrant fierce adventure. Delayed by the heavy roads and flooding streams, the Fifth Corps was not in position until four o'clock in the afternoon.

General Sheridan planned for battle to have General Merritt display the cavalry divisions of Custer and Devens against the Confederate front and right, to convey the impression that that was the field from which his battle would be made, while he drew up and massed the Fifth Corps at the other end of the field for the real fight. The corps was arranged, Crawford's division in column on the right, Ayers's on Crawford's left, Griffin's division in support, Mackenzie's cavalry division on the right of the infantry column, at the White Oak road. The Fifth Corps was to wheel in close connection and assault against the face of the return of Confederate works, while the cavalry divisions in front were to assail on that line and the right of the works.

The march and wheel of the Fifth Corps were made in tactical order, and the lines advanced in courageous charge, but staggered and halted under the destructive infantry fire. The charge was repeated, but held in check until Crawford's division found a way under cover of a woodland beyond the Confederate works, and marched to that advantage.

Ransom drew his brigade from the intrenched line to meet that march, but it was one brigade against three—and those supported by part of Griffin's division.

Ransom's horse was killed, falling on him; his adjutant-general, Captain Gee, was killed, and the brigade was forced back.

This formidable move by open field to Pickett's rear made his position untenable. Feeling this, the veteran soldiers of the left brigades realized that their battle was irretrievable. Those who could find escape from that end of the works fell back in broken ranks, while many others, finding the enemy closing in on their rear, thought it more soldierly to surrender to Ayres's brave assaulting columns, and not a few were the captives of Crawford's division.

It was not until that period that General Pickett knew, by the noise of battle, that it was on. He rode through the fire to his command, but his cavalry chief, riding later, was cut off from the field and failed to take part in the action. When Pickett got to the Forks, Colonel Pegram, of the artillery, had been mortally wounded, the battery commander was killed, and many of the cannoneers killed or wounded. He found an artillery sergeant and enough men to man one gun, and used it with effect until the axle broke.

The brigades of Steuart and Terry changed front and received the rolling battle. The cavalry assailants of the front and right had no decided success, but the infantry columns pressing their march, the Confederate brigades were pushed back to their extreme right, where in turn Corse's brigade changed front to receive the march, leaving W. H. F. Lee's cavalry to look to his right.

The Union cavalry essayed to charge the Confederate remnants to dismay, but the noble son of the noble sire seized opportunity to charge against the head of this threatening column before it could pass the swamp lands, drove back its head until Corse's brigade got back to cover of woodland, and night came to cover the disastrous field.*

The remnants of the command were collected as soon and as well as they could be in the dead of night and marched towards Exeter Mills, where Pickett proposed to cross the Appomattox and return to the army, but early movements of the next morning changed the face of the military zodiac.

The position was not of General Pickett's choosing, but of his orders, and from his orders he assumed that he would be reinforced. His execution was all that a skilful commander could apply. He reported as to his position and the movements of the enemy threatening to cut his command from the army, but no force came to guard his left. The reinforcements joined him after night, when his battle had been lost and his command disorganized. The cavalry of his left was in neglect in failing to report the advance of the enemy, but that was not for want of proper orders from his head-quarters. Though taken by surprise, there was no panic in any part of the command;

* This account is gathered from the evidence of officers of both sides, given before the Warren Court of Inquiry, which vindicated Warren and Pickett, though the court was inclined to coquette with the lieutenant-general, who, at that late day, was in high authority.

brigade after brigade changed front to the left and received the overwhelming battle as it rolled on, until crushed back to the next, before it could deploy out to aid the front,—or flank attack,—until the last right brigade of the brave Corse changed and stood alone on the left of W. H. F. Lee's cavalry, fronting at right angle against the enemy's cavalry columns.

It is not claiming too much for that grand division to say that, aided by the brigades of Ransom and Wallace, they could not have been dislodged from their intrenched position by parallel battle even by the great odds against them. As it was, Ayres's division staggered under the pelting blows that it met, and Crawford's drifted off from the blows against it, until it thus found the key of the battle away beyond the Confederate limits.

In generalship Pickett was not a bit below the "gay rider." His defensive battle was better organized, and it is possible that he would have gained the day if his cavalry had been diligent in giving information of the movements of the enemy.*

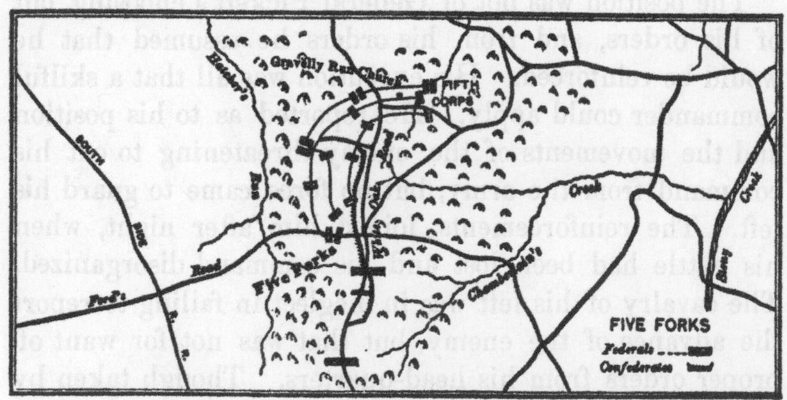

The losses are not found in separate reports. Both sides suffered severely, Pickett losing two thousand. He

---

* He reported that he could have gained the day if the cavalry of his left had been as efficient as that of his right.

had nine thousand men of all arms. His adversary had twenty-six thousand.

Reinforcements of Hunton's brigade, and Lieutenant-General R. H. Anderson with the other brigades of B. R. Johnson, were sent him too late, and a telegram came for me at Richmond to march a division to Petersburg to report to General Lee. The hour at which the telegram was received was not noted. As the operations at Five Forks were not decisive until after five o'clock, the telegram may have been received about seven P.M. Field's division was ordered to the railway station, and the quartermaster was sent in advance to have the cars ready to move it.

To give the troops the benefit of our limited transportation I rode with the staff by the dirt road.

CHAPTER XLII.

PETERSBURG.

The Fierce Concerted Assault by the Federals—Death of A. P. Hill—General Lee announces to Richmond Authorities that he must retreat—Reception of the News by President Davis at Church Service—Federals take Forts Gregg and Whitworth—The Retreat harassed by Continuous Fighting—Longstreet saves High Bridge, a Vital Point—Ewell and Others compelled to surrender—General Mahone's Account of Interesting Scenes—Magnitude of the Disaster—"Is the Army dissolving?"—General Reed mortally wounded—Panic occurs, but Order is restored—General Gregg and Part of his Cavalry Command captured by Rosser and Munford.

THE blackness of night spread over us when we crossed James River by the pontoon bridge, but before long land and water batteries lifted their bombs over their lazy curves, screaming shells came through the freighted night to light our ride, and signal sky-rockets gave momentary illumination. Our noble beasts peered through the loaded air and sniffed the coming battle; night-birds fluttered from their startled cover, and the solid pounding upon Mahone's defensive walls drove the foxes from their lairs. If tears and prayers could have put out the light it would not have passed Petersburg,—but it passed by twenty miles. A hundred guns and more added their lightning and thunder to the storm of war that carried consternation to thousands of long-apprehensive people.

The cause was lost, but the end was not yet. The noble Army of Northern Virginia, once, twice conqueror of empire, must bite the dust before its formidable adversary.

The impulse was to stop and guard Mahone, but some of his men had been called to assist in guarding elsewhere, which, with our imperative orders, admonished us that he must be left to his fate, and Weitzel's fire upon the lines we had just left told of his orders to be prepared for the grand enveloping charge. But the order for Weitzel's part in the general charge was afterwards suspended until enough troops could be sent to assure his success. Had General Grant known that Field's division was withdrawn during the night, Weitzel's assault would have gone in the general move of the morning of the 2d, and Richmond, with the Confederate authorities, would have been taken before noon.

As morning approached the combat was heavier. The rolling thunder of the heavy metal reverberated along the line, and its bursting blaze spread afar to light the doom of the army once so proud to meet the foe,—matchless Army of Northern Virginia!

General Grant had ordered assault for four o'clock, but it was near five before there was light enough for the men to see their way across the line and over the works. Our night-ride was beyond range of the enemy's batteries. Crossing the Appomattox, we rode through the streets of Petersburg for General Lee's head-quarters, some miles farther west. As no part of the command had reached the station when we passed, orders were left for the detachments to march as soon as they landed.

Before the first rays of morning we found general head-quarters. Some members of the staff were up and dressed, but the general was yet on his couch. When told of my presence, he called me to a seat at his bedside, and gave orders for our march to support the broken forces about Five Forks. He had no censure for any one, but mentioned the great numbers of the enemy and the superior repeating rifles of his cavalry. He was ill, suffering from the rheumatic ailment that he had been afflicted with for years, but keener trouble of mind made him in a measure superior to the shooting pains of his disease.

From the line gained by the Sixth Corps on the 25th it was a run of but two or three minutes across to the Confederate works.

At 4.45, General Wright advanced as the signal for general assault. General Lee was not through with his instructions for our march when a staff-officer came in and reported that the lines in front of his head-quarters were broken. Drawing his wrapper about him, he walked with me to the front door and saw, as far as the eye could cover the field, a line of skirmishers in quiet march towards us. It was hardly light enough to distinguish the blue from the gray.

General Wright drove in our picket line, and in desperate charges crowned the Confederate works. General Gibbon followed the move with his divisions of the Twenty-fourth and Twenty-fifth Corps, one of his brigades (Harris's) carrying part of the Confederate works. The troops, weary of their all-night watch and early battle, halted to close their ranks and wait for the skirmish line to open up the field. General Lee appealed to have me interpose and stop the march, but not a man of my command was there, nor had we notice that any of them had reached the station at Petersburg.

All staff-officers mounted and rode to find the parts of Heth's and Wilcox's divisions that had been forced from their lines. The display of officers riding in many directions seemed to admonish the skirmishers to delay under cover of an intervening swale. The alarm reached General A. P. Hill, of the Third Corps, who rode off to find his troops, but instead came suddenly upon the enemy's skirmishers in their concealment. He wheeled and made a dash to escape, but the Federal fire had deadly effect, the gallant general fell, and the Southern service lost a sword made bright by brave work upon many heavy fields.

General Humphreys, of the Second, followed the move of the Sixth Corps, and General Parke assaulted on the Bermuda Hundred front and at Petersburg. He had partial success at the former, but was repulsed when he met Mahone's strong line. At Petersburg he had more success, capturing twelve guns.

General Sheridan, reinforced by Miles's division, was ordered to follow up his work on the right bank. The reinforcements sent under Lieutenant-General Anderson joined General Pickett at night of the 1st, and the combined forces succeeded in getting out of the way of the Union infantry, and they gave the cavalry a severe trial a little before night at Amazon Creek, where the pursuit rested; but the Union forces made some important captures of artillery and prisoners. The divisions of Heth and Wilcox moved to the right and left to collect their broken files. General Wright wheeled to the right and massed the Sixth Corps for its march to Petersburg, and was joined by General Gibbon.

Not venturing to hope, I looked towards Petersburg and saw General Benning, with his Rock brigade, winding in rapid march around the near hill. He had but six hundred of his men. I asked for two hundred, and led them off to the canal on our right, which was a weak point, threatened by a small body of skirmishers, and ordered the balance of his troops deployed as skirmishers in front of the enemy's main force.

I rode then to Benning's line of skirmishers, and at the middle point turned and rode at a walk to the top of the hill, took out my glasses, and had a careful view of the enemy's formidable masses. I thought I recognized General Gibbon, and raised my hat, but he was busy and did not see me. There were two forts at our line of works,—Gregg and Whitworth. General Grant rode over the captured works and ordered the forts taken. Upon withdrawing my glasses I looked to the right and left, and saw Benning's four hundred standing in even line with me, viewing the masses preparing for their march to meet us.

During a few moments of quiet, General Lee despatched

to Richmond of affairs at Petersburg, and to advise that our troops must abandon their lines and march in retreat as soon as night could cover the move.

It was eleven o'clock of the morning when the despatch reached Richmond. It was the Sabbath-day. The city was at profound worship. The President was at St. Paul's Church. My wife was there (rest her spirit!) and heard the pastor, Mr. Minnegerode, read, "*The Lord is in his holy temple: let all the earth keep silence before him.*" The full congregation rose, but the air whispered silence. The solemnity was broken as a swift despatch-bearer entered the portals and walked with quiet but rapid steps up the aisle to the chancel. He handed the President a sealed envelope. After reading, the President took his hat and walked with dignity down the aisle. Service was resumed, but presently came another messenger for some of the ladies, then another, and still another, and in a few moments the congregation, followed by the minister, giving up the sacred service, passed out and to their homes to prepare, in silent resignation, for whatever was to come.

The tragic scenes of the south side, in a different way, were as impressive as these. General Gibbon prepared his divisions under Foster and Turner for assault upon Forts Gregg and Whitworth, and when the Sixth Corps lined up with him, he ordered the divisions to their work. As they advanced the other brigades of Field's division came up, were aligned before the enemy's heavy massing forces, and ordered to intrench. General Foster found his work at Fort Gregg called for all the force and skill that he could apply. He made desperate assault, but was checked, and charged again and again, even to the bayonet, before he could mount the parapets and claim the fort. It had been manned by part of Harris's brigade (Twelfth Mississippi Regiment, under Captain J. H. Duncan, three hundred men of Mahone's division). Fifty-five dead were found in the fort; two hundred and fifty, including wounded, were prisoners.

General Turner attacked at Fort Whitworth, and had easier work. General Wilcox, thinking it a useless sacrifice to try to hold it, ordered his troops withdrawn, and many got out in time to escape the heavy assault, but many were taken prisoners. General Gibbon lost ten officers and one hundred and twelve men killed, twenty-seven officers and five hundred and sixty-five men wounded; two pieces of artillery and several colors were captured.

It was my time next. General Meade called Miles's division back to the Second Corps, and prepared to march down upon Petersburg, but General Grant thought that the work might prove hazardous of delay to his plans for the next day; that General Lee was obliged to pull away from his lines during the night to find escape, and standing as he was he would have the start, while at Petersburg he would be behind him. He therefore ordered all things in readiness for his march westward at early light of the next morning.

After A. P. Hill fell his staff and corps were assigned as part of my command. Heth's and Wilcox's divisions were much broken by the losses of the day. Mahone had repulsed the attack made upon his position, and had his division in good order and spirits, except the part of Harris's brigade that was at Fort Gregg.

General Lee's order for retreat was out in time to have the troops take up the march as soon as night came. The troops at Petersburg were to cross the Appomattox at the bridge there, Mahone's division to march to Chesterfield Court-House and cover the march of the troops from the north side. General Ewell, commanding on the north side, was to cross his divisions, one at the lower bridge, the other at Richmond. Lieutenant-General Anderson and Major-General Pickett, with the cavalry, were to march up the south bank of the Appomattox.

Field's division and parts of Heth's and Wilcox's crossed the river soon after dark, and were followed by the Second Corps, which wrecked the bridge behind it. G. W. C. Lee's division, including the garrison at Chapin's Bluff, crossed the James at the lower bridge, breaking it when they had passed. The sailors and marines at Drury's Bluff, on the south side, failed to receive orders, but, under advice from General Mahone, got off in good season and marched through Chesterfield Court-House to join G. W. C. Lee's division in its after-march. General Kershaw crossed at Richmond. As the division came over the bridge the structure was fired (supposedly by an incendiary), and Kershaw had to go through the flames at double-quick time. Ewell's command was united near Manchester and pursued its march. General Mahone marched on his line just mentioned.

After a tramp of sixteen miles through mud, my column halted for a short rest, and marched to Goode's Bridge on the 3d. Field's and Wilcox's divisions were put across the Appomattox to guard against threatening moves of cavalry. In the forenoon of the 4th, Mahone's division crossed,—also a part of Heth's that had been cut off, and had marched up on the south side,—and our march was continued to Amelia Court-House, the enemy's cavalry constantly threatening our left flank. At the Court-House the cavalry was more demonstrative and seemed ready to offer battle. Field, Heth, Wilcox, and the artillery were put in position and looked for opportunity to strike the head of the enemy's column and delay his march. But it proved to be only the purpose of the cavalry to delay our march while the enemy was passing his heavier column by us to Jetersville.

Orders had been sent for provisions to meet us at the Court-House, but they were not there, so we lost the greater part of a day gathering supplies from the farmers.

Our purpose had been to march through Burkeville to join our forces to those of General J. E. Johnston in North Carolina, but at Jetersville, on the 5th, we found the enemy square across the route in force and intrenching, where our cavalry under General W. H. F. Lee engaged him. General Field put out a strong line of skirmishers to support the cavalry. Field's, Heth's, and Wilcox's divisions and artillery were prepared for action and awaited orders. General Meade was in front of us with the Second and Fifth Corps and Sheridan's cavalry, but his Sixth Corps was not up. General Fitzhugh Lee had been sent by the Painesville road with the balance of his cavalry to guard the trains raided by detachments of the enemy, which latter made some important captures.

General Lee was with us at Jetersville, and, after careful reconnoissance, thought the enemy's position too strong to warrant aggressive battle. He sent for some of the farmers to get more definite information of the country and the strength of the position in front of us, but they knew nothing beyond the roads and by-roads from place to place. General Meade, finding that his Sixth Corps could not join him till a late hour, decided to wait till next morning for his attack. General Ord rested his column for the night at Burkeville. The enemy was quiet at Jetersville, except for a light exchange of cavalry fire. No orders came, the afternoon was passing, further delay seemed perilous. I drew the command off and filed to the right to cross Flat Creek to march for Farmville. The other infantry and trains and artillery followed and kept the march until a late hour, halting for a short rest before daylight.

Early on the 6th, General Meade advanced for battle, and, not finding us at Jetersville, started towards Amelia Court-House to look for us, but General Humphreys, of his Second Corps, learned that our rear-guard was on the north side of Flat Creek on the westward march.

General Griffin, of the Fifth Corps, also had information of troops in march west, and General Meade, therefore, changed direction to pursue with his Second and Sixth Corps, putting the Fifth on the Painesville road. General Sheridan despatched General Ord that we had broken away from him and were marching direct for Burkeville. The latter prepared to receive us, but soon learned that we had taken another route. He had previously detached two regiments of infantry (five hundred men), under Colonel Washburn, with orders to make rapid march and burn High Bridge. To this force he afterwards sent eighty cavalrymen, under Brigadier-General Theodore Reed, of his staff, who conducted the column, and put his command in march to follow by the road through Rice's Station.

After repairing the bridge at Flat Creek, General Humphreys marched in hot pursuit of our rear-guard, followed by the Sixth Corps, Merritt's and Crook's cavalry moving on the left of our column as we marched. General Humphreys, in his account of the pursuit, says,—

> "A sharp and running fight commenced at once with Gordon's corps which was continued over a distance of fourteen miles, during which several partially-intrenched positions were carried." *

My column marched before daylight on the 6th. The design from the night we left Petersburg was that its service should be to press on and prevent the enemy's infantry columns from passing and standing across our march.

At Sailor's Creek the road forks,—one road to the High Bridge crossing of Appomattox River, the other by Rice's Station to Farmville. We had information of Ord's column moving towards Rice's Station, and I moved over to that point to meet it, the other columns to follow the trains over the bridge. At Rice's Station the

* Virginia Campaigns.

command was prepared for action,—Field's division across the road of Ord's march, Wilcox on Field's right; both ordered to intrench, artillery in battery. Heth's division was put in support of Wilcox, Mahone to support Field. Just then I learned that Ord's detachment of bridge-burners had passed out of sight when the head of my command arrived. I had no cavalry, and the head of Ord's command was approaching in sight; but directly General Rosser reported with his division of cavalry. He was ordered to follow after the bridge-burners and capture or destroy the detachment, *if it took the last man of his command to do it.* General Ord came on and drove in my line of skirmishers, but I rode to meet them, marched them back to the line, with orders to hold it till *called in.* Ord's force proved to be the head of his column, and he was not prepared to press for general engagement.

General T. T. Munford reported with his cavalry and was ordered to follow Rosser, with similar directions. Gary's cavalry came and reported to me. High Bridge was a vital point, for over it the trains were to pass, and I was under the impression that General Lee was there, passing with the rest of his army, but hearing our troops engaged at Rice's Station, he had ridden to us and was waiting near Mahone's division. Ord's command was not up till near night, and he only engaged with desultory fire of skirmishers and occasional exchange of battery practice, arranging to make his attack the next morning.

General Ewell's column was up when we left Amelia Court-House, and followed Anderson's by Amelia Springs, where he was detained some little time defending trains threatened by cavalry; at the same time our rear-guard was near him, followed by the enemy. Near Deatonville Crook's cavalry got in on our trains and caused delay of several hours to Anderson's march. Crook was joined by part of Merritt's cavalry and repeated the attack on the trains, but Ewell was up in time to aid in repelling the attack, and the march was resumed, the enemy's cavalry moving on their left flank.

Anderson crossed Sailor's Creek, closely followed by Ewell. The route by which they were to march was by High Bridge, but they were on strange ground, without maps, or instructions, or commander. In the absence of orders Anderson thought to march for the noise of battle, at Rice's Station. They had no artillery or cavalry. The chief of cavalry was there, but his troopers were elsewhere, and he rode away, advising the force to follow him. The rear-guard came up rapidly and essayed to deploy for defence, but the close pursuit of Humphreys's corps forced its continued march for High Bridge, letting the pursuit in upon Ewell's rear. As Anderson marched he found Merritt's cavalry square across his route. Humphreys was close upon Ewell, but the former awaited battle for the arrival of the Sixth Corps.

There was yet a way of escape from the closing clutches of the enemy by filing to their right and marching to the rear of the command at Rice's Station; but they were true soldiers, and decided to fight, even to sacrifice their commands if necessary, to break or delay the pursuit until the trains and rear-guard could find safety beyond High Bridge.

Ewell deployed his divisions, Kershaw's on the right, G. W. C. Lee's on the left. Their plan was, that Anderson should attack and open the way while Ewell defended the rear. As Anderson attacked, Wright's corps was up, Humphreys had matured his plans, and the attack of Anderson hastened that of the enemy upon the Confederate rear. Anderson had some success, and Ewell received the assaults with resolute coolness, and at one moment pushed his fight to aggressive return, but the enemy, finding that there was no artillery with the Confederates, dashed their batteries into closer range, putting in artillery and infantry fire, front and flanks, until the

Confederate rear was crushed to fragments. General Ewell surrendered; so also did General G. W. C. Lee with his division. General Kershaw advised such of his men as could to make their escape, and surrendered with his division. General Anderson got away with the greater part of B. R. Johnson's division, and Pickett with six hundred men. Generals Corse and Hunton and others of Pickett's men were captured. About two hundred of Kershaw's division got away.

General R. S. Ewell and General R. H. Anderson are barely known in the retreat, but their stand and fight on that trying march were among the most soldier-like of the many noble deeds of the war.

While waiting near my rear, General Lee received information, through Colonel Venable, of his staff, as to the disaster at Sailor's Creek. He drew Mahone's division away, and took it back to find the field. General Mahone writes of the scenes that he witnessed as follows:

"As we were moving up in line of battle, General Lee riding with me and remonstrating about the severity of my note in respect to Colonel Marshall's interference with my division the night before, up rode Colonel Venable, of General Lee's staff, and wanted to know if he, General Lee, had received his message. General Lee replied 'No,' when Colonel Venable informed him that the enemy had captured the wagon-trains at Sailor's Creek. General Lee exclaimed, 'Where is Anderson? Where is Ewell? It is strange I can't hear from them.' Then turning to me, he said, 'General Mahone, I have no other troops, will you take your division to Sailor's Creek?' and I promptly gave the order by the left flank, and off we were for Sailor's Creek, where the disaster had occurred. General Lee rode with me, Colonel Venable a little in the rear. On reaching the south crest of the high ground at the crossing of the river road overlooking Sailor's Creek, the disaster which had overtaken our army was in full view, and the scene beggars description,—hurrying teamsters with their teams and dangling traces (no wagons), retreating infantry without guns, many without hats, a harmless mob, with the massive columns of the enemy moving orderly on. At this spectacle General Lee straightened himself in his saddle, and, looking more the soldier than ever, exclaimed, as if talking to himself, 'My God! has the army dissolved?' As quickly as I could control my own voice I replied, 'No, general, here are troops ready to do their duty;' when, in a mellowed voice, he replied, 'Yes, general, there are some true men left. Will you please keep those people back?' As I was placing my division in position to 'keep those people back,' the retiring herd just referred to had crowded around General Lee while he sat on his horse with a Confederate battle-flag in his hand. I rode up and requested him to give me the flag, which he did.

"It was near dusk, and he wanted to know of me how to get away. I replied, 'Let General Longstreet move by the river road to Farmville, and cross the river there, and I will go through the woods to the High Bridge (railroad bridge) and cross there.' To this he assented. I asked him then, after crossing at the High Bridge, what I should do, and his reply was, to exercise my judgment. I wanted to know what should be done with the bridge after crossing it. He said, 'Set fire to it,' and I replied that the destruction of a span would as well retard the enemy as the destruction of the whole half mile of bridge, and asked him to call up Colonel Talcott, of the Engineers' Regiment, and personally direct him in the matter, which he did."

General Mahone withdrew at eleven o'clock at night through the wood, found the bridge, had the fragments of commands over before daylight, and crossed High Bridge. The parties called to fire the bridge failed to appear. He sent a brigade back to do the work, and had a sharp skirmish in checking the enemy long enough to start the fire, after which he withdrew as far as Cumberland Church and deployed for battle, Poague's artillery on his right. General Rosser got up with the detachment sent to burn the bridge, and attacked. General Reed, seeing his approach, found a defensive position, and arranged the command to receive battle. General Munford got up and deployed his troopers, dismounted, on Rosser's left. Nothing daunted, General Reed received the attack, and in gallant fight made one or two counter-charges with his small cavalry force, but ere long he was mortally wounded, as was Colonel Washburn. Most of his cavalry officers and many of his infantry were killed or wounded, and the rest surrendered. Reed's fight was as gallant and skilful as a soldier could make, and its noise in rear of Sailor's Creek may have served to increase the confusion there. The result shows the work of these remnants of Confederate veterans as skilful and worthy of their old chief who fell at Yellow Tavern.

I heard nothing of the affair at Sailor's Creek, nor from General Lee, until next morning. Our work at Rice's Station was not very serious, but was continued until night, when we marched and crossed the Appomattox at Farmville without loss, some of Rosser's and Munford's cavalry following. We crossed early in the morning and received two days' rations,—the first regular issue since we left Richmond,—halted our wagons, made fires, got out cooking utensils, and were just ready to prepare a good breakfast. We had not heard of the disasters on the other route and the hasty retreat, and were looking for a little quiet to prepare breakfast, when General Lee rode up and said that the bridges had been fired before his cavalry crossed, that part of that command was cut off and lost, and that the troops should hurry on to position at Cumberland Church.

I reminded him that there were fords over which his cavalry could cross, and that they knew of or would surely find them. Everything except the food was ordered back to the wagons and dumped in.

Meanwhile, the alarm had spread, and our teamsters, frightened by reports of cavalry trouble and approaching fire of artillery, joined in the panic, put whips to their teams as quick as the camp-kettles were tumbled over the tail-boards of the wagons, and rushed through the woods to find a road somewhere in front of them. The command was ordered under arms and put in quick march, but General Lee urged double-quick. Our cavalry was then engaged near Farmville, and presently came a reckless charge of Gregg's troopers towards parts of Rosser's and Munford's commands. Heth's division of infantry was sent to support them. As the balance of the command marched, General Lee took the head of the column and led it on the double-quick.

I thought it better to let them pass me, and, to quiet their apprehensions a little, rode at a walk. General Mahone received the attack of part of the enemy's Second Corps, like Gregg's cavalry making reckless attack. The enemy seemed to think they had another Sailor's Creek affair, and part of their attack got in as far as Poague's battery, but Mahone recovered it, and then drove off an attack against his front. General Gregg and a considerable part of his command were captured by Rosser and Munford. At Cumberland Church the command deployed on the right of Poague's battery, but Mahone reported a move by part of Miles's division to turn his left which might dislodge him. G. T. Anderson's brigade of Field's division was sent with orders to get around the threatening force and break it up. Mahone so directed them through a woodland that they succeeded in over-reaching the threatened march, and took in some three hundred prisoners,* the last of our trouble for the day. General Lee stopped at a cottage near my line, where I joined him after night; the trains and other parts of his army had moved on towards Appomattox Court-House.

---

* General Mahone claimed seven hundred in all.

CHAPTER XLIII.

APPOMATTOX.

Some of General Lee's Officers say to him that "Further Resistance is Hopeless"—Longstreet does not approve—General Grant calls for Surrender—"Not yet"—The Confederate Chieftain asks Terms—His Response to his Officers as represented by General Pendleton—Correspondence of Generals Lee and Grant—Morning of April 9—General Lee rides to meet the Federal Commander, while Longstreet orders the Last Line of Battle—Longstreet endeavors to recall his Chief, hearing of a Break where the Confederate Troops could pass—Custer demands Surrender of Longstreet—Reminded of Irregularity, and that he was "in the Enemy's Lines"—Meeting with General Grant—Capitulation—Last Scenes.

THE beginning of the end was now at hand,—not perhaps necessarily, but, at least, as the sequence of cause and effect actually followed.

"An event occurred on the 7th," says General Long, "which must not be omitted from the narrative. Perceiving the difficulties that surrounded the army, and believing its extrication hopeless, a number of the principal officers, from a feeling of affection and sympathy for the commander-in-chief, and with a wish to lighten his responsibility and soften the pain of defeat, volunteered to inform him that, in their opinion, the struggle had reached a point where further resistance was hopeless, and that the contest should be terminated and negotiations opened for a surrender of the army. The delivery of this opinion was confided to General Pendleton, who, both by his character and devotion to General Lee, was well qualified for such an office. The names of Longstreet and some others, who did not coincide in the opinion of their associates, did not appear in the list presented by Pendleton."*

A little after nightfall a flag of truce appeared under

* Memoirs of General Lee, A. L. Long.

torchlight in front of Mahone's line bearing a note to General Lee:

"HEAD-QUARTERS ARMIES OF THE UNITED STATES,
"5 P.M., April 7, 1865.

"GENERAL R. E. LEE,
"*Commanding Confederate States Army:*

"GENERAL,—The results of the last week must convince you of the hopelessness of further resistance on the part of the Army of Northern Virginia in this struggle. I feel that it is so, and regard it as my duty to shift from myself the responsibility of any further effusion of blood by asking of you the surrender of that portion of the Confederate army known as the Army of Northern Virginia.

"Very respectfully, your obedient servant,
"U. S. GRANT,
"*Lieutenant-General, Commanding Armies of the United States.*"

I was sitting at his side when the note was delivered. He read it and handed it to me without referring to its contents. After reading it I gave it back, saying, "*Not yet.*"

General Lee wrote in reply,—

"April 7, 1865.

"GENERAL,—I have received your note of this day. Though not entertaining the opinion you express on the hopelessness of further resistance on the part of the Army of Northern Virginia, I reciprocate your desire to avoid useless effusion of blood, and therefore, before considering your proposition, ask the terms you will offer on condition of its surrender.

"R. E. LEE,
"*General.*

"LIEUTENANT-GENERAL GRANT,
"*Commanding Armies of the United States.*"

I was not informed of the contents of the return note, but thought, from the orders of the night, it did not mean surrender. General Lee ordered my command from forward- to rear-guard, and his cavalry in rear of the march. The road was clear at eleven o'clock, and we marched at twelve. The enemy left us to a quiet day's march on the

8th, nothing disturbing the rear-guard, and our left flank being but little annoyed, but our animals were worn and reduced in strength by the heavy haul through rain and mud during the march from Petersburg, and the troops of our broken columns were troubled and faint of heart.

We passed abandoned wagons in flames, and limbers and caissons of artillery burning sometimes in the middle of the road. One of my battery commanders reported his horses too weak to haul his guns. He was ordered to bury the guns and cover their burial-places with old leaves and brushwood. Many weary soldiers were picked up, and many came to the column from the woodlands, some with, many without, arms,—all asking for food.

General Grant renewed efforts on the 8th to find a way to strike across the head of our march by his cavalry, the Army of the James and the Fifth Corps pursuing our rear-guard with the Second and Sixth Corps of the Army of the Potomac.

In the forenoon, General Pendleton came to me and reported the proceedings of the self-constituted council of war of the night before, and stated that he had been requested to make the report and ask to have me bear it to General Lee, in the name of the members of the council. Much surprised, I turned and asked if he did not know that the Articles of War provided that officers or soldiers who asked commanding officers to surrender should be shot, and said,—

"If General Lee doesn't know when to surrender until I tell him, he will never know."

It seems that General Pendleton then went to General Lee and made the report. General Long's account of the interview, as reported by Pendleton, is as follows:

"General Lee was lying on the ground. No others heard the conversation between him and myself. He received my communication with the reply, 'Oh, no, I trust that it has not come to that,' and added, 'General, we have yet too many bold men to think of laying down our arms. The enemy do not fight with spirit, while our boys still do. Besides, if I were to say a word to the Federal commander, he would regard it as such a confession of weakness as to make it the condition of demanding an unconditional surrender, a proposal to which I will never listen. . . . I have never believed we could, against the gigantic combination for our subjugation, make good, in the long run, our independence, unless foreign powers should, directly or indirectly, assist us. . . . But such considerations really make with me no difference. We had, I was satisfied, sacred principles to maintain, and rights to defend, for which we were in duty bound to do our best, even if we perished in the endeavor.'

"Such were, as nearly as I can recall them, the exact words of General Lee on that most critical occasion. You see in them the soul of the man. Where his conscience dictated and his judgment decided, there his heart was." *

The delicate affection that prompted the knights of later days to offer to relieve the grand commander of his official obligations and take upon themselves responsibility to disarm us and turn us over to the enemy is somewhat pathetic, but when to it are applied the stern rules of a soldier's duty upon a field of emergency, when the commander most needs steady hands and brave hearts, their proceeding would not stand the test of a military tribunal. The interesting part of the interview is that in it our great leader left a sufficient testimonial as a legacy to the soldiers of his column of the right. Though commanders of other columns were mutinous, he had confidence that we were firm and steady in waiting to execute his last command.

During the day General Grant wrote General Lee in reply to his note of the 7th inquiring as to terms of surrender,—

"April 8, 1865.

"General R. E. Lee,

"*Commanding Confederate States Army:*

"General,—Your note of last evening in reply to mine of the same date, asking the conditions on which I will accept surrender

* Memoirs of Robert E. Lee, A. L. Long.

of the Army of Northern Virginia, is just received. In reply I would say that, peace being my great desire, there is but one condition I would insist upon,—namely, that the men and officers surrendered shall be disqualified for taking up arms again against the government of the United States until properly exchanged. I will meet you, or will designate officers to meet any officers you might name for the same purpose, at any point agreeable to you, for the purpose of arranging definitely the terms upon which the surrender of the Army of Northern Virginia will be received.

"U. S. GRANT,
"*Lieutenant-General.*"

In reply, General Lee wrote,—

"April 8, 1865.

"GENERAL,—I received at a late hour your note of to-day. In mine of yesterday I did not intend to propose the surrender of the Army of Northern Virginia, but to ask the terms of your proposition. To be frank, I do not think the emergency has arisen to call for the surrender of this army, but as the restoration of peace should be the sole object of all, I desired to know whether your proposals would lead to that end. I cannot, therefore, meet you with a view to the surrender of the Army of Northern Virginia; but as far as your proposal may affect the Confederate States forces under my command and tend to the restoration of peace, I should be pleased to meet you at ten A.M. to-morrow on the old stage road to Richmond, between the picket lines of the two armies.

"R. E. LEE,
"*General.*"

The enemy's movements of the day were impressive of his desire to get by our left flank and make a strong stand across the route of our head of column. At Prospect Station, General Sheridan was informed of four trains of cars at Appomattox Station loaded with provisions for General Lee's army. He gave notice to Merritt's and Crook's cavalry, and rode twenty-eight miles in time for Custer's division to pass the station, cut off the trains, and drive back the guard advancing to protect them. He helped himself to the provisions, and captured besides twenty-five pieces of artillery and a wagon and hospital train.

At night General Lee made his head-quarters near the rear-guard, and spread his couch about a hundred feet from the saddle and blanket that were my pillow and spread for the night. If he had a more comfortable bed than mine I do not know, but I think not.

He sent for his cavalry commander, and gave orders for him to transfer his troopers from the rear to the advanced guard, and called General Gordon, commanding in front, for report and orders. The advance was then at Appomattox Court-House, Wallace's brigade resting in the village. His orders were to march at one o'clock in the morning, the trains and advanced forces to push through the village in time for my column to stand and prepare to defend at that point in case of close pursuit. General Gordon reported, as I remember, less than two thousand men. (General Fitzhugh Lee puts it at sixteen hundred, but he may have overlooked Wallace's brigade, which joined the advance on that day.) My column was about as it was when it marched from Petersburg. Parts of Ewell's, Anderson's, and Pickett's commands not captured on the march were near us, and reported to me, except Wallace's brigade.

On the 9th the rear-guard marched as ordered, but soon came upon standing trains of wagons in the road and still in park alongside. The command was halted, deployed into position, and ordered to intrench against the pursuing army.

It was five o'clock when the advance commands moved, —four hours after the time ordered. To these General Long's batteries of thirty guns were attached. They met Sheridan's cavalry advancing across their route. The column was deployed, the cavalry on the right of the artillery and infantry, as they advanced to clear the way. They reported some success, capturing two pieces of artillery, when General Ord's column came up. He had, besides his Army of the James, the Fifth Army Corps.

These commands, with the cavalry, pushed the Confederates back a little, while the two corps of the Army of the Potomac were advancing against my rear-guard.

Of the early hours of this, the last day of active existence of the Army of Northern Virginia, Colonel Venable, of General Lee's staff, wrote thus :

"At three o'clock on the morning of that fatal day, General Lee rode forward, still hoping that he might break through the countless hordes of the enemy, who hemmed us in. Halting a short distance in rear of our vanguard, he sent me on to General Gordon to ask him if he could break through the enemy. I found General Gordon and General Fitz Lee on their front line in the dim light of the morning, arranging our attack. Gordon's reply to the message (I give the expressive phrase of the gallant Georgian) was this : 'Tell General Lee I have fought my corps to a frazzle, and I fear I can do nothing unless I am heavily supported by Longstreet's corps.'

"When I bore the message back to General Lee, he said, 'Then there is nothing left me but to go and see General Grant, and I would rather die a thousand deaths.'

"Convulsed with passionate grief, many were the wild words which we spoke as we stood around him. Said one, 'Oh, general, what will history say of the surrender of the army in the field?'

"He replied, 'Yes, I know they will say hard things of us; they will not understand how we are overwhelmed by numbers. But that is not the question, colonel; the question is, "Is it right to surrender this army?" If it is right, then I will take all the responsibility!' " *

Presently General Lee called to have me ride forward to him. He was dressed in a suit of new uniform, sword and sash, a handsomely embroidered belt, boots, and a pair of gold spurs. At first approach his compact figure appeared as a man in the flush vigor of forty summers, but as I drew near, the handsome apparel and brave bearing failed to conceal his profound depression. He stood near the embers of some burned rails, received me

* Memoirs of Robert E. Lee, A. L. Long.

GENERAL ALEXANDER ARRANGING THE LAST LINE OF BATTLE FORMED IN THE ARMY OF NORTHERN VIRGINIA.

with graceful salutation, and spoke at once of affairs in front and the loss of his subsistence stores. He remarked that the advanced columns stood against a very formidable force, which he could not break through, while General Meade was at my rear ready to call for all the work that the rear-guard could do, and, closing with the expression that it was not possible for him to get along, requested my view. I asked if the bloody sacrifice of his army could in any way help the cause in other quarters. He thought not. Then, I said, your situation speaks for itself.

He called up General Mahone, and made to him a similar statement of affairs. The early morning was raw and damp. General Mahone was chilled standing in wait without fire. He pushed up the embers and said to the general he did not want him to think he was scared, he was only chilled. General Mahone sometimes liked to talk a little on questions of moment, and asked several questions. My attention was called to messages from the troops for a time, so that I failed to hear all of the conversation, but I heard enough of it to know that General Mahone thought it time to see General Grant. Appeal was made to me to affirm that judgment, and it was promptly approved.

General Grant had been riding with his column in our rear during the correspondence of the 7th and 8th. So General Lee, upon mounting Traveller, his favorite horse, rode to our rear to meet him, leaving his advanced forces engaged in a lively skirmish. He did not think to send them notice of his intended ride, nor did he authorize me to call a truce. He passed my rear under flag, but General Grant's orders were that his correspondence with General Lee should not interrupt or delay the operations of any of his forces. Our advance troops were in action, and General Humphreys was up with the Second Corps of the Army of the Potomac, preparing for action against our rear-guard. The situation was embarrassing. It was plain enough that I should attack the Second Corps before others could be up and prepare for action, though our truce forbade. It could not prevail, however, to call me to quiet while the enemy in plain view was preparing for attack, so we continued at our work constructing our best line of defence, and when strong enough I ordered parts of the rear-guard forward to support the advanced forces, and directed General Alexander to establish them with part of his batteries in the best position for support or rallying line in case the front lines were forced back. That was the last line of battle formed in the Army of Northern Virginia.

While this formation was proceeding, report came from our front that a break had been found through which we could force passage. I called for a swift courier, but not one could be found. Colonel J. C. Haskell had a blooded mare that had been carefully led from Petersburg. Appreciating the signs of the times, he had ordered her saddled, intending a desperate ride to escape impending humiliation, but, learning my need of a swift courier, he came and offered his services and his mare. He was asked to take the information just brought in to General Lee, and as he mounted was told to kill his mare but bring General Lee back. He rode like the wind.

General Lee had passed out and dismounted beyond a turn of the road, and was not seen until the gallant rider had dashed by him. The steed swept onward some distance before the rider could pull up. As Colonel Haskell rode back, General Lee walked to meet him, exclaiming, "You have ruined your beautiful mare! why did you do so?" The swift despatch was too late. General Lee's note to General Grant asking an interview had gone beyond recall.

As my troops marched to form the last line a message came from General Lee saying he had not thought to give notice of the intended ride to meet General Grant, and asked to have me send his message to that effect to General Gordon, and it was duly sent by Captain Sims, of the Third Corps staff, serving at my head-quarters since the fall of A. P. Hill.

After delivering the message, Captain Sims, through some informality, was sent to call the truce. The firing ceased. General Custer rode to Captain Sims to know his authority, and, upon finding that he was of my staff, asked to be conducted to my head-quarters, and down they came in fast gallop, General Custer's flaxen locks flowing over his shoulders, and in brusk, excited manner, he said,—

"In the name of General Sheridan I demand the unconditional surrender of this army."

He was reminded that I was not the commander of the army, that he was within the lines of the enemy without authority, addressing a superior officer, and in disrespect to General Grant as well as myself; that if I was the commander of the army I would not receive the message of General Sheridan.

He then became more moderate, saying it would be a pity to have more blood upon that field. Then I suggested that the truce be respected, and said,—

"As you are now more reasonable, I will say that General Lee has gone to meet General Grant, and it is for them to determine the future of the armies."

He was satisfied, and rode back to his command.

General Grant rode away from the Army of the Potomac on the morning of the 9th to join his troops near Appomattox Court-House, so General Lee's note was sent around to him. When advised of the change, General Lee rode back to his front to await there the answer to his note. While waiting, General Lee expressed apprehension that his refusal to meet General Grant's first proposition might cause him to demand harsh terms.

I assured him that I knew General Grant well enough

to say that the terms would be such as he would demand under similar circumstances, but he yet had doubts. The conversation continued in broken sentences until the bearer of the return despatch approached. As he still seemed apprehensive of humiliating demands, I suggested that in that event he should break off the interview and tell General Grant to do his worst. The thought of another round seemed to brace him, and he rode with Colonel Marshall, of his staff, to meet the Union commander.

The status of affairs spread through the advance troops of the army, but the work of preparation on my rear line was continued. General Field inquired of a passing officer, "What's up?" but, seeing arrangements going on for attack in our rear, he continued his work of preparation to receive it.

General Grant was found prepared to offer as liberal terms as General Lee could expect, and, to obviate a collision between his army of the rear with ours, ordered an officer sent to give notice of the truce. A ride around the lines would consume time, and he asked to have the officer conducted through our lines. Colonel Fairfax was sent with him. When they reached our rear line it was still at work on the trenches. The officer expressed surprise at the work of preparation, as not proper under truce. Colonel Fairfax ordered the work discontinued, and claimed that a truce between belligerents can only be recognized by mutual consent. As the object of the ride was to make the first announcement of properly authorized truce, the work of preparation between the lines was no violation of the usages of war, particularly when it was borne in mind that the orders of General Grant were that the correspondence should not delay or interrupt military operations.

As General Lee rode back to his army the officers and soldiers of his troops about the front lines assembled in promiscuous crowds of all arms and grades in anxious wait for their loved commander. From force of habit a burst of salutations greeted him, but it quieted as suddenly as it arose. The road was packed by standing troops as he approached, the men with hats off, heads and hearts bowed down. As he passed they raised their heads and looked upon him with swimming eyes. Those who could find voice said good-by, those who could not speak, and were near, passed their hands gently over the sides of Traveller. He rode with his hat off, and had sufficient control to fix his eyes on a line between the ears of Traveller and look neither to right nor left until he reached a large white-oak tree, where he dismounted to make his last head-quarters, and finally talked a little.

The shock was most severe upon Field's division. Seasoned by four years of battle triumphant, the veterans in that body stood at Appomattox when the sun rose on the 9th day of April, 1865, as invincible of valor as on the morning of the 31st of August, 1862, after breaking up the Union lines of the second field of Manassas. They had learned little of the disasters about Petersburg, less of that at Sailor's Creek, and surrender had not had time to enter their minds until it was announced accomplished!

The reported opportunity to break through the enemy's lines proved a mistake. General Munford, suspecting surrender from the sudden quiet of the front, made a dashing ride, and passed the enemy's lines with his division of cavalry, and that caused the impression that we would be able to march on.

Soon after General Lee's return ride his chief of ordnance reported a large amount of United States currency in his possession. In doubt as to the proper disposition of the funds, General Lee sent the officer to ask my opinion. As it was not known or included in the conditions of capitulation, and was due (and ten times more) to the faithful troops, I suggested a *pro rata* distribution of it.

The officer afterwards brought three hundred dollars as my part. I took one hundred, and asked to have the balance distributed among Field's division,—the troops most distant from their homes.

The commissioners appointed to formulate details of the capitulation were assigned a room in the McLean residence. The way to it led through the room occupied as General Grant's head-quarters.

As I was passing through the room, as one of the commissioners, General Grant looked up, recognized me, rose, and with his old-time cheerful greeting gave me his hand, and after passing a few remarks offered a cigar, which was gratefully received.

The first step under capitulation was to deliver to the Union army some fifteen hundred prisoners, taken since we left Petersburg, not all of them by my infantry, Rosser's and Munford's cavalry having taken more than half of them. Besides these I delivered to General Grant all of the Confederate soldiers left under my care by General Lee, except about two hundred lost in the affairs about Petersburg, Amelia Court-House, Jetersville, Rice's Station, and Cumberland Church. None were reported killed except the gallant officers Brigadier-General Dearing, of Rosser's cavalry, Colonel Bostan, of Munford's cavalry, and Major Thompson, of Stuart's horse artillery, in the desperate and gallant fight to which they were ordered against the bridge-burning party.

General Grant's artillery prepared to fire a salute in honor of the surrender, but he ordered it stopped.

As the world continues to look at and study the grand combinations and strategy of General Grant, the higher will be his award as a great soldier. Confederates should be foremost in crediting him with all that his admirers so justly claim, and ask at the same time that his great adversary be measured by the same high standards.

On the 12th of April the Army of Northern Virginia

marched to the field in front of Appomattox Court-House, and by divisions and parts of divisions deployed into line, stacked their arms, folded their colors, and walked empty-handed to find their distant, blighted homes.

There were "surrendered and paroled" on the last day of our military history over twenty-eight thousand officers and men,—viz.:

General Lee and staff	15
Longstreet's corps *	14,833
Gordon's corps †	7,200
Ewell's corps	287
Cavalry corps	1,786
Artillery	2,586
Detachments	1,649
Total	28,356

In glancing backward over the period of the war, and the tremendous and terrible events with which it was fraught, the reflection irresistibly arises, that it might perhaps have been avoided and without dishonor. The flag and the fame of the nation could have suffered no reproach had General Scott's advice, before the outbreak, been followed,—"Wayward sisters, depart in peace." The Southern States would have found their way back to the Union without war far earlier than they did by war. The reclaiming bonds would then have been those only of love, and the theory of government formulated by George Washington would have experienced no fracture. But the inflexible fiat of fate seemingly went forth for war; and so for four long years the history of this great nation was written in the blood of its strong men.

* Including the parts of the Third Corps attached after the fall of A. P. Hill, and about five thousand that reported on the 7th, 8th, and 9th in bands and squads from the columns broken up at Sailor's Creek.

† Including five thousand two hundred of fragments dispersed at Petersburg and during the rearward march, that joined us in retreat.

CHAPTER XLIV.

POST-BELLUM PENDANT.

Old Friends and their Kindness—General Grant—His Characteristic Letter of Introduction to President Johnson—In Business in New Orleans—Political Unfriendliness—Cause of Criticism of Military Career—Appointed Surveyor of Customs—The Old Nurse.

Some weeks after the surrender the newspapers announced that I was to visit Washington City. My old company commander, Bradford R. Alden, who had resigned from the army some years before the war, came down from New York to meet me. Not finding me, he sent to tell me of his trip, that he was anxious about me, lest I might be in need of assistance; that in that event I should draw on him for such amount as I wanted. When I was ready to return his favor he was not in the country, and it was only through a mutual friend, General Alvord, that his address in Europe was found and the amount returned. A more noble, lovable character never descended from the people of Plymouth Rock.

About the 1st of November, 1865, business of personal nature called me to Washington. I stopped at the Metropolitan Hotel. Upon seeing the arrival in the morning papers, General W. A. Nichols, of the United States army, called and insisted that my visit should be with him and his family. The request was declined with the suggestion that the war-feeling was too warm for an officer of the army to entertain a prominent Confederate, but he insisted and urged that his good wife would not be satisfied unless the visit was made. So it was settled, and I became his guest. He was on duty at the time as assistant adjutant-general at the War Department. As I was stopping with an officer of the army, the usages of military life required that I should call upon the commanding general.

The next morning I walked with General Nichols to make an official call on General Grant. He recognized us as we entered his office, rose and walked to meet us. After the usual brief call, we rose to take leave, when he asked to have us call on his family during the evening. Most of those whom we met during the evening were old-time personal friends, especially the father-in-law, Mr. Dent. When leaving, after a pleasant evening, General Grant walked with us to the gate and asked if I cared to have my pardon. I pleaded not guilty of an offence that required pardon. He said that he meant amnesty,—that he wished to know if I cared to have it. I told him that I intended to live in the country, and would prefer to have the privileges of citizenship. He told me to call at his office at noon next day; that in the mean time he would see the Secretary of War and the President in regard to the matter.

The next day he gave me a letter to the President, and said that he had seen him and thought the matter was arranged; that I should first see the Secretary of War, then the President. His strong and characteristic letter to the President was as follows:

"HEAD-QUARTERS ARMIES OF THE UNITED STATES,
"WASHINGTON, D. C., November 7, 1865.

"HIS EXCELLENCY A. JOHNSON,
"*President:*

"Knowing that General Longstreet, late of the army which was in rebellion against the authority of the United States, is in the city, and presuming that he intends asking executive clemency before leaving, I beg to say a word in his favor.

"General Longstreet comes under the third, fifth, and eighth exceptions made in your proclamation of the 29th of May, 1865. I believe I can safely say that there is nowhere among the exceptions a more honorable class of men than those embraced in the fifth and eighth of these, nor a class that will more faithfully observe any obligation which they may take upon themselves.

General Longstreet, in my opinion, stands high among this class. I have known him well for more than twenty-six years, first as a cadet at West Point and afterwards as an officer of the army. For five years from my graduation we served together, a portion of the time in the same regiment. I speak of him, therefore, from actual personal acquaintance.

"In the late rebellion, I think, not one single charge was ever brought against General Longstreet for persecution of prisoners of war or of persons for their political opinions. If such charges were ever made, I never heard them. I have no hesitation, therefore, in recommending General Longstreet to your Excellency for pardon. I will further state that my opinion of him is such that I shall feel it as a personal favor to myself if this pardon is granted.

"Very respectfully, your obedient servant,

"U. S. GRANT,

"*Lieutenant-General.*"

Supported by this generous endorsement, I called on the Secretary of War, who referred me to the President. After a lengthy interview the President asked to have the matter put off until next day, when I should call at noon. The next day he was still unprepared to make decision, but, after a long, pleasant talk, he said,—

"There are three persons of the South who can never receive amnesty: Mr. Davis, General Lee, and yourself. You have given the Union cause too much trouble."

I replied, "You know, Mr. President, that those who are forgiven most love the most."

"Yes," he said, "you have very high authority for that, but you can't have amnesty."

During a subsequent session of Congress, General Pope sent in a list of names from Georgia for whom he asked relief from their political disabilities. General Grant, after approving it, made request to one of his friends in Congress to have my name put on the list, and I was extended relief soon after it was given to General R. E. Lee.

In January, 1866, I engaged in business in New Or-

leans with the Owen brothers,—William, Miller, and Edward, old soldiers of the Washington Artillery,—as cotton factors, and speedily found fair prosperity. Before the year was out I was asked to take position in an insurance company, but declined, and repeated applications were refused under plea of limited business experience, but, under promise of ample and competent assistance, I accepted the place with a salary of five thousand dollars, and my affairs were more than prosperous until I was asked an opinion upon the political crisis of 1867.

As the whole animus of the latter-day adverse criticisms upon, and uncritical assertions in regard to, the commander of the First Corps of the Army of Northern Virginia had its origin in this matter of politics, a brief review of the circumstances is in order.

As will be readily recalled by my older readers (while for the younger it is a matter of history), President Johnson, after the war, adopted a reconstruction policy of his own, and some of the States were reorganized under it with Democratic governors and legislatures, and all would have followed. But Congress, being largely Republican, was not satisfied, and enacted that the States could not be accepted unless they provided in their new constitutions for *negro suffrage.* In case they would not, the State governments should be removed and the States placed in the hands of general officers of the army as military governors, who should see that the States were reorganized and restored to the Union under the laws.

Under the severe ordeal one of the city papers of New Orleans called upon the generals of Confederate service to advise the people of the course that they should pursue,—naming the officers. I thought it better policy to hold the States, as they were organized, under the President's policy, shape their constitutions as directed by Congress, and have the States not yet reorganized follow the same course. My letter upon the subject was as follows:

"NEW ORLEANS, LA., June 3, 1867.

"J. M. G. PARKER, ESQ.:

"DEAR SIR,—Your esteemed favor of the 15th ultimo was duly received.

"I was much pleased to have the opportunity to hear Senator Wilson, and was agreeably surprised to meet such fairness and frankness from a politician whom I had been taught to believe harsh in his feelings towards the people of the South.

"I have considered your suggestion to wisely unite in efforts to restore Louisiana to her former position in the Union 'through the party now in power.' My letter of the 6th of April, to which you refer, clearly indicates a desire for practical reconstruction and reconciliation. There is only one route left open, which practical men cannot fail to see.

"The serious difficulty arises from want of that wisdom so important for the great work in hand. Still, I will be happy to work in any harness that promises relief to our discomfited people and harmony to the nation, whether bearing the mantle of Mr. Davis or Mr. Sumner.

"It is fair to assume that the strongest laws are those established by the sword. The ideas that divided political parties before the war—upon the rights of the States—were thoroughly discussed by our wisest statesmen, and eventually appealed to the arbitrament of the sword. The decision was in favor of the North, so that her construction becomes the law, and should be so accepted.

"The military bill and amendments are the only peace-offerings they have for us, and should be accepted as the starting-point for future issues.

"Like others of the South not previously connected with politics, I naturally acquiesced in the ways of Democracy, but, so far as I can judge, there is nothing tangible in them, beyond the issues that were put to test in the war and there lost. As there is nothing left to take hold of except prejudice, which cannot be worked for good for any one, it seems proper and right that we should seek some standing which may encourage hope for the future.

"If I appreciate the issues of Democracy at this moment, they are the enfranchisement of the negro and the rights of Congress in the premises, but the acts have been passed, are parts of the laws of the land, and no power but Congress can remove them.

"Besides, if we now accept the doctrine that the States only can legislate on suffrage, we will fix the negro vote upon us, for he is

now a suffragan, and his vote, with the vote that will go with him, will hold to his rights, while, by recognizing the acts of Congress, we may, after a fair trial, if negro suffrage proves a mistake, appeal and have Congress correct the error. It will accord better with wise policy to insist that the negro shall vote in the Northern as well as the Southern States.

"If every one will meet the crisis with proper appreciation of our condition and obligations, the sun will rise to-morrow on a happy people. Our fields will again begin to yield their increase, our railways and waters will teem with abundant commerce, our towns and cities will resound with the tumult of trade, and we will be reinvigorated by the blessings of Almighty God.

"Very respectfully yours,

"James Longstreet."

I might have added that not less forceful than the grounds I gave were the obligations under which we were placed by the terms of our paroles,—"To respect the laws of Congress,"—but the letter was enough.

The afternoon of the day upon which my letter was published the paper that had called for advice published a column of editorial calling me traitor! deserter of my friends! and accusing me of joining the enemy! but did not publish a line of the letter upon which it based the charges! Other papers of the Democracy took up the garbled representation of this journal and spread it broadcast, not even giving the letter upon which they based their evil attacks upon me.

Up to that time the First Corps, in all of its parts, in all of its history, was above reproach. I was in successful business in New Orleans as cotton factor, with a salary from an insurance company of five thousand dollars per year.

The day after the announcement old comrades passed me on the streets without speaking. Business began to grow dull. General Hood (the only one of my old comrades who occasionally visited me) thought that he could save the insurance business, and in a few weeks I found myself at leisure.

Two years after that period, on March 4, 1869, General Grant was inaugurated President of the United States, and in the bigness of his generous heart called me to Washington. Before I found opportunity to see him he sent my name to the Senate for confirmation as surveyor of customs at New Orleans. I was duly confirmed, and held the office until 1873, when I resigned. Since that time I have lived in New Orleans, Louisiana, and in Gainesville, Georgia, surrounded by a few of my old friends, and in occasional appreciative touch with others, South and North.

Of all the people alive I still know and meet, probably no one carries me farther back in recollections of my long life than does my "old nurse." Most of the family servants were discharged after the war at Macon, Mississippi, where some of them still reside, among them this old man, Daniel, who still claims the family name, but at times uses another. He calls promptly when I visit Macon and looks for "something to remember you by." During my last visit he seemed more concerned for me than usual, and on one of his calls asked,—

"Marse Jim, do you belong to any church?"

"Oh, yes," I said, "I try to be a good Christian."

He laughed loud and long, and said,—

"Something must have scared you mighty bad; to change you so from what you was when I had to care for you."

In a recent letter he sent a message to say that he is getting to be a little feeble.

Blessings on his brave heart!

Lexington Va: 19 Jan '66

My dear Genl

Upon my return from Richmond, where I have been for a week, on business connected with Washington College, I found your letter of the 26 Ulto. I regret very much that you never recd my first letter, as you might then perhaps have given me the information I desired, with more ease to yourself, & with more expedition than now. I did not know how to address it, but sent it to a friend in Richmond, who gave it to one of our officers going South, who transferred it to another &c, & after travelling many weary miles, has been recently returned to me. I start it again in pursuit of you, though you did not tell me how to address you. I have almost forgotten what it contained, but I hope it will inform you of my purpose in writing a history of the Campaigns in Va & of the object that I have in view, so that you may give me all the information in your power. I shall be in no hurry in publishing, & will not do so, until I feel satisfied that

I have got the true story, as my only object is to disseminate the truth. I am very sorry to hear that your records were destroyed too, but I hope Sorrel & Latrobe will be able to supply you with all you require. I wish to detail the acts of all the Corps of the Army of N. Va. wherever they did duty, & do not wish to omit so important a one as yours. I will therefore wait as long as I can.

I shall be very glad to receive anything you may give to Mr Washington McLean, as I know you recommend no one but those who deserve your good opinion.

I am delighted to hear that your arm is still improving & hope it will soon be restored. You are however becoming so accomplished with your left hand, as not to need it. You must remember me very kindly to Mrs Longstreet & all your children. I have not had an opportunity yet to return the compliment she paid me. I had while in Richmond a great many enquiries after you, & learned that you intended commencing business in New Orleans. If you become as good a merchant as you were a soldier I shall be content. No one will then excel you, & no one can wish you more success & more happiness than I. My interest & affection for you will never cease, & my prayers are always offered for your prosperity—

I am most truly yours

R E Lee

Genl J. Longstreet

APPENDIX.

LETTERS OF GENERAL ROBERT E. LEE AND GENERAL LONGSTREET.

I.

Lee to Anderson on Conduct of the First Corps.

June 16, 1864.

LIEUTENANT-GENERAL R. H. ANDERSON,
Commanding Longstreet's Corps:

GENERAL,—I take great pleasure in presenting to you my congratulations upon the conduct of the men of your corps. I believe that they will carry anything they are put against. We tried very hard to stop Pickett's men from capturing the breast-works of the enemy, but could not do it. I hope his loss has been small.

I am, with respect, your obedient servant,

R. E. LEE,
General.

II.

Lee to Longstreet congratulating him on his Convalescence and anticipating Return.

CAMP PETERSBURG, August 29, 1864.

GENERAL J. LONGSTREET:

MY DEAR GENERAL,—I received yesterday your letter of the 23d, and am much gratified at your improvement. You will soon be as well as ever, and we shall all be rejoiced at your return. You must not, however, become impatient at the gradual progress you must necessarily make, but be content with the steady advance you are making to health and strength. Your progress will be the more certain and your recovery more confirmed. Do not let Sherman capture you, and I will endeavor to hold Grant till you come. I am glad to hear such good accounts of my little namesake. Good lungs are a great blessing, and nothing expands them better than a full, hearty yell. I hope Mrs. Longstreet is well, and that she is enjoying the good peaches and melons of Georgia. We have but little enjoyment here. Our enemy is very cautious, and he has become so proficient in intrenching that he seems to march with a system already prepared. He threatens dreadful things every day, but, thank God, he has not expunged us yet.

All your army friends inquire for you anxiously, and will be delighted to hear of your improvement. We shall not object to your chirography, so you must practise it often, and let me hear of your progress and well-doing. Please present my kindest regards to Mrs. Longstreet, and love to my namesake. The gentlemen of my staff are very grateful for your remembrance, and unite with me in sincere wishes for your welfare and happiness. I am sure the rest of this army would join did they know of the opportunity.

With great regard, very truly yours,

R. E. LEE.

III.

Longstreet to Lee.

HEAD-QUARTERS ARMY CORPS,
November 24, 1864.

GENERAL R. E. LEE,
Commanding:

GENERAL,—From the report of scouts received yesterday, it seems that the Tenth Corps is still on this side, or if it went over to the south side, has returned. The information, too, seems to indicate the arrival of the Sixth Corps from the Valley.

Under these circumstances it will be necessary for me to force the enemy to develop the extent of his move on this side before taking any more of my troops to the south side. This I shall do, of course, as rapidly as possible. I am going to have the roads leading from White Oak Swamp to the Williamsburg road well broken up with subsoil ploughs. I think that the enemy will then have to build a corduroy there as he moves. He surely will, if I can have a good gentle rain after the roads are thoroughly ploughed. Can't you apply this idea to advantage on your side on the roads that General Grant will be obliged to travel if he goes to Burkeville? I don't know, however, but that it would be better for us to go to Burkeville and block the roads behind him. If the roads that General Sherman must travel to get to Charleston

or Savannah can be thoroughly ploughed and the trees felled over them, I think that General Sherman will not be able to get to his destination in fifty days, as the Northern papers expect; and it is not thought to be possible that he can collect more than fifty days' rations before reaching the coast. If the parties are properly organized, I think that they might destroy or injure all of the roads so as to break down General Sherman's animals, and result in the capture of most of his forces.

I remain, very respectfully, yours most obediently,

J. LONGSTREET,
Lieutenant-General.

IV.

Longstreet to Lee on Impressment of Gold and Measures for Final Campaign.

[Confidential.]

HEAD-QUARTERS, February 14, 1865.

GENERAL R. E. LEE,
Commanding:

GENERAL,—Recent developments of the enemy's designs seem to indicate an early concentration of his armies against Richmond. This, of course, would involve a like concentration on our part, or the abandonment of our capital. The latter emergency would, I think, be almost fatal,—probably quite so, after our recent reverses. To concentrate here in time to meet the movements of the enemy we will be obliged to use the little of our Southern railroad that is left us in transporting our troops, so that we cannot haul provisions over that route. I fear, therefore, that we will not be able to feed our troops unless we adopt extraordinary efforts and measures. I think that there is enough of the necessaries of life left in Virginia and North Carolina to help us through our troubles if we can only reach them. Impressing officers, however, nor collectors of taxes in kind, nor any other plan heretofore employed, is likely to get those supplies in time or in quantities to meet our necessities. The citizens will not give their supplies up and permit their families and servants to suffer for the necessaries of life without some strong inducement. For each one may naturally think that the little that he would supply by denying himself and family would go but little way where so much is needed. He does not want Confederate money, for his meat and bread will buy him clothes, etc., for his family more readily and in larger quantities than the money that the government would pay. The only thing that will insure our rations and

national existence is *gold*. Send out the gold through Virginia and North Carolina and pay liberal prices, and my conviction is that we shall have no more distress for want of food. The winter is about over, and the families can and will subsist on molasses, bread, and vegetables for the balance of the year if they can get gold for their supplies. There is a great deal of meat and bread inside the enemy's lines that our people would bring us for gold; but they won't go to that trouble for Confederate money. They can keep gold so much safer than they can meat and bread, and it is always food and clothing.

If the government has not the gold, it must impress it, or if there is no law for the impressment, the gold must be taken without the law. Necessity does not know or wait for law. If we stop to make laws in order that we may reach the gold it will disappear the day that the law is mentioned in Congress. To secure it no one should suspect that we are after it until we knock at the doors of the vaults that contain it, and we must then have guards to be sure that it is not made away with.

It seems to my mind that our prospects will be brighter than they have been if we can only get food for our men; and I think that the plan that I have proposed will secure the food.

There seem to be many reasons for the opinion that the enemy deems our capital essential to him. To get the capital he will concentrate here everything that he has, and we will be better able to fight him when we shall have concentrated than when we are in detachments. The Army of the Mississippi will get new life and spirits as soon as it finds itself alongside of this, and we will feel more comfortable ourselves to know that all are under one eye and one head that is able to handle them.

I remain, most respectfully and truly, your obedient servant,

J. LONGSTREET,

Lieutenant-General.

V.

Lee to Longstreet on Plans for Campaign.

[Confidential.]

HEAD-QUARTERS CONFEDERATE STATES ARMIES,
February 22, 1865.

LIEUTENANT-GENERAL J. LONGSTREET,
Commanding, etc.:

GENERAL,—Your letter of the 14th instant is received. It arrived during my absence in Richmond, and has not been overlooked. I agree with you entirely in believing that if we had gold we could get sufficient supplies for our army, but the great difficulty is to obtain the gold. It is not in the coffers of the government or the banks, but is principally hoarded by individuals throughout the country, and is inaccessible to us. I hope, under the reorganization of the commissary department, if we can maintain possession of our communications, that the army will be better supplied than heretofore, and that we can accumulate some provisions ahead. As regards the concentration of our troops near the capital, the effect would be to produce a like concentration of the enemy, and an increase of our difficulties in obtaining food and forage. But this, whether for good or evil, is now being accomplished by the enemy, who seems to be forcing Generals Beauregard and Bragg in this direction. If Sherman marches his army to Richmond, as General Beauregard reports it is his intention to do, and General Schofield is able to unite with him, we shall have to abandon our position on the James River, as lamentable as it is on every account. The want of supplies alone would force us to withdraw when the enemy reaches the Roanoke. Our line is so long, extending nearly from the Chickahominy to the Nottoway, and the enemy is so close upon us, that if we are obliged to withdraw we cannot concentrate all our troops nearer than some point on the line of railroad between Richmond and Danville. Should a necessity, therefore, arise, I propose to concentrate at or near Burkeville. The route for the troops north of James River would have to be through Richmond, on the road to Amelia Court-House, the cavalry passing up the north branch of the river, and crossing at some point above Richmond. Pickett's division would take the route through Chesterfield Court-House, crossing the Appomattox at Goode's Bridge. With the army concentrated at or near Burkeville, our communications north and south would be by that railroad, and west by the Southside Railroad. We might also seize the opportunity of striking at Grant, should he pursue us rapidly, or at Sherman, before they could unite. I wish you to consider this subject, and give me your views. I desire you also to make every preparation to take the field at a moment's notice, and to accumulate all the supplies you can. General Grant seems to be preparing to move out by his left flank. He is accumulating near Hatcher's Run depots of supplies, and apparently concentrating a strong force in that quarter. Yesterday and to-day trains have passed from his right to his left loaded with troops, which may be the body of eight thousand which you report having left Signal Hill yesterday. I cannot tell whether it is his intention to maintain his position until his other columns approach nearer, or to anticipate any movement by us which he might suppose would then become necessary. I wish you would watch closely his movements on the north side of the river, and try and ascertain whether he is diminishing his force. If he makes the move which appearances now indicate, he may draw out his whole force, abandoning his lines of defence, or hold them partially and move with the remainder of his troops.

I should like very much to confer with you on these subjects, but I fear it will be impossible for me to go north of James River, and I do not know that it will be convenient for you to come here.

Very respectfully, your obedient servant,

R. E. LEE,
General.

P.S.—Can you not return Pickett's brigade to him in order that I may withdraw Grimes's brigade from his line, its division having been ordered to our right?

R. E. L.

VI.

Longstreet to Lee on Impressment of Men.

[Confidential.]

HEAD-QUARTERS, February 23, 1865.

GENERAL R. E. LEE,
Commanding, etc. :

GENERAL,—Your letter of yesterday is received. I think you did not understand my letter of the 14th instant. My effort was to express conviction that Sherman's move was aimed at Richmond, and that Grant's concentration here would force us to do the same thing; and, that we might be able to do so, it was necessary that we should have gold, by impressment, to purchase our produce supplies. I think that it is not too late yet. We can surely get the gold by sending impressing officers with guards to the vaults in which it is stored.

I understand that there are twelve hundred men in Lynchburg already organized, and that we may get eight or ten thousand men in Richmond by taking everybody who is able to bear arms. The staff-officers about Richmond would be nearly enough to officer this force. If such a force can be raised and put in my lines, it can hold them, I think, and my corps can move down to the relief of Beauregard, or it may be moved over to our right, and hold Grant in check, so that Sherman will be obliged to unite with him or seek a base at New-Berne or at Wilmington. This would give Beauregard and Bragg time to unite their forces to meet Sherman and Schofield here or wherever they may appear. We shall lose more men by a move than by a battle. It is true that we may be compelled to move after the battle, but I think not. If we fight Sherman as I suggest, we shall surely drive him to the water for fresh supplies, even if we are not otherwise successful. Then we may have time to concentrate as soon as Grant, and re-open the line of communication with the South.

The local and other troops that we may get from Richmond and Lynchburg will have tolerably comfortable huts, and there will be enough old soldiers amongst them to teach them picket duty. There are also some cavalrymen who can aid them.

I should think that Grant, if he moves, can only make a partial move, similar to his last, and that would not injure us very materially.

In preparing to take the field, in view of the abandonment of Richmond, is it your desire to keep our wagons about our camps that we may move at once? Our wagons are out all the time gathering supplies, and at times some distance; so that a very sudden move would leave them behind. Shall we continue to send them or keep them with us? . . .

Your obedient servant,

J. LONGSTREET,

Lieutenant-General.

VII.

Lee to Longstreet.

HEAD-QUARTERS, February 25, 1865.

GENERAL,—I have received your letters of the 23d and 24th insts. I fear I did not entirely comprehend your views expressed in your letter of the 14th. I think, however, my reply meets your supposition, in the event of concentration by the enemy. I shall in that case unite all the forces possible. I think you are misinformed as to the number of men in Lynchburg. At my last call upon General Colston, commissary there, he said he had not one hundred men, and they were unarmed. I am very glad to hear that General Ewell can get force enough from Richmond to man the lines north of James River. I know him to be a brave old soldier, ready to attempt anything, but I do not know where he will find the men. Please see him and get a definite statement, for if that can be done it will lighten our labor considerably. You cannot afford to keep your wagons by you. They will have to be kept collecting provisions, forage, etc., or you will starve. I am making great efforts to gather supplies, and send you some documents which will show what the commissary-general is doing in addition to the operations of the officers of his department. It will be a grievous thing to be obliged to abandon our position, and I hope the necessity will never arise, but it would be more grievous to lose our army. I am fully alive to the benefits of procuring gold, but fear it cannot be obtained in the way you suggest; still, I will try. I am much gratified by the earnestness and zeal you display in our operations; and were our whole population animated by the same spirit, we should be invincible. The last reports from S. C. indicated that Sherman was turning eastward. It may be to reach the Pedee in search of supplies.

Very respectfully, your obedient servant,

R. E. LEE,
General.

GENERAL LONGSTREET,
Commanding, etc.

VIII.

Longstreet to Lee on Impressment of Gold.

HEAD-QUARTERS FIRST CORPS,
February 26, 1865.

GENERAL R. E. LEE,
Commanding:

GENERAL,—I have just heard from General Ewell indirectly that he can raise force enough at Richmond to hold the lines on this side, so that my corps may be withdrawn temporarily to your right, that is, if you can put a part of the Second Corps in place of Pickett's division. This arrangement will give you force enough to meet any move that the enemy may make upon your right. If he makes no move, then you can, when the proper moment arrives, detach a force to the aid of General Beauregard, and if the enemy should then press you, you can abandon Petersburg and hold your line here, and take up the line of the Appomattox. But I think that the enemy will be forced to move a force south the moment that he finds that you are reinforcing against Sherman, else he will encounter the risk of losing Sherman as well as Richmond. There is some hazard in the plan, but nothing can be accomplished in war without risk.

The other important question is provisions. We are doing

tolerably well by hauling from the country and paying market prices in Confederate money. If you would give us gold I have reason to believe that we could get an abundant supply for four months, and by that time we ought to be able to reopen our communication with the South. The gold is here, and we should take it. We have been impressing food and all of the necessaries of life from women and children, and have been the means of driving thousands from their homes in destitute conditions. Should we hesitate, then, about putting a few who have made immense fortunes at our expense to a little inconvenience by impressing their gold? It is necessary for us, and I do not think that we should let our capital fall into the enemy's hands for fear of injuring the feelings or interests of a few individuals. We have expended too much of blood and treasure in holding it for the last four years to allow it to go now by default. I think that it may be saved. If it can, we should not leave any possible contingency untried.

I think, however, that the enemy's positions are so well selected and fortified that we must either wait for an opportunity to draw him off from here or await his attack. For even a successful assault would cripple us so much that we could get no advantage commensurate with our loss.

I remain with great respect, and truly, your obedient servant,

J. LONGSTREET,
Lieutenant-General.

IX.

Longstreet to Lee on his "Peace" Interview with General Ord.

HEAD-QUARTERS FIRST ARMY CORPS,
March 1, 1865.

GENERAL R. E. LEE,
Commanding:

GENERAL,—I had another interview with Major-General Ord yesterday, and expressed the opinions that were spoken of in our interview at the President's mansion on Sabbath last. He acceded promptly to my proposition that the war must cease if we are to go to work to try to make peace, and to the proposal for a military convention. I further claimed that we could not go into convention upon any more favorable basis than an earnest desire to arrange plans for peace that should be equally honorable for both parties. To this also I understood him to give his unqualified consent. He says that General Grant has the authority to meet you if you have authority to appoint a military convention, and proposed that you should indicate your desire to meet General Grant, if you felt authorized to do so. As he made this proposition before mine, to the effect that General Grant should express his desire to meet you, and as the interview between General Ord and myself had been brought on at the request of General Ord, I did not feel that I could well do otherwise than promise to write to you of the disposition on their part to have the interview. If you think it worth your time to invite General Grant to an interview, it might be upon some other as the ostensible grounds, and this matter might be brought up incidentally. I presume that General Grant's first proposition will be to go into convention upon the basis of reconstruction; but if I have not misunderstood General Ord's conversation, General Grant will agree to take the matter up without requiring any principle as a basis further than the general principle of desiring to make peace upon terms that are equally honorable for both sides. I would suggest that the interview take place on this side, and at the place of meeting between General Ord and myself; because there are several little points upon which you should be posted before the interview, and I do not see that I can well do that by writing. Besides, as "the ice has already been broken" on this side, your interview would be relieved in a measure of the formality incident to such occasions. If it should be on this side, I hope that you will give me two or three days' notice. General Stevens is of the opinion that one thousand negro laborers on this line during this month will so strengthen our position that we will be able to spare a division, and I am satisfied that we can do so if we can have the work completed, and can get the aid that General Ewell promises us.

I remain, very respectfully, your obedient servant,

J. LONGSTREET,
Lieutenant-General.

X.

Longstreet to Lee on Exchange of Political Prisoners.

HEAD-QUARTERS FIRST ARMY CORPS,
March 1, 1865.

GENERAL R. E. LEE,
Commanding:

GENERAL,—I neglected to mention in my letter just finished that General Ord expressed some apprehension for General Grant lest there might be some misunderstanding in regard to the exchange of political prisoners. The terms were general for the exchange of this class of prisoners, but were not intended by him, he says, to include such as were under charges for capital offences. General Grant desired that you should be advised of this construction of the terms.

I remain, respectfully, your most obedient servant,

J. LONGSTREET,
Lieutenant-General.

XI.

Lee to Longstreet on Interview with General Grant.

HEAD QUARTERS,
March 2, 1865.

GENERAL,—I have received to-day your letter of the 1st instant, and concluded to propose an interview to General Grant. As you desired to have two or three days' notice, I have appointed Monday next, 6th instant, at eleven A.M., at the point suggested by you. Will you send my letter to General Grant, and arrange with General Ord for the interview? If you will ride in to my quarters on Saturday next, 4th instant, by ten A.M., in Richmond, I shall be happy to see you, when you can enlighten me on the points you referred to in your letter.

I hope some good may result from the interview.

Very truly yours,

R. E. LEE,
General.

GENERAL J. LONGSTREET,
Commanding, etc.:

P.S.—Seal the letter to General Grant before transmitting.

R. E. L.

XII.

Longstreet to Lee urging Use of Gold.

HEAD-QUARTERS FIRST ARMY CORPS,
March 7, 1865.

GENERAL R. E. LEE,
Commanding:

GENERAL,—I received a letter yesterday from a friend in the interior of North Carolina assuring me that there are large quantities of provisions in the State; that many have two and three years' supply on hand, and that gold will bring anything that we need to our armies. The gold is in the country, and most of it is lying idle. Let us take it at once and save Richmond, and end the war. If we hold Richmond and keep our cotton, the war cannot last more than a year longer. If we give up Richmond we shall never be recognized by foreign powers until the government of the United States sees fit to recognize us. If we hold Richmond and let the enemy have our cotton, it seems to me that we shall furnish him the means to carry on the war against us. It looks to me as though the enemy had found that our policy of destroying the cotton rather than let it fall into their hands would break them down, and that it has forced them to the policy of sending on here to make a contract to feed and clothe our armies in order that they may get the means of carrying on the war of subjugation. If we will keep our cotton and use our gold our work will be comparatively easy.

I remain, respectfully, your obedient servant,

J. LONGSTREET,
Lieutenant-General.

XIII.

Longstreet to Lee on guarding the Danville Railroad.

HEAD-QUARTERS FIRST ARMY CORPS,
March 20, 1865.

GENERAL R. E. LEE,
Commanding:

GENERAL,—I presume that the enemy's next move will be to raid against the Danville Railroad, and think that it would be well if we begin at once to make our arrangements to meet it. In order that we may get the troops that may be necessary to meet such a move, would suggest that we collect all the dismounted men of Generals Fitz Lee, Rosser, and Lomax, and put them behind our strongest lines, and draw out a corps of infantry and hold it in readiness for the raid. General W. H. F. Lee's dismounts might also be used behind our works to great advantage. With a cavalry force of two or three thousand men to hold the enemy in check, I think that our infantry may be able to overtake the raiding column. If we can get a large cavalry force I think that we would surely be able to destroy the raiding force.

I remain your obedient servant,

J. LONGSTREET,
Lieutenant-General.

XIV.

Longstreet to Assistant Adjutant-General Taylor on Suppression of Desertion.

Head-quarters First Army Corps,
March 25, 1865.

Lieutenant-Colonel W. H. Taylor,
Assistant Adjutant-General:

The impression prevails amongst the Georgia troops of this command that persons at home having authority to raise local organizations are writing and sending messages to the men in the ranks here, offering inducements to them to quit our ranks and go home and join the home organizations. The large and increasing number of desertions, particularly amongst the Georgia troops, induces me to believe that some such outside influence must be operating upon our men. Nearly all of the parties of deserters seem to go home, and it must be under the influence of some promise, such as being received in the local forces. I would suggest, therefore, the publication of a general order warning all officers or persons authorized to raise local organizations against receiving such deserters or in any way harboring them, and cautioning all such parties that they shall be punished for such crimes under the twenty-second and twenty-third Articles of War. It may be well to publish the articles in the order, and to send the order South to be published in all the Southern papers. If the order is published, I would suggest that copies be sent to the Southern papers by special messenger or by parties going South who will take pains to have it published, otherwise I fear it may miscarry or be delayed by our irregular mails. Another growing evil seems to trouble us now in the shape of applications to raise negro companies, regiments, brigades, etc. The desire for promotion seems to have taken possession of our army, and it seems that nearly all the officers and men think that they could gain a grade or more if allowed to go home. I presume that many may try to go merely because they get furloughs. I would suggest, therefore, that some regulation be published upon this subject, and it seems to me that it should require the companies to be mustered in as non-commissioned officers and privates by the enrolling officers, and that all of the officers (general, field, and company) shall be selected from the officers, non-commissioned officers, and privates on duty with the armies of the Con-

federacy. If these matters are not speedily taken hold of by a *firm* hand, I fear that we shall be seriously damaged by them.

I remain, very respectfully, your most obedient servant,

(Signed) J. LONGSTREET,

Lieutenant-General.

XV.

Longstreet to Lee on Sheridan's Operations.

HEAD-QUARTERS FIRST ARMY CORPS,
March 28, 1865.

GENERAL R. E. LEE,
Commanding, etc.:

Your telegram asking if we can spare General Pickett's division as a supporting force to our cavalry is received. I suggested that it should be sent on that service because I was apprehensive that our railroad would be in danger of being broken up behind us, leaving us without supplies sufficient to hold Richmond until our communications south could be re-established, or in case Sheridan went to N. C., his mounted force would be too formidable for that of General Johnston's, and that General Johnston would be in great danger if we shall not reinforce him. I do not think that we can well spare the division. But I think that we would choose a lesser risk by sparing it in case Sheridan's cavalry makes either of these moves contemplated than we would by holding him here to await the result of these operations. The enemy seems now to count upon taking Richmond by raiding upon our lines of communication, and not by attacking our lines of work. I think, therefore, we should endeavor to put a force in the field that can contend against that of the enemy. If Grant sends off his cavalry, he can hardly intend to make any general move of his main army until its return. In every aspect of affairs, so far as I am advised, I think that the greater danger is from keeping too close within our trenches. If we can remain where we are independently of the railroad, and if General Johnston would be safe with such a force as Sheridan's operating against him, in addition to Sherman's, we had better keep the division here. You know much more about all those points than I do, and are much better able to decide upon them. My supply train is in from Northern Neck, and starts back to-morrow for other provisions. If there is any impropriety in sending it back, please telegraph me as soon as you receive this, that I may recall it. We have about one hundred thousand pounds of meat near

Dublin and eighteen thousand at New Boston. The C. S. complains that the railroad agents will not ship the meat unless it is boxed. This cannot always be done. If you can in any way aid us in this matter, we shall do very well for some time to come.

I remain, very respectfully, your most obedient servant,

(Signed) J. Longstreet,

Lieutenant-General.

XVI.

Longstreet to Adjutant-General Taylor on Policy towards New Organizations.

Head-quarters First Army Corps,
March 30, 1865.

Lieutenant-Colonel W. H. Taylor,
Assistant Adjutant-General:

Your letter expressing the views of the commander-in-chief in reference to the policy to be pursued in raising negro troops is received. I am apprehensive that we shall have applications and evidence enough to take from us more men than we can well spare at this critical moment in our affairs. It seems to me that any person who has the influence to raise a company or a regiment by going home could do so as well by letters to his friends at home. If I am right in this opinion, an order announcing that the officers of the companies and regiments of colored troops would be appointed from the officers, non-commissioned officers, and privates *on duty* with our armies would have the effect of bringing back more absentees than we should lose by making the appointments. If we may judge of our future success in getting up new organizations by the past, we may rely upon it that many will furnish the necessary evidence, and go home and there remain for eight and ten and twelve months. I think it would be well to publish a general order, explaining more clearly the policy indicated in your letter, in order that a better general understanding may exist amongst the parties who may desire to furnish evidence of their ability to get up new organizations. Otherwise I may adopt rules which would not be as favorable to the officers and men of this command as those of other commands.

I remain very respectfully, your obedient servant,

(Signed) J. Longstreet,

Lieutenant-General.

XVII.

Lee to Longstreet on Proposed Publication of a History of Virginia Campaigns.

LEXINGTON, VA., January 19, 1866.

GENERAL J. LONGSTREET:

MY DEAR GENERAL,—Upon my return from Richmond, where I have been for a week on business connected with Washington College, I found your letter of the 26th ultimo. I regret very much that you never received my first letter, as you might then, perhaps, have given me the information I desired, with more ease to yourself and with more expedition than now. I did not know how to address it, but sent it to a friend in Richmond, who gave it to one of our officers going south, who transferred it to another, etc., and after travelling many weary miles, has been recently returned to me. I start it again in pursuit of you, though you did not tell me how to address you. I have almost forgotten what it contained, but I hope it will inform you of my purpose in writing a history of the campaigns in Virginia, and of the object that I have in view, so that you may give me all the information in your power. I shall be in no hurry in publishing, and will not do so until I feel satisfied that I have got the true story, as my only object is to disseminate the truth. I am very sorry to hear that your records were destroyed too; but I hope Sorrel and Latrobe will be able to supply you with all you require. I wish to relate the acts of all the corps of the Army of Northern Virginia wherever they did duty, and do not wish to omit so important a one as yours. I will therefore wait as long as I can.

I shall be very glad to receive anything you may give to Mr. Washington McLean, as I know you recommend no one but those who deserve your good opinion.

I am delighted to hear that your arm is still improving, and hope it will soon be restored. You are, however, becoming so accomplished with your left hand as not to need it. You must remember me very kindly to Mrs. Longstreet and all your children. I have not had an opportunity yet to return the compliment she paid me. I had, while in Richmond, a great many inquiries after you, and learned that you intended commencing business in New Orleans. If you become as good a merchant as you were a soldier, I shall be content. No one will then excel you, and no one can wish you more success and more happiness than I. My interest and affection for you will never cease, and my prayers are always offered for your prosperity.

I am most truly yours,

R. E. LEE.

XVIII.

Lee to Longstreet—Congratulations.

LEXINGTON, VA., January 26, 1866.

LONGSTREET, OWEN & CO.,
New Orleans:

GENTLEMEN,—I am much obliged to you for your business card, and the pleasure it has afforded me to know that you have entered into partnership. I know you will do your work well, and please myself, therefore, with the prospect of your great success.

I wrote to your senior a few days since, at Macon, Mississippi, and hope he will receive my letter. I do not consider my partnership with him yet dissolved, and shall not let go him during life.

Wishing you all happiness and prosperity, I am, with great affection, your obedient servant,

R. E. LEE.

XIX.

Lee to Longstreet, suggesting the Preparation of his Memoirs.

LEXINGTON, VA., March 9, 1866.

GENERAL J. LONGSTREET:

MY DEAR GENERAL,—Your son Garland handed me a few days since your letter of the 15th of January, with the copies of your reports of operations in East Tennessee, Wilderness, Virginia, and of some of my official letters to you. I hope you will be able to send me a report of your operations around Suffolk and Richmond previous to the evacuation of that city, and of any of my general orders which you may be able to collect.

Can you not occupy your leisure time in preparing your memoirs of the war? Every officer whose position and character would give weight to his statements ought to do so. It is the only way in which we may hope that fragments of truth will reach posterity. Mrs. Longstreet will act as your amanuensis. I am very sorry that your arm improves so slowly. I trust it will be eventually restored to you. You must present my kindest regards to Mrs. Longstreet. I hope your home in New Orleans will be happy; that your life, which is dear to me, may be long and prosperous.

Most truly yours,

R. E. Lee.

XX.

Longstreet to Lee on Battle of Gaines's Mill.

New Orleans, La., March 20, 1866.

General R. E. Lee,

Lexington, Va.:

My dear General,—Your favor of the 9th instant is received. The papers or copies sent by Garland contain everything that I have or can get in the shape of your letters and orders. I shall be able to give you an account of movements, etc., connected with the Suffolk campaign and the siege of Richmond when I can get our diaries,—that is, Sorrel's, Latrobe's, and my own. But I fear that I shall not be able to do so in time to meet your desires. I shall send all that I can gather together to your house as soon as I can. I have sometimes thought that I would make the effort to write at some future time, but begin to despair of my arm. It is too much labor to write with my left hand, and it gives me inconvenience, indeed pain, to keep my right hand in the constrained position necessary in writing. Our business affairs occupy my days from nine till four P.M., so I am glad to give my arm rest after that time. Mrs. Longstreet would be rather a poor amanuensis in the evening, my only spare time, as her two little boys, Lee and Jim, occupy most of her time. She is trying to get a picture of Lee to send you. I delivered your message that you "regretted that you had not been able to return the compliment." To go back to history and the war. There is one portion of our records as written that I should like corrected,—the battle of Gaines's Mill. Your report of that battle does not recognize the fact that the line in my front, that is, the enemy's line, was broken by the troops that were under my orders and handling. A part of Jackson's command, being astray, reported to me just as I was moving my column of attack forward,—Whiting's division,—and I put it in my column of attack, as stated in my report. I think that you must have overlooked my report on this point, and have been guided by Jackson's. Jackson knew nothing of the matter of my having his troops, I suppose, and merely made his report from riding over the ground after the battle. I presume that he was not within one mile of the division when I put it in, and had no idea of its whereabouts. General Whiting reported to me that he had lost his way, and did not know where to find General Jackson, and offered his troops if I had use for them. I was then moving to assault, and put Whiting in a little behind Pickett's brigade. The commands made the assault together, and broke the enemy's line. Anderson's brigade followed and secured it, the assaulting columns being somewhat broken in making the charge. Just after breaking his lines the enemy made a severe attack, and would have recovered his position, I think, but for the timely support of Anderson's and Kemper's brigades at this point. Another fact should not be lost sight of in this connection. A. P. Hill had made several formidable attacks at the same point, and had fought manfully against it for several hours, and though not entirely successful, he must have made a decided impression, and have injured the enemy as much as he was himself injured, and thus weakened the enemy's lines so as to enable us to break them. It is quite common to give those credit only who show results, but it frequently happens, as in this case, that there are others who merit as much who are not known by results,—that is, who are not seen by others than those on the ground.

If you can come across my son when you have an idle moment, I hope that you will give him a few words of kindly advice and encouragement. He is taught to look up to you as superior to others. Mrs. Longstreet joins me in affectionate salutations.

I remain very truly yours,

J. LONGSTREET.

XXI.

Lee to Longstreet—Situation and Prospects.

LEXINGTON, VA., May 25, 1866.

GENERAL J. LONGSTREET:

MY DEAR GENERAL,—I was very glad to receive your letter of the 18th, but you told me so little of yourself that I presume you intend writing to me again shortly. But what you did say was very satisfactory, and I am much pleased to know that your prospects in a commercial point of view are good and progressive. I hope they may regularly and surely advance. I feel much obliged by your kind proposition as regards myself. For the present I must remain where I am. When I see that I have done all the good that I can accomplish for Washington College I may find it necessary to do something that will enable me to procure a competence for my family. I will then turn my hand to whatever may offer. For myself I want nothing but my food and clothes. I send in compliance with your request a number of autographs, enough, I should think, to last for all time; but if they will be of any service to you I will send more. Mr. Lowe has not yet reached Lexington. It will give me pleasure to see him when he does, as he comes from you. As you did not mention your arm, I hope that is improving too. You must never omit to mention it, Mrs. Longstreet, and your children when you write. I see Garland very often in my walks, but very rarely at my house. . . All unite in kindest regards to yourself and family.

Most truly yours,

R. E. LEE.

XXII.

The following letter appears in the Records of the Rebellion as from General Lee:

HEAD-QUARTERS ARMY OF NORTHERN VIRGINIA,
CHAMBERSBURG, June 28, 1863, 7.30 A.M.

LIEUTENANT-GENERAL R. S. EWELL,
Commanding Corps:

GENERAL,—I wrote you last night stating that General Hooker was reported to have crossed the Potomac and is advancing by the way of Middletown, the head of his column being at that point in Frederick County. I directed you in that letter to move your forces to this point. If you have not already progressed on that road, and if you have no good reason against it, I desire you to move in the direction of Gettysburg *via* Heidlersburg, where you will have a turnpike most of the way, and you can thus join your other divisions to Early's, which is east of the mountains. I think it preferable to keep on the east side of the mountains.

R. E. LEE,
General.

This letter was taken from General Lee's letter-book, but in that book it is noted *that the record is made from memory,* and that point is also mentioned in the Records of the Rebellion. The inference, therefore, is that the original draught of the letter was lost or misplaced.

That the letter as recorded is not correctly dated is proved by all contemporaneous orders and movements.

General Lee's orders for the 29th, issued on the 28th, were for the advance of his army against Harrisburg. The orders were changed after night upon the report of the scout. When about to march on the 29th, under his original orders, General Ewell

received the orders issued after the scout made his report, which called for concentration at Cashtown, in conjunction with the orders issued for the other commands.

The body of the above letter is as far from the movements made as the date is from other orders, for it indicates a march of the Second in a body, while its divisions marched separately,—E. Johnson's back on the Chambersburg road to Green Village or Scotland, thence east to the Chambersburg-Gettysburg road, near Greenwood; Rodes's division marched *via* Heidlersburg, and Early's *via* Hunterstown. The historian should be careful, therefore, when he comes to consider this letter, for it will put to confusion all facts with which it is connected. Errors in history are heart-rending. Truth may be mortifying, but it passes the glories of Libanus and the beauties of Carmel and Sharon.

APPENDIX TO CHAPTER XXIII.

THE UNION ARMY AT FREDERICKSBURG, VA.

ARMY OF THE POTOMAC, MAJOR-GENERAL AMBROSE E. BURNSIDE.

Escort, etc.: Oneida (N. Y.) Cav., Capt. Daniel P. Mann; 1st U. S. Cav. (detachment), Capt. Marcus A. Reno; A and E, 4th U. S. Cav., Capt. James B. McIntyre. *Provost Guard*, Brig.-Gen. Marsena R. Patrick; A and B, McClellan (Ill.) Dragoons, Capts. George W. Shears and David C. Brown; G, 9th N. Y., Capt. Charles Child; 93d N. Y., Col. John S. Crocker; 2d U. S. Cav., Maj. Charles J. Whiting; 8th U. S., Capt. Royal T. Frank. *Volunteer Engineer Brigade*, Brig.-Gen. Daniel P. Woodbury; 15th N. Y., Maj. James A. Magruder; 50th N. Y., Maj. Ira Spaulding. *Battalion U. S. Engineers*, Lieut. Charles E. Cross.

ARTILLERY, Brig.-Gen. Henry J. Hunt:—*Artillery Reserve*, Lieut.-Col. William Hays; 5th N. Y., Capt. Elijah D. Taft; A, 1st Batt. N. Y., Capt. Otto Diederichs; B, 1st Batt. N. Y., Capt. Adolph Voegelee; C, 1st Batt. N. Y., Lieut. Bernhard Wever; D, 1st Batt. N. Y., Capt. Charles Kusserow; K, 1st U. S., Capt. William M. Graham; A, 2d U. S., Capt. John C. Tidball; G, 4th U. S., Lieut. Marcus P. Miller; K, 5th U. S., Lieut. David H. Kinzie; C, 32d Mass. (train guard), Capt. Josiah C. Fuller. *Unattached Artillery*, Maj. Thomas S. Trumbull; B, 1st Conn. Heavy, Capt. Albert F. Brooker; M, 1st Conn. Heavy, Capt. Franklin A. Pratt.

RIGHT GRAND DIVISION, MAJOR-GENERAL EDWIN V. SUMNER.

SECOND ARMY CORPS, MAJOR-GENERAL DARIUS N. COUCH.

FIRST DIVISION, Brig.-Gen. Winfield S. Hancock:—*First Brigade*, Brig.-Gen. John C. Caldwell, Col. George W. von Schack; 5th N. H., Col. Edward E. Cross, Maj. E. E. Sturtevant, Capt. James E. Larkin, Capt. Horace T. H. Pierce; 7th N. Y., Col. George W. von Schack, Capt. G. A. von Bransen; 61st N. Y., Col. Nelson A. Miles;* 64th N. Y., Lieut.-Col. Enos C. Brooks;* 81st Pa., Col. H. Boyd McKean, Capt. William Wilson; 145th Pa., Col. Hiram L. Brown, Lieut.-Col. David B. McCreary. *Second Brigade*, Brig.-Gen. Thomas F. Meagher; 28th Mass., Col. Richard Byrnes; 63d N. Y., Maj. Joseph O'Neill, Capt. Patrick J. Condon; 69th N. Y., Col. Robert Nugent, Capt. James Saunders; 88th N. Y., Col. Patrick Kelly; 116th Pa., Col. Dennis Heenan, Lieut.-Col. St. Clair A. Mulholland, Lieut. Francis T. Quinlan. *Third Brigade*, Col. Samuel K. Zook; 27th Conn., Col. Richard S. Bosswick; 2d Del., Col. William P. Baily; 52d N. Y., Col. Paul Frank; 57th

* Commanded 61st and 64th N. Y., consolidated.

N. Y., Lieut.-Col. Alford B. Chapman, Major N. Garrow Throop, Capt. James W. Britt; 66th N. Y., Lieut.-Col. James H. Bull, Capt. Julius Wehle, Capt. John S. Hammell, Lieut. James G. Derrickson; 53d Pa., Col. John R. Brooke. *Artillery*, B, 1st N. Y., Capt. Rufus D. Pettit; C, 4th U. S., Lieut. Evan Thomas.

SECOND DIVISION, Brig.-Gen. Oliver O. Howard:—*First Brigade*, Brig.-Gen. Alfred Sully; 19th Me., Col. Frederick D. Sewall, Lieut.-Col. Francis E. Heath; 15th Mass., Major Chase Philbrick, Capt. John Murkland, Capt. Charles H. Watson; 1st Co. Mass. Sharp-shooters, Capt. William Plumer; 1st Minn., Col. George N. Morgan; 2d Co. Minn. Sharp-shooters, Capt. William F. Russell; 34th N. Y., Col. James A. Suiter; 82d N. Y. (2d Militia), Lieut.-Col. James Huston. *Second Brigade*, Col. Joshua T. Owen; 69th Pa., Lieut.-Col. Dennis O'Kane; 71st Pa., Lieut.-Col. John Markoe; 72d Pa., Col. De Witt C. Baxter; 106th Pa., Col. Turner G. Morehead. *Third Brigade*, Col. Norman J. Hall; 19th Massachusetts, Capt. H. G. O. Weymouth; 20th Mass., Capt. George N. Macy; 7th Mich., Lieut.-Col. Henry Baxter, Maj. Thomas H. Hunt; 42d N. Y., Lieut.-Col. George N. Bomford; 59th N. Y., Lieut.-Col. William Northedge; 127th Pa., Col. William W. Jennings. *Artillery*, A, 1st R. I., Capt. William A. Arnold; B, 1st R. I., Capt. John G. Hazard.

THIRD DIVISION, Brig.-Gen. William H. French:—*First Brigade*, Brig.-Gen. Nathan Kimball, Col. John S. Mason; 14th Ind., Maj. Elijah H. C. Cavins; 24th N. J., Col. William B. Robertson; 28th N. J., Col. Moses N. Wisewell, Lieut.-Col. E. A. L. Roberts; 4th Ohio, Col. John S. Mason, Lieut.-Colonel James H. Godman, Capt. Gordon A. Stewart; 8th Ohio, Lieut.-Col. Franklin Sawyer; 7th W. Va., Col. Joseph Snider, Lieut.-Col. Jonathan H. Lockwood. *Second Brigade*, Col. Oliver H. Palmer; 14th Conn., Lieut.-Col. Sanford H. Perkins, Capt. Samuel H. Davis; 108th N. Y, Lieut.-Col. Charles J. Powers; 130th Pa., Col. Henry I. Zinn, Captain William M. Porter. *Third Brigade*, Col. John W. Andrews, Lieut.-Col. William Jameson, Lieut.-Col. John W. Marshall; 1st Del., Maj. Thomas A. Smyth; 4th N. Y., Col. John D. MacGregor, Lieut.-Col. William Jameson, Maj. Charles W. Kruger; 10th N. Y., Col. John E. Benedix, Capt. Salmon Winchester, Capt. George F. Hopper; 132d Pa., Lieut.-Col. Charles Albright. *Artillery*, G, 1st N. Y., Capt. John D. Frank; G, 1st R. I., Capt. Charles D. Owen.

ARTILLERY RESERVE, Capt. Charles H. Morgan; I, 1st U. S., Lieut. Edmund Kirby; A, 4th U. S., Lieut. Rufus King, Jr.

NINTH ARMY CORPS, BRIGADIER-GENERAL ORLANDO B. WILLCOX. *Escort*, B, 6th N. Y. Cav., Capt. Hillman A. Hall; C, 6th N. Y. Cav., Capt. William L. Heermance.

FIRST DIVISION, Brig.-Gen. William W. Burns:—*First Brigade*, Col. Orlando M. Poe; 2d Mich., Lieut.-Col. Louis Dillman; 17th Mich., Col. William H. Withington; 20th Mich., Col. Adolphus W. Williams; 79th N. Y., Lieut.-Col. David Morrison. *Second Brigade*, Col. Benjamin C. Christ; 29th Mass., Lieut.-Col. Joseph H. Barnes; 8th Mich., Maj. Ralph Ely; 27th N. J., Col. George W. Mindil; 46th N. Y., Lieut.-Col. Joseph Gerhardt; 50th Pa., Lieut.-Col. Thomas S. Brenholtz. *Third Brigade*, Col. Daniel Leasure; 36th Mass., Col. Henry Bowman; 45th Pa., Col.

Thomas Welsh; 100th Pa., Lieut.-Col. David A. Leckey. *Artillery*, D, 1st N. Y., Capt. Thomas W. Osburn; L and M, 3d U. S., Lieut. Horace J. Hayden.

SECOND DIVISION, Brig.-Gen. Samuel D. Sturgis:—*First Brigade*, Brig.-Gen. James Nagle; 2d Md., Col. Thomas B. Allard; 6th N. H., Col. Simon G. Griffin; 9th N. H., Lieut.-Col. John W. Babbitt; 48th Pa., Col. Joshua K. Sigfried; 7th R. I., Col. Zenas R. Bliss; 12th R. I., Col. George H. Browne. *Second Brigade*, Brig.-Gen. Edward Ferrero; 21st Mass., Col. William S. Clark; 35th Mass., Maj. Sidney Willard, Capt. Stephen H. Andrews; 11th N. H., Col. Walter Harriman; 51st N. Y., Col. Robert B. Potter; 51st Pa., Col. John F. Hartranft. *Artillery*, L, 2d N. Y., Capt. Jacob Roemer; D, Pa., Capt. George W. Durell; D, 1st R. I., Capt. William W. Buckley; E, 4th U. S., Lieut. George Dickenson, Lieut. John Egan.

THIRD DIVISION, Brig.-Gen. George W. Getty:—*First Brigade*, Col. Rush C. Hawkins; 10th N. H., Col. Michael T. Donohoe; 13th N. H., Col. Aaron F. Stevens; 25th N. J., Col. Andrew Derrom; 9th N. Y., Lieut.-Col. Edgar A. Kimball; 89th N. Y., Col. Harrison S. Fairchild; 103d N. Y., Col. Benjamin Ringold. *Second Brigade*, Col. Edward Harland; 8th Conn., Maj. John E. Ward, Capt. Henry M. Hoyt; 11th Conn., Col. Griffin A. Stedman, Jr.; 15th Conn., Lieut.-Col. Samuel Tolles; 16th Conn., Capt. Charles L. Upham; 21st Conn., Col. Arthur H. Dutton; 4th R. I., Lieut.-Col. Joseph B. Curtis, Maj. Martin P. Buffum. *Artillery*, E, 2d U. S., Lieut. Samuel N. Benjamin; A, 5th U. S., Lieut. James Gilliss.

CAVALRY DIVISION, Brig.-Gen. Alfred Pleasonton:—*First Brigade*, Brig.-Gen. John F. Farnsworth; 8th Ill., Col. William Gamble; 3d Ind., Maj. George H. Chapman; 8th N. Y., Col. Benjamin F. Davis. *Second Brigade*, Col. David McM. Gregg, Col. Thomas C. Devin; 6th N. Y., Col. Thomas C. Devin, Lieut.-Col. Duncan McVicar; 8th Pa., Lieut.-Col. Amos E. Griffiths; 6th U. S., Capt. George C. Cram. *Artillery*, M, 2d U. S., Lieut. Alexander C. M. Pennington, Jr.

CENTRE GRAND DIVISION, MAJOR-GENERAL JOSEPH HOOKER.

THIRD ARMY CORPS, BRIGADIER-GENERAL GEORGE STONEMAN.

FIRST DIVISION, Brig.-Gen. David B. Birney:—*First Brigade*, Brig.-Gen. John C. Robinson; 20th Ind., Col. John Van Valkenburg; 63d Pa., Maj. John A. Danks; 68th Pa., Col. Andrew H. Tippin; 105th Pa., Col. Amor A. McKnight; 114th Pa., Col. Charles H. T. Collis; 141st Pa., Col. Henry J. Madill. *Second Brigade*, Brig.-Gen. J. H. Hobart Ward; 3d Me., Col. Moses B. Lakeman; 4th Me., Col. Elijah Walker; 38th N. Y., Lieut.-Col. William Birney; 40th N. Y., Lieut.-Col. Nelson A. Gesner; 55th N. Y., Col. P. Regis de Trobriand; 57th Pa., Col. Charles T. Campbell, Lieut.-Col. Peter Sides; 99th Pa., Col. Asher S. Leidy, Lieut.-Col. Edwin R. Biles. *Third Brigade*, Brig.-Gen. Hiram G. Berry; 17th Me., Col. Thomas A. Roberts; 3d Mich., Maj. Moses B. Houghton; 5th Mich., Lieut.-Col. John Gilluly, Maj. Edward T. Sherlock; 1st N. Y., Col. J. Frederick Pierson; 37th N. Y., Col. Samuel B. Hayman; 101st N. Y., Col. George F. Chester. *Artillery*, Capt. George

E. Randolph; E, 1st R. I., Lieut. Pardon S. Jastram; F and K, 3d U. S., Lieut. John G. Turnbull.

SECOND DIVISION, Brig.-Gen. Daniel E. Sickles:—*First Brigade*, Brig.-Gen. Joseph B. Carr; 1st Mass., Lieut.-Col. Clark B. Baldwin, Col. Napoleon B. McLaughlen; 11th Mass., Col. William Blaisdell; 16th Mass., Col. Thomas R. Tannatt; 2d N. H., Col. Gilman Marston; 11th N. J., Col. Robert McAllister; 26th Pa., Lieut.-Col. Benjamin C. Tilghman. *Second Brigade*, Col. George B. Hall; 70th N. Y., Col. J. Egbert Farnum; 71st N. Y., Maj. Thomas Rafferty; 72d N.Y., Col. William O. Stevens; 73d N. Y., Col. William R. Brewster; 74th N. Y., Lieut.-Col. William H. Lounsbury; 120th N. Y., Col. George H. Sharpe. *Third Brigade*, Brig.-Gen. Joseph W. Revere; 5th N. J., Col. William J. Sewell; 6th N. J., Col. George C. Burling; 7th N. J., Col. Louis R. Francine; 8th N. J., Col. Adolphus J. Johnson; 2d N. Y., Col. Sidney W. Park; 115th Pa., Lieut.-Col. William A. Olmsted. *Artillery*, Capt. James E. Smith; 2d N. J., Capt. A. Judson Clark; 4th N. Y., Lieut. Joseph E. Nairn; H, 1st U. S., Lieut. Justin E. Dimick; K, 4th U. S., Lieut. Francis W. Seeley.

THIRD DIVISION, Brig.-Gen. Amiel W. Whipple:—*First Brigade*, Brig.-Gen. A. Sanders Piatt, Col. Emlen Franklin; 86th N. Y., Lieut.-Col. Barna J. Chapin; 124th N. Y., Col. A. Van Horne Ellis; 122d Pa., Col. Emlen Franklin. *Second Brigade*, Col. Samuel S. Carroll; 12th N. H., Col. Joseph H. Potter; 163d N. Y., Maj. James J. Byrne; 84th Pa., Col. Samuel M. Bowman; 110th Pa., Lieut.-Col. James Crowther. *Artillery*, 10th N. Y., Capt. John T. Bruen; 11th N. Y., Capt. Albert A. von Puttkammer; H, 1st Ohio, Lieut. George W. Norton.

FIFTH ARMY CORPS, BRIGADIER-GENERAL DANIEL BUTTERFIELD.

FIRST DIVISION, Brig.-Gen. Charles Griffin:—*First Brigade*, Col. James Barnes; 2d Me., Lieut.-Col. George Varney, Maj. Daniel F. Sargent; 2d Co. Mass. Sharp-shooters, Capt. Lewis E. Wentworth; 18th Mass., Lieut.-Col. Joseph Hayes; 22d Mass., Lieut.-Col. William S. Tilton; 1st Mich., Lieut.-Col. Ira C. Abbott; 13th N. Y., Col. Elisha G. Marshall, Lieut.-Col. Francis A. Schoeffel; 25th N. Y., Capt. Patrick Connelly; 118th Pa., Lieut.-Col. James Gwyn. *Second Brigade*, Col. Jacob B. Sweitzer; 9th Mass., Col. Patrick R. Guiney; 32d Mass., Col. Francis J. Parker; 4th Mich., Lieut.-Col. George W. Lumbard; 14th N. Y., Lieut.-Col. Thomas M. Davies; 62d Pa., Lieut.-Col. James C. Hull. *Third Brigade*, Col. T. B. W. Stockton; 20th Me., Col. Adelbert Ames; Brady's Co. Mich. Sharp-shooters, Lieut. Jonas H. Titus, Jr.; 16th Mich., Lieut.-Col. Norval E. Welch; 12th N. Y., Lieut.-Col. Robert M. Richardson; 17th N. Y., Capt. John Vickers; 44th N. Y., Lieut.-Col. Freeman Conner, Maj. Edward B. Knox; 83d Pa., Col. Strong Vincent. *Artillery*, 3d Mass., Capt. Augustus P. Martin; 5th Mass., Capt. Charles A. Phillips; C, 1st R. I., Capt. Richard Waterman; D, 5th U. S., Lieut. Charles E. Hazlett. *Sharp-shooters*, 1st U. S., Lieut.-Col. Casper Trepp.

SECOND DIVISION, Brig.-Gen. George Sykes:—*First Brigade*, Lieut.-Col. Robert C. Buchanan; 3d U. S., Capt. John D. Wilkins; 4th U. S., Capt. Hiram Dryer; 1st Battn., 12th U. S., Capt. Matthew M. Blunt;

2d Battn., 12th U. S., Capt. Thomas M. Anderson; 1st Battn., 14th U. S., Capt. John D. O'Connell; 2d Battn., 14th U. S., Capt. Giles B. Overton. *Second Brigade*, Maj. George L. Andrews, Maj. Charles S. Lovell; 1st and 2d U. S. (battn.), Capt. Salem S. Marsh; 6th U. S., Capt. Levi C. Bootes; 7th U. S. (battn.), Capt. David P. Hancock; 10th U. S., Capt. Henry E. Maynadier; 11th U. S., Capt. Charles S. Russell; 17th and 19th U. S. (battn.), Capt. John P. Wales. *Third Brigade*, Brig.-Gen. Gouverneur K. Warren; 5th N. Y., Col. Cleveland Winslow; 140th N. Y., Col. Patrick H. O'Rorke; 146th N. Y., Col. Kenner Garrard. *Artillery*, L, 1st Ohio, Lieut. Frederick Dorries; I, 5th U. S., Lieut. Malbone F. Watson.

THIRD DIVISION, Brig.-Gen. Andrew A. Humphreys:—*First Brigade*, Brig.-Gen. Erastus B. Tyler; 91st Pa., Col. Edgar M. Gregory; 126th Pa., Col. James G. Elder, Lieut.-Col. David W. Rowe; 129th Pa., Col. Jacob G. Frick; 134th Pa., Lieut.-Col. Edward O'Brien. *Second Brigade*, Col. Peter H. Allabach; 123d Pa., Col. John B. Clark; 131st Pa., Lieut.-Col. William B. Shaut; 133d Pa., Col. Franklin B. Speakman; 155th Pa., Col. Edward J. Allen. *Artillery*, C, 1st N. Y., Lieut. William H. Phillips; E and G, 1st U. S., Capt. Alanson M. Randol.

CAVALRY BRIGADE, Brig.-Gen. William W. Averell; 1st Mass., Col. Horace B. Sargent; 3d Pa., Lieut.-Col. Edward S. Jones; 4th Pa., Col. James K. Kerr; 5th U. S., Capt. James E. Harrison. *Artillery*, B and L, 2d U. S., Capt. James M. Robertson.

LEFT GRAND DIVISION, MAJOR-GENERAL WILLIAM B. FRANKLIN. *Escort*, 6th Pa. Cav., Col. Richard H. Rush.

FIRST ARMY CORPS, MAJOR-GENERAL JOHN F. REYNOLDS. *Escort*, L, 1st Me. Cav., Capt. Constantine Taylor.

FIRST DIVISION, Brig.-Gen. Abner Doubleday:—*First Brigade*, Col. Walter Phelps, Jr.; 22d N. Y., Lieut.-Col. John McKie, Jr.; 24th N. Y., Lieut.-Col. Samuel R. Beardsley; 30th N. Y., Lieut.-Col. Morgan H. Chrysler; 84th N. Y. (14th Militia), Lieut.-Col. William H. de Bevoise; 2d U. S. Sharp-shooters, Maj. Homer R. Stoughton. *Second Brigade*, Col. James Gavin; 7th Ind., Lieut.-Col. John F. Cheek; 76th N. Y., Col. William P. Wainwright; 95th N. Y., Col. George H. Biddle; 56th Pa., Lieut.-Col. J. William Hofmann. *Third Brigade*, Col. William F. Rogers; 21st N. Y., Capt. George N. Layton; 23d N. Y., Col. Henry C. Hoffman; 35th N. Y., Col. Newton B. Lord; 80th N. Y. (20th Militia), Lieut.-Col. Jacob B. Hardenbergh. *Fourth Brigade*, Brig.-Gen. Solomon Meredith, Col. Lysander Cutler; 19th Ind., Lieut.-Col. Samuel J. Williams; 24th Mich., Col. Henry A. Morrow; 2d Wis., Col. Lucius Fairchild; 6th Wis., Col. Lysander Cutler, Lieut.-Col. Edward S. Bragg; 7th Wis., Col. William W. Robinson. *Artillery*, Capt. George A. Gerrish, Capt. John A. Reynolds; 1st N. H., Lieut. Frederick M. Edgell; L, 1st N. Y., Capt. John A. Reynolds; B, 4th U. S., Lieut. James Stewart.

SECOND DIVISION, Brig.-Gen. John Gibbon, Brig.-Gen. Nelson Taylor:—*First Brigade*, Col. Adrian R. Root; 16th Me., Lieut.-Col. Charles W. Tilden; 94th N. Y., Maj. John A. Kress; 104th N. Y., Maj. Gilbert G. Prey; 105th N. Y., Maj. Daniel A. Sharp, Capt. Abraham Moore;

107th Pa., Col. Thomas F. McCoy. *Second Brigade*, Col. Peter Lyle; 12th Mass., Col. James L. Bates; 26th N. Y., Lieut.-Col. Gilbert S. Jennings, Maj. Ezra F. Wetmore; 90th Pa., Lieut.-Col. William A. Leech; 136th Pa., Col. Thomas M. Bayne. *Third Brigade*, Brig.-Gen. Nelson Taylor, Col. Samuel H. Leonard; 13th Mass., Col. Samuel H. Leonard, Lieut.-Col. N. Walter Batchelder; 83d N. Y. (9th Militia), Capt. John Hendrickson, Capt. Joseph A. Moesch, Lieut. Isaac E. Hoagland; 97th N. Y., Col. Charles Wheelock; 11th Pa., Col. Richard Coulter, Capt. Christian Kuhn; 88th Pa., Maj. David A. Griffith. *Artillery*, Capt. George F. Leppien; 2d Me., Capt. James A. Hall; 5th Me., Capt. George F. Leppien; C, Pa., Capt. James Thompson; F, 1st Pa., Lieut. R. Bruce Ricketts.

THIRD DIVISION, Maj.-Gen. George G. Meade:—*First Brigade*, Col. William Sinclair, Col. William McCandless; 1st Pa. Reserves, Capt. William C. Talley; 2d Pa. Reserves, Col. William McCandless, Capt. Timothy Mealey; 6th Pa. Reserves, Maj. Wellington H. Ent; 13th Pa. Reserves (1st Rifles), Capt. Charles F. Taylor; 121st Pa., Col. Chapman Biddle. *Second Brigade*, Col. Albert L. Magilton; 3d Pa. Reserves, Col. Horatio G. Sickel; 4th Pa. Reserves, Lieut.-Col. Richard H. Woolworth; 7th Pa. Reserves, Col. Henry C. Bolinger; 8th Pa. Reserves, Maj. Silas M. Baily; 142d Pa., Col. Robert P. Cummins. *Third Brigade*, Brig.-Gen. C. Feger Jackson, Col. Joseph W. Fisher, Lieut.-Col. Robert Anderson; 5th Pa. Reserves, Col. Joseph W. Fisher, Lieut.-Col. George Dare; 9th Pa. Reserves, Lieut.-Col. Robert Anderson, Maj. James McK. Snodgrass; 10th Pa. Reserves, Maj. James B. Knox; 11th Pa. Reserves, Lieut.-Col. Samuel M. Jackson; 12th Pa. Reserves, Capt. Richard Gustin. *Artillery*, A, 1st Pa., Lieut. John G. Simpson; B, 1st Pa., Capt. James H. Cooper; G, 1st Pa., Capt. Frank P. Amsden; C, 5th U. S., Capt. Dunbar R. Ransom.

SIXTH ARMY CORPS, MAJOR-GENERAL WILLIAM F. SMITH. *Escort*, L, 10th N. Y. Cav., Lieut. George Vanderbilt; I, 6th Pa. Cav., Capt. James Starr; K, 6th Pa. Cav., Capt. Frederick C. Newhall.

FIRST DIVISION, Brig.-Gen. William T. H. Brooks:—*First Brigade*, Col. Alfred T. A. Torbert; 1st N. J., Lieut.-Col. Mark W. Collet; 2d N. J., Col. Samuel L. Buck; 3d N. J., Col. Henry W. Brown; 4th N. J., Col. William B. Hatch, Lieut.-Col. James N. Duffy; 15th N. J., Lieut.-Col. Edward L. Campbell; 23d N. J., Col. Henry O. Ryerson. *Second Brigade*, Col. Henry L. Cake; 5th Me., Col. Edward A. Scammon; 16th N. Y., Col. Joel J. Seaver; 27th N. Y., Col. Alexander D. Adams; 121st N. Y., Col. Emory Upton; 96th Pa., Lieut.-Col. Peter A. Filbert. *Third Brigade*, Brig.-Gen. David A. Russell; 18th N. Y., Col. George R. Myers; 31st N. Y., Lieut.-Col. Leopold C. Newman; 32d N. Y., Capt. Charles Hubbs; 95th Pa., Lieut. Col. Elisha Hall. *Artillery*, A, Md., Capt. John W. Wolcott; 1st Mass., Capt. William H. McCartney; 1st N. J., Capt. William Hexamer; D, 2d U. S., Lieut. Edward B. Williston.

SECOND DIVISION, Brig.-Gen. Albion P. Howe:—*First Brigade*, Brig.-Gen. Calvin E. Pratt; 6th Me., Col. Hiram Burnham; 43d N. Y., Col. Benjamin F. Baker; 49th Pa., Col. William H. Irwin; 119th Pa., Col.

Peter C. Ellmaker; 5th Wis., Col. Amasa Cobb. *Second Brigade*, Col. Henry Whiting; 26th N. J., Col. Andrew J. Morrison; 2d Vt., Lieut.-Col. Charles H. Joyce; 3d Vt., Col. Breed N. Hyde; 4th Vt., Col. Charles B. Stoughton; 5th Vt., Col. Lewis A. Grant; 6th Vt., Col. Nathan Lord, Jr. *Third Brigade*, Brig.-Gen. Francis L. Vinton, Col. Robert F. Taylor, Brig.-Gen. Thomas H. Neill; 21st N. J., Col. Gilliam Van Houten; 20th N. Y., Col. Ernst von Vegesack; 33d N. Y., Col. Robert F. Taylor; 49th N. Y., Col. Daniel D. Bidwell; 77th N. Y., Lieut.-Col. Winsor B. French. *Artillery*, B, Md., Capt. Alonzo Snow; 1st N. Y., Capt. Andrew Cowan; 3d N. Y., Lieut. William A. Harn; F, 5th U. S., Lieut. Leonard Martin.

THIRD DIVISION, Brig.-Gen. John Newton:—*First Brigade*, Brig.-Gen. John Cochrane; 65th N. Y., Col. Alexander Shaler; 67th N. Y., Col. Nelson Cross; 122d N. Y., Col. Silas Titus; 23d Pa., Maj. John F. Glenn; 61st Pa., Col. George C. Spear; 82d Pa., Col. David H. Williams. *Second Brigade*, Brig.-Gen. Charles Devens, Jr.; 7th Mass., Lieut.-Col. Franklin P. Harlow; 10th Mass., Col. Henry L. Eustis; 37th Mass., Col. Oliver Edwards; 36th N. Y., Col. William H. Browne; 2d R. I., Col. Frank Wheaton, Lieut.-Col. Nelson Viall. *Third Brigade*, Col. Thomas A. Rowley, Brig.-Gen. Frank Wheaton; 62d N. Y., Maj. Wilson Hubbell; 93d Pa., Maj. John M. Mark; 98th Pa., Lieut.-Col. Adolph Mehler; 102d Pa., Lieut.-Col. Joseph M. Kinkead; 139th Pa., Lieut.-Col. James D. Owens. *Artillery*, C, 1st Pa., Capt. Jeremiah McCarthy; D, 1st Pa., Capt. Michael Hall; G, 2d U. S., Lieut. John H. Butler.

CAVALRY BRIGADE, Brig.-Gen. George D. Bayard, Col. David McM. Gregg; Indep't Co., D. C., Lieut. Williams H. Orton; 1st Me., Lieut.-Col. Calvin S. Douty; 1st N. J., Lieut.-Col. Joseph Kargé; 2d N. Y., Maj. Henry E. Davies; 10th N. Y., Lieut.-Col. William Irvine; 1st Pa., Col. Owen Jones. *Artillery*, C, 3d U. S., Capt. Horatio G. Gibson.

INDEX